PHILIP'S

STREET A...
Liverpool
and Merseyside

www.philips-maps.co.uk
First published in 1997 by
Philip's, a division of
Octopus Publishing Group Ltd
www.octopusbooks.co.uk
Endeavour House, 189 Shaftesbury Avenue
London WC2H 8JY
An Hachette UK Company
www.hachette.co.uk

Fourth edition 2007
Fourth impression 2011
MERDA

978-1-84907-047-8 (spiral)

© Philip's 2007

Ordnance Survey®

This product includes mapping data licensed
from Ordnance Survey® with the permission
of the Controller of Her Majesty's Stationery
Office. © Crown copyright 2007. All rights
reserved. Licence number 100011710.

While every reasonable effort has been made
to ensure that the information compiled in
this atlas is accurate, complete and up-to-
date at the time of publication, some of this
information is subject to change and the
Publisher cannot guarantee its correctness or
completeness.

The information in this atlas is provided with-
out any representation or warranty, express
or implied and the Publisher cannot be held
liable for any loss or damage due to any use or
reliance on the information in this atlas, nor for
any errors, omissions or subsequent changes
in such information.

The representation in this atlas of a road, track
or path is no evidence of the existence of a
right of way.

Ordnance Survey and the OS Symbol are
registered trademarks of Ordnance Survey, the
national mapping agency of Great Britain.

Speed camera data provided by
PocketGPSWorld.com Ltd

Printed in China

Contents

Digital Data

The exceptionally high-quality mapping found in this atlas is available as digital data in TIFF format, which is easily convertible to other bitmapped (raster) image formats.

The index is also available in digital form as a standard database table. It contains all the details found in the printed index together with the National Grid reference for the map square in which each entry is named.

For further information and to discuss your requirements, please contact
philips@mapsinternational.co.uk

Mobile speed cameras

The vast majority of speed cameras used on Britain's roads are operated by safety camera partnerships. These comprise local authorities, the police, Her Majesty's Court Service (HMCS) and the Highways Agency.

This table lists the sites where each safety camera partnership may enforce speed limits through the use of mobile cameras or detectors. These are usually set up on the roadside or a bridge spanning the road and operated by a police or civilian enforcement officer. The speed limit at each site (if available) is shown in red type, followed by the approximate location in black type.

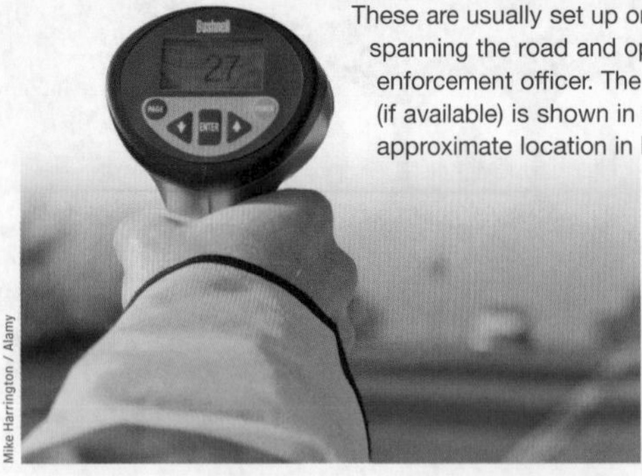

Mike Harrington / Alamy

A57
Liverpool, East Prescot Rd

A58
St Helens, Prescot Rd

A506
Liverpool, Longmoor Lane

A551
Wirral, Leasowe Rd

A553
Wirral, Laird Street

A561
Liverpool, Speke Rd/Speke Boulevard

A562
Liverpool, Parliament Street/Upper Parliament Street

A572
St Helens, Common Rd

A580
Liverpool, Townsend Avenue

St Helens, East Lancashire Rd

A5038
Sefton, Southport Rd/ Liverpool Boundary to Oxford Rd

Sefton, Southport Rd/Oxford Rd to Northfield Rd

A5080
Liverpool, Bowring Park Rd/Roby Rd

A5098
Liverpool, Hornby Rd

B5136
Wirral, New Chester Rd

UNCLASSIFIED
Liverpool, Great Homer Street

Liverpool, Green Lane

Liverpool, Lower House Lane/Dwerry House Lane

Liverpool, Muirhead Avenue

Liverpool, Netherfield Rd North

Liverpool, Utting Avenue East

Sefton, Park Lane

Symbol	Description
	Motorway with junction number
	Primary route – dual/single carriageway
	A road – dual/single carriageway
	B road – dual/single carriageway
	Minor road – dual/single carriageway
	Other minor road – dual/single carriageway
	Road under construction
	Tunnel, covered road
	Speed cameras - single, multiple
	Rural track, private road or narrow road in urban area
	Gate or obstruction to traffic (restrictions may not apply at all times or to all vehicles)
	Path, bridleway, byway open to all traffic, road used as a public path
	Pedestrianised area
DY7	**Postcode boundaries**
	County and unitary authority boundaries
	Railway, tunnel, railway under construction
	Tramway, tramway under construction
	Miniature railway
Walsall	**Railway station**
	Private railway station
South Shields	**Metro station**
	Tram stop, tram stop under construction
	Bus, coach station

Symbol	Description
♦	**Ambulance station**
♦	**Coastguard station**
♦	**Fire station**
♦	**Police station**
✚	**Accident and Emergency entrance to hospital**
H	**Hospital**
+	**Place of worship**
i	**Information Centre** (open all year)
	Shopping Centre
P P&R	**Parking, Park and Ride**
PO	**Post Office**
Å ⌂	**Camping site, caravan site**
▶ ✕	**Golf course, picnic site**
Prim Sch	**Important buildings, schools, colleges, universities and hospitals**
	Built up area
	Woods
River Medway	**Water name**
	River, weir, stream
	Canal, lock, tunnel
	Water
	Tidal water
Church	**Non-Roman antiquity**
ROMAN FORT	**Roman antiquity**
87	**Adjoining page indicators and overlap bands**
237	The colour of the arrow and the band indicates the scale of the adjoining or overlapping page (see scales below)

Enlarged mapping only

Symbol	Description
	Railway or bus station building
	Place of interest
	Parkland

Acad	**Academy**	Inst	**Institute**	Recn Gd	**Recreation Ground**
Allot Gdns	**Allotments**	Ct	**Law Court**		
Cemy	**Cemetery**	L Ctr	**Leisure Centre**	Resr	**Reservoir**
C Ctr	**Civic Centre**	LC	**Level Crossing**	Ret Pk	**Retail Park**
CH	**Club House**	Liby	**Library**	Sch	**School**
Coll	**College**	Mkt	**Market**	Sh Ctr	**Shopping Centre**
Crem	**Crematorium**	Meml	**Memorial**	TH	**Town Hall/House**
Ent	**Enterprise**	Mon	**Monument**	Trad Est	**Trading Estate**
Ex H	**Exhibition Hall**	Mus	**Museum**	Univ	**University**
Ind Est	**Industrial Estate**	Obsy	**Observatory**	W Twr	**Water Tower**
IRB Sta	**Inshore Rescue Boat Station**	Pal	**Royal Palace**	Wks	**Works**
		PH	**Public House**	YH	**Youth Hostel**

■ The small numbers around the edges of the maps identify the 1 kilometre National Grid lines

■ The dark grey border on the inside edge of some pages indicates that the mapping does not continue onto the adjacent page

The scale of the maps on the pages numbered in blue is 5.52 cm to 1 km • 3½ inches to 1 mile • 1: 18103	0 — ¼ — ½ — ¾ — 1 mile 0 — 250 m — 500 m — 750 m — 1 kilometre
The scale of the maps on pages numbered in red is 11.04 cm to 1 km • 7 inches to 1 mile • 1: 9051	0 — 220 yards — 440 yards — 660 yards — ½ mile 0 — 125 m — 250 m — 375 m — ½ kilometre

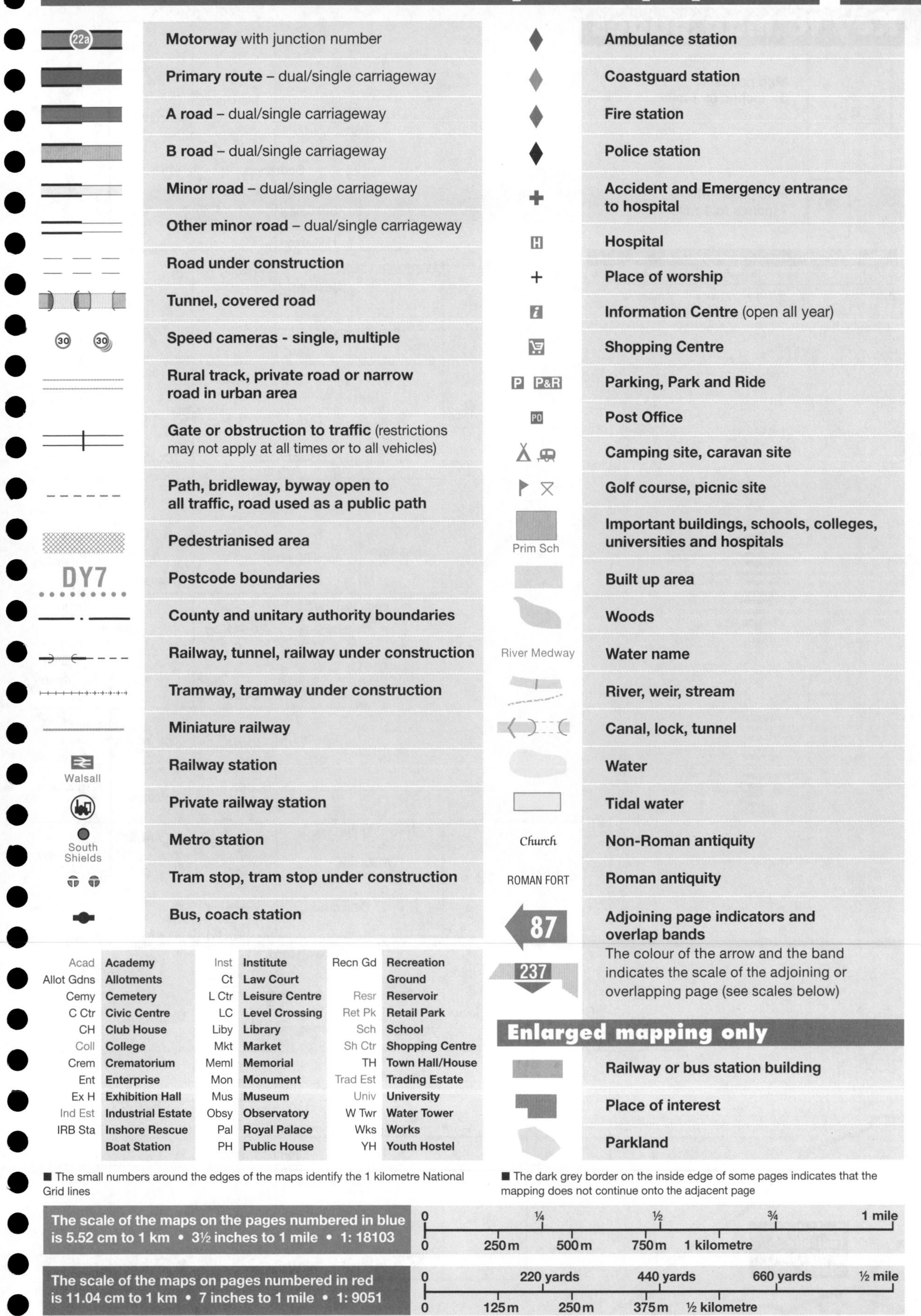

IV

Key to map pages

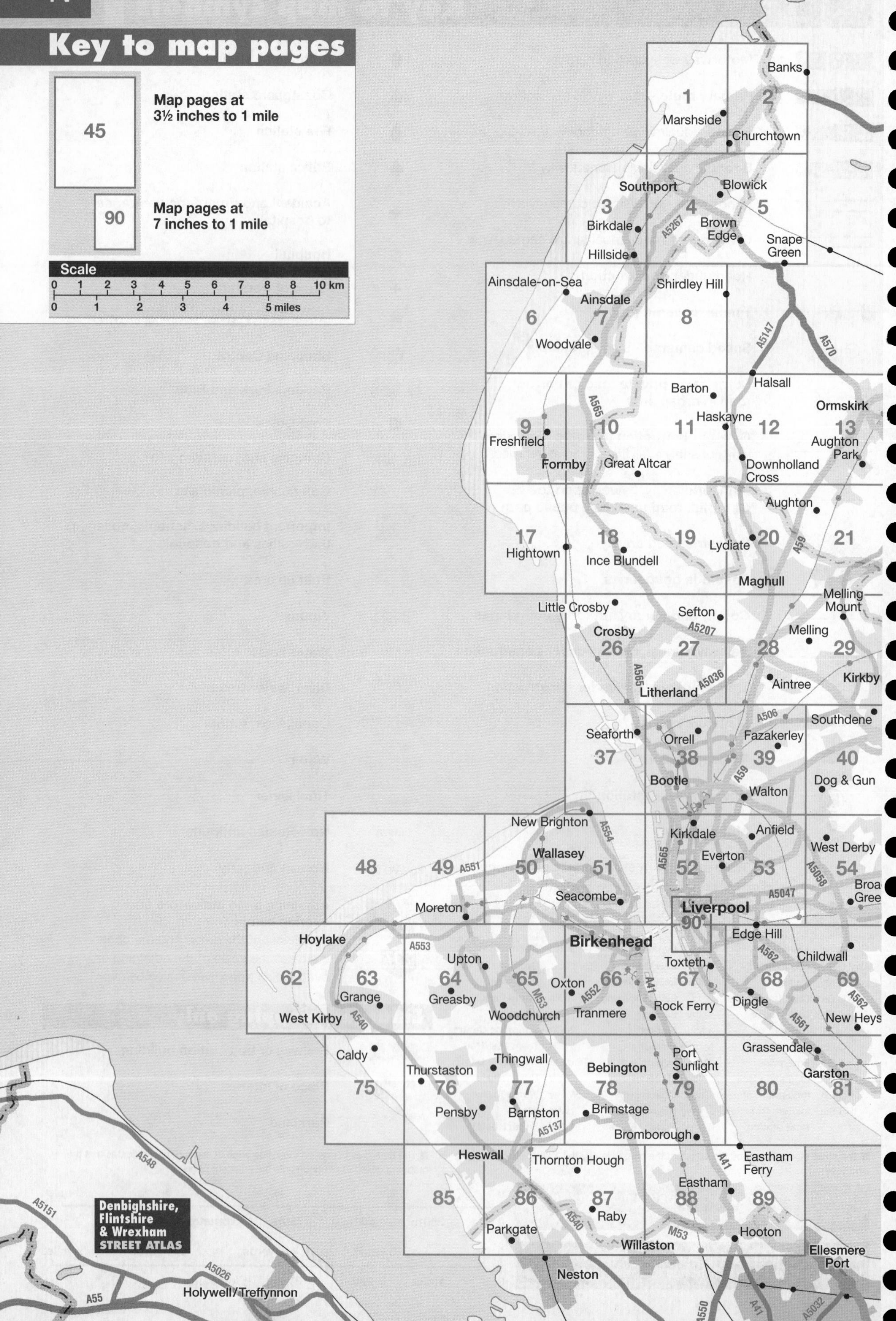

| 45 | Map pages at 3½ inches to 1 mile |
| 90 | Map pages at 7 inches to 1 mile |

Scale

0 1 2 3 4 5 6 7 8 8 10 km
0   1   2   3   4   5 miles

1 Banks
Marshside **2** Churchtown

3 Southport Birkdale Hillside **4** Blowick Brown Edge **5** Snape Green A5267

Ainsdale-on-Sea **6** **7** Ainsdale Woodvale Shirdley Hill **8** A5147 A570

9 Freshfield Formby **10** A565 Barton **11** Haskayne Great Altcar **12** Halsall Downholland Cross **13** Ormskirk Aughton Park

17 Hightown **18** Ince Blundell **19** Aughton Lydiate **20** A59 **21** Maghull

Little Crosby **26** Crosby Sefton A5207 **27** **28** Melling Melling Mount **29**
Litherland A565 A5036 Aintree Kirkby

Seaforth **37** Orrell **38** Bootle A565 Fazakerley **39** A59 Walton A506 Southdene **40** Dog & Gun

New Brighton A564 **48** **49** A551 Wallasey **50** Seacombe **51** Kirkdale **52** A565 Everton Anfield **53** West Derby A5058 **54** Broa Gree A5047

Hoylake A553 Upton **62** **63** Grange West Kirby A540 **64** Greasby **65** M53 Woodchurch Oxton **66** A552 Tranmere Birkenhead Rock Ferry A41 Toxteth **67** Edge Hill A562 Dingle **68** Childwall **69** A561 New Heys A562

Caldy **75** Thurstaston **76** Pensby Thingwall **77** Barnston A5137 Bebington **78** Brimstage Port Sunlight **79** Bromborough Grassendale **80** Garston **81**

Heswall **85** **86** A540 Thornton Hough Raby **87** Eastham **88** Eastham Ferry M41 Hooton **89** M53
Parkgate Willaston Neston Ellesmere Port

Liverpool 90

A548 A5151 A5026 A55
Denbighshire, Flintshire & Wrexham STREET ATLAS
Holywell/Treffynnon

A550 A41 A5032

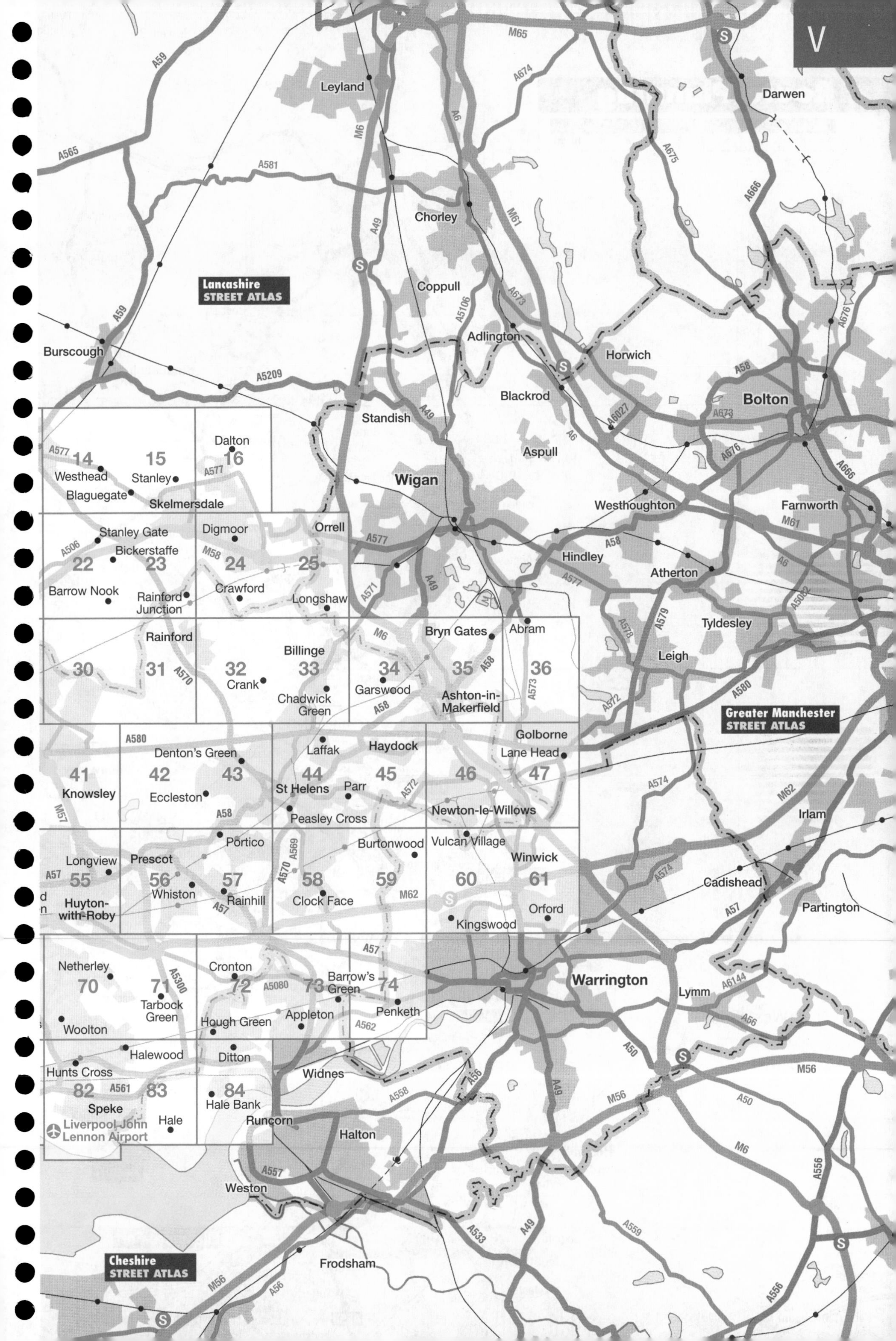

M65
S
Darwen
A59
A674
A675
A666
Leyland
A565
A581
M6
A6
Chorley
A49
M61
A673
Coppull
Lancashire STREET ATLAS
Adlington
A5106
Burscough
Horwich
S
A6027
Blackrod
S
Bolton
Standish
A5209
Aspull
A58
A673
A676
Wigan
A49
A6
Westhoughton
Farnworth
M61
Dalton
Hindley
A58
A6
A577
14   15   16
A577
Westhead   Stanley
Blaguegate
Skelmersdale
Orrell
A577
Atherton
A5082
Digmoor
Stanley Gate
A506
Bickerstaffe
M58
24   25
Tyldesley
Greater Manchester STREET ATLAS
22   23
A571
A49
Leigh
A579
A580
Barrow Nook
Crawford
Longshaw
Rainford Junction
M6
Bryn Gates   Abram
A578
A572
Rainford
Billinge
A58
A580
30   31   32   33   34   35   36
A570
Crank
Chadwick Green
Garswood
Ashton-in-Makerfield
A573
A574
A580
Golborne
A580
Denton's Green
Laffak   Haydock
Lane Head
Irlam
41   42   43   44   45   46   47
M62
Knowsley
Eccleston
St Helens   Parr
M57
A58
A572
Newton-le-Willows
Peasley Cross
Cadishead
A574
A57
Partington
Portico
Burtonwood
Vulcan Village
Longview   Prescot
A569
Winwick
A57
55   56   57   58   59   60   61
A570
Huyton-with-Roby
Whiston   Rainhill
Clock Face
M62
Orford
A57
A57
S
Kingswood
A57
Netherley
Cronton
Barrow's Green
Warrington
70   71   72   73   74
A5300
A5080
Lymm
A6144
Tarbock Green
Appleton
Penketh
A56
Woolton
Hough Green
A562
A50
S
Halewood
Ditton
M56
Hunts Cross
A561
Widnes
M56
82   83   84
A558
A50
Speke
Hale Bank
A49
M56
Liverpool John Lennon Airport
Runcorn
Hale
Halton
M6
A557
A556
Weston
Cheshire STREET ATLAS
A559
M56
A56
Frodsham
A533
A556
S

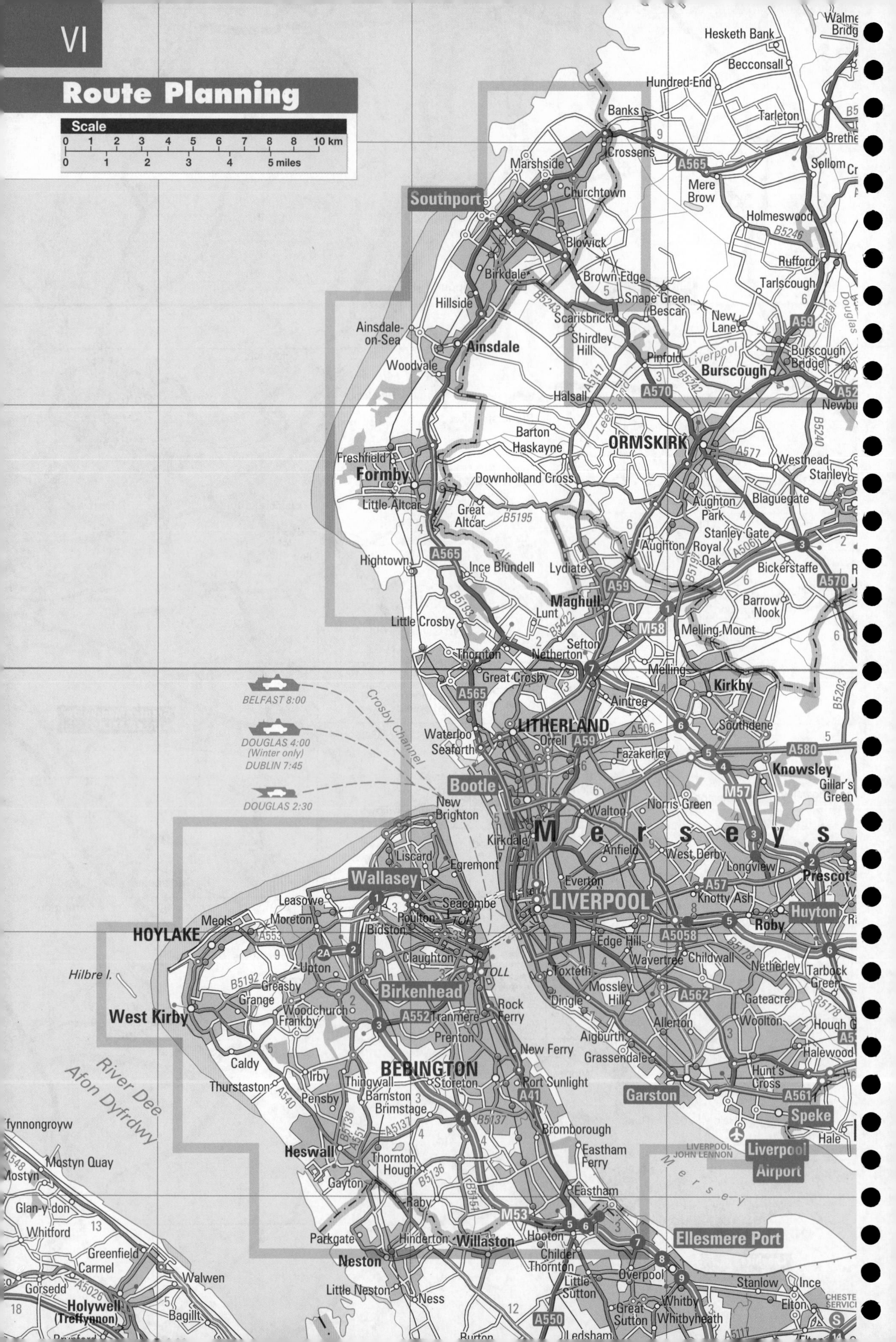

Route Planning

Scale

0 1 2 3 4 5 6 7 8 8 10 km
0 1 2 3 4 5 miles

Southport
Marshside
Churchtown
Blowick
Birkdale
Hillside
Ainsdale-on-Sea
Ainsdale
Woodvale
Scarisbrick
Shirdley Hill
Halsall
Barton
Haskayne
Downholland Cross
Freshfield
Formby
Little Altcar
Great Altcar
Hightown
Ince Blundell
Little Crosby
Thornton
Great Crosby
Waterloo
Seaforth
New Brighton
Liscard
Wallasey
Leasowe
Meols
Moreton
Seacombe
Poulton
Bidston
Claughton
Upton
Greasby
Grange
Woodchurch
Frankby
Birkenhead
Tranmere
Prenton
Rock Ferry
New Ferry
Port Sunlight
Bromborough
Eastham
Ferry
Eastham
Hilbre I.
West Kirby
Caldy
Irby
Thurstaston
Pensby
Thingwall
Barnston
Brimstage
Heswall
Thornton
Hough
Gayton
Raby
Parkgate
Hinderton
Willaston
Neston
Little Neston
Ness

BELFAST 8:00
DOUGLAS 4:00
(Winter only)
DUBLIN 7:45
DOUGLAS 2:30

Crosby Channel

Hesketh Bank
Becconsall
Hundred-End
Banks
Crossens
Mere Brow
Holmeswood
Rufford
Tarlscough
New Lane
Burscough
Bescar
Snape Green
Pinfold
Burscough Bridge
ORMSKIRK
Westhead
Stanley
Aughton Park
Blaguegate
Stanley Gate
Royal Oak
Bickerstaffe
Barrow Nook
Melling Mount
Kirkby
Southdene
Knowsley
Gillar's Green
Melling
Aintree
Litherland
Orrell
Fazakerley
Walton
Norris Green
West Derby
Longview
Prescot
Knotty Ash
Huyton
Roby
Edge Hill
Wavertree
Childwall
Netherley
Tarbock Green
Toxteth
Mossley Hill
Gateacre
Dingle
Allerton
Woolton
Hough
Aigburth
Grassendale
Hunt's Cross
Halewood
Garston
Speke
Hale
Liverpool John Lennon Airport
Mersey
Ellesmere Port
Hooton
Childer Thornton
Overpool
Stanlow
Ince
Little Sutton
Great Sutton
Whitby
Whitbyheath
Elton
CHESTER SERVICES

Tarleton
Sollom
Brethe
Newbu
Aughton
Lydiate
Maghull
Lunt
Sefton
Netherton
Melling
Anfield
Everton
LIVERPOOL
Bootle
Kirkdale
Egremont
TOLL
TOLL
Bebington
Storeton
Hoylake
Mersey

River Dee
Afon Dyfrdwy

fynnongroyw
Mostyn Quay
Mostyn
Glan-y-don
Whitford
Greenfield
Carmel
Gorsedd
Holywell
(Treffynnon)
Walwen
Bagillt
18
13

MERSEYSIDE

LIVERPOOL

A565
A570
A59
A577
A580
A57
M58
M57
M53
M58
A5058
A562
A561
A41
A550
A552
A553
A540
A548
A5026

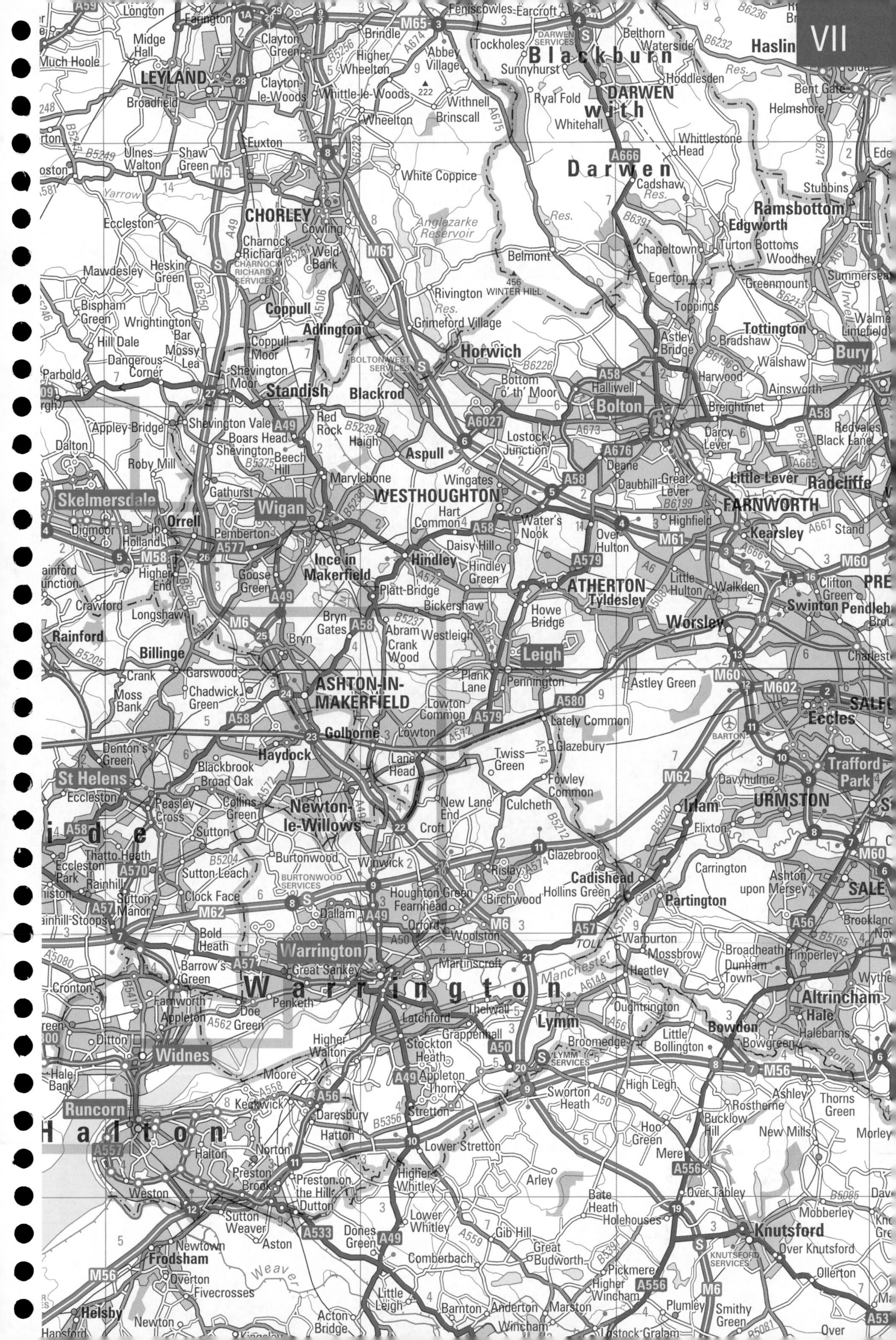
Longton
Farington
Feniscowles
Earcroft
Midge Hall
Much Hoole
LEYLAND
Clayton Green
Brindle
Abbey Village
Higher Wheelton
Tockholes
DARWEN SERVICES
Blackburn
Belthorn
Waterside
Haslin
Hoddlesden
Sunnyhurst
Ryal Fold
DARWEN
with
Whitehall
Broadfield
Clayton-le-Woods
Whittle-le-Woods
Withnell
Brinscall
Wheelton
Bent Gate
Helmshore
Euxton
Ulnes Walton
Shaw Green
White Coppice
Whittlestone Head
Darwen
Cadshaw
Stubbins
Ramsbottom
Edgworth
CHORLEY
Eccleston
Cowling
Anglezarke Reservoir
Charnock Richard
Weld Bank
Chapeltown
Turton Bottoms
Woodhey
Mawdesley
Heskin Green
CHARNOCK RICHARD SERVICES
Belmont
Egerton
Summerseat
WINTER HILL
Greenmount
Bispham Green
Wrightington Bar
Coppull
Rivington
Toppings
Hill Dale
Adlington
Grimeford Village
Tottington
Mossy Lea
Dangerous Corner
Coppull Moor
Astley Bridge
Bradshaw
Bury
Parbold
Shevington Moor
BOLTON WEST SERVICES
Horwich
Walshaw
Harwood
Standish
Blackrod
Bottom o' th' Moor
Halliwell
Ainsworth
Bolton
Breightmet
Appley Bridge
Shevington Vale
Red Rock
Haigh
Redvales
Black Lane
Dalton
Boars Head
Shevington
Beech Hill
Aspull
Lostock Junction
Darcy Lever
Roby Mill
Marylebone
Wingates
Deane
Little Lever
Radcliffe
Gathurst
WESTHOUGHTON
Daubhill
Great Lever
Skelmersdale
Wigan
Hart Common
Water's Nook
FARNWORTH
Highfield
Digmoor
Up Holland
Orrell
Pemberton
Over Hulton
Kearsley
Stand
Daisy Hill
Ince in Makerfield
Hindley
Hindley Green
Higher End
Goose Green
ATHERTON
Little Hulton
Walkden
Clifton Green
Swinton
Pendlebury
Crawford
Platt Bridge
Tyldesley
Howe Bridge
Longshaw
Bryn Gates
Abram
Bickershaw
Worsley
Rainford
Bryn
Westleigh
Crank Wood
Billinge
Leigh
Charlestown
Crank
Garswood
Plank Lane
Pennington
Astley Green
Moss Bank
Chadwick Green
ASHTON-IN-MAKERFIELD
Lowton Common
Eccles
SALFORD
Lately Common
Golborne
Lowton
BARTON
Denton's Green
Haydock
Twiss Green
Glazebury
Trafford Park
St Helens
Blackbrook
Broad Oak
Lane Head
Davyhulme
Eccleston
Peasley Cross
Collins Green
Fowley Common
URMSTON
Newton-le-Willows
New Lane End
Culcheth
Irlam
Sutton
Croft
Flixton
Thatto Heath
Eccleston Park
Burtonwood
Winwick
Glazebrook
Carrington
Sutton Leach
BURTONWOOD SERVICES
Risley
Cadishead
Ashton upon Mersey
Rainhill
Clock Face
Houghton Green
Hollins Green
SALE
Sutton Manor
Fearnhead
Birchwood
Partington
Rainhill Stoops
Dallam
Orford
Brooklands
Bold Heath
Woolston
Warburton
Broadheath
Timperley
Warrington
Mossbrow
Dunham Town
Barrow's Green
Great Sankey
Martinscroft
Heatley
Cronton
Manchester Ship Canal
Wythenshawe
Warrington
Farnworth
Penketh
Thelwall
Oughtrington
Altrincham
Appleton
Doe Green
Latchford
Lymm
Hale
Bowdon
Ditton
Higher Walton
Grappenhall
Broomedge
Little Bollington
Halebarns
Widnes
Stockton Heath
LYMM SERVICES
Bowgreen
Hale Bank
Moore
Appleton Thorn
High Legh
Ashley
Thorns Green
Keckwick
Swerton Heath
Rostherne
Runcorn
Daresbury
Stretton
Bucklow Hill
New Mills
Morley
Halton
Hatton
Hoo Green
Norton
Lower Stretton
Mere
Preston Brook
Higher Whitley
Arley
Weston
Preston on the Hill
Dutton
Bate Heath
Over Tabley
Holehouses
Mobberley
Sutton Weaver
Lower Whitley
Knutsford
Newtown
Aston
Dones Green
Gib Hill
Great Budworth
Over Knutsford
KNUTSFORD SERVICES
Frodsham
Comberbach
Pickmere
Ollerton
Overton
Fivecrosses
Weaver
Higher Wincham
Little Leigh
Helsby
Acton Bridge
Barnton
Anderton
Marston
Plumley
Smithy Green
Newton
Wincham
Lostock Gralam
Over
Halton

Major administrative and Postcode boundaries

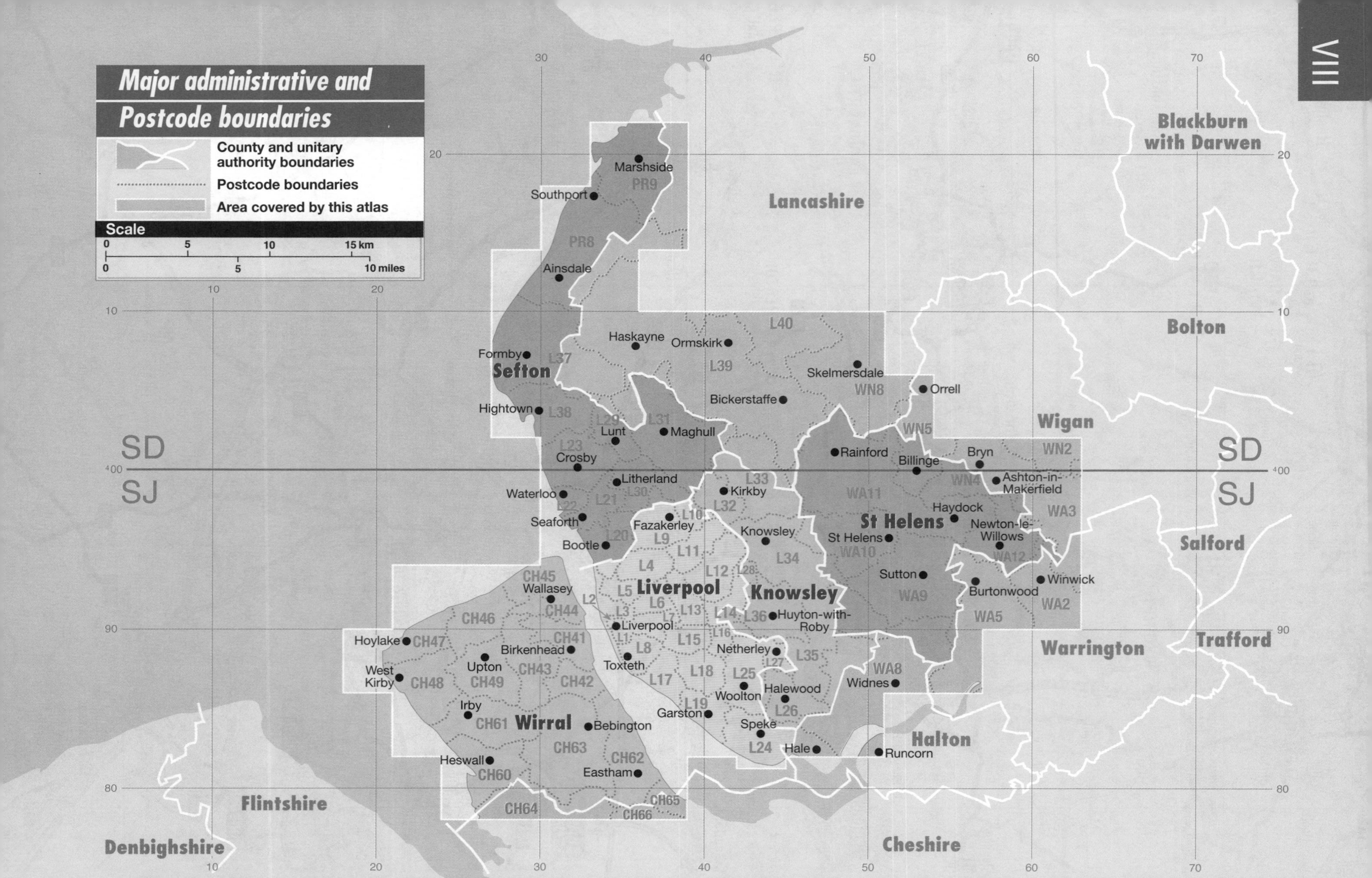

Scale

| 0 | 5 | 10 | 15 km |

| 0 | 5 | 10 miles |

- County and unitary authority boundaries
- Postcode boundaries
- Area covered by this atlas

Blackburn with Darwen

Bolton

Salford

Trafford

Wigan

Warrington

Lancashire

Halton

Cheshire

St Helens

Knowsley

Liverpool

Sefton

Wirral

Flintshire

Denbighshire

SD
SJ

SD
SJ

WN2

WN4

WN5

WN8

WA3
WA2
WA12
WA5
WA9
WA11
WA10
WA8

Orrell
Bryn
Billinge
Rainford
Ashton-in-Makerfield
Haydock
Newton-le-Willows
Winwick
Burtonwood
Sutton
St Helens
Widnes
Runcorn
Hale

Skelmersdale
Bickerstaffe
Ormskirk
Haskayne
Maghull
Lunt
Crosby
Litherland
Waterloo
Seaforth
Bootle
Fazakerley
Knowsley
Kirkby
Huyton-with-Roby
Netherley
Halewood
Wooton
Speke
Garston
Toxteth
Bebington
Eastham
Heswall
Irby
Upton
Birkenhead
Wallasey
Hoylake
West Kirby

Marshside
Southport
Ainsdale
Formby
Hightown

L40
L39
L37
L38
L31
L30
L29
L23
L22
L21
L20
L9
L10
L11
L12
L32
L33
L34
L35
L36
L14
L28
L13
L6
L4
L5
L3
L2
L7
L1
L8
L17
L18
L15
L16
L25
L26
L24
L19
L27

PR9
PR8

CH45
CH44
CH41
CH46
CH47
CH48
CH49
CH43
CH42
CH62
CH63
CH61
CH60
CH64
CH65
CH66
CH51

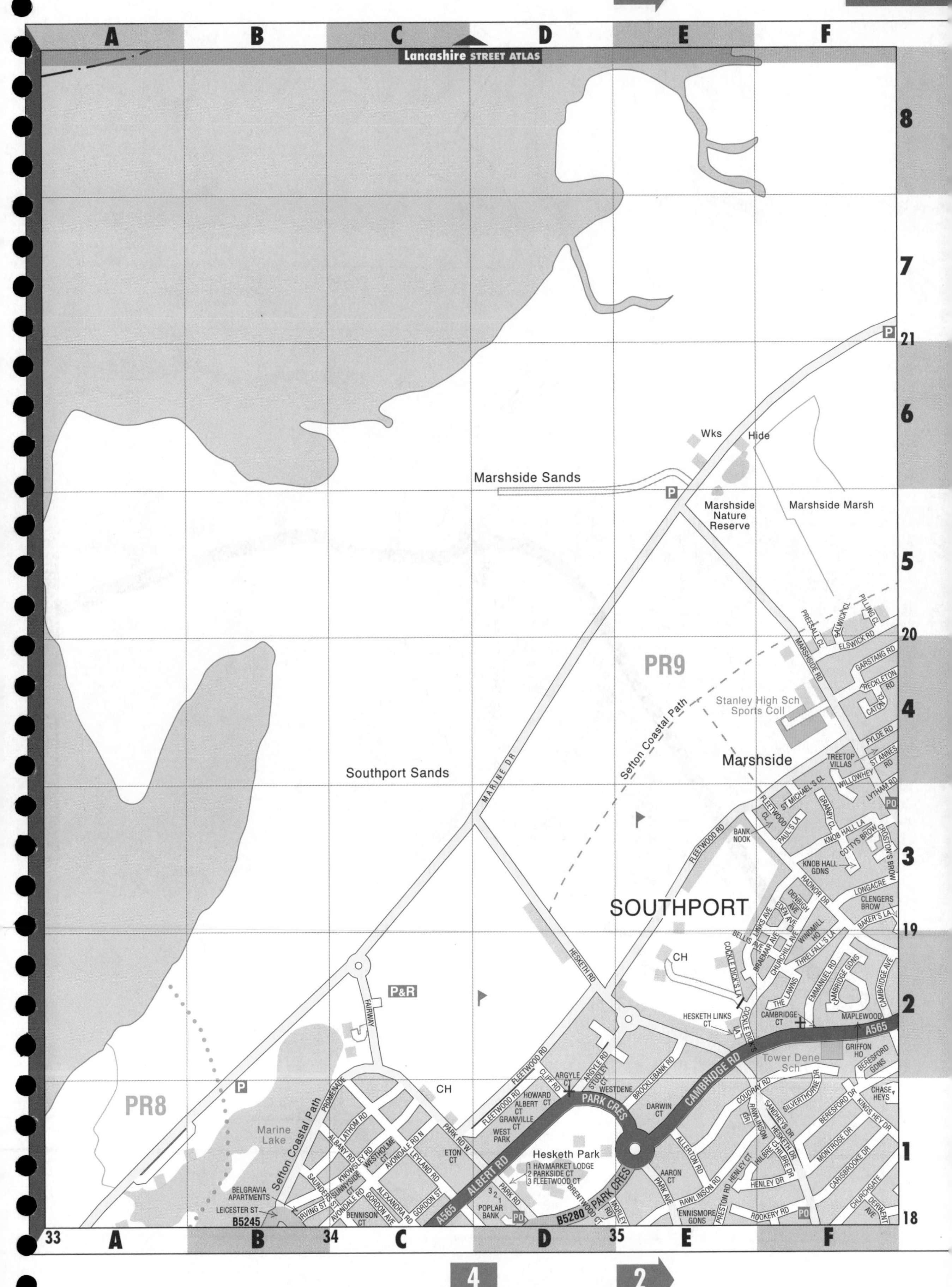

Lancashire STREET ATLAS

A B C D E F

8

7

21

6

Wks   Hide

Marshside Sands

P

Marshside
Nature
Reserve

Marshside Marsh

5

PR9

PRESTALL CT
SALWICK CL
PILLING CT
ELSWICK RD

MARSHSIDE RD

GARSTANG RD
PRECKLETON
CATON

20

Stanley High Sch
Sports Coll

FYLDE RD

4

Southport Sands

MARINE DR

Sefton Coastal Path

Marshside

TREETOP
VILLAS
WILLOWHEY

ST ANNES
RD
LYTHAM RD

PO

ST MICHAEL'S CL
FLEETWOOD RD
GRANBY CL
PAUL'S LA

KNOB HALL LA
COTTY'S BROW

CROSTON'S BROW

3

BANK
NOOK

KNOB HALL
GDNS

LONGACRE

CLENGERS
BROW

BAKER'S LA

SOUTHPORT

DENVER
RD
RAYMOND RD
ELM AVE

WINDMILL
HO

19

HESKETH RD

CH

BELLIS AVE
BRABANT RD

COCKLE DICK'S LA

THRELFALL'S LA
CHURCHILL AVE

EMMANUEL RD

CAMBRIDGE GDNS
CAMBRIDGE AVE

2

P&R

FAIRWAY

THE
LAWNS

HESKETH LINKS
CT

COCKLE DICK'S

CAMBRIDGE
RD

CAMBRIDGE
+

MAPLEWOOD

A565

P

CH

FLEETWOOD RD

CLIFF RD

ARGYLE
CT

WESTDENE

BROCKBANK RD

GRIFFON
HO

BERESFORD
GDNS

Tower Dene
Sch

PR8

P

PROMENADE

CH

HOWARD
ALBERT   CT
GRANVILLE
CT

WEST
PARK

PARK CRES

DARWIN
CT

COUDRAY RD

SILVERTHORNE

BERESFORD DR

CHASE
HEYS

KINGS HEY DR

1

Marine
Lake

Sefton Coastal Path

SALING
CT

BANKS RD
LATHOM RD

SUNNYSIDE
AVONDALE RD
WESTHOLME
CT

LEYLAND RD

PARK RD W

ETON
CT

FLEETWOOD RD

ALBERT   RD

Hesketh Park
1 HAYMARKET LODGE
2 PARKSIDE CT
3 FLEETWOOD CT

AARON
CT

ALLERTON RD

HENLEY CT

PARK RD

SANDYE DR

RAWLINSON RD

HESKETH DR

WILBRECK DR

MONTROSE DR

CARISBROOKE DR

HENLEY DR

CHURCHGATE

18

BELGRAVIA
APARTMENTS

LEICESTER ST

B5245

IRVING ST
AVONDALE
CT

BENNISON
CT

GORDON AVE

ALEXANDRA RD

GORDON ST

3 2
1

POPLAR
BANK

PO

Hesketh Park
A565

B5280

MORLEY

PARK CRES

BRENTWOOD

PRESTON RD

RAWLINSON RD
ENNISMORE
GDNS

ROOKERY RD

CHURCHGATE
AVE

PO

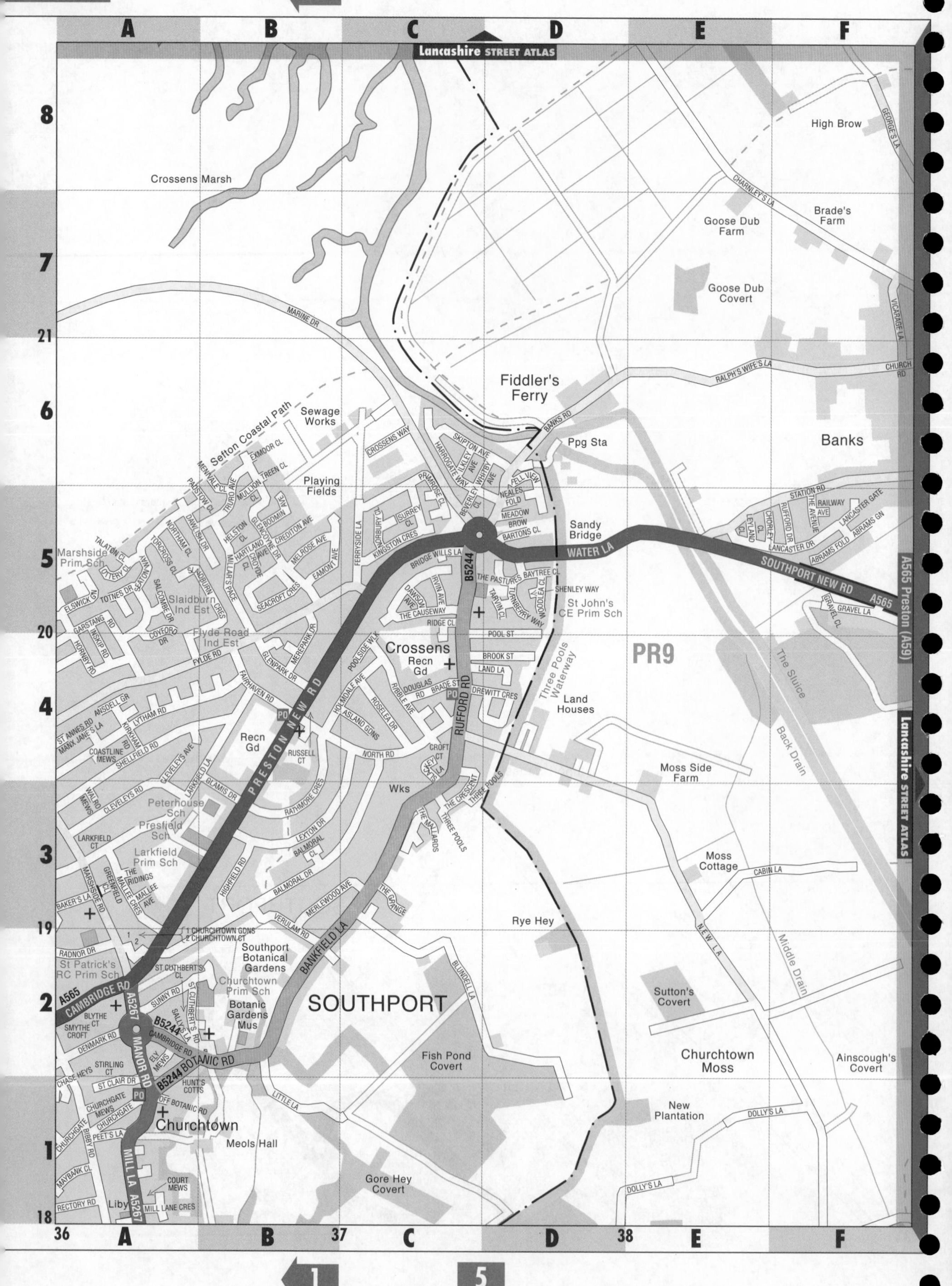

Lancashire STREET ATLAS

Crossens Marsh

High Brow

Brade's Farm

CHARNLEY'S LA

Goose Dub Farm

Goose Dub Covert

GEORGE'S LA

VICARAGE LA

MARINE DR

Sefton Coastal Path

Sewage Works

Playing Fields

Fiddler's Ferry

Ppg Sta

RALPH'S WIFE'S LA

Banks

CHURCH RD

STATION RD

RAILWAY

THE AVENUE

RUFFORD RD

LANCASTER GATE

CHORLEY

LEYLAND

LANCASTER DR

ABRAMS FOLD

ABRAMS GN

Sandy Bridge

WATER LA

SOUTHPORT NEW RD

A565

A565 Preston (A59)

Marshside Prim Sch

B5244

The Pastures

St John's CE Prim Sch

SHENLEY WAY

GRAVEL LA

Slaidburn Ind Est

Crossens Recn Gd

POOL ST

BROOK ST

LAND LA

Three Pools Waterway

PR9

Flyde Road Ind Est

Recn Gd

Douglas

DREWITT CRES

Land Houses

The Sluice

Back Drain

Wks

Three Pools

Moss Side Farm

Peterhouse Sch

Presfield Sch

Larkfield Prim Sch

The Ridings

The Gange

Rye Hey

Moss Cottage

CABIN LA

Middle Drain

NEW LA

T CHURCHTOWN GDNS

CHURCHTOWN CT

Southport Botanical Gardens

Churchtown Prim Sch

BANKFIELD LA

BLUNDELL LA

Sutton's Covert

St Patrick's RC Prim Sch

A565

CAMBRIDGE RD

Botanic Gardens Mus

SOUTHPORT

Churchtown Moss

Ainscough's Covert

A5267

MANOR RD

B5244 BOTANIC RD

Fish Pond Covert

HUNT'S COTTS

OFF BOTANIC RD

LITTLE LA

New Plantation

DOLLY'S LA

Churchtown

Meols Hall

Gore Hey Covert

DOLLY'S LA

MILL LA A5267

Lib

COURT MEWS

MILL LANE CRES

RECTORY RD

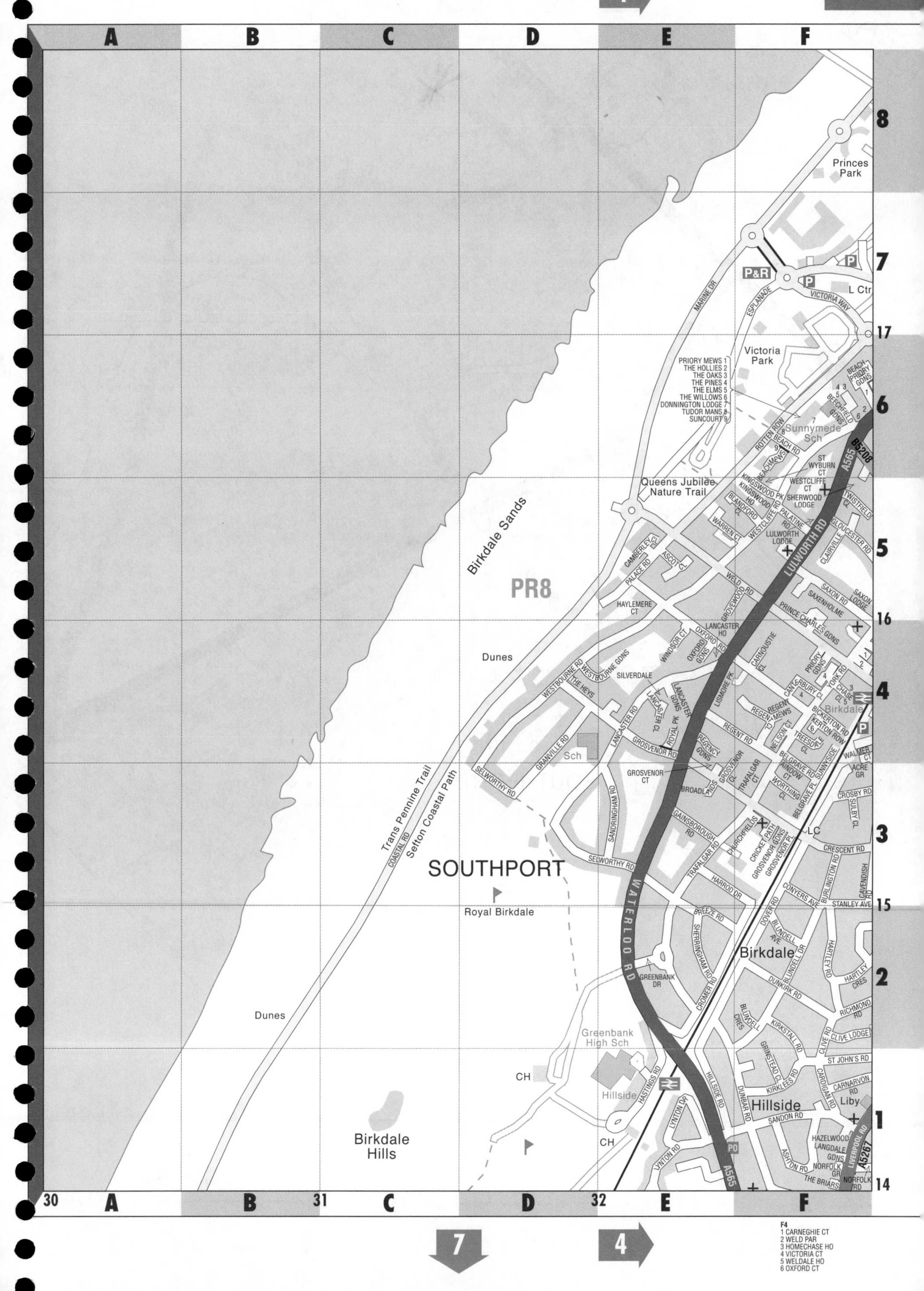

F4
1 CARNEGHIE CT
2 WELD PAR
3 HOMECHASE HO
4 VICTORIA CT
5 WELDALE HO
6 OXFORD CT

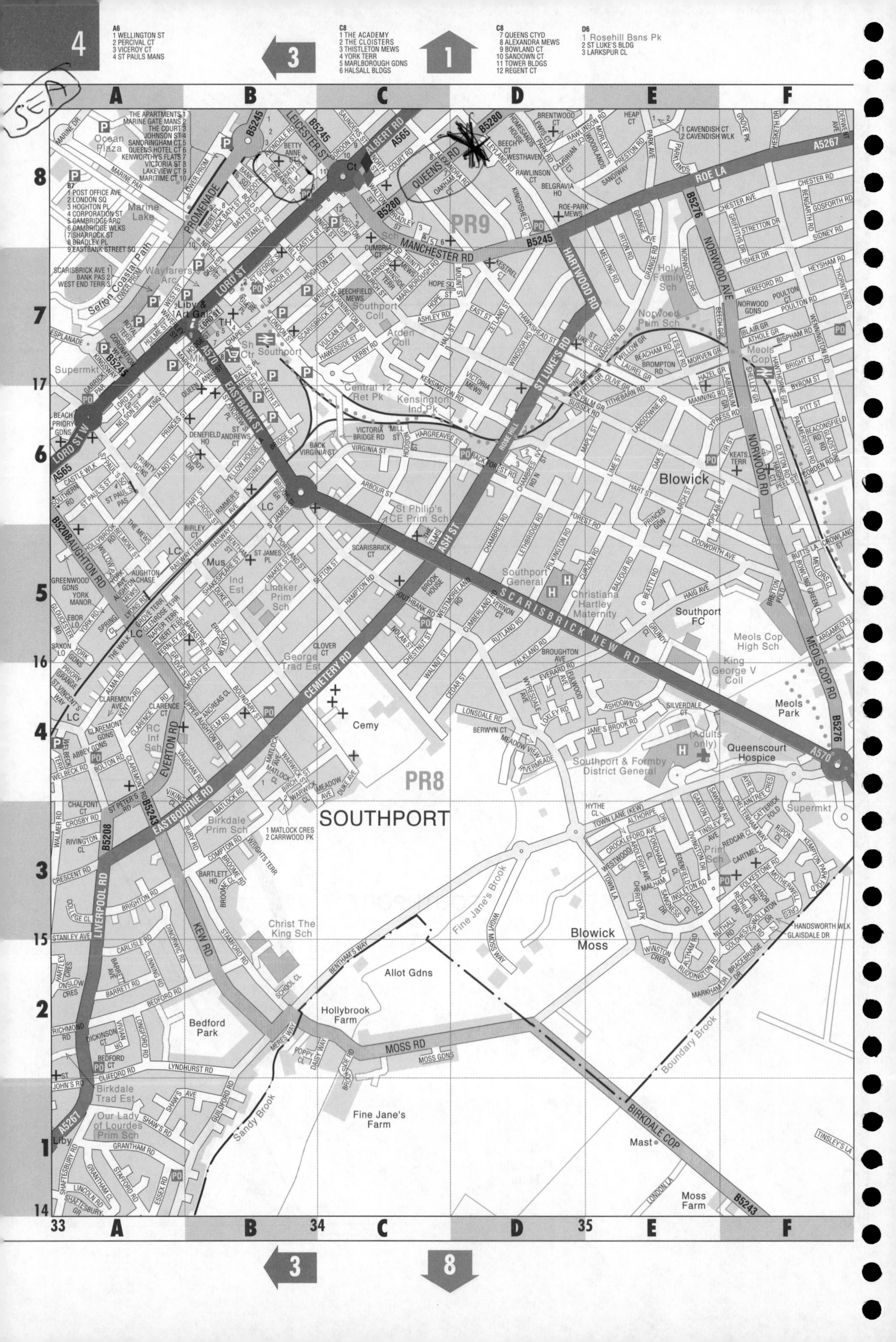

4
A6
1 WELLINGTON ST
2 PERCIVAL CT
3 VICEROY CT
4 ST PAULS MANS
3
C8
1 THE ACADEMY
2 THE CLOISTERS
3 THISTLETON MEWS
4 YORK TERR
5 MARLBOROUGH GDNS
6 HALSALL BLDGS
1
C8
7 QUEENS CTYD
8 ALEXANDRA MEWS
9 BOWLAND CT
10 SANDOWN CT
11 TOWER BLDGS
12 REGENT CT
D6
1 Rosehill Bsns Pk
2 ST LUKE'S BLDG
3 LARKSPUR CL
A
B
C
D
E
F
THE APARTMENTS 1
MARINE GATE MANS 2
THE COURT 3
JOHNSON ST 4
SANDRINGHAM CT 5
QUEENS HOTEL CT 6
KENWORTHYS FLATS 7
VICTORIA ST 8
LAKEVIEW CT 9
MARITIME CT 10
B7
1 POST OFFICE AVE
2 LONDON SQ
3 HOGHTON PL
4 CORPORATION ST
5 CAMBRIDGE ARC
6 CAMBRIDGE WLKS
7 SHARROCK ST
8 BRADLEY PL
9 EASTBANK STREET SQ
SCARISBRICK AVE 1
BANK PAS 2
WEST END TERR 3
Ocean Plaza
Marine Lake
Sefton Coastal Path
Wayfarers Arc
Liby & Art Gal
TH
Sh Ctr
Southport
Supermkt
Southport Coll
Arden Coll
Central 12 Ret Pk
Kensington Ind Pk
PR9
Holy Family Sch
Norwood Prim Sch
Meols Cop
Blowick
St Philip's CE Prim Sch
Mus
Ind Est
Linaker Prim Sch
Southport General
Christiana Hartley Maternity
Southport FC
Meols Cop High Sch
King George V Coll
Meols Park
George Trad Est
Cemy
PR8
SOUTHPORT
(Adults only)
Queenscourt Hospice
Southport & Formby District General
Supermkt
RC Inf Sch
Birkdale Prim Sch
1 MATLOCK CRES
2 CARRWOOD PK
Christ The King Sch
Allot Gdns
Blowick Moss
Hollybrook Farm
Bedford Park
Birkdale Trad Est
Our Lady of Lourdes Prim Sch
Fine Jane's Farm
Fine Jane's Brook
Boundary Brook
Sandy Brook
Mast
Moss Farm
Liby
LORD ST
LORD ST W
EASTBANK ST
SCARISBRICK NEW RD
MANCHESTER RD
ROE LA
NORWOOD AVE
NORWOOD RD
MEOLS COP RD
HARTWOOD RD
ST LUKE'S RD
ASH ST
CEMETERY RD
EASTBOURNE RD
LIVERPOOL RD
KEW RD
MOSS RD
BIRKDALE COP
AUGHTON RD
EVERTON RD
PROMENADE
A565
A570
A5267
B5245
B5280
B5276
B5208
B5243
8
7
6
5
4
3
2
1
17
16
15
14
33
34
35
8

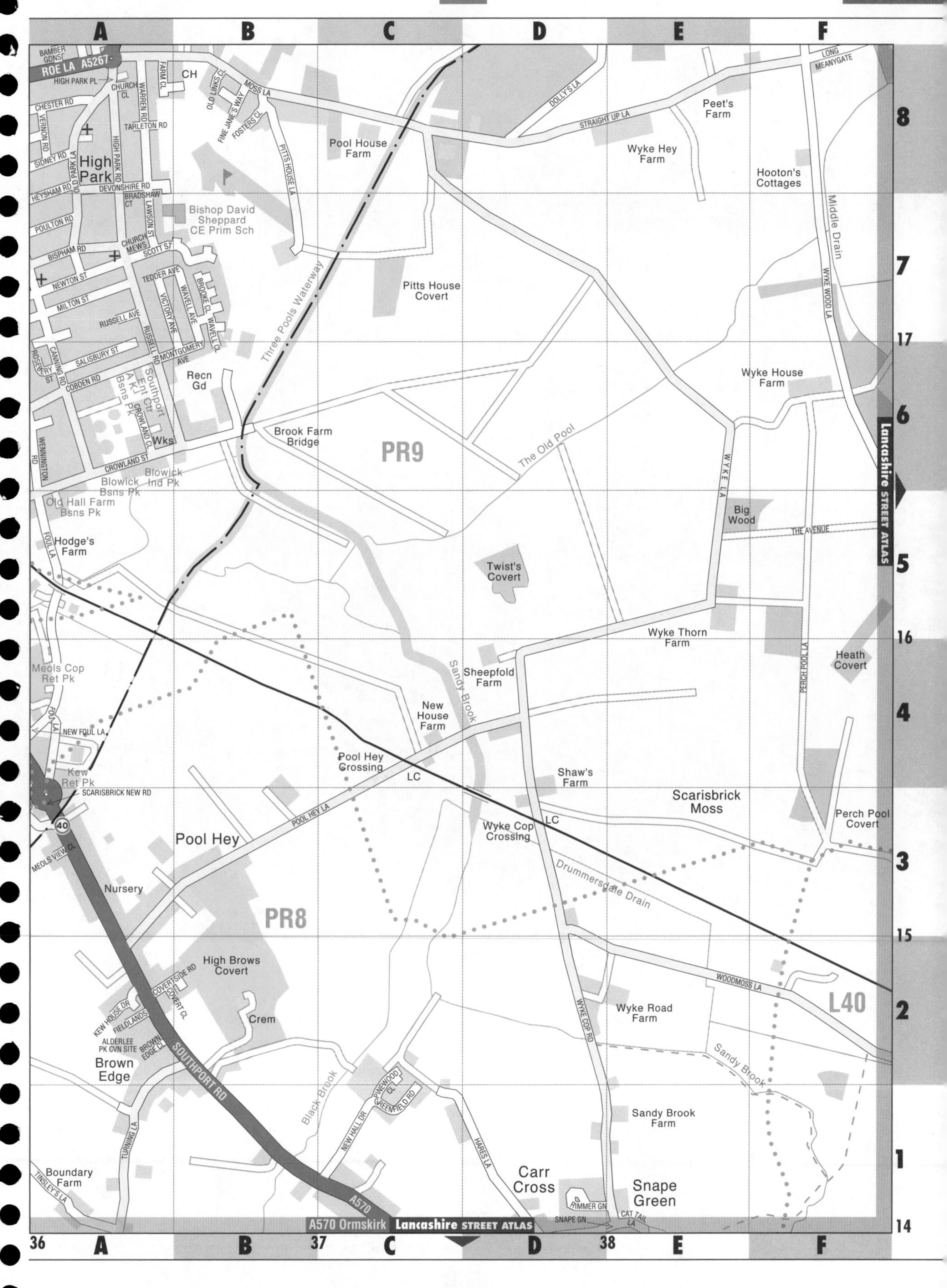
2
A
B
C
D
E
F
ROE LA A5267
BAMBER GDNS
HIGH PARK PL
CHURCH CL
CHESTER RD
High Park
TARLETON RD
DEVONSHIRE RD
Bishop David Sheppard CE Prim Sch
Pool House Farm
Pitts House Covert
Three Pools Waterway
STRAIGHT UP LA
DOLLY'S LA
Peet's Farm
Wyke Hey Farm
Hooton's Cottages
Middle Drain
WYKE WOOD LA
LONG MEANYGATE
Wyke House Farm
Recn Gd
Brook Farm Bridge
PR9
The Old Pool
WYKE LA
Big Wood
THE AVENUE
Twist's Covert
Blowick Bsns Pk
Blowick Ind Pk
Old Hall Farm Bsns Pk
Hodge's Farm
Wyke Thorn Farm
Heath Covert
PERCH POOL LA
Meols Cop Ret Pk
Sheepfold Farm
Sandy Brook
New House Farm
Pool Hey Crossing
LC
Shaw's Farm
Scarisbrick Moss
Kew Ret Pk
SCARISBRICK NEW RD
Wyke Cop Crossing
Perch Pool Covert
Pool Hey
POOL HEY LA
Drummersdale Drain
Nursery
PR8
High Brows Covert
WOODMOSS LA
L40
Crem
Wyke Road Farm
WYKE COP RD
Brown Edge
SOUTHPORT RD
Black Brook
Sandy Brook Farm
Boundary Farm
Carr Cross
Snape Green
A570
A570 Ormskirk
Lancashire STREET ATLAS
36
37
38
14
15
16
17
1
2
3
4
5
6
7
8

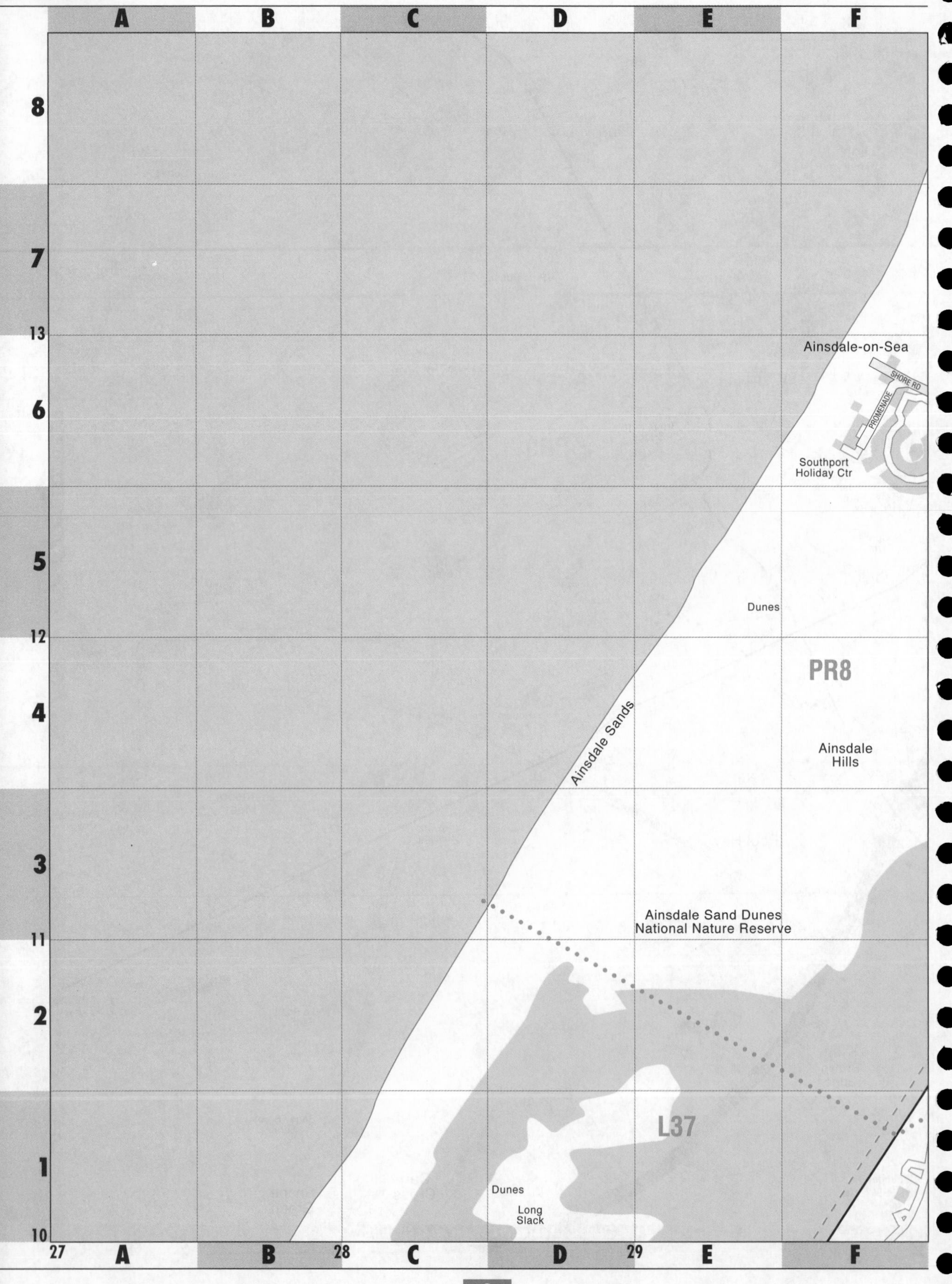

Ainsdale-on-Sea

SHORE RD

PROMENADE

Southport
Holiday Ctr

Dunes

PR8

Ainsdale Sands

Ainsdale
Hills

Ainsdale Sand Dunes
National Nature Reserve

L37

Dunes

Long
Slack

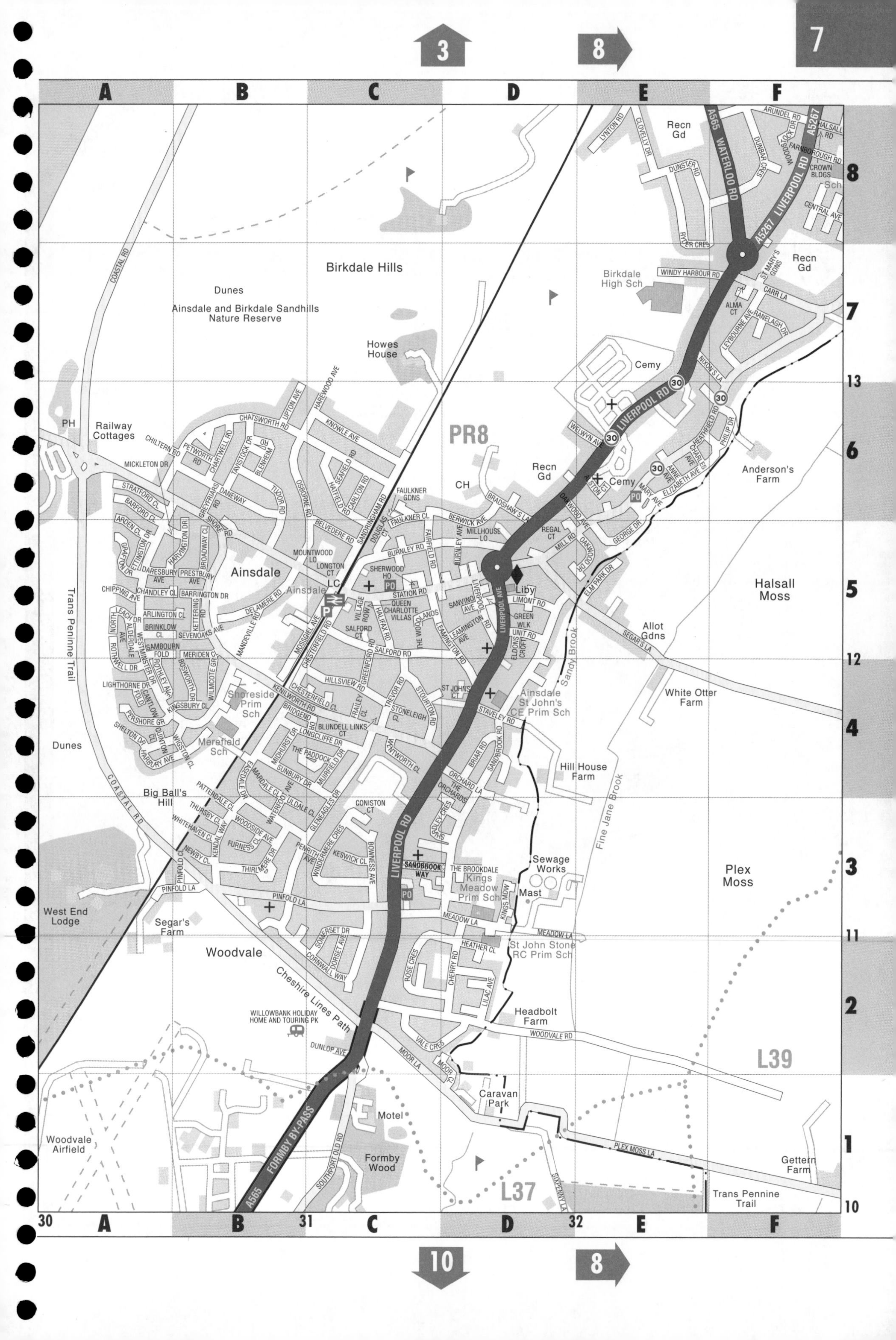
3
8
A
B
C
D
E
F
Birkdale Hills
Dunes
Ainsdale and Birkdale Sandhills Nature Reserve
Howes House
COASTAL RD
Recn Gd
A565 WATERLOO RD
A5267 LIVERPOOL RD
A5267
ARUNDEL RD
HALSALL RD
FARNBOROUGH RD
CROWN BLDGS
Sch
CENTRAL AVE
LYNTON RD
CLOVELLY DR
DUNSTER RD
DUNBAR CRES
RYDER CRES
Birkdale High Sch
WINDY HARBOUR RD
ST MARY'S GDNS
CARR LA
ALMA CT
RANELAGH DR
LEYBOURNE AVE
NIXON'S LA
Cemy
LIVERPOOL RD
WELWYN AVE
HEATHFIELD RD
PHILIP DR
Anderson's Farm
PR8
Recn Gd
CH
ALSTON CT
Cemy
PO
MARY AVE
ELIZABETH AVE
ANNE AVE
CHARLES CT
GEORGE DR
OAKWOOD AVE
BRADSHAW'S LA
REGAL CT
MILL RD
OAKWOOD DR
ELM PARK DR
Halsall Moss
PH
Railway Cottages
CHILTERN RD
MICKLETON DR
PETWORTH RD
CHARTWELL RD
TAVISTOCK DR
BLENHEIM RD
CHATSWORTH RD
UPTON AVE
HAREWOOD AVE
KNOWLE AVE
SEAFIELD RD
HATFIELD RD
CARLTON RD
FAULKNER GDNS
FAULKNER CL
STRATFORD CL
BARFORD CL
ARDEN CL
GRAFTON DR
DANEWAY
GREYFRIARS RD
TUDOR RD
OSBORNE RD
BELVEDERE RD
SANDRINGHAM RD
DOUGLAS CT
BERWICK AVE
MILLHOUSE LO
SHORE RD
HARVINGTON DR
BROADWAY CL
MOUNTWOOD LO
LONGTON CT
BURNLEY RD
FAIRFIELD RD
BURNLEY AVE
Ainsdale
DARESBURY AVE
PRESTBURY AVE
CHIPPING AVE
CHANDLEY CL
BARRINGTON DR
ARLINGTON CL
BRINKLOW CL
SEVENOAKS AVE
SAMBOURN FOLD
MERIDEN CL
KETTERING RD
DELAMERE RD
MANDEVILLE RD
Ainsdale
LC
SHERWOOD HO
PO
STATION RD
QUEEN CHARLOTTE VILLAS
VILLAGE ROW
HALIFAX RD
SALFORD CT
SALFORD RD
THE WOODLANDS
SANVINO AVE
LEAMINGTON AVE
LEAMINGTON RD
LIVERPOOL AVE
Liby
LIMONT RD
GREEN WLK
UNIT RD
ELDONS CROFT
Allot Gdns
SEGAR'S LA
Trans Pennine Trail
WESTMINSTER DR
ROTHLEY AVE
BOSWORTH DR
WILMCOTE GR
LIGHTHORNE DR
CANTLOW FOLD
KINGSBURY CL
Shoreside Prim Sch
KENILWORTH RD
CHESTERFIELD CL
CHESTERFIELD RD
MOSSGIEL AVE
HILLSVIEW RD
GREENFORD RD
TREVOR RD
STOURTON RD
STONELEIGH CL
ST JOHN'S CT
Sandy Brook
Ainsdale St John's CE Prim Sch
White Otter Farm
BRIDGEND
BLUNDELL LINKS CT
FRAILEY CL
STAVELEY RD
PERSHORE GR
SHELTON DR
QUINTON CL
HARBURY AVE
WIGSTON CL
Merefield Sch
LONGCLIFFE DR
MIDHURST DR
THE PADDOCK
SUNBURY DR
MUIRFIELD RD
WENTWORTH CL
BRIAR RD
SANDBROOK RD
ORCHARD LA
THE ORCHARDS
Hill House Farm
Dunes
Big Ball's Hill
PATTERDALE CL
EASEDALE DR
MARDALE CL
THURSBY CL
WHITEHAVEN CL
KENDAL WAY
WOODSIDE AVE
WATERLOO AVE
ULDALE CL
GLENEAGLES DR
CONISTON CT
HADLEY CRES
Fine Jane Brook
FURNESS CL
THIRLMERE DR
NEWBY CL
PENRITH AVE
WINDERMERE CRES
KESWICK CL
BOWNESS AVE
LIVERPOOL RD
SANDBROOK WAY
THE BROOKDALE
Kings Meadow Prim Sch
Sewage Works
Mast
Plex Moss
PINFOLD CL
PINFOLD LA
PINFOLD LA
PO
KINGS MDW
MEADOW LA
MEADOW LA
West End Lodge
Segar's Farm
Woodvale
SOMERSET DR
DORSET AVE
CORNWALL WAY
ROSE CRES
CHERRY RD
HEATHER CL
LILAC AVE
St John Stone RC Prim Sch
Cheshire Lines Path
Headbolt Farm
WILLOWBANK HOLIDAY HOME AND TOURING PK
WOODVALE RD
DUNLOP AVE
VALE CRES
MOOR LA
MOOR CL
L39
Caravan Park
Motel
A565 FORMBY BY-PASS
Woodvale Airfield
SOUTHPORT OLD RD
Formby Wood
PLEX MOSS LA
Gettern Farm
L37
SIXPENNY LA
Trans Pennine Trail
30
31
32
8
7
13
6
5
12
4
3
11
2
1
10
10
8

A B C D E F

BIRKDALE COP
HEATHEY LA
B5243

White Moss
Farm

Hodge's
Farm

PR8

8

Farnborough Road
Inf & Jun Schs

SHAFTESBURY AVE
SUFFOLK RD
ESSEX RD
HALSALL RD
BLYTHE MEWS
CENTRAL AVE
GUILDFORD RD
NEW CUT CL

Gorsehill
Farm

Fine Jane's Brook

Boundary Brook

HEADBOLT LA

LONDON LA

7

East Crantum
Farm

London
Farm

Renacres
Moss

13

King's
Covert

The
Willows

NEW CUT LA

Shirdley
Hill
SHAW CL

6

New
Moss

Short Ranks
Farm

SHAWS
GARTH

RENACRES LA

Old Canal

Halsall
Moss

CABIN LA

BARLOW'S LA

Manor House
Farm

5

Olverston
House

12

L39

HEADBOLT LA

4

SEGAR'S LA

New Cut Brook

Rain
Bag

Barn House
Farm

Front
Covert

SPENCER'S LA

3

MICHAEL'S LA

11

Heather
Farm

Green Kettle
House

2

Plex
Moss

Gettern Mere
Farm

CARR MOSS LA

PLUMPTON LA

Colonel's
Holt

1

Holt
Farm

Carr
Moss

10

PLEX MOSS LA

33 A B 34 C D 35 E F

Lancashire STREET ATLAS

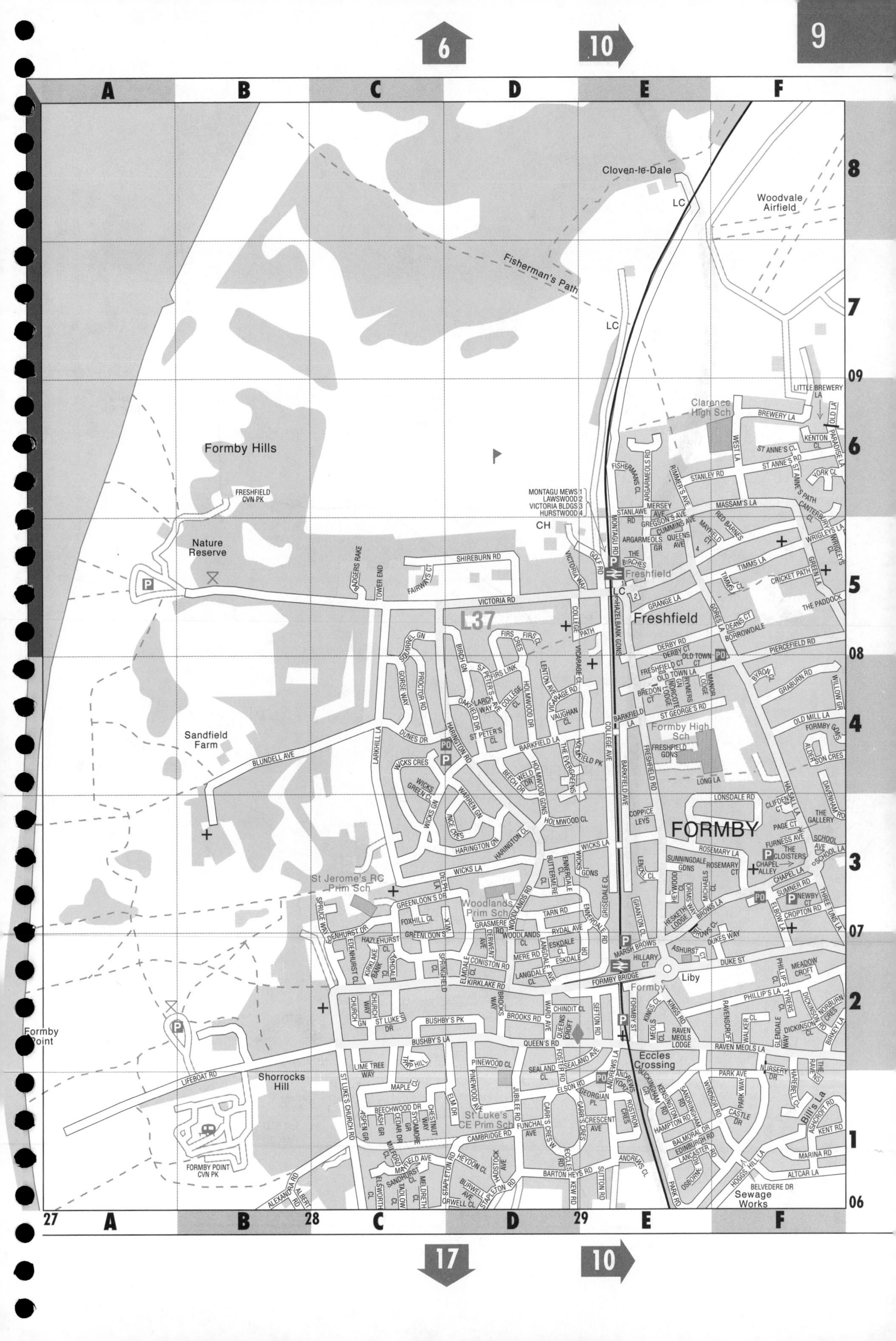
6
10
A
B
C
D
E
F
Cloven-le-Dale
LC
Woodvale Airfield
8
Fisherman's Path
7
09
Formby Hills
Clarence High Sch
LITTLE BREWERY LA
BREWERY LA
OLD LA
KENTON CL
PARADISE LA
ST ANNE'S CL
ST ANNE'S RD
WEST LA
6
FISHERMANS CL
ARGARMEOLS RD
RIMMER'S AVE
STANLEY RD
YORK CL
ST ANNE'S PATH
FRESHFIELD CVN PK
MONTAGU MEWS 1
LAWSWOOD 2
VICTORIA BLDGS 3
HURSTWOOD 4
CH
STANLAWE RD
MERSEY AVE
GREGSON'S AVE
CUMMINS AVE
MASSAM'S LA
CANTERBURY CL
MONTAGU RD
ARGARMEOLS GR
QUEENS AVE
MAYFIELD CT
RED BARNES
WRIGLEY'S LA
WRIGLEYS CL
Nature Reserve
SHIREBURN RD
RODGERS RAKE
TOWER END
FAIRWAYS CT
VICTORIA WAY
GOLF RD
THE BIRCHES
Freshfield
TIMMS LA
TIMMS CL
CRICKET PATH
GREEN LA
5
VICTORIA RD
L37
HAZELBANK GDNS
GRANGE LA
Freshfield
GORES LA
DEANS CT
BORROWDALE
THE PADDOCK
COLLEGE PATH
FIRS CRES
FIRS CL
SQUIRREL GN
BIRCH GN
ST PETER'S AVE
FIRS LINK
DERBY RD
DERBY CT
OLD TOWN CT
PO
PIERCEFIELD RD
08
VICARAGE CL
GORSE WAY
PROCTOR RD
LARCH WAY
COLLEGE CL
HOLMWOOD DR
LENTON AVE
VICARAGE RD
FRESHFIELD CT
OLD TOWN LA
BREDON CL
NORCOTE LODGE
RYMERS GN
MANOR LODGE
BYRON CL
GRABURN RD
WILLOW GR
OAKFIELD DR
VAUGHAN CL
BARKFIELD LA
ST GEORGE'S RD
OLD MILL LA
Sandfield Farm
DUNES DR
HARINGTON RD
ST PETER'S CL
COLLEGE AVE
Formby High Sch
FORMBY GDNS
4
LARKHILL LA
BARKFIELD LA
THE EVERGREENS
HOLYFIELD PK
FRESHFIELD GDNS
ALDERSON CRES
BLUNDELL AVE
WICKS CRES
WELD DR
BEECH DR
HOLMWOOD GDNS
FRESHFIELD RD
BARKFIELD AVE
LONG LA
WICKS GREEN CL
WARREN GN
LONSDALE RD
CLIFDEN CT
DAVENHAM RD
INCE CRES
WICKS GN
HOLMWOOD CL
COPPICE LEYS
FORMBY
THE GALLERY
HALSALL LA
PAGE CT
SCHOOL AVE
HARINGTON GN
HARINGTON CL
WICKS LA
ROSEMARY LA
FURNESS AVE
SCHOOL LA
THE CLOISTERS
3
WICKS LA
WICKS GDNS
LENDEL CL
SUNNINGDALE GDNS
ROSEMARY CT
CHAPEL ALLEY
St Jerome's RC Prim Sch
DELPH LA
ENNERDALE CL
BUTTERMERE CL
CHAPEL LA
SPRUCE WAY
GREENLOON'S DR
Woodlands Prim Sch
WOODLANDS RD
HEYWOOD CL
DRAMS WAY
MICHAELS CL
SUMNER RD
NEWBY CT
ELBOW LA
FOXHILL CL
KIRK CL
GRISEDALE CL
GRANTON CL
HESKETH LODGE
BROWS LA
CROPTON RD
THREE TUNS LA
DENHURST DR
TARN RD
HAZLEHURST CL
GREENLOON'S
GRASMERE RD
RYDAL AVE
ENNERDALE RD
BROWS CL
DUKES WAY
07
EDENHURST CL
KIRKLAKE BANK
ASHDALE CL
DERWENT AVE
WOODLANDS CL
ESKDALE CL
MARSH BROWS
HILLARY CT
ASHURST CL
SPRINGFIELD CL
ELMDALE CL
CONISTON RD
MERE RD
LANGDALE AVE
ESKDALE DR
DUKE ST
MEADOW CROFT
LANGDALE CL
KIRKLAKE RD
FORMBY BRIDGE
Formby
Liby
PHILLIP'S CL
2
CHURCH GN
CHURCH WAY
ST LUKE'S DR
BROOKS WAY
WARD AVE
CHINDIT CL
SEFTON RD
FORMBY ST
KINGS CL
KINGS RD
RAVENSCROFT
PHILLIP'S LA
TYRERS CL
DICKINSON RD
NORBURN CRES
BUSHBY'S PK
BROOKS RD
CROFT
ENGLEFIELD
MEOLS CL
RAVEN MEOLS LODGE
WALKER CL
GLENDALE WAY
DICKINSON CL
BIRKEY LA
Formby Point
BUSHBY'S LA
QUEEN'S RD
Eccles Crossing
RAVEN MEOLS LA
LIME TREE WAY
TRAP HILL
PINEWOOD CL
SEALAND CL
SEALAND AVE
FOSTER RD
ANDREWS LA
ANDREWS YORK
NURSERY DR
THE RAVENS
LIFEBOAT RD
Shorrocks Hill
MAPLE CL
PINEWOOD AVE
ELSON RD
GEORGIAN PL
BUCKINGHAM GR
KENSINGTON RD
WINDSOR RD
PARK AVE
PARK WAY
HAREBELL CL
Bill's La
ASHCROFT RD
BEECHWOOD DR
CHESTNUT WAY
ELM DR
ROSTRON CRES
ST LUKE'S CHURCH RD
ASPEN GR
ASH GR
CEDAR DR
SYCAMORE GR
St Luke's CE Prim Sch
JUBILEE RD
FUNCHAL AVE
CARR'S CRES W
CARR'S CRES
CRESCENT AVE
HAMPTON RD
SANDRINGHAM RD
BALMORAL DR
CASTLE DR
KENT RD
1
CAMBRIDGE RD
EDINBURGH RD
MARINA RD
MILFORD CL
MAYFIELD AVE
HEYDON CL
HADSTOCK AVE
ECCLES RD
ANDREWS CL
LANCASTER RD
OSBORNE
HOGGS HILL LA
ALTCAR LA
FORMBY POINT CVN PK
ALEXANDRA RD
ALBERT RD
ELSWORTH CL
SANDHURST CL
TADLOW CL
MELDRETH CL
STAPLETON RD
BURWELL AVE
ORWELL CL
BURWELL CL
BARTON HEYS RD
KEW RD
SUTTON RD
PARK RD
BELVEDERE DR
Sewage Works
06
27
28
29
17
10

A · B · C · D · E · F

8

Woodvale Airfield

Formby Hall

Formby Hall Farm

Golf Driving Range

Camp Site

CH

A565

Formby Moss

7

Sandy Brook

Broad La

Trans Pennine Trail

White Grass

Fine Jane Brook

09

Eight Acre La

North Moss La

North Moss Farm

Shalom

GORSEY LA

Fine Jane Pumping Sta

Sixteen Acre La

Rose Farm

CHESHIRE LINES PATH

6

The Rydinge · Dales Wlk · Hawksworth Dr · Hawksworth · Tushore · Longton Dr · Dorsefield · Deansgate La · Brackenway · Croft Wats · Heapey · Spymers

South Moss Farm

L39

5

Wrigleys La · The Paddock · Piercefield Ct · Ryeground La · New Rd · Clifton Rd

SOUTHPORT RD · B5424

Trinity St Peter's CE Prim Sch

Primrose Cl · Mount House Cl · Deansgate La · Mount House Rd · FORMBY BY-PASS

Warren Farm

HEATHER CL

Pasture La

Downholland Brook

MOSS LA

08

Freshfield Prim Sch

MOSS SIDE

LITTLE HEY LA

L37

DOWNHOLLAND MOSS LA

Thirty Acre La

Downholland Moss

4

Old Mill La · Cable St · Dobbs Dr · Hayward Ct · Watchyard La · Smithy Gn

Southern Heys Farm

Altcar La

CHURCH RD

Whitehouse La · Whitehouse Ave · Cattan Gn · Moss Cl · Shaw Cres · Gardner Rd · Devon Farms La · Norris Way · Mawdsley

FORMBY

MITTEN'S LA

Davenham Rd · Church Cl · Church Close Ct · Kenyon's La

SCHOOL LA

Bull Cop

Formby Moss

3

Flaxfield Rd · Priesthouse La · Freshfield Rd · Chapel House · Burlington Ave · Lowes Gn · Glenmarsh Way

Our Lady of Compassion RC Prim Sch

Formby Bsns Pk

STEPHENSON WAY

Formby's Farm

YORK RD · Rosebay Cl · B5424

CROSS GN · B5195

ALTCAR RD

07

Cross Grn · Cross Path · Whalley Dr · Bolton Rd · Esson · Roman's La · Byland Ct · Buckfast

Rose Nursery

BROAD LA

2

The Nurseries · Hawthorne Cres · Ditchfield · Marshal La · Seafield · Redgate · Redcar · Cartmel Dr · Abbey Cl · Altars · Friars Wlk

Superstore

1 BATTLE WAY
2 CLEVE WAY
3 CROWLAND WAY
4 KIRKSTALL DR
5 FORMBY LA
6 CLOISTER GN

Sutton's Farm

Tyrer's Farm

LORD SEFTON WAY

BROAD LA

Coronation Ave · Conifer Ct · Raven Meols La · Thirlmere Ave

Redgate Prim Sch

Priory Cl · Tintern Ave · Abbot's Way · Royal Cres · Royal Cl

Altcar Hall

Tatlock's Farm

ASPINALL CRES

BROAD LA · B5195

1

LIVERPOOL RD · Kent Ave · Kent Rd · Marina Rd · Altcar La

Mayflower Ind Est · Gable Mews · Monks Cl · Monks Dr · River Cl · Saxon Hook

PO

NEW CSWY

ENGINE LA

DOCTOR'S LA

Great Altcar

LIGHTHOUSE LA

B5424

A565

Little Altcar

06

30 · A · B · 31 · C · D · 32 · E · F

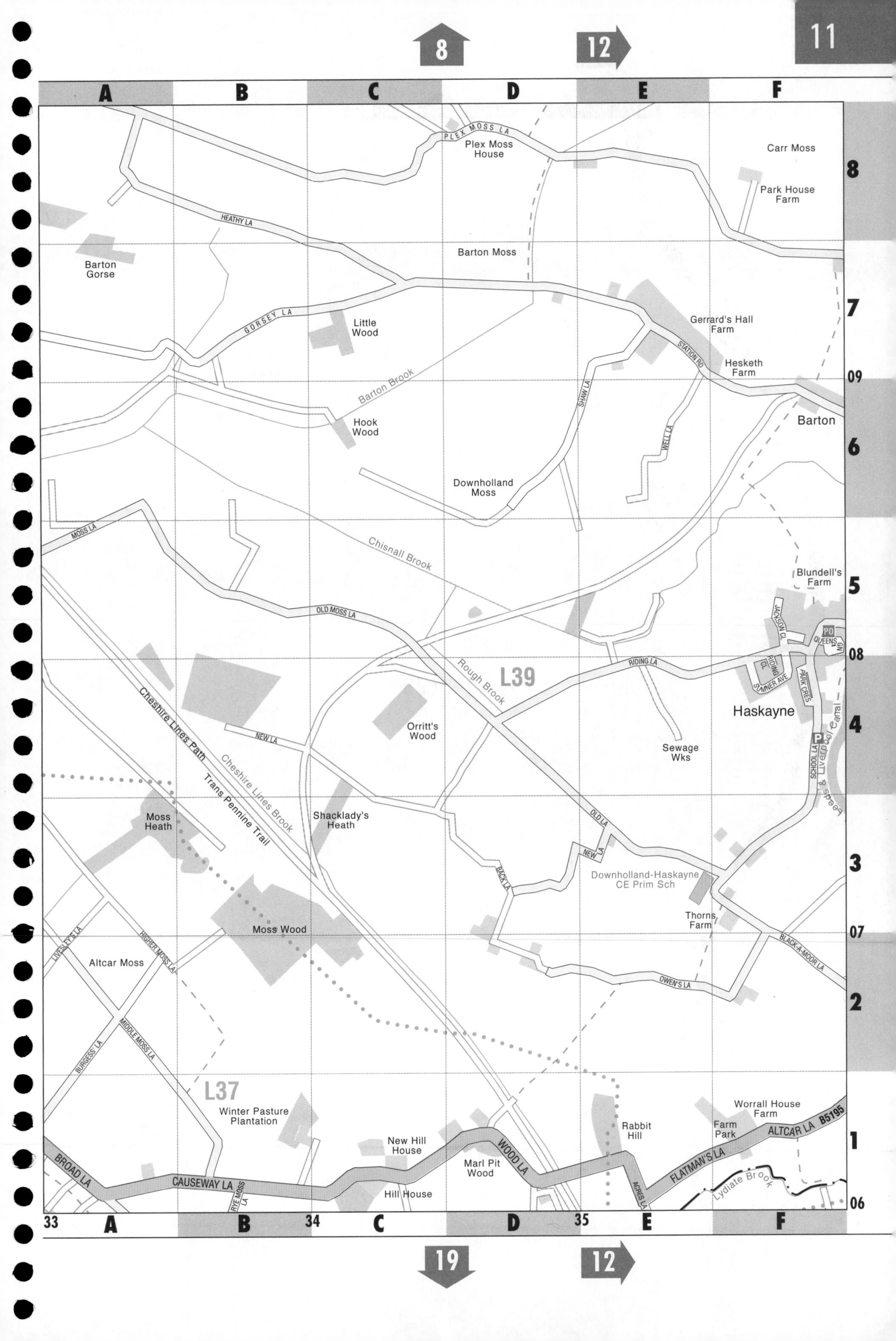

A   B   C   D   E   F

8

Carr Moss

Park House
Farm

Plex Moss
House

PLEX MOSS LA

HEATHY LA

Barton Moss

7

Barton
Gorse

Gerrard's Hall
Farm

Hesketh
Farm

09

GORSEY LA

Little
Wood

Barton Brook

SHAW LA

STATION RD

WELL LA

Barton

6

Hook
Wood

Downholland
Moss

MOSS LA

Chisnall Brook

Blundell's
Farm

5

OLD MOSS LA

L39

Rough Brook

RIDING LA

JACKSON CL

PO
QUEENS

GW

08

Cheshire Lines Path

NEW LA

Orritt's
Wood

SUMNER AVE

PARK CRES

SCHOOL LA

Haskayne

4

Trans Pennine Trail

Cheshire Lines Brook

Shacklady's
Heath

Sewage
Wks

OLD LA

P

Leeds & Liverpool Canal

Moss
Heath

BACK LA

NEW LA

Downholland-Haskayne
CE Prim Sch

3

07

HIGHER MOSS LA

Moss Wood

Thorns
Farm

BLACK-A-MOOR LA

Altcar Moss

OWEN'S LA

2

LIVESLEY'S LA

MIDDLE MOSS LA

Worrall House
Farm

BURGESS LA

L37

Winter Pasture
Plantation

Rabbit
Hill

Farm
Park

ALTCAR LA B5195

1

New Hill
House

WOOD LA

Marl Pit
Wood

FLATMAN'S LA

ACRES LA

Lydiate Brook

BROAD LA

CAUSEWAY LA

RYE MOSS LA

Hill House

06

33   A   B   34   C   D   35   E   F

11

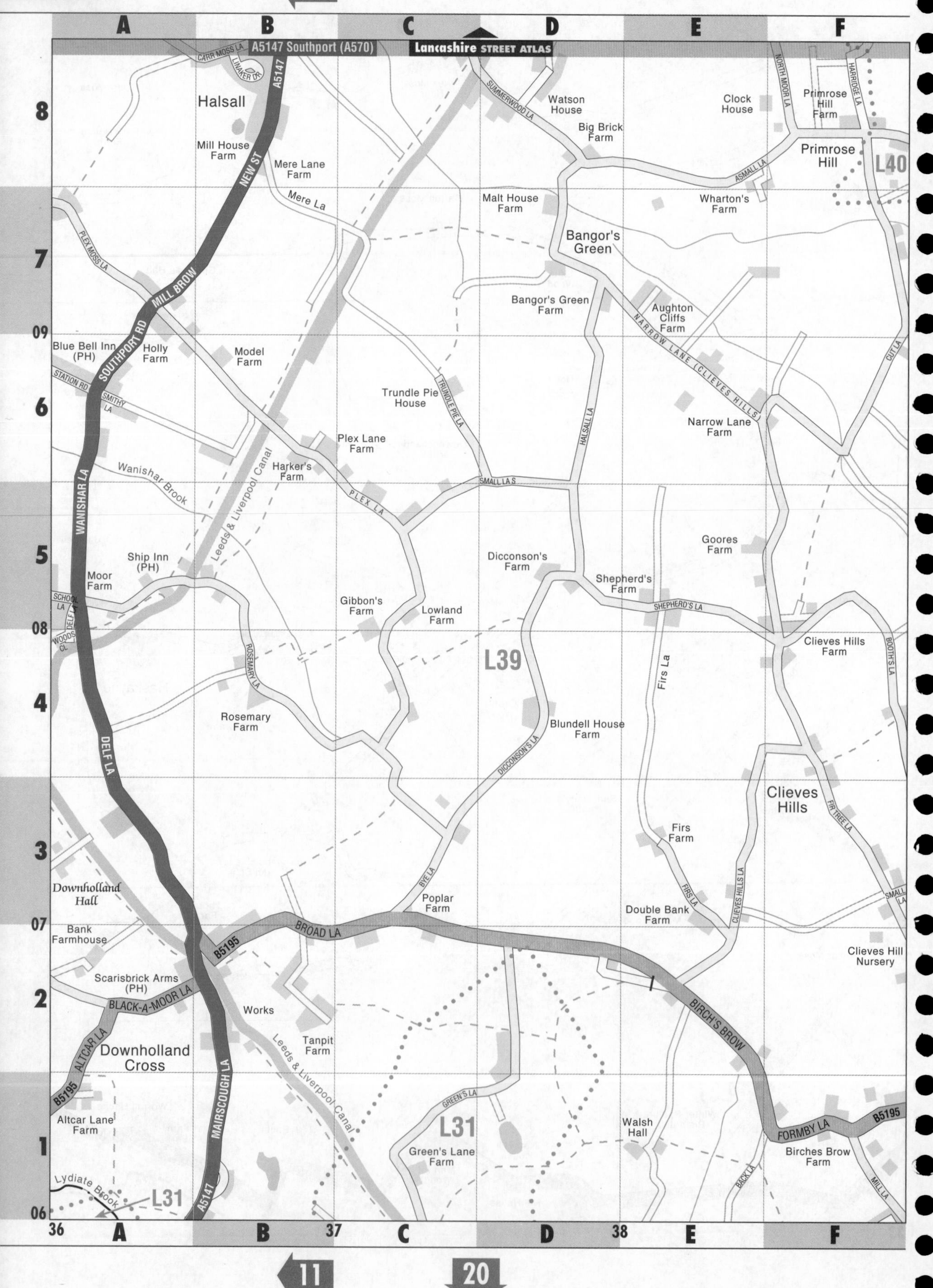
A5147 Southport (A570)
Lancashire STREET ATLAS
Halsall
Mill House Farm
Mere Lane Farm
Mere La
Watson House
Big Brick Farm
Clock House
Primrose Hill Farm
Primrose Hill
L40
Malt House Farm
Wharton's Farm
Bangor's Green
Bangor's Green Farm
Aughton Cliffs Farm
NARROW LANE (CLIEVES HILLS)
Blue Bell Inn (PH)
Holly Farm
Model Farm
Trundle Pie House
Narrow Lane Farm
Plex Lane Farm
Harker's Farm
Wanishar Brook
Leeds & Liverpool Canal
Goores Farm
Ship Inn (PH)
Moor Farm
Dicconson's Farm
Shepherd's Farm
Gibbon's Farm
Lowland Farm
L39
Clieves Hills Farm
Firs La
Rosemary Farm
Blundell House Farm
Clieves Hills
Firs Farm
Downholland Hall
Poplar Farm
Double Bank Farm
Bank Farmhouse
BROAD LA
Clieves Hill Nursery
Scarisbrick Arms (PH)
BLACK-A-MOOR LA
Works
BIRCH'S BROW
Tanpit Farm
Downholland Cross
Altcar Lane Farm
L31
Walsh Hall
FORMBY LA
B5195
Green's Lane Farm
Birches Brow Farm
Lydiate Brook
MAIRSCOUGH LA
A5147
NEW ST
MILL BROW
SOUTHPORT RD
WANISHAR LA
DELF LA
PLEX LA
PLEX MOSS LA
HALSALL LA
DICCONSON'S LA
SHEPHERD'S LA
ROSEMARY LA
TRUNDLE PIE LA
SMALL LA S
SUMMERWOOD LA
NORTH MOOR LA
HARRIDGE LA
ASMALL LA
CUT LA
BOOTH'S LA
FIR TREE LA
CLIEVES HILLS LA
FIRS LA
BYE LA
GREEN'S LA
BACK LA
MILL LA
ALTCAR LA
STATION RD
SMITHY LA
SCHOOL LA
WOODS CL
CARR MOSS LA
LINAKER DR
A B C D E F
8 7 6 5 4 3 2 1
09 08 07 06
36 37 38

11
20

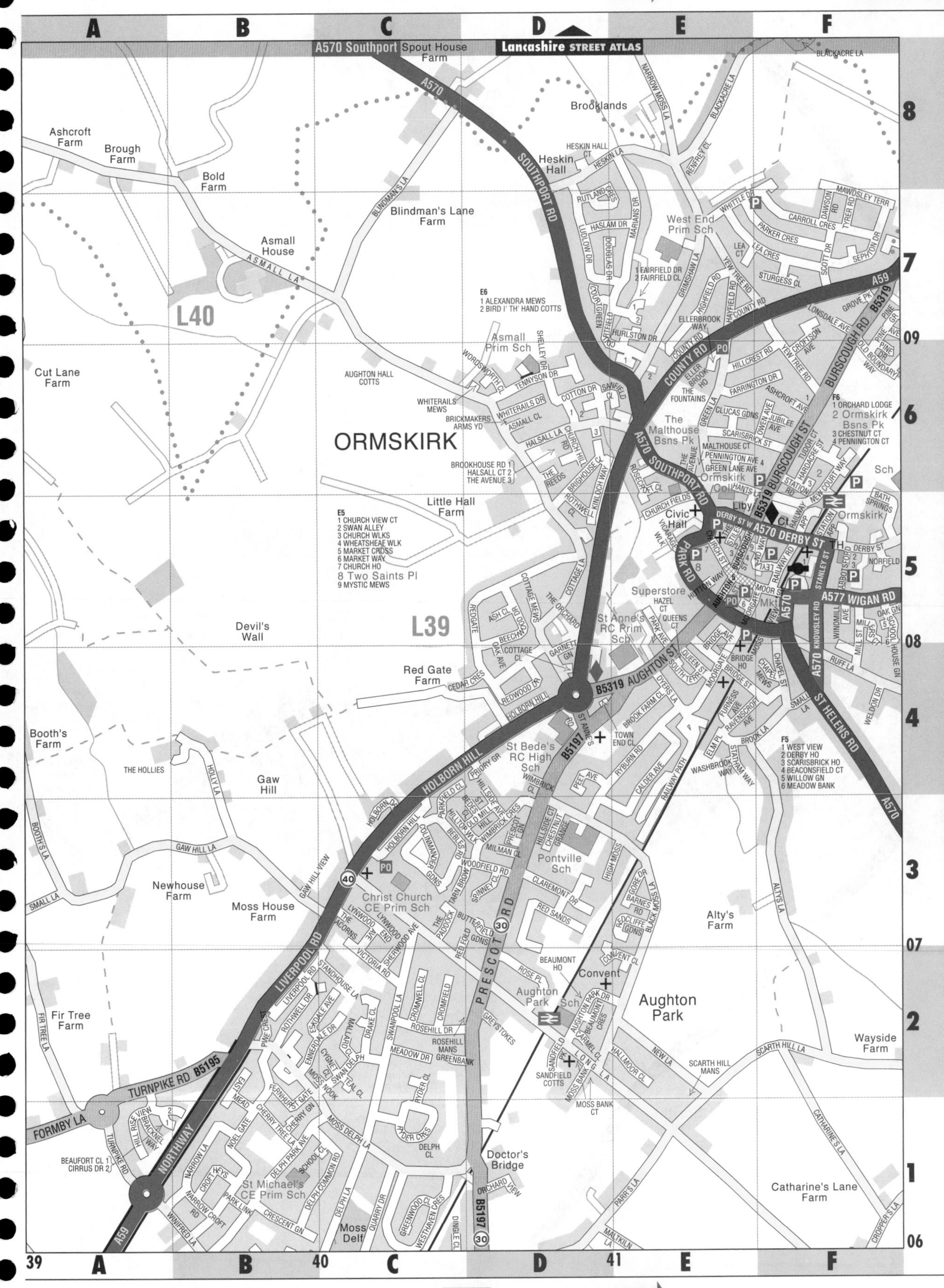
A570 Southport
Lancashire STREET ATLAS
Spout House Farm
Brooklands
Ashcroft Farm
Brough Farm
Bold Farm
Heskin Hall
Blindman's Lane Farm
Asmall House
L40
West End Prim Sch
Cut Lane Farm
Asmall Prim Sch
ORMSKIRK
The Malthouse Bsns Pk
Ormskirk Coll
Civic Hall
Little Hall Farm
Ormskirk
Devil's Wall
L39
Superstore
St Anne's RC Prim Sch
Red Gate Farm
Booth's Farm
St Bede's RC High Sch
Gaw Hill
Pontville Sch
Newhouse Farm
Moss House Farm
Christ Church CE Prim Sch
Alty's Farm
Fir Tree Farm
Convent
Aughton Park
Aughton Park Sch
Wayside Farm
Doctor's Bridge
St Michael's CE Prim Sch
Catharine's Lane Farm
Moss Delf
E6 1 ALEXANDRA MEWS 2 BIRD I' TH' HAND COTTS
E5 1 CHURCH VIEW CT 2 SWAN ALLEY 3 CHURCH WLKS 4 WHEATSHEAF WLK 5 MARKET CROSS 6 MARKET WAY 7 CHURCH HO 8 Two Saints Pl 9 MYSTIC MEWS
F6 1 ORCHARD LODGE 2 Ormskirk Bsns Pk 3 CHESTNUT CT 4 PENNINGTON CT
F5 1 WEST VIEW 2 DERBY HO 3 SCARISBRICK HO 4 BEACONSFIELD CT 5 WILLOW GN 6 MEADOW BANK
1 FAIRFIELD DR 2 FAIRFIELD CL
BROOKHOUSE RD 1 HALSALL CT 2 THE AVENUE 3
BEAUFORT CL 1 CIRRUS DR 2
A570 DERBY ST
A577 WIGAN RD
B5319 BURSCOUGH ST
B5319 AUGHTON ST
SOUTHPORT RD
COUNTY RD
HOLBORN HILL
LIVERPOOL RD
PRESCOT RD
ST HELENS RD
TURNPIKE RD B5195
NORTHWAY
A59
39
40
41
06
07
08
09

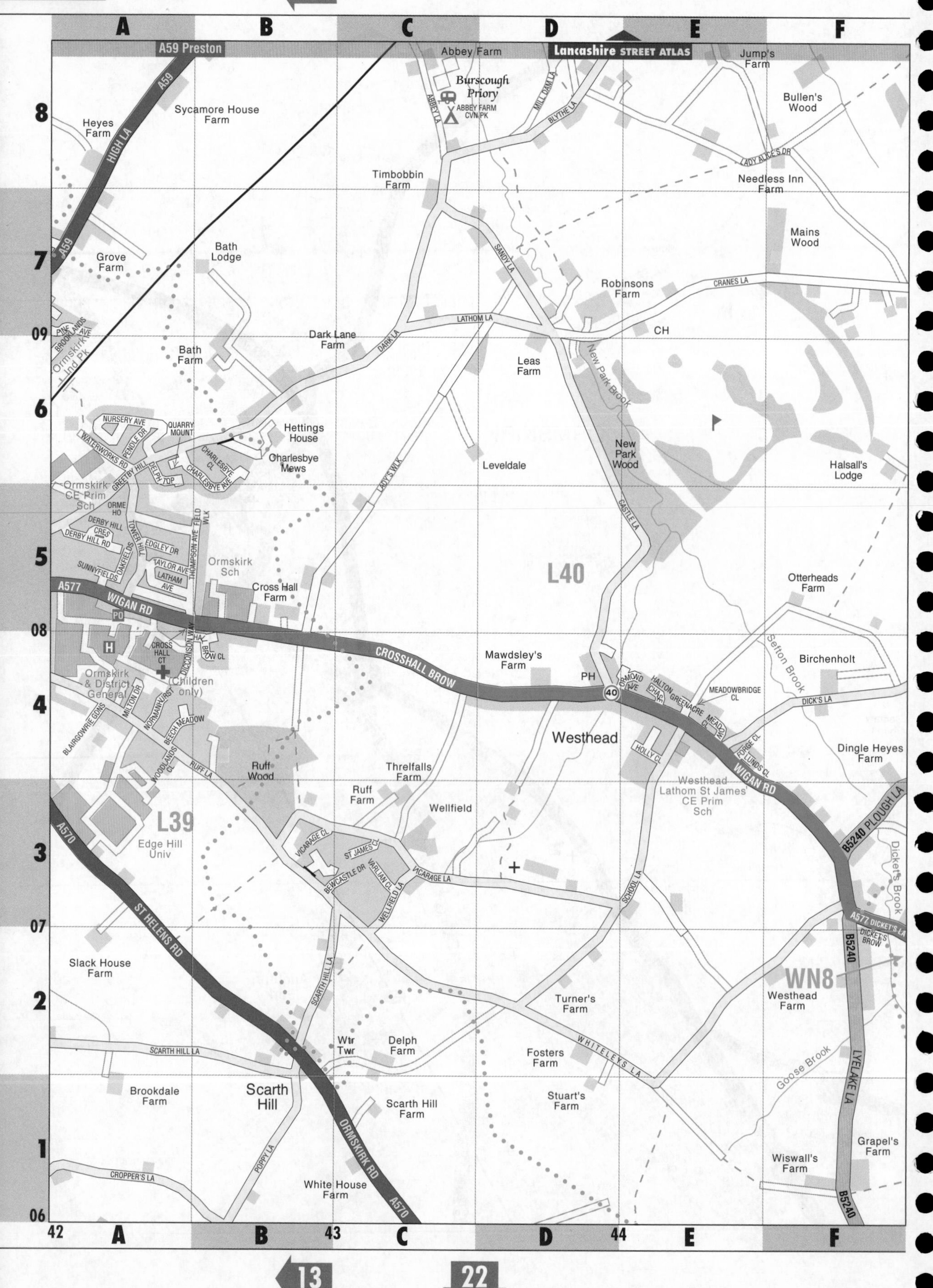

A B C D E F

Lancashire STREET ATLAS

8

7

09

6

5

08

4

3

07

2

1

06

42 A | B 43 C | D 44 E | F

A59 Preston

Heyes Farm

HIGH LA

A59

Sycamore House Farm

Abbey Farm

Burscough Priory

ABBEY LA

MILL DAM LA

Jump's Farm

Bullen's Wood

BLYTHE LA

LADY ALICE'S DR

Needless Inn Farm

Mains Wood

Timbobbin Farm

Bath Lodge

Grove Farm

A59

PINE AVE

BROADLANDS AVE

Ormskirk Trad Ind Pk

Bath Farm

Dark Lane Farm

DARK LA

SANDY LA

LATHOM LA

Robinsons Farm

CRANES LA

CH

New Park Brook

Leas Farm

Leveldale

New Park Wood

Halsall's Lodge

NURSERY AVE

QUARRY MOUNT

Hettings House

Charlesbye Mews

WATERWORKS RD

PENDLE DR

GREETBY HILL

DELPH TOP

CHARLESBYE CL

CHARLESBYE AVE

Ormskirk CE Prim Sch

ORME HO

DERBY HILL CRES

DERBY HILL RD

ORME HILL

TOWER HILL

EDGLEY DR

FIELD WLK

THOMPSON AVE

LADY'S WLK

CASTLE LA

L40

Otterheads Farm

SUNNYFIELDS

DIXKFIELDS

TAYLOR AVE

LATHAM AVE

Ormskirk Sch

Cross Hall Farm

Sefton Brook

Birchenholt

A577

WIGAN RD

PO

H

Ormskirk & District General

CROSS HALL CT

(Children only)

DICCONSON WAY

CHAC

BROW CL

CROSSHALL BROW

Mawdsley's Farm

PH

PH 40

DAVID AVE

CHAC

HALTON GREENACRE

MEADOWBRIDGE CL

MEADOW CL

DICK'S LA

Dingle Heyes Farm

BLAIRGOWRIE GDNS

MILL TOW DR

NORMAN WAY

BEECH MEADOW

Ruff Wood

WOODLANDS CL

RUFF LA

Ruff Farm

Threlfalls Farm

Wellfield

Westhead

HOLLY CL

Westhead Lathom St James CE Prim Sch

FORGE CL

LUNDS CL

WIGAN RD

B5240 PLOUGH LA

Dicket's Brook

L39

A570

Edge Hill Univ

VICARAGE CL

ST JAMES CL

BLNCASTLE DR

WELLAN CL

VICARAGE LA

WELLFIELD LA

SCHOOL LA

A577 DICKET'S LA

B5240

DICKET'S BROW

WN8

ST HELENS RD

Slack House Farm

SCARTH HILL LA

Turner's Farm

Westhead Farm

SCARTH HILL LA

Wtr Twr

Delph Farm

WHITELEYS LA

Fosters Farm

Stuart's Farm

Goose Brook

L'YELAKE LA

Brookdale Farm

Scarth Hill

POPPY LA

ORMSKIRK RD

Scarth Hill Farm

A570

White House Farm

Wiswall's Farm

Grapel's Farm

B5240

CROPPER'S LA

SCARTH HILL LA

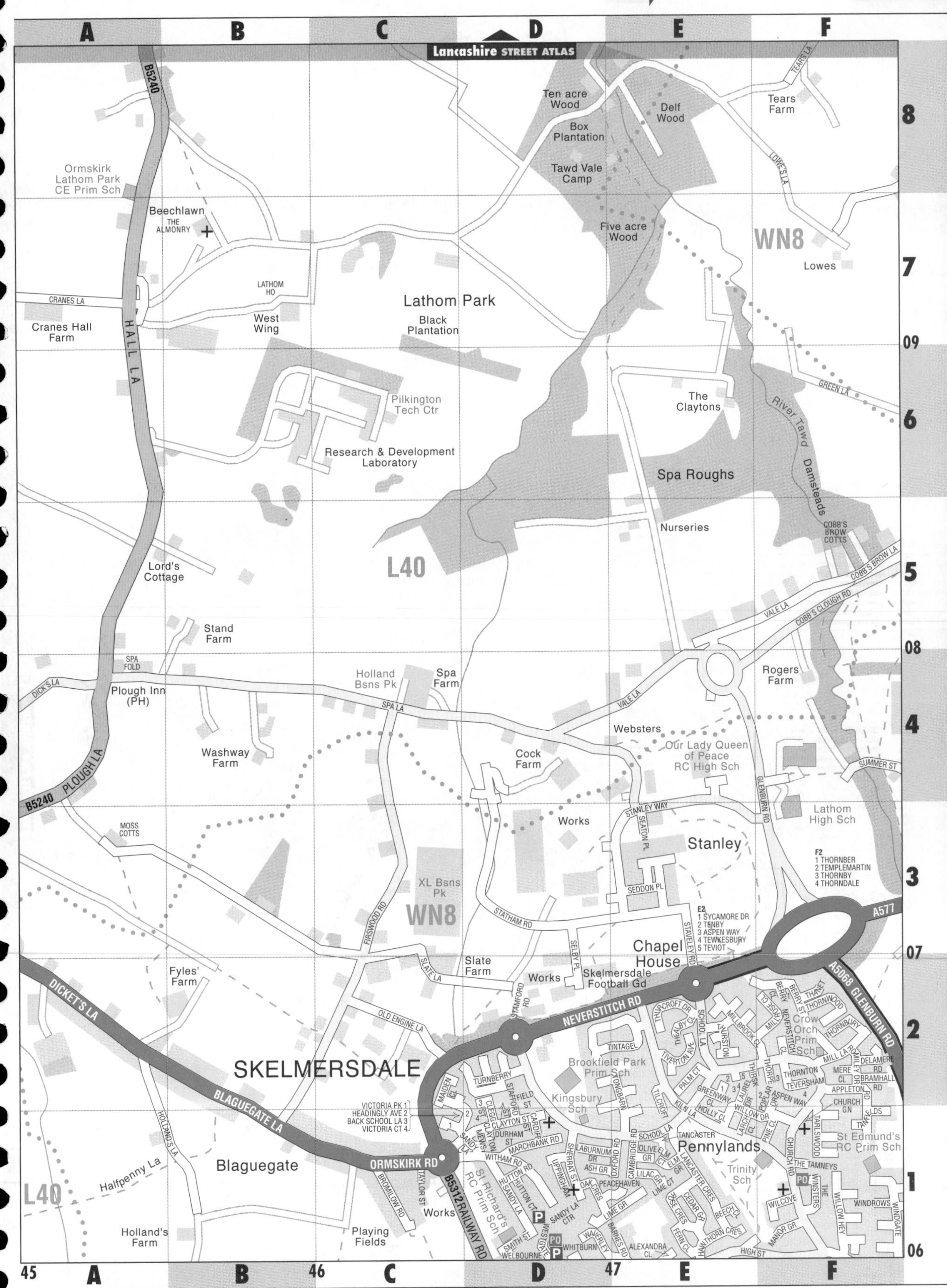

Lancashire STREET ATLAS

A   B   C   D   E   F

8

B5240

Ten acre Wood

Delf Wood

Tears Farm

Ormskirk Lathom Park CE Prim Sch

Box Plantation

Beechlawn
THE ALMONRY

Tawd Vale Camp

LOWES LA

WN8

7

LATHOM HO

CRANES LA

West Wing

Five acre Wood

Lowes

HALL LA

Cranes Hall Farm

Lathom Park

Black Plantation

09

GREEN LA

River Tawd

6

Pilkington Tech Ctr

The Claytons

Damsteads

Research & Development Laboratory

Spa Roughs

COBB'S BROW COTTS

Lord's Cottage

L40

Nurseries

COBB'S BROW LA

5

Stand Farm

VALE LA

COBB'S CLOUGH RD

SPA FOLD

08

DICK'S LA

Plough Inn (PH)

Holland Bsns Pk

Spa Farm

Rogers Farm

SPA LA

VALE LA

4

Websters

SUMMER ST

B5240 PLOUGH LA

Washway Farm

Cock Farm

Our Lady Queen of Peace RC High Sch

MOSS COTTS

Works

Lathom High Sch

STANLEY WAY

SEATON PL

Stanley

GLENBURN RD

F2
1 THORNBER
2 TEMPLEMARTIN
3 THORNBY
4 THORNDALE

3

XL Bsns Pk

FRISWOOD RD

SEDDON PL

WN8

STATHAM RD

E2
1 SYCAMORE DR
2 TENBY
3 ASPEN WAY
4 TEWKESBURY
5 TEVIOT

A577

A5068 GLENBURN RD

07

Fyles' Farm

SLATE LA

Slate Farm

SELBY PL

Chapel House

THORNCROFT DR

CROW ORCH PRIM SCH

DICKET'S LA

Works

STAMFORD RD

Skelmersdale Football Gd

NEVERSTITCH RD

SCHOOL LA

MILLBROOK

Crow Orch Prim Sch

2

OLD ENGINE LA

Brookfield Park Prim Sch

TINTAGEL

TIVERTON CT

Kingsbury Sch

THORNE

TEVERSHAM

SKELMERSDALE

TURNBERRY

STAFFORD

GREENWAY

THORNTON

MERE CL

DELAMERE RD

BLAGUEGATE LA

VICTORIA PK 1
HEADINGLY AVE 2
BACK SCHOOL LA 3
VICTORIA CT 4

MAIDEN

CLEGG ST

CLAYTON ST

CARDIFF ST

HOLLY GR

WILLOW CR

APPLETON

BRAMHALL

CHURCH

St Edmund's RC Prim Sch

TAYLOR ST

MARCHBANK RD

LABURNUM DR

OLIVE GR

SCHOOL LA

TANCASTER

TARLSWOOD

1

Blaguegate

ORMSKIRK RD

WITHAM RD

SANDY LA

ASH GR

LILAC

LANCASTER CRES

THE TAMNEYS

THE WISTERS

L40

Halfpenny La

B5312 RAILWAY RD

St Richard's RC Prim Sch

HUTTON CT

SHERRAT ST

UPPINGHAM

LIME GR

CAMBRIDGE

Pennylands

Trinity Sch

WILLOW HEY

WILCOVE

Holland's Farm

Works

SMITH ST

SANDY LA REC CTR

DAK

PEACEHAVEN

BEECH

CEDAR GR

CLOSE CRES

FERN

WINDROWS

WINDGATE

HOLLAND'S LA

BROMILOW RD

Playing Fields

WELBOURNE

WHITBURN

ALEXANDRA CL

HIGH ST

MANOR GR

06

45   A   46   B   C   47   D   E   F

15

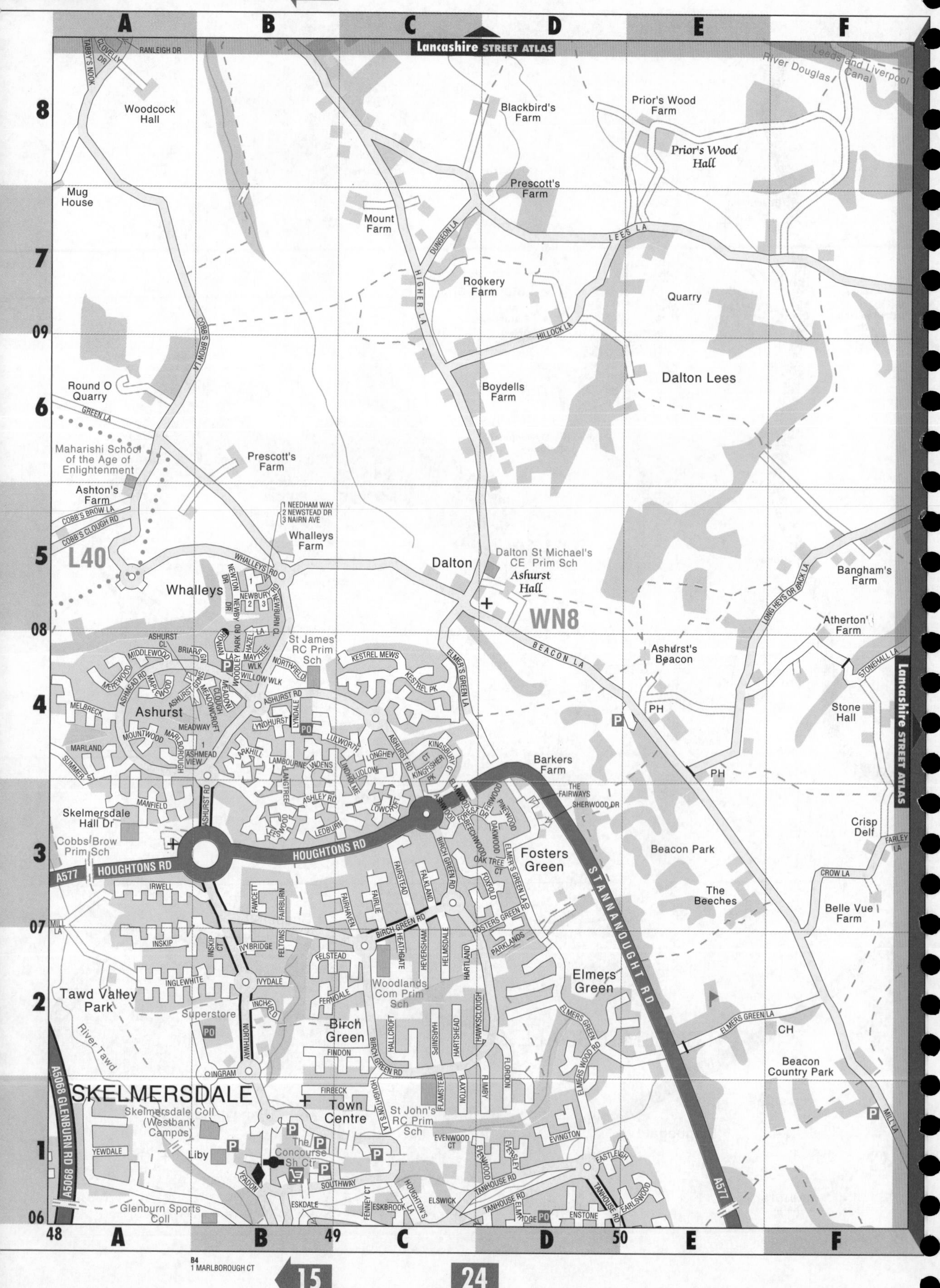
Lancashire STREET ATLAS
A
B
C
D
E
F
8
7
09
6
5
08
4
3
07
2
1
06
48
49
50
Woodcock Hall
Mug House
Blackbird's Farm
Prior's Wood Farm
Prior's Wood Hall
River Douglas
Leeds and Liverpool Canal
Prescott's Farm
Mount Farm
Lees La
Rookery Farm
Quarry
Hillock La
Higher La
Dungeon La
Cobb's Brow La
Round O Quarry
Green La
Boydells Farm
Dalton Lees
Maharishi School of the Age of Enlightenment
Ashton's Farm
Prescott's Farm
Whalleys Farm
Cobb's Brow La
Cobb's Clough Rd
L40
Whalleys
Dalton
Dalton St Michael's CE Prim Sch
Ashurst Hall
WN8
Bangham's Farm
Atherton's Farm
Ashurst's Beacon
Beacon La
Long Heys or Back La
Stonehall La
Stone Hall
St James' RC Prim Sch
Ashurst
Kestrel Mews
Elmer's Green La
Barkers Farm
PH
Skelmersdale Hall Dr
Cobbs Brow Prim Sch
Houghtons Rd
A577
Fosters Green
Stannanought Rd
Beacon Park
The Beeches
Crisp Delf
Farley La
Crow La
Belle Vue Farm
Tawd Valley Park
River Tawd
Superstore
Woodlands Com Prim Sch
Birch Green
Elmers Green
Elmers Green La
CH
Beacon Country Park
Mill La
A5068 Glenburn Rd
SKELMERSDALE
Skelmersdale Coll (Westbank Campus)
Town Centre
St John's RC Prim Sch
Liby
The Concourse Sh Ctr
Glenburn Sports Coll
Tanhouse Rd
1 Needham Way
2 Newstead Dr
3 Nairn Ave
B4
1 Marlborough Ct

15
24

A B C D E F

8

7

05

6

5

04

4

3

03

2

1

02

Mount
Pleasant

ALEXANDRA RD

ALBERT RD

ELSWORTH CL

STAPLETON RD

ST LUKE'S CHURCH RD

L37

Marsh
Farm

Range
High Sch

Raven Meols Hills

Raven Meols Hills
Nature Reserve

Sefton Coastal Path

DANGER AREA

Cambrai
Cottage

Battery
Cottage

Altcar Rifle Range

DANGER AREA

L38

DANGER AREA

DANGER AREA

Formby
Bank

Liverpool Bay

PARK CL
FOGGS HILL
LA

Sewage
Works

Works

Grange
Farm

Altcar Training
Camp

GRANGE RD

River Alt

LC

FLOODGATES RD

ST GEORGE'S RD

MARK RD

ST STEPHEN RD

HESTER CL

LAKE WAY

LOWER ALT RD

PO

ALT RD

NORTH
DUNES

WEST WAY

TUDOR
GDNS

RATHBONE
RD

VILLAGE WAY

THE
OUTLOOK

RIVERSIDE

SANDILANDS
GR

BLUNDELL
AVE

THE ROUND

WIGNALLS
MOW

BARNSIDE

SANDHILLS

MOORHOUSES

BRIARY CROFT

THORNBECK AVE

LARKHILL
GR

OLD ACRE

WITHINS FIELD

BLUNDELL GR

Hightown

ALTON CL

BRENTWOOD CL

WHITEFIELD CL

LANGLEY CL

OAKFIELD CL

RICHMOND CL

BLUNDELL RD

MAYFAIR CL

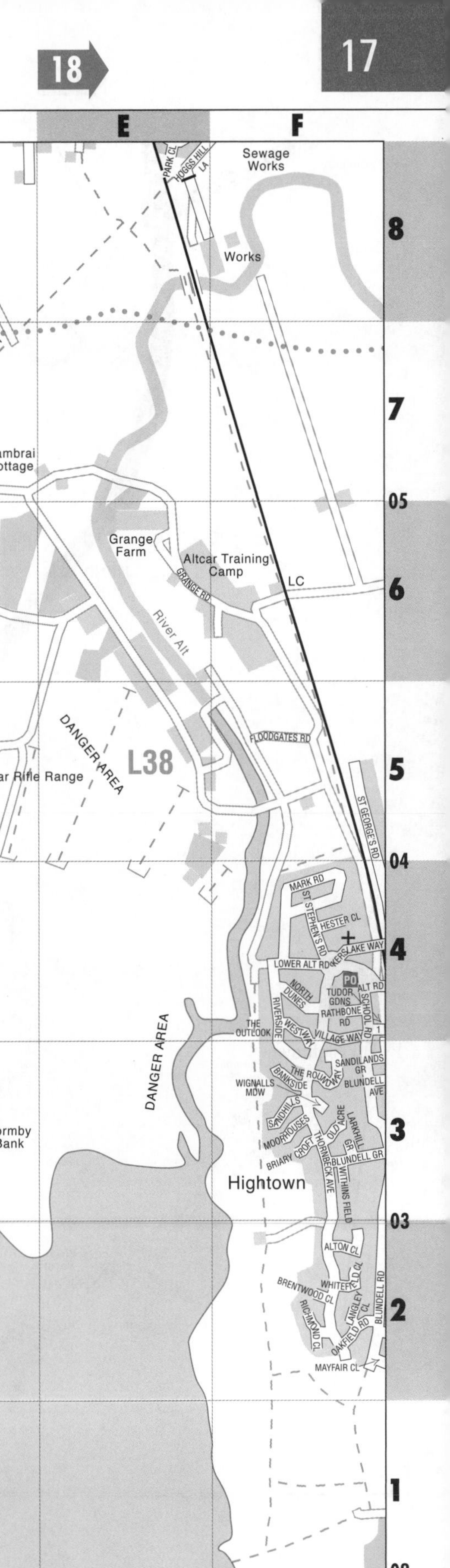

17

10

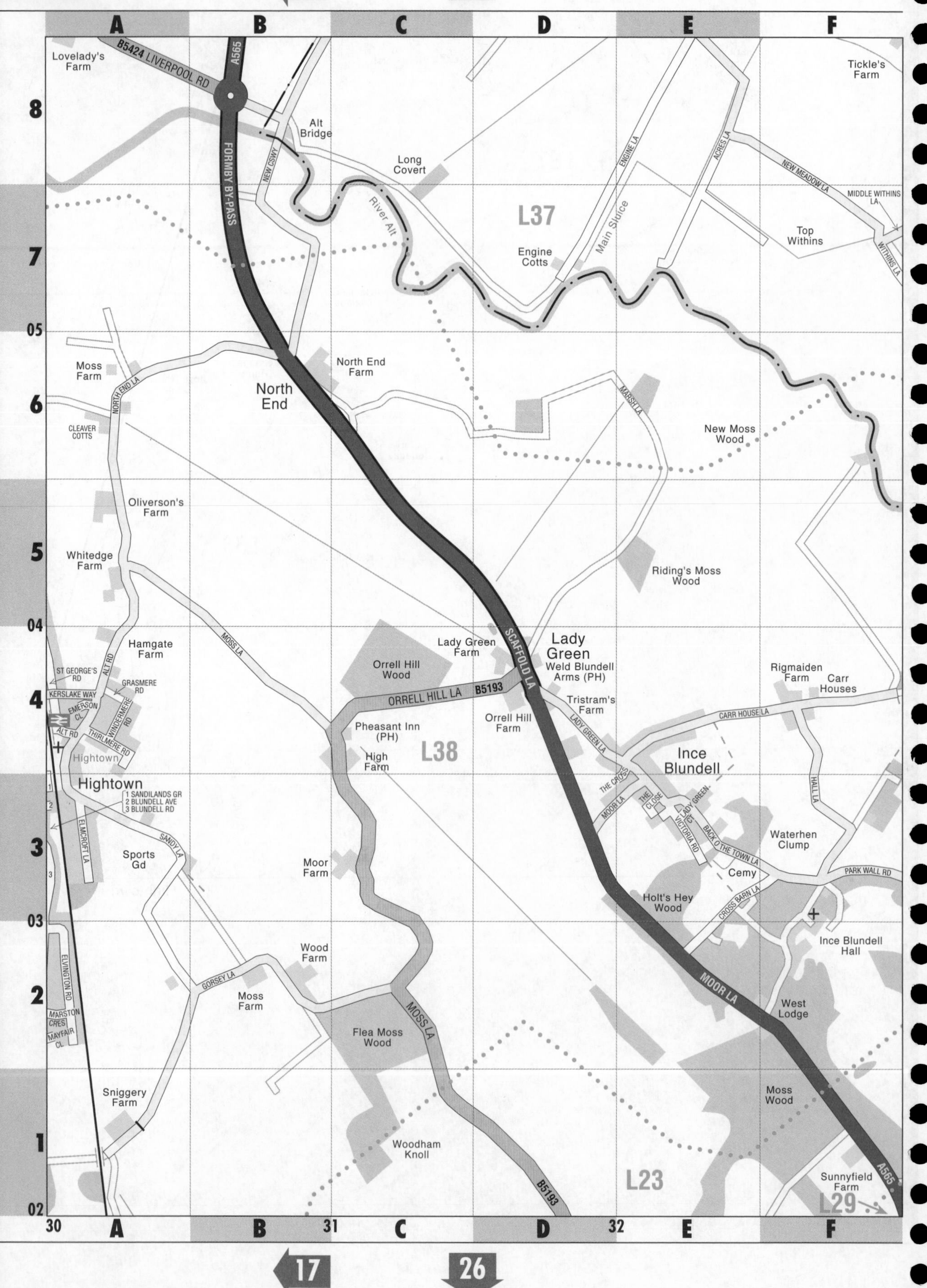

Lovelady's Farm
B5424 LIVERPOOL RD
A565
FORMBY BY-PASS
Alt Bridge
NEW CSWY
Long Covert
River Alt
L37
Engine Cotts
ENGINE LA
Main Sluice
ACRES LA
NEW MEADOW LA
MIDDLE WITHINS LA
Tickle's Farm
Top Withins
WITHINS LA
Moss Farm
NORTH END LA
North End
North End Farm
CLEAVER COTTS
MARSH LA
New Moss Wood
Oliverson's Farm
Whitedge Farm
Riding's Moss Wood
MOSS LA
Hamgate Farm
ALT RD
Lady Green Farm
Lady Green
Weld Blundell Arms (PH)
SCAFFOLD LA
Orrell Hill Wood
ORRELL HILL LA
B5193
Orrell Hill Farm
Tristram's Farm
Rigmaiden Farm
Carr Houses
CARR HOUSE LA
ST GEORGE'S RD
GRASMERE RD
KERSLAKE WAY
EMERSON CL
WINDERMERE RD
THIRLMERE RD
Hightown
Pheasant Inn (PH)
High Farm
L38
LADY GREEN LA
Ince Blundell
THE CROSS
MOOR LA
THE CLOSE
LADY GREEN CT
VICTORIA RD
BACK O'THE TOWN LA
HALL LA
1 SANDILANDS GR
2 BLUNDELL AVE
3 BLUNDELL RD
ELMCROFT LA
SANDY LA
Sports Gd
Moor Farm
Waterhen Clump
Cemy
PARK WALL RD
Holt's Hey Wood
CROSS BARN LA
Ince Blundell Hall
ELVINGTON RD
Wood Farm
GORSEY LA
Moss Farm
MOSS LA
MOOR LA
West Lodge
MARSTON CRES
MAYFAIR CL
Flea Moss Wood
Sniggery Farm
Moss Wood
Woodham Knoll
L23
B5193
Sunnyfield Farm
A565
L29

17

26

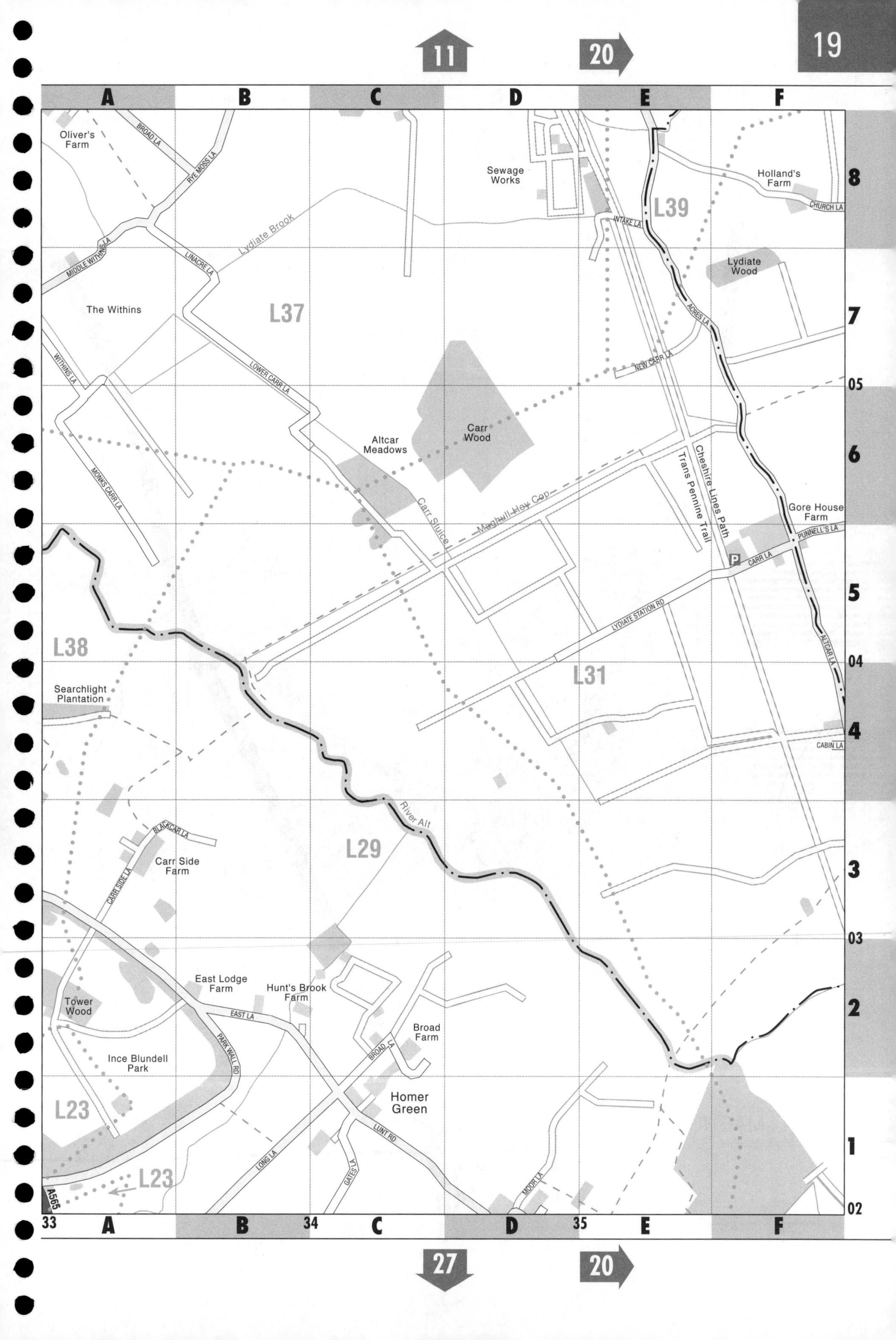

A   B   C   D   E   F

Oliver's Farm

Sewage Works

Holland's Farm

L39

Lydiate Wood

BROAD LA
RYE MOSS LA
LINACRE LA
Lydiate Brook
CHURCH LA
INTAKE LA
ACRES LA

8

MIDDLE WITHINS LA

The Withins

L37

7

05

WITHINS LA
LOWER CARR LA
NEW CARR LA

Altcar Meadows

Carr Wood

6

MONKS CARR LA

Cheshire Lines Path
Trans Pennine Trail

Gore House Farm

PUNNELL'S LA

Carr Sluice

Maghull Hey Cop

P   CARR LA

5

L38

Searchlight Plantation

Lydiate Station Rd

L31

ALTCAR LA

04

4

CABIN LA

River Alt

L29

3

03

BLACKCAR LA

Carr Side Farm

CARR SIDE LA

East Lodge Farm

Hunt's Brook Farm

EAST LA

Broad Farm

2

Tower Wood

PARK WALL RD

BROAD LA

Ince Blundell Park

Homer Green

L23

1

L23

LONG LA

GATES LA

LUNT RD

MOOR LA

A565

02

33   A   B   34   C   D   35   E   F

19
12

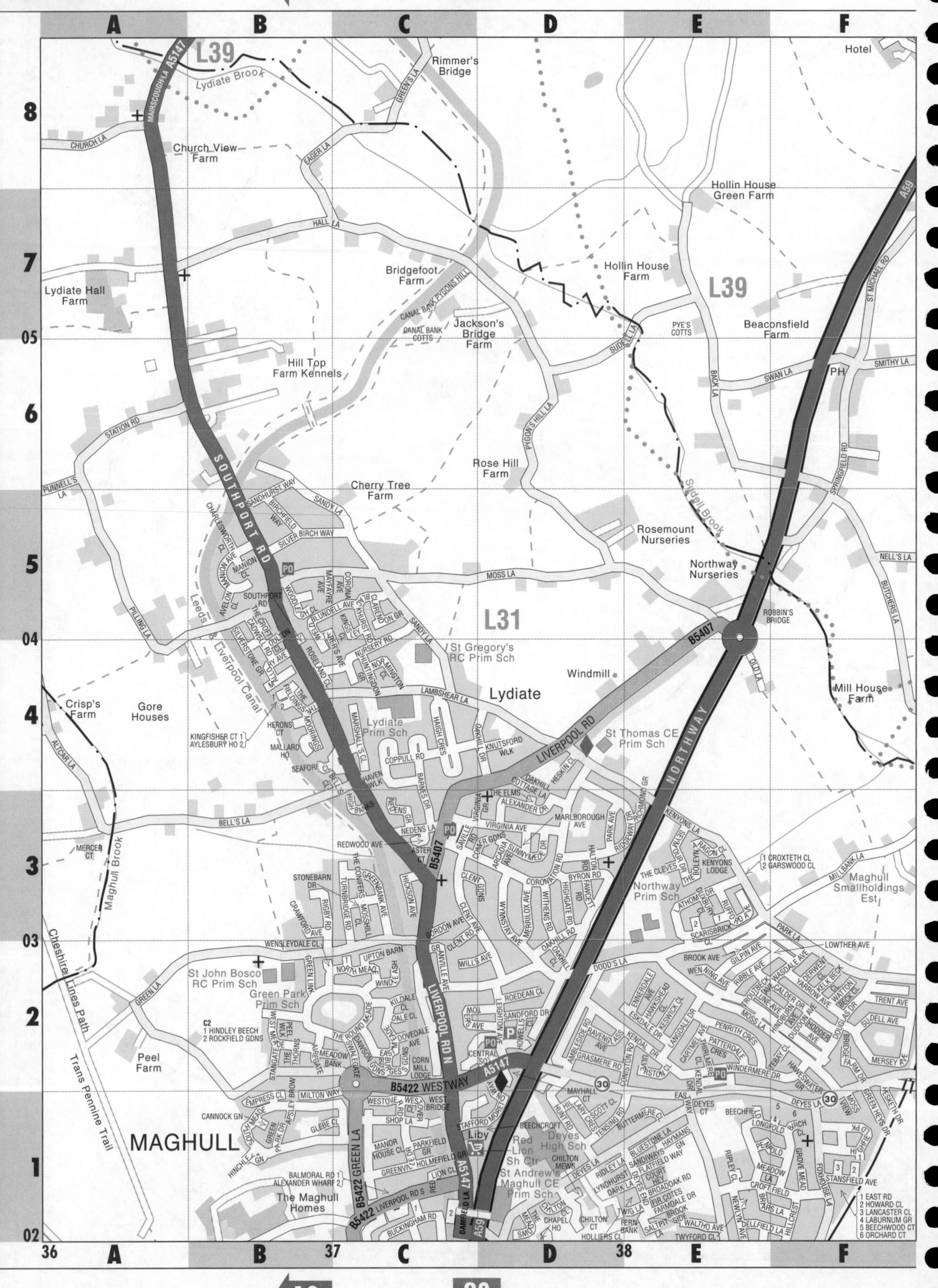
A
B
C
D
E
F
8
7
05
6
5
04
4
3
03
2
1
02
36
37
38
L39
Lydiate Brook
MARSCOUGH LA
A5147
Rimmer's Bridge
GREEN'S LA
Hotel
CHURCH LA
Church View Farm
EAGER LA
Hollin House Green Farm
A59
HALL LA
Bridgefoot Farm
Hollin House Farm
Lydiate Hall Farm
L39
ST MICHAEL RD
CANAL BANK
PYGONS HILL
Jackson's Bridge Farm
CANAL BANK COTTS
PYE'S COTTS
Beaconsfield Farm
SUDELL LA
Hill Top Farm Kennels
SWAN LA
BACK LA
PH
SMITHY LA
STATION RD
SOUTHPORT RD
PYGON'S HILL LA
Rose Hill Farm
SPRINGFIELD RD
PUNNELL'S LA
Cherry Tree Farm
SANDHURST WAY
SANDY LA
BIRCHFIELD WAY
SILVER BIRCH WAY
Sudell Brook
Rosemount Nurseries
Northway Nurseries
NELL'S LA
PO
MOSS LA
Leeds & Liverpool Canal
L31
PILLING LA
AVELON CL
SOUTHPORT RD
ROBBIN'S BRIDGE
BUTCHERS LA
B5407
St Gregory's RC Prim Sch
Windmill
OLD LA
Lydiate
LAMBSHEAR LA
Mill House Farm
Crisp's Farm
Gore Houses
Lydiate Prim Sch
KINGFISHER CT
AYLESBURY HO
HERONS CT
MALLARD HO
LIVERPOOL RD
St Thomas CE Prim Sch
NORTHWAY
ALTCAR LA
SEAFORE CL
COPPULL RD
KNUTSFORD WLK
HESKIN CL
BELL'S LA
THE ELMS
MARLBOROUGH AVE
KENYONS LA
MERCER CT
REDWOOD AVE
VIRGINIA AVE
1 CROXTETH CL
2 GARSWOOD CL
MILLBANK LA
Maghull Brook
STONEBARN DR
THE CLEVES
KENYONS LODGE
Maghull Smallholdings Est
Northway Prim Sch
Cheshire Lines Path
WENSLEYDALE CL
PARK LA
LOWTHER AVE
DODD'S LA
BROOK AVE
St John Bosco RC Prim Sch
Green Park Prim Sch
GREEN LA
LIVERPOOL RD N
TRENT AVE
C2
1 HINDLEY BEECH
2 ROCKFIELD GDNS
MOSS LA
Trans Pennine Trail
Peel Farm
B5422 WESTWAY
A5147
WINDERMERE DR
MERSEY AVE
MILTON WAY
DEYES LA
CANNOCK GN
MAGHULL
Liby
Red Lion Sh Ctr
Deyes High Sch
St Andrew's Maghull CE Prim Sch
BALMORAL RD
ALEXANDER WHARF
B5422 GREEN LA
The Maghull Homes
LIVERPOOL RD S
STANSFIELD AVE
1 EAST RD
2 HOWARD CL
3 LANCASTER CL
4 LABURNUM GR
5 BEECHWOOD AVE
6 ORCHARD CT
BUCKINGHAM RD
DAMFIELD LA
CHILTON CT
HOLLIERS CL
TWYFORD CL
A59

19
28

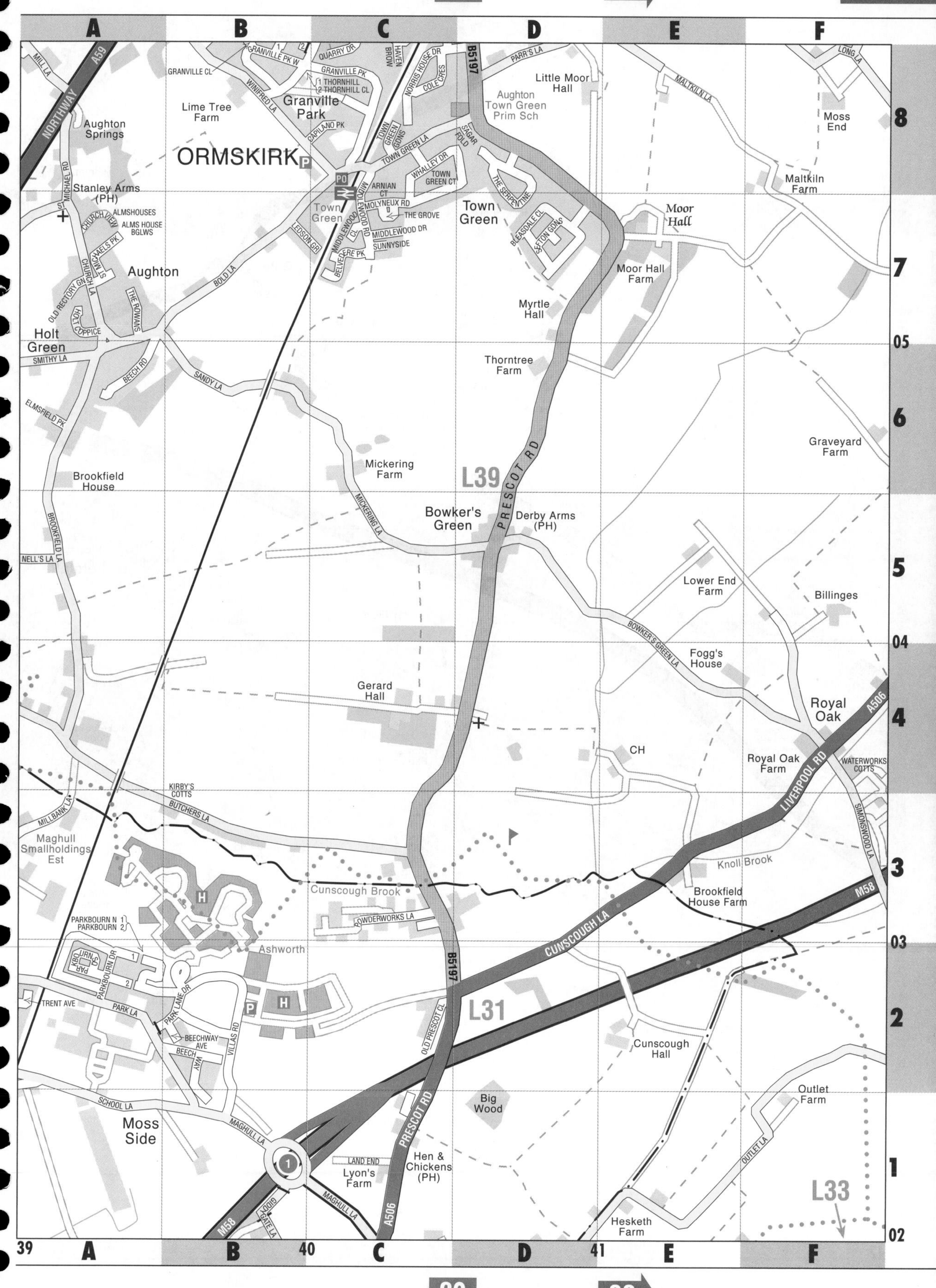
13
22
22
29
ORMSKIRK
Granville Park
Aughton Springs
Lime Tree Farm
Stanley Arms (PH)
Aughton
Holt Green
Town Green
Little Moor Hall
Aughton Town Green Prim Sch
Moss End
Maltkiln Farm
Moor Hall
Moor Hall Farm
Myrtle Hall
Thorntree Farm
Graveyard Farm
Mickering Farm
Brookfield House
Bowker's Green
Derby Arms (PH)
Lower End Farm
Billinges
Fogg's House
Gerard Hall
Royal Oak
Royal Oak Farm
CH
Maghull Smallholdings Est
Knoll Brook
Cunscough Brook
Brookfield House Farm
Ashworth
Cunscough Hall
Outlet Farm
Big Wood
Moss Side
Hen & Chickens (PH)
Lyon's Farm
Hesketh Farm
L39
L31
L33
PRESCOT RD
LIVERPOOL RD
CUNSCOUGH LA
BOWKER'S GREEN LA
MICKERING LA
SANDY LA
BOLD LA
BROOKFIELD LA
BUTCHERS LA
MAGHULL LA
SCHOOL LA
PARK LA
SIMONSWOOD LA
OUTLET LA
NORTHWAY
A59
A506
B5197
M58

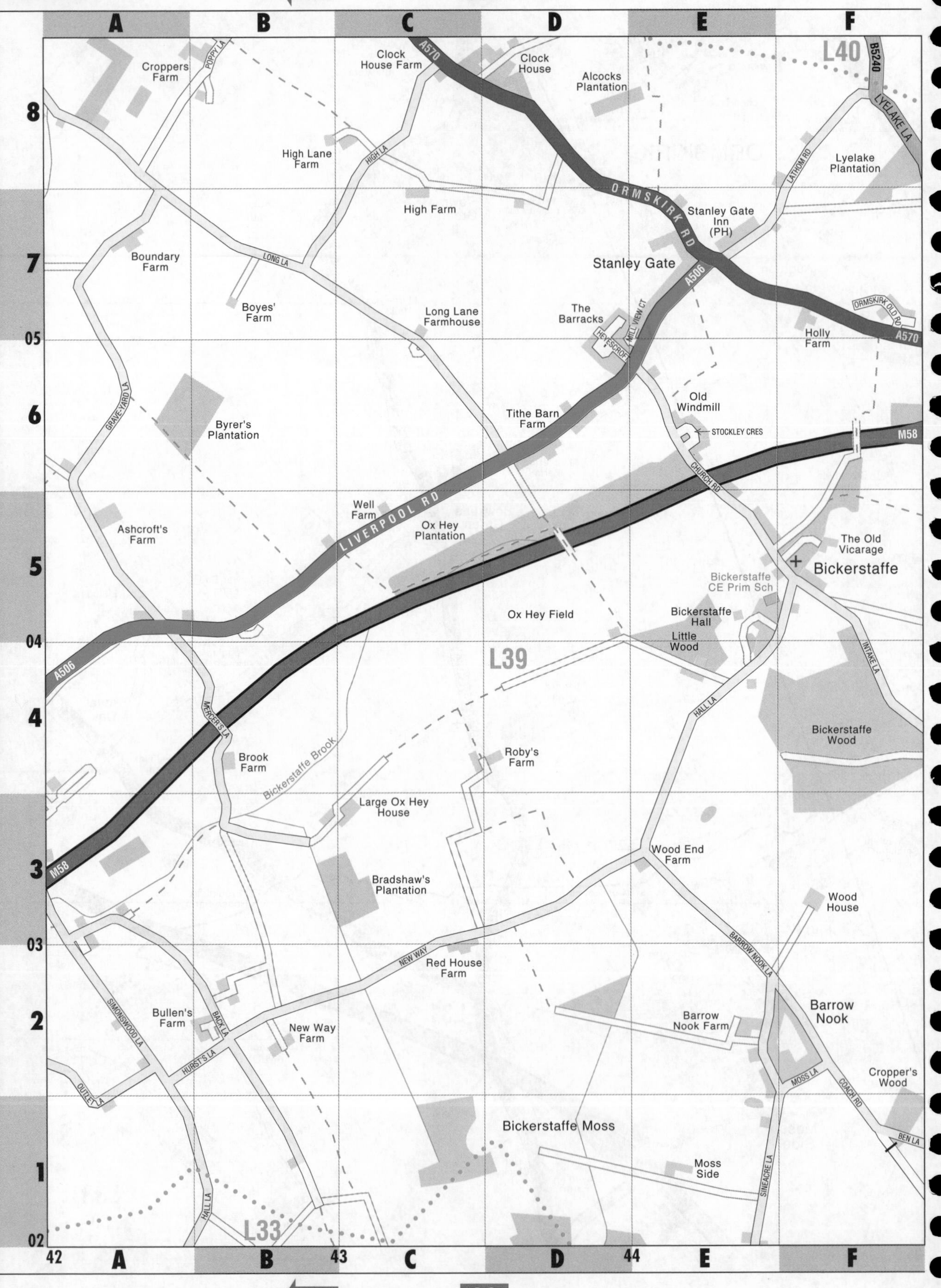

21
14

A   B   C   D   E   F

L40
B5240

8

Croppers Farm
POPPY LA
Clock House Farm
A570
Clock House
Alcocks Plantation
LYELAKE LA

High Lane Farm
HIGH LA
Lyelake Plantation
LATHOM RD

High Farm
ORMSKIRK RD
Stanley Gate Inn (PH)
Stanley Gate

7

Boundary Farm
LONG LA
A506
ORMSKIRK OLD RD
A570

05

Boyes' Farm
Long Lane Farmhouse
The Barracks
MILL VIEW CT
HEYESCROF
Holly Farm

6

GRAVEYARD LA
Byrer's Plantation
Tithe Barn Farm
Old Windmill
STOCKLEY CRES
M58

Well Farm
CHURCH RD

Ashcroft's Farm
LIVERPOOL RD
Ox Hey Plantation
The Old Vicarage

5

Ox Hey Field
Bickerstaffe CE Prim Sch
Bickerstaffe

04

A506
Bickerstaffe Hall
Little Wood
INTAKE LA

L39
HALL LA
Bickerstaffe Wood

4

MERCER'S LA
Brook Farm
Bickerstaffe Brook
Roby's Farm

3

Large Ox Hey House
Wood End Farm
Wood House

03

Bradshaw's Plantation
NEW WAY
Red House Farm
BARROW NOOK LA

M58

SIMONSWOOD LA
Bullen's Farm
BACK LA
New Way Farm
Barrow Nook Farm
Barrow Nook

2

HURST'S LA
OUTLET LA
MOSS LA
COACH RD
Cropper's Wood
BEN LA

1

Bickerstaffe Moss
Moss Side
SINEACRE LA

HALL LA

02

L33

42   A   B   43   C   D   44   E   F

15

24

A
B
C
D
E
F
L40
Blaguegate Moss
Primrose Farm
Lyelake Farm
LYELAKE LA
Four Lane Ends
B5240
B5312
Stanley Farm
SKELMERSDALE RD
LIVERPOOL RD
KERFOOT'S LA
DERBY RD
PARKSIDE AVE 1
STANDSIDE PK 2
OLD TOWN CL 3
OLD TOWN WAY 4
VILLAGE WAY 5
WEST PARK CL 6
WELBOURNE
SWIFT'S FOLD
VILLAGE CL
WHITE MOSS RD
WHITE MOSS RD S
WESTGATE
WAVERLEY
ASHWALL ST
WALDRON
JUBILEE DR
BARNES RD
BIRCH ST
WHITEHEY
WALLCROFT ST
WHEATACRE
HIGH ST
WHITE STOCK
WOODROW
WOODCROFT
WINSTANLEY RD
WOLVERTON
WIGAN RD
WINDGATE
B5312
RAILWAY RD
GLADDEN PL
GARDINERS PL
West Gillibrands Ind Est
West Gillibrands
GREENHEY PL
GILLIBRANDS RD
GERRARD PL
GLENBURN RD
A5068
Peel Farm
SKELMERSDALE
WN8
White Moss
4
M58
05
MOSS LANE VIEW
MARLE VIEW
MOSS LA
Whitemoss Bsns Pk
Moss Lane Farm
Colliery Plantation
A570
3
Wash Farm
RAINFORD RD
Rose Farm
Bickerstaffe Moss
Ivy House
Higherend Farm
Hey's Crossing
04
Ferny Knoll
L39
Holly Lane Farm
Brookdale
COAL PIT LA
Barker's Brook
HOLLY LA
Big Ferny Knoll Farm
FERNY KNOLL RD
HOLLY FOLD LA
Long Plantation
RAINFORD RD
Intake Farm
Holly Fold Farm
WA11
03
INTAKE LA
Ben Lane Farm
BEN LANE CT
Park Hill
ORMSKIRK RD
KESWICK WAY 1
CONISTON WAY 2
WINDERMERE DR
NEWS LA
Rainford Junction
Rainford
PH
PO
BUTTERMERE CRES
RAIL CL
KENDAL CL
KENDAL DR
SPRING FIELD
BUSHEY LA
PH
Lodge Farm
BEN LA
Red Delph Farm
LODGE LA
Bridge Farm
Kenyon's Wood
RED DELPH LA
Moss House Farm
SIDING LA
JUNCTION RD
COACH RD
Rigby's Wood
B5203
02
8
7
6
5
4
3
2
1
45
46
47

31

24

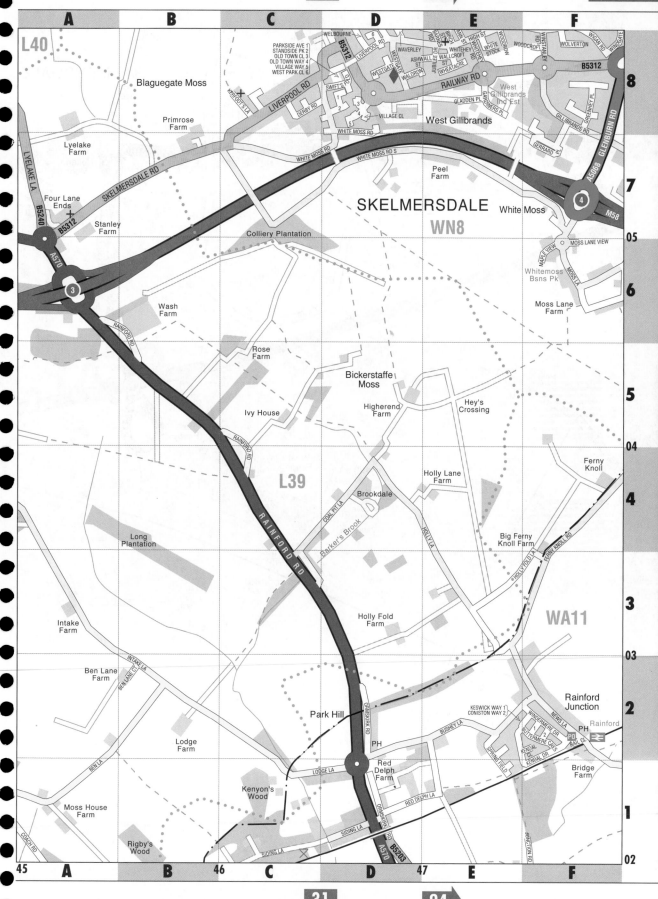

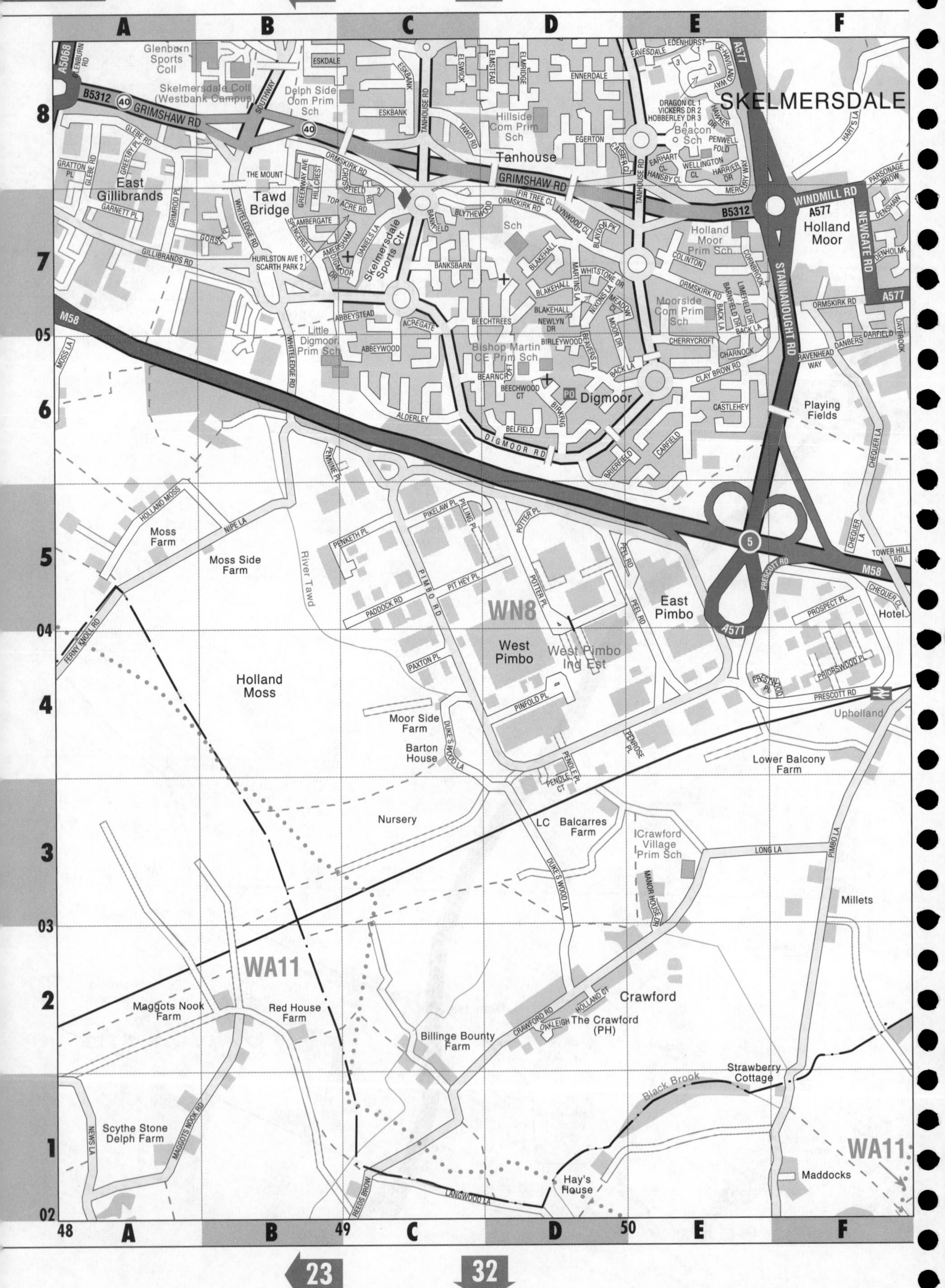

SKELMERSDALE

Glenburn Sports Coll

B5312 GRIMSHAW RD

Skelmersdale Coll (Westbank Campus)

Delph Side Com Prim Sch

East Gillibrands

Tawd Bridge

Tanhouse

Hillside Com Prim Sch

Egerton

Dragon CL 1
Vickers DR 2
Hobberley DR 3

Beacon Sch

WINDMILL RD

A577 Holland Moor

Holland Moor Prim Sch

GRIMSHAW RD

Hurlston Ave 1
Scarth Park 2

Skelmersdale Sports Ctr

Banksbarn

Blakehall

Moorside Com Prim Sch

Little Digmoor Prim Sch

Abbeystead

Acregate

Abbeywood

Bishop Martin CE Prim Sch

Bearncroft

Beechwood CT

PO Digmoor

Cherrycroft

Charnock

Clay Brow RD

Castlehey

Playing Fields

Alderley

Belfield

DIGMOOR RD

Brierfield

Garfield

Moss Farm

Moss Side Farm

River Tawd

Penketh PL

Pikelaw PL

Pilling PL

Potter PL

WN8

West Pimbo

West Pimbo Ind Est

East Pimbo

Paddock RD

Paxton PL

Pinfold PL

Hotel

Holland Moss

Moor Side Farm

Barton House

Lower Balcony Farm

Upholland

Nursery

LC Balcarres Farm

Crawford Village Prim Sch

Long La

Millets

WA11

Maggots Nook Farm

Red House Farm

Billinge Bounty Farm

Crawford

The Crawford (PH)

Strawberry Cottage

Black Brook

Scythe Stone Delph Farm

Hay's House

WA11

Maddocks

Reeds Brow

LANGWOOD LA

A7
1 DENHOLME
2 FIELDVIEW
3 MEADOWFIELD

E5
1 COSGATE CL
2 MIDDLECOT CL
3 THE ORCHARDS

F7
1 THIRLMERE AVE
2 LATIMER CL
3 BYRON CL
4 WINCHESTER CL

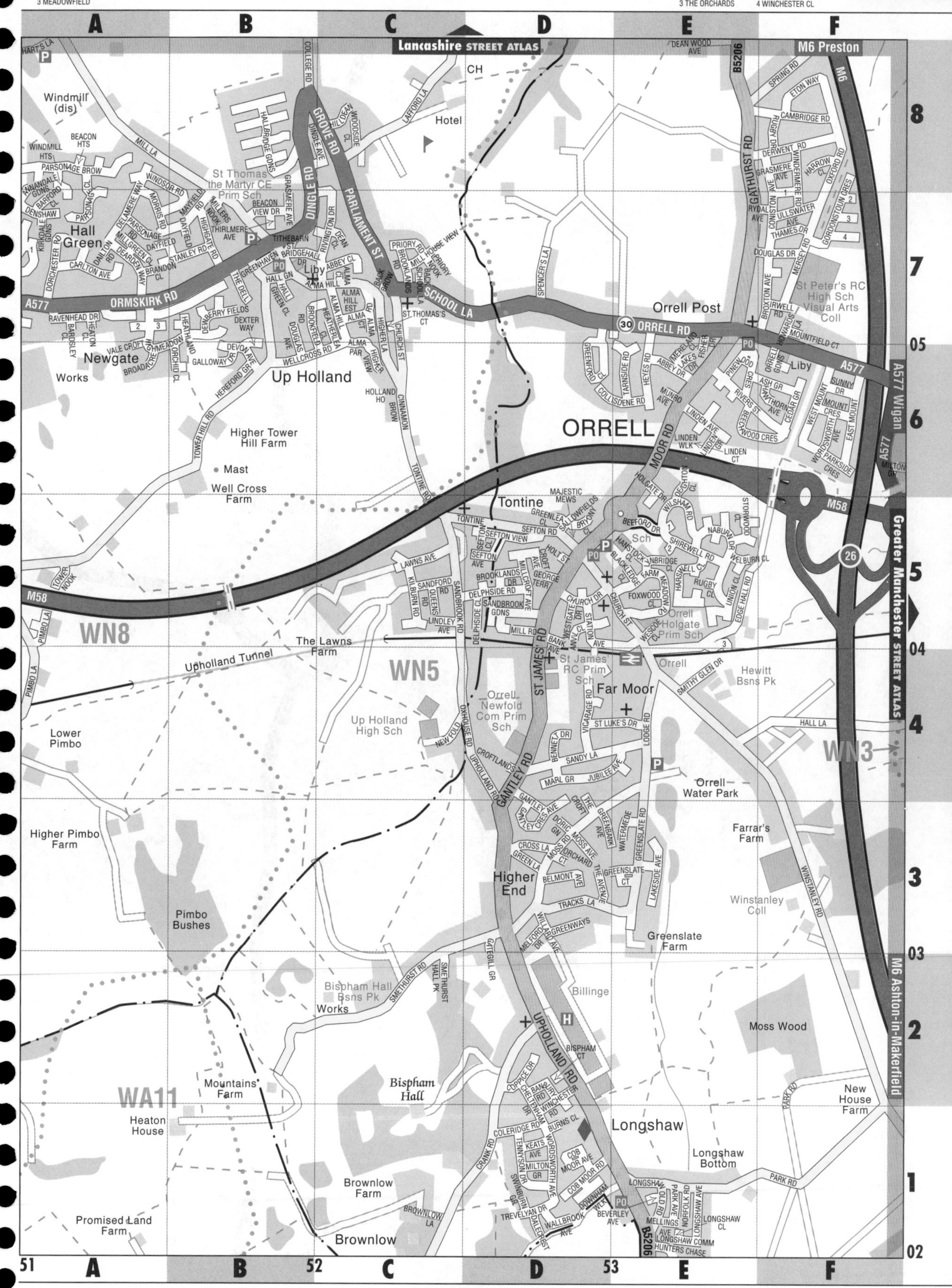

33

C4
1 HOMEDOVE HO
2 SANDHURST
3 FORTON LODGE

18

D5
1 CLAREMONT TERR
2 SPRINGFIELD COTTS
3 PINFOLD CT

E4
1 CHURCH RD
2 CENTRAL BLDGS
3 CROWN BLDGS
4 THE PRECINCTS

E5
1 ALLENGATE
2 GLENN BLDGS
3 TELEGRAPH HO
4 MOOR HO
5 RICHMOND CT

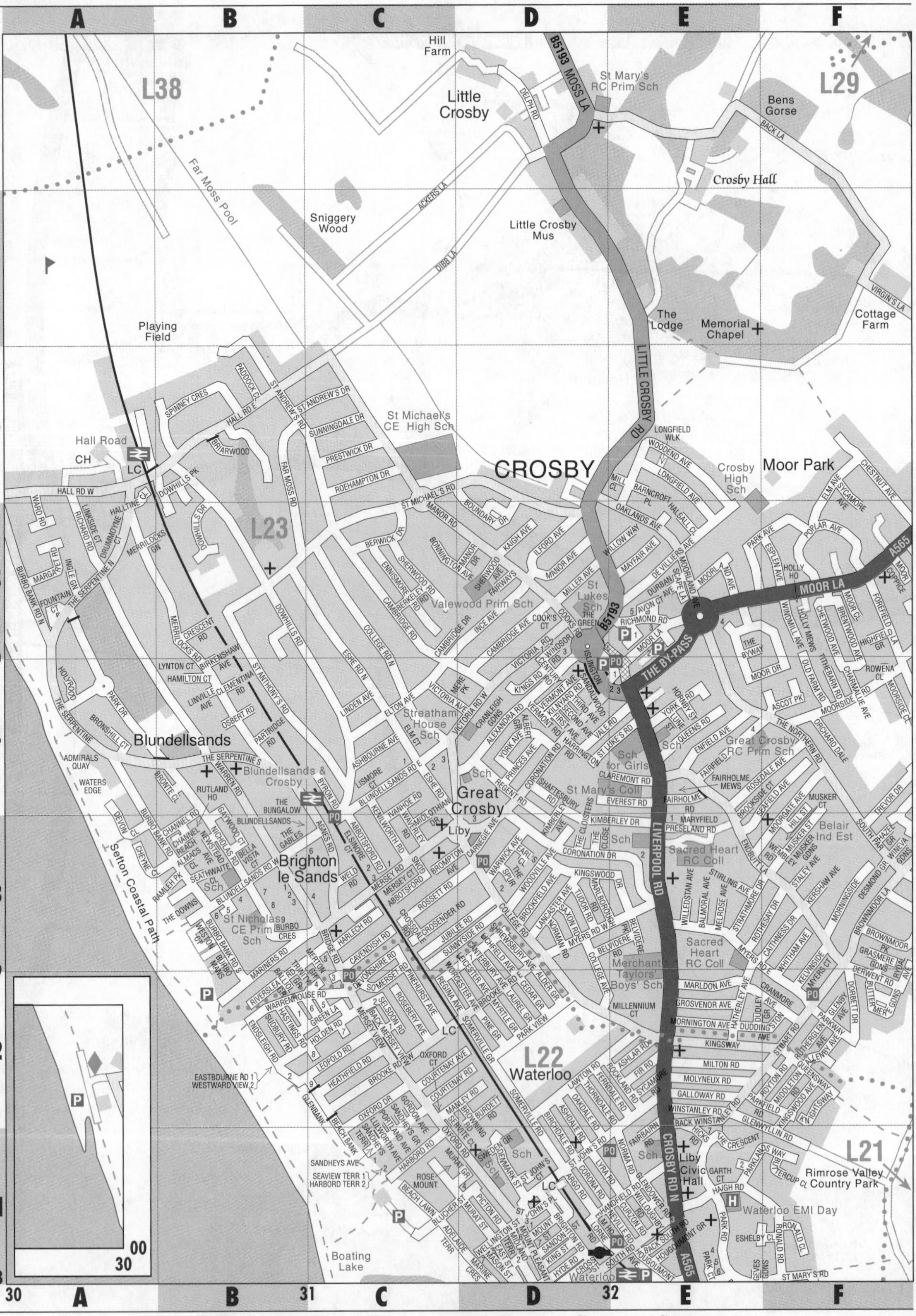

A B C D E F
8 7 01 6 5 00 4 3 99 2 1 98
30 31 32 00
L38
L29
L23
L22
L21
Hill Farm
Little Crosby
St Mary's RC Prim Sch
Bens Gorse
Crosby Hall
Far Moss Pool
Sniggery Wood
Little Crosby Mus
The Lodge
Memorial Chapel
Cottage Farm
Playing Field
St Michael's CE High Sch
CROSBY
Crosby High Sch
Moor Park
Hall Road
Valewood Prim Sch
St Lukes Sch
Streatham House Sch
Blundellsands
Blundellsands & Crosby
Great Crosby
Great Crosby RC Prim Sch
Sch for Girls
St Mary's Coll
Belair Ind Est
Sacred Heart RC Coll
Brighton le Sands
St Nicholas CE Prim Sch
Sefton Coastal Path
Merchant Taylors' Boys' Sch
Waterloo
Liby Civic Hall
Waterloo EMI Day
Rimrose Valley Country Park
Boating Lake
B5193 MOSS LA
LITTLE CROSBY RD
LIVERPOOL RD
CROSBY RD N
THE BY-PASS
MOOR LA
A565

B3
1 LINDEN CT
2 WARRENHURST CT
3 GLENDOWER CT
4 BLUNDELLSANDS CT
5 THE KNOWLE
6 THE LAWNS
7 INVERCLYDE CT
8 NICHOLAS CT
9 SOMERFORD HO

C2
1 PURLEY RD
2 HOLDEN RD E
3 SANDPIPERS CT
4 BRIGHTON VALE
5 SUSSEX ST
6 WORTHING ST
7 HOLDEN GR
8 HOLDEN TERR
9 RIVER VIEW

C3
1 INGLESIDE CT
2 HOMEWOOD
3 ABBOTSFORD CT
4 WARREN CT
5 BACK BRIDGE RD
6 FORMBY LODGE

37

D1
1 BACK MOUNT ST
2 CANNING ST
3 WELBECK CT
4 GREENACRES
5 WELLINGTON GDNS
6 MOUNT PLEASANT FLATS
7 SANDON CT

D3
1 WINCHESTER AVE
2 COLLEGE GN
3 ALEXANDRA CT

E1
1 WINSTANLEY HO
2 BLUEBELL CL
3 CREMONA CNR
4 PARKHOLME
5 PARK CT
6 LEESWOOD
7 KENMORE

E3
1 THE MEWS
2 ARGYLE CT

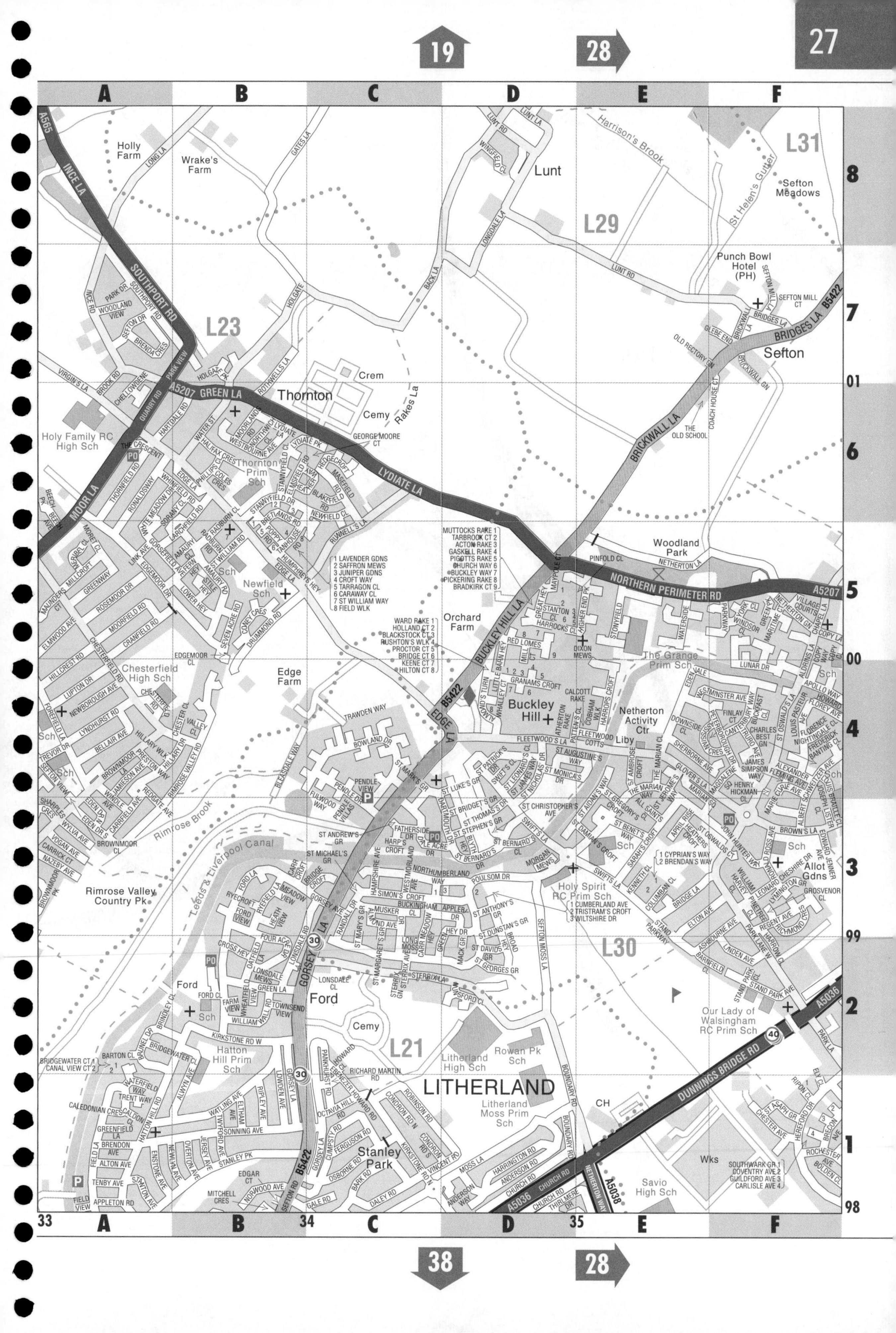

19
28
A
B
C
D
E
F
Holly Farm
Wrake's Farm
Lunt
L31
Sefton Meadows
L29
Harrison's Brook
St Helen's Gutter
Punch Bowl Hotel (PH)
L23
Sefton
Thornton
Crem
Cemy
Rakes La
A5207 GREEN LA
LYDIATE LA
BRICKWALL LA
BRIDGES LA
B5422
SOUTHPORT RD
INCE LA
A565
MOOR LA
LUNT RD
LONGDALE LA
BACK LA
HOLGATE
GATES LA
LONG LA
THE OLD SCHOOL
COACH HOUSE CT
OLD RECTORY GN
GLEBE END
Holy Family RC High Sch
Thornton Prim Sch
Newfield Sch
Woodland Park
NORTHERN PERIMETER RD
NETHERTON LA
PINFOLD CL
Orchard Farm
Edge Farm
BUCKLEY HILL LA
EDGE LA
Buckley Hill
Netherton Activity Ctr
Liby
The Grange Prim Sch
Chesterfield High Sch
Rimrose Brook
Leeds & Liverpool Canal
Rimrose Valley Country Pk
Holy Spirit RC Prim Sch
Allot Gdns
L30
GORSEY LA
Ford
Cemy
L21
Hatton Hill Prim Sch
Litherland High Sch
Rowan Pk Sch
LITHERLAND
Litherland Moss Prim Sch
Stanley Park
CH
Wks
Savio High Sch
Our Lady of Walsingham RC Prim Sch
DUNNINGS BRIDGE RD
A5036
A5038
SEFTON MOSS LA
BOUNDARY RD
CHURCH RD
8
7
01
6
5
00
4
3
99
2
1
98
33
34
35
38
28

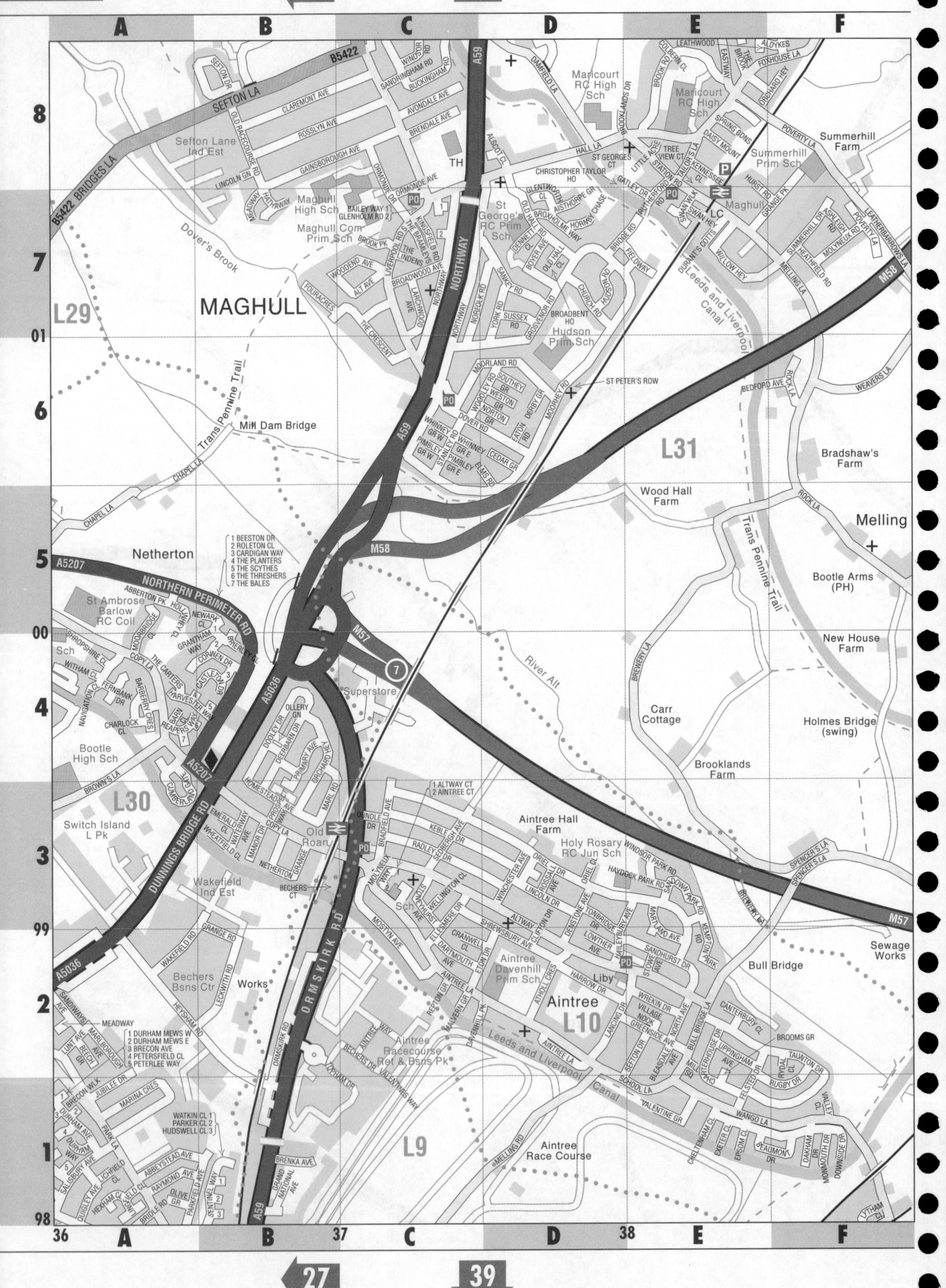
27
20
A
B
C
D
E
F
8
7
01
6
5
00
4
3
99
2
1
98
36
37
38
27
39
MAGHULL
L29
L30
L31
L10
L9
B5422
SEFTON LA
B5422 BRIDGES LA
Sefton Lane Ind Est
CLAREMONT AVE
ROSSLYN AVE
GAINSBOROUGH AVE
LINCOLN GN
OLD RACECOURSE RD
SEFTON DR
SANDRINGHAM RD
BUCKINGHAM RD
WINDSOR RD
AVONDALE AVE
BRENDALE AVE
ORMONDE AVE
ORMONDE DR
Maghull High Sch
Maghull Com Prim Sch
BAILEY WAY 1
GLENHOLM RD 2
BROOK PK
KINGSFIELD RD
THE BRAMBLES
LIVERPOOL RD S
THE LINDENS
WOODEND AVE
ALT AVE
BROADWOOD AVE
LARCHWOOD AVE
FOURACRES
THE CRESCENT
Dover's Brook
TH
A59
NORTHWAY
DAMFIELD LA
Maricourt RC High Sch
BROOKLANDS DR
HALL LA
ST GEORGES CT
CHRISTOPHER TAYLOR HO
ALSCOT CL
St George's RC Prim Sch
GLENTWORTH CL
OLD HALL RD
BROXHOLME WAY
AISTHORPE GR
HORNBY CHASE
DENNETT CL
BOYER AVE
OLD HALL CL
SANKEY RD
NORFOLK RD
YORK RD
SUSSEX RD
GROSVENOR RD
CHURCH RD
HUDSON RD
BROADBENT HO
Hudson Prim Sch
LITTLE ACRE
TREE VIEW CT
GATLEY DR
RUTHERFORD RD
BRIDGE RD
FIELDWAY
LEATHWOOD
COLBERN CL
BROOK RD
EASTWAY
THE BROOK
ALDYKES
FOXHOUSE LA
ORCHARD HEY
SPRING GDNS
DAISY MOUNT
TAILOR'S LA
STATION RD
KENNESSEE CL
SWAN WALK
SWAN HEY
Maghull
LC
DURANT'S COTTS
WILLOW HEY
Leeds and Liverpool Canal
POVERTY LA
Summerhill Farm
Summerhill Prim Sch
HURST RD
GRANGE PK
SUMMERHILL DR
ASHLEIGH RD
MOLYNEUX RD
HEATHFIELD RD
MELLING LA
LEATHERBARROWS LA
M58
MOORLAND RD
SOUTHEY GR
WOODLEY RD
WESTON GR
NORTON GR
DERBY GR
EATON RD
MOORHEY RD
ST PETER'S ROW
DOVER RD
WHINNEY GR W
WHINNEY GR E
STANLEY RD
PIMBLEY GR W
PIMBLEY GR E
CEDAR GR
ELMS RD
BEDFORD AVE
ROCK LA
WEAVERS LA
Mill Dam Bridge
Trans Pennine Trail
CHAPEL LA
Wood Hall Farm
Bradshaw's Farm
Melling
Bootle Arms (PH)
New House Farm
Holmes Bridge (swing)
1 BEESTON DR
2 ROLETON CL
3 CARDIGAN WAY
4 THE PLANTERS
5 THE SCYTHES
6 THE THRESHERS
7 THE BALES
Netherton
A5207
NORTHERN PERIMETER RD
ABBERTON PK
St Ambrose Barlow RC Coll
HOLLYHEY CL
NEWARK CL
GRANTHAM WAY
CORWEN DR
BRIERLEY CL
CASTLETON DR
THE CARTERS
HARVESTER WAY
MOORBRIDGE CL
SHROPSHIRE CL
COPY LA
WITHAM CL
Sch
FERNBANK DR
BARBERRY CRES
NAVIGATION CL
CHARLOCK CL
REAPERS WAY
BARN CL
Bootle High Sch
BROWN'S LA
CUMBERLAND GATE
M57
7
A5036
Superstore
OLLERY GN
DOOLEY DR
DEERBARN DR
PRIMARY AVE
ORCHARD HEY
HOMESTEAD AVE
PROSPECT WAY
MARL RD
River Alt
BREWERY LA
Carr Cottage
Brooklands Farm
EMERALD CL
WATERWAY AVE
COPY LA
MANOR DR
WHEATFIELD CL
NETHERTON GRANGE
DUNNINGS BRIDGE RD
Switch Island L Pk
Wakefield Ind Est
Old Roan
1 ALTWAY CT
2 AINTREE CT
OUNDLE DR
BRADFIELD AVE
KEBLE DR
SEDBERGH AVE
RADLEY DR
WINCHESTER AVE
ORIEL DR
ROSSALL AVE
LINCOLN DR
ORIEL CL
WINDSOR PARK RD
HAYDOCK PARK RD
SANDOWN PARK RD
KEMPTON PARK RD
Aintree Hall Farm
Holy Rosary RC Jun Sch
SPENCER'S LA
BREWERY LA
MOLYNEUX WAY
BECHERS CT
PO
Sch
HEYHURST AVE
WELLINGTON CL
ELLESMERE DR
CRANWELL CL
DARTMOUTH AVE
SHREWSBURY AVE
ALTWAY
CLIFTON DR
DENSTONE AVE
TONBRIDGE DR
HAILEYBURY AVE
MARYLAND AVE
LOWTHER AVE
SANDHURST DR
STOWE AVE
HARROW DR
Liby
ETON DR
Aintree Davenhill Prim Sch
ATHOLL CRES
MOSTYN AVE
Aintree
Bull Bridge
Sewage Works
GRANGE RD
WAKEFIELD RD
LECKWITH RD
Bechers Bsns Ctr
Works
HEYSHAM RD
ORMSKIRK RD
AINTREE LA
REPTON GR
MALVERN GR
DAVENHILL PK
LANCING DR
WREKIN DR
VILLAGE NOOK
GREENSIDE AVE
NORTH AVE
BULL BRIDGE LA
CANTERBURY CL
BROOMS GR
TAUNTON DR
RYDAL CL
UPPINGHAM AVE
RUGBY DR
CHARTERHOUSE DR
FELSTED DR
MILL SQ
BLEASDALE AVE
SEFTON DR
SCHOOL LA
VALENTINE GR
WANGO LA
VALLEY CL
Leeds and Liverpool Canal
AINTREE LA
AINTREE WAY
Aintree Racecourse Ret & Bsns Pk
BECHERS DR
VALENTINES WAY
TOPHAM DR
MEADWAY
SANDIWAYS AVE
1 DURHAM MEWS W
2 DURHAM MEWS E
3 BRECON AVE
4 PETERSFIELD CL
5 PETERLEE WAY
LUNT AVE
BEECH GR
MARLBOROUGH AVE
BRECON WLK
JUBILEE DR
MARINA CRES
DURHAM AVE
DURHAM WAY
PARK LA
SALISBURY AVE
LICHFIELD CL
QUIGLEY AVE
HEXHAM CL
LINGFIELD CL
RAYMOND AVE
ABBEYSTEAD AVE
OLIVE GR
BRIDLE RD
PARKFIELD AVE
SENTINEL WAY
WATKIN CL 1
PARKER CL 2
HUDSWELL CL 3
BRENKA AVE
GRAND NATIONAL AVE
MELLING RD
Aintree Race Course
CHELTENHAM CL
EXETER CL
EPSOM CL
BEAUMONT DR
OAKHAM DR
MONMOUTH DR
DOWNSIDE DR
LYTHAM CL

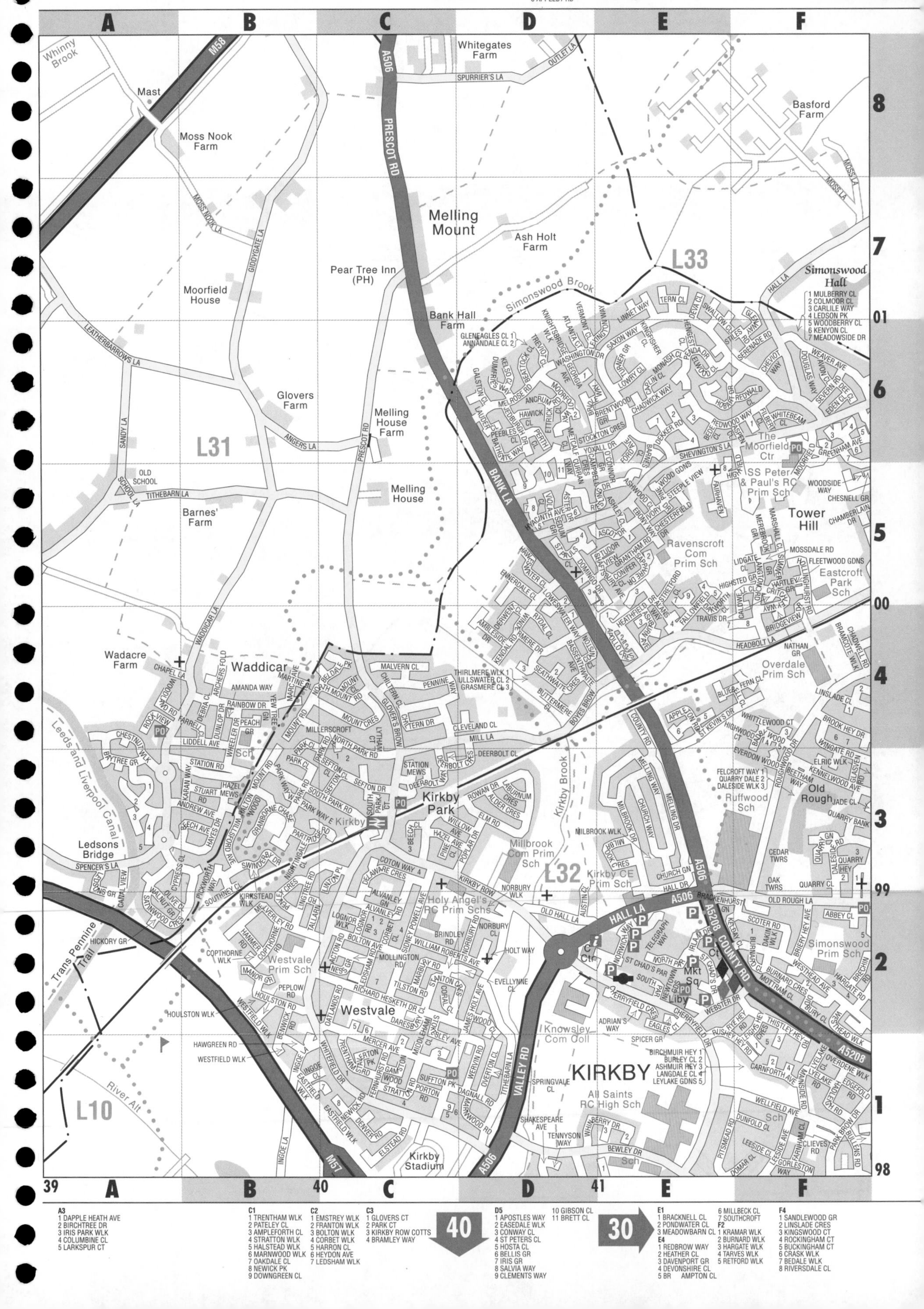

21

30

E5
1 ST PATRICK'S CL
2 WINDMILL CL
3 REDMOOR CRES
4 SANDRINGHAM CL
5 BALMORAL CL
6 APPLEBY RD

E5
7 FARNWORTH GR
8 ST ANDREW'S VIEW
9 FAIRLAWNE CL

E6
1 HORTON CL
2 KERR CL
3 FRANKLIN GR
4 LEWIS WLK

L33

L31

L32

L10

KIRKBY

A3
1 DAPPLE HEATH AVE
2 BIRCHTREE DR
3 IRIS PARK WLK
4 COLUMBINE CL
5 LARKSPUR CT

C1
1 TRENTHAM WLK
2 PATELEY CL
3 AMPLEFORTH CL
4 STRATTON WLK
5 HALSTEAD WLK
6 MARNWOOD WLK
7 OAKDALE CL
8 NEWICK PK
9 DOWNGREEN CL

C2
1 EMSTREY WLK
2 FRANTON WLK
3 BOLTON WLK
4 CORBET WLK
5 HARRON CL
6 HEYDON AVE
7 LEDSHAM CL

C3
1 GLOVERS CT
2 PARK CT
3 KIRKBY ROW COTTS
4 BRAMLEY WAY

D5
1 APOSTLES WAY
2 EASEDALE WLK
3 CONWAY CL
4 ST PETERS CL
5 HOSTA CL
6 BELLIS GR
7 IRIS GR
8 SALVIA WAY
9 CLEMENTS WAY

10 GIBSON CL
11 BRETT CL

E1
1 BRACKNELL CL
2 PONDWATER CL
3 MEADOWBARN CL
E4
1 REDBROW WAY
2 HEATHER CL
3 DAVENPORT CL
4 DEVONSHIRE CL
5 BRAMPTON CL

6 MILLBECK CL
7 SOUTHCROFT
F2
1 KRAMAR WLK
2 BURNARD WLK
3 HARGATE WLK
4 TARVES WLK
5 RETFORD WLK

F4
1 SANDLEWOOD GR
2 LINSLADE CRES
3 KINGSWOOD CT
4 BUCKINGHAM CT
5 CRASK WLK
6 BEDALE WLK
7 RIVERSDALE CL

29
22

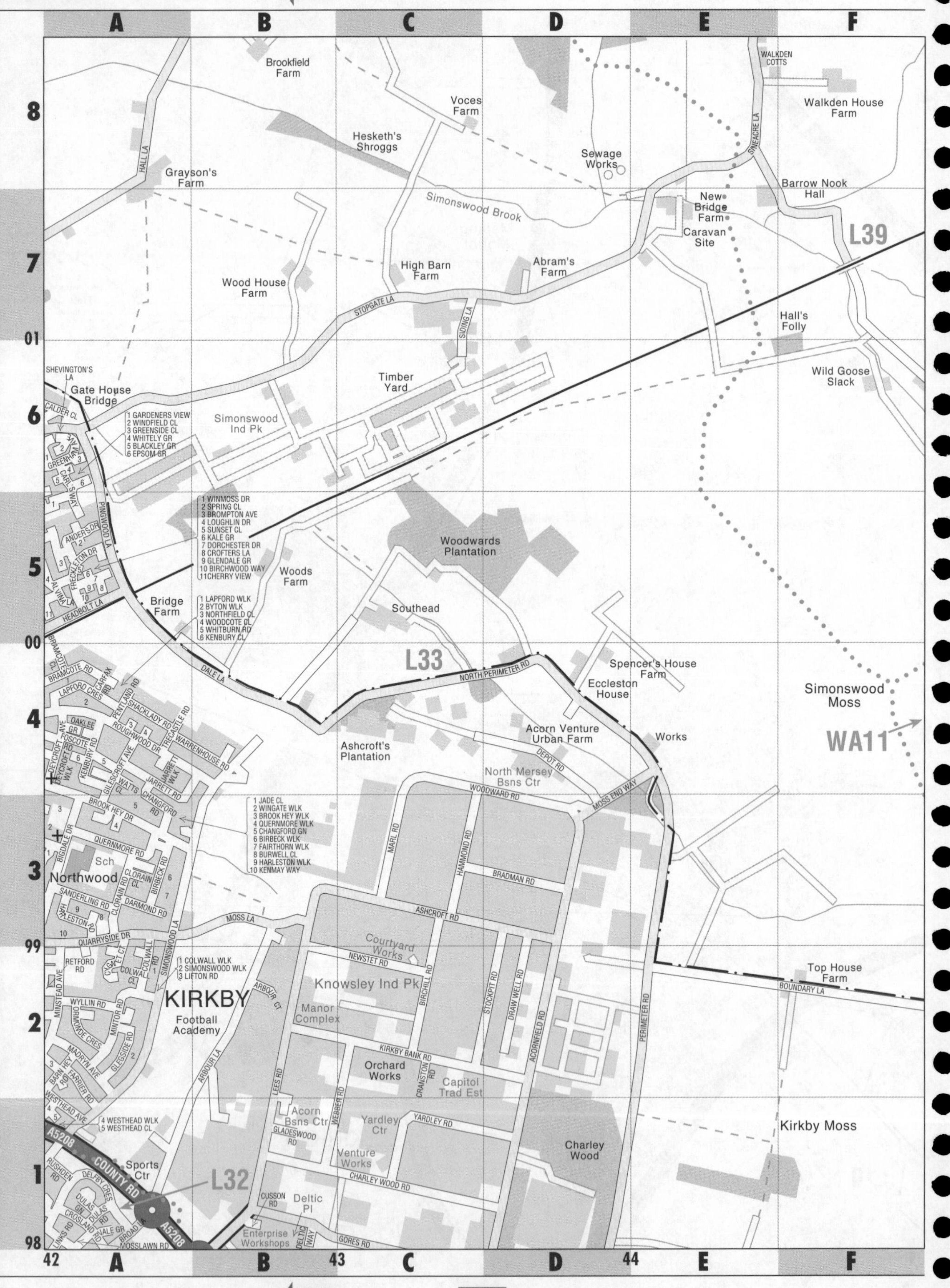
Brookfield Farm
Voces Farm
Hesketh's Shroggs
Grayson's Farm
Sewage Works
Walkden House Farm
WALKDEN COTTS
Barrow Nook Hall
New Bridge Farm
Caravan Site
Simonswood Brook
L39
High Barn Farm
Abram's Farm
Wood House Farm
STOPGATE LA
SIDING LA
Hall's Folly
Wild Goose Slack
Timber Yard
Gate House Bridge
Simonswood Ind Pk
Woodwards Plantation
Woods Farm
Southead
Bridge Farm
L33
Spencer's House Farm
Eccleston House
Simonswood Moss
WA11
Acorn Venture Urban Farm
Works
Ashcroft's Plantation
North Mersey Bsns Ctr
Northwood
Sch
Courtyard Works
Knowsley Ind Pk
Manor Complex
KIRKBY
Football Academy
Top House Farm
BOUNDARY LA
Orchard Works
Capitol Trad Est
Acorn Bsns Ctr
Yardley Ctr
Venture Works
Kirkby Moss
Charley Wood
Sports Ctr
L32
Deltic Pl
Enterprise Workshops
A5208
COUNTY RD
PERIMETER RD
NORTH PERIMETER RD
MOSS END WAY
MOSS LA
DALE LA
HEADBOLT LA
PINGWOOD LA
SIMONSWOOD LA
ARBOUR LA
1 GARDENERS VIEW
2 WINDFIELD CL
3 GREENSIDE CL
4 WHITELY GR
5 BLACKLEY GR
6 EPSOM GR
1 WINMOSS DR
2 SPRING CL
3 BROMPTON AVE
4 LOUGHLIN DR
5 SUNSET CL
6 KALE GR
7 DORCHESTER DR
8 CROFTERS LA
9 GLENDALE GR
10 BIRCHWOOD WAY
11 CHERRY VIEW
1 LAPFORD WLK
2 BYTON WLK
3 NORTHFIELD CL
4 WOODCOTE CL
5 WHITBURN RD
6 KENBURY CL
1 JADE CL
2 WINGATE WLK
3 BROOK HEY WLK
4 QUERNMORE WLK
5 CHANGFORD GN
6 BIRBECK WLK
7 FAIRTHORN WLK
8 BURWELL CL
9 HARLESTON WLK
10 KENMAY WAY
1 COLWALL WLK
2 SIMONSWOOD WLK
3 LIFTON RD
4 WESTHEAD WLK
5 WESTHEAD CL

29
41

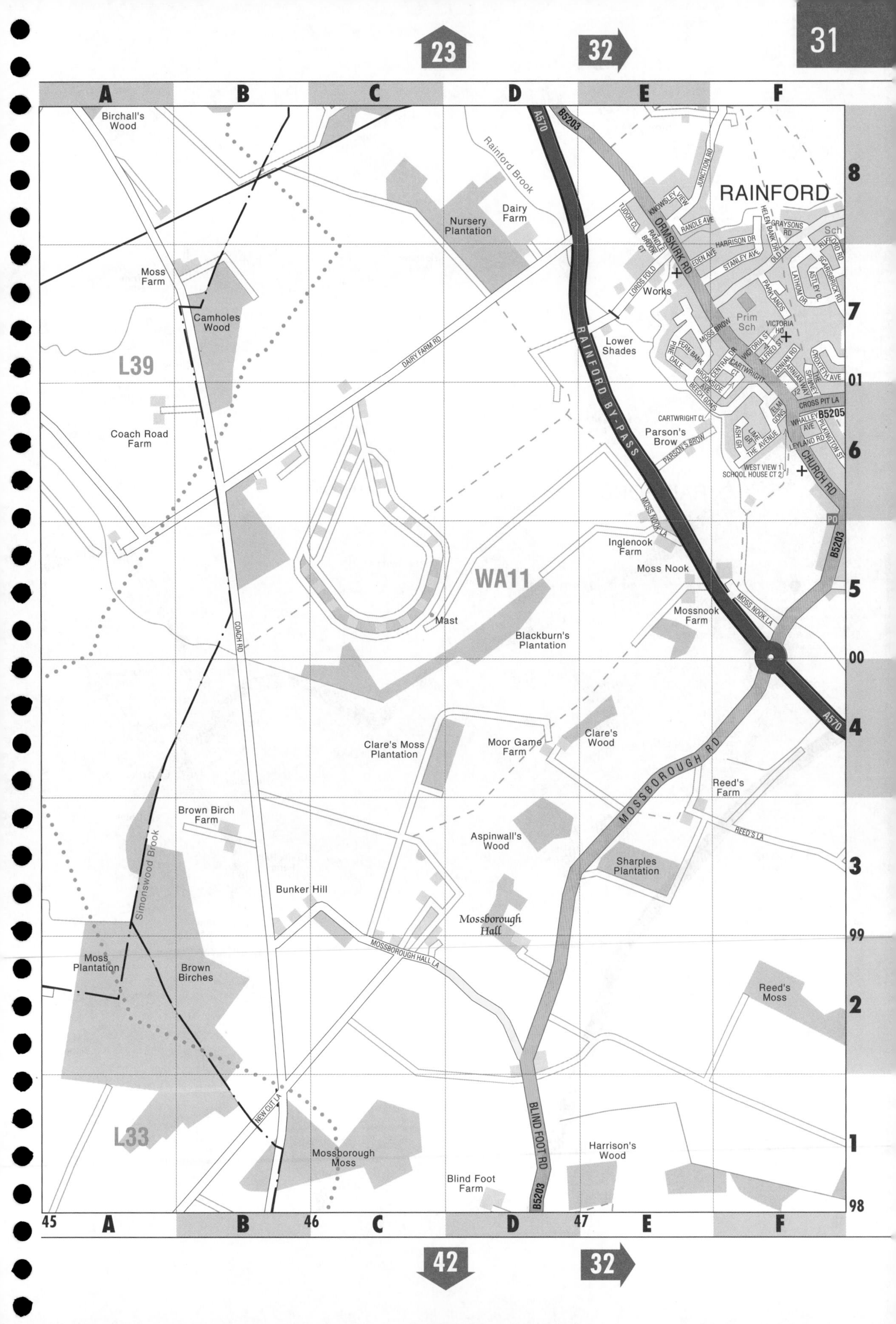

A B C D E F

RAINFORD

L39

Birchall's Wood

Moss Farm

Camholes Wood

Coach Road Farm

Dairy Farm Rd

Nursery Plantation

Dairy Farm

Rainford Brook

B5203

A570

ORMSKIRK RD

Works

Lower Shades

Prim Sch

Parson's Brow

Parson's Brow

Cartwright Cl

WEST VIEW 1
SCHOOL HOUSE CT 2

CHURCH RD

B5205

B5203

PO

WA11

Mast

Blackburn's Plantation

Inglenook Farm

Moss Nook

Mossnook Farm

MOSS NOOK LA

RAINFORD BY-PASS

Clare's Moss Plantation

Moor Game Farm

Clare's Wood

MOSSBOROUGH RD

Reed's Farm

REED'S LA

Brown Birch Farm

Aspinwall's Wood

Sharples Plantation

A570

Simonswood Brook

COACH RD

Bunker Hill

Mossborough Hall

MOSSBOROUGH HALL LA

Moss Plantation

Brown Birches

Reed's Moss

L33

NEW CUT LA

Mossborough Moss

Blind Foot Farm

BLIND FOOT RD

B5203

Harrison's Wood

45 A B 46 C D 47 E F

8 8 7 01 6 5 00 4 3 99 2 1 98

31
24

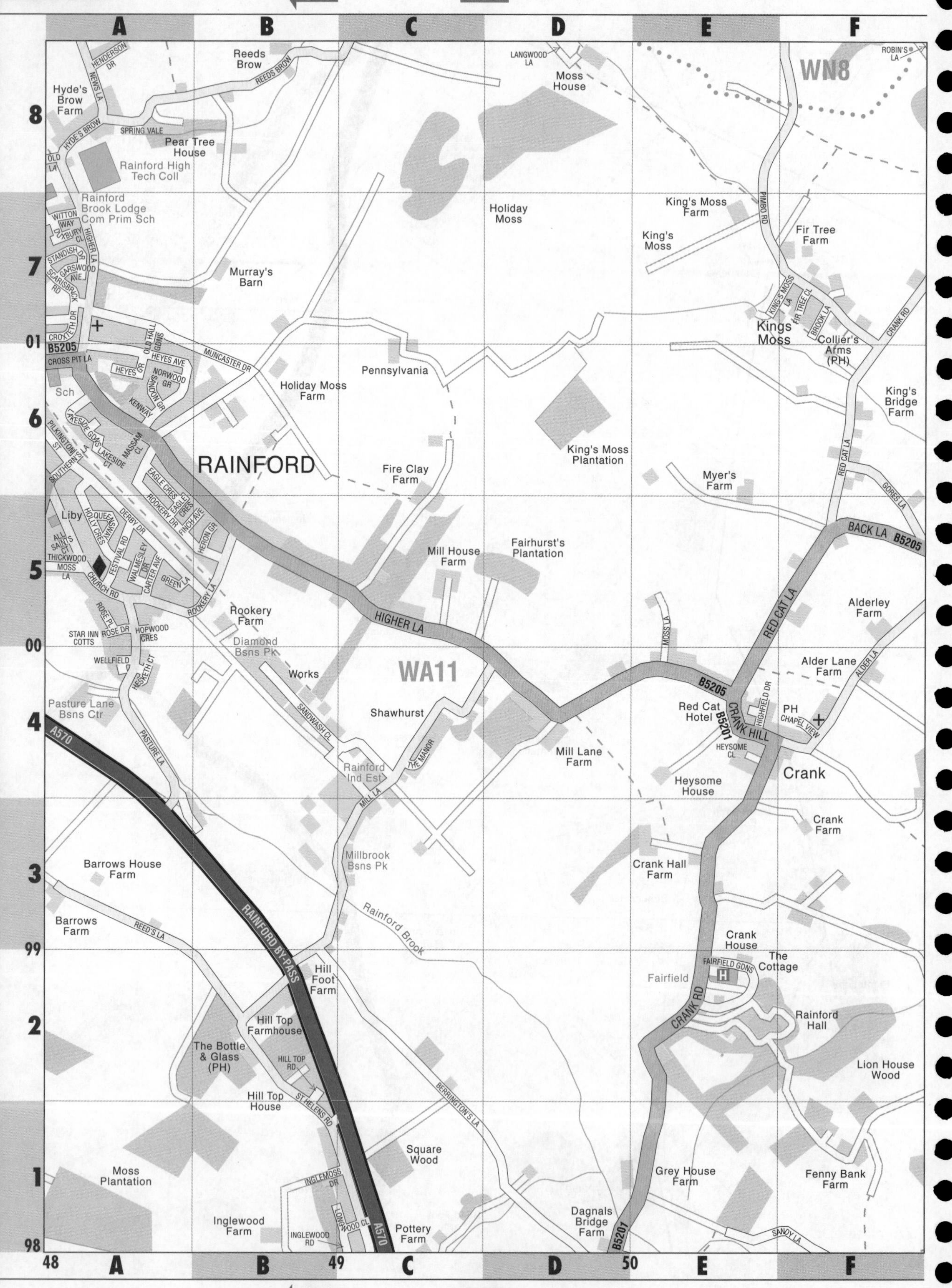
A
B
C
D
E
F
RAINFORD
WA11
WN8
Reeds Brow
Hyde's Brow Farm
Pear Tree House
Rainford High Tech Coll
Rainford Brook Lodge Com Prim Sch
Moss House
Holiday Moss
King's Moss Farm
King's Moss
Fir Tree Farm
Murray's Barn
Kings Moss
Collier's Arms (PH)
King's Bridge Farm
Pennsylvania
Holiday Moss Farm
King's Moss Plantation
Fire Clay Farm
Myer's Farm
Liby
Mill House Farm
Fairhurst's Plantation
Alderley Farm
Rookery Farm
Diamond Bsns Pk
Works
Shawhurst
Red Cat Hotel
PH
Alder Lane Farm
Pasture Lane Bsns Ctr
Mill Lane Farm
Rainford Ind Est
Heysome House
Crank
Crank Farm
Barrows House Farm
Millbrook Bsns Pk
Crank Hall Farm
Rainford Brook
Barrows Farm
Crank House
The Cottage
Fairfield
Hill Foot Farm
Hill Top Farmhouse
Rainford Hall
The Bottle & Glass (PH)
Lion House Wood
Hill Top House
Square Wood
Moss Plantation
Grey House Farm
Fenny Bank Farm
Inglewood Farm
Dagnals Bridge Farm
Pottery Farm
HIGHER LA
B5205
B5201
BACK LA
RED CAT LA
CRANK HILL
CRANK RD
A570
RAINFORD BY-PASS
REED'S LA
BERRINGTON'S LA
SANDY LA
MILL LA
PIMBO RD
CROSS PIT LA
MUNCASTER DR
CHURCH RD
PASTURE LA
8
7
01
6
5
00
4
3
99
2
1
98
48
49
50

31
43

25
34

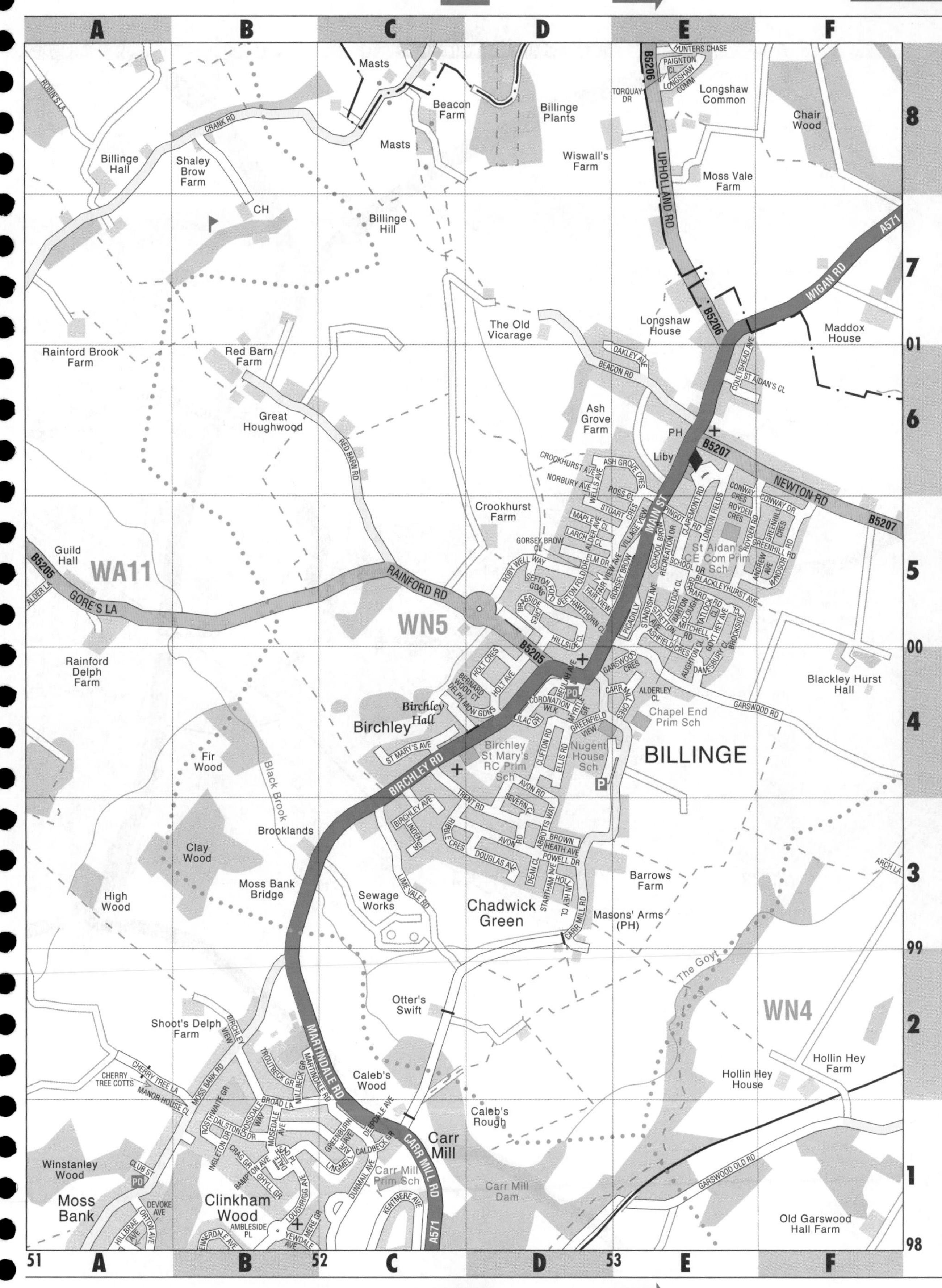
Masts
Beacon Farm
Billinge Plants
Longshaw Common
Chair Wood
Billinge Hall
Shaley Brow Farm
CH
Billinge Hill
Wiswall's Farm
Moss Vale Farm
The Old Vicarage
Longshaw House
Maddox House
Rainford Brook Farm
Red Barn Farm
Great Houghwood
Ash Grove Farm
Liby
PH
Crookhurst Farm
Guild Hall
WA11
WN5
St Aidan's CE Com Prim Sch
Rainford Delph Farm
Blackley Hurst Hall
Birchley Hall
Birchley
Chapel End Prim Sch
BILLINGE
Birchley St Mary's RC Prim Sch
Nugent House Sch
Fir Wood
Black Brook
Brooklands
Clay Wood
Barrows Farm
High Wood
Moss Bank Bridge
Sewage Works
Chadwick Green
Masons' Arms (PH)
The Goyt
Otter's Swift
WN4
Shoot's Delph Farm
Hollin Hey Farm
Hollin Hey House
Caleb's Wood
Caleb's Rough
Carr Mill
Winstanley Wood
Carr Mill Prim Sch
Carr Mill Dam
Moss Bank
Clinkham Wood
Old Garswood Hall Farm
RAINFORD RD
GORE'S LA
B5205
B5206
B5207
A571
UPHOLLAND RD
WIGAN RD
NEWTON RD
MAIN ST
BIRCHLEY RD
MARTINDALE RD
CARR MILL RD
GARSWOOD RD
GARSWOOD OLD RD
CRANK RD
RED BARN RD
ROBIN'S LA
ARCH LA
A B C D E F
8 7 6 5 4 3 2 1
01 00 99 98
51 52 53

44
34

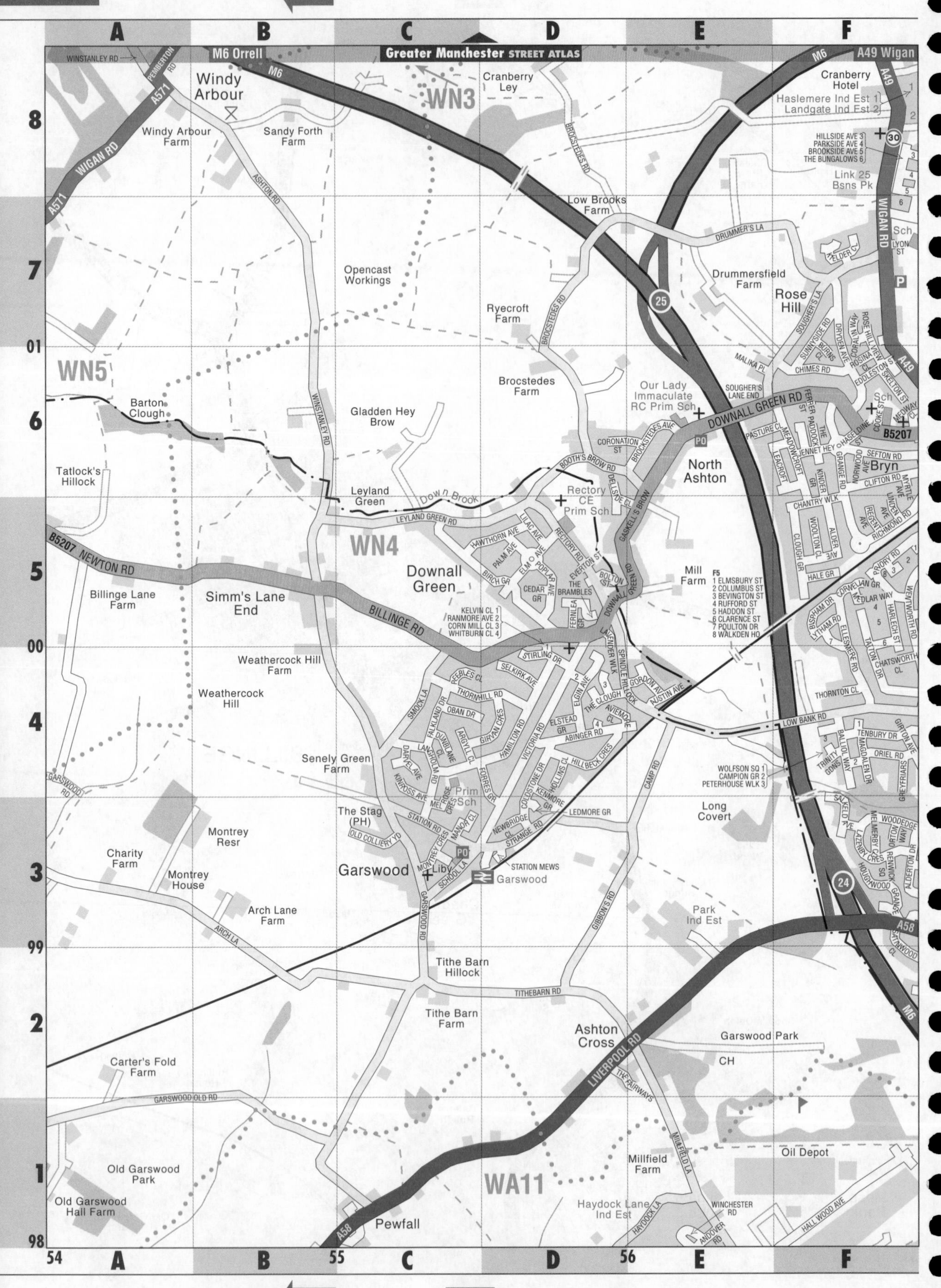

Greater Manchester STREET ATLAS

A   B   C   D   E   F

WINSTANLEY RD

M6 Orrell

Windy Arbour

WN3

Cranberry Ley

M6

A49 Wigan

Cranberry Hotel

Haslemere Ind Est 1
Landgate Ind Est 2

HILLSIDE AVE 3
PARKSIDE AVE 4
BROOKSIDE AVE 5
THE BUNGALOWS 6

Link 25 Bsns Pk

Sch

LYON ST

P

Windy Arbour Farm

Sandy Forth Farm

WIGAN RD

A571

ASHTON RD

Low Brooks Farm

DRUMMER'S LA

Drummersfield Farm

Rose Hill

SOUGHER'S LA

ZELDER ST

WIGAN RD

A49

8

Opencast Workings

Ryecroft Farm

BROCSTEDES RD

Our Lady Immaculate RC Prim Sch

SOUGHER'S LANE END

DOWNALL GREEN RD

FERRER PADDOCK

PASTURE LA

MEADOWCROFT

JENNET HEY

Bryn

B5207

Sch

SUNNYSIDE RD

DRYDEN AVE

CHIMES RD

MALIKA PL

7

01

WN5

Barton Clough

Gladden Hey Brow

WINSTANLEY RD

Brocstedes Farm

CORONATION ST

BROCSTEDES AVE

BOOTH'S BROW RD

Rectory CE Prim Sch

GASKELL'S BROW

North Ashton

PO

GRANGE RD

CLIFTON AVE

CHANTRY WLK

WOOLTON GR

ALDER AVE

RICHMOND RD

6

Tatlock's Hillock

Leyland Green

Down Brook

LEYLAND GREEN RD

LILAC AVE

RECTORY RD

BOLTON

DELLSIDE CL

Mill Farm

F5

1 ELMSBURY ST
2 COLUMBUS ST
3 BEVINGTON ST
4 RUFFORD ST
5 HADDON ST
6 CLARENCE ST
7 POULTON DR
8 WALKDEN HO

HALE GR

5

B5207 NEWTON RD

Billinge Lane Farm

Simm's Lane End

WN4

Downall Green

HAWTHORN AVE

PALM AVE

ELMO AVE

POPLAR AVE

BIRCH GR

CEDAR GR

THE BRAMBLES

FERNLEA

KELVIN CL 1
RANMORE AVE 2
CORN MILL CL 3
WHITBURN CL 4

DOWNALL GREEN RD

DOLAR WAY

HARLECH CL

TAXTON

ELLESMERE RD

CHATSWORTH CL

00

BILLINGE RD

Weathercock Hill Farm

STIRLING DR

LAVENDER WLK

SPINDLE HILL CL

GORDON AVE

AUSTIN AVE

THORNTON CL

BSPHAM DR

ORNELLAN CL

4

Weathercock Hill

SMOCK LA

PEEBLES AVE

THORNHILL RD

OBAN DR

FALKLAND GR

SELKIRK AVE

ELGIN AVE

THE CLOUGH

AVIEMORE

ELSTEAD GR

ABINGER RD

LOW BANK RD

TENBURY DR

TRINITY BUNGALOW

BALLOT WAY

ORIEL RD

MAGDALEN DR

GIRTON

Senely Green Farm

ARGYLL CL

DARYL AVE

LANGFORM LA

KINROSS AVE

HAMILTON RD

VICTORIA RD

FORRES DR

ELGIN AVE

KEMMORE

HOLLINS CL

HILLBECK CRES

Camp Rd

WOLFSON SQ 1
CAMPION GR 2
PETERHOUSE WLK 3

Long Covert

SALFORD AVE

WOODEDGE

MELMERBY CRES

MALVERN GROVE

3

Charity Farm

Montrey Resr

Montrey House

The Stag (PH)

Prim Sch

STATION RD

OLD COLLIERY YD

MOTREY CRES

SCHOOL LA

NEWBRIDGE

STRANGE RD

MANOR

LEDMORE GR

Park Ind Est

A58

24

99

Arch Lane Farm

ARCH LA

PO

Libr

Garswood

Garswood

STATION MEWS

GIBBON'S RD

Tithe Barn Hillock

2

Carter's Fold Farm

GARSWOOD OLD RD

Tithe Barn Farm

TITHEBARN RD

Ashton Cross

LIVERPOOL RD

Garswood Park

CH

M6

1

Old Garswood Park

Old Garswood Hall Farm

WA11

THE FAIRWAYS

HAYDOCK LANE

Millfield Farm

Haydock Lane Ind Est

WINCHESTER RD

ANDOVER

MILFIELD LA

Oil Depot

HALL WOOD AVE

98

54   A   B   55   C   D   56   E   F

36

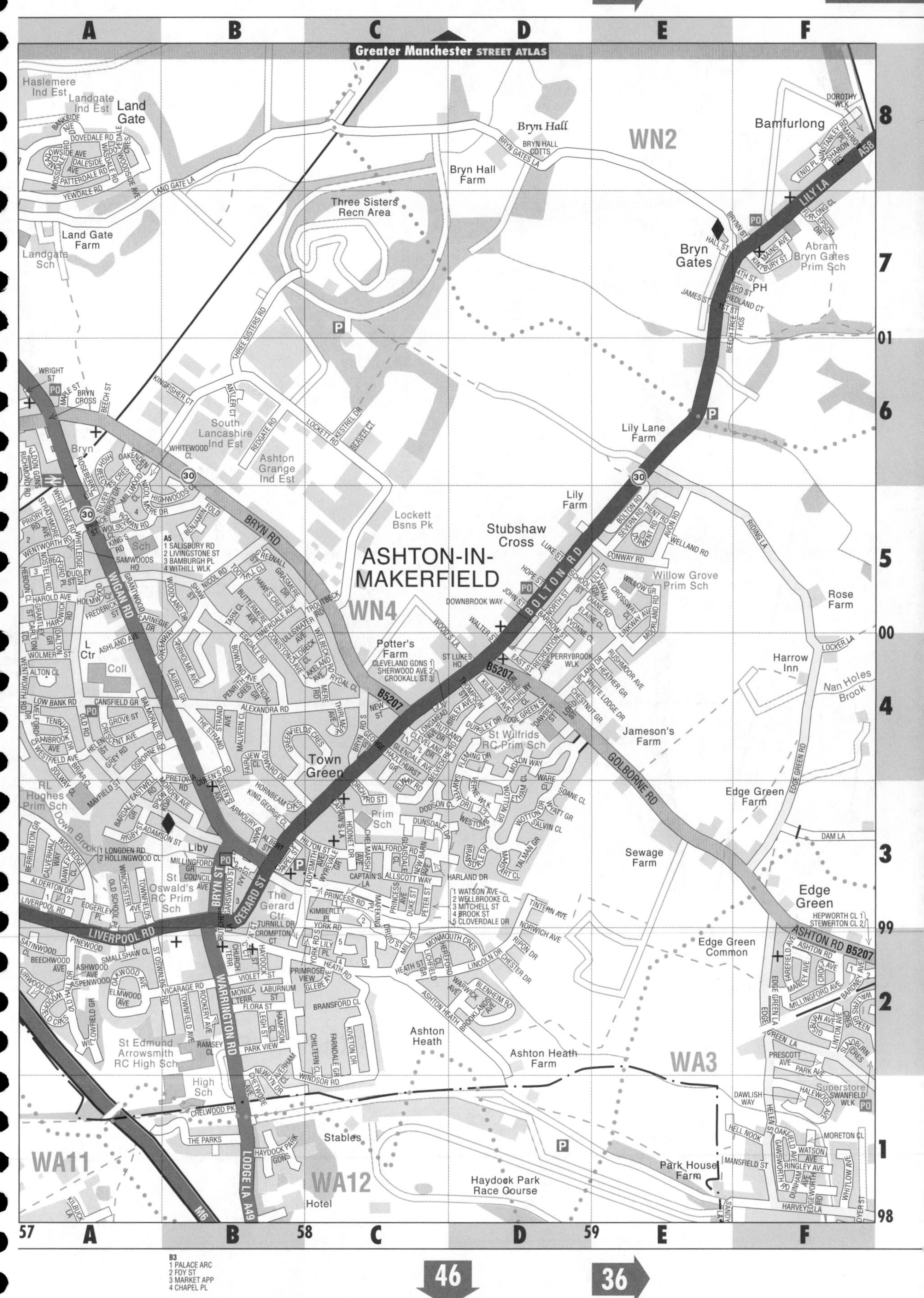

B3
1 PALACE ARC
2 FOY ST
3 MARKET APP
4 CHAPEL PL

46

36

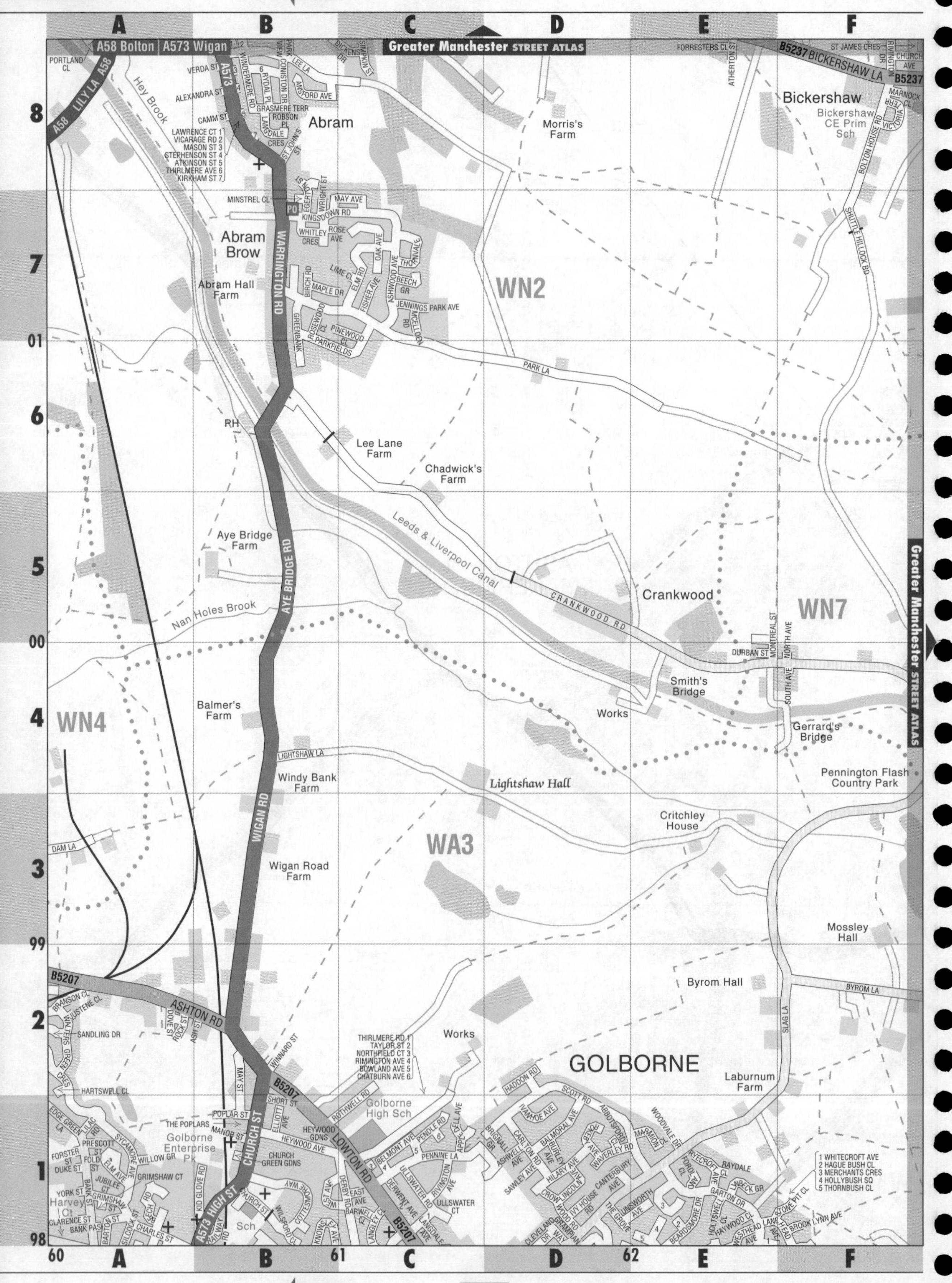

A58 Bolton | A573 Wigan

Greater Manchester STREET ATLAS

Bickershaw

Bickershaw
CE Prim
Sch

Abram

Morris's
Farm

WN2

Abram
Brow

Abram Hall
Farm

RH

Lee Lane
Farm

Chadwick's
Farm

Leeds & Liverpool Canal

Aye Bridge
Farm

Crankwood

WN7

Nan Holes Brook

CRANKWOOD RD

Smith's
Bridge

Works

WN4

Balmer's
Farm

Gerrard's
Bridge

Pennington Flash
Country Park

Windy Bank
Farm

Lightshaw Hall

Critchley
House

Mossley
Hall

Wigan Road
Farm

WA3

B5207

Byrom Hall

BYROM LA

ASHTON RD

B5207

Works

Laburnum
Farm

GOLBORNE

THIRLMERE RD 1
TAYLOR ST 2
NORTHFIELD CT 3
RIMINGTON AVE 4
BOWLAND AVE 5
CHATBURN AVE 6.

Golborne
High Sch

THE POPLARS

Golborne
Enterprise
Pk

Church
Green Gdns

1 WHITECROFT AVE
2 HAGUE BUSH CL
3 MERCHANTS CRES
4 HOLLYBUSH SQ
5 THORNBUSH CL.

Harvey
Ct

26
38

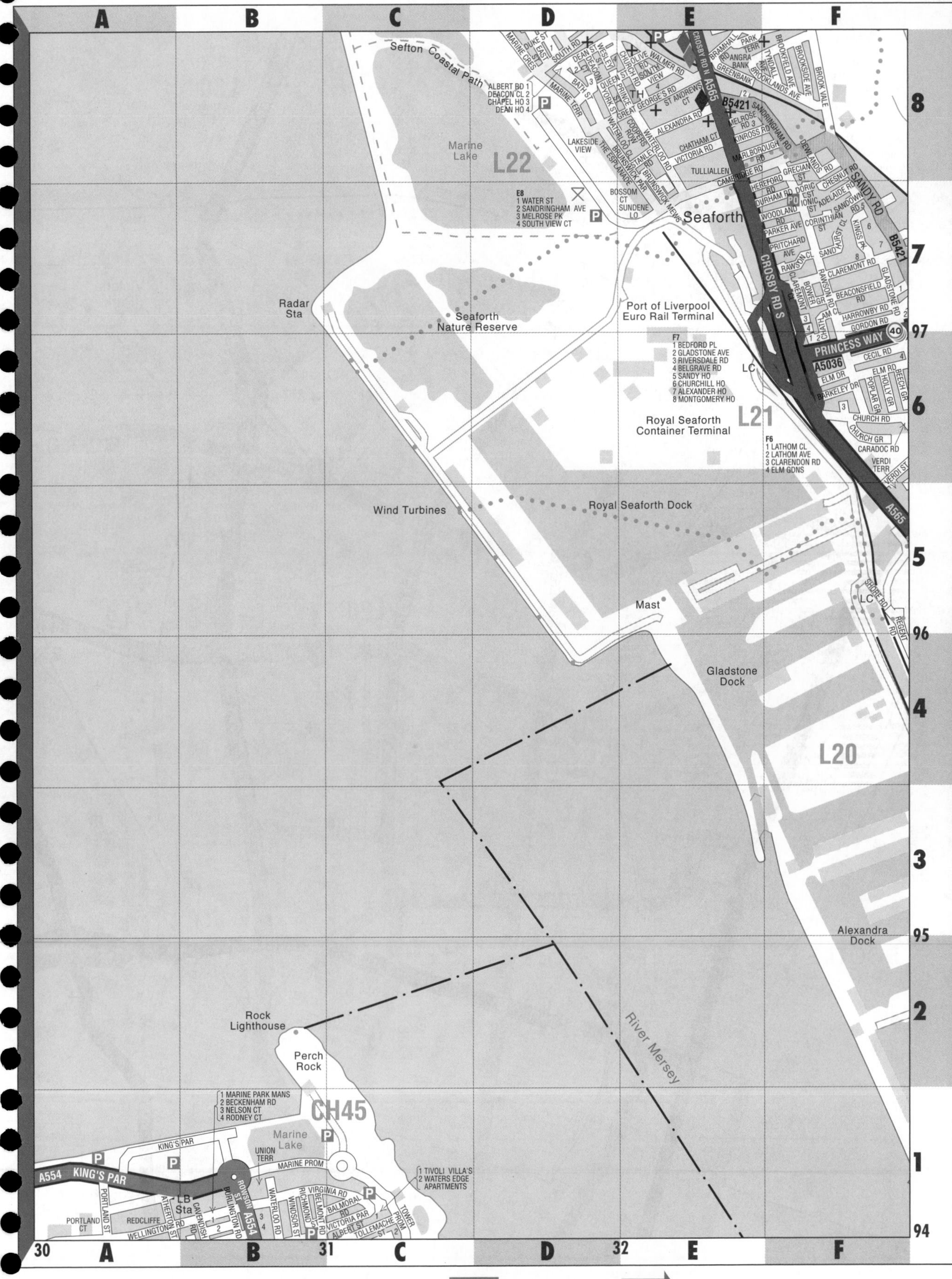
A
B
C
D
E
F
8
7
97
6
5
96
4
3
95
2
1
94
30
31
32
Sefton Coastal Path
Marine Lake
L22
ALBERT RD 1
DEACON CL 2
CHAPEL HO 3
DEAN HO 4
E8
1 WATER ST
2 SANDRINGHAM AVE
3 MELROSE PK
4 SOUTH VIEW CT
LAKESIDE VIEW
BOSSOM CT
SUNDENE LO
Seaforth
TH
CROSBY RD N
A565
B5421
SANDRINGHAM RD
ALEXANDRA RD
CHATHAM CT
VICTORIA RD
TULLIALLEN
MARLBOROUGH RD
CROSBY RD S
SANDY RD
PRINCESS WAY
A5036
40
Radar Sta
Seaforth Nature Reserve
Port of Liverpool Euro Rail Terminal
F7
1 BEDFORD PL
2 GLADSTONE AVE
3 RIVERSDALE RD
4 BELGRAVE RD
5 SANDY HO
6 CHURCHILL HO
7 ALEXANDER HO
8 MONTGOMERY HO
LC
Royal Seaforth Container Terminal
L21
F6
1 LATHOM CL
2 LATHOM AVE
3 CLARENDON RD
4 ELM GDNS
Wind Turbines
Royal Seaforth Dock
Mast
Gladstone Dock
L20
Alexandra Dock
River Mersey
Rock Lighthouse
Perch Rock
CH45
Marine Lake
1 MARINE PARK MANS
2 BECKENHAM RD
3 NELSON CT
4 RODNEY CT
KING'S PAR
A554
MARINE PROM
UNION TERR
LB Sta
1 TIVOLI VILLA'S
2 WATERS EDGE APARTMENTS
PORTLAND ST
PORTLAND CT
REDCLIFFE
WELLINGTON RD
VIRGINIA RD
VICTORIA PAR
TOWER PROM

51
38

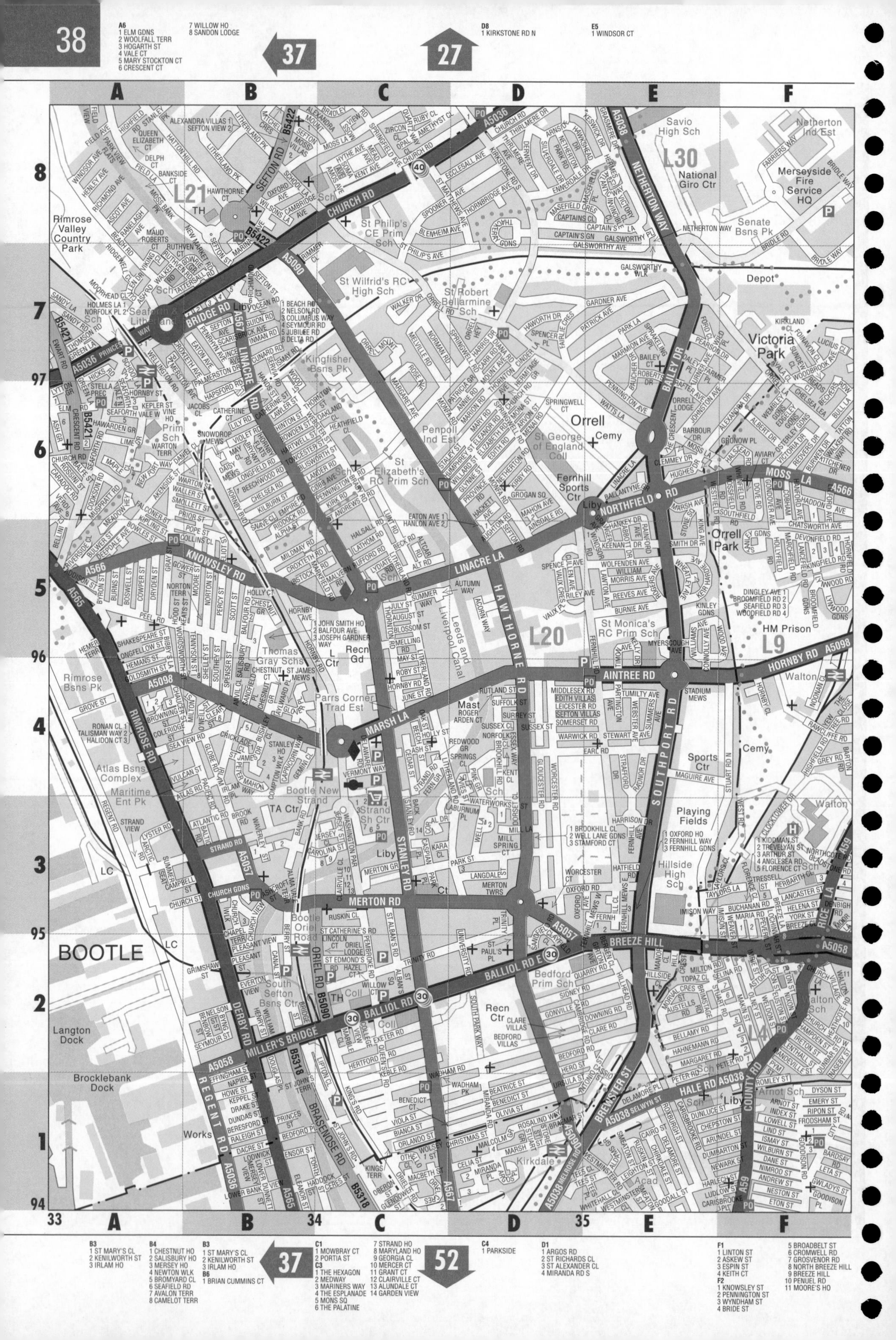
A6
1 ELM GDNS
2 WOOLFALL TERR
3 HOGARTH ST
4 VALE CT
5 MARY STOCKTON CT
6 CRESCENT CT
7 WILLOW HO
8 SANDON LODGE
37
27
D8
1 KIRKSTONE RD N
E5
1 WINDSOR CT
A
B
C
D
E
F
8
7
97
6
5
96
4
3
95
2
1
94
33
34
35
L21
L30
L20
L9
Rimrose Valley Country Park
Savio High Sch
National Giro Ctr
Netherton Ind Est
Merseyside Fire Service HQ
Senate Bsns Pk
St Philip's CE Prim Sch
St Wilfrid's RC High Sch
St Robert Bellarmine Sch
Seaforth & Litherland
Kingfisher Bsns Pk
Victoria Park
Orrell
St George of England Coll
Penpoll Ind Est
St Elizabeth's RC Prim Sch
Fernhill Sports Ctr
Orrell Park
Leeds and Liverpool Canal
St Monica's RC Prim Sch
HM Prison
Thomas Gray Schs
Recn Gd
Rimrose Bsns Pk
Parrs Corner Trad Est
Atlas Bsns Complex
Maritime Ent Pk
Bootle New Strand
Strand Sh Ctr
TA Ctr
Sports Ctr
Playing Fields
Hillside High Sch
Bootle Oriel Road
BOOTLE
South Sefton Bsns Ctr
Bedford Prim Sch
Recn Ctr
Langton Dock
Brocklebank Dock
Works
Kirkdale
Walton
NETHERTON WAY
CHURCH RD
BRIDGE RD
LINACRE RD
LINACRE LA
KNOWSLEY RD
HAWTHORNE RD
AINTREE RD
HORNBY RD
MARSH LA
STANLEY RD
MERTON RD
RIMROSE RD
DERBY RD
BREEZE HILL
BALLIOL RD
MILLER'S BRIDGE
SOUTHPORT RD
BAILEY DR
NORTHFIELD RD
MOSS LA
HALE RD
COUNTY RD
REGENT RD
BRASENOSE RD
B3
1 ST MARY'S CL
2 KENILWORTH ST
3 IRLAM HO
B4
1 CHESTNUT HO
2 SALISBURY HO
3 MERSEY HO
4 NEWTON WLK
5 BROMYARD CL
6 SEAFIELD RD
7 AVALON TERR
8 CAMELOT TERR
B3
1 ST MARY'S CL
2 KENILWORTH ST
3 IRLAM HO
B6
1 BRIAN CUMMINS CT
37
C1
1 MOWBRAY CT
2 PORTIA ST
C3
1 THE HEXAGON
2 MEDWAY
3 MARINERS WAY
4 THE ESPLANADE
5 MONS SQ
6 THE PALATINE
7 STRAND HO
8 MARYLAND HO
9 GEORGIA CL
10 MERCER CT
11 GRANT CT
12 CLAIRVILLE CT
13 ALUNDALE CT
14 GARDEN VIEW
52
C4
1 PARKSIDE
D1
1 ARGOS RD
2 ST RICHARDS CL
3 ST ALEXANDER CL
4 MIRANDA RD S
F1
1 LINTON ST
2 ASKEW ST
3 ESPIN ST
4 KEITH CT
F2
1 KNOWSLEY ST
2 PENNINGTON ST
3 WYNDHAM ST
4 BRIDE ST
5 BROADBELT ST
6 CROMWELL RD
7 GROSVENOR RD
8 NORTH BREEZE HILL
9 BREEZE HILL
10 PENUEL RD
11 MOORE'S HO

28 40

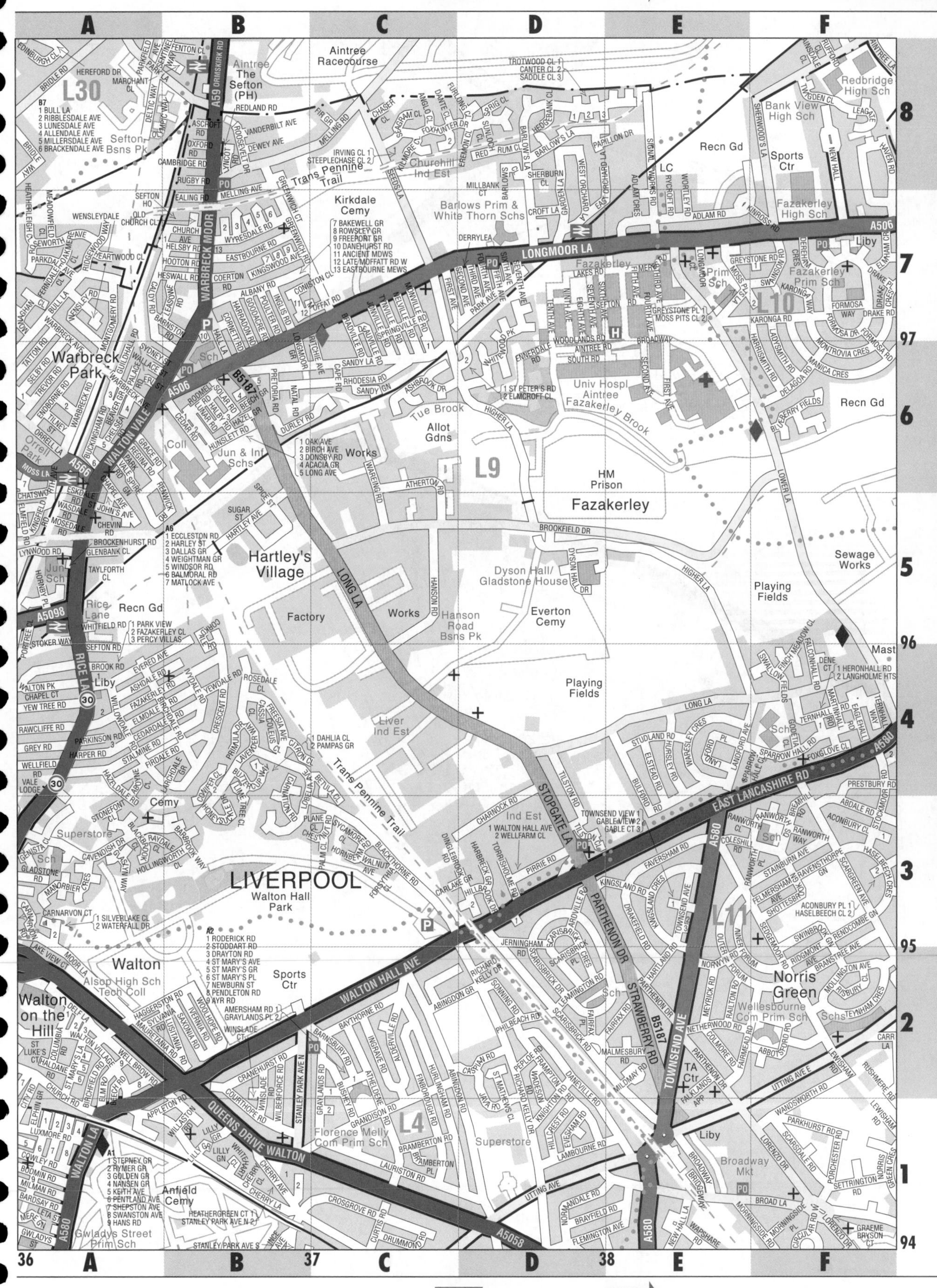
A
B
C
D
E
F
8
7
97
6
5
96
4
3
95
2
1
94
36
37
38
Aintree Racecourse
Aintree
The Sefton (PH)
L30
Sefton Bsns Pk
ORMSKIRK RD
A59
REDLAND RD
WARBRECK MOOR
Kirkdale Cemy
Trans Pennine Trail
Churchill Ind Est
Barlows Prim & White Thorn Schs
LONGMOOR LA
A506
Recn Gd
Bank View High Sch
Redbridge High Sch
Sports Ctr
Fazakerley High Sch
Fazakerley Prim Sch
L10
Liby
Warbreck Park
WALTON VALE
Orrell Park
Coll
Jun & Inf Schs
Works
Allot Gdns
Tue Brook
L9
HM Prison
Fazakerley
Univ Hospl Aintree
Fazakerley Brook
Recn Gd
BROOKFIELD DR
Hartley's Village
LONG LA
Factory
Works
Hanson Road Bsns Pk
Dyson Hall/ Gladstone House
Everton Cemy
Sewage Works
Playing Fields
Mast
Rice Lane
Recn Gd
RICE LA
A5098
Liby
Playing Fields
Liver Ind Est
Cemy
Superstore
LIVERPOOL
Walton Hall Park
STOPGATE LA
Ind Est
EAST LANCASHIRE RD
A580
L11
Walton
Alsop High Sch Tech Coll
Walton on the Hill
Sports Ctr
WALTON HALL AVE
PARTHENON DR
STRAWBERRY RD
B5187
TOWNSEND AVE
Norris Green
Wellesbourne Com Prim Sch
Schs
TA Ctr
QUEENS DRIVE WALTON
L4
Florence Melly Com Prim Sch
Superstore
Anfield Cemy
Gwladys Street Prim Sch
WALTON LA
A5058
Liby
Broadway Mkt
BROADWAY
UTTING AVE

53 40

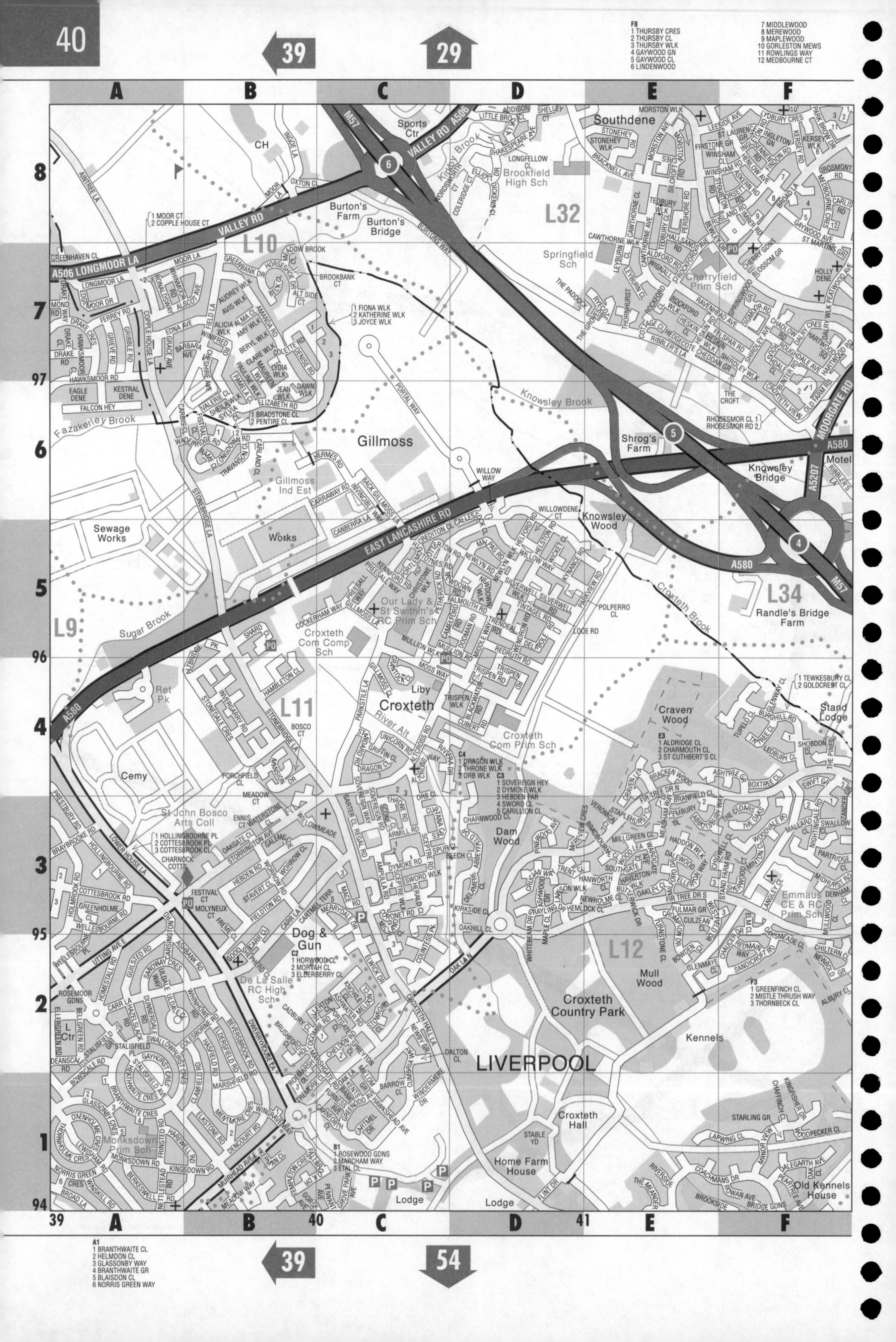

40
39
29
F8
1 THURSBY CRES
2 THURSBY CL
3 THURSBY WLK
4 GAYWOOD GN
5 GAYWOOD CL
6 LINDENWOOD
7 MIDDLEWOOD
8 MEREWOOD
9 MAPLEWOOD
10 GORLESTON MEWS
11 ROWLINGS WAY
12 MEDBOURNE CT
A
B
C
D
E
F
8
7
97
6
5
96
4
3
95
2
1
94
39
40
41
Southdene
Sports Ctr
VALLEY RD
A506
M57
Burton's Farm
Burton's Bridge
Brookfield High Sch
L32
L10
Springfield Sch
Cherryfield Prim Sch
1 MOOR CT
2 COPPLE HOUSE CT
A506 LONGMOOR LA
1 FIONA WLK
2 KATHERINE WLK
3 JOYCE WLK
Fazakerley Brook
Knowsley Brook
1 BRADSTONE CL
2 PENTIRE CL
Gillmoss
Gillmoss Ind Est
Shrog's Farm
Knowsley Bridge
Motel
A580
A5207
MOORGATE RD
RHOSESMOR CL 1
RHOSESMOR RD 2
Sewage Works
Works
EAST LANCASHIRE RD
Knowsley Wood
L34
Randle's Bridge Farm
Croxteth Brook
L9
Sugar Brook
Our Lady & St Swithin's RC Prim Sch
Croxteth Com Comp Sch
Ret Pk
L11
Croxteth
Liby
River Alt
Croxteth Com Prim Sch
Craven Wood
1 TEWKESBURY CL
2 GOLDCREST CL
Stand Lodge
C4
1 DRAGON WLK
2 THRONE WLK
3 ORB WLK
C3
1 SOVEREIGN HEY
2 DYMOKE WLK
3 HEBDEN PAR
4 SWORD CL
5 CARILLION CL
E3
1 ALDRIDGE CL
2 CHARMOUTH CL
3 ST CUTHBERT'S CL
Cemy
St John Bosco Arts Coll
1 HOLLINGBOURNE PL
2 COTTESBROOK PL
3 COTTESBROOK CL
Dam Wood
Emmaus CE & RC Prim Sch
Dog & Gun
C2
1 HORWOOD CL
2 MORVAH CL
3 ELDERBERRY CL
De La Salle RC High Sch
L12
Mull Wood
Croxteth Country Park
F3
1 GREENFINCH CL
2 MISTLE THRUSH WAY
3 THORNBECK CL
Kennels
LIVERPOOL
L Ctr
Croxteth Hall
Monksdown Prim Sch
Home Farm House
B1
1 ROSEWOOD GDNS
2 MARCHAM WAY
3 ETAL CL
Lodge
Old Kennels House
A1
1 BRANTHWAITE CL
2 HELMDON CL
3 GLASSONBY WAY
4 BRANTHWAITE GR
5 BLAISDON CL
6 NORRIS GREEN WAY
39
54

30 42

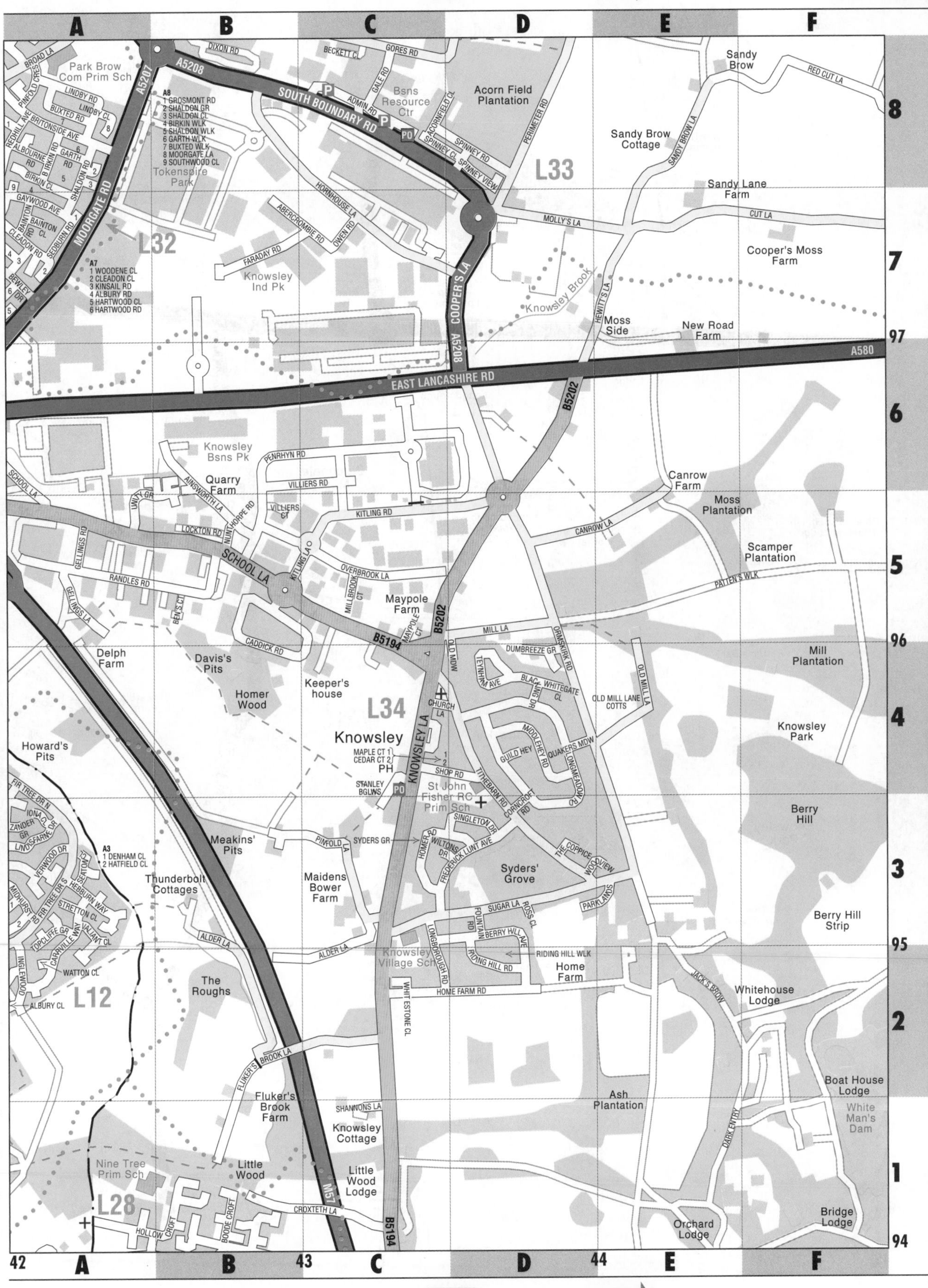
A
B
C
D
E
F
Park Brow
Com Prim Sch
BROAD LA
LINDBY RD
LINDBY CL
BUXTED RD
BRITONSIDE AVE
REDHILL AVE
ALBOURNE RD
BIRKIN RD
GARTH RD
SHALDON RD
BIRKIN CL
GAYWOOD AVE
BAINTON RD
BAINTON CL
CLEADON RD
SEDBURN RD
BEWLEY DR
MOORGATE RD
A5207
A5208
DIXON RD
BECKETT CL
GORES RD
SOUTH BOUNDARY RD
ADMIN RD
GALE RD
Bsns
Resource
Ctr
PO
A8
1 GROSMONT RD
2 SHALDON GR
3 SHALDON CL
4 BIRKIN WLK
5 SHALDON WLK
6 GARTH WLK
7 BUXTED WLK
8 MOORGATE LA
9 SOUTHWOOD CL
Tokenspire
Park
L32
A7
1 WOODENE CL
2 CLEADON CL
3 KINSAIL RD
4 ALBURY RD
5 HARTWOOD CL
6 HARTWOOD RD
ABERCROMBIE RD
HORNHOUSE LA
OWEN RD
FARADAY RD
Knowsley
Ind Pk
ACORNFIELD CL
SPINNEY CL
SPINNEY RD
SPINNEY VIEW
Acorn Field
Plantation
PERIMETER RD
L33
COOPER'S LA
A5208
Sandy
Brow
RED CUT LA
Sandy Brow
Cottage
SANDY BROW LA
Sandy Lane
Farm
MOLLY'S LA
CUT LA
Cooper's Moss
Farm
Knowsley Brook
HEWITT'S LA
Moss
Side
New Road
Farm
97
A580
EAST LANCASHIRE RD
B5202
6
Knowsley
Bsns Pk
PENRHYN RD
Quarry
Farm
VILLIERS RD
VILLIERS CT
KITLING RD
SCHOOL LA
UNITY GR
AINSWORTH LA
NUNTHORPE RD
LOCKTON RD
GELLINGS RD
RANDLES RD
KITLING LA
OVERBROOK LA
MILLBROOK CT
Maypole
Farm
MAYPOLE CT
B5202
B5194
GELLINGS LA
BEN'S CT
CADDICK RD
Canrow
Farm
Moss
Plantation
CANROW LA
Scamper
Plantation
PATTEN'S WLK
5
MILL LA
OLD MDW
DUMBREEZE GR
TEYNHAM AVE
BLACKWATER DR
WHITEGATE CL
ORMSKIRK RD
OLD MILL LANE
COTTS
OLD MILL LA
Mill
Plantation
96
Delph
Farm
Davis's
Pits
Homer
Wood
Keeper's
house
L34
CHURCH LA
Knowsley
MAPLE CT
CEDAR CT
PH
KNOWSLEY LA
SHOP RD
MIDDLEHEY RD
GUILD HEY
QUAKERS MDW
LONGMEADOW RD
TITHEBARN RD
4
Knowsley
Park
Howard's
Pits
STANLEY BGLWS
St John
Fisher RC
Prim Sch
CORNCROFT RD
SINGLETON DR
Berry
Hill
FIR TREE DR N
IONA CL
ZANDER GR
LINDISFARNE DR
VERWOOD DR
SEATON
A3
1 DENHAM CL
2 HATFIELD CL
Meakins'
Pits
PINFOLD LA
SYDERS GR
HOMER RD
WILTONS DR
FREDERICK LUNT AVE
THE COPPICE
WOODVIEW
Syders'
Grove
3
MIDHURST RD
FIR TREE DR S
HEBBURN WAY
STRETTON CL
TOPCLIFFE GR
VALIANT CL
CARRVILLE WAY
Thunderbolt
Cottages
Maidens
Bower
Farm
SUGAR LA
ROSS CL
PARKLANDS
FOUNTAIN RD
BERRY HILL AVE
Berry Hill
Strip
ALDER LA
Knowsley
Village Sch
LONGBOROUGH RD
RIDING HILL RD
RIDING HILL WLK
Home
Farm
95
INGLEWOOD
WATTON CL
ALBURY CL
L12
The
Roughs
HOME FARM RD
WHITESTONE CL
JACK'S BROW
Whitehouse
Lodge
2
BROOK LA
FLUKER'S
Fluker's
Brook
Farm
SHANNONS LA
Knowsley
Cottage
Ash
Plantation
DARK ENTRY
Boat House
Lodge
White
Man's
Dam
Nine Tree
Prim Sch
Little
Wood
Little
Wood
Lodge
M57
1
L28
HOLLOW CROFT
BOODE CROFT
CROXTETH LA
B5194
Orchard
Lodge
Bridge
Lodge
94
8
7
42
43
44

55 42

41
31

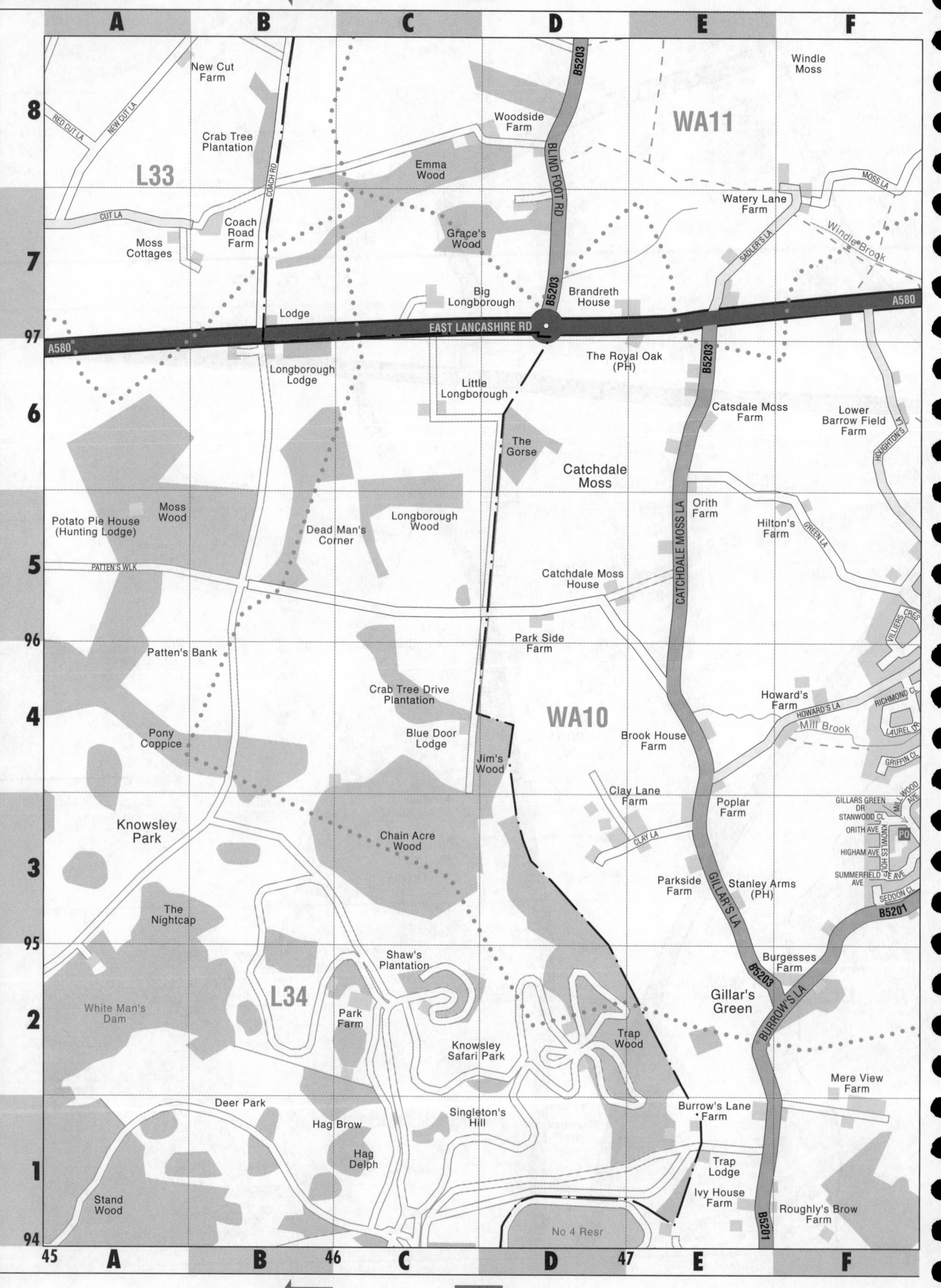
A
B
C
D
E
F
8
7
97
6
5
96
4
3
95
2
1
94
45
46
47
L33
L34
WA11
WA10
New Cut Farm
RED CUT LA
NEW CUT LA
Crab Tree Plantation
COACH RD
CUT LA
Coach Road Farm
Moss Cottages
Woodside Farm
Emma Wood
Grace's Wood
BLIND FOOT RD
B5203
Windle Moss
Watery Lane Farm
MOSS LA
SADLER'S LA
Windle Brook
Big Longborough
Brandreth House
Lodge
A580
EAST LANCASHIRE RD
The Royal Oak (PH)
Longborough Lodge
Little Longborough
Catsdale Moss Farm
Lower Barrow Field Farm
HOUGHTON'S LA
The Gorse
Catchdale Moss
Orith Farm
Hilton's Farm
GREEN LA
Potato Pie House (Hunting Lodge)
Moss Wood
Dead Man's Corner
Longborough Wood
CATCHDALE MOSS LA
PATTEN'S WLK
Catchdale Moss House
VILLIERS CRES
Park Side Farm
Patten's Bank
Crab Tree Drive Plantation
Howard's Farm
HOWARD'S LA
RICHMOND CL
Mill Brook
LAUREL DR
Pony Coppice
Blue Door Lodge
Brook House Farm
Jim's Wood
GRIFFIN CL
Clay Lane Farm
Poplar Farm
GILLARS GREEN DR
STANWOOD CL
MILL WOOD AVE
ORITH AVE
KNOWLES HOUSE AVE
PO
HIGHAM AVE
SUMMERFIELD AVE
Knowsley Park
Chain Acre Wood
CLAY LA
Parkside Farm
Stanley Arms (PH)
GILLAR'S LA
SEDDON CL
B5201
The Nightcap
Shaw's Plantation
Burgesses Farm
White Man's Dam
Park Farm
Gillar's Green
BURROW'S LA
Trap Wood
Knowsley Safari Park
Mere View Farm
Deer Park
Hag Brow
Singleton's Hill
Burrow's Lane Farm
Hag Delph
Trap Lodge
Ivy House Farm
Stand Wood
Roughly's Brow Farm
No 4 Resr

41
56

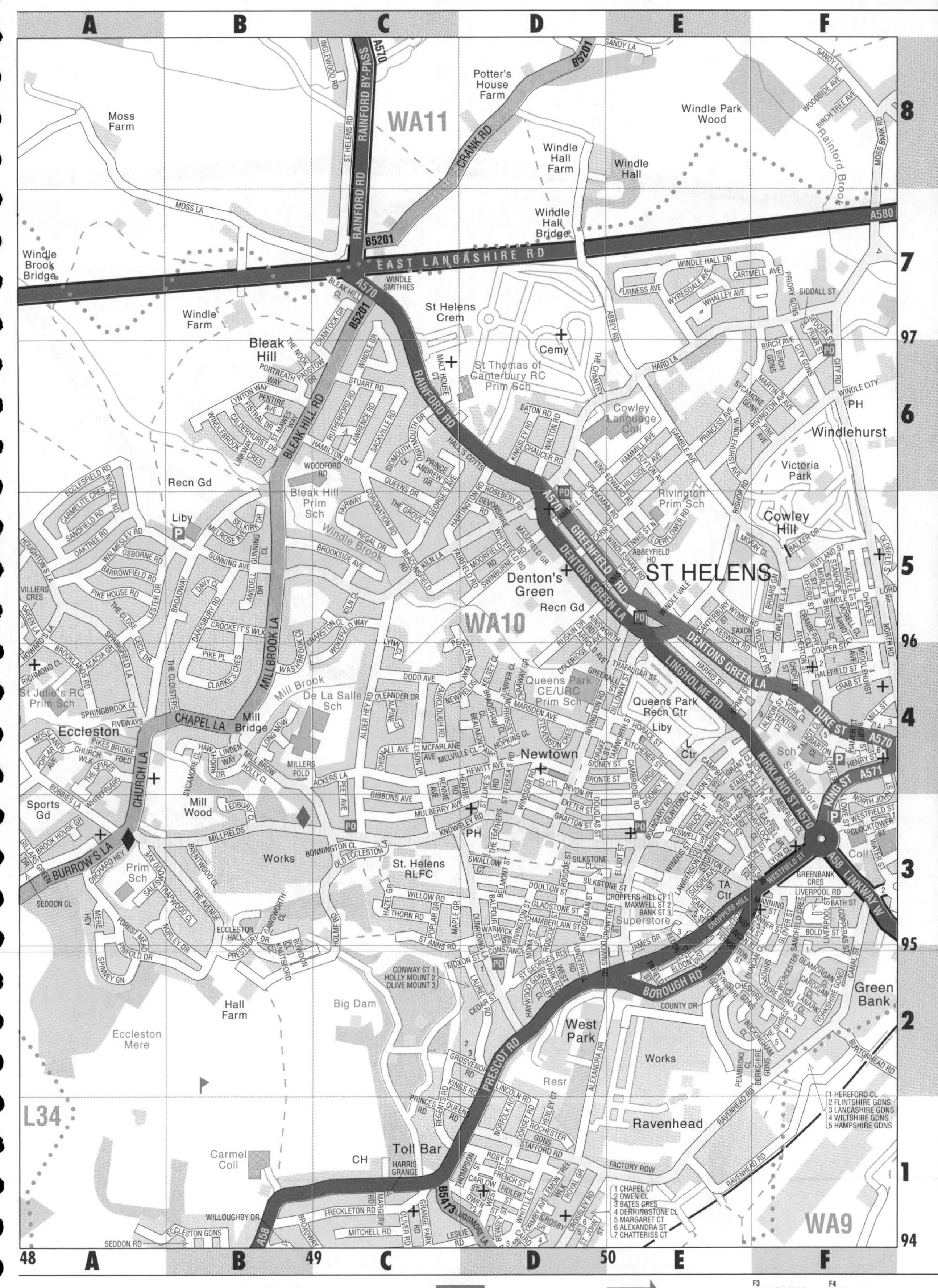

F3
1 NEW CROSS ST
2 CHALON WAY W
3 BANNER WLK

F4
1 MORLEY WAY
2 OXFORD ST
3 VOLUNTEER ST
4 LEACH ST
5 RANDON GR
6 NEW CROSS ST
7 PALMER CL
8 BURNELL CL
9 PATRICIA CT

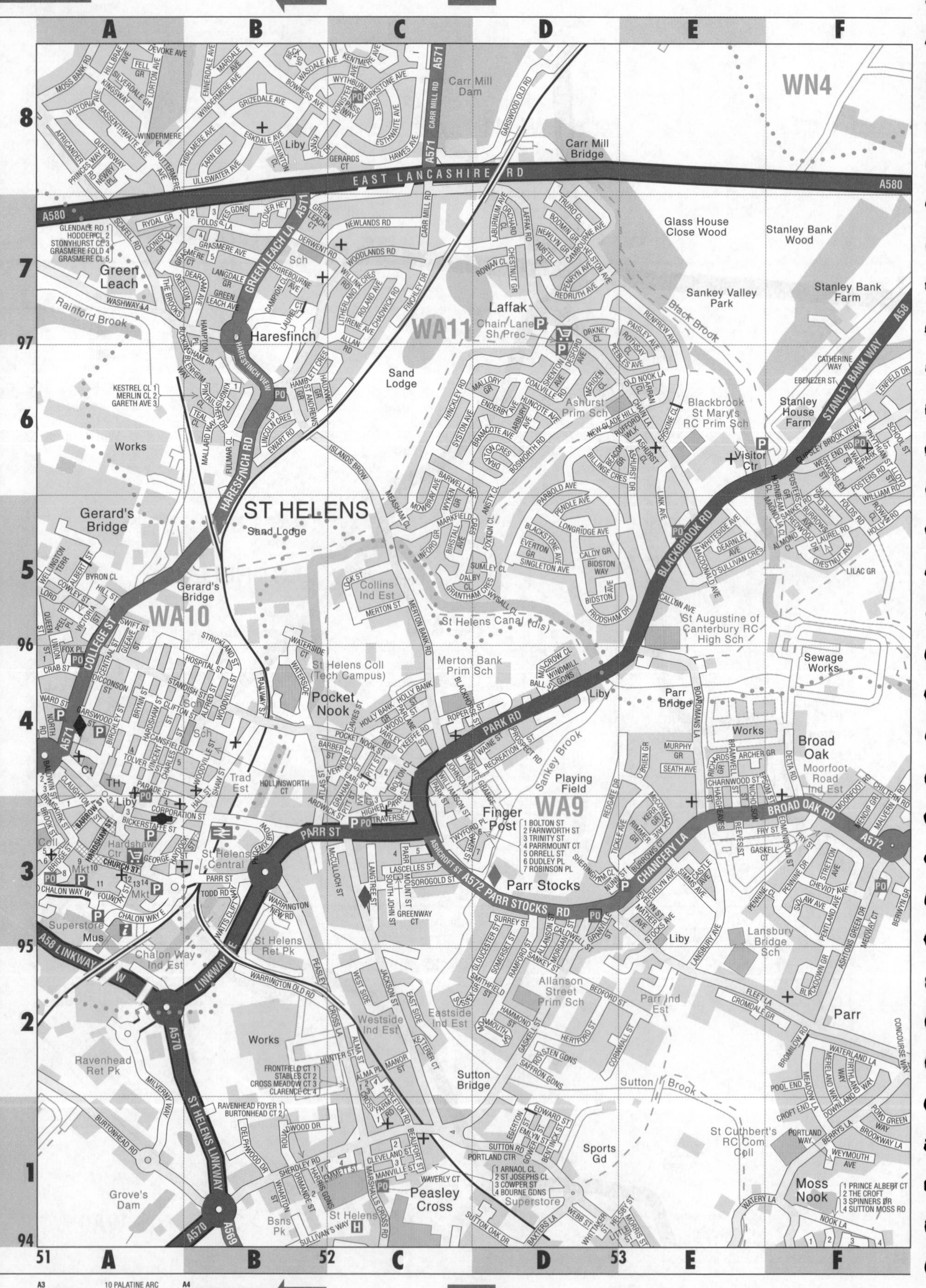

A3
1 COTHAM ST
2 VICTORIA SQ
3 LIBRARY ST
4 CATAPULT TOO
5 WATERLOO ST
6 CROSS ST
7 MILK ST
8 EXCHANGE ST
9 LAGRANGE ARC
10 PALATINE ARC
11 MARKET ST
12 CHURCH SQ
13 ST MARY'S ARC
14 BROWNLOW ARC

A4
1 NORMAN SALISBURY CT
2 WILLIAM ST
3 NORTH JOHN ST
4 TOLVER HO
5 PROVIDENCE CT

34
46

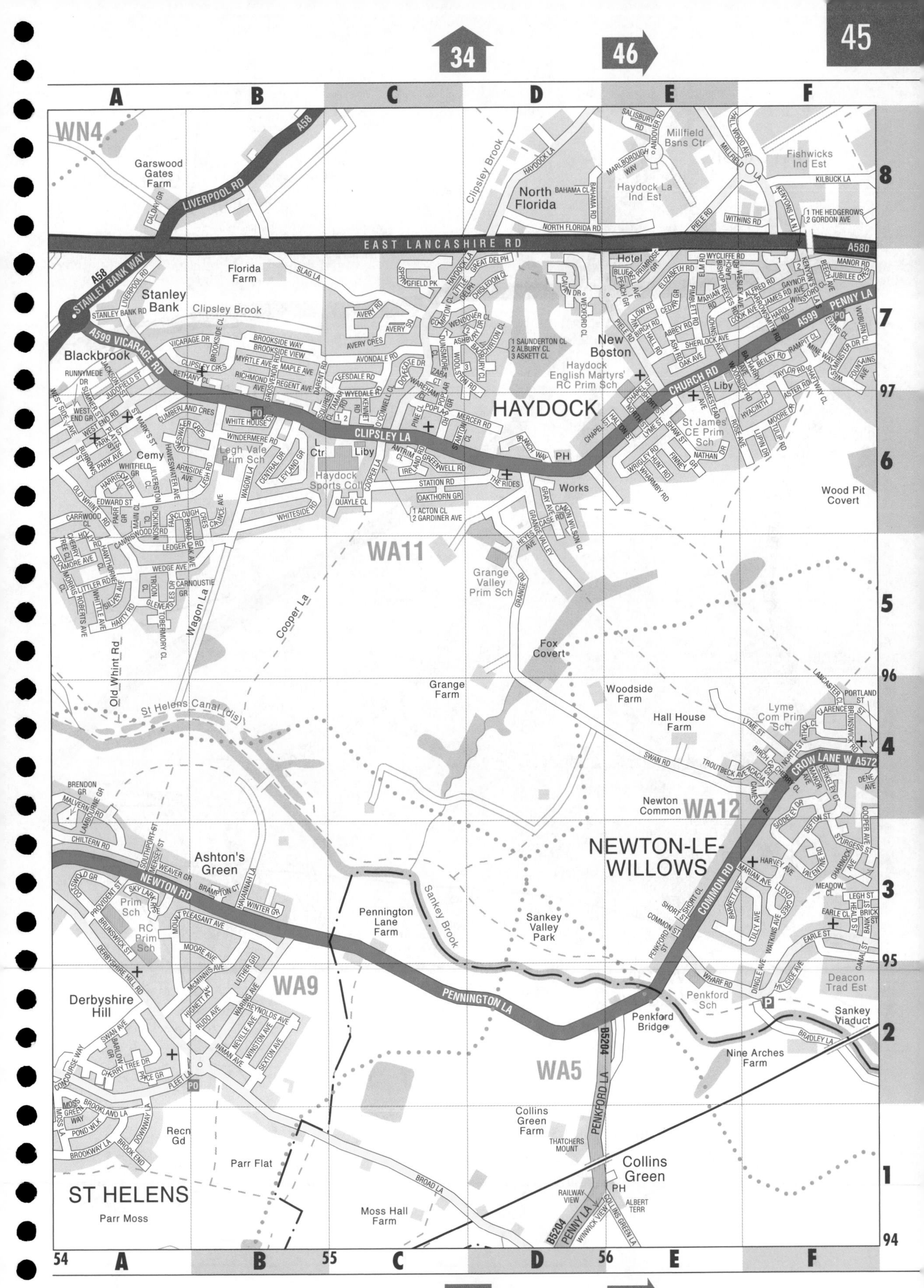
HAYDOCK
NEWTON-LE-
WILLOWS
ST HELENS
EAST LANCASHIRE RD
A580
WN4
WA11
WA12
WA9
WA5
Garswood
Gates
Farm
Florida
Farm
Stanley
Bank
Blackbrook
North
Florida
Millfield
Bsns Ctr
Fishwicks
Ind Est
Haydock La
Ind Est
New
Boston
Haydock
English Martyrs'
RC Prim Sch
St James
CE Prim
Sch
Legh Vale
Prim Sch
Haydock
Sports Coll
Grange
Valley
Prim Sch
Fox
Covert
Wood Pit
Covert
Grange
Farm
Woodside
Farm
Hall House
Farm
Lyme
Com Prim
Sch
Newton
Common
Ashton's
Green
Pennington
Lane
Farm
Sankey
Valley
Park
Derbyshire
Hill
Penkford
Bridge
Penkford
Sch
Deacon
Trad Est
Sankey
Viaduct
Nine Arches
Farm
Collins
Green
Farm
Collins
Green
Recn
Gd
Parr Flat
Parr Moss
Moss Hall
Farm
Clipsley Brook
Sankey Brook
St Helens Canal (dis)
Cooper La
Wagon La
Old Whint Rd
LIVERPOOL RD
STANLEY BANK WAY
A58
A599 VICARAGE RD
CLIPSLEY LA
CHURCH RD
A599 PENNY LA
CROW LANE W A572
COMMON RD
NEWTON RD
PENNINGTON LA
PENKFORD LA
B5204
BROAD LA
SWAN RD
1 SAUNDERTON CL
2 ALBURY CL
3 ASKETT CL
1 ACTON CL
2 GARDINER AVE
1 THE HEDGEROWS
2 GORDON AVE
A
B
C
D
E
F
8
7
6
5
4
3
2
1
97
96
95
94
54
55
56

59
46

45
35

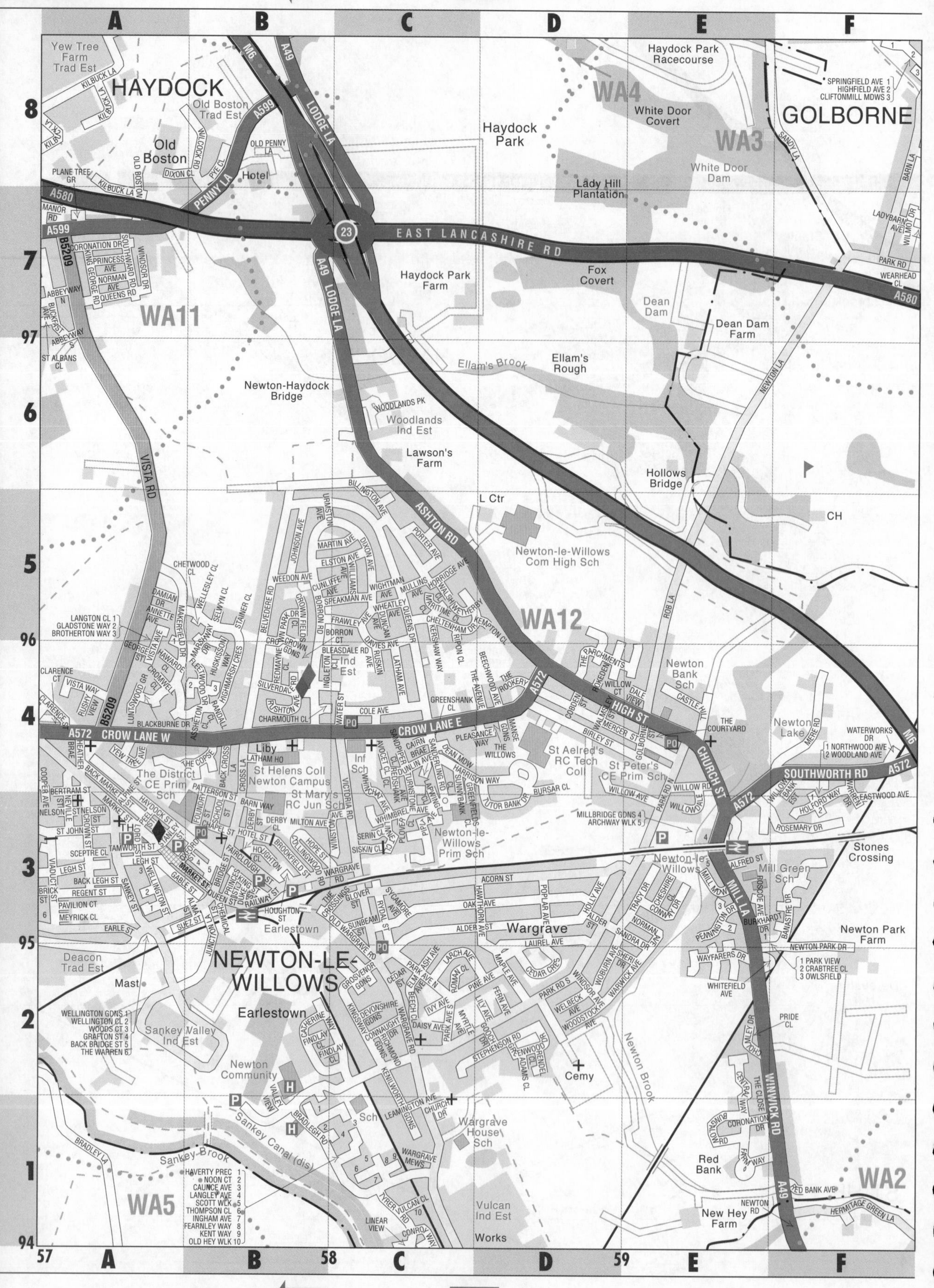
HAYDOCK
GOLBORNE
NEWTON-LE-WILLOWS
Haydock Park Racecourse
White Door Covert
Haydock Park
Old Boston
Old Boston Trad Est
Yew Tree Farm Trad Est
Lady Hill Plantation
White Door Dam
EAST LANCASHIRE RD
Haydock Park Farm
Fox Covert
Dean Dam
Dean Dam Farm
Ellam's Brook
Ellam's Rough
Newton-Haydock Bridge
Woodlands Ind Est
Lawson's Farm
Hollows Bridge
Newton-le-Willows Com High Sch
WA11
WA12
WA4
WA3
WA5
WA2
CROW LANE W
CROW LANE E
HIGH ST
CHURCH ST
SOUTHWORTH RD
ASHTON RD
LODGE LA
VISTA RD
St Helens Coll Newton Campus
St Mary's RC Jun Sch
The District CE Prim Sch
St Aelred's RC Tech Coll
St Peter's CE Prim Sch
Newton-le-Willows Prim Sch
Newton Bank Sch
Newton Lake
Stones Crossing
Mill Green Sch
Newton Park Farm
Wargrave
Earlestown
Deacon Trad Est
Sankey Valley Ind Est
Newton Community
Sankey Canal (dis)
Sankey Brook
Wargrave House Sch
Vulcan Ind Est
Works
Red Bank
New Hey Farm
Newton Brook
Cemy
WINWICK RD
MILL LA

45
60

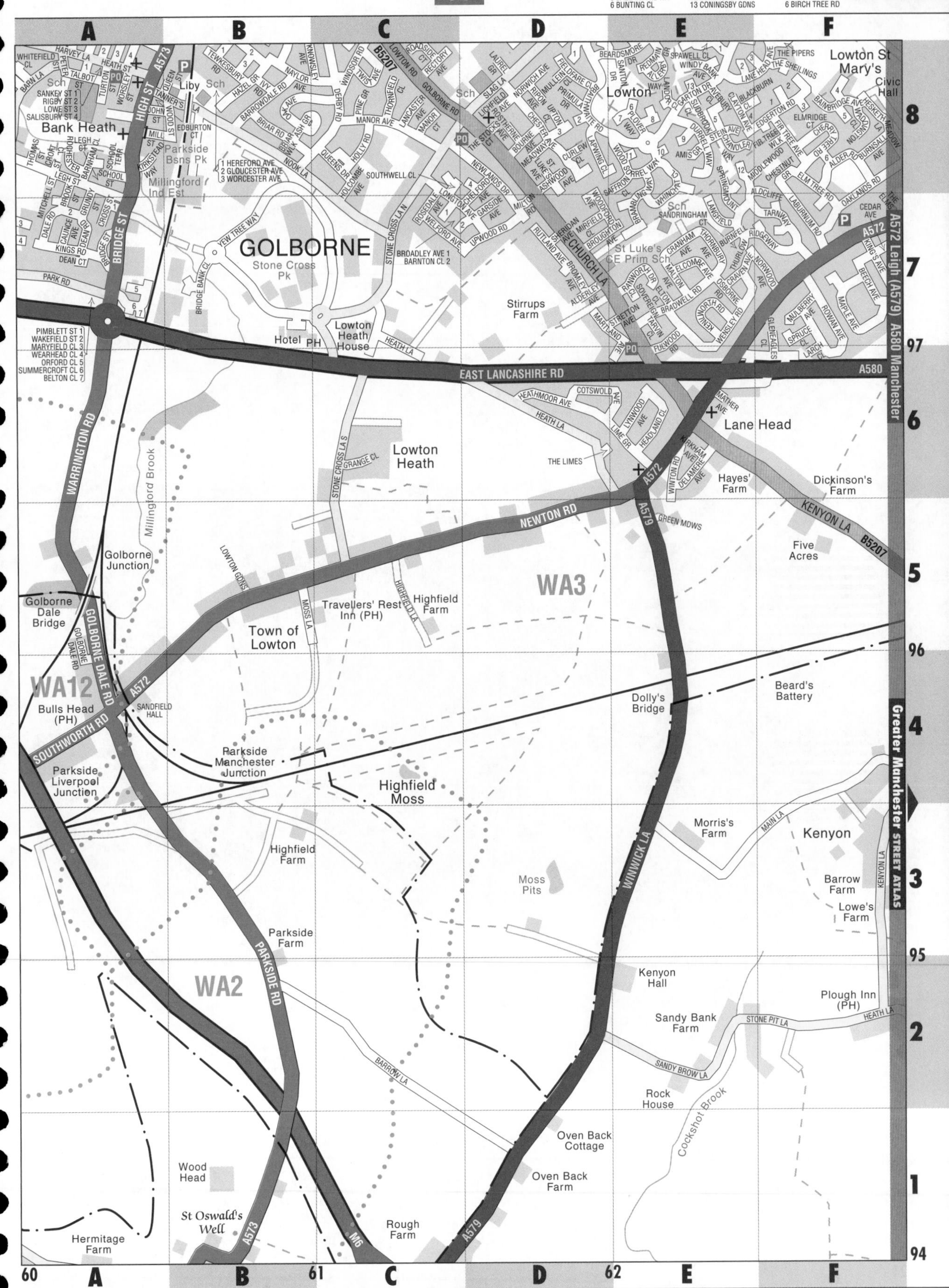

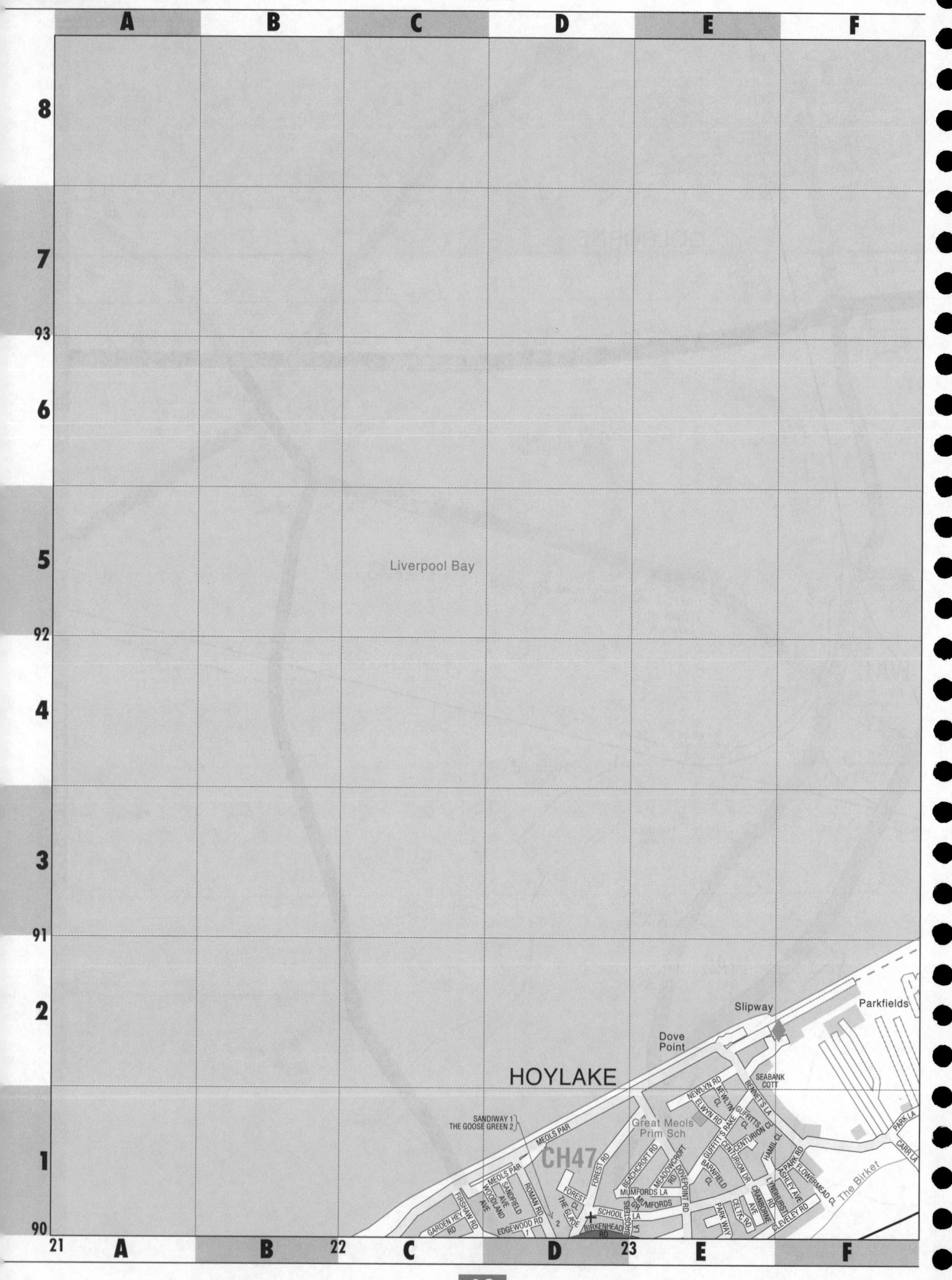

Liverpool Bay

Slipway

Parkfields

Dove
Point

HOYLAKE

SEABANK
COTT

SANDIWAY 1
THE GOOSE GREEN 2

MEOLS PAR

Great Meols
Prim Sch

CH47

The Birket

50

A
B
C
D
E
F
8
7
6
5
4
3
2
1
93
92
91
90
24
25
26
Liverpool Bay
North Wirral Coastal Park
Wallasey Embankment
Leasowe Castle Hotel
Caravan Pk
CH
1 SHANNON HO
2 LAGAN HO
3 CAUSEWAY HO
COASTAL POINT
CASTLEFIELDS
A551
LEASOWE RD
Leasowe Common
Caravan Site
Lighthouse (dis)
The Birket
Parkfield House
Lingham Farm
LINGHAM LA
MEREHEATH GDNS
Ditton Lane Nature Area
DITTON LA
WALLASEY
Works
Leasowe Hotel (PH)
PASTURE RD
Moreton
STATION APP
CH46
CH47
Arrowe Brook
PARK LA
WASTDALE CT 1
WASTDALE MEWS 2
LC
CARR LA
TANWORTH GR
Moreton
E1
1 GARDEN LA
2 OAKENHOLT RD
Lingham Prim Sch
Eastway Prim Sch
Sacred Heart RC Prim Sch
HOYLAKE RD
A553
Liby
BLACKHEATH DR
TWICKENHAM DR
BIRKET AVE
BIRKET SQ
REEDVILLE GR
ROSSALL CT
PASTURE AVE
FAIRMEAD RD
MARYLAND LA
TARRAN WAY N
TARRAN WAY S
SUNNYSIDE
BERRYLANDS RD
MEADFOOT RD
HARVEST LA
FELICITY GR
CURLEW WAY
TERN WAY
WASTDALE DR
MALLARD WAY
TOWN MEADOW LA
LESKDALE AVE
BRADMAN RD
GLASIER RD
ELEANOR RD
HEATHMOOR RD
FLAXHILL
CHELTENHAM CRES
GOODWOOD DR
DUNSTALL CL
REEDS LA
GREENHEATH WAY
FARNWORTH AVE
CRONTON AVE
WEST WAY
EAST WAY
YEW WAY
SAXON RD
DANESWELL DR
AVONDALE AVE
KNUTSFORD GN
BURNLEY GR
STUART AVE

64
50

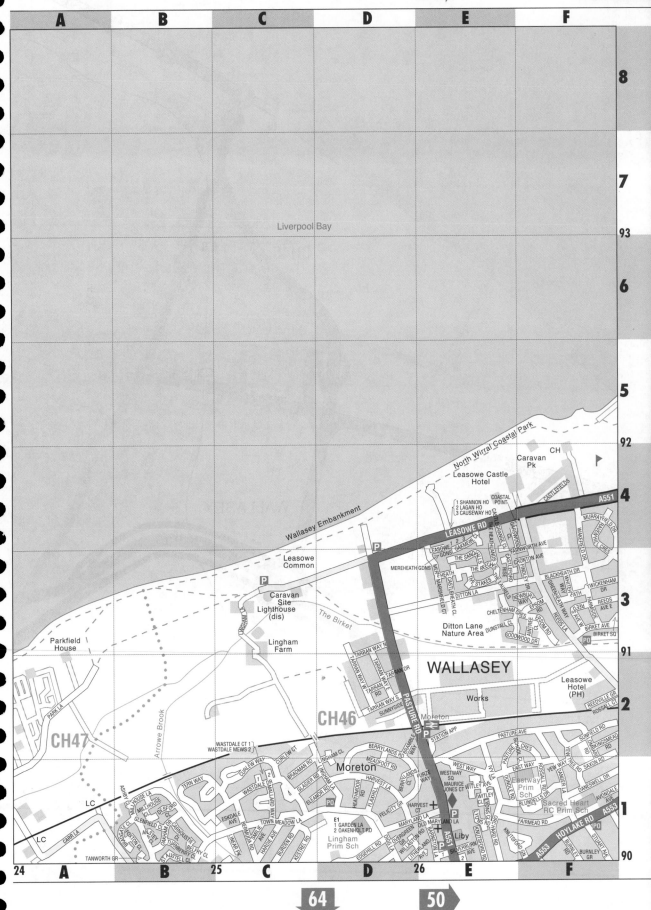

49

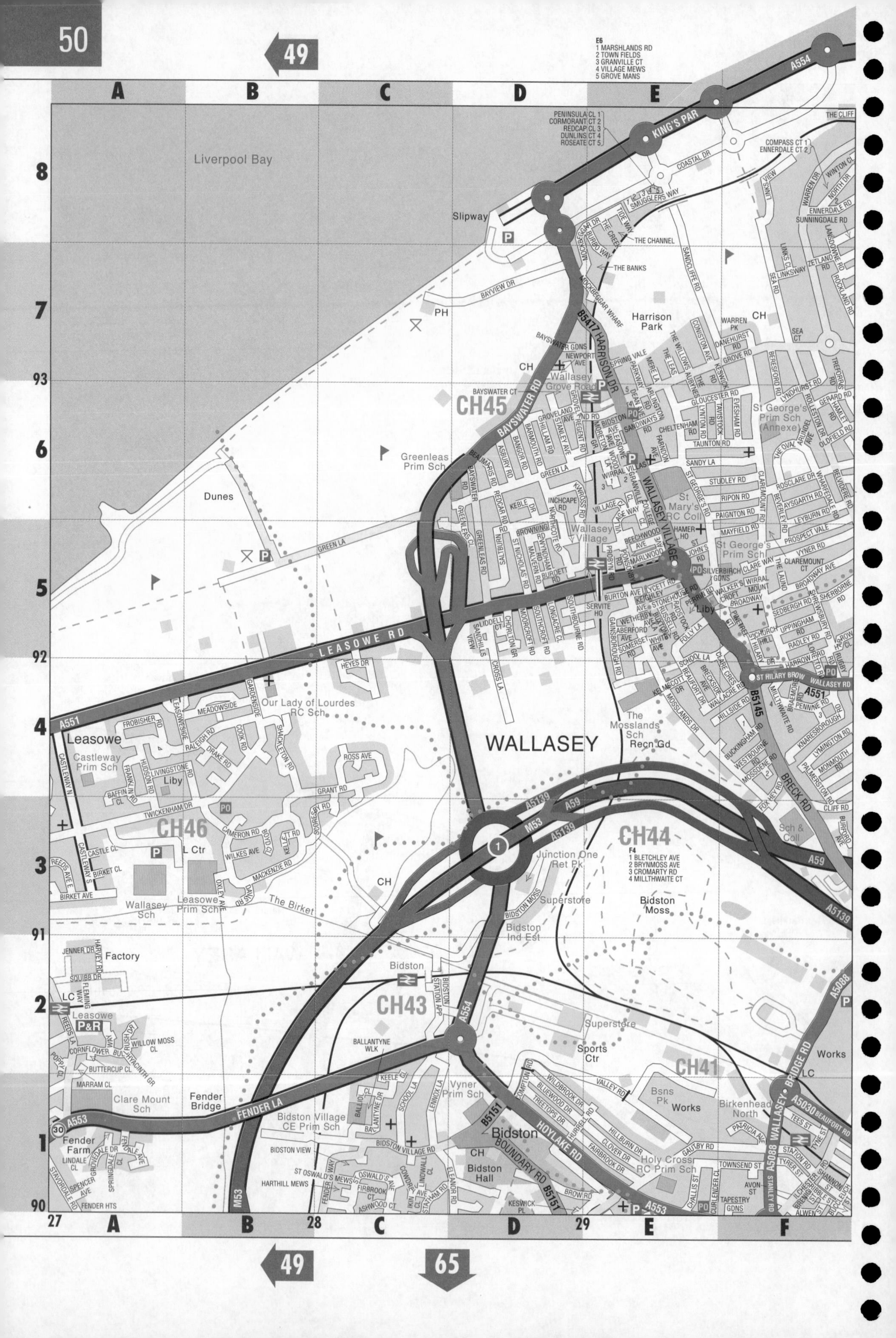
E6
1 MARSHLANDS RD
2 TOWN FIELDS
3 GRANVILLE CT
4 VILLAGE MEWS
5 GROVE MANS
A
B
C
D
E
F
8
7
6
5
4
3
2
1
93
92
91
90
27
28
29
Liverpool Bay
PENINSULA CL 1
CORMORANT CT 2
REDCAP CL 3
DUNLINS CT 4
ROSEATE CT 5
KING'S PAR
A554
THE CLIFF
COMPASS CT 1
ENNERDALE CT 2
COASTAL DR
SMUGGLERS WAY
Slipway
THE CHANNEL
THE BANKS
BAYVIEW DR
PH
MOCKBEGGAR WHARF
B5477 HARRISON DR
Harrison Park
WARREN PK
CH
SUNNINGDALE RD
LINKSWAY
SEA RD
SANDCLIFFE RD
BAYSWATER GDNS
NEWPORT AVE
Wallasey Grove Road
BAYSWATER CT
CH45
BAYSWATER RD
Greenleas Prim Sch
Dunes
GREEN LA
St George's Prim Sch (Annexe)
St Mary's RC Coll
Wallasey Village
WALLASEY VILLAGE
St George's Prim Sch
SERVITE HO
LEASOWE RD
A551
Leasowe
Castleway Prim Sch
Liby
Our Lady of Lourdes RC Sch
WALLASEY
The Mosslands Sch
Recn Gd
ST HILARY BROW
WALLASEY RD
B5145
BRECK RD
CH46
L Ctr
A5139
A59
M53
Junction One Ret Pk
CH44
F4
1 BLETCHLEY AVE
2 BRYNMOSS AVE
3 CROMARTY RD
4 MILLTHWAITE CT
Sch & Coll
Wallasey Sch
Leasowe Prim Sch
The Birket
Superstore
Bidston Moss
Bidston Ind Est
Factory
Bidston
CH43
LC
Leasowe
P&R
Superstore
Sports Ctr
CH41
Works
Clare Mount Sch
Fender Bridge
FENDER LA
A553
Fender Farm
Bidston Village CE Prim Sch
Vyner Prim Sch
Bsns Pk
Birkenhead North
Bidston
CH
Bidston Hall
B5151
HOYLAKE RD
BOUNDARY RD
Holy Cross RC Prim Sch
WALLASEY BRIDGE RD
A5088
A5030
FENDER HTS
KESWICK PL
STANLEY RD

49
65

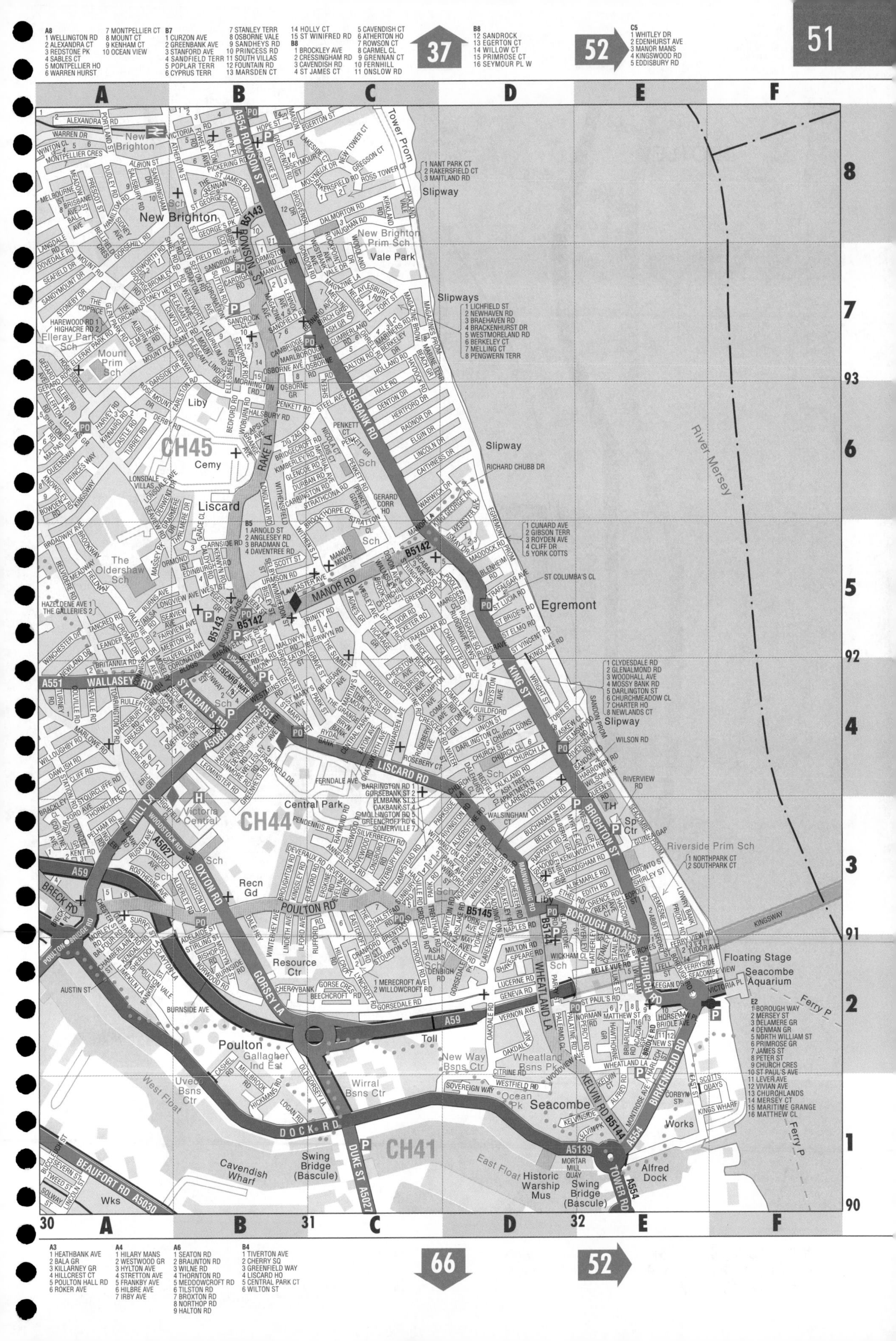
A8
1 WELLINGTON RD
2 ALEXANDRA CT
3 REDSTONE PK
4 SABLES CT
5 MONTPELLIER HO
6 WARREN HURST
7 MONTPELLIER CT
8 MOUNT CT
9 KENHAM CT
10 OCEAN VIEW
B7
1 CURZON AVE
2 GREENBANK AVE
3 STANFORD AVE
4 SANDFIELD TERR
5 POPLAR TERR
6 CYPRUS TERR
7 STANLEY TERR
8 OSBORNE VALE
9 SANDHEYS RD
10 PRINCESS RD
11 SOUTH VILLAS
12 FOUNTAIN RD
13 MARSDEN CT
14 HOLLY CT
15 ST WINIFRED RD
B8
1 BROCKLEY AVE
2 CRESSINGHAM RD
3 CAVENDISH RD
4 ST JAMES CT
5 CAVENDISH CT
6 ATHERTON HO
7 ROWSON CT
8 CARMEL CL
9 GRENNAN CT
10 FERNHILL
11 ONSLOW RD
37
B8
12 SANDROCK
13 EGERTON CT
14 WILLOW CT
15 PRIMROSE CT
16 SEYMOUR PL W
52
C5
1 WHITLEY DR
2 EDENHURST AVE
3 MANOR MANS
4 KINGSWOOD RD
5 EDDISBURY RD
A
B
C
D
E
F
8
7
93
6
5
92
4
3
91
2
1
90
30
31
32
New Brighton
Liscard
Egremont
Poulton
Seacombe
CH45
CH44
CH41
River Mersey
Central Park
Vale Park
Slipway
Slipways
Floating Stage
Seacombe Aquarium
Alfred Dock
Cavendish Wharf
Historic Warship Mus
Swing Bridge (Bascule)
West Float
East Float
Riverside Prim Sch
New Brighton Prim Sch
The Oldershaw Sch
Mount Prim Sch
Elleray Park Sch
Victoria Central
Gallagher Ind Est
Uveco Bsns Ctr
Wirral Bsns Ctr
New Way Bsns Ctr
Wheatland Bsns Pk
Resource Ctr
Recn Gd
Toll
Works
Wks
KINGSWAY
Ferry P
A554
A551
A59
A5027
A5030
A5088
A5139
B5142
B5143
B5144
B5145
SEABANK RD
KING ST
BRIGHTON ST
ROWSON ST
RAKE LA
MANOR RD
LISCARD RD
WALLASEY RD
POULTON RD
BOROUGH RD
DOCK RD
DUKE ST
GORSEY LA
OXTON RD
BIRKENHEAD RD
KELVIN RD
WHEATLAND LA
TOWER RD
BEAUFORT RD
CHURCH RD
MILL LA
1 NANT PARK CT
2 RAKERSFIELD CT
3 MAITLAND RD
1 LICHFIELD ST
2 NEWHAVEN RD
3 BRAEHAVEN RD
4 BRACKENHURST DR
5 WESTMORELAND RD
6 BERKELEY CT
7 MELLING CT
8 PENGWERN TERR
1 CUNARD AVE
2 GIBSON TERR
3 ROYDEN AVE
4 CLIFF DR
5 YORK COTTS
B5
1 ARNOLD ST
2 ANGLESEY RD
3 BRADMAN CL
4 DAVENTREE RD
1 CLYDESDALE RD
2 GLENALMOND RD
3 WOODHALL AVE
4 MOSSY BANK RD
5 DARLINGTON ST
6 CHURCHMEADOW CL
7 CHARTER HO
8 NEWLANDS CT
1 BARRINGTON RD
2 GORSEBANK ST
3 ELMBANK ST
4 OAKBANK ST
5 MOLLINGTON RD
6 GREENCROFT RD
7 SOMERVILLE
1 NORTHPARK CT
2 SOUTHPARK CT
1 MERECROFT AVE
2 WILLOWCROFT RD
E2
1 BOROUGH WAY
2 MERSEY ST
3 DELAMERE GR
4 DENMAN GR
5 NORTH WILLIAM ST
6 PRIMROSE GR
7 JAMES ST
8 PETER ST
9 CHURCH CRES
10 ST PAUL'S AVE
11 LEVER AVE
12 VIVIAN AVE
13 CHURCHLANDS
14 MERSEY CT
15 MARITIME GRANGE
16 MATTHEW CL
66
52
A3
1 HEATHBANK AVE
2 BALA GR
3 KILLARNEY GR
4 HILLCREST CT
5 POULTON HALL RD
6 ROKER AVE
A4
1 HILARY MANS
2 WESTWOOD GR
3 HYLTON AVE
4 STRETTON AVE
5 FRANKBY AVE
6 HILBRE AVE
7 IRBY AVE
A6
1 SEATON RD
2 BRAUNTON RD
3 WILNE RD
4 THORNTON RD
5 MEDDOWCROFT RD
6 TILSTON RD
7 BROXTON RD
8 NORTHOP RD
9 HALTON RD
B4
1 TIVERTON AVE
2 CHERRY SQ
3 GREENFIELD WAY
4 LISCARD HO
5 CENTRAL PARK CT
6 WILTON ST

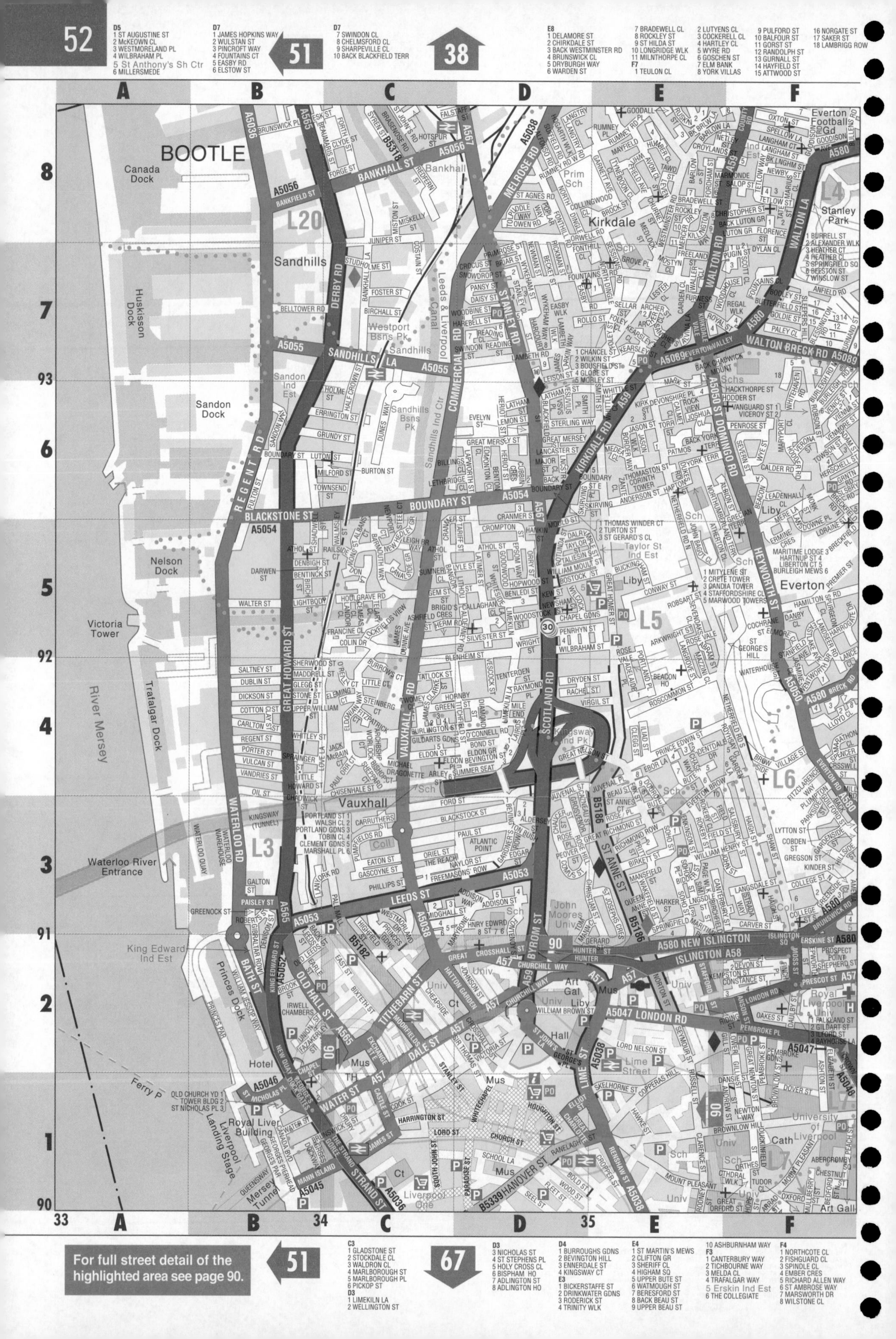

52
D5
1 ST AUGUSTINE ST
2 McKEOWN CL
3 WESTMORELAND PL
4 WILBRAHAM PL
5 St Anthony's Sh Ctr
6 MILLERSMEDE
D7
1 JAMES HOPKINS WAY
2 WULSTAN ST
3 PINCROFT WAY
4 FOUNTAINS CT
5 EASBY RD
6 ELSTOW ST
51
D7
7 SWINDON CL
8 CHELMSFORD CL
9 SHARPEVILLE CL
10 BACK BLACKFIELD TERR
38
E8
1 DELAMORE ST
2 CHIRKDALE ST
3 BACK WESTMINSTER RD
4 BRUNSWICK CL
5 DRYBURGH WAY
6 WARDEN ST
7 BRADEWELL CL
8 ROCKLEY ST
9 ST HILDA ST
10 LONGRIDGE WLK
11 MILNTHORPE CL
F7
1 TEULON CL
2 LUTYENS CL
3 COCKERELL CL
4 HARTLEY CL
5 WYRE RD
6 GOSCHEN ST
7 ELM BANK
8 YORK VILLAS
9 PULFORD ST
10 BALFOUR ST
11 GORST ST
12 RANDOLPH ST
13 GURNALL ST
14 HAYFIELD ST
15 ATTWOOD ST
16 NORGATE ST
17 SAKER ST
18 LAMBRIGG ROW
A
B
C
D
E
F
BOOTLE
Canada Dock
L20
Sandhills
Huskisson Dock
Sandon Dock
Nelson Dock
Victoria Tower
River Mersey
Trafalgar Dock
Waterloo River Entrance
King Edward Ind Est
Princes Dock
Royal Liver Building
Liverpool Landing Stage
Mersey Tunnel
Kirkdale
Everton Football Gd
Stanley Park
Everton
Vauxhall
Leeds & Liverpool Canal
L3
L4
L5
L6
L7
REGENT RD
WATERLOO RD
GREAT HOWARD ST
DERBY RD
COMMERCIAL RD
VAUXHALL RD
SCOTLAND RD
KIRKDALE RD
STANLEY RD
MELROSE RD
WALTON LA
WALTON RD
WALTON BRECK RD A5089
ST DOMINGO RD
HEYWORTH ST
BOUNDARY ST
BLACKSTONE ST
BANKHALL ST
SANDHILLS LA
LEEDS ST
BYROM ST
A580 NEW ISLINGTON
ISLINGTON A58
A5047 LONDON RD
DALE ST
TITHEBARN ST
OLD HALL ST
WATER ST
STRAND ST
LIME ST
ST ANNE ST
EVERTON VALLEY
University of Liverpool
Royal Liverpool Univ
Liverpool One
8
7
93
6
5
92
4
3
91
2
1
90
33
34
35
For full street detail of the highlighted area see page 90.
51
67
C3
1 GLADSTONE ST
2 STOCKDALE CL
3 WALDRON CL
4 MARLBOROUGH ST
5 MARLBOROUGH PL
6 PICKOP ST
D3
1 LIMEKILN LA
2 WELLINGTON ST
D3
3 NICHOLAS ST
4 ST STEPHENS PL
5 HOLY CROSS CL
6 BISPHAM HO
7 ADLINGTON ST
8 ADLINGTON HO
D4
1 BURROUGHS GDNS
2 BEVINGTON HILL
3 ENNERDALE ST
4 KINGSWAY CT
E3
1 BICKERSTAFFE ST
2 DRINKWATER GDNS
3 RODERICK ST
4 TRINITY WLK
E4
1 ST MARTIN'S MEWS
2 CLIFTON GR
3 SHERIFF CL
4 HIGHAM SQ
5 UPPER BUTE ST
6 WATMOUGH ST
7 BERESFORD ST
8 BACK BEAU ST
9 UPPER BEAU ST
10 ASHBURNHAM WAY
F3
1 CANTERBURY WAY
2 TICHBOURNE WAY
3 MELDA CL
4 TRAFALGAR WAY
5 Erskin Ind Est
6 THE COLLEGIATE
F4
1 NORTHCOTE CL
2 FISHGUARD CL
3 SPINDLE CL
4 EMBER CRES
5 RICHARD ALLEN WAY
6 ST AMBROSE WAY
7 MARSWORTH DR
8 WILSTONE CL

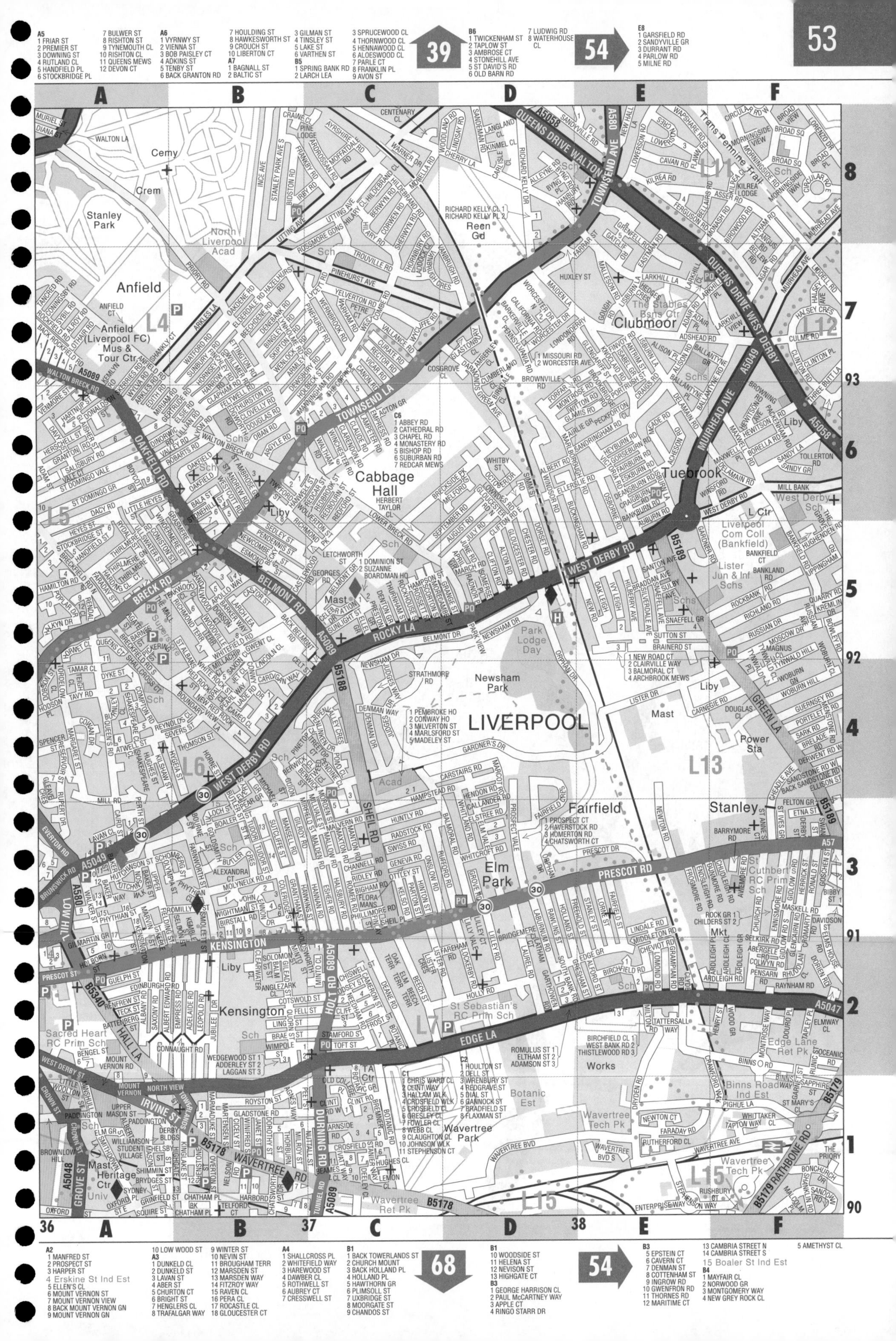
A5
1 FRIAR ST
2 PREMIER ST
3 DOWNING ST
4 RUTLAND CL
5 HANDFIELD PL
6 STOCKBRIDGE PL
7 BULWER ST
8 RISHTON ST
9 TYNEMOUTH CL
10 RISHTON CL
11 QUEENS MEWS
12 DEVON CT
A6
1 VYRNWY ST
2 VIENNA ST
3 BOB PAISLEY CT
4 ADKINS ST
5 TENBY ST
6 BACK GRANTON RD
7 HOULDING ST
8 HAWKESWORTH ST
9 CROUCH ST
10 LIBERTON CT
A7
1 BAGNALL ST
2 BALTIC ST
3 GILMAN ST
4 TINSLEY ST
5 LAKE ST
6 VARTHEN ST
B5
1 SPRING BANK RD
2 LARCH LEA
3 SPRUCEWOOD CL
4 THORNWOOD CL
5 HENNAWOOD CL
6 ALOESWOOD CL
7 PARLE CT
8 FRANKLIN PL
9 AVON ST
39
B6
1 TWICKENHAM ST
2 TAPLOW ST
3 AMBROSE CT
4 STONEHILL AVE
5 ST DAVID'S RD
6 OLD BARN RD
7 LUDWIG RD
8 WATERHOUSE CL
54
E8
1 GARSFIELD RD
2 SANDYVILLE GR
3 DURRANT RD
4 PARLOW RD
5 MILNE RD
A B C D E F
8 7 93 6 5 92 4 3 91 2 1 90
36 37 38
Anfield
Stanley Park
Cemy
Crem
North Liverpool Acad
Anfield (Liverpool FC) Mus & Tour Ctr
Reen Gd
Clubmoor
Cabbage Hall
Tuebrook
Newsham Park
Park Lodge Day
LIVERPOOL
Fairfield
Stanley
Elm Park
Kensington
Sacred Heart RC Prim Sch
St Sebastian's RC Prim Sch
Edge Lane Ret Pk
Binns Road Ind Est
Botanic Est
Wavertree Tech Pk
Wavertree Park
Wavertree Ret Pk
Liverpool Com Coll (Bankfield)
Lister Jun & Inf Schs
St Cuthbert's RC Prim Sch
Power Sta
Heritage Ctr
Univ
QUEENS DRIVE WALTON
QUEENS DRIVE WEST DERBY
TOWNSEND LA
TOWNSEND AVE
WEST DERBY RD
BELMONT RD
BRECK RD
OAKFIELD RD
ROCKY LA
MUIRHEAD AVE
PRESCOT RD
KENSINGTON
EDGE LA
WAVERTREE RD
DURNING RD
HOLT RD
SHEIL RD
GREEN LA
LOW HILL
EVERTON RD
A2
1 MANFRED ST
2 PROSPECT ST
3 HARPER ST
4 Erskine St Ind Est
5 ELLEN'S CL
6 MOUNT VERNON ST
7 MOUNT VERNON VIEW
8 BACK MOUNT VERNON GN
9 MOUNT VERNON GN
10 LOW WOOD ST
A3
1 DUNKELD CL
2 DUNKELD ST
3 LAVAN ST
4 ABER ST
5 CHURTON CT
6 BRIGHT ST
7 HENGLERS CL
8 TRAFALGAR WAY
9 WINTER ST
10 NEVIN ST
11 BROUGHAM TERR
12 MARSDEN ST
13 MARSDEN WAY
14 FITZROY WAY
15 RAVEN CL
16 PERA CL
17 ROCASTLE CL
18 GLOUCESTER CT
A4
1 SHALLCROSS PL
2 WHITEFIELD WAY
3 HAREWOOD ST
4 DAWBER CL
5 ROTHWELL ST
6 AUBREY CT
7 CRESSWELL ST
B1
1 BACK TOWERLANDS ST
2 CHURCH MOUNT
3 BACK HOLLAND PL
4 HOLLAND PL
5 HAWTHORN GR
6 PLIMSOLL ST
7 UXBRIDGE ST
8 MOORGATE ST
9 CHANDOS ST
68
B1
10 WOODSIDE ST
11 HELENA ST
12 NEVISON ST
13 HIGHGATE CT
B3
1 GEORGE HARRISON CL
2 PAUL McCARTNEY WAY
3 APPLE CT
4 RINGO STARR DR
54
B3
5 EPSTEIN CT
6 CAVERN CT
7 DENMAN ST
8 COTTENHAM ST
9 INGROW RD
10 GWENFRON RD
11 THORNES RD
12 MARITIME CT
13 CAMBRIA STREET N
14 CAMBRIA STREET S
15 Boaler St Ind Est
B4
1 MAYFAIR CL
2 NORWOOD GR
3 MONTGOMERY WAY
4 NEW GREY ROCK CL
5 AMETHYST CL

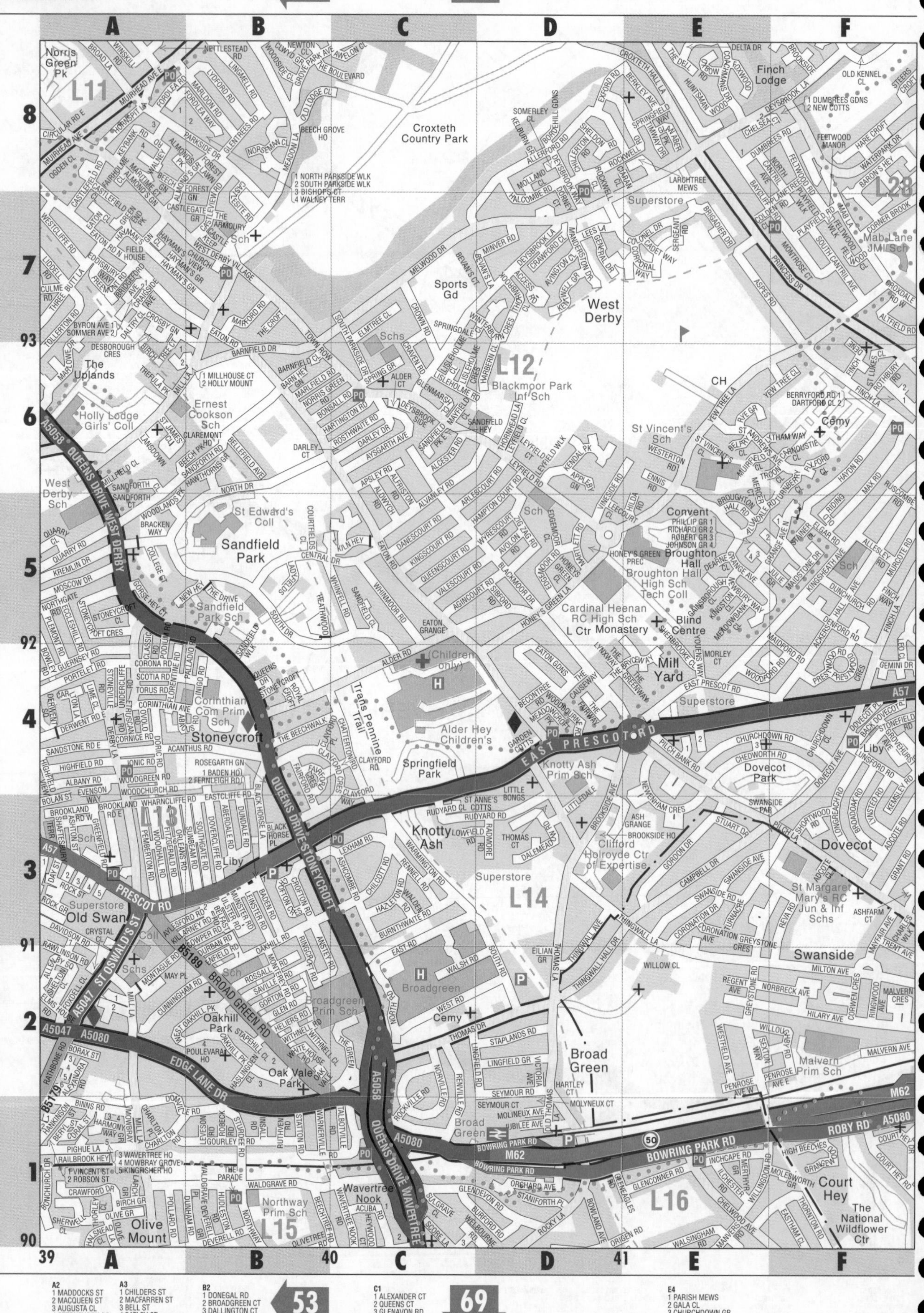

A2
1 MADDOCKS ST
2 MACQUEEN ST
3 AUGUSTA CL
4 STEPHENSON RD
5 ARMOUR GR
6 WILTON GR

A3
1 CHILDERS ST
2 MACFARREN ST
3 BELL ST
4 BATLEY ST
5 BOOTH ST
6 RAVENSWOOD RD
7 BEATTY RD

B2
1 DONEGAL RD
2 BROADGREEN CT
3 DALLINGTON CT
4 MULRANKIN CT

C1
1 ALEXANDER CT
2 QUEENS CT
3 GLENAVON RD

E4
1 PARISH MEWS
2 GALA CL
3 CHURCHDOWN GR

41 56

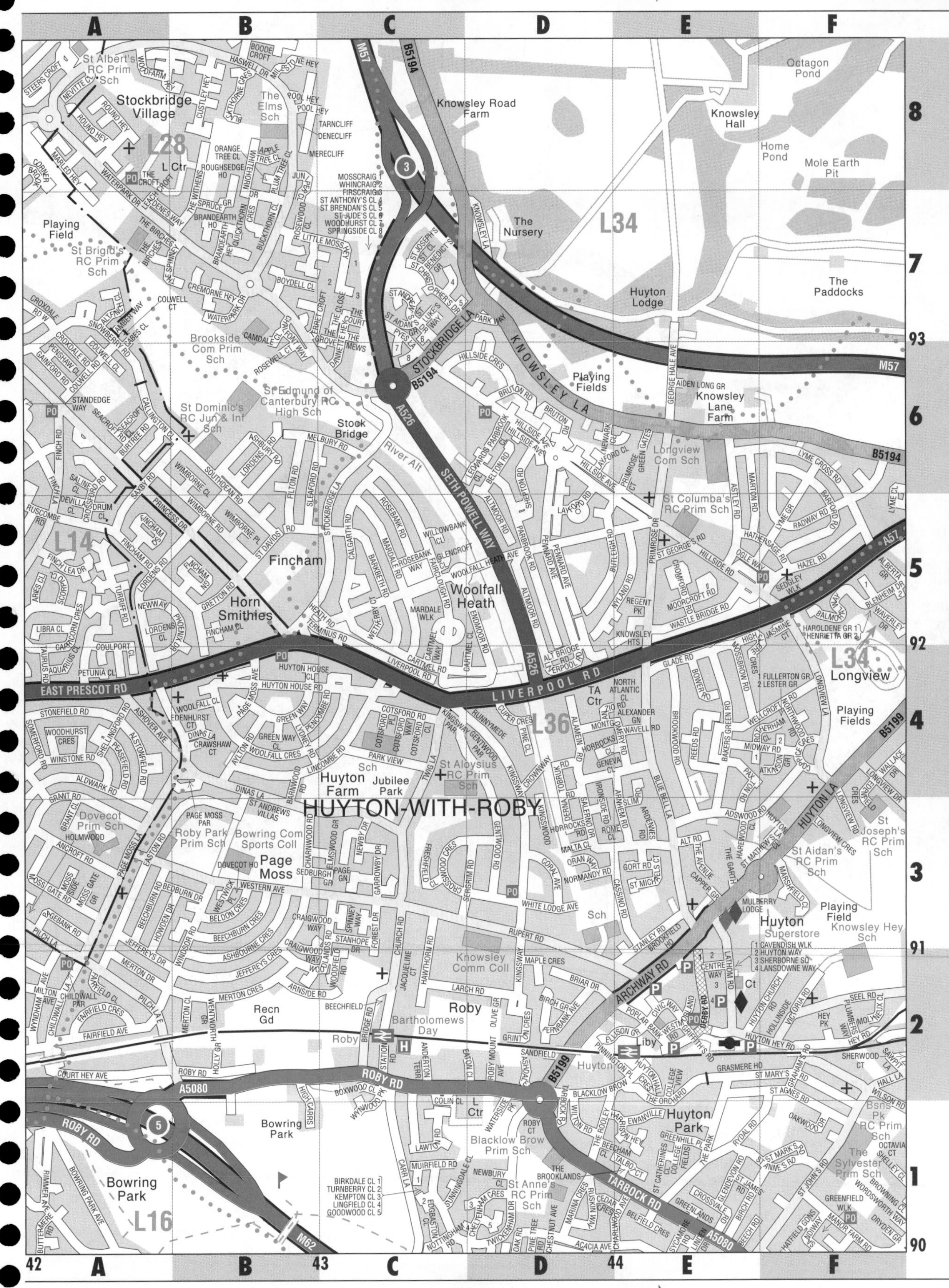
A
B
C
D
E
F
8
7
93
6
5
92
4
3
91
2
1
90
42
43
44
Stockbridge Village
St Albert's RC Prim Sch
L28
L Ctr
The Elms Sch
Knowsley Road Farm
Octagon Pond
Knowsley Hall
Home Pond
Mole Earth Pit
The Nursery
L34
The Paddocks
Huyton Lodge
Playing Field
St Brigid's RC Prim Sch
Brookside Com Prim Sch
St Edmund of Canterbury RC High Sch
St Dominic's RC Jun & Inf Sch
Stock Bridge
River Alt
SETH POWELL WAY
STOCKBRIDGE LA
KNOWSLEY LA
Playing Fields
Knowsley Lane Farm
Longview Com Sch
St Columba's RC Prim Sch
M57
B5194
A526
A57
L14
Fincham
Horn Smithies
Woolfall Heath
EAST PRESCOT RD
LIVERPOOL RD
L36
TA Ctr
L34
Longview
Playing Fields
B5199
HUYTON-WITH-ROBY
Huyton Farm
Jubilee Park
St Aloysius RC Prim Sch
Dovecot Prim Sch
Roby Park Prim Sch
Bowring Com Sports Coll
Page Moss
St Joseph's RC Prim Sch
St Aidan's RC Prim Sch
Huyton
Superstore
Playing Field
Knowsley Hey Sch
Knowsley Comm Coll
Recn Gd
Roby
Bartholomews Day
Liby
Ct
HUYTON LA
ARCHWAY RD
ROBY RD
A5080
Bowring Park
L16
M62
Huyton Park
Bsns Pk RC Prim Sch
The Sylvester Prim Sch
Blacklow Brow Prim Sch
St Anne's RC Prim Sch
TARBOCK RD

70 56

55
42

D6
1 SEDDONS CT
2 WYCHERLEY ST
3 SALISBURY ST
4 DUKE ST
5 CARLTON ST
6 STONE ST
7 HILL ST
8 LEYLAND ST
9 ATHERTON ST
10 CHAPEL ST
11 ACKERS ST
12 VICTORIA HO
13 BEACONSFIELD
14 Prescot Sh Ctr
15 GREENALL CT

E6
1 POTTERY FIELDS
2 SMITH ST
3 TINLING CL
4 HUNTER CT
5 MENAI MEWS
6 OLIVER LYME HO
7 LAVENDER CRES
8 DERBY SQ
9 PEMBERTONS CT
10 FAIRHURST TERR

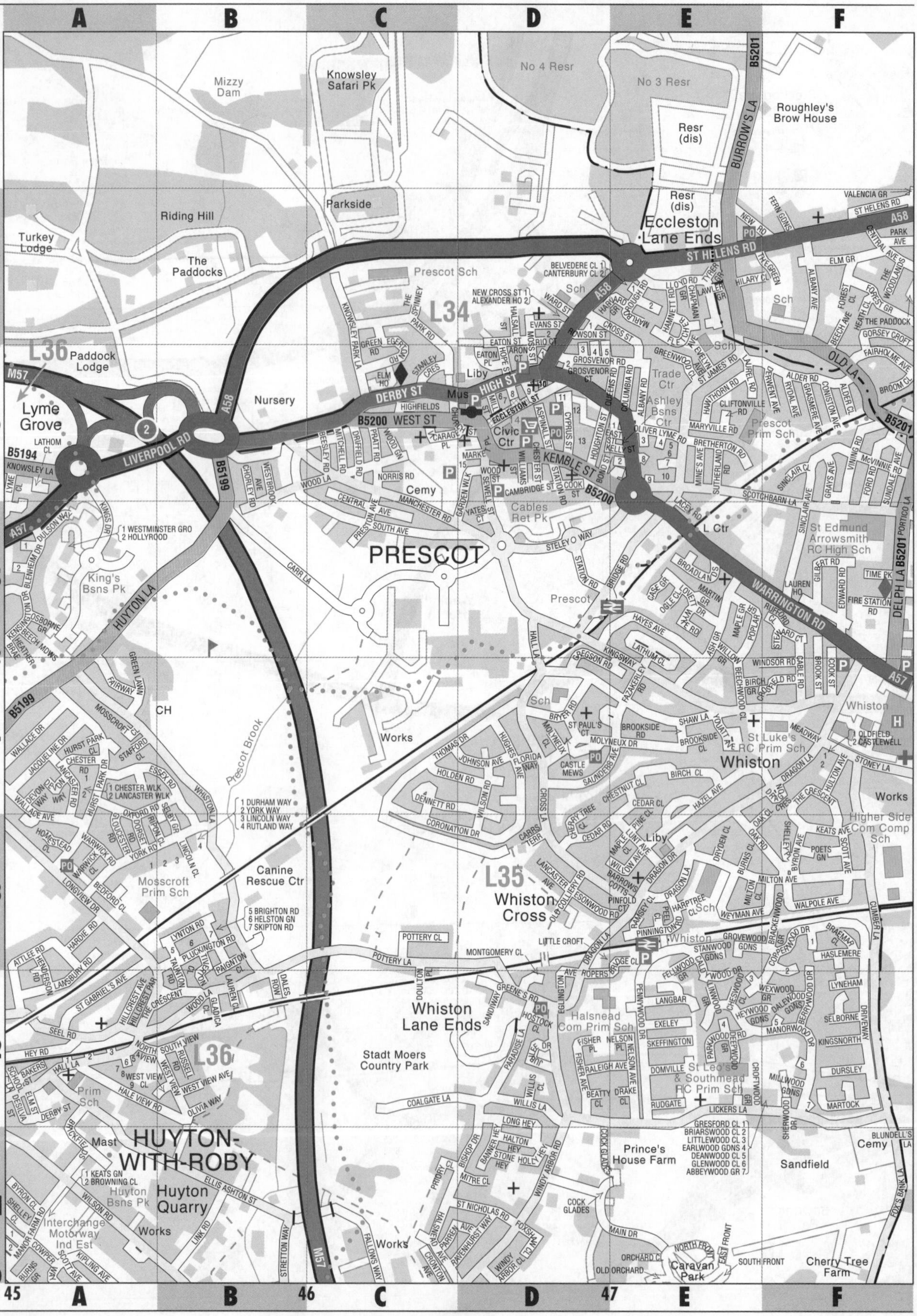

A2
1 ROOFERS WAY
2 STATION WAY
3 POPLAR WAY
4 OLIVIA MANS
5 ALEXANDER MANS
6 QUARRY WAY
7 ALAMORA HO
8 RIO HO
9 GRANITE TERR

55
71

43
58

A
B
C
D
E
F
8
7
93
6
5
92
4
3
91
2
1
90
48
49
50
ST HELENS
Thatto Heath
Grange Park
WA10
WA9
L34
L35
Portico
Valencia Farm
Eccleston Park
Playing Fields
Hospice
The Lodge
CH
Brown Edge
Sutton Heath
Nutgrove
Scott Clinic
Lea Green
Glasshouse Farm
Lowfield Ind Est
Elton Head Hall Farm
Holt
Longton Lane Com Prim Sch
Stoney La Ind Est
Rainhill
Sports Ground
Pendlebury Brook
Lea Green Ind Est
Lea Green Bsns Pk
Micklehead Farm
Micklehead Green Farm
Brookhouse Bridge
Home Farm
Rainhill High Sch
Loyola Hall
Chapel House Farm
Wood's House Farm
Rainhill Stoops
St Bartholomew's RC Prim Sch
Blundell's Hill
Willis Hall Farm
Shirebrook
Rainhill Hall Farm
Tower Coll
Oakdene Prim Sch
Depot
Thatto Heath Com Prim Sch
St Austin's RC Prim Sch
Nutgrove Meth Prim Sch
Liby
Sch
PO
FB
PRESCOT RD
ST HELENS RD
B5413 THATTO HEATH RD
NUTGROVE RD
ELTON HEAD RD
B5204
RAINHILL RD
WARRINGTON RD
ST HELENS LINKWAY
A570
A58
A57
M62
Two Butt La
BLUNDELL'S LA
CHAPEL LA
SCHOOL LA
MILL LA
1 CROWN ST
2 COMMON ST
3 GORSEFIELD
4 OAKFIELD CL
5 BILLINGHAM RD
1 SUDBURY GDNS
2 GOODWOOD CT
3 HOLKHAM GDNS
1 OULTON GDNS
2 SURLINGHAM GDNS
3 ROLLESBY GDNS
4 ORMESBY GDNS
5 HICKLING GDNS
6 SALHOUSE GDNS
7 RANWORTH GDNS
1 HOLLEY CT
2 BRAITHWAITE CL
3 Victoria Trad Est
4 STATION ST
5 STATION RD
6 HOUGHTON ST
1 WIDDALE AVE
2 KINGSDALE AVE
1 ALVA RD
2 ELGIN CT
TOFTWOOD GDNS 1
ANDERSON CL 2
OAK MEADOWS CT 1
NORBURY FOLD 2

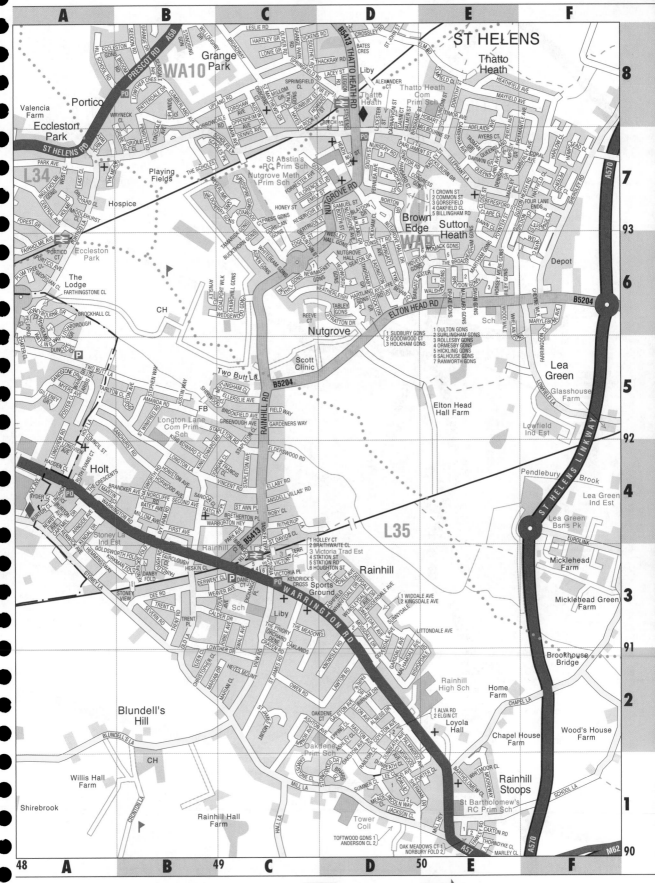

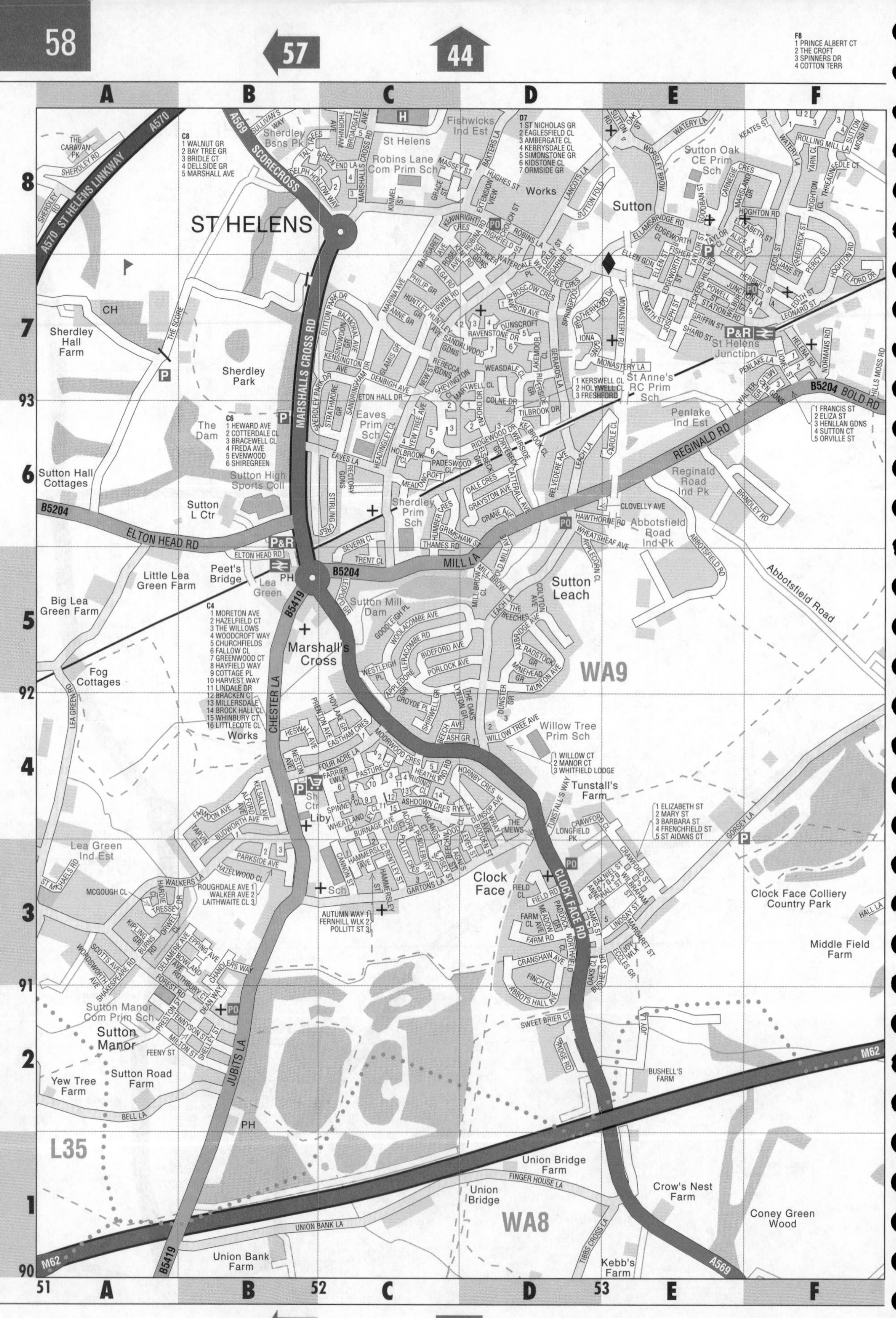
57
44
F8
1 PRINCE ALBERT CT
2 THE CROFT
3 SPINNERS DR
4 COTTON TERR
A
B
C
D
E
F
ST HELENS
Sherdley Bsns Pk
St Helens
Robins Lane Com Prim Sch
Fishwicks Ind Est
Works
Sutton
Sutton Oak CE Prim Sch
C8
1 WALNUT GR
2 BAY TREE GR
3 BRIDLE CT
4 DELLSIDE GR
5 MARSHALL AVE
D7
1 ST NICHOLAS GR
2 EAGLESFIELD CL
3 AMBERGATE CL
4 KERRYSDALE CL
5 SIMONSTONE GR
6 KIDSTONE CL
7 ORMSIDE GR
A570 ST HELENS LINKWAY
A569 SCORECROSS
MARSHALLS CROSS RD
THE CARAVAN PK
CH
Sherdley Hall Farm
Sherdley Park
The Dam
C6
1 HEWARD AVE
2 COTTERDALE CL
3 BRACEWELL CL
4 FREDA AVE
5 EVENWOOD
6 SHIREGREEN
Eaves Prim Sch
Sutton Hall Cottages
Sutton High Sports Coll
Sutton L Ctr
Sherdley Prim Sch
1 KERSWELL CL
2 HOLYWELL CL
3 FRESHFORD
St Anne's RC Prim Sch
St Helens Junction
Penlake Ind Est
Reginald Road Ind Pk
1 FRANCIS ST
2 ELIZA ST
3 HENLLAN GDNS
4 SUTTON CT
5 ORVILLE ST
B5204 BOLD RD
REGINALD RD
B5204
ELTON HEAD RD
MILL LA
Abbotsfield Road Ind Pk
Abbotsfield Road
Little Lea Green Farm
Peet's Bridge
Lea Green
PH
Big Lea Green Farm
Sutton Mill Dam
Sutton Leach
C4
1 MORETON AVE
2 HAZELFIELD CT
3 THE WILLOWS
4 WOODCROFT WAY
5 CHURCHFIELDS
6 FALLOW CL
7 GREENWOOD CT
8 HAYFIELD WAY
9 COTTAGE PL
10 HARVEST WAY
11 LINDALE DR
12 BRACKEN CT
13 MILLERSDALE
14 BROCK HALL CL
15 WHINBURY CT
16 LITTLECOTE CL
Marshall's Cross
Fog Cottages
WA9
Works
Willow Tree Prim Sch
1 WILLOW CT
2 MANOR CT
3 WHITFIELD LODGE
Tunstall's Farm
CHESTER LA
B5419
1 ELIZABETH ST
2 MARY ST
3 BARBARA ST
4 FRENCHFIELD ST
5 ST AIDANS CT
Lea Green Ind Est
Clock Face
CLOCK FACE RD
Clock Face Colliery Country Park
Middle Field Farm
ROUGHDALE AVE 1
WALKER AVE 2
LAITHWAITE CL 3
AUTUMN WAY 1
FERNHILL WLK 2
POLLITT ST 3
Sutton Manor Com Prim Sch
Sutton Manor
Yew Tree Farm
Sutton Road Farm
JUBITS LA
BUSHELL'S FARM
M62
L35
Union Bridge Farm
FINGER HOUSE LA
Union Bridge
Crow's Nest Farm
Coney Green Wood
WA8
UNION BANK LA
Union Bank Farm
Kebb's Farm
A569
8
7
93
6
5
92
4
3
91
2
1
90
51
52
53
57
73

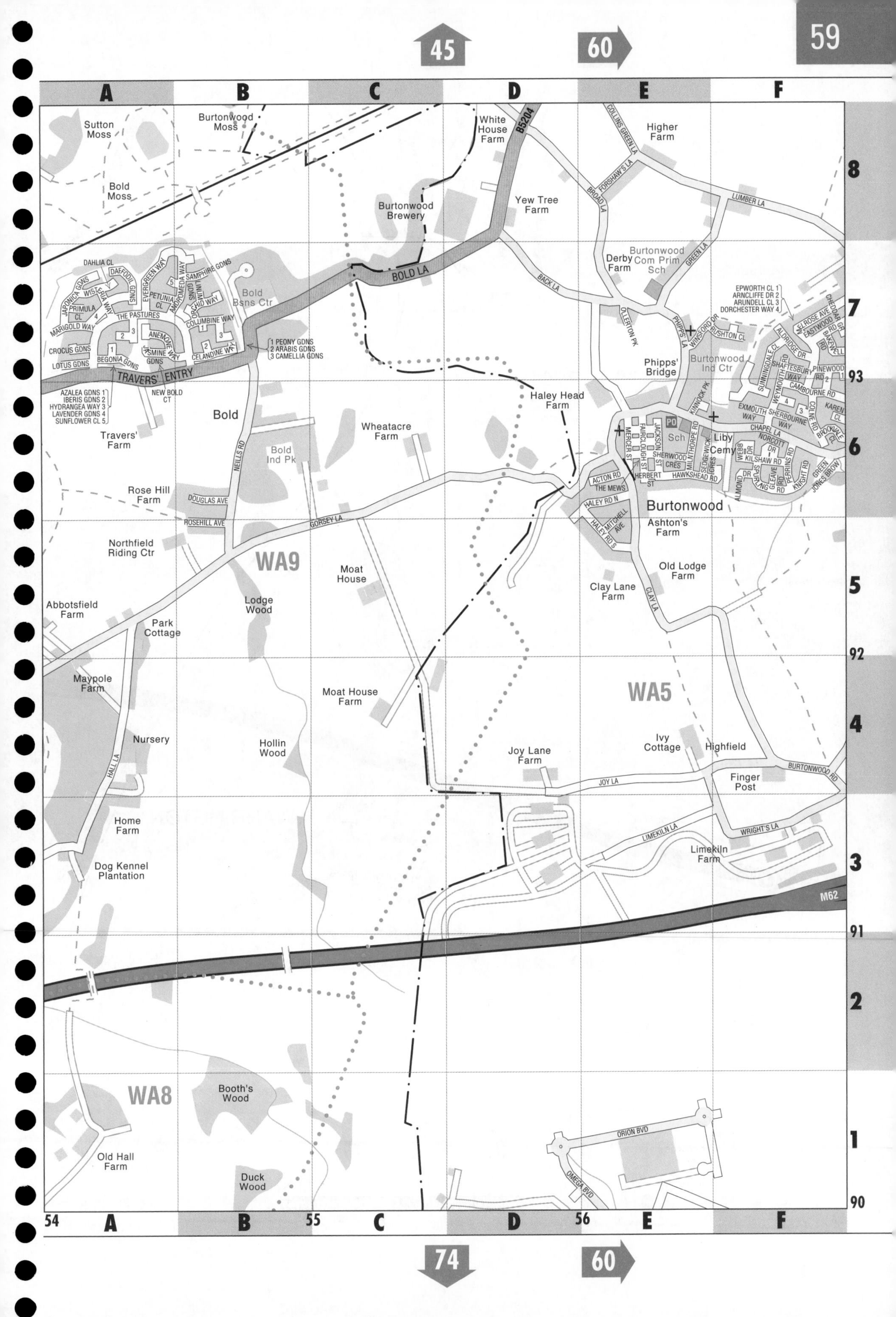

A B C D E F

8

7

93

6

5

92

4

3

91

2

1

90

Sutton
Moss

Burtonwood
Moss

White
House
Farm

B5204

Higher
Farm

Bold
Moss

Burtonwood
Brewery

Yew Tree
Farm

BACK LA

COLLINS GREEN LA

FORSHAW'S LA

BROAD LA

LUMBER LA

DAHLIA CL
DAFFODIL
GDNS
EVERGREEN WAY
SAMPHIRE GDNS
VERONICA
GDNS
WISTA
PRIMULA
CL
PETUNIA
CL
ALMOND WAY
SNOWDROP WAY
ORCHID WAY
COLUMBINE WAY
MARIGOLD WAY
THE PASTURES
ANEMONE WAY
JASMINE WAY
CELANDINE WAY
CROCUS GDNS
LOTUS GDNS
BEGONIA GDNS

Bold
Bsns Ctr

BOLD LA

Derby
Farm

Burtonwood
Com Prim
Sch

GREEN LA

EPWORTH CL 1
ARNCLIFFE DR 2
ARUNDELL CL 3
DORCHESTER WAY 4

ROSE AVE
EASTWOOD RD
CHERITON
ALDRIDGE DR
BLACKWELL
MAXWELL

1 PEONY GDNS
2 ARABIS GDNS
3 CAMELLIA GDNS

TRAVERS' ENTRY

OLLERTON PK

PHIPPS LA

Phipps'
Bridge

WINSFORD CL
RUSHTON CL
SUNNINGDALE CL

Burtonwood
Ind Ctr

WEYMOUTH CL

SHAFTESBURY
WAY
CAMBOURNE
WAY
PINEWOOD
RD
KAREN
CL

AZALEA GDNS 1
IBERIS GDNS 2
HYDRANGEA WAY 3
LAVENDER GDNS 4
SUNFLOWER CL 5

NEW BOLD
CT

Bold

Travers'
Farm

Haley Head
Farm

KINNOCK PK

EXMOUTH
WAY
SHERBOURNE
WAY

COLNE RD
NORCOTT
DR

BROOKVALE

Rose Hill
Farm

NEILL'S RD

Wheatacre
Farm

Bold
Ind Pk

MERCER ST
JACKSON
ST
FAIRCLOUGH ST
SHERWOOD
CRES
SEDGWICK RD
MILNTHORPE RD

PO
Sch

Liby
Cemy

KILSHAW RD

ALMOND DR
SPURLING RD

WEBB DR
GLEAVE RD
PERKINS RD
KNIGHT RD

GREEN
JONES BROW

Northfield
Riding Ctr

DOUGLAS AVE

GORSEY LA

HERBERT
ST

The Mews
Acton Rd

Ashton's
Farm

HAWKSHEAD RD

Burtonwood

Abbotsfield
Farm

ROSEHILL AVE

WA9

Moat
House

HALEY RD N
HALEY RD S
MITCHELL
AVE

Clay Lane
Farm

Old Lodge
Farm

CLAY LA

WA5

Park
Cottage

Lodge
Wood

Maypole
Farm

Moat House
Farm

Ivy
Cottage

Highfield

BURTONWOOD RD

Nursery

Hollin
Wood

Joy Lane
Farm

Finger
Post

HALL LA

JOY LA

Home
Farm

LIMEKILN LA

WRIGHT'S LA

Limekiln
Farm

Dog Kennel
Plantation

M62

WA8

Booth's
Wood

ORION BVD

Old Hall
Farm

Duck
Wood

OMEGA BVD

59
46

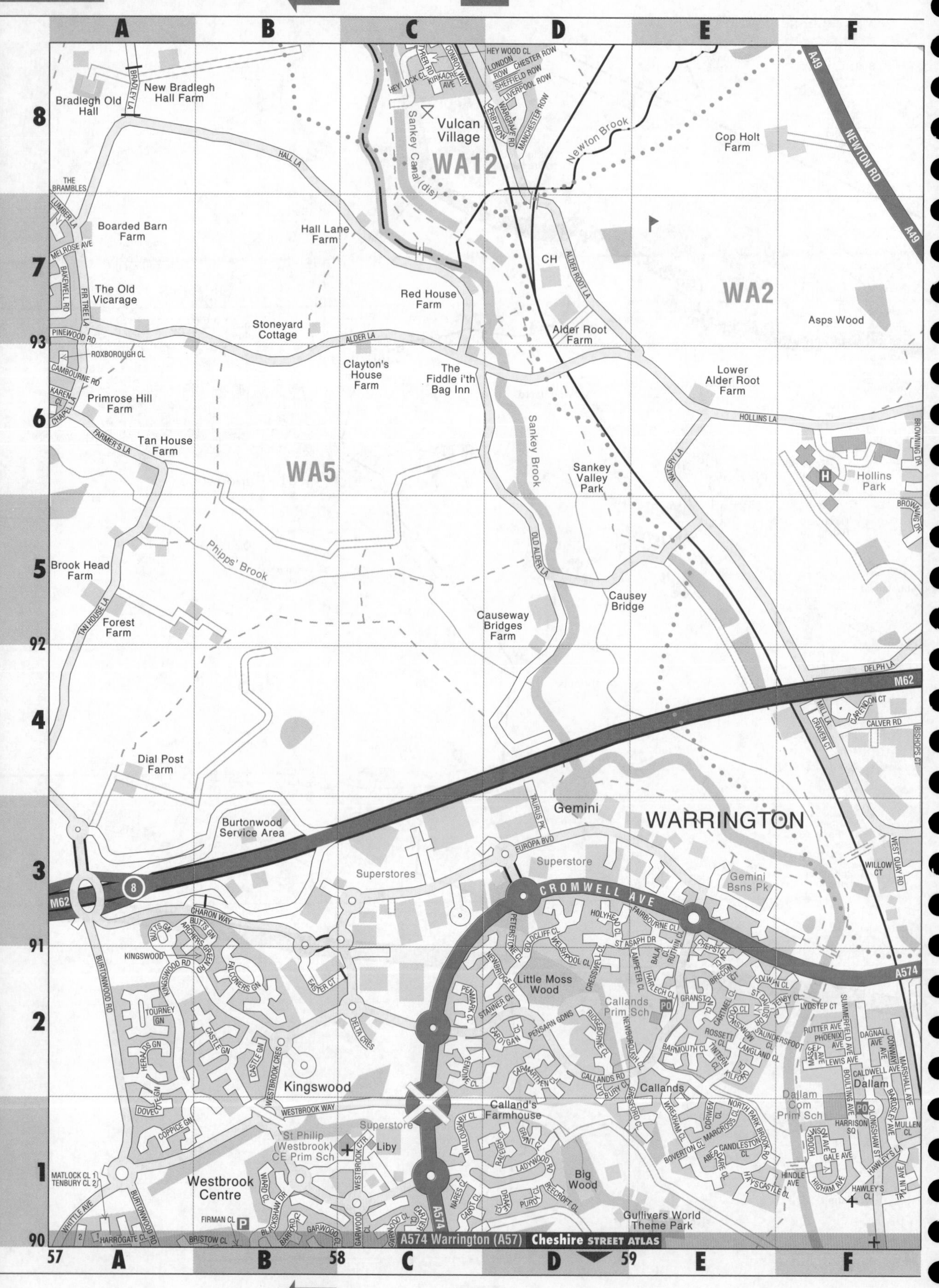
Bradlegh Old Hall
New Bradlegh Hall Farm
Vulcan Village
WA12
Sankey Canal (dis)
Newton Brook
Cop Holt Farm
NEWTON RD
A49
Boarded Barn Farm
Hall Lane Farm
The Old Vicarage
Red House Farm
CH
WA2
Asps Wood
Stoneyard Cottage
Alder Root Farm
ALDER LA
Clayton's House Farm
The Fiddle i'th Bag Inn
Lower Alder Root Farm
Primrose Hill Farm
HOLLINS LA
Tan House Farm
WA5
Sankey Brook
Sankey Valley Park
Hollins Park
Phipps' Brook
Brook Head Farm
Causey Bridge
Forest Farm
Causeway Bridges Farm
Dial Post Farm
M62
Gemini
WARRINGTON
Burtonwood Service Area
Superstores
Superstore
Gemini Bsns Pk
CROMWELL AVE
A574
Little Moss Wood
Callands Prim Sch
Kingswood
Callands
Dallam
Dallam Com Prim Sch
Calland's Farmhouse
Superstore
St Philip (Westbrook) CE Prim Sch
Liby
Westbrook Centre
Big Wood
Gullivers World Theme Park
A574 Warrington (A57)

59

47

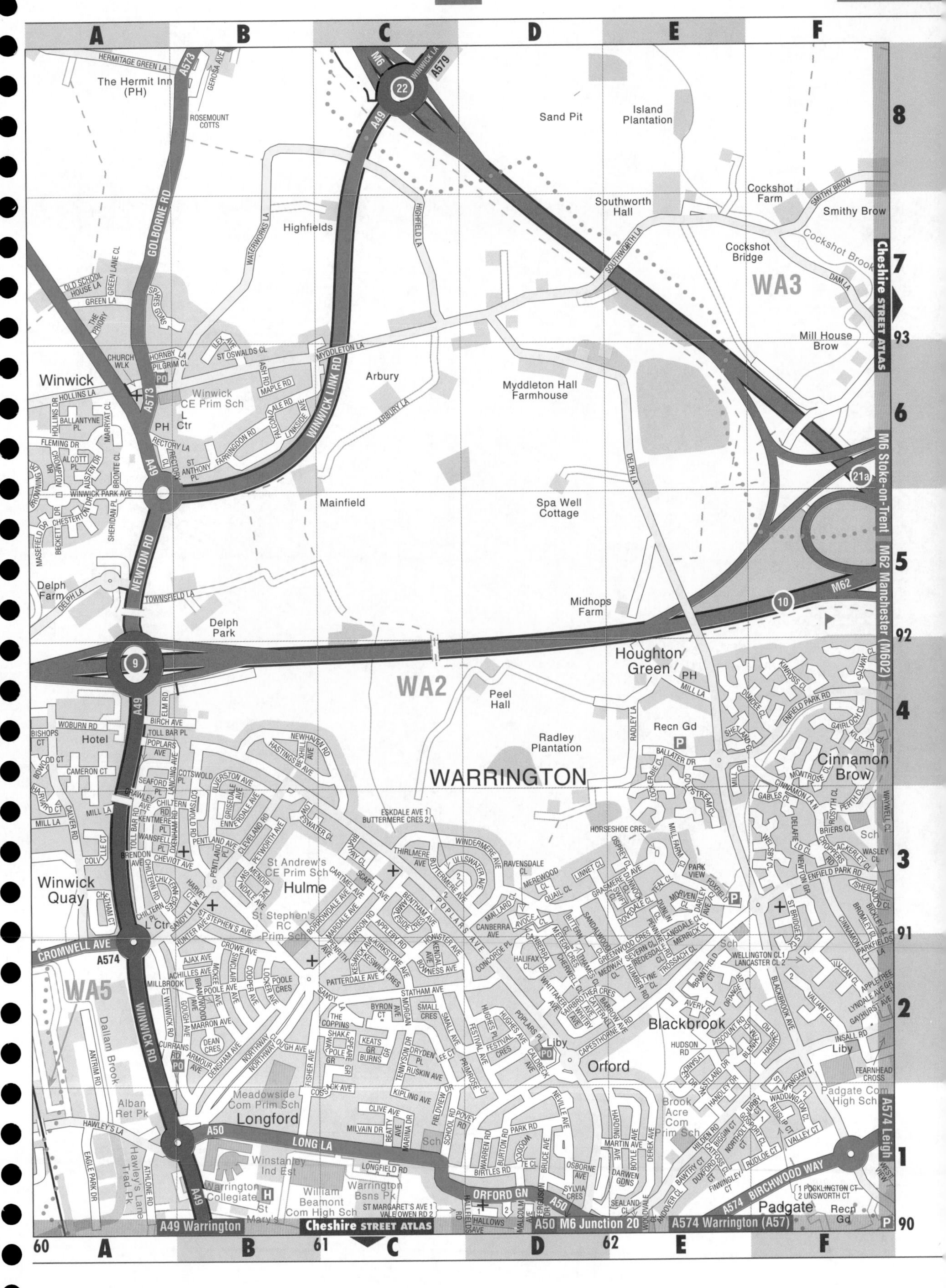

A
B
C
D
E
F
8
7
6
5
4
3
2
1
93
92
91
90
60
61
62
HERMITAGE GREEN LA
The Hermit Inn (PH)
A573
GEROSA AVE
ROSEMOUNT COTTS
M6
WINWICK LA
A579
22
A49
Sand Pit
Island Plantation
Cockshot Farm
SMITHY BROW
Smithy Brow
Southworth Hall
Highfields
HIGHFIELD LA
WATERWORKS LA
GOLBORNE RD
SOUTHWORTH LA
Cockshot Bridge
Cockshot Brook
WA3
DAM LA
Mill House Brow
GREEN LANE CL
OLD SCHOOL HOUSE LA
GREEN LA
THE PRIORY
SPIRES GDNS
CHURCH WLK
HORNBY LA
PILGRIM CL
ILEX AVE
ST OSWALDS CL
MYDDLETON LA
Winwick
HOLLINS LA
Winwick CE Prim Sch
Arbury
ARBURY LA
Myddleton Hall Farmhouse
ASH RD
MAPLE RD
FALCON DALE RD
LINKSIDE AVE
WINWICK LINK RD
BALLANTYNE PL
MARRYAT CL
HOLLINS DR
PH
L Ctr
FLEMING DR
CROMPTON DR
ALCOTT PL
AUSTEN DR
BRONTE CL
RECTORY LA
FARRINGDON RD
ST ANTHONY PL
DELPH LA
WINWICK PARK AVE
Mainfield
Spa Well Cottage
21a
M6 Stoke-on-Trent
BROWNING DR
CHESTERTON DR
SHERIDAN PL
MASEFIELD DR
BECKETT DR
NEWTON RD
Delph Farm
TOWNSFIELD LA
Midhops Farm
10
M62
M62 Manchester (M602)
Delph Park
9
Houghton Green
PH
MILL LA
WA2
Peel Hall
KINROSS CL
SOLWAY CL
DUNDEE CL
ENFIELD PARK RD
ELM RD
BIRCH AVE
WOBURN RD
BISHOPS CT
Hotel
TOLL BAR PL
POPLARS AVE
NEWHAVEN RD
HASTINGS AVE
RADLEY LA
Radley Plantation
Recn Gd
BALLATER DR
SHETLAND CL
GAIRLOCH CL
KILSYTH CL
Cinnamon Brow
CAMERON CT
SEAFORD PL
COTSWOLD PL
ULVERSTON AVE
WARRINGTON
LOCKERBIE CL
COLDSTREAM CL
MONTROSE CL
CINNAMON LA N
GABLES CL
PERTH CL
CRAWLEY AVE
CHILTERN PL
GRISEDALE AVE
ENNERDALE AVE
ESKDALE AVE 1
BUTTERMERE CRES 2
MILL LA
KENTMERE PL
CLEVELAND RD
HORSESHOE CRES
MILL FARM CL
ROSYTH CL
DELAFIELD CL
WAYWELL CL
TOLL BAR RD
WANSFELL PL
PENTLAND AVE
PETWORTH AVE
SWATER CL
WINDERMERE AVE
BRIERS CL
Sch
WASLEY CL
MILL LA
THIRLMERE AVE
ULLSWATER AVE
RAVENSDALE CL
LINNET CL
OSPREY CL
PARK VIEW
ACKERLEY CL
ENFIELD PARK RD
BRENDON AVE
CHEVIOT AVE
St Andrew's CE Prim Sch
MEREWOOD CL
QUAIL CL
FOXFIELD
Winwick Quay
HARVEY CT
Hulme
CARTMEL AVE
SCAFELL AVE
BUTTERMERE AVE
MALLARD CL
GRASMERE AVE
TEAL CL
MORVEN CL
P
ST BRIDGETS CL
CHILTERN RD
SANDY LA W
ST STEPHEN'S AVE
St Stephen's RC Prim Sch
BORROWDALE AVE
HOWSON RD
APPLEBY RD
BENTHAM AVE
POPLARS AVE
CANBERRA AVE
AVOCET CL
SANDALWOOD
DOVEDALE CL
DUNLIN CL
DARLEY AVE
91
CROMWELL AVE
A574
CROWE AVE
HUNTER AVE
AJAX AVE
ACHILLES AVE
COOPER AVE
LOCKER AVE
POOLE CRES
PENRITH AVE
KESWICK AVE
KIRKSTONE AVE
HONISTER AVE
KENDAL AVE
BOWNESS AVE
CONCORDE PL
HALIFAX CL
GREENWOOD CRES
SEVERN CL
REDESDALE CL
TYNE CL
TROSSACH CL
MERRICK CL
WELLINGTON CL 1
LANCASTER CL 2
PARKFIELDS LA
WA5
MILLBROOK CT
WINWICK RD
POOLE AVE
PATTERDALE AVE
KESWICK CRES
STATHAM AVE
BRANTFIELD CT
AVERY CL
BLACKBROOK AVE
VALIANT CL
APPLETREE
LYNDALE AVE
GAYHURST AVE
MARRON AVE
BYRON CT
SMALL CRES
SMALL AVE
HUGHES PL
HUGHES AVE
POPLARS PL
FAIRBROTHER CRES
Blackbrook
INSALL RD
Dallam Brook
GOUGH AVE
DEAN CRES
THE COPPINS
SHAKESPEARE GR
KEATS GR
BURNS GR
MORGAN AVE
FESTIVAL CRES
FESTIVAL AVE
Liby
PO
CAPESTHORNE RD
HUDSON RD
Liby
CURRANS RD
ARMOUR AVE
DENSHAM AVE
NORTHWAY
CLOUGH AVE
TENNYSON DR
DRYDEN PL
LEE CT
RUSKIN AVE
PRIMROSE CL
CALDBECK AVE
Orford
FEARNHEAD CROSS
ANTRIM RD
COSSACK AVE
KIPLING AVE
FIELDVIEW DR
Brook Acre Com Prim Sch
Padgate Com High Sch
Meadowside Com Prim Sch
FISHER AVE
CLIVE AVE
SCHOOL RD
POVEY RD
HARDING AVE
HANDLEY DR
WADDINGTON CL
Alban Ret Pk
Longford
HAWLEY'S LA
MILVAIN DR
BEATTY AVE
MARINA DR
Sch
PARK RD
NEVILLE AVE
MARTIN AVE
BOYLE AVE
DEREK AVE
HILDEN RD
VALLEY CT
EAGLE PARK DR
Hawley's Lane Trad Pk
ATHLONE RD
A50
LONG LA
WARREN RD
BURTON RD
BIRTLES RD
BRUCE AVE
OSBORNE AVE
DARWEN GDNS
BAWTRY CT
DUXFORD CT
FINNINGLEY CT
BIGGIN CT
NORTHOLT CT
RUDLOE CT
WEST VIEW
Winstanley Ind Est
LONGFIELD RD
ORFORD GN
SYLVIA CRES
SEALAND CL
A574 BIRCHWOOD WAY
1 POCKLINGTON CT
2 UNSWORTH CT
Warrington Collegiate
H
William Beamont Com High Sch
Warrington Bsns Pk
ST MARGARET'S AVE 1
VALE OWEN RD 2
HALLOWS AVE
MALCOLM AVE
FERGUSON AVE
A50
WOODVALE
ANDOVER CL
Padgate
Recn Gd
St Mary's
A49 Warrington
Cheshire STREET ATLAS
A50 M6 Junction 20
A574 Warrington (A57)
A574 Leigh

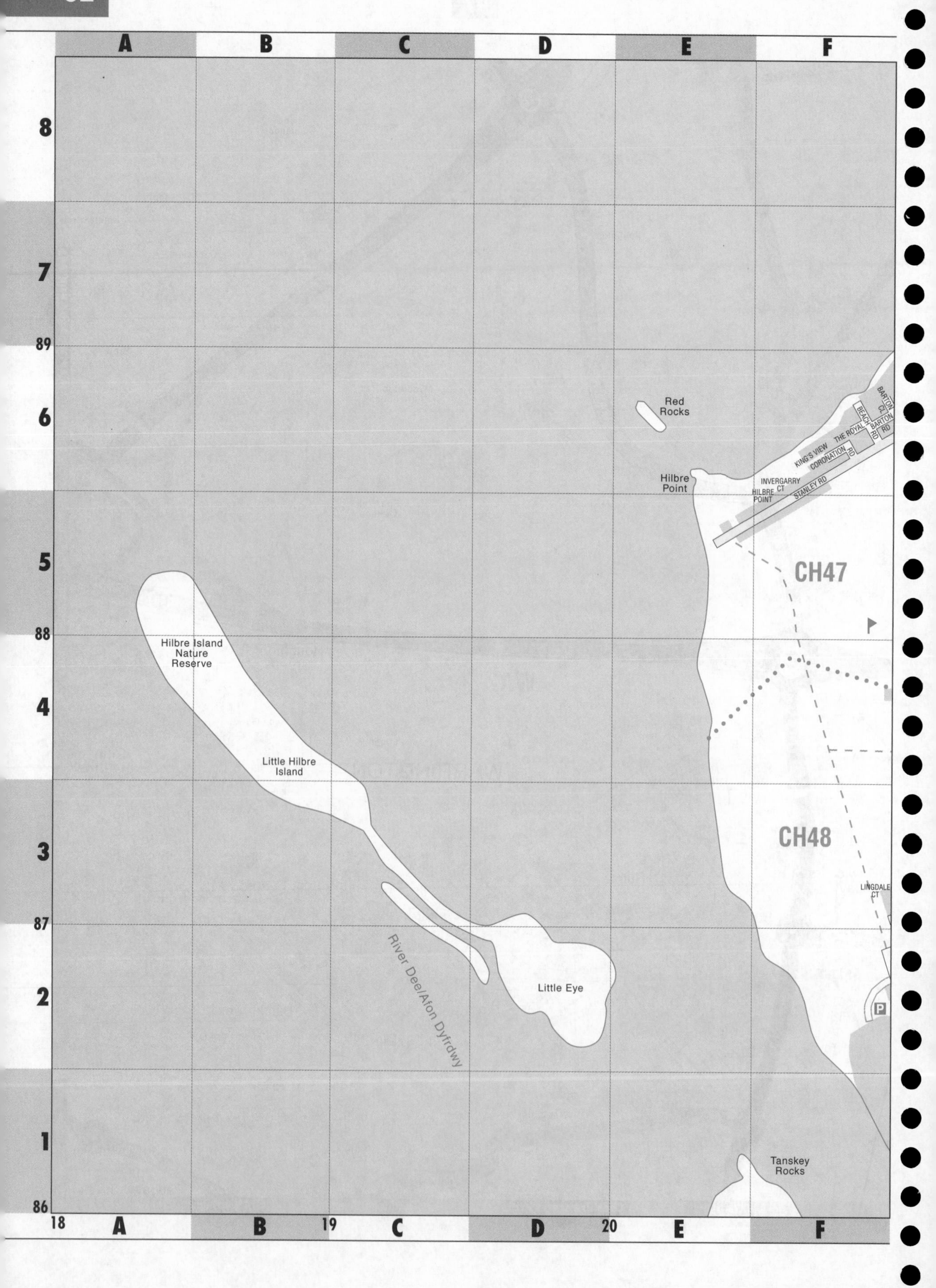
A
B
C
D
E
F
8
7
89
6
5
88
4
3
87
2
1
86
18
19
20
Red Rocks
Hilbre Point
BARTON CL
BEACH RD
BARTON RD
THE ROYAL
KING'S VIEW
CORONATION RD
INVERGARRY CT
HILBRE POINT
STANLEY RD
CH47
Hilbre Island Nature Reserve
Little Hilbre Island
CH48
LINGDALE CT
River Dee/Afon Dyfrdwy
Little Eye
Tanskey Rocks

48
64

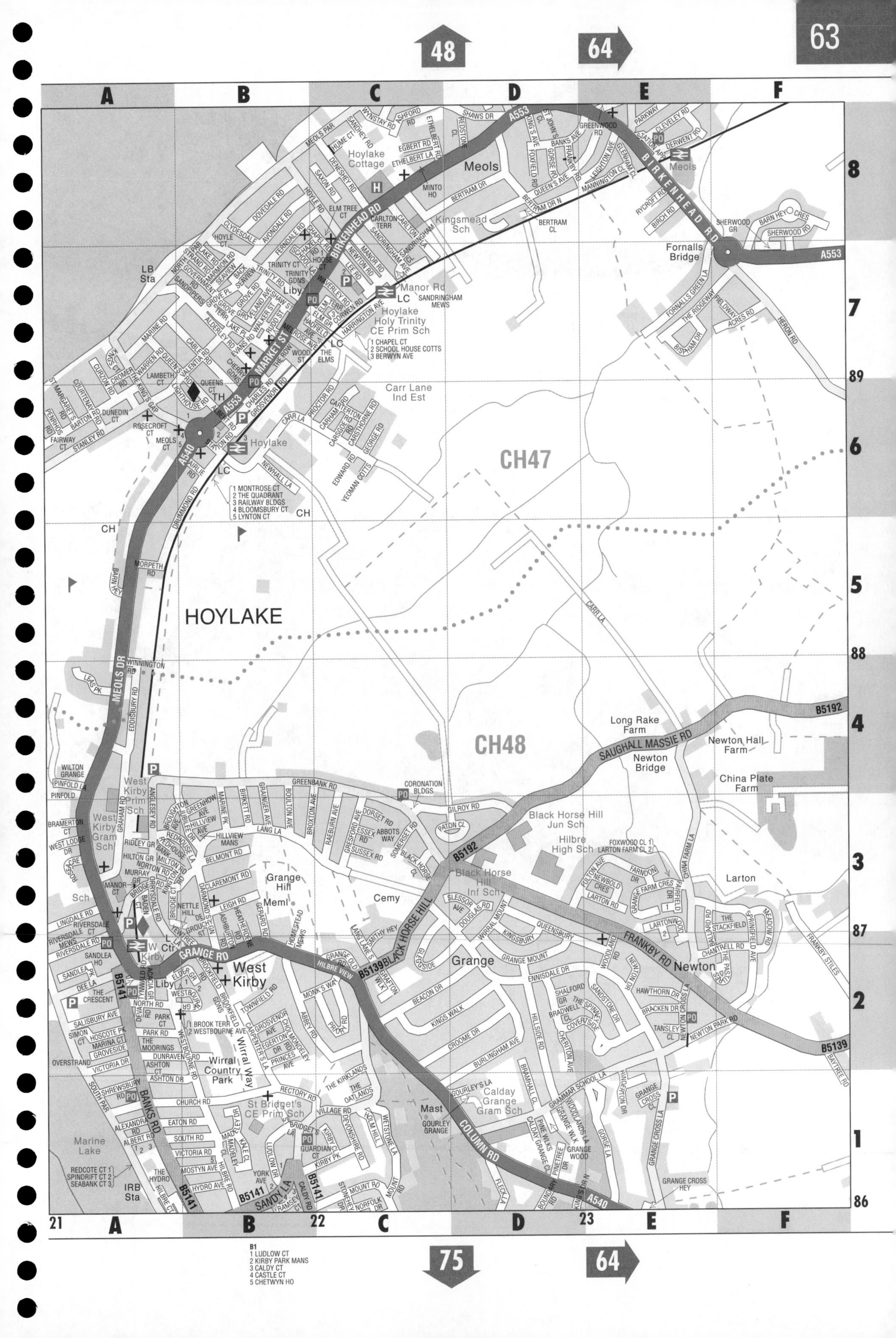

B1
1 LUDLOW CT
2 KIRBY PARK MANS
3 CALDY CT
4 CASTLE CT
5 CHETWYN HO

75
64

63
49

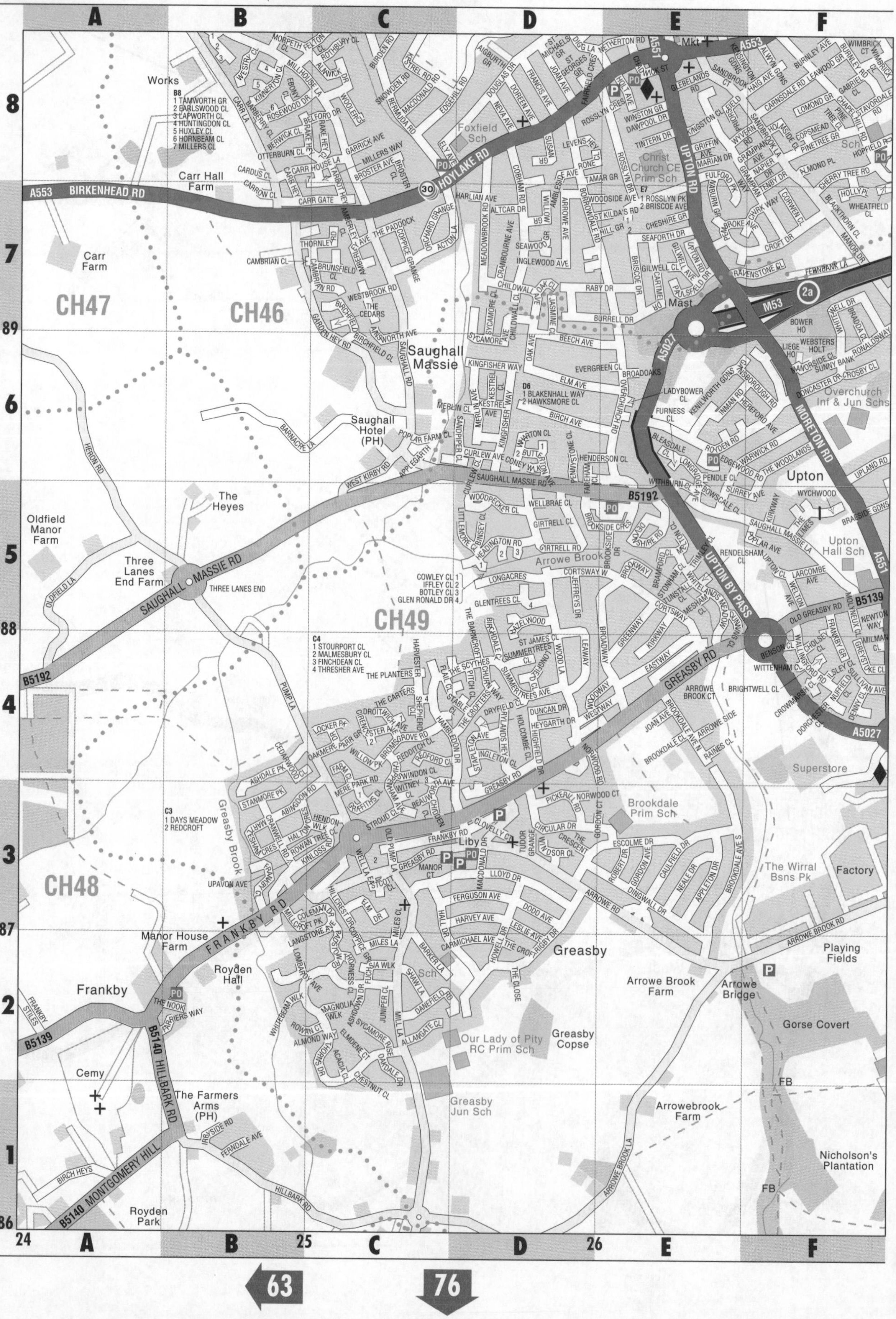
A
B
C
D
E
F
8
7
89
6
5
88
4
3
87
2
1
86
24
25
26
CH47
CH46
CH49
CH48
Works
B8
1 TAMWORTH GR
2 EARLSWOOD CL
3 LAPWORTH CL
4 HUNTINGDON CL
5 HUXLEY CL
6 HORNBEAM CL
7 MILLERS CL
Carr Hall Farm
A553 BIRKENHEAD RD
HOYLAKE RD
Carr Farm
Foxfield Sch
Christ Church CE Prim Sch
E7
1 ROSSLYN PK
2 BRISCOE AVE
UPTON RD
M53
Mast
Saughall Massie
D6
1 BLAKENHALL WAY
2 HAWKSMORE CL
Saughall Hotel (PH)
SAUGHALL MASSIE RD
B5192
The Heyes
Oldfield Manor Farm
Three Lanes End Farm
THREE LANES END
Arrowe Brook
COWLEY CL 1
IFFLEY CL 2
BOTLEY CL 3
GLEN RONALD DR 4
C4
1 STOURPORT CL
2 MALMESBURY CL
3 FINCHDEAN CL
4 THRESHER AVE
Upton
Upton Hall Sch
Overchurch Inf & Jun Schs
MORETON RD
UPTON BY PASS
A5027
A551
B5139
GREASBY RD
Superstore
Brookdale Prim Sch
C3
1 DAYS MEADOW
2 REDCROFT
Greasby Brook
FRANKBY RD
Liby
The Wirral Bsns Pk
Factory
Greasby
Manor House Farm
Royden Hall
Frankby
Arrowe Brook Farm
Arrowe Bridge
Playing Fields
Gorse Covert
Our Lady of Pity RC Prim Sch
Greasby Copse
Cemy
The Farmers Arms (PH)
B5140 HILLBARK RD
B5140 MONTGOMERY HILL
Greasby Jun Sch
Arrowebrook Farm
Nicholson's Plantation
Royden Park
FB
ARROWE BROOK RD
HILLBARK RD

63
76

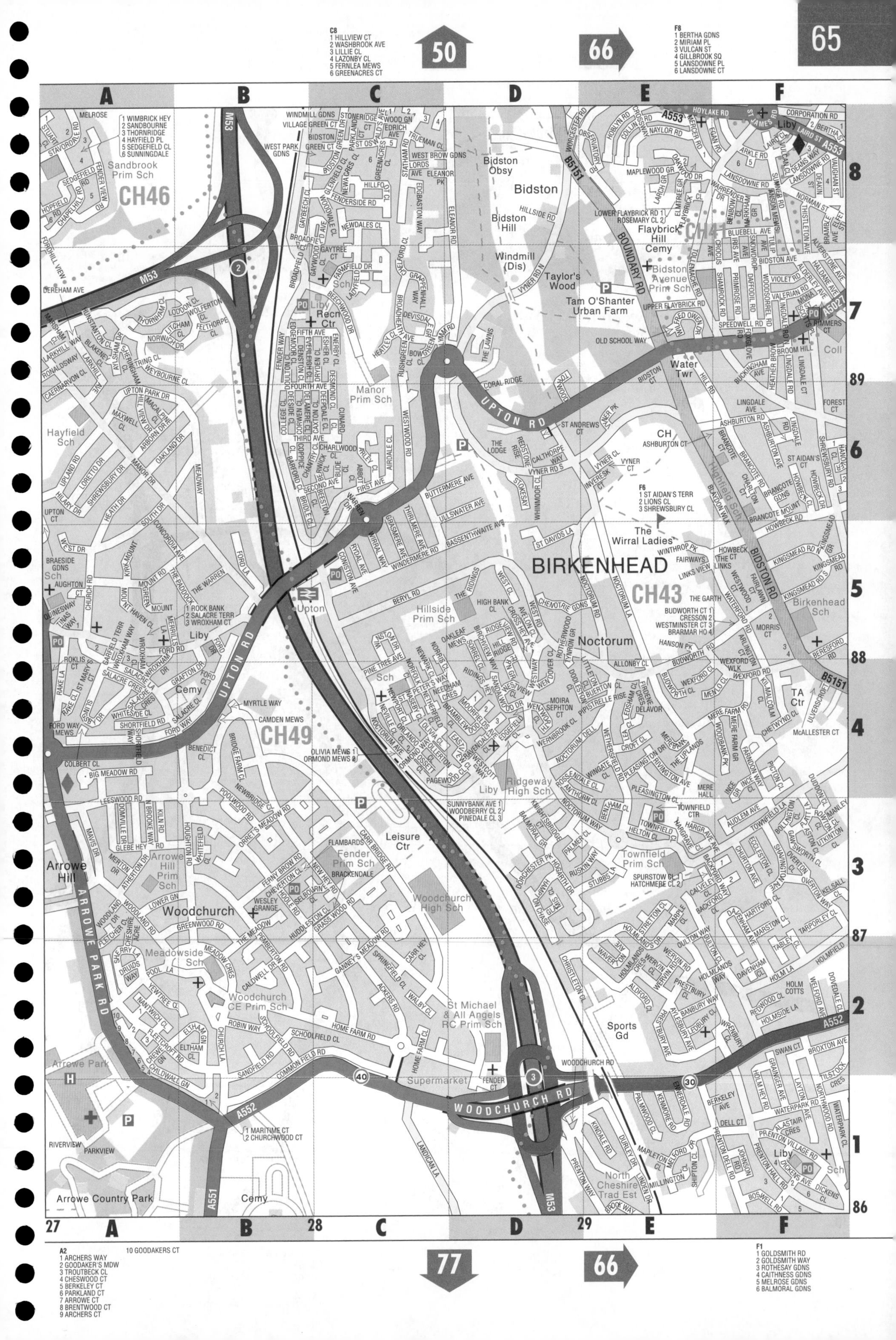
C8
1 HILLVIEW CT
2 WASHBROOK AVE
3 LILLIE CL
4 LAZONBY CL
5 FERNLEA MEWS
6 GREENACRES CT
50
66
F8
1 BERTHA GDNS
2 MIRIAM PL
3 VULCAN ST
4 GILLBROOK SQ
5 LANSDOWNE PL
6 LANSDOWNE CT
65
A
B
C
D
E
F
8
7
89
6
5
88
4
3
87
2
1
86
27
28
29
CH46
CH41
CH43
CH49
BIRKENHEAD
Bidston
Bidston Obsy
Bidston Hill
Windmill (Dis)
Taylor's Wood
Tam O'Shanter Urban Farm
Flaybrick Hill Cemy
Bidston Avenue Prim Sch
Sandbrook Prim Sch
Hayfield Sch
Manor Prim Sch
Recn Ctr
Water Twr
The Wirral Ladies'
Noctorum
Hillside Prim Sch
Upton
Cemy
Ridgeway High Sch
Leisure Ctr
Fender Prim Sch
Woodchurch High Sch
Arrowe Hill Prim Sch
Arrowe Hill
Woodchurch
Meadowside Sch
Woodchurch CE Prim Sch
St Michael & All Angels RC Prim Sch
Townfield Prim Sch
Sports Gd
Birkenhead Sch
TA Ctr
Highfield Sch
North Cheshire Trad Est
Arrowe Park
Arrowe Country Park
Supermarket
M53
A553
A5027
B5151
A552
A551
UPTON RD
WOODCHURCH RD
ARROWE PARK RD
BOUNDARY RD
BIDSTON RD
HOYLAKE RD
A2
1 ARCHERS WAY
2 GOODAKER'S MDW
3 TROUTBECK CL
4 CHESWOOD CT
5 BERKELEY CT
6 PARKLAND CT
7 ARROWE CT
8 BRENTWOOD CT
9 ARCHERS CT
10 GOODAKERS CT
77
66
F1
1 GOLDSMITH RD
2 GOLDSMITH WAY
3 ROTHESAY GDNS
4 CAITHNESS GDNS
5 MELROSE GDNS
6 BALMORAL GDNS

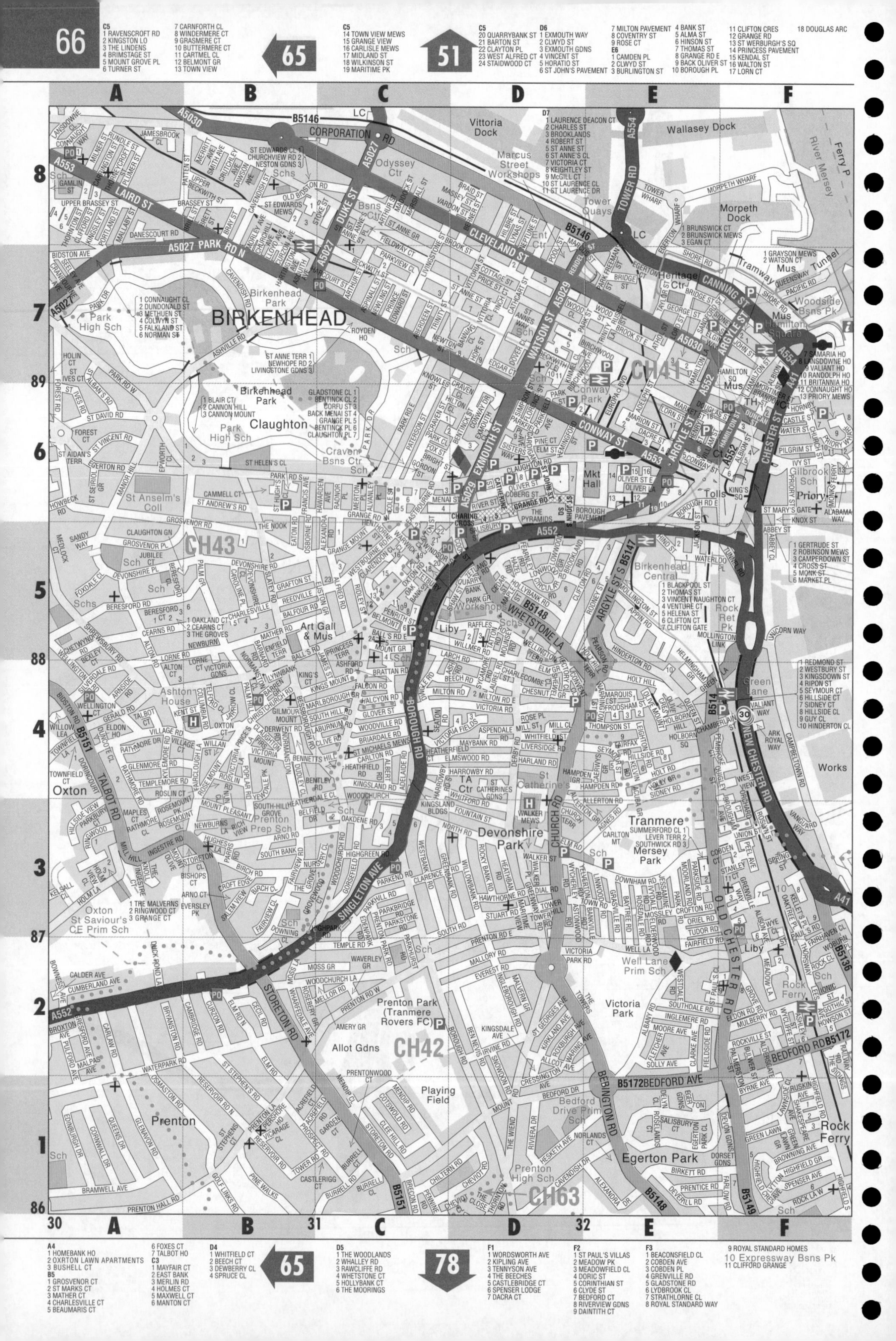

66
C5
1 RAVENSCROFT RD
2 KINGSTON LO
3 THE LINDENS
4 BRIMSTAGE ST
5 MOUNT GROVE PL
6 TURNER ST
7 CARNFORTH CL
8 WINDERMERE CT
9 GRASMERE CT
10 BUTTERMERE CT
11 CARTMEL CL
12 BELMONT GR
13 TOWN VIEW
65
C5
14 TOWN VIEW MEWS
15 GRANGE VIEW
16 CARLISLE MEWS
17 MIDLAND ST
18 WILKINSON ST
19 MARITIME PK
51
C5
20 QUARRYBANK ST
21 BARTON ST
22 CLAYTON PL
23 WEST ALFRED CT
24 STAIDWOOD CT
D6
1 EXMOUTH WAY
2 CLWYD ST
3 EXMOUTH GDNS
4 VINCENT ST
5 HORATIO ST
6 ST JOHN'S PAVEMENT
7 MILTON PAVEMENT
8 COVENTRY ST
9 ROSE CT
E6
1 CAMDEN PL
2 CLWYD ST
3 BURLINGTON ST
4 BANK ST
5 ALMA ST
6 HINSON ST
7 THOMAS ST
8 GRANGE RD E
9 BACK OLIVER ST
10 BOROUGH PL
11 CLIFTON CRES
12 GRANGE RD
13 ST WERBURGH'S SQ
14 PRINCESS PAVEMENT
15 KENDAL ST
16 WALTON ST
17 LORN CT
18 DOUGLAS ARC
A
B
C
D
E
F
8
7
89
6
5
88
4
3
87
2
1
86
30
31
32
BIRKENHEAD
Claughton
Oxton
Prenton
Tranmere
Rock Ferry
Devonshire Park
Egerton Park
Victoria Park
Mersey Park
Birkenhead Park
Wallasey Dock
Vittoria Dock
Morpeth Dock
River Mersey
CH41
CH42
CH43
CH63
Birkenhead Central
Prenton Park (Tranmere Rovers FC)
Allot Gdns
Playing Field
Art Gall & Mus
Mkt Hall
Conway Park
Green Lane
Hamilton Square
Woodside Bsns Pk
Queensway Tunnel
LAIRD ST
PARK RD N
CLEVELAND ST
CONWAY ST
CORPORATION RD
BOROUGH RD
SINGLETON AVE
WHETSTONE LA
CHURCH RD
BEBINGTON RD
OLD CHESTER RD
NEW CHESTER RD
CHESTER ST
ARGYLE ST
ARGYLE ST S
TALBOT RD
STORETON RD
BEDFORD AVE
BEDFORD RD
GRANGE RD
A41
A552
A553
A5027
A5029
A5030
A554
B5146
B5147
B5148
B5149
B5151
B5136
B5172
A4
1 HOMEBANK HO
2 OXTRON LAWN APARTMENTS
3 BUSHELL CT
B5
1 GROSVENOR CT
2 ST MARKS CT
3 MATHER CT
4 CHARLESVILLE CT
5 BEAUMARIS CT
6 FOXES CT
7 TALBOT HO
C3
1 MAYFAIR CT
2 EAST BANK
3 MERLIN RD
4 HOLMES CT
5 MAXWELL CT
6 MANTON CT
D4
1 WHITFIELD CT
2 BEECH CT
3 DEWBERRY CL
4 SPRUCE CL
65
D5
1 THE WOODLANDS
2 WHALLEY RD
3 RAWCLIFFE RD
4 WHETSTONE CT
5 HOLLYBANK CT
6 THE MOORINGS
78
F1
1 WORDSWORTH AVE
2 KIPLING AVE
3 TENNYSON AVE
4 THE BEECHES
5 CASTLEBRIDGE CT
6 SPENSER LODGE
7 DACRA CT
F2
1 ST PAUL'S VILLAS
2 MEADOW PK
3 MEADOWFIELD CL
4 DORIC ST
5 CORINTHIAN ST
6 CLYDE ST
7 BEDFORD CT
8 RIVERVIEW GDNS
9 DAINTITH CT
F3
1 BEACONSFIELD CL
2 COBDEN AVE
3 COBDEN PL
4 GRENVILLE RD
5 GLADSTONE RD
6 LYDBROOK CL
7 STRATHLORNE CL
8 ROYAL STANDARD WAY
9 ROYAL STANDARD HOMES
10 Expressway Bsns Pk
11 CLIFFORD GRANGE

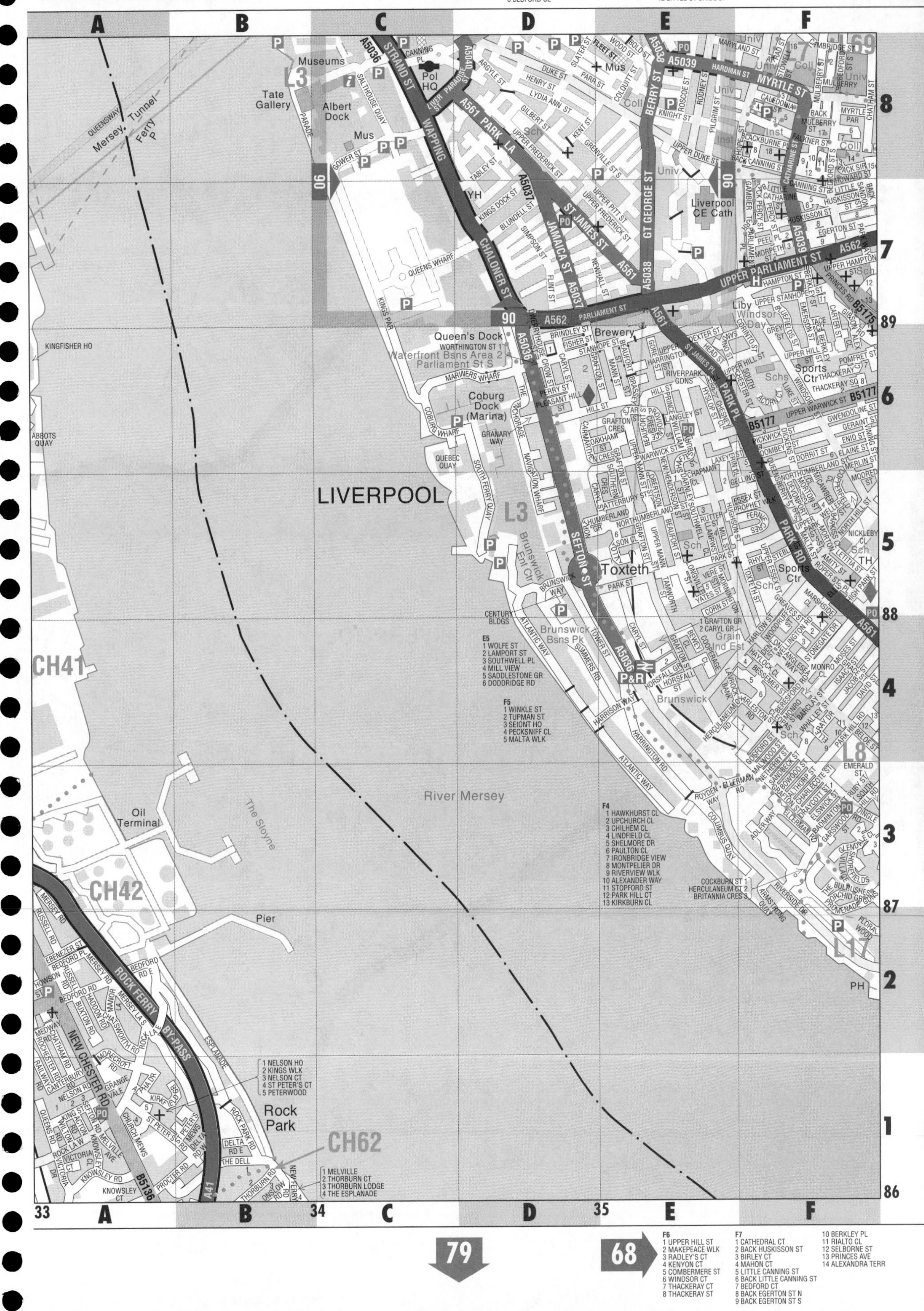

52

F8
1 SOUTH HUNTER ST
2 BACK BEDFORD ST
3 SUGNALL ST
4 UPPER HOPE PL
5 PHILHARMONIC CT
6 BEDFORD CL

68

F8
7 BEDFORD WLK
8 HOPE WAY
9 BACK CATHARINE ST
10 ST BRIDE ST
11 BACK ST BRIDE ST
12 LITTLE ST BRIDE ST

13 SIR HOWARD ST
14 SIR HOWARD WAY
15 SANDON ST
16 CAMBRIDGE CT
17 AGNES JONES HO
18 BLACKBURNE TERR

F6
1 UPPER HILL ST
2 MAKEPEACE WLK
3 RADLEY'S CT
4 KENYON ST
5 COMBERMERE ST
6 WINDSOR CT
7 THACKERAY CT
8 THACKERAY ST

F7
1 CATHEDRAL CT
2 BACK HUSKISSON ST
3 BIRLEY CT
4 MAHON CT
5 LITTLE CANNING ST
6 BACK LITTLE CANNING ST
7 BEDFORD CT
8 BACK EGERTON ST N
9 BACK EGERTON ST S

10 BERKLEY PL
11 RIALTO CL
12 SELBORNE ST
13 PRINCES AVE
14 ALEXANDRA TERR

E5
1 WOLFE ST
2 LAMPORT ST
3 SOUTHWELL PL
4 MILL VIEW
5 SADDLESTONE GR
6 DODDRIDGE RD

F5
1 WINKLE ST
2 TUPMAN ST
3 SEIONT HO
4 PECKSNIFF CL
5 MALTA WLK

F4
1 HAWKHURST CL
2 UPCHURCH CL
3 CHILHEM CL
4 LINDFIELD CL
5 SHELMORE DR
6 PAULTON CL
7 IRONBRIDGE VIEW
8 MONTPELIER DR
9 RIVERVIEW WLK
10 ALEXANDER WAY
11 STOPFORD ST
12 PARK HILL CT
13 KIRKBURN CL

1 GRAFTON GR
2 CARYL GR

COCKBURN ST 1
HERCULANEUM CT 2
BRITANNIA CRES 3

1 NELSON HO
2 KINGS WLK
3 NELSON CT
4 ST PETER'S CT
5 PETERWOOD

1 MELVILLE
2 THORBURN CT
3 THORBURN LODGE
4 THE ESPLANADE

LIVERPOOL

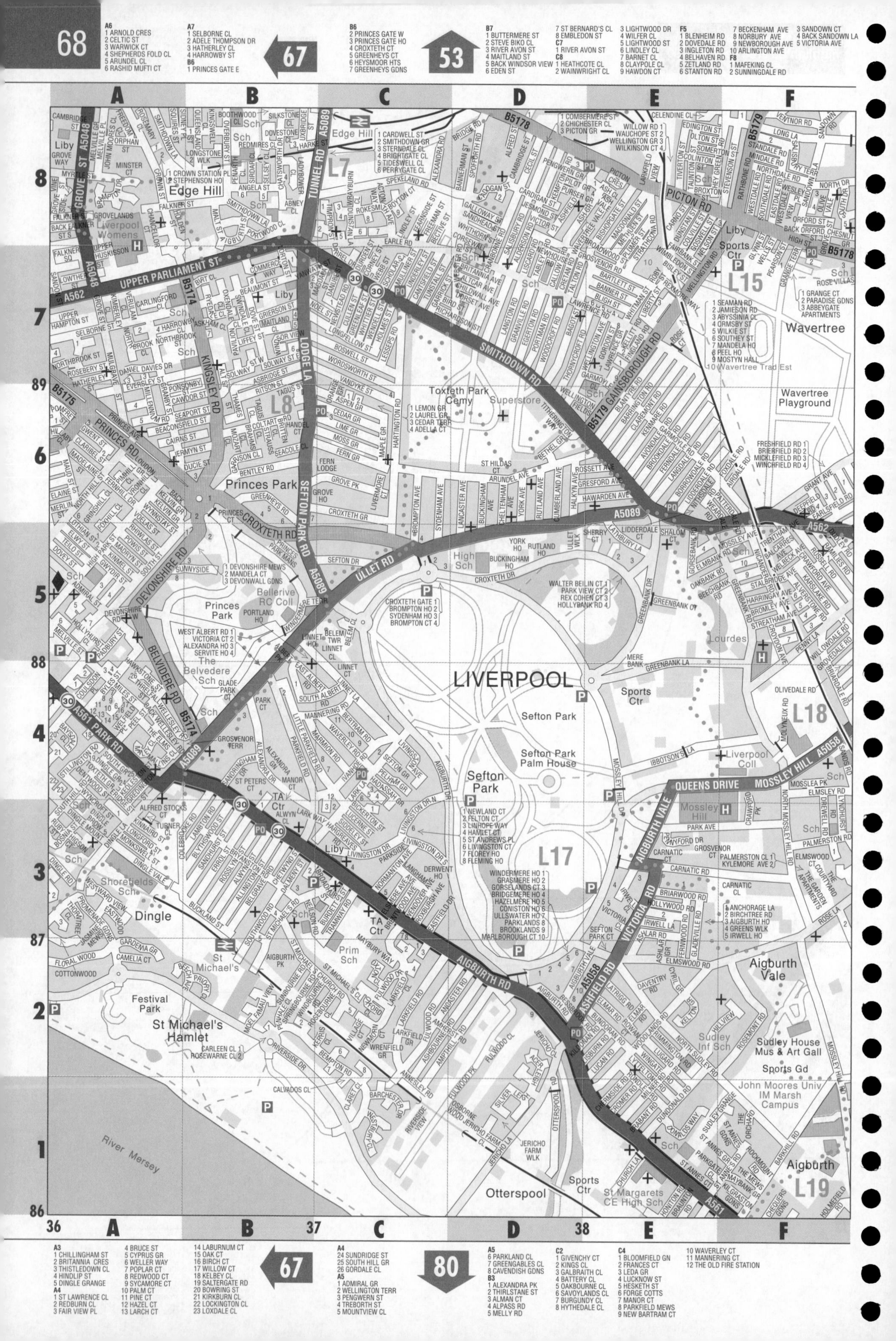
68
A6
1 ARNOLD CRES
2 CELTIC ST
3 WARWICK CT
4 SHEPHERDS FOLD CL
5 ARUNDEL CL
6 RASHID MUFTI CT
A7
1 SELBORNE CL
2 ADELE THOMPSON DR
3 HATHERLEY CL
4 HARROWBY ST
B6
1 PRINCES GATE E
67
B6
2 PRINCES GATE W
3 PRINCES GATE HO
4 CROXTETH CT
5 GREENHEYS CT
6 HEYSMOOR HTS
7 GREENHEYS GDNS
53
B7
1 BUTTERMERE ST
2 STEVE BIKO CL
3 RIVER AVON ST
4 MAITLAND ST
5 BACK WINDSOR VIEW
6 EDEN ST
7 ST BERNARD'S CL
8 EMBLEDON ST
C7
1 RIVER AVON ST
C8
1 HEATHCOTE CL
2 WAINWRIGHT CL
3 LIGHTWOOD DR
4 WILFER CL
5 LIGHTWOOD ST
6 LINDLEY CL
7 BARNET CL
8 CLAYPOLE CL
9 HAWDON CT
F5
1 BLENHEIM RD
2 DOVEDALE RD
3 INGLETON RD
4 BELHAVEN RD
5 ZETLAND RD
6 STANTON RD
7 BECKENHAM AVE
8 NORBURY AVE
9 NEWBOROUGH AVE
10 ARLINGTON AVE
F8
1 MAFEKING CL
2 SUNNINGDALE RD
3 SANDOWN CT
4 BACK SANDOWN LA
5 VICTORIA AVE
Edge Hill
L7
L8
L15
L17
L18
L19
LIVERPOOL
Toxteth Park Cemy
Superstore
Princes Park
Sefton Park
Sefton Park Palm House
Wavertree
Wavertree Playground
Liverpool Womens
Lourdes
Mossley Hill
Liverpool Coll
Bellerive RC Coll
The Belvedere Sch
Shorefields Sch
Dingle
St Michael's
Festival Park
St Michael's Hamlet
River Mersey
Aigburth Vale
Sudley Inf Sch
Sudley House Mus & Art Gall
Sports Gd
John Moores Univ IM Marsh Campus
Aigburth
Otterspool
St Margarets CE High Sch
Prim Sch
UPPER PARLIAMENT ST
SMITHDOWN RD
PICTON RD
LODGE LA
SEFTON PARK RD
ULLET RD
PRINCES RD
DEVONSHIRE RD
BELVIDERE RD
PARK RD
AIGBURTH RD
AIGBURTH VALE
QUEENS DRIVE
MOSSLEY HILL
GAINSBOROUGH RD
TUNNEL RD
GROVE ST
KINGSLEY RD
CROXTETH RD
ASHFIELD RD
VICTORIA RD
86
36
A
B
37
C
D
38
E
F
A3
1 CHILLINGHAM ST
2 BRITANNIA CRES
3 THISTLEDOWN CL
4 HINDLIP ST
5 DINGLE GRANGE
A4
1 ST LAWRENCE CL
2 REDBURN CL
3 FAIR VIEW PL
4 BRUCE ST
5 CYPRUS GR
6 WELLER WAY
7 POPLAR CT
8 REDWOOD CT
9 SYCAMORE CT
10 PALM CT
11 PINE CT
12 HAZEL CT
13 LARCH CT
14 LABURNUM CT
15 OAK CT
16 BIRCH CT
17 WILLOW CT
18 KELBEY CL
19 SALTERGATE RD
20 BOWRING ST
21 KIRKBURN CL
22 LOCKINGTON CL
23 LOXDALE CL
67
A4
24 SUNDRIDGE ST
25 SOUTH HILL GR
26 GORDALE CL
A5
1 ADMIRAL GR
2 WELLINGTON TERR
3 PENGWERN ST
4 TREBORTH ST
5 MOUNTVIEW CL
80
A5
6 PARKLAND CL
7 GREENGABLES CL
8 CAVENDISH GDNS
B3
1 ALEXANDRA PK
2 THIRLSTANE ST
3 ALMAN CT
4 ALPASS RD
5 MELLY RD
C2
1 GIVENCHY CT
2 KINGS CL
3 GALBRAITH CL
4 BATTERY CL
5 OAKBOURNE CL
6 SAVOYLANDS CL
7 BURGUNDY CL
8 HYTHEDALE CL
C4
1 BLOOMFIELD GN
2 FRANCES CT
3 LEDA GR
4 LUCKNOW ST
5 HESKETH ST
6 FORGE COTTS
7 MANOR CT
8 PARKFIELD MEWS
9 NEW BARTRAM CT
10 WAVERLEY CT
11 MANNERING CT
12 THE OLD FIRE STATION

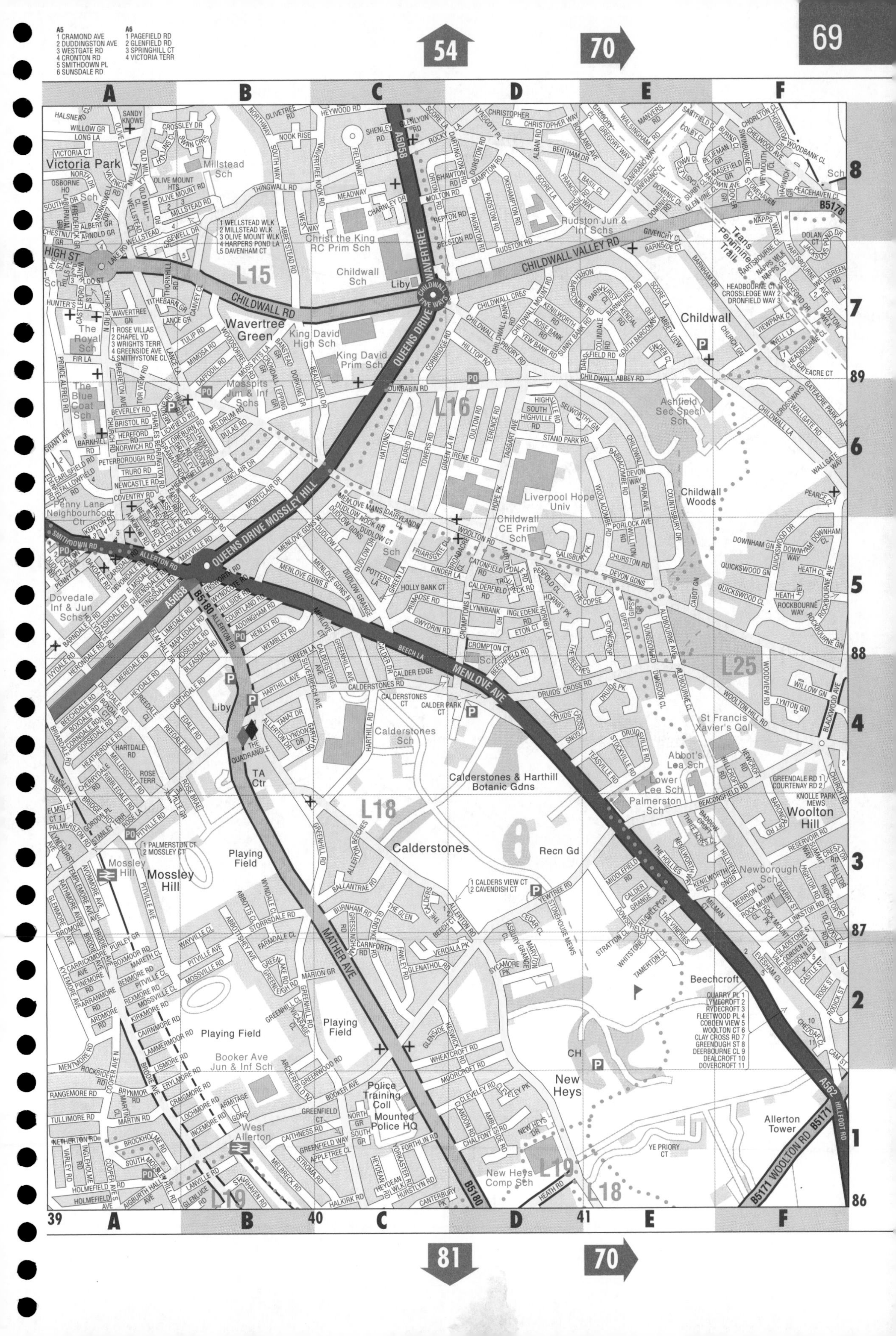
A5
1 CRAMOND AVE
2 DUDDINGSTON AVE
3 WESTGATE RD
4 CRONTON RD
5 SMITHDOWN PL
6 SUNSDALE RD
A6
1 PAGEFIELD RD
2 GLENFIELD RD
3 SPRINGHILL CT
4 VICTORIA TERR
54
70
A
B
C
D
E
F
8
7
89
6
5
88
4
3
87
2
1
86
39
40
41
Victoria Park
Millstead Sch
1 WELLSTEAD WLK
2 MILLSTEAD WLK
3 OLIVE MOUNT WLK
4 HARPERS POND LA
5 DAVENHAM CT
Christ the King RC Prim Sch
Childwall Sch
Liby
L15
HIGH ST
CHILDWALL RD
WAVERTREE
A5058
CHILDWALL FIVE WAYS
CHILDWALL VALLEY RD
Rudston Jun & Inf Schs
Trans Pennine Trail
B5178
HEADBOURNE CT 1
CROSSLEDGE WAY 2
DRONFIELD WAY 3
Childwall
The Royal Sch
1 ROSE VILLAS
2 CHAPEL YD
3 WRIGHTS TERR
4 GREENSIDE AVE
5 SMITHYSTONE CL
Wavertree Green
King David High Sch
King David Prim Sch
QUEENS DRIVE
Mosspits Jun & Inf Schs
The Blue Coat Sch
L16
CHILDWALL ABBEY RD
Ashfield Sec Spec Sch
QUEENS DRIVE MOSSLEY HILL
Penny Lane Neighbourhood Ctr
Liverpool Hope Univ
Childwall CE Prim Sch
Childwall Woods
SMITHDOWN RD
ALLERTON RD
WOOLTON RD
Dovedale Inf & Jun Schs
B5180
MENLOVE AVE
L25
St Francis Xavier's Coll
Calderstones Sch
Liby
TA Ctr
Abbot's Lea Sch
Lower Lee Sch
Calderstones & Harthill Botanic Gdns
Palmerston Sch
Woolton Hill
L18
Calderstones
Recn Gd
Mossley Hill
Mossley Hill
1 PALMERSTON CT
2 MOSSLEY CT
Playing Field
1 CALDERS VIEW CT
2 CAVENDISH CT
Newborough Sch
MATHER AVE
Beechcroft
QUARRY PL 1
LYMECROFT 2
RYDECROFT 3
FLEETWOOD PL 4
COBDEN VIEW 5
WOOLTON CT 6
CLAY CROSS RD 7
GREENOUGH ST 8
DEERBOURNE CL 9
DEALCROFT 10
DOVERCROFT 11
Playing Field
Playing Field
Booker Ave Jun & Inf Sch
CH
New Heys
Police Training Coll
Mounted Police HQ
A562
West Allerton
Allerton Tower
B5171 WOOLTON RD
New Heys Comp Sch
L19
L18
L19
81
70

69
55

A B C D E F

8

L16

Sports Gd

HUYTON-WITH-ROBY

L36

7

Wheathill
Farm

Hope Sch

CH

89

L27 Wheathills
Ind Est

6

Our Lady of the
Assumption
RC Prim Sch

CHILDWALL VALLEY RD

Belle Vale

Belle Vale
Sh Ctr

Superstore

PH

Sewage
Works

L35

NETHERLEY RD

5

Dunlin
Ct

Gateacre
Com Comp
Sch

Gateacre

BELLE VALE RD

CALDWAY DR

Blue Jay Cl

Swallow Cl

88

Netherley

Norman
Pannell Sch

CH

Cross Farm
Prim Sch

4

Trans Pennine Trail

GATEACRE BROW

LIVERPOOL

Woodlands

Gerrard's
Farm

3

Woolton
Park

L25

Woolton
Jun & Inf
Schs

North End

Foxhill
House

87

Bishop Martin
CE Prim Sch

Superstore

Halewood
Way

Halewood Farm
House

L26

2

Superstore

Liby

HIGH ST

Woolton

Halewood Country Pk

1

Woolton
Manor

Woolton
Wood

St Julie's
RC High Sch

Holy Family
RC Prim Sch

86

42 A B 43 C D 44 E F

56
72

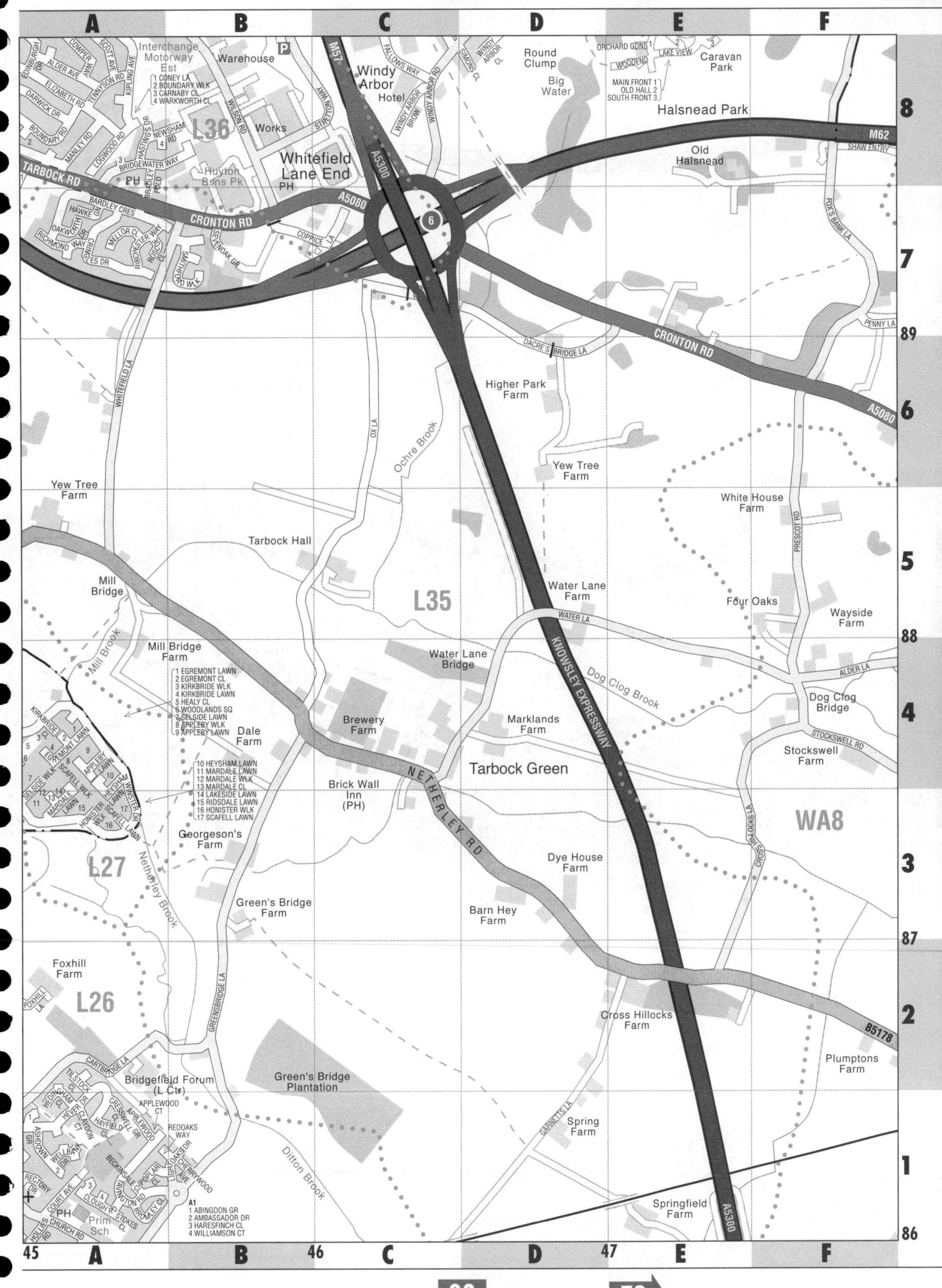
A B C D E F
Interchange Motorway Est
Warehouse
Windy Arbor
Hotel
Round Clump
Big Water
Caravan Park
Halsnead Park
M62
Old Halsnead
SHAW ENTRY
L36
Works
Whitefield Lane End
Huyton Bsns Pk
PH
TARBOCK RD
CRONTON RD
A5080
A5300
M57
COPPICE LA
FOX'S BANK LA
CRONTON RD
DACRE'S BRIDGE LA
PENNY LA
Higher Park Farm
OX LA
Ochre Brook
Yew Tree Farm
WHITEFIELD LA
White House Farm
PRESCOT RD
Tarbock Hall
L35
Mill Bridge
Water Lane Farm
WATER LA
Four Oaks
Wayside Farm
Mill Bridge Farm
Water Lane Bridge
KNOWSLEY EXPRESSWAY
Dog Clog Brook
ALDER LA
Dog Clog Bridge
Mill Brook
1 EGREMONT LAWN
2 EGREMONT CL
3 KIRKBRIDE WLK
4 KIRKBRIDE LAWN
5 HEALY CL
6 WOODLANDS SQ
7 SELSIDE LAWN
8 APPLEBY WLK
9 APPLEBY LAWN
Dale Farm
Brewery Farm
Marklands Farm
STOCKSWELL RD
Stockswell Farm
Tarbock Green
10 HEYSHAM LAWN
11 MARDALE LAWN
12 MARDALE WLK
13 MARDALE CL
14 LAKESIDE LAWN
15 RIDSDALE LAWN
16 HONISTER WLK
17 SCAFELL LAWN
Brick Wall Inn (PH)
NETHERLEY RD
CROSS HILLOCKS LA
WA8
Georgeson's Farm
L27
Netherley Brook
Dye House Farm
Green's Bridge Farm
Barn Hey Farm
Foxhill Farm
L26
GREENSBRIDGE LA
Cross Hillocks Farm
B5178
Green's Bridge Plantation
Plumptons Farm
Bridgefield Forum (L Ctr)
APPLEWOOD CT
REDOAKS WAY
GARNETTS LA
Spring Farm
Ditton Brook
Springfield Farm
A1
1 ABINGDON GR
2 AMBASSADOR DR
3 HARESFINCH CL
4 WILLIAMSON CT
PH
Prim Sch
CHURCH RD
8 7 89 6 5 88 4 3 87 2 1 86
45 46 47

83
72

71 57

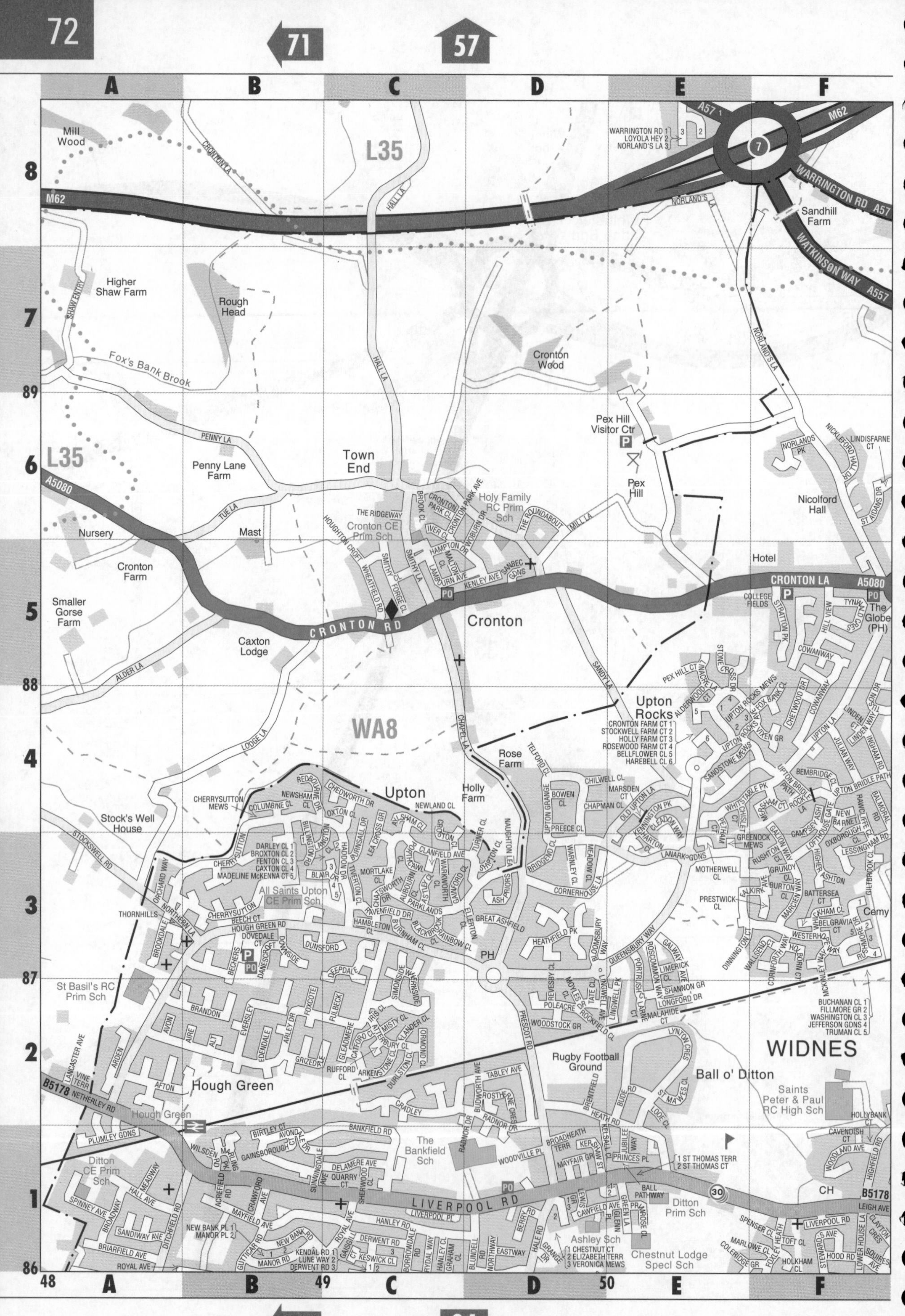
A
B
C
D
E
F
8
7
89
6
5
88
4
3
87
2
1
86
48
49
50
M62
A57
L35
Mill Wood
CRONTON LA
HALL LA
WARRINGTON RD 1
LOYOLA HEY 2
NORLAND'S LA 3
WARRINGTON RD
NORLAND'S LA
Sandhill Farm
WATKINSON WAY
A557
Higher Shaw Farm
SHAW ENTRY
Rough Head
Fox's Bank Brook
Cronton Wood
PENNY LA
Penny Lane Farm
Pex Hill Visitor Ctr
Pex Hill
Town End
Holy Family RC Prim Sch
Cronton CE Prim Sch
A5080
TUE LA
Mast
Nursery
Cronton Farm
Smaller Gorse Farm
THE RIDGEWAY
HOUGHTON CROFT
BROOK CL
CRONTON PARK AVE
WOBURN DR
THE ROUNDABOUT
MILL LA
HAMPTON DR
MALTON CL
KENLEY AVE
SMITHY LA
WHEATFIELD RD
CRONTON RD
Caxton Lodge
Cronton
Hotel
CRONTON LA
COLLEGE FIELDS
STRATTON PK
The Globe (PH)
Nicolford Hall
NORLANDS PK
LINDISFARNE CT
ST AIDANS DR
ALDER LA
SANDY LA
Upton Rocks
CRONTON FARM CT 1
STOCKWELL FARM CT 2
HOLLY FARM CT 3
ROSEWOOD FARM CT 4
BELLFLOWER CL 5
HAREBELL CL 6
PEX HILL CT
UPTON ROCKS MEWS
FOX BANK CL
VIXEN GR
CHETWOOD DR
COWAN WAY
LINDEN WAY
INGHAM RD
JULIAN WAY
UPTON LA
WA8
CHAPEL LA
LODGE LA
Rose Farm
Holly Farm
Upton
TELFORD CL
CHILWELL CL
MARSDEN CT
BOWEN CL
CHAPMAN CL
PREECE CL
UPTON GRANGE
OLD UPTON LA
KENNINGTON PK
CLEADON WAY
SANDSTONE MEWS
WHITSTABLE PK
BEMBRIDGE CL
UPTON BRIDLE PATH
BALMORAL RD
NEW BARNET
OXBOROUGH CL
LESSINGHAM RD
GREENOCK MEWS
GALLOWAY
RUSHTON
GRUNDY CL
LANARK GDNS
MOTHERWELL CL
PRESTWICK CL
FALKIRK AVE
BATTERSEA CT
Cemy
CHERRYSUTTON MEWS
NEWSHAM CL
CHEDWORTH DR
OXTON CL
NEWLAND CL
Stock's Well House
STOCKSWELL RD
ORCHARD WAY
DARLEY CL 1
BROXTON CL 2
FENTON CL 3
CAXTON CL 4
MADELINE McKENNA CT 5
All Saints Upton CE Prim Sch
MORTLAKE CL
PARKLANDS
THORNHILLS
NORTHERN LA
CHERRYSUTTON
BEECH CT
HOUGH GREEN RD
DOVEDALE CT
RAVENFIELD DR
HAMBLETON CL
BURNHAM CL
RAINBOW CL
GREAT ASHFIELD
CORNERHOUSE LA
HEATHFIELD PK
BLOOMSBURY WAY
QUEENSBURY WAY
GALWAY AVE
LIMERICK CL
SHANNON GR
LONGFORD DR
MALAHIDE CT
DINNINGTON CT
WALLSEND CT
CORNFORTH WAY
HOLBORN CT
WESTERHOPE WAY
BELGRAVIA CT
BUCHANAN CL 1
FILLMORE GR 2
WASHINGTON CL 3
JEFFERSON GDNS 4
TRUMAN CL 5
PH
BROOKDALE
DUNSFORD
DEEPDALE
St Basil's RC Prim Sch
BRANDON
AVON
AIRE
ALT
EVERSLEY
EDENDALE
ARLEY DR
FOXCOTE
FULBECK
GLEADMERE
SIMONSIDE
WARNSIDE
ORMOND CL
GRIZEDALE
RUFFORD CL
ARKENSTONE CL
DURLSTON CL
PRESCOT RD
WOODSTOCK GR
POLEACRE
ROCKFIELD CL
Rugby Football Ground
LYNTON CRES
WIDNES
Ball o' Ditton
Saints Peter & Paul RC High Sch
LANCASTER AVE
ARDEN
VINE TERR
AFTON
Hough Green
B5178
NETHERLEY RD
PLUMLEY GDNS
BIRTLEY CT
AVONDALE DR
BANKFIELD RD
CRADLEY
TABLEY AVE
ROSTHERNE CRES
RADNOR DR
BUDWORTH AVE
BRENTFIELD
HEATH RD
BUDE RD
ST MAWES CL
LOOE CL
HOLLYBANK
CAVENDISH CT
WOODLAND AVE
HIGHFIELD RD
Ditton CE Prim Sch
WILSDEN RD
MARLING PK
GAINSBOROUGH RD
SUNNINGDALE AVE
DELAMERE AVE
QUARRY CT
SHERWOOD CL
The Bankfield Sch
WOODVILLE PL
BROADHEATH TERR
KERSHAW ST
MAYFAIR GR
PRINCES PL
1 ST THOMAS TERR
2 ST THOMAS CT
BALL PATHWAY
Ditton Prim Sch
CH
B5178
LEIGH AVE
MEADWAY
HALL AVE
SPINNEY AVE
BROADWAY
SANDIWAY AVE
DITCHFIELD RD
BRIARFIELD AVE
ROYAL AVE
ACREFIELD RD
CRAWFORD AVE
MAYFIELD AVE
LIVERPOOL RD
LIVERPOOL PL
HANLEY RD
NEW BANK PL 1
MANOR PL 2
GUTTICAR RD
MANOR RD
NEW BANK RD
KENDAL RD 1
LUNE WAY 2
DERWENT RD 3
ROYAL AVE
DERWENT RD
KESWICK CL
BORROWDALE RD
RYDAL WAY
HANLEY CL
GRAHAM CL
BLUNDELL RD
NORTHWAY
EASTWAY
HALE RD
GRANGE RD
BERRY RD
CAWFIELD AVE
GLENN PL
PRIMROSE CL
Ashley Sch
1 CHESTNUT CT
2 ELIZABETH TERR
3 VERONICA MEWS
Chestnut Lodge Specl Sch
SPENSER CL
MARLOWE CL
COLERIDGE GR
FOXLEY HEATH
TOFT CL
HOLKHAM CL
STEWARDS AVE
HOOD RD
LOWER HOUSE LA
CLAYTON CRES
SQUIRES AVE

71 84

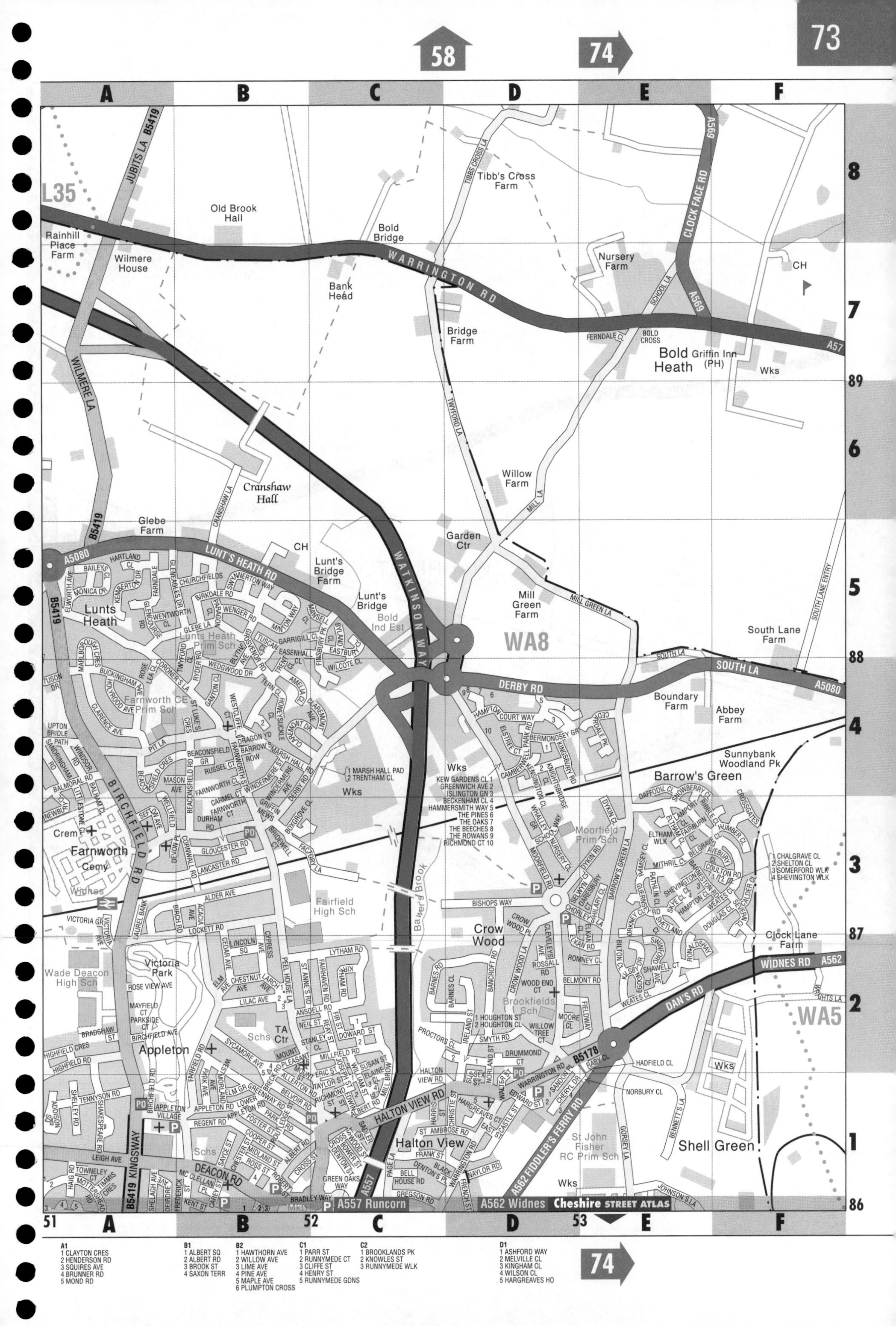

73
58
74
A
B
C
D
E
F
8
7
6
5
4
3
2
1
89
88
87
86
51
52
53
L35
WA8
WA5
JUBITS LA
B5419
Old Brook Hall
Rainhill Place Farm
Wilmere House
Bold Bridge
WARRINGTON RD
Bank Head
Tibb's Cross Farm
TIBBS CROSS LA
Nursery Farm
CLOCK FACE RD
A569
SCHOOL LA
CH
Bridge Farm
FERNDALE CL
BOLD CROSS
Bold Heath
Griffin Inn (PH)
Wks
A57
WILMERE LA
TWYFORD LA
Willow Farm
MILL LA
Cranshaw Hall
CRANSHAW LA
Glebe Farm
A5080
LUNT'S HEATH RD
Lunt's Bridge Farm
Lunt's Bridge
Bold Ind Est
WATKINSON WAY
Garden Ctr
Mill Green Farm
MILL GREEN LA
South Lane Farm
SOUTH LANE ENTRY
SOUTH LA
DERBY RD
Lunts Heath
Lunts Heath Prim Sch
Farnworth CE Prim Sch
Boundary Farm
Abbey Farm
Sunnybank Woodland Pk
Barrow's Green
1 MARSH HALL PAD
2 TRENTHAM CL
Wks
KEW GARDENS CL 1
GREENWICH AVE 2
ISLINGTON GN 3
BECKENHAM CL 4
HAMMERSMITH WAY 5
THE PINES 6
THE OAKS 7
THE BEECHES 8
THE ROWANS 9
RICHMOND CT 10
Moorfield Prim Sch
1 CHALGRAVE CL
2 SHELTON CL
3 SOMERFORD WLK
4 SHEVINGTON WLK
Crem
Farnworth
Cemy
Widnes
BIRCHFIELD RD
Fairfield High Sch
Bowers Brook
BISHOPS WAY
Crow Wood
Clock Lane Farm
WIDNES RD
A562
DAN'S RD
Wade Deacon High Sch
Victoria Park
Brookfields Sch
Appleton
Schs
TA Ctr
HALTON VIEW RD
Halton View
B5178
A562 FIDDLER'S FERRY RD
St John Fisher RC Prim Sch
Shell Green
Wks
B5419 KINGSWAY
DEACON RD
A557
A557 Runcorn
A562 Widnes
Cheshire STREET ATLAS
A1
1 CLAYTON CRES
2 HENDERSON RD
3 SQUIRES AVE
4 BRUNNER RD
5 MOND RD
B1
1 ALBERT SQ
2 ALBERT RD
3 BROOK ST
4 SAXON TERR
B2
1 HAWTHORN AVE
2 WILLOW AVE
3 LIME AVE
4 PINE AVE
5 MAPLE AVE
6 PLUMPTON CROSS
C1
1 PARR ST
2 RUNNYMEDE CT
3 CLIFFE ST
4 HENRY ST
5 RUNNYMEDE GDNS
C2
1 BROOKLANDS PK
2 KNOWLES ST
3 RUNNYMEDE WLK
D1
1 ASHFORD WAY
2 MELVILLE CL
3 KINGHAM CL
4 WILSON CL
5 HARGREAVES HO

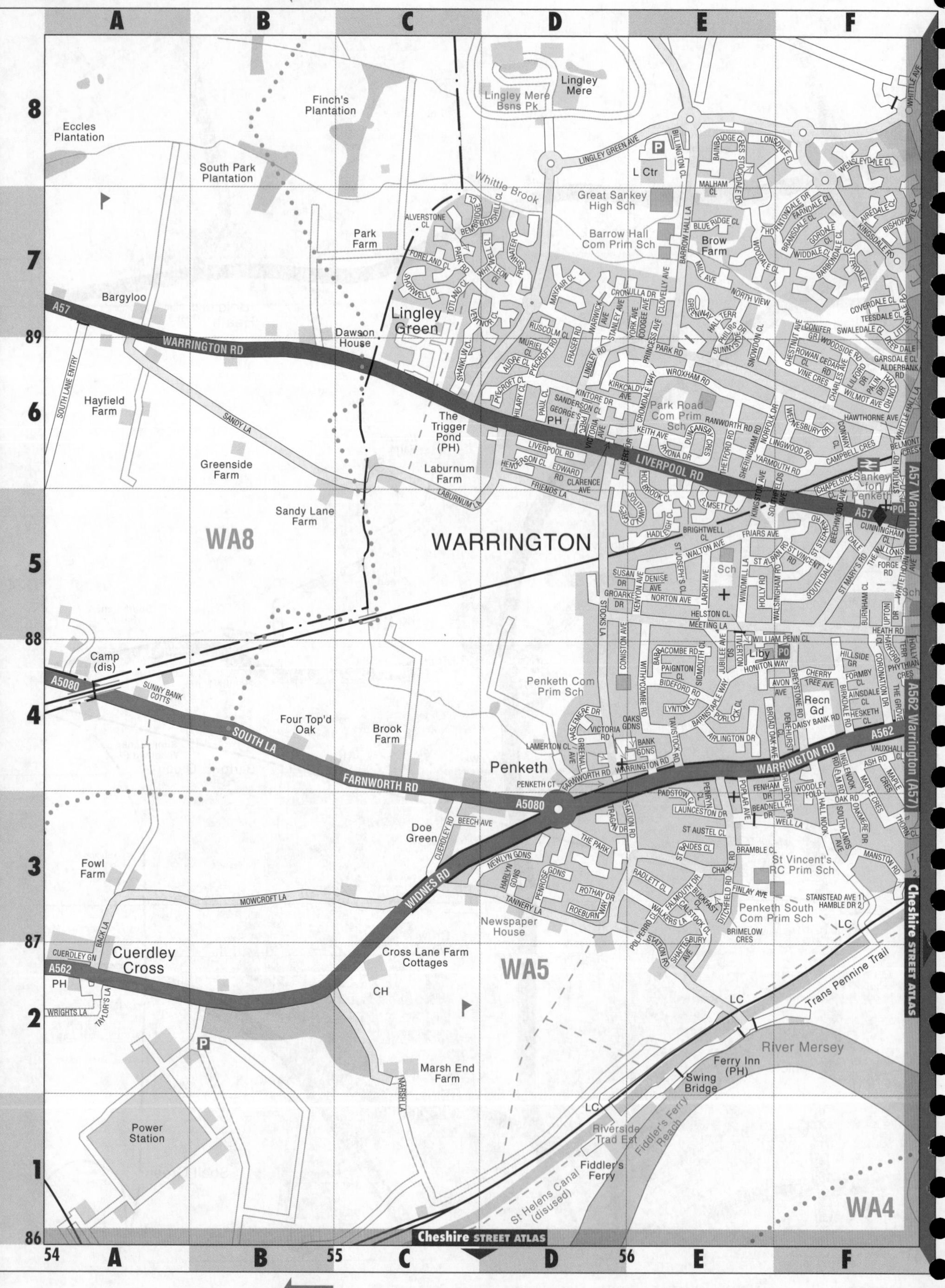

A B C D E F

8

7

89

6

Eccles
Plantation

South Park
Plantation

Finch's
Plantation

Lingley Mere
Bsns Pk

Lingley
Mere

Whittle Brook

L Ctr

Great Sankey
High Sch

Barrow Hall
Com Prim Sch

Brow
Farm

Bargyloo

A57

WARRINGTON RD

Park
Farm

ALVERSTONE
CL

Dawson
House

Lingley
Green

FORELAND CL

The
Trigger
Pond
(PH)

LIVERPOOL RD

Sankey
for
Penketh

A57 Warrington

5

WA8

Hayfield
Farm

Greenside
Farm

Sandy Lane
Farm

WARRINGTON

Laburnum
Farm

LABURNUM

Park Road
Com Prim
Sch

Sch

A562 Warrington (A57)

88

4

Camp
(dis)

A5080

SUNNY BANK
COTTS

SOUTH LA

Four Top'd
Oak

Brook
Farm

Penketh Com
Prim Sch

Penketh

FARNWORTH RD

PENKETH CT

A5080

Lby

Recn
Gd

WARRINGTON RD

A562

3

Fowl
Farm

MOWCROFT LA

Doe
Green

BEECH AVE

CUERDLEY RD

WIDNES RD

MENLYN GDNS

Newspaper
House

TANNERY LA

St Vincent's
RC Prim Sch

Penketh South
Com Prim Sch

LC

87

2

Cuerdley
Cross

CUERDLEY GN

A562

PH

TAYLOR'S LA

WRIGHTS LA

BACK LA

Cross Lane Farm
Cottages

CH

WA5

MARSH LA

Marsh End
Farm

LC

Ferry Inn
(PH)

Swing
Bridge

River Mersey

Trans Pennine Trail

LC

Cheshire STREET ATLAS

1

Power
Station

Fiddler's
Ferry

St Helens Canal
(disused)

Riverside
Trad Est

Fiddler's Ferry
Reach

WA4

86

63
76

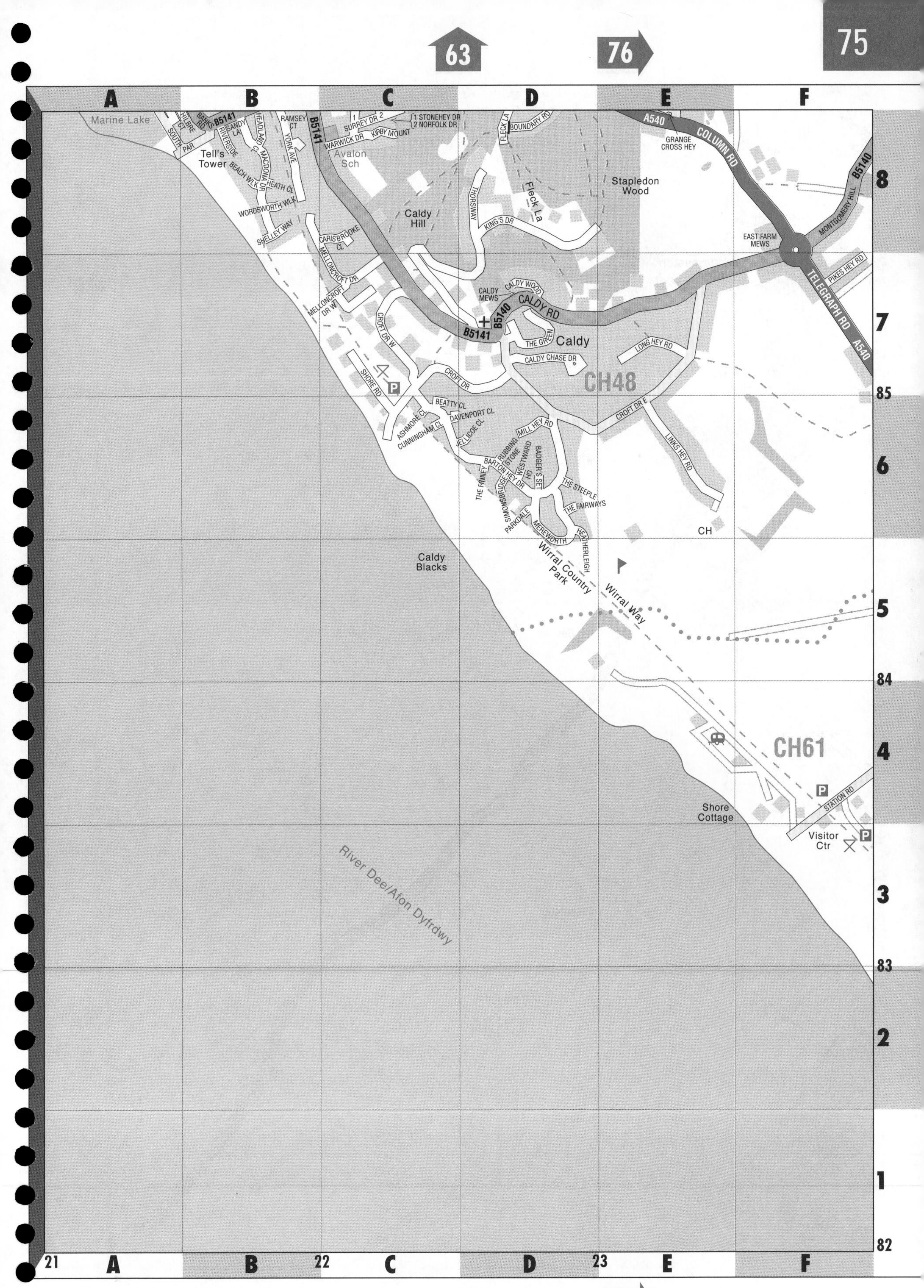
A
B
C
D
E
F
Marine Lake
Tell's Tower
Avalon Sch
Caldy Hill
Fleck La
Stapledon Wood
Caldy
CH48
Caldy Blacks
Wirral Country Park
Wirral Way
CH
CH61
Shore Cottage
Visitor Ctr
River Dee/Afon Dyfrdwy
B5141
B5140
A540
COLUMN RD
TELEGRAPH RD
CALDY RD
CROFT DR
CROFT DR W
CROFT DR E
SHORE RD
STATION RD
LINKS HEY RD
LONG HEY RD
MILL HEY RD
KING'S DR
THORSWAY
BOUNDARY RD
GRANGE CROSS HEY
EAST FARM MEWS
MONTGOMERY HILL
PIKES HEY RD
1 STONEHEY DR
2 NORFOLK DR
SURREY DR
WARWICK DR
KIRBY MOUNT
RAMSEY CT
YORK AVE
HEADLAND CL
MACDONA DR
HEATH CL
SANDY LA
RIVERSIDE
BANKS RD
HILBRE CT
SOUTH PAR
BEACH WLK
WORDSWORTH WLK
SHELLEY WAY
CARISBROOKE CL
MELLONCROFT DR
MELLONCROFT DR W
CALDY MEWS
CALDY WOOD
THE GREEN
CALDY CHASE DR
BEATTY CL
DAVENPORT CL
JELLICOE CL
ASHMORE CL
CUNNINGHAM CL
RUBBING STONE
WESTWARD HO
BADGER'S SET
BARTON HEY DR
THE FINNEY
SIMONSBRIDGE
PARKDALE
MEREWORTH
HEATHERLEIGH
THE STEEPLE
THE FAIRWAYS
8
7
6
5
4
3
2
1
85
84
83
82
21
22
23

76

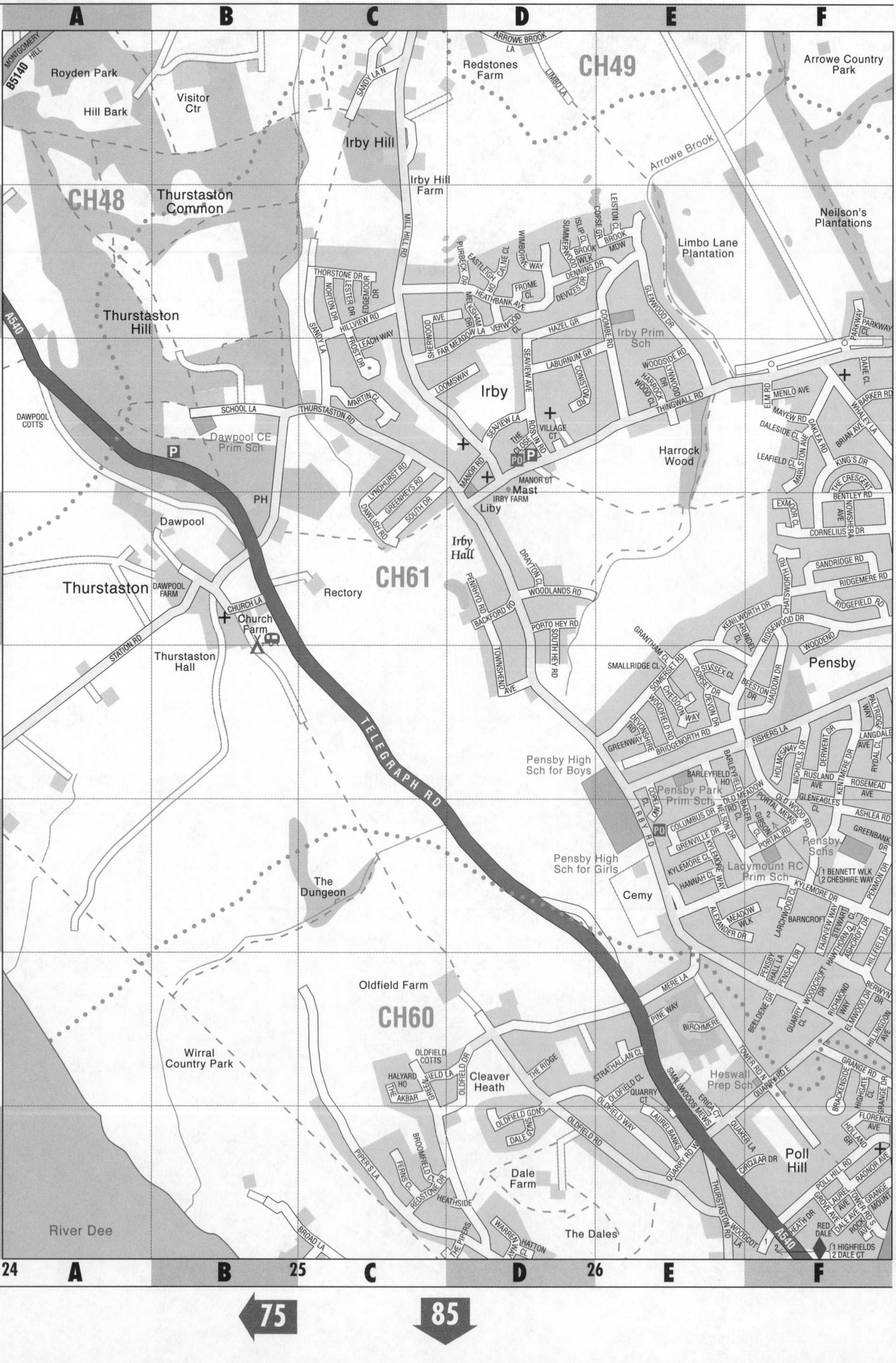
A
B
C
D
E
F
8
7
85
6
5
84
4
3
83
2
1
82
24
25
26
Royden Park
Hill Bark
Visitor Ctr
Redstones Farm
CH49
Arrowe Country Park
Irby Hill
Irby Hill Farm
Arrowe Brook
CH48
Thurstaston Common
Neilson's Plantations
Limbo Lane Plantation
Thurstaston Hill
Irby Prim Sch
Irby
DAWPOOL COTTS
Dawpool CE Prim Sch
Harrock Wood
Mast
Liby
PH
Dawpool
Irby Hall
CH61
Thurstaston
DAWPOOL FARM
Rectory
Church Farm
Thurstaston Hall
Pensby
Pensby High Sch for Boys
Pensby Park Prim Sch
Pensby Schs
Ladymount RC Prim Sch
Pensby High Sch for Girls
Cemy
The Dungeon
Oldfield Farm
CH60
Wirral Country Park
Cleaver Heath
Heswall Prep Sch
Poll Hill
Dale Farm
River Dee
The Dales
TELEGRAPH RD
A540
B5140
MONTGOMERY HILL
ARROWE BROOK LA
LIMBO LA
SANDY LA N
MILL HILL RD
THORSTONE DR
NORTON DR
LESTER DR
EDGEMOOR DR
SANDY LA
HILLVIEW RD
LEACH WAY
FROST DR
MARTIN CL
SCHOOL LA
THURSTASTON RD
LYNDHURST RD
GREENHEYS RD
DAWLISH RD
SOUTH DR
MANOR RD
MANOR CT
IRBY FARM
PURBECK DR
EASTLEIGH DR
CALNE CL
WIMBORNE WAY
HEATHBANK AVE
FROME CL
MELKSHAM DR
VERWOOD DR
SHERWOOD AVE
FAR MEADOW LA
LOOMSWAY
HAZEL GR
LABURNUM GR
CONISTON RD
SEAVIEW AVE
SEAVIEW LA
THE CLOSE
ROSLIN RD
VILLAGE CT
SUMMERWOOD
ISLIP CL
BROOK WLK
COPSE GR
DENNING DR
DEVIZES DR
LEISTON CL
BROOK MDW
COOMBE RD
GLENWOOD DR
WOODSIDE RD
HARROCK WOOD CL
LYNWOOD DR
THINGWALL RD
ELM RD
MENLO AVE
PARKWAY
DANE CL
WHALEY LA
BARKER RD
MAYEW RD
DALESIDE CL
OAKLEA RD
BRIAN AVE
MARLSTON AVE
LEAFIELD CL
KING'S DR
THE CRESCENT
BENTLEY RD
EXMOOR CL
NOWSHERA AVE
CORNELIUS DR
SANDRIDGE RD
RIDGEMERE RD
RIDGEFIELD RD
CHATSWORTH RD
KENILWORTH DR
ARUNDEL CL
RIDGEWOOD DR
WOODEND
GRANTHAM CL
SMALLRIDGE CL
SOMERSET RD
SUSSEX CL
DORSET DR
DEVON DR
BEESTON DR
HADDON DR
CHEDDON WAY
WOODFIELD RD
DEVONSHIRE RD
GREENWAY
BRIDGENORTH RD
FISHERS LA
HOLMESWAY
NICHOLLS DR
DERWENT DR
KENTMERE DR
LANGDALE AVE
RYDAL CL
PALTRIDGE WAY
RUSLAND AVE
ROSEMEAD AVE
GLENEAGLES CL
ASHLEA RD
GREENBANK DR
PENMON DR
BARLEYFIELD HO
BARLEYFIELD RD
BADGER CL
OLD MEADOW RD
NELSON DR
GIBSON CL
PORTAL MEWS
PORTAL RD
OLD WOOD RD
COPELAND CL
IRBY RD
COLUMBUS DR
GRENVILLE DR
KYLEMORE CL
KYLEMORE WAY
KYLEMORE DR
HANNAH CL
ALEXANDER DR
MEADOW WLK
LARCHWOOD CL
BARNCROFT
STEWART CL
FAIRVIEW WAY
HAWTHORN CL
ASHCROFT DR
HILLFIELD DR
1 BENNETT WLK
2 CHESHIRE WAY
PENSBY HALL LA
PENSALL DR
WOODCROFT DR
RICHMOND WAY
BERWYN DR
ELMWOOD DR
HILLINGDON AVE
BEELDENE GR
QUARRY CL
TOWER RD N
QUARRY RD E
GRANGE RD
BRACKENSIDE
HIGHGATE CL
GRANGE DR
FLORENCE AVE
HOLLAND GR
RADNOR AVE
POLL HILL RD
GROVE AVE
LAUREL AVE
DALE AVE
TOWER RD S
ROCK AVE
GRANGE MOUNT
HEATH DR
RED DALE
1 HIGHFIELDS
2 DALE CT
CIRCULAR DR
QUAKER LA
ERICA CT
SMALLWOODS MEWS
LAUREL BANKS
QUARRY RD W
THURSTASTON RD
WOODCOT LA
MERE LA
PINE WAY
BIRCHMERE
STRATHALLAN CL
OLDFIELD CL
QUARRY CT
OLDFIELD WAY
OLDFIELD RD
THE RIDGE
OLDFIELD GDNS
DALE GDNS
OLDFIELD COTTS
OLDFIELD DR
HALYARD HO
GREENFIELD LA
THE AKBAR
BROOMFIELD CL
FERNS CL
REDSTONE DR
HEATHSIDE
PIPER'S LA
BROAD LA
THE PIPERS
WARREN WAY
HATTON CL
DRAYTON CL
WOODLANDS RD
PENRHYD RD
BACKFORD RD
PORTO HEY RD
SOUTH HEY RD
TOWNSHEND AVE
CHURCH LA
STATION RD

65
78

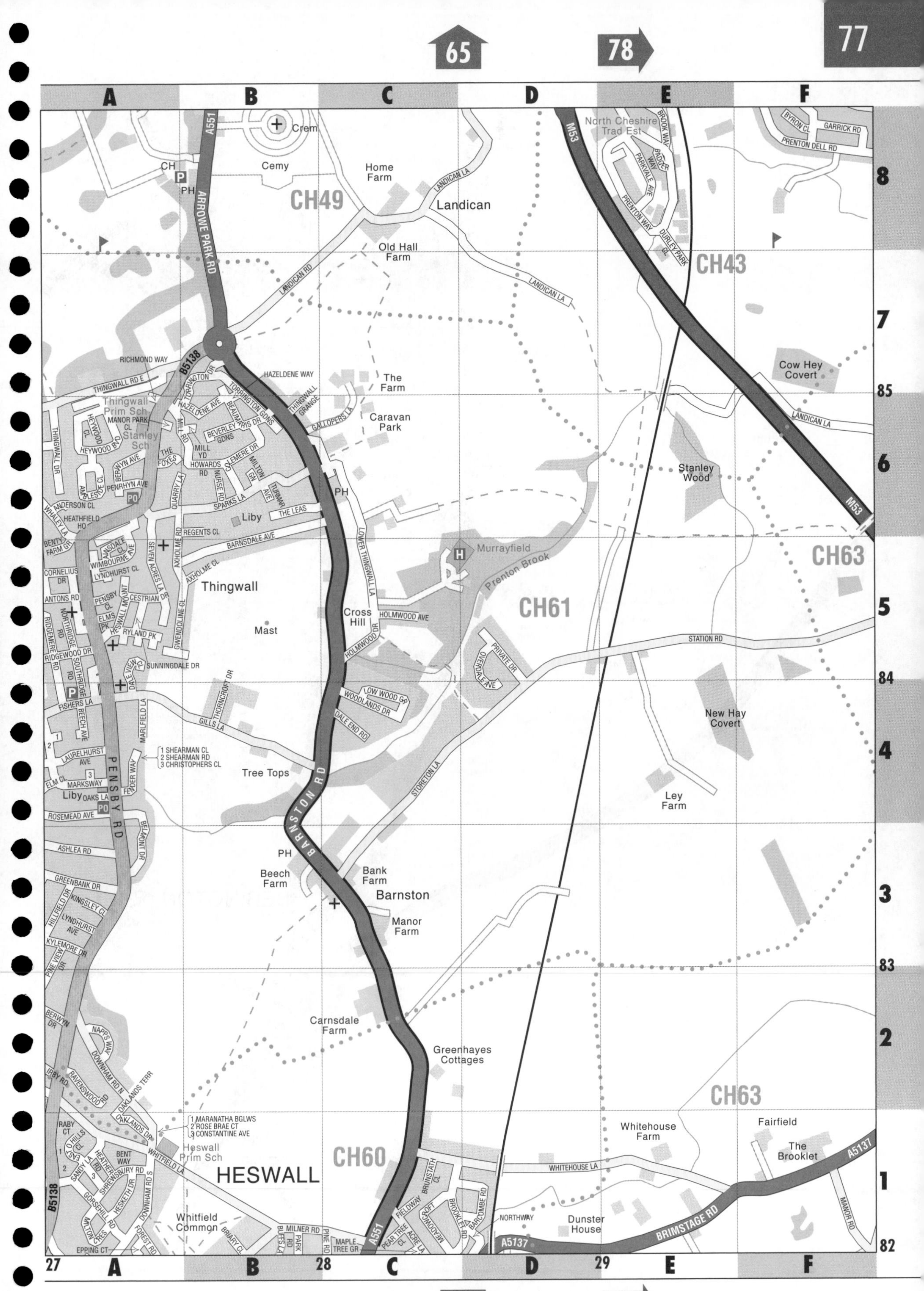

A
B
C
D
E
F
Crem
Cemy
CH
PH
Home Farm
Landican
CH49
North Cheshire Trad Est
CH43
ARROWE PARK RD
A551
M53
LANDICAN RD
LANDICAN LA
Old Hall Farm
RICHMOND WAY
THINGWALL RD E
HAZELDENE WAY
Thingwall Prim Sch
Stanley Sch
The Farm
Caravan Park
Cow Hey Covert
Stanley Wood
PH
Liby
Murrayfield
Prenton Brook
CH61
CH63
Thingwall
Cross Hill
Mast
STATION RD
New Hay Covert
Tree Tops
Ley Farm
BARNSTON RD
PENSBY RD
PH
Beech Farm
Bank Farm
Barnston
Manor Farm
Carnsdale Farm
Greenhayes Cottages
CH63
Whitehouse Farm
Fairfield
The Brooklet
HESWALL
CH60
Heswall Prim Sch
Whitfield Common
Dunster House
BRIMSTAGE RD
A5137
B5138
WHITEHOUSE LA
1 SHEARMAN CL
2 SHEARMAN RD
3 CHRISTOPHERS CL
1 MARANATHA BGLWS
2 ROSE BRAE CT
3 CONSTANTINE AVE
27
28
29
8
7
85
6
5
84
4
3
83
2
1
82

86
78

A B C D E F

CH43

CH42

CH63

Prenton Hall Rd
Burrell Rd
Prenton Ave
Prenton Dell Av
Pren on Farm Rd
Prenton Village Rd
Roman Rd
Golf Links Rd
Fairway's Rd
Pine Walks
CH
Mount Wood Rd
Brecon Rd
Heswall Av
Pennine Rd
Harley Ave
B5151
Raby
Gr
Richardson Rd
CH42
Autumn
B5148
B5149
Ravenscroft Av

Marsh Hey Covert
Stanley Ave
Pinewalks Ridge
Thornton Rd
Brimstage Ave
Kingsbrook Rd
The Coverts
Dacre Hill
Rock Ferry High Sch
Bryony Way
Woodhey Ct

Regents Way
The Ridgeway
Broadway
Kirkway
Mountway
Claremont Gr
Hognton Gr
Gayton Av
Thornton Ave
Withert Av
Bickerton Av
Conville Bvd
Princes Bvd
Berwyn Bvd
Garth Bvd
King's La
Buckingham Ave
Woodfield Ave
Old Chester Rd
B5150
B5149
Oak Rd

Lever Cswy
Roman Rd
Marsh La
Linkside
Beckett Gr
Bentfield Gdns
Kings Rd
Portia Gdns
Miranda Ave 1
Cressida Ave 2
Juliet Av
Beatrice Av
Rosemary Av
Portia Ave
Juliet Gdns
Playing Field
St John's RC Jun & Inf Schs
The Oval Sports Ctr

85

Little Storeton
Heather Bank
Millwood Rd
Rotherwood Av
Well La
Anbury Way
Bramley Av
Carey Ave
Asterfield Av
Rossfield Av
Sherwood Dr
Town La
Woodhey Cemy
St Andrew's CE Prim Sch

6

Grange Cotts
Landican La
Little Storeton La
Storeton Hill
Mill View Dr
Millbut Cl
King's Brow
Mersey View
Village Rd
Richard
Acorn Cl
30 Jun Sch
PO
1 Roland
Higher Bebington
Rec Gnd
Bebington High Sports Coll
Greenlea Cl
Kenyon La
Anscot Av

Storeton Hall Farm
Resthill Rd
Millbut
B5150
Village Rd
Liby
1 Sandfield Rd
2 Sandfield Cl
3 Elm Ct
4 Willow Ct
5 Rowan Ct
Oakleigh Gr
Greaves Rd
Richmond Cl
Higher Bebington Rd
Holmville Rd
Acreville Rd
Tudorville Rd
Greenville Rd

5

Storeton House Farm
Storeton
Keepers La
Hillside Farm
Glenmarsh
Shallmarsh Rd
School La
Mithe
Teehey La
Conway Cl
Waterfield Cl
Calder Rd
Derwent Rd
Stan
Kennet Rd
Kingsville Rd
Gorseyville Rd
Sch
Sch
Heathcote Gdns
St Edmu
Heath Rd
High Cft

84

Red Hill Rd
Clatter Brook
Mast
Elmure Av
Bracken La
CH
Mount Rd
Heather Rd
Lime Ave
Laurel Ave
Cedar Ave
Yew Tree
Plane Tree Rd
Welland Rd
Ferns Rd
Ivy Rd
Holloway
St Anne
Wirral Grammar Schs
Claremount Dr 1
Cornwall Ct 2
Conway Ct 3
Rothesay Ct 4
Caernarvon Ct 5
Chester Ct 6
Harlech Ct 7
Hawarden Ct 8
Kirket La
Quarry Ave

4

Rake Hey Covert
Hillside Cottage
Brackenwood Rd
Langdale Rd
Borrowdale Rd
Teesdale Rd
Peter Price's La
Stanton Rd
Patterdale Rd
Kempson Terr
Corrie Rd

3

Brimstage Plantation
Brimstage La
Umberstone Covert
BEBINGTON
B5137
B5151
Kevelioc Cl
Delves Ave
Brynsule Rd
Mynsule Rd
Myleton Rd
B5137
Beechway
Firs Ave
Pine Ave
Holly Ave

83

Brimstage
Green Bank
Sitch Cottages
Brimstage Rd
A5137
4
B5137
Stevens
St Hensham
Gilbert Rd
Weymoor Dr
Windrth
Box Dr

2

Talbot Ave
A5137
Brimstage Hall Courtyard (Craft Ctr)
Mount Rd
B5151
Winfrith Cl 1
Broadstone Dr 2
Tyburn Cl 3
Walford Cl 4
Bellward Cl 5
Baumville Dr 6

Clatterbridge
H
Clatter Bridge
B5151 Clatterbridge Rd
M53
Mast

1

82

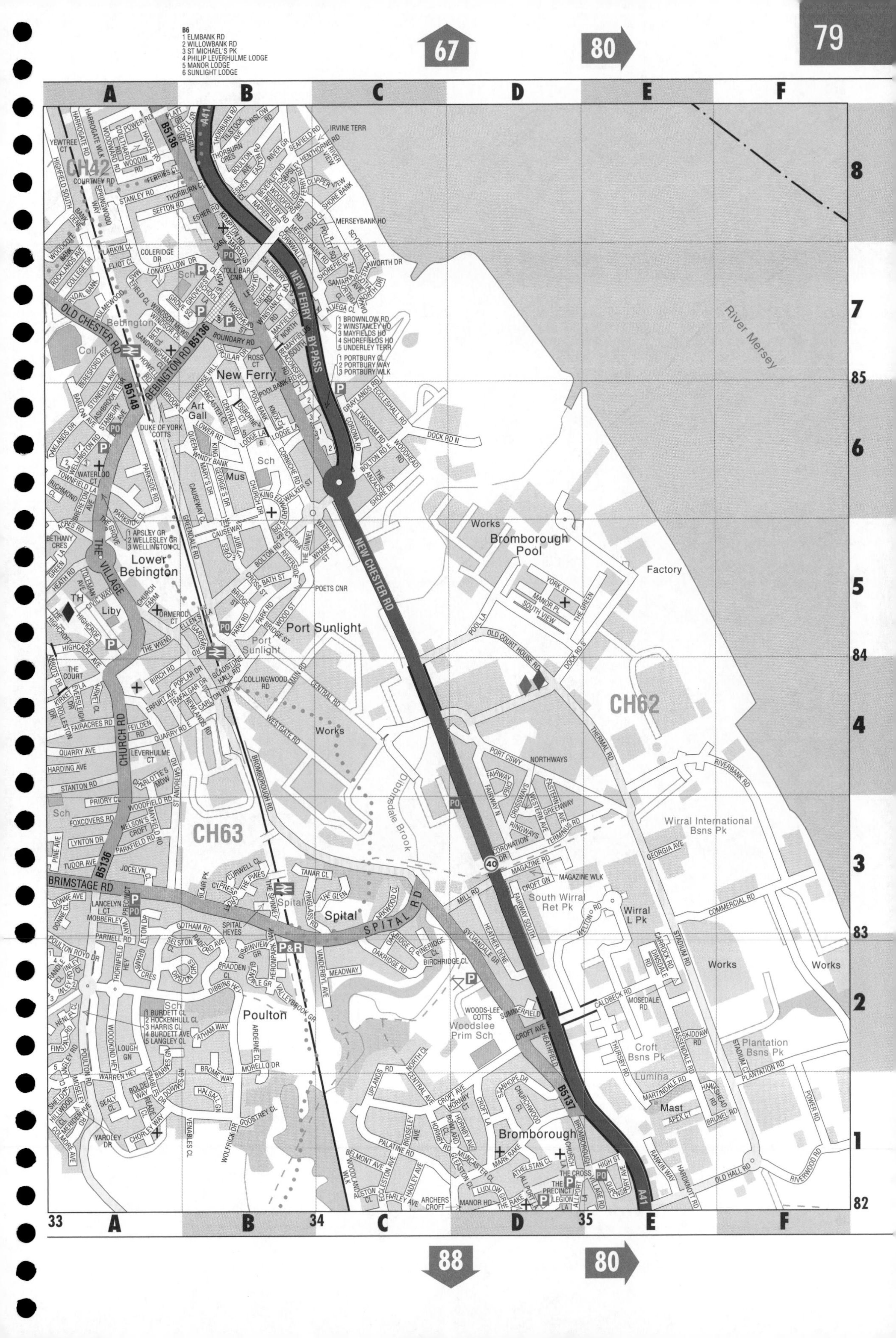
B6
1 ELMBANK RD
2 WILLOWBANK RD
3 ST MICHAEL'S PK
4 PHILIP LEVERHULME LODGE
5 MANOR LODGE
6 SUNLIGHT LODGE
67
80
A
B
C
D
E
F
8
7
85
6
5
84
4
3
83
2
1
82
33
34
35
88
80
CH42
CH62
CH63
River Mersey
New Ferry
NEW FERRY BY-PASS
NEW CHESTER RD
Bebington
Lower Bebington
Port Sunlight
Bromborough Pool
Bromborough
Spital
Poulton
Wirral International Bsns Pk
South Wirral Ret Pk
Wirral L Pk
Croft Bsns Pk
Plantation Bsns Pk
Lumina
Woodslee Prim Sch
Dibbinsdale Brook
Works
Factory
Mast
Coll
Sch
Art Gall
Mus
Liby
TH
BRIMSTAGE RD
OLD CHESTER RD
BEBINGTON RD
CHURCH RD
THE VILLAGE
SPITAL RD
THERMAL RD
RIVERBANK RD
COMMERCIAL RD
STADIUM RD
PLANTATION RD
OLD HALL RD
DOCK RD N
DOCK RD S
OLD COURT HOUSE RD
BROMBOROUGH RD
BROMBOROUGH VILLAGE RD
A41
B5136
B5137
B5148
1 BROWNLOW RD
2 WINSTANLEY HO
3 MAYFIELDS HO
4 SHOREFIELDS HO
5 UNDERLEY TERR
1 PORTBURY CL
2 PORTBURY WAY
3 PORTBURY WLK
1 APSLEY GR
2 WELLESLEY GR
3 WELLINGTON CL
1 BURDETT CL
2 HOCKENHULL CL
3 HARRIS CL
4 BURDETT AVE
5 LANGLEY CL

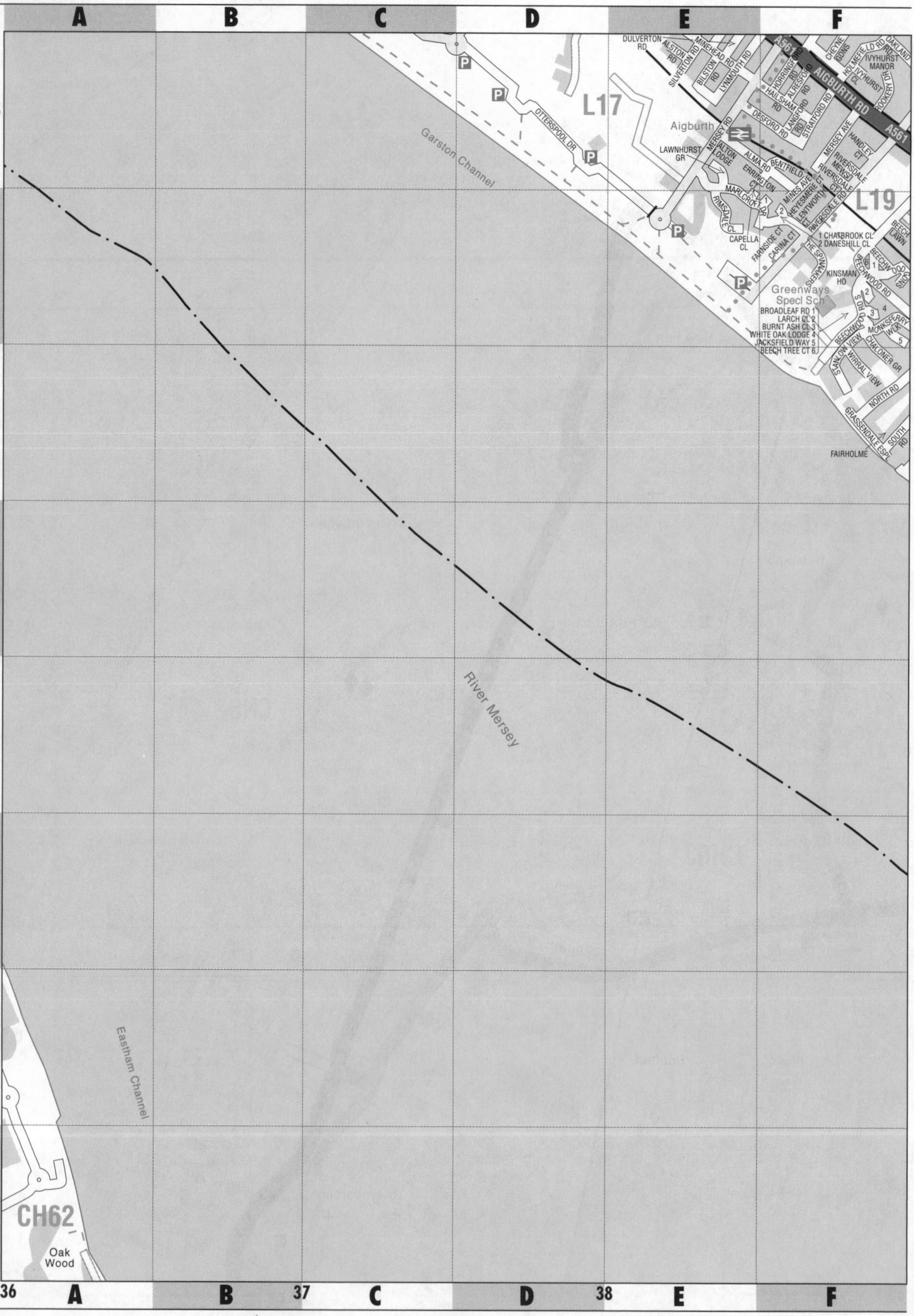

A B C D E F

8

7

85

6

5

84

4

3

83

2

1

82

36 A B 37 C D 38 E F

Garston Channel

Otterspool Dr

L17

Aigburth

LAWNHURST GR

Greenways Spec Sch

BROADLEAF RD 1
LARCH CL 2
BURNT ASH CL 3
WHITE OAK LODGE 4
JACKSFIELD WAY 5
BEECH TREE CT 6

DULVERTON RD

AIGBURTH RD

A561

L19

1 CHATBROOK CL
2 DANESHILL CL

FAIRHOLME

River Mersey

Eastham Channel

CH62

Oak Wood

69
82

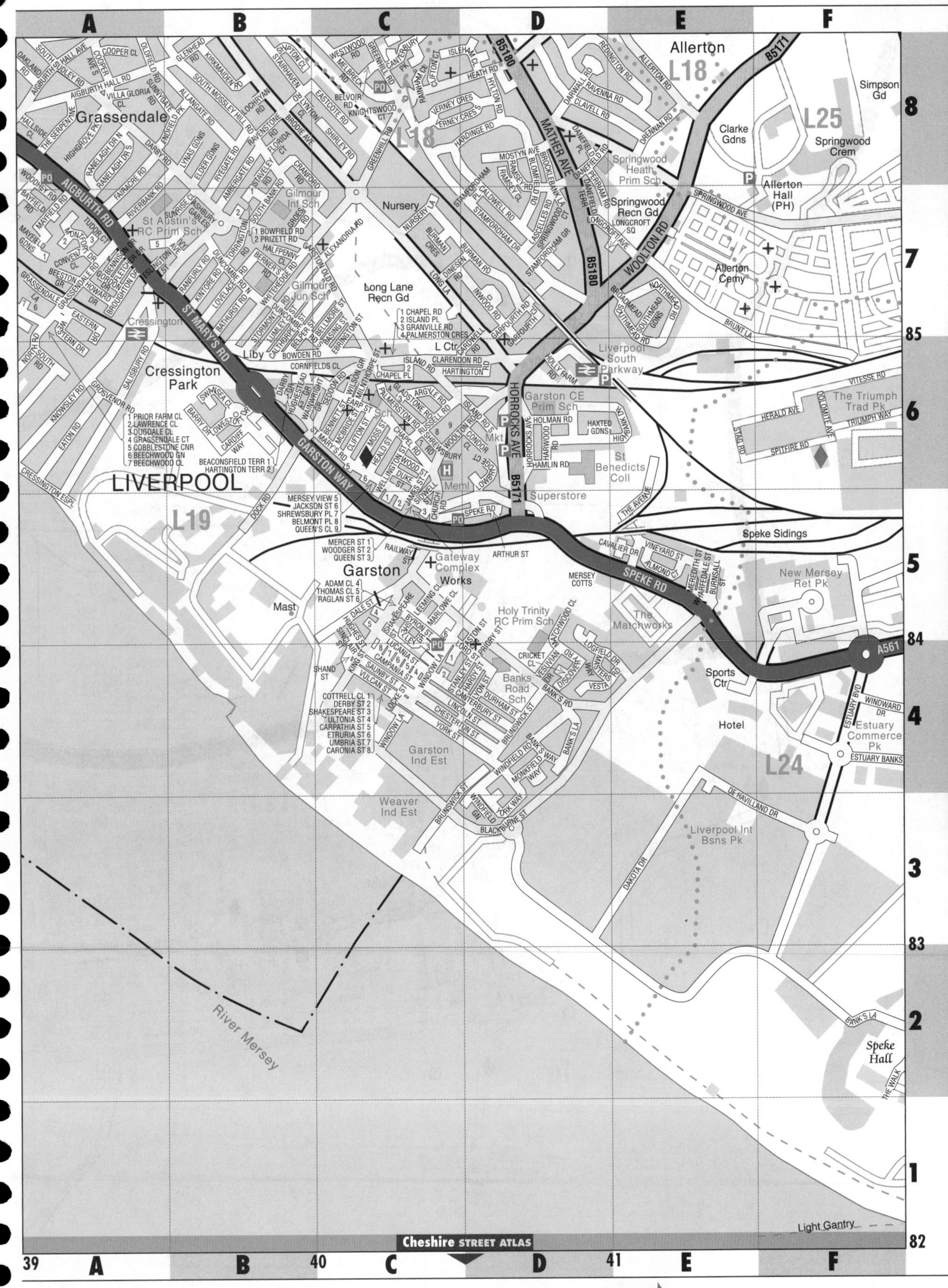
A
B
C
D
E
F
8
7
85
6
5
84
4
3
83
2
1
82
39
40
41
Allerton
L18
Simpson Gd
L25
Clarke Gdns
Springwood Crem
Allerton Hall (PH)
Springwood Heath Prim Sch
Springwood Recn Gd
Allerton Cemy
Grassendale
Gilmour Inf Sch
St Austin's RC Prim Sch
Nursery
Long Lane Recn Gd
Gilmour Jun Sch
Cressington
Cressington Park
Liby
L Ctr
Liverpool South Parkway
The Triumph Trad Pk
Garston CE Prim Sch
St Benedicts Coll
Mkt
Meml
Superstore
LIVERPOOL
L19
Speke Sidings
Garston
Gateway Complex
Works
Mast
Holy Trinity RC Prim Sch
The Matchworks
New Mersey Ret Pk
Sports Ctr
Hotel
Banks Road Sch
Estuary Commerce Pk
L24
Garston Ind Est
Weaver Ind Est
Liverpool Int Bsns Pk
River Mersey
Speke Hall
Light Gantry
AIGBURTH RD
ST MARY'S RD
GARSTON WAY
SPEKE RD
WOOLTON RD
MATHER AVE
HORROCKS AVE
B5180
B5171
A561
BLACKBURNE ST
DE HAVILLAND DR
DAKOTA DR
ESTUARY BVD
WINDWARD DR
ESTUARY BANKS
BANK'S LA
THE WALK
VITESSE RD
HERALD AVE
DOLOMITE AVE
TRIUMPH WAY
SPITFIRE RD
STAG RD
CRESSINGTON ESPL
DOCK RD
BRUNT LA
SPRINGWOOD AVE
1 PRIOR FARM CL
2 LAWRENCE CL
3 DUGDALE CL
4 GRASSENDALE CT
5 COBBLESTONE CNR
6 BEECHWOOD GN
7 BEECHWOOD CL
BEACONSFIELD TERR 1
HARTINGTON TERR 2
MERSEY VIEW 5
JACKSON ST 6
SHREWSBURY PL 7
BELMONT PL 8
QUEEN'S CL 9
MERCER ST 1
WOODGER ST 2
QUEEN ST 3
ADAM CL 4
THOMAS CL 5
RAGLAN ST 6
COTTRELL CL 1
DERBY ST 2
SHAKESPEARE ST 3
ULTONIA ST 4
CARPATHIA ST 5
ETRURIA ST 6
UMBRIA ST 7
CARONIA ST 8
1 CHAPEL RD
2 ISLAND PL
3 GRANVILLE RD
4 PALMERSTON CRES
1 BOWFIELD RD
2 PRIZETT RD

A B C D E F

9
8
85
7
84
6
84
5
83
4
83
3
82
2
82
1

LIVERPOOL

L25

L26

L24

Camp Hill

Halewood

Halewood 'Triangle' Country Park

Visitor Ctr

Plantation Prim Sch

Halewood Coll

Greengates Com Prim Sch

Hunt's Cross

St Andrew RC Prim Sch

Charlton Ct

St Christopher's RC Prim Sch

Speke

Austin Rawlinson Sports Ctr

Parklands High Sch

Middlefield Com Prim Sch

Stockton Wood Com Prim Sch

Edwards Lane Ind Est

Bridge Ind Est

Opco Complex

Venture Point West

Sports Gd

Viscount Ctr

Factory

Works

Boulevard Ind Pk

Works

The Hunts Cross Sh Pk

The Triumph Trad Pk

Estuary Banks Bsns Pk

Ind Est

Stockton's Wood

Speke Home Farm

Pegasus (PH)

Liverpool John Lennon Airport

River Mersey

The Red Brow

Oglet

Yew Tree Farm

Oglet Point

Dungeon Point

HILLFOOT RD
HILLFOOT AVE
SPEKE HALL RD
SPEKE BLVD
HIGHER RD
A562
A561

Cemy

Oak Farm

Camp Hill

Doe Park Ctyd

Railway Cotts

Sports Gd

Church Mews

Cartwrights Farm Rd

71
84
A
B
C
D
E
F
8
7
6
5
4
3
2
1
85
84
83
82
45
46
47
L35
L26
L24
WA8
Halewood Village
Halewood
Speke
Hale
Hale Heath
Hale Cliff
River Mersey
Yew Tree Farm
Caravan Site
Ireland Farm
Ditton Fold Farm
Brook House Farm
Wellbrook Farm
Finch Farm
New Farm Bungalows
Bosco Hall Farm
Ditton Brook
A5300 KNOWSLEY EXPRESSWAY
A562
A561
SPEKE RD
HIGHER RD
SPEKE BVD
Works
RSPCA Home
Highfield Sch
St Mark's RC Prim Sch
Sports Ctr
Manor Farm
Linner Farm
The Beehive Inn (PH)
Ramsbrook Farm
Burnt Mill Farm
Sewage Works
Mast
Ramsbrook Bridge
Mill Wood
Ram's Brook
Little Boar's Wood
Big Boar's Wood
Clamley Park Plantation
Alder Plantation
St Ambrose RC Prim Sch
Lenox Farm
Hoghton Towers Farm
Marsh Bridge
Hale Gate Farm
Ciss Green
Brook Farm
Trans Pennine Trail
Old Plantation
Recn Gd
Parsonage Green
Manor Farm
Hale CE Prim Sch
1 STAPELEY GDNS
2 HASLINGTON GR
3 WINTERLEA DR
4 BURLAND RD
5 WILLASTON DR
6 HATHERTON GR
7 WESTON GR
8 CALVELEY RD
1 MILLWOOD CT
2 RAMSFIELD RD
1 BANDON CL
2 GREENORE DR
IVY FARM CT 3
THE GREEN 4
1 ROSSALL CL
2 MEOLS CL
3 ORFORD CL
4 ST MARYS CL
5 JOHN MIDDLETON CL
6 TURTON CL
7 ASSHETON WLK
8 CLAMLEY GDNS
9 LUMLEY WLK
10 CRAB TREE CL
11 PEACH TREE CL
12 THORN TREE CL
13 ALMOND TREE CL
14 CHERRY TREE CL
15 APPLE TREE CL
16 PEAR TREE CL
Cheshire STREET ATLAS

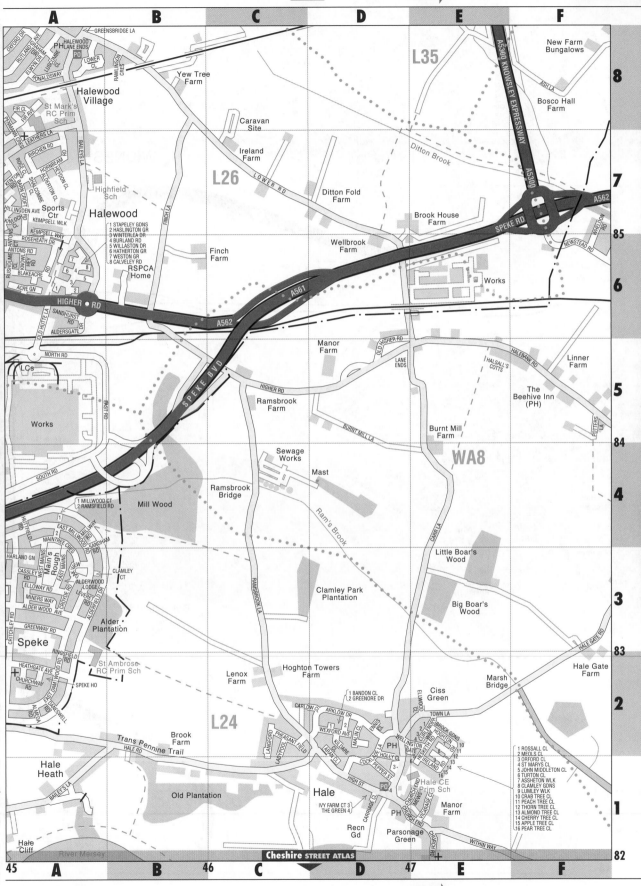

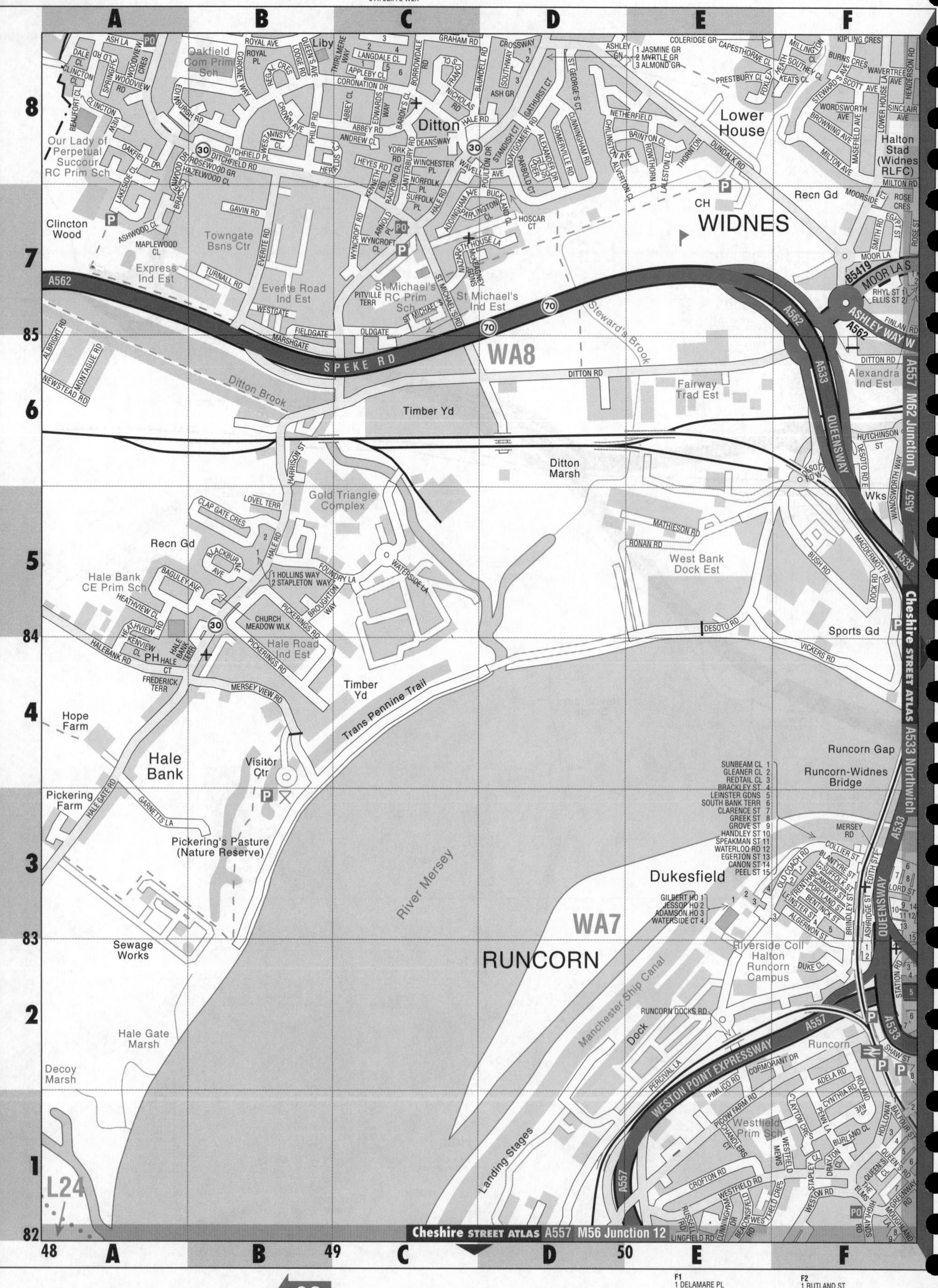

C8
1 LEVENS WAY
2 RIDSDALE
3 LONSDALE CL
4 LEIGH GREEN CL
5 APPLEBY WLK
6 AYCLIFFE WLK

SUNBEAM CL 1
GLEANER CL 2
REDTAIL CL 3
BRACKLEY ST 4
LEINSTER GDNS 5
SOUTH BANK TERR 6
CLARENCE ST 7
GREEK ST 8
GROVE ST 9
HANDLEY ST 10
SPEAKMAN ST 11
WATERLOO RD 12
EGERTON ST 13
CANON ST 14
PEEL ST 15

GILBERT HO 1
JESSOP HO 2
ADAMSON HO 3
WATERSIDE CT 4

F1
1 DELAMARE PL
2 PICOW ST
3 ELAINE PRICE CT
4 HAVERGAL ST
5 CURZON ST
6 LIGHTBURN ST
7 STANLEY VILLAS
8 SOUTHLANDS MEWS
9 SOUTHLANDS CT

F2
1 RUTLAND ST
2 HANKEY ST
3 WATERLOO RD
4 HIGH ST
5 DARESBURY EXPRESSWAY
6 LOWLANDS RD
7 CAVENDISH ST
8 ARTHUR ST

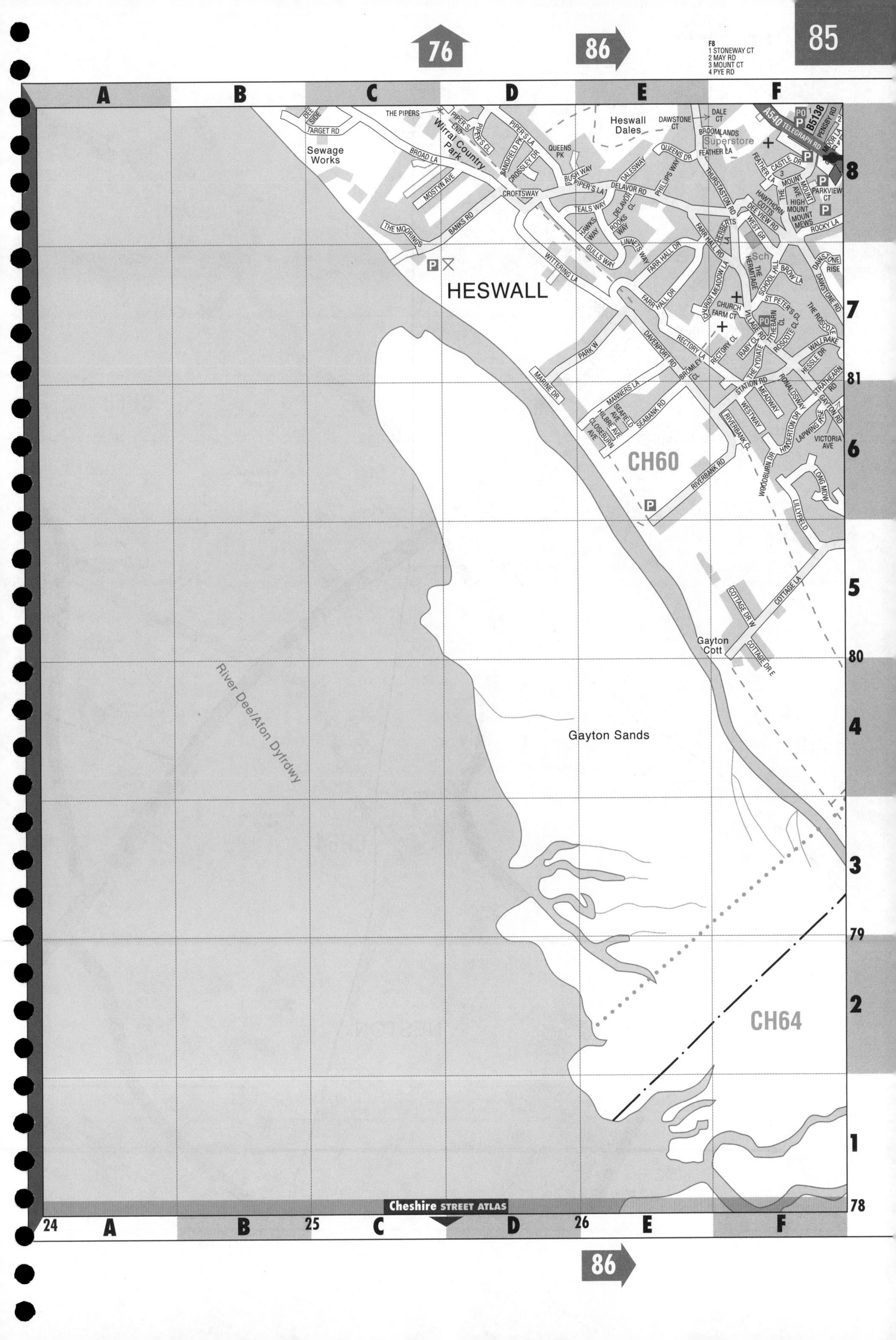
76
86
F8
1 STONEWAY CT
2 MAY RD
3 MOUNT CT
4 PYE RD
A
B
C
D
E
F
HESWALL
Heswall Dales
Sewage Works
Wirral Country Park
Superstore
CH60
CH64
Gayton Cott
Gayton Sands
River Dee/Afon Dyfrdwy
THE PIPERS
TARGET RD
BROAD LA
MOSTYN AVE
BANKS RD
THE MOORINGS
CROFTSWAY
SANDFIELD PK
CROSSLEY DR
QUEENS PK
BUSH WAY
DALESWAY
DELAVOR RD
TEALS WAY
HAWKS WAY
ROOKS WAY
GULLS WAY
LINNETS WAY
WITTERING LA
FARR HALL DR
FARR HALL RD
PHILLIPS WAY
QUEENS DR
THURSTASTON RD
DAWSTONE CT
DALE CT
BROOMLANDS
FEATHER LA
A540 TELEGRAPH RD
B5138
PENSBY RD
MOOR LA
CASTLE DR
PARKVIEW CT
ROCKY LA
DEE VIEW RD
HAWTHORN COTTS
HIGH MOUNT
MOUNT MEWS
SCHOOL HILL
BROW LA
DAWSTONE RISE
DAWSTONE RD
THE HERMITAGE
CHURCH MEADOW LA
CHURCH FARM CT
VILLAGE RD
ST PETER'S CL
TITHEBARN CL
ROSCOTE CL
THE ROSCOTE
WALLRAKE
HESSLE DR
STRATHEARN RD
GAYTON RD
LAPWING RISE
VICTORIA AVE
RABY CL
THE LYDIATE
RECTORY LA
RECTORY CL
STATION RD
RONALDSWAY
MEADWAY
WESTWAY
HINDERTON DR
WOODBURN DR
LONG MDW
LILLYFIELD
RIVERBANK CL
RIVERBANK RD
PARK W
MARINE DR
DAVENPORT RD
BROMLEY CL
MANNERS LA
SEAFIELD AVE
HILBRE AVE
CLOSEBURN AVE
SEABANK RD
COTTAGE LA
COTTAGE DR W
COTTAGE DR E
8
7
6
5
4
3
2
1
81
80
79
78
24
25
26
Cheshire STREET ATLAS

A8
1 DOWNHAM CT
2 BIRCHES HO
3 CHERRY TREE MEWS
4 BEACON CT
5 THE CHASE
6 YEW TREE CT
7 HESWALL POINT

85
77

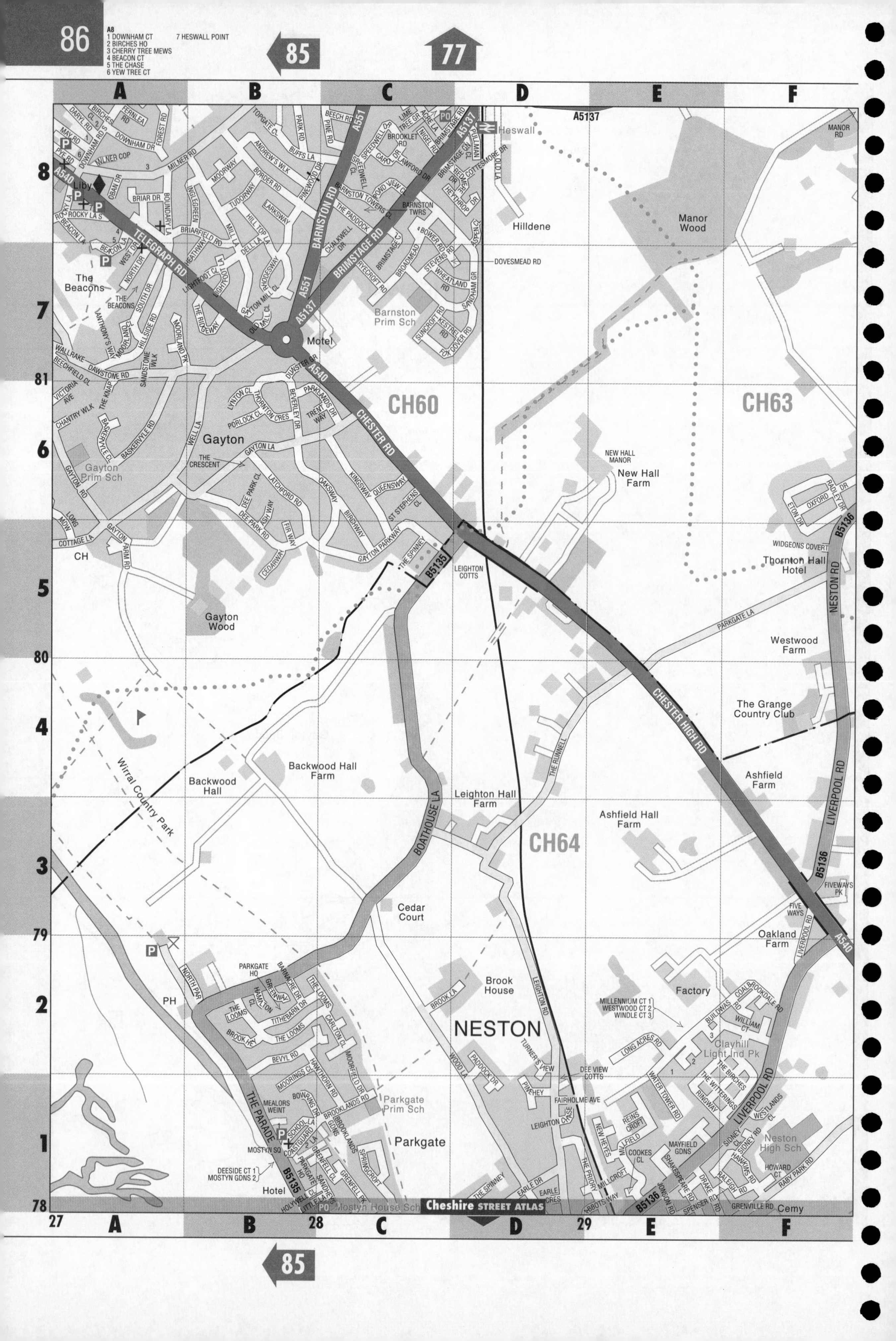

85

78
88

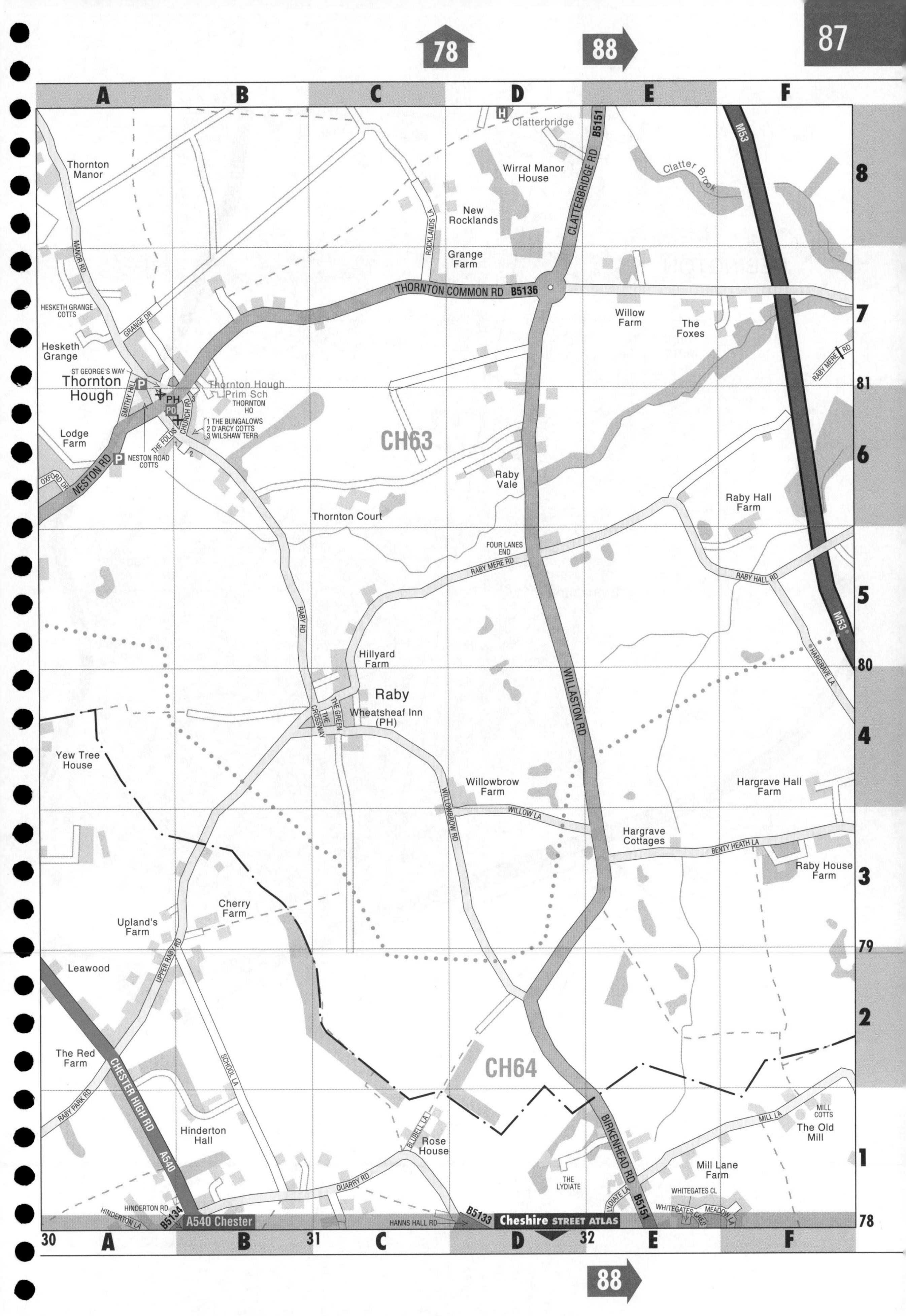
A
B
C
D
E
F
Clatterbridge
Thornton Manor
Wirral Manor House
CLATTERBRIDGE RD
B5151
Clatter Brook
M53
New Rocklands
ROCKLANDS LA
Grange Farm
MANOR RD
THORNTON COMMON RD
B5136
Willow Farm
The Foxes
HESKETH GRANGE COTTS
GRANGE DR
Hesketh Grange
ST GEORGE'S WAY
Thornton Hough
SMITHY HILL
PH
PO
Thornton Hough Prim Sch
THORNTON HO
CHURCH RD
THE FOLDS
1 THE BUNGALOWS
2 D'ARCY COTTS
3 WILSHAW TERR
RABY MERE RD
Lodge Farm
NESTON RD
NESTON ROAD COTTS
OXFORD DR
CH63
Raby Vale
Raby Hall Farm
Thornton Court
FOUR LANES END
RABY MERE RD
RABY HALL RD
RABY RD
Hillyard Farm
Raby
THE CROSSWAY
THE GREEN
Wheatsheaf Inn (PH)
WILLASTON RD
HARGRAVE LA
Yew Tree House
Willowbrow Farm
WILLOWBROW RD
WILLOW LA
Hargrave Hall Farm
Hargrave Cottages
BENTY HEATH LA
Raby House Farm
Cherry Farm
Upland's Farm
UPPER RABY RD
Leawood
SCHOOL LA
The Red Farm
CHESTER HIGH RD
A540
CH64
RABY PARK RD
Hinderton Hall
BLUEBELL LA
Rose House
BIRKENHEAD RD
MILL LA
MILL COTTS
The Old Mill
Mill Lane Farm
THE LYDIATE
QUARRY RD
LYDIATE LA
WHITEGATES CL
WHITEGATES CRES
MEADOW LA
HINDERTON RD
HINDERTON LA
B5134
A540 Chester
HANNS HALL RD
B5133
Cheshire STREET ATLAS
8
7
81
6
5
80
4
3
79
2
1
78
30
31
32

88

87
79

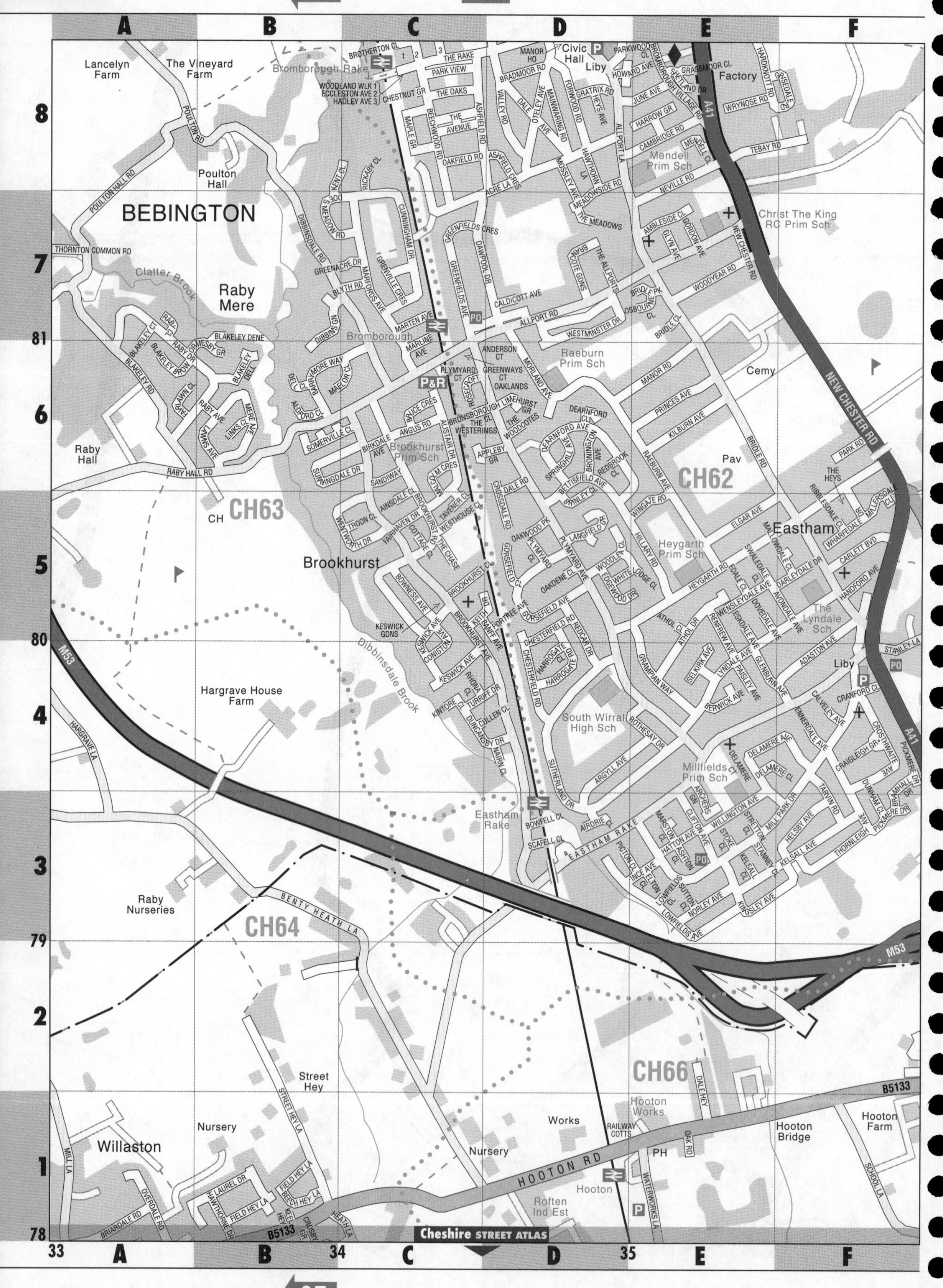
BEBINGTON
Lancelyn Farm
The Vineyard Farm
Poulton Hall
Raby Mere
Raby Hall
CH63
Brookhurst
Bromborough Rake
Bromborough
Civic Hall
Factory
Mendell Prim Sch
Christ The King RC Prim Sch
Raeburn Prim Sch
Brookhurst Prim Sch
CH62
Eastham
Heygarth Prim Sch
The Lyndale Sch
South Wirral High Sch
Millfields Prim Sch
Eastham Rake
Hargrave House Farm
Raby Nurseries
CH64
Street Hey
Nursery
Willaston
CH66
Hooton Works
Works
Hooton
Hooton Bridge
Hooton Farm
Roften Ind Est
HOOTON RD
NEW CHESTER RD
M53
A41
B5133
Cheshire STREET ATLAS

87

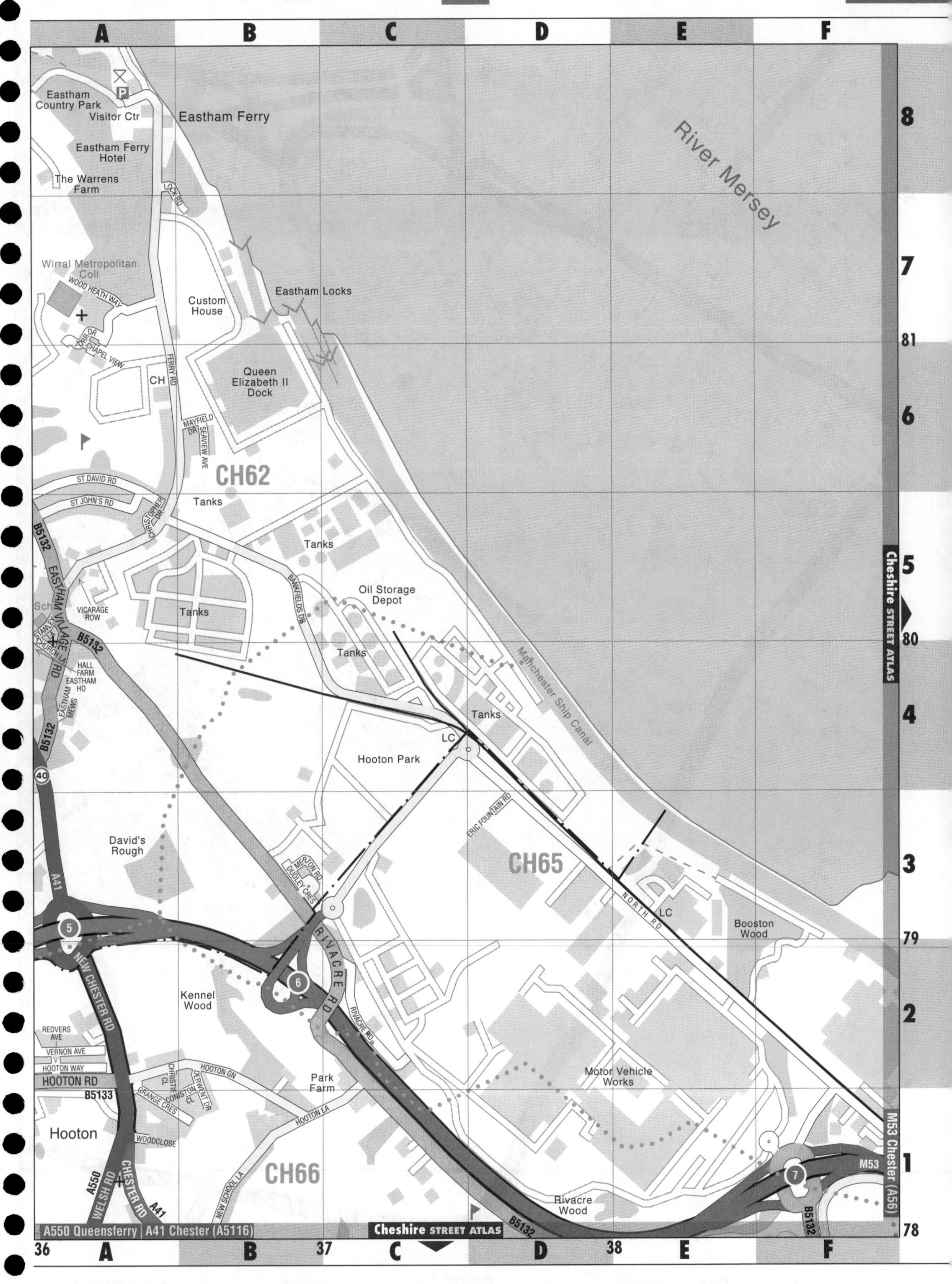

A   B   C   D   E   F

8

Eastham
Country Park
Visitor Ctr

Eastham Ferry

7

Eastham Ferry
Hotel

River Mersey

The Warrens
Farm

81

Wirral Metropolitan
Coll

Custom
House

Eastham Locks

6

WOOD HEATH WAY

CHAPEL VIEW

CH

Queen
Elizabeth II
Dock

ST DAVID RD

CH62

Cheshire STREET ATLAS

5

ST JOHN'S RD

Tanks

80

B5132

Tanks

EASTHAM VILLAGE RD

Tanks

Oil Storage
Depot

BANKFIELDS DR

VICARAGE
ROW

Sch

STANLEY RD

Tanks

CHURCH RD

Manchester Ship Canal

B5132

HALL
FARM
EASTHAM
HO

Tanks

4

EASTHAM MEWS

Tanks

LC

Hooton Park

40

David's
Rough

ERIC FOUNTAIN RD

A41

MERTON RD

CH65

3

DUDLEY CRES

NORTH RD

LC

Booston
Wood

79

5

RIVACRE RD

NEW CHESTER RD

6

Kennel
Wood

RIVACRE RD

2

REDVERS
AVE

CHRISTIE CL

VERNON AVE

HOOTON GN

DERWENT CL

GRANGE CONISTON CRES CL

Motor Vehicle
Works

HOOTON WAY

HOOTON RD

Park
Farm

B5133

HOOTON LA

WOODCLOSE

Hooton

A550

WELSH RD

CHESTER RD

NEW SCHOOL LA

CH66

1

A41

7

M53

Rivacre
Wood

M53 Chester (A56)

B5132

B5132

78

36   A   B   37   C   D   38   E   F

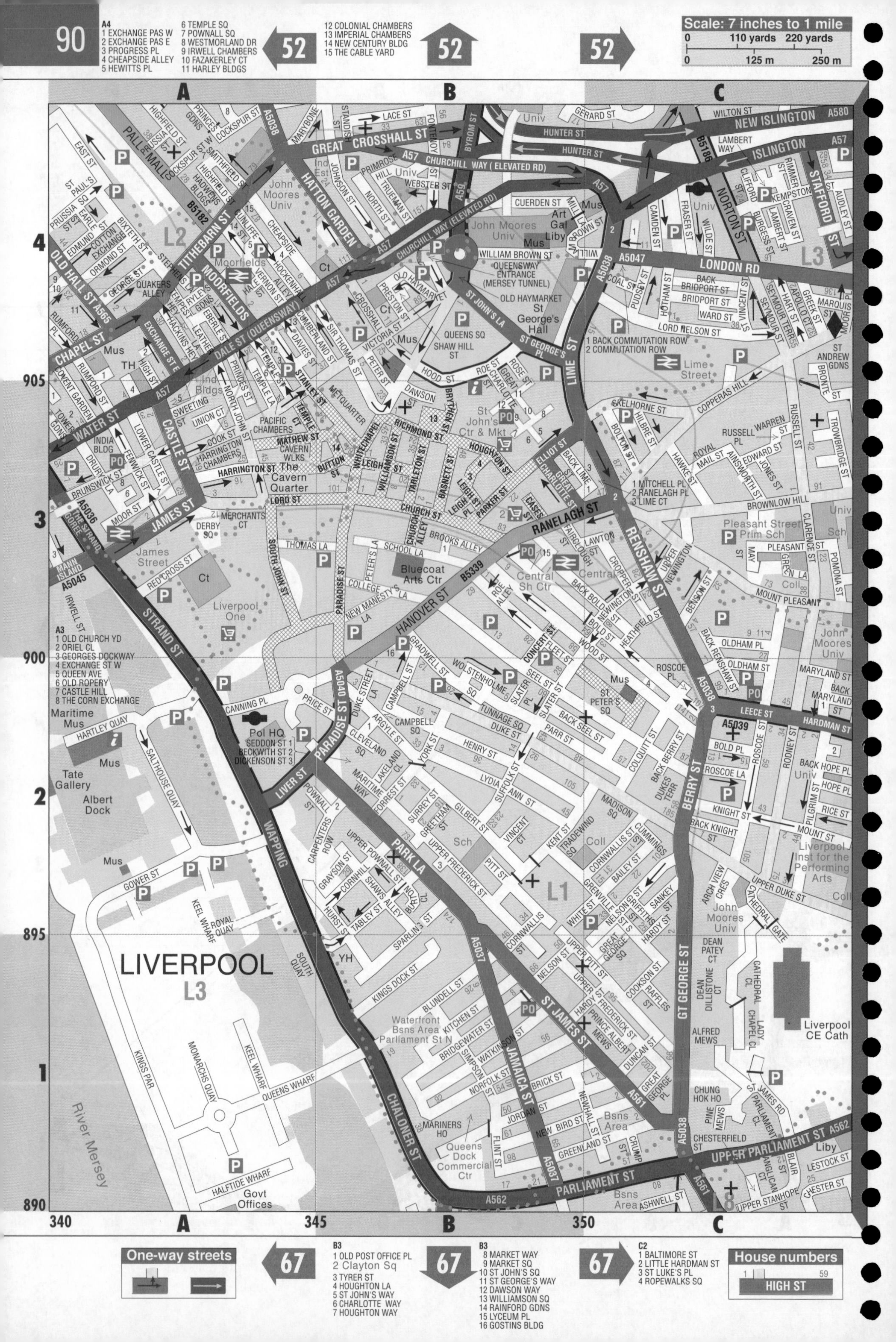

90
A4
1 EXCHANGE PAS W
2 EXCHANGE PAS E
3 PROGRESS PL
4 CHEAPSIDE ALLEY
5 HEWITTS PL
6 TEMPLE SQ
7 POWNALL SQ
8 WESTMORLAND DR
9 IRWELL CHAMBERS
10 FAZAKERLEY CT
11 HARLEY BLDGS
52
12 COLONIAL CHAMBERS
13 IMPERIAL CHAMBERS
14 NEW CENTURY BLDG
15 THE CABLE YARD
52
52
Scale: 7 inches to 1 mile
0
110 yards
220 yards
0
125 m
250 m
A
B
C
4
905
3
900
2
895
1
890
340
345
350
LIVERPOOL
L1
L2
L3
L8
River Mersey
GREAT CROSSHALL ST
CHURCHILL WAY (ELEVATED RD)
NEW ISLINGTON
ISLINGTON
HUNTER ST
LONDON RD
LIME ST
RENSHAW ST
BERRY ST
GT GEORGE ST
STRAND ST
WAPPING
CHALONER ST
PARK LA
ST JAMES ST
JAMAICA ST
PARLIAMENT ST
UPPER PARLIAMENT ST
HANOVER ST
RANELAGH ST
DALE ST (QUEENSWAY)
TITHEBARN ST
MOORFIELDS
OLD HALL ST
CHAPEL ST
WATER ST
CASTLE ST
JAMES ST
LORD ST
CHURCH ST
BOLD ST
DUKE ST
PARADISE ST
HATTON GARDEN
NORTON ST
LEECE ST
HARDMAN ST
MOUNT PLEASANT
BROWNLOW HILL
COPPERAS HILL
A3
1 OLD CHURCH YD
2 ORIEL CL
3 GEORGES DOCKWAY
4 EXCHANGE ST W
5 QUEEN AVE
6 OLD ROPERY
7 CASTLE HILL
8 THE CORN EXCHANGE
1 BACK COMMUTATION ROW
2 COMMUTATION ROW
1 MITCHELL PL
2 RANELAGH PL
3 LIME CT
SEDDON ST 1
BECKWITH ST 2
DICKENSON ST 3
John Moores Univ
Art Gal Liby
St George's Hall
Lime Street
Central
Central Sh Ctr
Bluecoat Arts Ctr
Liverpool One
The Cavern Quarter
Maritime Mus
Tate Gallery
Albert Dock
Pol HQ
Liverpool CE Cath
Liverpool Inst for the Performing Arts
Waterfront Bsns Area Parliament St N
Queens Dock Commercial Ctr
Govt Offices
One-way streets
67
B3
1 OLD POST OFFICE PL
2 Clayton Sq
3 TYRER ST
4 HOUGHTON LA
5 ST JOHN'S WAY
6 CHARLOTTE WAY
7 HOUGHTON WAY
67
B3
8 MARKET WAY
9 MARKET SQ
10 ST JOHN'S SQ
11 ST GEORGE'S WAY
12 DAWSON WAY
13 WILLIAMSON SQ
14 RAINFORD GDNS
15 LYCEUM PL
16 GOSTINS BLDG
67
C2
1 BALTIMORE ST
2 LITTLE HARDMAN ST
3 ST LUKE'S PL
4 ROPEWALKS SQ
House numbers
1
59
HIGH ST

Index

Place name May be abbreviated on the map

→ Church Rd **6** Beckenham BR2.........**53** C6

Location number Present when a number indicates the place's position in a crowded area of mapping

Locality, town or village Shown when more than one place has the same name

Postcode district District for the indexed place

Page and grid square Page number and grid reference for the standard mapping

Cities, towns and villages are listed in CAPITAL LETTERS

Public and commercial buildings are highlighted in magenta   **Places of interest** are highlighted in blue with a star★

Abbreviations used in the index

Acad	Academy	Comm	Common	Gd	Ground	L	Leisure	Prom	Promenade
App	Approach	Cott	Cottage	Gdn	Garden	La	Lane	Rd	Road
Arc	Arcade	Cres	Crescent	Gn	Green	Liby	Library	Recn	Recreation
Ave	Avenue	Cswy	Causeway	Gr	Grove	Mdw	Meadow	Ret	Retail
Bglw	Bungalow	Ct	Court	H	Hall	Meml	Memorial	Sh	Shopping
Bldg	Building	Ctr	Centre	Ho	House	Mkt	Market	Sq	Square
Bsns, Bus	Business	Ctry	Country	Hospl	Hospital	Mus	Museum	St	Street
Bvd	Boulevard	Cty	County	HQ	Headquarters	Orch	Orchard	Sta	Station
Cath	Cathedral	Dr	Drive	Hts	Heights	Pal	Palace	Terr	Terrace
Cir	Circus	Dro	Drove	Ind	Industrial	Par	Parade	TH	Town Hall
Cl	Close	Ed	Education	Inst	Institute	Pas	Passage	Univ	University
Cnr	Corner	Emb	Embankment	Int	International	Pk	Park	Wk, Wlk	Walk
Coll	College	Est	Estate	Intc	Interchange	Pl	Place	Wr	Water
Com	Community	Ex	Exhibition	Junc	Junction	Prec	Precinct	Yd	Yard

Index of towns, villages, streets, hospitals, industrial estates, railway stations, schools, shopping centres, universities and places of interest

1st St WN2.............. 35 E7
3rd St WN2.............. 35 E7
4th St WN2.............. 35 F7

A

Aaron Ct PR9...............1 E1
Abacus Rd L13........... 54 B4
Abberley Cl WA10....... 43 F3
Abberley Rd L25........ 82 D8
Abberton Pk L30....... 28 A5
Abbey Cl
  Birkenhead CH41...... 66 F5
  Formby L37............ 10 B2
  Kirkby L33............ 29 F2
  Up Holland WN8....... 25 C7
  Widnes WA8........... 84 C8
Abbey Ct L25............ 70 B2
Abbey Dr WN5.......... 25 E6
Abbey Farm Cvn Pk
  L40.................. 14 C8
Abbeyfield Dr L12..... 40 D3
Abbeyfield Ho WA10... 43 E5
Abbeygate Apartments
  L15.................. 68 F7
Abbey Gdns PR8......... 4 A4
Abbey La L40........... 14 C8
Abbey Rd
  Haydock WA11........ 45 E7
  1 Liverpool L6....... 53 C6
  St Helens WA10...... 43 E7
  West Kirby CH48..... 63 B2
  Widnes WA8.......... 84 C8
Abbey St CH41......... 66 F5
Abbeystead WN8....... 24 C7
Abbeystead Ave L30... 28 A1
Abbeystead Rd L15.... 69 B7
Abbeyvale Dr L25..... 70 C6
Abbey View L16........ 69 E7
Abbeyway N WA11..... 46 A7
Abbeyway S WA11..... 46 A7
Abbeywood WN8....... 24 C6
Abbeywood Gr L35.... 56 F2
Abbot Cl CH43......... 65 C6
Abbotsbury Way L12.. 40 E3
Abbots Cl L37......... 10 A1
Abbots Dr CH63....... 78 F5
Abbotsfield Rd WA9... 58 E5
Abbotsfield Rd Ind Pk
  WA9................. 58 E6
Abbotsford L39........ 13 F5
Abbotsford Cl WA3.... 36 D1

Abbotsford Ct **3** L23.. 26 C3
Abbotsford Gdns L23.. 26 C3
Abbotsford Rd
  Crosby L23........... 26 C3
  Liverpool L11........ 39 F2
Abbotsford St CH44... 51 E2
Abbots Hall Ave WA9.. 58 D2
Abbots Quay CH41.... 67 A6
Abbots Way
  Formby L37.......... 10 B1
  Neston CH64......... 86 E1
  West Kirby CH48..... 63 C3
Abbott Dr L20......... 38 E5
Abbotts Cl L18........ 69 B3
Abbottshey Ave L18... 69 B2
Abbotts Way WN5..... 33 D3
Abdale Rd L11......... 39 F3
Abercrombie Rd L33... 41 C7
Abercromby Sq L7.... 52 F1
Aberdale Rd L13....... 54 B3
Aberdare Cl WA5...... 60 E1
Aberdeen St CH41.... 66 C7
Aberford Ave CH45... 50 E5
Abergele Rd L13....... 53 F2
Aber St **4** L6........ 53 A3
Abingdon Gr
  1 Halewood L26... 71 A1
  Liverpool, Walton L4. 39 C2
Abingdon Rd
  Birkenhead CH49.... 64 B3
  Liverpool L4......... 39 C2
Abinger Rd WN4....... 34 D4
Abney Cl L7........... 68 B8
Aboyne Cl L9.......... 39 A4
ABRAM................ 36 B8
ABRAM BROW......... 36 B7
Abram Bryn Gates Prim
  Sch WN2............ 35 F7
Abrams Fold PR9......2 F5
Abrams Gn PR9........2 F5
Abram St L5........... 52 E5
Abratio St CH41....... 66 D6
Abyssinia Cl L15..... 68 E7
Acacia Ave
  Huyton-w-R L36..... 55 D1
  Widnes WA8......... 73 B3
Acacia Cl CH49........ 64 C2
Acacia Gr
  Liverpool L9......... 39 B6
  St Helens WA10..... 43 A4
  Wallasey CH44...... 51 E2
  West Kirby CH48.... 63 A2

Acacia St WA12........ 45 F4
Academy The **1** PR9... 4 C8
Acad of St Francis of
  Assisi The L6....... 53 C4
Acanthus Rd L13...... 54 B4
Access Rd L12......... 54 D7
Acer Leigh L17........ 68 D2
Acheson Rd L13....... 53 E6
Achilles Ave WA2..... 61 B2
Ackerley Cl WA2...... 61 F3
Ackers Hall Ave L14.. 54 F5
Ackers La
  Crosby L23.......... 26 C7
  St Helens WA10..... 43 C4
Ackers Rd CH49....... 65 C2
Ackers St **11** L34..... 56 D6
Acland Rd CH44....... 51 B4
Aconbury Cl L11...... 39 F3
Aconbury Pl L11...... 39 F3
Acorn Bsns Ctr L33... 30 B1
Acorn Cl
  Bebington CH63..... 78 D6
  St Helens WA9...... 58 C4
Acorn Ct L8........... 67 F6
Acornfield Cl L33..... 41 C8
Acornfield Rd L33.... 30 D2
Acorn St WA12........ 46 D3
Acorns The L39....... 13 C3
Acorn Venture Urban
  Farm★ L33......... 30 D4
Acorn Way L20........ 38 D5
Acrefield Ct CH42.... 66 B1
Acrefield Pk L25...... 70 A3
Acrefield Rd
  Birkenhead CH42.... 66 C1
  Liverpool L25....... 70 A3
  Widnes WA8......... 72 B1
Acregate WN8......... 24 C7
Acre Gn L26.......... 83 A6
Acre Gr PR8...........3 F3
Acre La
  Bebington CH62..... 88 D8
  Heswall CH60....... 77 C1
Acres Cl L25.......... 70 A6
Acresgate Ct L25..... 70 A6
Acres La
  Great Altcar L37.... 18 E8
  Maghull L31, L39.... 19 E7
Acres Rd
  Bebington CH63..... 78 F6
  Hoylake CH47....... 63 F7
Acreville Rd CH63.... 78 F5
'A' Ct WN4............ 35 B2

Acton Cl WA11........ 45 C6
Acton Gr L6........... 53 C6
Acton La CH46........ 64 C7
Acton Rake L30....... 27 D5
Acton Rd
  Birkenhead CH42.... 67 A1
  Burtonwood WA5.... 59 E6
  Kirkby L32.......... 29 C2
Acton Way L7......... 68 C8
Acton Way CH46...... 64 D8
Acuba Gr CH42........ 66 E4
Acuba Rd L15......... 54 C1
Adair Pl L13.......... 53 E7
Adair Rd L13.......... 53 E7
Adam Cl L19.......... 81 C5
Adams Cl WA12....... 46 D2
Adamson Ho WA7..... 84 E3
Adamson St
  Ashton-in-M WN4... 35 A3
  Liverpool L7........ 53 D2
Adam St L5........... 52 F6
Adaston Ave CH62.... 88 F4
Adcote Cl L14........ 54 F3
Adcote Rd L14........ 54 F3
Addenbrooke Dr L24.. 82 C7
Adderley St L7....... 53 B2
Addingham Ave WA8.. 84 C7
Addingham Rd L18.... 69 B5
Addington St CH44... 51 D3
Addison Cl L32....... 40 D8
Addison Sq WA8...... 73 A1
Addison St
  Bootle L20.......... 38 A5
  Liverpool L3........ 52 D3
Addison Way L3...... 52 D3
Adelaide Ave WA9.... 57 E7
Adelaide Pl L5........ 52 E4
Adelaide Rd
  Birkenhead CH42.... 66 C4
  Liverpool L7........ 53 B2
  Seaforth L21........ 37 F7
Adelaide St CH44..... 51 B3
Adelaide Terr L22.... 26 C1
Adela Rd WA7........ 84 F2
Adele Thompson Dr **2**
  L8.................. 68 A7
Adella Ct L17......... 68 C6
Adelphi St CH41...... 66 E6
Adkins St **4** L5..... 53 A6
Adlam Cres L9........ 39 E7
Adlam Rd L10, L9..... 39 E7
Adler Way L3......... 67 F3
Adlington Ho **8** L3.. 52 D3
Adlington St **7** L3.. 52 D3

1st–Ain 91

Admin Rd L33......... 41 C8
Admiral Gr **1** L8.... 68 A5
Admirals Quay L23... 26 A4
Admiral St L8......... 68 A5
Adrian's Way L32..... 29 D2
Adshead Rd L13...... 53 E7
Adstone Rd L25...... 70 C5
Adswood Rd L36...... 55 E3
Africander Rd WA11.. 44 A8
Afton WA8............ 72 A2
Agar Rd L11.......... 53 F7
Agate St L5........... 53 A5
Agincourt Rd L12..... 54 C5
Agnes Gr CH44, CH45. 51 C5
Agnes Jones Ho **17** L7,
  L8................. 67 F8
Agnes Rd
  Birkenhead CH42.... 66 E3
  Crosby L23.......... 26 C3
Agnes St WA9........ 58 C3
Agnes Way L7........ 53 B1
Aiden Long Gr L34... 55 E6
AIGBURTH............ 68 F1
Aigburth Dr L17...... 68 C4
Aigburth Hall Ave L19,
  L18................ 81 A8
Aigburth Hall Rd L19. 81 A8
Aigburth Ho L17...... 68 E3
Aigburth Pk L17...... 68 B2
Aigburth Rd L17, L8.. 68 D2
Aigburth St L7........ 68 B8
Aigburth Sta L17..... 80 E8
AIGBURTH VALE...... 68 F2
Aigburth Vale
  Liverpool L17....... 68 D2
  Liverpool L17, L18.. 68 E3
Ailsa Rd CH45........ 51 A5
Aindow Ct PR8.........3 F3
AINSDALE.............7 B5
Ainsdale & Birkdale
  Sandhills Nature
  Reserve★ PR8...... 7 B7
Ainsdale Cl
  Bebington CH63..... 88 C5
  Heswall CH61....... 77 A5
  Liverpool L10....... 39 D4
AINSDALE-ON-SEA.....6 F6
Ainsdale Rd L20...... 38 D6

Appleton Rd *continued*
Litherland L21 27 A1
Liverpool L4 39 A1
Skelmersdale WN8 15 F2
St Helens WA9 44 C1
Widnes WA8 73 B1
Appleton Village WA8 73 B1
Appletree Cl L18 69 C1
Apple Tree Cl
Hale L24 83 E1
Huyton-w-R L28 55 B8
Appletree Gr WA2 61 F2
Applewood Ct L26 71 A1
Applewood Gr L26 71 A1
April Gr L6 53 D5
April Rise L30 27 E3
Apsley Ave CH45 51 B6
Apsley Brow L31 20 B1
Apsley Gr CH63 79 A6
Apsley Rd
Bebington CH62 79 B8
Liverpool L12 54 C6
Aquarius Cl L14 55 A4
Arabis Gdns WA9 59 B7
Aragon Cl L31 20 E3
Aran Cl L24 83 D1
Arborn Dr CH49 65 A6
Arbour Ct L33 30 B2
Arbour La L33 30 B2
Arbour St PR8 4 C6
Arbury Ave WA11 44 D6
Arbury La WA2 61 C6
Arcadia Ave L31 20 D3
Archbishop Beck RC Sports Coll L9 39 B6
Archbishop Blanch CE High Sch L7 53 A1
Archbishop Warlock Ct L3 52 C4
Archbrook Mews L13 53 E5
Archer Cl L4 52 E7
Archerfield Rd L18 69 B1
Archer Gr WA9 44 E4
Archers Croft CH62 79 D1
Archers Ct [9] CH49 65 A2
Archers Fold L31 29 B4
Archers Gn CH62 88 E3
Archers Green Rd WA5 60 B3
Archer St L4 52 E7
Archers Way [1] CH49 65 A2
Arch La WN4 34 B3
Arch View Cres L1 90 C2
Archway Rd L36 55 E2
Archway Wlk WA12 46 E3
Arctic Rd L20 38 A3
Arden WA8 72 A2
Arden Cl PR8 7 A5
Arden Coll PR9 4 C7
Ardennes Rd L36 55 E3
Arderne Cl CH63 79 B2
Ardleigh Ave PR8 4 E3
Ardleigh Cl L13 53 F2
Ardleigh Gr L13 53 F2
Ardleigh Pl L13 53 F2
Ardleigh Rd L13 53 F2
Ardmore Rd L18 69 A2
Ardrossan Rd L4 53 C8
Ardville Rd L11 39 D3
Ardwick Rd L24 82 F4
Ardwick St WA9 44 C3
Argameols Cl PR8 4 F5
Argarmeols Gr L37 9 E5
Argarmeols Rd L37 9 E6
Argo Rd L22 26 D1
Argos Pl L20 38 D1
Argos Rd [1] L20 38 D1
Argyle Ct
[2] Crosby L23 26 E3
Southport PR9 1 D1
Argyle Rd
Liverpool, Cabbage Hall L4 53 B6
Liverpool, Garston L19 81 C6
Southport PR9 1 D2
Argyle St S CH41 66 E5
Argyle St
Birkenhead CH41 66 E6
Liverpool L1 90 B2
St Helens WA10 43 F5
Argyle Street Hamilton Sq CH41 66 E7
Argyll Ave CH62 88 D4
Argyll Cl WN4 34 C4
Ariel Wlk [4] WA3 47 E8
Aries Cl L14 55 A5
Ariss Gr L35 57 A5
Arkenstone Cl WA8 72 C2
Arkle Rd CH43 65 F8
Arkles La L4 53 B7
Arkles Rd L4 53 A6
Arklow Dr L24 83 D2
Ark Royal Way CH41 66 F4
Arkwood Cl CH62 79 C3
Arkwright St L5 52 E5
Arlescourt Rd L12 54 D6
Arley Cl CH43 65 C6
Arley Dr WA8 72 B2
Arley St L3 52 C4
Arlington Ave [10] L18 68 F5
Arlington Cl PR8 7 A5
Arlington Ct CH43 65 F5
Arlington Dr WA5 74 E4
Arlington Rd CH45 50 E6
Armill Rd L11 40 C3
Armitage Gdns L18 69 B1
Armley Rd L4 53 B7
Armour Ave WA2 61 B2
Armour Gr [5] L13 54 A2
Armoury Bank WN4 35 B3
Armoury The L12 54 B7
Armscot Cl L25 82 B8
Armscot Pl L25 82 B8
Armstrong Quay L3 67 F3
Arncliffe Dr WA5 59 F6
Arncliffe Rd L25 82 D9
Arnhem Rd L36 55 E3
Arnian Ct L39 21 C7
Arnian Rd WA11 31 F7
Arnian Way WA11 31 F7
Arno Ct CH43 66 B3
Arnold Ave WA10 43 D5
Arnold Cl WA9 44 C1
Arnold Cres [1] L8 68 A6
Arnold Gr L15 69 A8
Arnold Pl WA8 84 C7
Arnold St [1] CH45 51 B5
Arno Rd CH42, CH43 66 B3
Arnot Cl WA10 43 F5
Arnot Com Prim Sch L4 38 F1
Arnot St L4 38 F1
Arnot Way CH63 78 D7
Arnside L21 38 D8
Arnside Ave
Haydock WA11 45 B6
Rainhill L35 57 A4
Arnside Rd
Birkenhead CH43 66 A4
Huyton-w-R L36 55 B2
Liverpool L7 53 C1
Southport PR9 4 C7
Wallasey CH45 51 B5
Arnside Terr PR9 4 C7
Aron Ct L34 56 D6
Arrad St L1, L7 67 F8
Arran Cl WA11 44 E6
Arranmore Rd L18 69 A2
Arrowe Ave CH46 64 D7
Arrowe Brook Ct CH49 64 E4
Arrowe Brook La CH49 64 E1
Arrowe Brook Rd CH49 64 F3
Arrowe Ct [7] CH49 65 A2
Arrowe Ctry Pk* CH49 65 A1
ARROWE HILL 65 A3
Arrowe Hill Prim Sch CH49 65 A3
Arrowe Park Hospl CH49 65 A2
Arrowe Park Rd CH49 65 A2
Arrowe Rd CH49 64 E3
Arrowe Side CH49 64 E4
Arrowsmith Rd WA11 45 F7
Arthur St
Birkenhead CH41 66 C7
Birkenhead CH41 66 C8
Liverpool, Garston L19 81 D5
Liverpool, Walton L9 38 F3
[8] Runcorn WA7 84 F2
Arundel Ave
Liverpool L17 68 D6
Wallasey CH45 50 F6
Arundel Cl
Heswall CH61 76 E5
[5] Liverpool L8 68 A6
Arundell Cl WA5 59 F6
Arundel Rd PR8 7 F8
Arundel St L4 38 F1
Arvon St L20 38 D6
Asbridge St L8 68 B7
Asbury Cl L18 69 D3
Asbury Rd CH45 50 D6
Ascot Ave L21 38 A8
Ascot Cl PR8 3 E5
Ascot Dr
Bebington CH63 78 F5
Kirkby L33 29 E5
Ascot Gr CH63 78 F5
Ascot Pk L23 26 F4
Ascroft Rd L9 39 B8
Ash Ave WA12 46 C2
Ashbank Rd L11 40 B2
Ashbourne Ave
Crosby L23 26 C4
Litherland L30 27 E2
Ashbourne Cres L36 55 B3
Ashbourne Rd L17 68 C2
Ashbrook Dr L9 39 C6
Ashbrook Terr CH63 79 A6
Ashburn Ave L33 29 E4
Ashburnham Way [10] L5 52 E4
Ashburton Ave CH43 65 F6
Ashburton Ct CH43 65 E6
Ashburton Rd
Birkenhead CH43 65 F6
Wallasey CH44 51 B4
West Kirby CH48 63 B2
Ashbury Dr WA11 45 D7
Ashbury Gables L19 81 B7
Ashbury Rd L14 55 B6
Ashby Cl CH46 49 B1
Ash Cl
Liverpool L15 68 E8
Ormskirk L39 13 D5
Ashcombe Rd L14 54 C3
Ash Cres L36 70 E8
Ashcroft Ave L39 13 F6
Ashcroft Dr CH61 76 F3
Ashcroft Rd
Formby L37 9 F1
Kirkby L33 30 C3
Ashcroft St
Bootle L20 38 B3
St Helens WA9 44 C3
Ashdale L36 55 D2
Ashdale Cl L37 9 C2
Ashdale Pk CH49 64 B4
Ashdale Rd
Crosby L22 26 D2
Liverpool, Hartley's Village L9 39 A4
Liverpool, Mossley Hill L18 69 A5
Ashdown Cl PR8 4 E4
Ashdown Cres WA9 58 C4
Ashdown Dr CH49 64 C2
Ashdown Gr L26 71 A1
Ashfarm Ct L14 54 F3
Ashfield
Liverpool L15 68 D8
Rainhill L35 57 D3
Ashfield Cres
Bebington CH62 88 D8
Billinge WN5 33 E4
Ashfield Rd
Bebington CH62 88 C8
Liverpool L17 68 E2
Ashfield Sec Specl Sch L16 69 E6
Ashfield St L5 52 C5
Ashford Cl L26 82 E8
Ashford Rd
Birkenhead CH41, CH42 66 C4
Hoylake CH47 63 C8
Ashford Way [1] WA8 73 D1
Ash Gr
Formby L37 9 C1
Golborne WA3 47 B8
Liverpool L15 68 D8
Orrell WN5 25 F6
Prescot L35 56 E5
Rainford WA11 31 F6
Seaforth L21 38 A6
Skelmersdale WN8 15 D1
St Helens WA9 58 C4
Wallasey CH45 51 C7
Widnes WA8 84 D8
Ash Grange L14 54 E3
Ash Grove Cres WN5 33 E6
Ash La WA8 84 A8
Ashland Ave WN4 35 A4
Ashlar Gr L17 68 E2
Ashlar Rd
Crosby L22 26 E2
Liverpool L17 68 E3
Ashlea Rd CH61 77 A3
Ashleigh Rd L31 28 F7
Ashley Ave CH47 48 F1
Ashley Bsns Ctr L34 56 E6
Ashley Cl
Kirkby L33 29 E5
Rainhill L35 57 D2
Ashley Gn WA8 84 D8
Ashley Rd
Skelmersdale WN8 16 B3
Southport PR9 4 C7
Ashley Sch WA8 72 D1
Ashley St CH42 66 F2
Ashley Way W WA8 84 F7
Ashmead Rd WN8 16 A4
Ashmead View WN8 16 A4
Ashmore Cl CH48 75 C6
Ashmuir Hey L32 29 F1
Ashover Ave L14 55 A4
Ash Priors WA8 72 D3
Ash Rd
Bebington CH63 78 F7
Birkenhead CH42 66 D4
Haydock WA11 45 E7
Litherland L21 38 A7
Warrington WA5 74 F4
Winwick WA2 61 B6
Ashridge St WA7 84 F3
Ash St
Bootle L20 38 C4
Golborne WA3 36 B2
Southport PR8 4 C5
Ashton Ave L35 57 C2
Ashton Cl CH62 88 E3
ASHTON CROSS 34 D2
Ashton Ct CH48 63 A2
Ashton Dr
Liverpool L25 82 C8
West Kirby CH48 63 A1
Ashton Grange Ind Est WN4 35 B6
Ashton Heath WN4 35 C2
Ashton House Hospl CH43 66 B4
ASHTON-IN-MAKERFIELD 35 C5
Ashton Pk L25 82 D9
Ashton Rd
Golborne WA3 36 A2
Newton-le-W WA12 46 C5
Southport PR8 3 F1
Windy Arbour WN5 34 B8
ASHTON'S GREEN 45 B3
Ashtons Green Dr WA9 44 F3
Ashton Sq L25 70 B1
Ashton St
Liverpool L3 52 F1
Liverpool, Stanley L13 54 A3
Ash Tree Apartments CH44 51 D3
Ashtree Gr L12 40 F4
ASHURST 16 A4
Ashurst Cl
Liverpool L25 70 B4
Skelmersdale WN8 16 A4
St Helens WA11 44 E6
Ashurst Ct L37 9 E2
Ashurst Dr WA11 44 E6
Ashurst Gdns WN8 16 B4
Ashurst Prim Sch WA11 44 D6
Ashurst Rd WN8 16 B4
Ash Vale L15 68 E8
Ash Villas CH44 51 C2
Ashville Rd
Birkenhead CH41, CH43 66 B7
Wallasey CH44 51 D2
Ashwall St WN8 23 E8
Ashwater Rd L12 40 C2
Ash Way CH60 86 B6
Ashwell Ave WA3 36 D1
Ashwell St L8 90 C1
Ashwood WN8 16 C3
Ashwood Ave
Abram Brow WN2 36 C7
Ashton-in-M WN4 35 A2
Golborne WA3 47 D8
Ashwood Cl
Kirkby L33 29 E5
Liverpool L27 70 E5
Widnes WA8 84 A7
Ashwood Ct CH43 50 C1
Ashwood Dr L12 40 D3
Ashworth Hospl L31 21 B2
Askern Rd L32 40 F8
Askett Cl WA11 45 C7
Askew Cl CH44 51 D4
Askew St [2] L4 38 F1
Askham Cl L8 68 B7
Asland Gdns PR9 2 C4
Asmall Cl L39 13 D6
Asmall La
Haskayne L39, L40 12 E8
Ormskirk L39, L40 13 B7
Asmall Prim Sch L39 13 D6
Aspen Cl
Heswall CH60 86 D8
Kirkby L33 29 F6
Aspendale Rd CH42 66 D4
Aspen Gdns WA9 57 C6
Aspen Gr
Formby L37 9 C1
Liverpool L8 68 C6
Aspen Way [3] WN8 15 E2
Aspenwood WN4 35 A2
Aspes Rd L12 54 E7
Aspinall Cres L37 10 F1
Aspinall St
Birkenhead CH41 66 C7
Prescot L34 56 D6
Asquith Ave CH41 66 B7
Asser Rd L11 53 F8
Assheton Cl WA12 46 B4
Assheton Wlk L24 83 E2
Assissian Cres L30 27 E4
Aster Ct L31 20 C3
Aster Dr L33 29 D5
Asterfield Ave CH63 78 E7
Aster Rd WA11 45 F7
Astley Cl
Rainford WA11 31 F7
Widnes WA8 72 C3
Astley Rd L36 55 E5
Aston Cl CH43 65 F3
Aston St L19 81 D5
Astonwood Rd CH42 66 D3
Astor St L4 38 F2
Atheldene Rd L4 39 C2
Athelstan Cl CH62 79 D1
Atherton Cl L5 52 E5
Atherton Dr CH49 65 A3
Atherton Ho [6] CH45 51 B8
Atherton House Sch L23 26 D4
Atherton Rake L30 27 D4
Atherton Rd L9 39 C6
Atherton St
Bickershaw WN2 36 E8
[9] Prescot L34 56 D6
St Helens WA10 43 F4
Wallasey CH45 51 B8
Athlone Rd WA2 61 A1
Athol Cl
Bebington CH62 88 E5
Newton-le-W WA12 45 F4
Athol Dr CH62 88 E5
Athole Gr PR9 4 F7
Atholl Cres L10 28 D2
Athol St
Birkenhead CH41 66 E7
Liverpool L5 52 B5
Liverpool L5 52 C5
Liverpool L5 52 D5
Atkinson Gr L36 55 F4
Atkinson St WN2 36 B8
Atlanta Ct L33 29 D6
Atlantic Point L3 52 D3
Atlantic Rd L20 38 B3
Atlantic Way
Bootle L30 38 E8
Liverpool L3 67 D4
Atlas Bsns Complex L20 38 A4
Atlas Rd L20 38 B4
Atlas St WA9 44 B4
Atterbury Cl WA8 72 C2
Atterbury St L8 67 E5
Attlee Rd L36 56 A3
Attwood St [15] L4 52 F7
Atwell St L6 53 A4
Aubourn Cl WA8 72 C3
Aubrey Ct [6] L6 53 A4
Auburn Rd
Liverpool L13 53 E6
Wallasey CH45 51 A7
Aubynes The CH45 50 E7
Audlem Ave CH43 65 F3
Audley St L3 90 C4
Audre Cl WA5 74 D6
Audrey Wlk L10 40 B7
AUGHTON 21 A7
Aughton Chase PR8 4 A5
Aughton Christ Church CE Prim Sch L39 13 C3
Aughton Cl WN5 33 E4
Aughton Ct CH49 65 A5
Aughton Hall Cotts L39 13 C6
Aughton Mews PR8 4 A5
AUGHTON PARK 13 E2
Aughton Park Dr L39 13 D2
Aughton Park Sta L39 13 D2
Aughton Rd
Bootle L20 38 D5
Southport PR8 4 A5
Aughton St Michael's CE Prim Sch L39 13 B1
Aughton St L39 13 E4
Aughton Town Green Prim Sch L39 21 D8
Augusta Cl [3] L13 54 A2
August Rd L6 53 D5
August St L20 38 C5
Aukland Gr WA9 57 D6
Aukland Rd L15, L18 69 A5
Aurorean Cl L27 70 D6
Austell Cl WA11 44 D7
Austen Dr WA2 61 A6
Austin Ave
Garswood WN4 34 E4
St Helens WA10 57 C8
Austin Cl L32 29 D2
Austin Rawlinson Sports Ctr L24 82 E4
Austin St CH44 51 A2
Autumn Gr CH42 78 E8
Autumn Way
Bootle L20 38 C5
St Helens WA9 58 C3
Avalon Sch CH48 75 C8
Avalon Terr [7] L20 38 B4
Avebury Cl
Golborne WA3 47 E8
Widnes WA8 73 F3
Avelon Cl
Birkenhead CH43 65 D5
Maghull L31 20 B5
Avenue The
Banks PR9 2 F5
Bebington CH62 88 C8
Halewood L26 82 E8
Huyton-w-R L36 55 E3
Liverpool, Garston L19 81 E5
Newton-le-W WA12 46 D4
Ormskirk L39 13 D6
Ormskirk L39 13 E6
Orrell WN5 25 D3
Rainford WA11 31 F6
Southport PR8 5 F5
St Helens WA10 43 B3
Averham Cl WN4 35 B2
Avery Cl WA2 61 E2
Avery Cres WA11 45 C7
Avery Rd WA11 45 C7
Avery Sq WA11 45 C7
Aviary Ct L9 38 F6
Aviemore Cl WN4 34 D4
Aviemore Rd L13 53 F3
Avington Cl L12 54 D7
Avis Wlk L10 40 B7
Avocet Cl
Newton-le-W WA12 46 C4
Warrington WA2 61 D3
Avolon Rd L12 54 D5
Avon WA8 72 A2
Avon Ave WA5 74 F4
Avon Cl
Kirkby L33 29 F6
Liverpool L4 52 E8
Avon Ct L23 26 E5
Avondale Ave
Bebington CH62 88 F5
Maghull L31 28 C8
Wallasey CH46 49 F1
Avondale Dr WA8 72 B1
Avondale Rd
Haydock WA11 45 C7
Hoylake CH47 63 B8
Liverpool L15 68 E6
Southport PR9 4 B8
Avondale Rd N PR9 1 C1
Avonmore Ave L18 69 A3
Avon Rd
Ashton-in-M WN4 35 E5
Billinge WN5 33 D3
Avon St
[9] Liverpool L6 53 B5
Wallasey CH41 50 F1
Awelon Cl L12 54 C8
Axbridge Ave WA9 58 D5
Axholme Cl CH61 77 B5
Axholme Rd CH61 77 A5
Ayala Cl L9 38 F7
Aycliffe Rd WA9 57 D6
Aycliffe Wlk [6] WA8 84 C8
Aye Bridge Rd WA3 36 B5
Ayers Ct WA9 57 E7
Aylesbury Ave CH43 65 E2
Aylesbury Ho L31 20 B4
Aylesbury Rd CH45 51 C7

Beaconsfield Terr L19 81 B6
Beacons The CH60 86 A7
Beacon View Dr WN8 25 B7
Beadnell Dr WA5 74 F3
Beames Cl L7 53 C1
Beardsmore Dr WA3 36 E1
Bearncroft WN8 24 D6
Beatles Story (Mus) The★ L3 90 A2
Beatrice Ave CH63 78 E7
Beatrice St L20 38 D1
Beattock Cl L33 29 D6
Beatty Ave WA2 61 C1
Beatty Cl
Prescot L35 56 D2
West Kirby CH48 75 C6
Beatty Rd
[7] Liverpool L13 54 A3
Southport PR8 4 E5
Beauclair Dr L15 69 C6
Beaufort L37 10 A2
Beaufort Cl
Ormskirk L39 13 A1
Widnes WA8 84 A8
Beaufort Dr CH44 50 E4
Beaufort Park Prim Sch L8 67 F5
Beaufort Rd CH41 51 A1
Beaufort St
Liverpool L8 67 E5
St Helens WA9 44 C1
Beaumaris Ct [5] CH43 66 B5
Beaumaris Dr CH61 77 B6
Beaumaris Rd CH45 50 D6
Beaumaris St L20 52 C8
Beaumont Ave WA10 43 D4
Beaumont Cres L39 13 D2
Beaumont Dr L10 28 F1
Beaumont Ho L39 13 D2
Beaumont St L8 68 B7
Beau St L3 52 E4
Beauworth Ave CH49 64 C3
Beaver Ct WN4 35 C6
Beaver Gr L9 39 A6
Beavers La WN8 24 D6
BEBINGTON 78 E3
Bebington High Sports Coll CH63 78 F6
Bebington Rd
Bebington CH62 79 A6
Birkenhead CH42 66 E1
Bebington Sta CH63 79 A7
Bebles Rd L39 13 C3
Bechers WA8 72 B3
Bechers Bsns Ctr L30 28 B2
Bechers Ct L9 28 B3
Bechers Dr L9 28 C2
Bechers Row L9 38 F6
Beck Cl L10 40 B7
Beckenham Ave [7] L18 68 F5
Beckenham Cl WA8 73 D4
Beckenham Rd CH45 37 B1
Becket St L4 52 D7
Beckett Cl L33 41 C8
Beckett Dr WA2 61 A5
Beckett Gr CH63 78 D7
Beck Gr WA11 44 B8
Beckinsale Cl L26 71 A1
Beck Rd L20 38 C5
Beckwith St E CH41 66 D7
Beckwith St
Birkenhead CH41 66 C7
Liverpool L1 90 B2
Becky St L6 53 B5
Becontree Rd L12 54 D4
Bective St L7 68 C8
Bedale Wlk [7] L33 29 F4
Bedburn Dr L36 55 B3
Bede Cl L33 29 E6
Bedford Ave
Birkenhead CH42 66 E1
Maghull L31 28 F6
Bedford Cl
Huyton-w-R L36 56 A3
[6] Liverpool L7 67 F8
Bedford Ct
[7] Birkenhead CH42 66 F2
[7] Liverpool L8 67 F7
Southport PR8 4 A2
Bedford Dr CH42 66 D1
Bedford Drive Prim Sch CH42 66 D1
Bedford Pl
Ashton-in-M WN4 35 A5
Birkenhead CH42 67 A2
Liverpool L20 38 B1
[1] Seaforth L21 37 F7
Bedford Prim Sch L20 38 D2
Bedford Rd
Birkenhead CH42 66 F2
Bootle L20, L4 38 D2
Southport PR8 4 A2
Wallasey CH45 51 B6
Bedford Rd E CH42 67 A2
Bedford St N L7 52 F1
Bedford St S L7, L8, L69 67 F8
Bedford St WA9 44 D2
Bedford Villas L20 38 D2
Bedford Wlk [7] L7 67 F8
Beecham Cl L36 55 D1
Beech Ave
Birkenhead CH49 64 D6
Crosby L23 27 A6
Golborne WA3 47 F7
Haydock WA11 45 F7
Heswall CH61 77 A4
Kirkby L31 29 B3
Liverpool L17 68 B2
Beech Ave *continued*
Prescot L34 56 F7
St Helens WA9 58 C4
Warrington WA5 74 C3
Beechbank Rd L18 68 F5
Beechburn Cres L36 55 B3
Beechburn Rd L36 55 A3
Beech Cl
Kirkby L32 29 C3
Liverpool L12 40 D3
Newton-le-W WA12 46 C2
Skelmersdale WN8 15 E1
Beechcroft L31 20 D1
Beechcroft Rd CH44 51 C2
Beech Ct
[2] Birkenhead CH42 66 D4
Liverpool L18 69 D3
Southport PR9 4 D8
Widnes WA8 72 B3
Beechdale Rd L18 69 A4
Beechdene Rd L4 53 B7
Beech Dr L37 9 D4
Beechenhurst Sch L18 69 D4
Beeches The
[4] Birkenhead CH42 66 F1
Liverpool L18 69 D4
St Helens WA9 58 D5
Wallasey CH46 49 E3
Widnes WA8 73 D4
Beechfield
Huyton-w-R L36 55 C2
Maghull L31 20 E1
Beechfield Cl
Heswall CH60 86 A7
Liverpool L26 82 E7
Beechfield Gdns PR8 3 F6
Beechfield Mews PR9 4 C7
Beechfield Rd L18 69 D4
Beech Gdns WA11 31 E6
Beech Gn L12 54 A8
Beech Gr
Abram Brow WN2 36 C7
Litherland L30 28 A2
Liverpool L9 39 B6
Seaforth L21 37 F6
Southport PR9 4 F7
Beech Grove Ho L12 54 B8
Beech Hey La CH64 88 B1
Beechill Cl L25 70 C4
Beech La L18 69 C5
Beech Lawn L19 80 F7
Beech Mdw L39 14 A4
Beech Mdws L34 56 A5
Beech Pk
Crosby L23 27 A6
Liverpool L12 54 A6
Beech Rd
Aughton L39 21 A6
Bebington CH63 78 F7
Birkenhead CH42 66 D4
Golborne WA3 36 A1
Heswall CH60 86 C8
Huyton-w-R L36 55 E1
Liverpool L4 39 A2
Beech St
Ashton-in-M WN4 35 A6
Bootle L20 38 C4
Liverpool L7 53 C2
St Helens WA10 57 D8
Beech Terr L7 53 C2
Beech Tree Ct L19 80 F7
Beech Tree Hos WN2 35 F7
Beechtree Rd L15 54 B1
Beechtrees WN8 24 D7
Beechurst Cl L25 70 B5
Beechurst Rd L25 70 B5
Beechwalk The L14 54 B4
Beechway
Bebington CH63 78 F3
Maghull L31 21 B2
Beechway Ave L31 21 B2
Beechwood WN8 16 C3
Beechwood Ave
Ashton-in-M WN4 35 A2
Liverpool L26 82 F8
Newton-le-W WA12 46 D4
Wallasey CH45 50 E5
Warrington WA5 74 F5
Beechwood Cl
Liverpool L19 81 A7
Prescot L35 56 E4
St Helens WA9 58 C4
Beechwood Cres WN5 25 E6
Beechwood Ct
Maghull L31 20 F1
Skelmersdale WN8 24 D6
Beechwood Dr
Birkenhead CH43 65 C7
Formby L37 9 C1
Ormskirk L39 13 D5
Beechwood Gdns L19 80 F7
Beechwood Gn L19 81 A7
Beechwood Rd
Bebington CH62 88 C8
Bootle L21 38 B6
Liverpool, Grassendale L19 80 F7
Beechwood Rd S L19 80 F7
Beecroft Cl WA5 60 D1
Beeford Dr WN5 25 E5
Beesands Cl L27 70 F4
Beesley Rd L34 56 C6
Beeston Cl CH43 65 C6
Beeston Dr
Heswall CH61 76 F4
Litherland L30 28 B5
Beeston Gr L19 81 A7
Beeston St L4 52 F8
Beetham Way L33 29 F3
Begonia Gdns WA9 59 A7
Beilby Rd WA11 45 E7
Belair Ind Est L23 26 F3
Beldale Pk L32 29 C4
Beldon Cres L36 55 B3
Belem Cl L17 68 C5
Belem Twr L17 68 C5
Belfast Rd L13 54 B3
Belfield WN8 24 D6
Belfield Cres L36 55 E1
Belfield Dr CH43 66 B3
Belford Dr CH46 64 C8
Belfort Rd L25 70 B4
Belfry Cl
Liverpool L12 54 E6
Wallasey CH46 49 B1
Belgrave Ave CH44 51 C4
Belgrave Cl WA8 73 E3
Belgrave Pl PR8 3 F3
Belgrave Rd
Liverpool L17 68 B3
[4] Seaforth L21 37 F7
Southport PR8 3 F3
Belgrave St CH44 51 C4
Belgravia Apartments PR9 1 B1
Belgravia Ct WA8 72 F3
Belgravia Ho PR9 4 D8
Belhaven Rd [4] L18 68 F5
Bellair Ave L23 27 A4
Bellairs Rd L11 53 E8
Bellamy Rd L4 38 E2
Bella Vista Ct L23 26 B3
Bell Cl L36 70 F8
Belldene Gr CH61 76 F2
Bellefield Ave L12 54 B6
Bellerive RC Coll L8 68 B5
BELLE VALE 70 C6
Belle Vale Com Prim Sch L25 70 B5
Belle Vale Rd L25 70 C5
Belle Vale Sh Ctr L25 70 B6
Belle Vue Rd
Liverpool L25 70 B4
Wallasey CH44 51 E2
Bellew Rd L11 53 F7
Bellfield Cres CH45 51 A8
Bellflower Cl WA8 72 E4
Bellgreen Rd L11 40 A2
Bell House Rd WA8 73 C1
Bellini Cl L21 38 A6
Bellis Ave PR9 1 F2
Bellis Gr [6] L33 29 D5
Bell La L35, WA9 58 A2
Bellmore St L19 81 C7
Bell Rd CH44 51 D3
Bell's Cl L31 20 C4
Bell's La L31 20 B3
Bell St [3] L13 54 A3
Belltower Rd L20 52 B7
Bellward Cl CH63 78 F2
Belmont CH41 66 C5
Belmont Ave
Bebington CH62 79 C1
Golborne WA3 36 C1
Orrell WN5 25 D3
Belmont Cres WA5 74 F6
Belmont Dr
Heswall CH61 77 A3
Liverpool L6 53 D5
Belmont Gr
[12] Birkenhead CH43 66 C5
Liverpool L6 53 C5
Belmont Pl L19 81 C6
Belmont Rd
Liverpool L6 53 B5
Wallasey CH45 37 B1
West Kirby CH48 63 B3
Widnes WA8 73 E2
Belmont St
Southport PR8 4 A5
St Helens WA10 43 D3
Beloe St L8 67 F4
Belper St L19 81 B7
Belsford Way L24 82 B5
Belston Rd L16 69 D8
Belton Cl WA3 47 A7
Belton Rd L36 55 D6
Belvedere Ave WA9 58 D6
Belvedere Cl L34 56 E7
Belvedere Dr L37 9 F1
Belvedere Pk L39 21 C7
Belvedere Rd
Ashton-in-M WN4 35 C4
Newton-le-W WA12 46 B5
Southport PR8 7 C5
Belvedere Sch (Girls Jun) L17 68 B4
Belvedere Sch The L8 68 A4
Belvidere Pk L23 26 E3
Belvidere Rd
Crosby L23 26 E3
Liverpool L8 68 A4
Wallasey CH45 51 A5
Belvoir Rd
Liverpool L18 81 C8
Widnes WA8 73 B1
Bembridge Cl
Warrington WA5 74 C7
Widnes WA8 72 F4
Bempton Rd L17 68 C2
Benbow Cl CH43 65 F8
Benbow St L20 38 B2
Benedict Cl CH49 65 B4
Benedict Ct L20 38 C1
Benedict's Gr L36 55 C7
Benedict St L20 38 D1
Bengarth Rd PR9 4 F8
Bengel St L7 53 A2
Benjamin Fold WN4 35 B5
Ben La L39 23 A1
Ben Lane Ct L39 23 B2
Benledi St L5 52 D5
Benmore Rd L18 69 A2
Bennet's La CH47 48 E1
Bennett Dr WN5 25 D4
Bennetts Hill CH43 66 B4
Bennett's La WA8 73 E1
Bennett St L19 81 C6
Bennett Wlk CH61 76 F3
Ben Nevis Rd CH42 66 D2
Bennison Ct PR9 1 C1
Bennison Dr L19 81 A7
Ben's Ct L34 41 B5
Benson Cl CH49 64 F4
Benson St L1 90 C3
Bentfield L17 80 F8
Bentfield Cl CH63 78 D7
Bentfield Gdns CH63 78 D7
Bentham Ave WA2 61 C3
Bentham Cl CH43 65 E3
Bentham Dr L16 69 D8
Bentham St PR8 4 B5
Bentham's Way PR8 4 C2
Bentinck Cl CH41 66 D6
Bentinck Pl CH41, CH43 66 C6
Bentinck St
Birkenhead CH41 66 D6
Liverpool L5 52 B5
Runcorn WA7 84 F3
St Helens WA9 44 D1
Bentley Rd
Birkenhead CH43 66 B4
Heswall CH61 76 F5
Liverpool L8 68 B6
Bentley St WA9 58 C3
Benton Cl L5 52 D6
Bent Way CH60 77 A1
Benty Cl CH63 78 E4
Benty Farm Gr CH61 77 A5
Benty Heath La CH64, CH66 88 B3
Benwick Rd L32 29 B2
Berbice Rd L15, L18 69 A5
Beresford Ave CH63 79 A7
Beresford Cl CH43 66 A5
Beresford Ct CH43 66 A5
Beresford Dr PR9 1 F1
Beresford Gdns PR9 1 F2
Beresford Rd
Birkenhead CH43 66 A5
Liverpool L8 67 F4
Wallasey CH45 50 F7
Beresford St
Bootle L20 38 B1
[7] Liverpool L5 52 E4
St Helens WA9 57 E7
Bergen Cl L20 38 E2
Berkeley Ave CH43 65 E1
Berkeley Ct
[5] Birkenhead CH49 65 A2
Newton-le-W WA12 45 F4
Wallasey CH45 51 C7
Berkeley Dr CH45 51 C7
Berkeley Rd L23 26 C5
Berkeswell Rd L11 40 A1
Berkley Ave L12 54 E8
Berkley Pl [10] L8 67 F7
Berkley St L8 67 F7
Berkshire Gdns WA10 43 F2
Bermondsey Gr WA8 73 D4
Bermuda Rd CH46 64 C8
Bernard Ave CH45 51 C7
Bernard Wood Ct WN5 33 D4
Berner's Rd L19 81 B7
Berner St CH41 66 D8
Berrington Gr WN4 35 A3
Berrington's La WA11 32 C1
Berry Cl WN8 15 F2
Berryford Rd L14 54 F6
Berry Hill Ave L34 41 D3
Berrylands Cl CH46 49 D1
Berrylands Rd CH46 49 D2
Berry Rd WA8 72 D1
Berrys La WA9 44 F1
Berry St
Bootle L20 38 B2
Liverpool L1 90 C2
Skelmersdale WN8 15 F2
Berrywood Dr L35 56 F2
Bertha Gdns [1] CH41 65 F8
Bertha St CH41 65 F8
Bertram Cl CH47 63 D8
Bertram Dr CH47 63 D8
Bertram Dr N CH47 63 D8
Bertram Rd L17 68 C4
Bertram St WA12 46 A4
Berwick Ave
Bebington CH62 88 E4
Southport PR8 7 D5
Berwick Cl
Birkenhead, Bidston CH43 65 C6
Birkenhead, Moreton CH46 64 B8
Liverpool L6 53 B4
Berwick Dr L23 26 C5
Berwick St L6 53 B4
Berwyn Ave
Heswall CH61 77 A6
Hoylake CH47 63 C7
Berwyn Bvd CH63 78 E8
Berwyn Ct PR8 4 D4
Berwyn Dr CH61 77 A2
Berwyn Gr WA9 44 F3
Berwyn Rd
Liverpool L4 53 C8
Wallasey CH44 51 C5
Beryl Rd CH43 65 C5
Beryl St L13 54 A1
Beryl Wlk L10 40 B7
Besford Ho L25 70 B5
Besford Rd L25 70 B5
Bessborough Rd CH43 66 B4
Bessbrook Rd L17 68 E2
Bessemer St L8 67 F4
Beta Cl CH62 79 A7
Bethany Cl WA11 45 B7
Bethany Cres CH63 79 A5
Bethel Gr L17 68 D6
Betjeman Gr L16 69 E8
Betony Cl L26 70 E1
Bettisfield Ave CH62 88 D6
Betty Anne Ct PR9 4 B8
Betula Cl L9 39 C4
Beulah Ave WN5 33 D4
Bevan Cl WA9 57 D6
Bevan's Ct L12 54 C7
Bevan's La L12 54 D7
Beverley Ave WN5 25 E1
Beverley Cl PR9 2 C5
Beverley Dr CH60 86 B6
Beverley Gdns CH61 77 B6
Beverley Rd
Bebington CH62 79 B8
Liverpool L15 69 A6
Wallasey CH45 50 F6
Beversbrook Rd L11 40 B2
Bevington Bush L3 52 D3
Bevington Hill [2] L3 52 D4
Bevington St
[3] Ashton-in-M WN4 34 F5
Liverpool L3 52 D4
Bevyl Rd CH64 86 B2
Bewcastle Dr L40 14 C3
Bewey Cl L8 67 E4
Bewley Dr L32 40 E8
Bewsey St WA10 43 D1
Bexhill Ave WA2 61 B4
Bexhill Cl L24 82 B5
Bexhill Gdns WA9 57 C6
Bexley Ct CH43 66 A5
Bianca St L20 38 C1
Bibby Rd PR9 2 A1
Bibby's La L20 38 A5
Bibby St L13 53 F3
BICKERSHAW 36 F8
Bickershaw CE Prim Sch WN2 36 F8
Bickershaw La WN2 36 F8
BICKERSTAFFE 22 F5
Bickerstaffe CE Prim Sch L39 22 E5
Bickerstaffe St
[1] Liverpool L3 52 E3
St Helens WA10 44 A3
Bickerton Ave CH63 78 D8
Bickerton Rd PR8 3 F4
Bickerton St L17 68 C3
Bickley Cl WA2 61 F3
Bidder St L3 52 E3
Bideford Ave WA9 58 C5
Bideford Rd WA5 74 E4
BIDSTON 50 D1
Bidston Ave
Birkenhead CH41 65 F7
St Helens WA11 44 D5
Wallasey CH45 50 E6
Bidston Avenue Prim Sch CH41 65 E7
Bidston Ct CH43 65 E7
Bidston Green Ct CH43 65 C8
Bidston Green Dr CH43 65 C8
Bidston Ind Est CH44 50 D3
Bidston Moss CH44 50 D3
Bidston Rd
Birkenhead CH43 65 F5
Liverpool L4 53 B8
Bidston Sta CH43 50 C2
Bidston Station App CH43 50 C2
Bidston View CH43 50 C1
Bidston Village CE Prim Sch CH43 50 C1
Bidston Village Rd CH43 50 C1
Bidston Way WA11 44 D5
Bigdale Dr L33 30 A3
Biggin Ct WA2 61 E1
Bigham Rd L6 53 C3
Biglands Dr L36 70 F8
Big Meadow Rd CH49 65 A4
BILLINGE 33 E4
Billinge Cres WA11 44 D6
Billinge Hospl WN5 25 D2
Billinge Rd WN4 34 C5
Billingham Rd WA9 57 D7
Billings Cl L5 52 D6
Billington Ave WA12 46 C5
Billington Cl WA5 74 E8
Billington Rd WA8 72 B3
Bilston Rd L17 80 E8
Bilton Cl WA8 73 E2
Bingley Rd L4 53 B7
Binns Rd L13, L7 53 F2
Binns Road Ind Est L13 53 F1
Binns Way L13 53 F1
Binsey Cl CH49 64 D5
Birbeck Rd L33 30 A3

Bowscale Cl CH49 .... 64 E5
Bowscale Rd L11 .... 40 A2
Boxdale Ct L18 .... 69 A4
Boxdale Rd L18 .... 69 A4
Boxgrove Cl WA8 .... 73 B3
Boxmoor Rd L18 .... 69 A2
Boxtree Cl L12 .... 40 F4
Boxwood Cl L36 .... 55 C2
Boycott St L5 .... 53 A6
Boyd Cl CH46 .... 50 B3
Boydell Cl L28 .... 55 B7
Boyer Ave L31 .... 28 D7
Boyes Brow L33 .... 29 D4
Boyle Ave WA2 .... 61 E1
Boyton Ct L7 .... 68 C8
Brabant Rd L17 .... 68 E1
Braby Rd L20, L21 .... 38 C6
Bracebridge Dr PR8 .... 4 F2
Bracewell Cl [3] WA9 .... 58 C6
Bracken Ct [12] WA9 .... 58 C4
Brackendale CH49 .... 65 C3
Brackendale Ave [6] L9 .... 39 B7
Bracken Dr CH48 .... 63 E2
Brackenhurst Dr CH45 ... 51 C7
Brackenhurst Gn L33 .... 29 E2
Bracken La CH63 .... 78 D5
Brackenside CH60 .... 76 F2
Brackenway L37 .... 10 A6
Bracken Way L12 .... 54 A5
Bracken Wood L12 .... 40 E4
Brackenwood Dr WA8 .... 84 A8
Brackenwood Gr L35 ..... 56 F3
Brackenwood Inf Sch
CH63 .... 78 F5
Brackenwood Jun Sch
CH63 .... 78 E5
Brackenwood Rd CH63 ... 78 E4
Brackley Cl CH44 .... 51 A3
Brackley St WA7 .... 84 F3
Bracknell Ave L32 .... 40 E8
Bracknell Cl [1] L32 .... 29 E1
Bracknel Way L39 .... 13 A1
Bradbourne Cl L12 ...... 40 E3
Bradda Cl CH49 .... 64 F7
Braddan Ave L13 .... 53 E5
Bradden Cl CH63 .... 79 B2
Brade St PR9 .... 2 C4
Bradewell Cl [7] L4 .... 52 E8
Bradfield Ave L10 .... 28 C3
Bradfield St [7] L7 .... 53 C2
Bradgate Cl CH46 .... 49 B1
Bradkirk Ct L30 .... 27 D5
Bradlegh Rd WA12 ...... 46 B1
Bradley Fold L35 .... 71 A8
Bradley La WA5, WA12 ... 46 A1
Bradley Pl [8] PR8 .... 4 B7
Bradley Rd L21 .... 38 C8
Bradley St PR9 .... 4 C8
Bradley Way WA8 .... 73 B1
Bradman Cl [3] CH45 ..... 51 B5
Bradman Rd
Kirkby L33 .... 30 D3
Wallasey CH46 .... 49 C1
Bradmoor Rd CH62 ...... 88 D8
Bradshaw Cl WA10 ...... 43 D4
Bradshaw Ct PR9 .... 5 A7
Bradshaw's La PR8 .... 7 D6
Bradshaw St WA8 .... 73 A2
Bradstone Cl L10 .... 40 B6
Bradville Rd L9 .... 39 C7
Bradwell Cl CH48 .... 63 D2
Bradwell Rd WA3 .... 47 E7
Braehaven Rd CH45 ..... 51 C7
Braemar Ave PR9 .... 1 E2
Braemar Cl L35 .... 56 F3
Braemar Ho CH43 .... 65 F5
Braemar St L20 .... 38 D1
Braemore Rd CH44 ...... 50 F4
Braeside Cres WN5 ...... 33 D5
Braeside Gdns CH49 .... 64 F5
Brae St L7 .... 53 B2
Brahms Cl L8 .... 68 B6
Braid St CH41 .... 66 D8
Braidwood Ct [24] CH42 .... 66 C5
Brainerd St L13 .... 53 E5
Braithwaite Cl L35 ...... 57 C3
Braithwaite Rd WA3 ..... 47 D8
Bramberton Pl L4 .... 39 C1
Bramberton Rd L4 .... 39 C1
Bramble Ave CH41 .... 65 F8
Bramble Cl WA5 .... 74 E3
Brambles The
Burtonwood WA5 .... 60 A7
Downall Green WN4 ..... 34 D5
Bramble Way CH46 ...... 49 D2
Bramblewood Cl L27 .... 70 E5
Brambling Pk L26 .... 70 E1
Brambling Way WA3 ..... 47 E7
Bramcote Ave WA11 ..... 44 D6
Bramcote Cl L33 .... 30 A4
Bramcote Rd L33 .... 30 A4
Bramcote Wlk L33 .... 29 F4
Bramerton Ct CH48 ..... 63 A3
Bramford Cl CH49 .... 64 E5
Bramhall Cl
Liverpool L24 .... 82 E3
West Kirby CH48 .... 63 D1
Bramhall Dr CH62 .... 88 F4
Bramhall Rd
Seaforth L22 .... 37 E8
Skelmersdale WN8 .... 15 F2
Bramley Ave CH63 .... 78 E7
Bramley Cl L27 .... 70 E5
Bramleys The L31 .... 28 C7
Bramley Way [4] L32 .... 29 C3
Bramley Wlk L24 .... 82 D3
Brampton Cl [5] L32 .... 29 E4
Brampton Ct WA9 .... 45 B3
Brampton Dr L8 .... 68 A8
Bramwell Ave CH43 ..... 66 A1
Bramwell St WA9 .... 44 E4
Branch Way WA11 .... 45 D6
Brancker Ave L35 .... 57 B4
Brancote Ct CH43 .... 65 F6
Brancote Gdns
Bebington CH62 .... 88 D7
Birkenhead CH43 .... 65 F6
Brancote Mount CH43 .... 65 F6
Brancote Rd CH43 .... 65 F6
Brandearth Hey L28 ..... 55 B7
Brandearth Ho L28 ...... 55 B7
Brandon WA8 .... 72 B2
Brandon Cl WN8 .... 25 A7
Brandon St CH41 .... 66 F6
Brandreth Cl L35 .... 57 C3
Brandwood Ave WA2 ..... 61 B2
Branfield Cl L12 .... 40 E3
Bransdale Cl WA5 .... 74 F7
Bransdale Dr WN4 ...... 35 D3
Bransford Cl WN4 .... 35 C2
Branson Cl WA3 .... 36 A2
Branstree Ave L11 ...... 39 F2
Brantfield Ct WA2 ...... 61 E2
Branthwaite Cl [1] L11 .... 40 A1
Branthwaite Cres L11 .... 40 A1
Branthwaite Gr [4] L11 .... 40 A1
Brasenose Rd L20 .... 38 C1
Brassey St
Birkenhead CH41 .... 66 B8
Liverpool L8 .... 67 E6
Brathay Cl WA2 .... 61 C3
Brattan Rd CH41 .... 66 C4
Braunton Rd
Liverpool L17 .... 68 E1
[2] Wallasey CH45 .... 51 A6
Braybrooke Rd L11 ...... 40 A3
Braydon Cl L25 .... 82 C7
Brayfield Rd L4 .... 39 D1
Bray Rd L24 .... 82 C5
Bray St CH41 .... 66 B8
Brechin Rd L33 .... 29 F2
Breckfield Pl L5 .... 52 F5
Breckfield Prim Sch
L5 .... 52 F6
Breckfield Rd N L5 ...... 53 A5
Breckfield Rd S L6 .... 53 A5
Breck Pl CH44 .... 51 A3
Breck Rd
Liverpool L6 .... 53 A5
Wallasey CH44 .... 50 F4
Widnes WA8 .... 73 B1
Breckside Ave CH44 ..... 50 E4
Breckside Pk L6 .... 53 D6
Brecon Ave L30 .... 27 F1
Brecon Ct WA5 .... 60 E2
Brecon Rd
Bebington CH42 .... 78 C8
Birkenhead CH42 .... 66 C1
Brecon Wlk L30 .... 28 A1
Bredon Ct L37 .... 9 E4
Breeze Cl L9 .... 38 F3
Breeze Hill
Bootle L20, L4 .... 38 E2
[9] Liverpool L4 .... 38 F2
Breeze La L9 .... 38 F3
Breeze Rd PR8 .... 3 E2
Brelade Rd L13 .... 53 F4
Bremhill Rd L11 .... 39 F3
Bremner Cl L7 .... 53 C1
Brenda Cres L23 .... 27 A7
Brendale Ave L31 .... 28 C8
Brendan's Way L30 ...... 27 E3
Brendon Ave
Litherland L21 .... 27 A1
Warrington WA2 .... 61 A3
Brendon Gr WA9 .... 45 A4
Brendor Rd L25 .... 70 B1
Brenig St CH41 .... 50 F1
Brenka Ave L9 .... 28 B1
Brentfield WA8 .... 72 D2
Brent Way L26 .... 82 F7
Brentwood Ave
Crosby L23 .... 26 F5
Liverpool L17 .... 68 C3
Brentwood Cl
Hightown L38 .... 17 F2
St Helens WA10 .... 43 B3
Brentwood Ct
[8] Birkenhead CH49 ...... 65 A2
Southport PR9 .... 1 D1
Brentwood Gr L33 .... 29 E6
Brentwood St CH44 ..... 51 C3
Brereton Ave
Bebington CH63 .... 79 A6
Liverpool L15 .... 69 A7
Bretherton Pl L35 .... 57 C4
Bretherton Rd L34 ...... 56 E6
Bretlands Rd L23 .... 27 B6
Brett Cl [11] L33 .... 29 D5
Bretton Fold PR8 .... 4 F5
Brett St CH41 .... 66 B8
Brewery La
Aintree L31 .... 28 E4
Formby L37 .... 9 F6
Brewster St L20, L4 ...... 38 E1
Breydon Gdns WA9 ...... 57 E6
Brian Ave CH61 .... 76 F6
Brian Cummings Ct [1]
L21 .... 38 B6
Briar Cl WN4 .... 35 A4
Briardale Rd
Bebington CH63 .... 78 F7
Birkenhead CH42 .... 66 C4
Liverpool L18 .... 69 A4
Wallasey CH44 .... 51 E2
Willaston CH64 .... 88 A1
Briar Dr
Heswall CH60 .... 86 A8
Huyton-w-R L36 .... 55 D2
Briarfield Ave WA8 ...... 72 A1
Briarfield Rd CH60 ...... 86 B8
Briar Rd
Golborne WA3 .... 47 B8
Southport PR8 .... 7 D4
Briars Cl L35 .... 57 D1
Briars Gn
Skelmersdale WN8 .... 16 B4
St Helens WA10 .... 43 F5
Briars La L31 .... 20 E1
Briar St L4, L5 .... 52 D7
Briars The PR8 .... 3 F1
Briarswood Cl
Bebington CH42 .... 78 F8
Prescot L35 .... 56 F3
Briar Wlk WA3 .... 47 B8
Briarwood L23 .... 26 B6
Briarwood Rd L17 .... 68 E3
Briary Cl CH60 .... 77 B1
Briary Croft L38 .... 17 F3
Brickfields L36 .... 56 A1
Brickmakers Arms Yd
L39 .... 13 D6
Brick St
Liverpool L1 .... 90 B1
Newton-le-W WA12 ...... 45 F3
Brickwall Gn L29 .... 27 F7
Brickwall La L29, L30 .... 27 E6
Bride St [4] L4 .... 38 F2
Bridewell Ct WA8 .... 73 B3
Bridge Ave L39 .... 13 E5
Bridge Bank Cl WA3 .... 47 B7
Bridge Croft L21, L30 .... 27 C3
Bridgecroft Rd CH45 .... 51 B6
Bridge Ct
Litherland L30 .... 27 D4
West Kirby CH48 .... 63 A3
Bridge Farm Cl CH49 .... 65 B4
Bridge Farm Dr L31 ..... 20 F2
Bridgefield Cl L25 ...... 70 B7
Bridgefield Forum (L Ctr)
L26 .... 71 A2
Bridgeford Ave L12 ..... 54 A7
Bridge Gdns L12 .... 40 F1
Bridge Gr PR8 .... 4 B6
Bridgehall Dr WN8 ...... 25 B7
Bridge Ho L39 .... 13 E4
Bridge Ind Est L24 ...... 82 B6
Bridge La L30 .... 27 E3
Bridgeman St WA10 ..... 43 D3
Bridgemere Cl L7 .... 53 D3
Bridgemere Ho L17 ...... 68 D2
Bridgend Cl WA8 .... 72 D3
Bridgend Dr PR8 .... 7 B4
Bridgenorth Rd CH61 .... 76 E4
Bridge Rd
Bootle L21 .... 38 B7
Crosby L23 .... 26 C3
Huyton-w-R L36 .... 55 C2
Liverpool L7 .... 68 D8
Liverpool, Mossley Hill
L18 .... 69 A3
Maghull L31 .... 28 D7
Prescot L34, L35 .... 56 E5
St Helens WA9 .... 58 D2
West Kirby CH48 .... 63 A3
Bridges La
Maghull L29, L31 .... 28 A8
Sefton L29 .... 27 F7
Bridge St
Bebington CH62 .... 79 B5
Birkenhead CH41 .... 66 E7
Bootle L20 .... 38 B2
Golborne WA3 .... 47 A7
Newton-le-W WA12 ...... 46 B3
Ormskirk L39 .... 13 E4
Southport PR8 .... 4 B6
St Helens WA10 .... 44 A3
Bridgeview Dr L33 ...... 29 F4
Bridgewater Cl L21 ...... 27 A2
Bridgewater Ct L21 ...... 27 A2
Bridgewater St L1 .... 90 B1
Bridgewater Way L36 .... 71 A8
Bridgeway L11 .... 39 E1
Bridge Wills La PR9 .... 2 C5
Bridle Ave CH44 .... 51 E2
Bridle Cl
Bebington CH62 .... 88 E7
Birkenhead CH43 .... 65 B6
Bridle Ct [3] WA9 .... 58 C8
Bridle Pk CH62 .... 88 E7
Bridle Rd
Bebington CH62 .... 88 E6
Bootle L30 .... 38 F8
Litherland L30 .... 28 A1
Wallasey CH44 .... 51 E2
Bridle Way
Bootle L30 .... 38 F7
Kirkby L33 .... 29 D6
Bridport St L3 .... 90 C4
Brierfield WN8 .... 24 D6
Brierfield Rd L15 .... 68 F6
Brierley Cl L30 .... 28 B4
Briers Cl WA2 .... 61 F3
Briery Hey Ave L33 ..... 29 F2
Brigadier Dr L12 .... 54 E7
Brighouse Cl L39 .... 13 D6
Brightgate Cl L7 .... 68 B8
BRIGHTON LE SANDS 26 B3
Brighton Rd
Crosby L22 .... 26 D1
Huyton-w-R L36 .... 56 B3
Southport PR8 .... 4 A3
Brighton St CH44 .... 51 E3
Brighton Vale [4] L22 ...... 26 C2
Bright St
Birkenhead CH41 .... 66 C6
[6] Liverpool L6 .... 53 A3
Southport PR9 .... 4 F7
Brightwell Cl
Birkenhead CH49 .... 64 F4
Warrington WA5 .... 74 E5
Brignall Gr WA3 .... 36 D1
Brill St CH41 .... 66 B8
Brimelow Cres WA5 ..... 74 E3
BRIMSTAGE 78 A2
Brimstage Ave CH63 .... 78 D8
Brimstage Cl CH60 ...... 86 C8
Brimstage Gn CH60 ..... 86 D8
Brimstage Hall Courtyard
(Craft Ctr)* CH63 ...... 78 A2
Brimstage La CH63 ...... 78 B3
Brimstage Rd
Bebington CH63 .... 78 D2
Heswall CH60 .... 86 C7
Liverpool L4 .... 38 E2
Brimstage St [4] CH41 .... 66 C5
Brindley Cl L21 .... 27 A2
Brindley Rd
Kirkby L32 .... 29 C2
St Helens WA9 .... 58 F6
Brindley St
Liverpool L8 .... 67 D6
Runcorn WA7 .... 84 F3
Brinklow Cl PR8 .... 7 A5
Brinley Cl CH62 .... 88 D5
Brinton Cl
Liverpool L27 .... 70 D6
Widnes WA8 .... 84 E8
Brisbane Ave CH45 ..... 51 A8
Brisbane St WA9 .... 57 D8
Briscoe Ave [2] CH46 ..... 64 E7
Briscoe Dr CH46 .... 64 E7
Bristol Ave CH44 .... 51 C4
Bristol Rd L15 .... 69 A6
Bristow Cl WA5 .... 60 B1
Britannia Ave L15 .... 68 D7
Britannia Cres [2] L8 ...... 68 A3
Britannia Ho CH41 ...... 66 F6
Britannia Rd CH45 ...... 51 A4
British Lawnmower Mus*
PR8 .... 4 B5
Britonside Ave L32 ...... 41 A8
Brittarge Brow L27 ...... 70 E4
Britten Cl L8 .... 68 B6
Broadacre WN8 .... 25 A6
Broadacre Cl L18 .... 69 D5
Broadbelt St [5] L4 .... 38 F2
Broadbent Ho L31 .... 28 D7
Broadfield Ave CH43 .... 65 C8
Broadfield Cl CH43 ..... 65 B8
Broadgate Ave WA9 ..... 58 C8
BROAD GREEN 54 D2
Broadgreen Ct [2] L13 ..... 54 B2
Broadgreen High Sch
Tech Coll L13 .... 54 C2
Broadgreen Hospl L14 ... 54 C2
Broadgreen Prim Sch
L13 .... 54 B2
Broad Green Rd L13 .... 54 B2
Broad Green Sta L14 .... 54 D1
Broadheath Ave CH43 ... 65 C7
Broadheath Terr WA8 .... 72 D1
Broad Hey L30 .... 27 D3
Broad Hey Cl L25 .... 70 B3
Broadhurst St L17 ...... 68 C3
Broad La
Billinge WA11 .... 33 B1
Burtonwood WA5 .... 59 E8
Formby L37 .... 10 E2
Great Altcar L37, L38 .... 19 A8
Haskayne L39 .... 12 B2
Haydock WA5, WA9 ...... 45 C1
Heswall CH60 .... 85 C8
Kirkby L32 .... 40 F8
Liverpool L11, L4 .... 39 F1
Maghull, Homer Green
L29 .... 19 C2
Broadlands
Prescot L35 .... 56 E5
Southport PR8 .... 3 E3
Broadleaf Rd L19 .... 80 F7
Broadley Ave WA3 ...... 47 C7
Broadmead
Heswall CH60 .... 86 C7
Liverpool L19 .... 81 E7
BROAD OAK 44 F4
Broad Oak Ave
Haydock WA11 .... 45 A6
Warrington WA5 .... 74 E4
Broad Oak Com Prim Sch
WA9 .... 45 A3
Broadoak Rd
Liverpool L14 .... 54 F3
Maghull L31 .... 20 E1
Broad Oak Rd WA9 ...... 44 F3
Broadoaks CH49 .... 64 E6
Broad Pl L11 .... 53 F8
Broad Sq L11 .... 53 F8
Broad Square Com Prim
Sch L11 .... 53 F8
Broads The WA9 .... 57 E6
Broadstone Dr CH63 .... 78 F2
Broad View L11 .... 53 F8
Broadway
Bebington CH63 .... 78 D7
Birkenhead CH49 .... 64 E4
Liverpool, Fazakerley L9 ... 39 E7
Liverpool, Norris Green
L11 .... 39 E1
St Helens, Grange Park
WA10 .... 57 C8
Broadway *continued*
St Helens, Windlehurst
WA10 .... 43 B5
Wallasey CH45 .... 50 F5
Widnes WA8 .... 72 A1
Broadway Ave CH45 ..... 50 F5
Broadway Cl PR8 .... 7 B5
Broadway Mkt L11 .... 39 E1
Broadwood Ave L31 ..... 28 C7
Broadwood St L15 .... 68 E7
Brockenhurst Rd L9 ..... 39 A5
Brock Gdns L24 .... 83 E2
Brockhall Cl L35 .... 57 A6
Brock Hall Cl [14] WA9 .... 58 C4
Brockholme Rd L18,
L19 .... 69 A1
Brocklebank La L19 ..... 81 D8
Brocklebank Rd PR9 ...... 1 E2
Brockley Ave [1] CH45 .... 51 B8
Brock St L4 .... 52 E8
Brockstedes Ave WN4 .... 34 E6
Brocstedes Rd WN4 ..... 34 D7
Brodie Ave L18, L19 ..... 69 A1
BROMBOROUGH 79 D1
BROMBOROUGH POOL
.... 79 D5
Bromborough Rake Sta
CH62 .... 88 C8
Bromborough Rd CH62,
CH63 .... 79 B4
Bromborough Sta
CH63 .... 88 C7
Bromborough Village Rd
CH62 .... 79 E1
Brome Way CH63 .... 79 B2
Bromilow Rd
Skelmersdale WN8 .... 15 C1
St Helens WA9 .... 44 F2
Bromley Ave
Golborne WA3 .... 47 D7
Liverpool L18 .... 68 F5
Bromley Cl
Heswall CH60 .... 85 E7
Liverpool L26 .... 71 A1
Warrington WA2 .... 61 F3
Bromley Rd CH45 .... 51 A7
Brompton Ave
Crosby L23 .... 26 C3
Kirkby L33 .... 30 A5
Liverpool L17 .... 68 C6
Wallasey CH44 .... 51 C4
Brompton Ct L17 .... 68 C5
Brompton Ho L17 .... 68 C5
Brompton Rd PR8 .... 4 E7
Bromsgrove Rd CH49 .... 64 C4
Bromyard Cl [5] L20 .... 38 B4
Bronington Ave CH62 .... 88 D6
Bronshill Ct L23 .... 26 A4
Bronte Cl
Crosby L23 .... 26 B4
Winwick WA2 .... 61 A6
Bronte St
Liverpool L3 .... 90 C4
St Helens WA10 .... 43 D4
Brook Acre Com Prim Sch
WA2 .... 61 E1
Brook Ave L31 .... 20 E2
Brookbank Ct L10 .... 40 B7
Brookbridge Rd L13 ..... 53 E6
Brook Cl
Cronton WA8 .... 72 C6
Wallasey CH44, CH45 .... 51 C5
Brookdale WA8 .... 72 A3
Brookdale Ave N CH49 ... 64 E4
Brookdale Ave S CH49 ... 64 E3
Brookdale Cl CH49 ...... 64 E4
Brookdale Prim Sch
CH49 .... 64 E3
Brookdale Rd L15 .... 68 E6
Brookdale The PR8 .... 7 D3
Brooke Cl PR9 .... 5 B7
Brook End WA9 .... 45 A1
Brooke Rd E L22, L23 .... 26 D2
Brooke Rd W L22 .... 26 C2
Brook Farm Cl L39 ...... 13 E4
Brookfield Ave
Crosby L23 .... 26 D3
Rainhill L35 .... 57 C5
Seaforth L22 .... 37 F8
Brookfield Dr L9 .... 39 D5
Brookfield Gdns CH48 .... 63 B2
Brookfield High Sch
L32 .... 40 D8
Brookfield Ho L36 .... 55 E3
Brookfield La L39 .... 21 A5
Brookfield Park Prim Sch
WN8 .... 15 D2
Brookfield Rd
Up Holland WN8 .... 25 B7
West Kirby CH48 .... 63 B2
Brookfields Sch WA8 .... 73 D2
Brookfield St WA12 ..... 46 B3
Brook Hey CH64 .... 86 B2
Brook Hey Dr L33 .... 30 A3
Brook Hey Wlk L33 ..... 30 A3
Brookhill Cl L20 .... 38 D3
Brookhill Rd L20 .... 38 D4
Brook Ho PR8 .... 4 C5
Brook House Gr WA10 ... 43 A3
Brookhouse Rd L39 ..... 13 D6
BROOKHURST 88 C5
Brookhurst Ave CH63 ... 88 C5
Brookhurst Cl CH63 ..... 88 C5
Brookhurst Prim Sch
CH63 .... 88 C6

Calderstones & Harthill Botanic Gdns★ L18 69 D4
Calderstones Rd L18 69 C4
Calderstones Sch L18 69 C4
Calders View Ct L18 69 C3
Calderwood Pk L27 70 D6
Caldicott Ave CH62 88 D7
Caldon Cl L21 27 A1
Caldway Dr L27 70 E6
Caldwell Ave WA5 60 F2
Caldwell Cl L33 29 F5
Caldwell Dr CH49 65 B2
Caldwell Rd L19 81 D7
Caldwell St WA9 44 D3
CALDY 75 D7
Caldy Chase Dr CH48 75 D7
Caldy Ct 3 CH48 63 B1
Caldy Gr WA11 44 D5
Caldy Mews CH48 75 D7
Caldy Rd
Liverpool L9 39 A7
Wallasey CH45 51 B5
West Kirby CH48 75 D7
Caldy Wood CH48 75 D7
Caldywood Dr L35 56 E3
Caledonian Cres L21 27 A1
Caledonia St L7, L8 67 F8
Calgarth Rd L36 55 C5
California Rd L13 53 D7
Callaghan Cl L5 52 D5
Callander Rd L6 53 D3
Callands Prim Sch WA5 60 E2
Callands Rd WA5 60 D2
Callard Cl L27 70 C6
Callestock Cl L11 40 D6
Callington Cl L14 55 A6
Callon Ave WA11 44 E5
Callow Rd L15 68 D7
Calmet Cl L5 52 E6
Calne Cl CH61 76 D7
Calstock Cl WA5 74 E3
Calthorpe St L19 81 B7
Calthorpe Way CH43 65 D6
Calton Ave L15, L18 69 A5
Calvados Cl L17 68 C1
Calveley Ave CH62 88 F4
Calveley Cl CH43 65 E3
Calveley Rd L26 83 A6
Calverhall Way WN4 35 A3
Calver Rd WA2 61 A3
Camberley Cl PR8 3 E5
Camberley Dr L25 82 D9
Camberwell Park Rd WA8 73 D4
Camborne Ave L25 70 C1
Cambourne Ave WA11 44 D7
Cambourne Rd WA5 59 F6
Cambrian Cl CH46 64 B7
Cambrian Ct PR9 4 D8
Cambrian Rd CH46 64 C7
Cambrian Way L25 70 B3
Cambria Street N 13 L6 53 B3
Cambria Street S 14 L6 53 B3
Cambridge Arc 5 PR8 4 B7
Cambridge Ave
Crosby L23 26 D5
Litherland L21 38 B8
Southport PR9 1 F2
Cambridge Ct
Liverpool L7 67 F8
Southport PR9 1 F2
Cambridge Dr
Crosby L23 26 C5
Liverpool L26 82 F9
Cambridge Gdns PR9 1 F2
Cambridge Rd
Bebington CH62 88 E8
Birkenhead CH42 66 B2
Bootle L20 38 D2
Crosby L23 26 C5
Formby L37 9 D1
Liverpool L9 39 B8
Orrell WN5 25 F8
Seaforth L21, L22 37 E8
Skelmersdale WN8 15 E1
Southport PR9 1 E2
St Helens WA10 43 E4
Wallasey CH45 51 B7
Cambridge St
16 Liverpool, Edge Hill L7, L69 67 F8
Liverpool, Wavertree L15 68 D8
Prescot L34 56 D6
Cambridge Wlks 6 PR8 4 B7
Camdale Cl L28 55 B7
Camden Mews CH49 65 B4
Camden Pl 1 CH41 66 E6
Camden St L3 90 C4
Camelford Rd L11 40 C5
Camelia Ct L17 68 A2
Camellia Gdns WA9 59 B7
Camelot Cl WA12 45 F4
Camelot Terr 8 L20 38 B4
Cameo Cl L6 53 B4
Cameron Ct WA2 61 A4
Cameron Rd CH46 50 B3
Cameron St L7 53 C2
Cammell Ct CH43 66 B6
Camm St WN2 36 B8
Campania St L19 81 C4
Campbell Cres
Kirkby L33 29 D6
Warrington WA5 74 F6
Campbell Dr L14 54 E3
Campbell Sq L1 90 B2
Campbell St
Bootle L20 38 B3
Liverpool L1 90 B2
St Helens WA10 43 E4
Campbeltown Rd CH41 66 F4
Camperdown St CH41 66 F6
Camphill Rd L25 82 A9
Campion Cl WA11 44 B7
Campion Gr WN4 34 F4
Campion Way L36 70 F7
Camp Rd
Garswood WN4 34 E4
Liverpool L25 70 B1
Campsey Ash WA8 72 F4
Cam St L25 69 F2
Canada Bvd L3 52 B1
Canal Bank Cotts L31 20 C7
Canal Bank Pygons Hill L31 20 C7
Canalside Gr L5 52 C5
Canal St
Bootle L20 38 B2
Newton-le-W WA12 45 F3
St Helens WA10 43 F2
Canal View L31 29 A3
Canal View Ct L21 27 A2
Canberra Ave
St Helens WA9 57 E8
Warrington WA2 61 D3
Canberra La L11 40 C5
Canberra Sq WA2 61 D2
Candia Twr L5 52 E6
Candleston Cl WA5 60 E1
Canning Pl L1 90 A2
Canning Rd PR9 5 A6
Canning St
Birkenhead CH41 66 F7
2 Crosby L22 26 D1
Liverpool L8 67 F7
Canniswood Rd WA11 45 A6
Cannock Gn L31 20 B1
Cannon Hill CH43 66 B6
Cannon Mount CH43 66 B6
Cannon St WA9 58 C3
Canon Rd L6 53 C7
Canon St WA7 84 F3
Canon Wilson Cl WA11 45 D6
Canova Cl L27 70 F4
Canrow La L34 41 E5
Cansfield Gr WN4 35 A4
Cansfield High Specialist Language Coll WN4 35 A4
Cansfield St WA10 44 A4
Canterbury Ave
Crosby L22 26 D3
Golborne WA3 36 D1
Canterbury Cl
Aintree L10 28 E2
Formby L37 9 F5
Prescot L34 56 E7
Southport PR8 3 F4
Canterbury Pk L18 81 C8
Canterbury Rd
Birkenhead CH42 67 A1
Wallasey CH44 51 C3
Widnes WA8 84 C8
Canterbury St
Liverpool, Garston L19 81 D4
Liverpool L3 52 E3
St Helens WA10 43 E5
Canterbury Way
Litherland L30 27 F4
1 Liverpool L3 52 F3
Canter Cl L9 39 D8
Cantlow Fold PR8 7 A4
Cantsfield St L7 68 C7
Canvey Cl L15 69 B7
Capella Cl L17 80 E7
Cape Rd L9 39 C6
Capesthorne Cl WA8 84 E8
Capesthorne Rd WA2 61 D2
Capilano Pk L39 21 C8
Capitol Trad Est L33 30 C2
Caplin Cl L33 29 E6
Capper Gr L36 55 E3
Capricorn Cres L14 55 A5
Capricorn Way L20 38 B4
Capstick Cres L25 70 B6
Captains Cl L30 38 D8
Captains Gn L30 38 D8
Captain's La
Ashton-in-M WN4 35 C3
Bootle L30 38 E8
Caradoc Rd L21 38 A6
Caravan Pk The WA9 58 A8
Caraway Cl L23 27 B5
Caraway Gr WA10 43 D4
Carbis Cl L10 40 B6
Carden Cl L4 52 E7
Cardiff St WN8 15 D1
Cardiff Way L19 81 B6
Cardigan Ave CH41 66 D6
Cardigan Cl
St Helens WA10 43 F2
Warrington WA5 60 D2
Cardigan Rd
Southport PR8 3 F1
Wallasey CH45 51 B7
Cardigan St L15 68 D8
Cardigan Way
Litherland L30 28 B4
Liverpool L6 53 B4
Cardinal Heenan RC High Sch L12 54 D5
Cardus Cl CH46 64 B8
Cardwell Rd L19 81 D6
Cardwell St L7 68 B8
Carey Ave CH63 78 D6
Carey St WA8 73 B1
Carfax Rd L33 30 A4
Carfield WN8 24 E6
Cargill Gr CH42 79 B8
Carham Rd CH47 63 C6
Carillion Cl L11 40 C3
Carina Ct L17 80 F7
Carisbrooke Cl CH48 75 C8
Carisbrooke Dr PR9 1 F1
Carisbrooke Pl L4 38 F1
Carisbrooke Rd L20, L4 38 E1
Carkington Rd L25 70 C1
Carlake Gr L9 39 D3
Carland Cl L10 40 B6
Carlaw Rd CH42 66 A2
Carleen Cl L17 68 B2
Carleton House Prep Sch L18 68 F3
Carlett Bvd CH62 88 F5
Carley Wlk L24 82 E3
Carlile Way L33 29 F6
Carlingford Cl L8 68 A7
Carlisle Ave L30 27 F1
Carlisle Cl L4 53 D8
Carlisle Mews 16 CH43 66 C5
Carlisle Rd PR8 4 A2
Carlis Rd L32 40 F8
Carlow Cl L24 83 D2
Carlow St WA10 43 D1
Carl's Way L33 30 A6
Carlton Ave WN8 25 A7
Carlton Cl
Ashton-in-M WN4 35 A5
Neston CH64 86 C2
Carlton La
Hoylake CH47 63 C8
Liverpool L13 54 A4
Carlton Mt CH42 66 E3
Carlton Rd
Bebington CH63 79 B4
Birkenhead CH42 66 C4
Golborne WA3 36 D1
Southport PR8 7 C6
Wallasey CH45 51 B7
Carlton St
Liverpool L3 52 B4
5 Prescot L34 56 D6
St Helens WA10 43 E3
Carlton Terr CH47 63 C8
Carlyon Way L26 82 E9
Carmarthen Cl WA5 60 D2
Carmarthen Cres L8 67 D6
Carmel Cl
Ormskirk L39 13 D2
8 Wallasey CH45 51 B8
Carmel Coll WA10 43 B1
Carmel Ct WA8 73 B4
Carmelite Cres WA10 43 A5
Carmichael Ave CH49 64 D2
Carnaby Cl L36 71 A8
Carnarvon Ct L9 39 A3
Carnarvon Rd
Liverpool L9 39 A3
Southport PR8 3 F1
Carnarvon St WA9 57 D8
Carnatic Cl L18 68 F3
Carnatic Ct L18 68 E3
Carnatic Rd L17, L18 68 E3
Carnation Rd L9 39 B3
Carneghie Ct 1 PR8 3 F4
Carnegie Ave L23 26 D3
Carnegie Cres WA9 58 E8
Carnegie Dr WN4 35 A5
Carnegie Rd L13 53 E4
Carnforth Ave L32 29 F1
Carnforth Cl
7 Birkenhead CH41 66 C5
Liverpool L12 40 C1
Carnforth Rd L18 69 C2
Carno St L15 68 E8
Carnoustie Cl
Liverpool L12 54 F6
Southport PR8 3 F4
Wallasey CH46 49 B1
Carnoustie Gr WA11 45 A5
Carnsdale Rd CH46 64 F8
Carol Dr CH60 86 C8
Carole Cl WA9 58 E6
Carolina St L20 38 C3
Caroline Pl CH43 66 B5
Caronia St L19 81 C4
Carpathia St L19 81 C4
Carpenter's La CH48 63 B2
Carpenters Row L1 90 B2
Carraway Rd L11 40 C6
Carr Bridge Rd CH49 65 C3
Carr Cl L11 40 B2
Carr Croft L21 27 B3
CARR CROSS 5 D1
Carrfield Ave L23 27 A3
Carr Gate CH46 64 C7
Carr Hey CH46 64 B7
Carr Hey Cl CH49 65 C2
Carr House La
Birkenhead CH46 64 B8
Ince Blundell L38 18 E4
Carriage Cl L24 83 D1
Carrick Ct L23 27 A3
Carrickmore Ave L18 69 A2
Carrington Rd CH45 51 C6
Carrington St CH41 66 A8
Carr La
Hale L24, WA8 83 E4
Hoylake CH47 63 B6
Huyton-w-R L36 55 C1
Liverpool L11 40 A2
Maghull L31 19 F5
Carr La *continued*
Prescot L34 56 B5
Southport PR8 7 F7
Wallasey CH46, CH47 49 A1
West Kirby CH48 63 E5
Carr La E L11 40 B3
Carr La Ind Est CH47 63 C6
Carr Meadow Hey L30 27 C3
CARR MILL 33 C1
Carr Mill Cres WN5 33 E4
Carr Mill Prim Sch WA11 33 C1
Carr Mill Rd
Billinge WA11, WN5 33 D3
St Helens WA11 44 C8
Carr Moss La
Haskayne L39 12 B8
Southport L39 8 D2
Carrock Rd CH62 79 E2
Carroll Cres L39 13 F7
Carrow Cl CH46 64 B7
Carr Rd L20 38 D7
Carr's Cres L37 9 E1
Carr's Cres W L37 9 D1
Carr Side La L29 19 A3
Carr St WA10 43 D5
Carrs Terr L35 56 D3
Carruthers St L3 52 C3
Carrville Way L12 41 A3
Carrwood Cl WA11 45 A6
Carrwood Pk PR8 4 B4
Carsdale Rd L18 69 A5
Carsgoe Rd CH47 63 C6
Carsington Rd L11 40 A2
Carstairs Rd L6 53 D4
Carsthorne Rd CH47 63 C6
Cartbridge La L26, L35 71 A2
Carter Ave WA11 32 A5
Carter St L8 67 F6
Carters The
Birkenhead CH49 64 C4
Litherland L30 28 A4
Carterton Rd CH47 63 C6
Cartier Cl WA5 60 C1
Cartmel Ave
Maghull L31 20 E2
Warrington WA2 61 C3
Cartmel Cl
11 Birkenhead CH41 66 C5
Huyton-w-R L36 55 D4
Southport PR8 4 F3
Warrington WA5 60 E2
Cartmel Dr
Birkenhead CH46 64 E7
Formby L37 10 B2
Liverpool L12 40 C1
Rainhill L35 57 A4
Cartmell Ave WA10 43 E7
Cartmel Rd L36 55 C4
Cartmel Terr L11 40 C3
Cartmel Way L36 55 C4
Cartwright Cl WA11 31 F6
Cartwright Ct WA11 31 F7
Cartwrights Farm Rd L24 82 A5
Carver St L3 52 F3
Caryl Gr L8 67 E4
Caryl St
Liverpool L8 67 D6
Liverpool L8 67 E4
Liverpool, Toxteth L8 67 D5
Cascade Rd L24 82 C7
Case Gr L35 56 E5
Case Rd WA11 45 D6
Cases St L1 90 B3
Cashel Rd CH44 51 B2
Caspian Pl L20 38 C3
Caspian Rd L4 39 D2
Cassia Cl L9 39 B4
Cassino Rd L36 55 E3
Cassio St L20 38 E2
Cassley Rd L24 83 A3
Cassville Rd L15, L18 69 A6
Castell Gr WA10 43 F3
Castle Ave WA9 44 E3
Castlebridge Ct 5 CH42 66 F1
Castle Cl CH46 50 A3
Castle Ct 4 CH48 63 B1
Castle Dr
Formby L37 9 F1
Heswall CH60 85 F8
Castlefield Cl L12 54 A7
Castlefield Rd L12 54 A8
Castlefields CH46 49 F4
Castleford Rise CH46 49 E3
Castleford St L15 69 A7
Castlegate Gr L12 54 B7
Castle Gn WA5 60 B2
Castlegrange Cl CH46 49 E4
Castleheath Cl CH46 49 E3
Castlehey WN8 24 E6
Castle Hill
7 Liverpool L2 90 A3
Newton-le-W WA12 46 E4
Castle Keep L12 54 B7
Castle La L40 14 E5
Castle Mews L35 56 D4
Castle Rd CH45 51 A6
Castlerigg Ct CH42 66 C1
Castlesite Rd L12 54 B7
Castle St
Birkenhead CH41 66 F6
Liverpool L2 90 A3
Liverpool, Woolton Hill L25 69 F2
Southport PR9 4 B8
Widnes WA8 73 D1
Castleton Dr L30 28 B4
Castletown Cl L16 69 E8
Castleview Rd L12 54 B7
Castleway N CH46 50 A4
Castleway Prim Sch CH46 50 A4
Castleway S CH46 50 A3
Castlewell L35 56 F4
Castle Wlk PR8 4 A6
Castlewood Rd L6 53 B5
Castor St L6 53 B5
Catapult Too 4 WA10 44 A3
Catchdale Moss La WA10 42 E5
Catford Cl WA8 72 C2
Catford Gn L24 82 F4
Catfoss Cl WA2 61 E1
Catharine's La L39 13 F1
Catharine St L8 67 F8
Cathcart St CH41 66 D7
Cathcart Street Prim Sch CH41 66 D7
Cath CE (Cathedral Church of Christ)★ L1 90 C1
Cathedral Cl L1 90 C1
Cathedral Ct 1 L8 67 F7
Cathedral Gate L1 90 C2
Cathedral Rd 2 L6 53 C6
Cathedral Wlk L3 52 F1
Catherine Ct L21 38 B6
Catherine St
Birkenhead CH41 66 D6
Bootle L21 38 B6
Catherine Way
Newton-le-W WA12 46 B2
St Helens WA11 44 F6
Catkin Rd L26 70 D2
Caton Cl PR9 1 F4
Catonfield Rd L18 69 D5
Cat Tail La PR8 5 E1
Cattan Gn L37 10 B3
Catterall Ave
St Helens WA9 58 D6
Warrington WA2 61 D2
Catterick Cl L26 82 F9
Catterick Fold PR8 4 F3
Caulfield Dr CH49 64 E3
Caunce Ave
Golborne WA3 47 A7
Haydock WA11 45 B6
Newton-le-W WA12 46 C1
Causeway Cl CH62 79 B6
Causeway Ho CH46 49 E4
Causeway La L37 11 B1
Causeway The
Bebington CH62 79 B5
Liverpool L12 54 D4
Southport PR9 2 C5
Cavalier Dr L19 81 E5
Cavan Dr WA11 45 D7
Cavan Rd L11 53 E8
Cavell Cl L25 70 A1
Cavendish Ct
Liverpool L18 69 D3
Southport PR9 4 E8
5 Wallasey CH45 51 B8
Widnes WA8 72 F1
Cavendish Dr
Birkenhead CH42 66 D1
Liverpool L9 39 A3
Cavendish Gdns 8 L8 68 A5
Cavendish Rd
Birkenhead CH41 66 B7
Crosby L23 26 C3
Southport PR8 3 F3
3 Wallasey CH45 51 B8
Cavendish St
Birkenhead CH41 66 B8
7 Runcorn WA7 84 F2
Cavendish Wlk
Huyton-w-R L36 55 E2
Southport PR9 4 E8
Cavern Ct 6 L6 53 B3
Cavern Wlks L2 90 A3
Cawdor St
Liverpool L8 68 A6
Runcorn WA7 84 F3
Cawfield Ave WA8 72 D1
Cawthorne Ave L32 40 E8
Cawthorne Cl L32 40 E8
Cawthorne Wlk L32 40 E8
Caxton Cl
Birkenhead CH43 65 C6
Widnes WA8 72 C3
Caxton Rd L35 57 E1
Cazneau St L3 52 D3
'C' Ct WN4 35 B2
Cearns Ct CH43 66 A5
Cearns Rd CH43 66 A5
Cecil Dr WA10 43 A4
Cecil Rd
Bebington CH62 79 B8
Birkenhead CH42 66 B2
Seaforth L21 37 F6
Wallasey CH44 51 B4
Cecil St
Liverpool L15 68 D8
St Helens WA9 58 F7
Cedar Ave
Bebington CH63 78 E4
Golborne WA3 47 F7
Widnes WA8 73 B2
Cedar Cl
Liverpool L18 69 D3

Cedar Cl *continued*
Prescot L35 56 E4
Cedar Cres
Huyton-w-R L36 55 D1
Newton-le-W WA12 46 D2
Ormskirk L39 13 D4
Cedar Ct L34 41 C4
Cedardale Pk WA8 73 E4
Cedardale Rd L9 39 A4
Cedar Dr L37 9 C1
Cedar Gr
Crosby L22 26 D2
Downall Green WN4 34 D5
Haydock WA11 45 E7
Liverpool L8 68 C6
Maghull L31 28 D6
Orrell WN5 25 F6
Skelmersdale WN8 15 E1
Cedar Rd
Liverpool L9 39 B6
Prescot L35 56 D3
Warrington WA5 74 F6
Cedar St
Birkenhead CH41 66 D5
Bootle L20 38 C4
Newton-le-W WA12 46 C2
Southport PR8 4 D4
St Helens WA10 43 D2
Cedars The
Birkenhead CH46 64 C7
Liverpool L12 40 F3
Cedar Terr L8 68 C6
Cedar Twrs L33 29 F3
Cedarway CH60 86 B5
Cedarwood Cl CH49 64 B4
Cedarwood Ct L36 70 E8
Celandine Way WA9 59 B7
Celebration Dr L6 53 C5
Celendine Cl L15 68 E8
Celia St L20 38 D1
Celtic Rd CH47 48 E1
Celtic St [2] L8 68 A6
Celt St L6 53 C4
Cemeas Cl L3 52 C5
Cemetery Rd PR8 4 C4
Centenary Cl L4 53 C8
Central 12 Ret Pk PR9 4 C6
Central Ave
Bebington CH62 79 C1
Eccleston Park L34 57 A7
Liverpool L24 82 D4
Prescot L34 56 C5
Southport PR8 7 F8
Central Bldgs [2] L23 26 E4
Central Dr
Haydock WA11 45 B6
Liverpool L12 54 B5
Rainford WA11 31 F7
Central Liverpool Coll of F Ed L1 90 C2
Central Par L24 82 E4
Central Park Ave CH44 51 C4
Central Park Ct [5] CH44 51 B4
Central Rd
Bebington, New Ferry CH62 79 B6
Bebington, Port Sunlight CH62 79 C4
Central Sh Ctr L1 90 B3
Central Sq L31 20 D2
Central St WA10 44 A4
Central Sta L1 90 B3
Central Way
Liverpool L24 82 F3
Newton-le-W WA12 46 E2
Centreville Rd L15, L18 69 A6
Centre Way L36 55 E2
Centurion Cl CH47 48 E1
Centurion Dr CH47 48 E1
Century Bldgs L3 67 D5
Century Rd L23 26 D4
Ceres St L20 38 C1
Cestrian Dr CH61 77 A5
Chadlow Rd L32 40 F7
Chadwell Rd L33 29 F4
CHADWICK GREEN 33 D3
Chadwick Rd WA11 44 C7
Chadwick St
Birkenhead CH46 64 E8
Liverpool L3 52 B3
Chadwick Way L33 29 E6
Chaffinch Cl L12 40 F1
Chaffinch Glade L26 70 E1
Chainhurst Cl L27 70 D5
Chain La WA11 44 E6
Chain Lane Sh Prec WA11 44 D7
Chalfont Ct PR8 4 A3
Chalfont Rd L18 69 D1
Chalfont Way L28 55 B7
Chalgrave Cl WA8 73 F3
Chalkwell Dr CH60 86 C7
Challis St CH41 50 E1
Challoner Cl L36 70 F8
Chaloner Gr L19 80 F6
Chaloner St L1 90 B1
Chalon Way E WA10 44 A3
Chalon Way Ind Est WA10 44 A2
Chalon Way W WA10 44 A3
Chamberlain Dr L33 29 F5
Chamberlain St
Birkenhead CH41 66 F4
St Helens WA10 43 D3
Chamberlain St *continued*
Wallasey CH44 51 A2
Chambres Rd PR8 4 D5
Chambres Rd N PR8 4 D6
Chancellor Ct L8 68 A8
Chancel St L4 52 E7
Chancery La WA9 44 E3
Chandlers Ct WA7 84 E1
Chandlers Way WA9 58 B3
Chandler Way WA3 47 E8
Chandley Cl PR8 7 A5
Chandos St [9] L7 53 B1
Changford Gn L33 30 A3
Changford Rd L33 30 A3
Channell Rd L6 53 C3
Channel Rd L23 26 B3
Channel Reach L23 26 B3
Channel The CH45 50 E8
Chantrell Rd CH48 63 F2
Chantry Cl CH43 65 C6
Chantry The WA10 43 D6
Chantry Wlk
Ashton-in-M WN4 34 F5
Heswall CH60 86 A6
Chapel Alley L37 9 F3
Chapel Ave L9 39 A5
Chapel Ct
Hoylake CH47 63 C7
Liverpool L9 39 A4
St Helens WA10 43 D1
Chapel End Prim Sch WN5 33 E4
Chapel Gdns L5 52 D5
Chapelhill Rd CH46 64 F8
Chapel Ho
Maghull L31 20 D1
Seaforth L22 37 D8
CHAPEL HOUSE 15 E2
Chapelhouse Wlk L37 10 A3
Chapel La
Burtonwood WA5 59 F6
Formby L37 9 F3
Kirkby L31 29 A4
Litherland L30 27 F5
Litherland, Netherton L30 28 A5
Rainhill L35, WA9 57 E2
St Helens, Eccleston WA10 43 B4
Widnes WA8 72 C4
Chapel Mews L39 13 F4
Chapel Pl
[4] Ashton-in-M WN4 35 B3
Liverpool L19 81 C6
Chapel Rd
Hoylake CH47 63 C8
[3] Liverpool, Cabbage Hall L6 53 C6
Liverpool, Garston L19 81 C6
Warrington WA5 74 E3
Chapel St
Ashton-in-M WN4 35 B3
Haydock WA11 45 E6
Liverpool L3 90 A4
Newton-le-W WA12 46 B3
Ormskirk L39 13 F4
[10] Prescot L34 56 D6
Southport PR8 4 B7
St Helens WA10 43 F5
Chapel Terr L20 38 B3
Chapel View
Bebington CH62 89 A6
Crank WA11 32 F4
Chapel Yd L15 69 A7
Chapman Cl
Liverpool L8 67 E5
Widnes WA8 72 D4
Chapman Gr L34 56 E7
Chardstock Dr L25 70 C4
Charlecombe St CH42 66 D4
Charlecote St L8 67 F3
Charles Ave
Southport PR8 7 E6
Warrington WA5 74 F6
Charles Berrington Rd L15 69 A6
Charles Best Gn L30 27 F4
Charlesbye Ave L39 14 B6
Charlesbye Cl L39 14 B6
Charles Rd CH47 63 B6
Charles St
[2] Birkenhead CH41 66 D7
Golborne WA3 36 A1
St Helens WA10 44 A4
Charleston Rd L8 67 F4
Charlesville CH43 66 B5
Charlesville Ct [4] CH43 66 B5
Charles Wlk L14 54 F3
Charlesworth Cl L31 20 B5
Charley Wood Rd L33 30 C1
Charlock Cl L30 28 A4
Charlotte Rd CH44 51 D5
Charlotte's Mdw CH63 79 A4
Charlotte Way [6] L1 90 B3
Charlton Ct
Birkenhead CH43 65 F6
Liverpool L25 82 D8
Charlton Pl L13 54 A1
Charlton Rd L13 54 A1
Charlwood Ave L36 55 E1
Charlwood Cl CH43 65 C6
Charmalue Ave L23 26 F4
Charmouth Cl
[2] Liverpool L12 40 E3
Newton-le-W WA12 46 B4
Charnley Dr L15 69 C8
Charnley's La PR9 2 E7
Charnock Ave WA12 45 F3
Charnock Cotts L11 40 A3
Charnock Rd L9 39 D3
Charnwood Cl L12 40 D3
Charnwood Rd L36 55 B3
Charnwood St WA9 44 E4
Charon Way WA5 60 B3
Charter Ho CH44 51 D4
Charterhouse Cl L25 70 B1
Charterhouse Dr L10 28 E2
Charterhouse Rd L25 70 B1
Chartmount Way L25 70 B4
Chartwell Gr L26 70 F1
Chartwell Rd PR8 7 B6
Chase Cl PR8 3 F4
Chase Heys PR9 2 A1
Chaser Cl L9 39 C8
Chase The
Bebington CH63 88 C5
[5] Heswall CH60 86 A8
Huyton-w-R L36 70 F8
Chase Way L5 52 E4
Chatbrook Cl L17 80 F7
Chatburn Ave WA3 36 C1
Chater Cl L35 57 A5
Chatham Cl L21 37 F7
Chatham Ct L22 37 E8
Chatham Pl L7 53 B1
Chatham Rd CH42 67 A2
Chatham St L7, L69 67 F8
Chatsworth Ave
Liverpool L9 38 F5
Wallasey CH44 51 C4
Chatsworth Cl WN4 34 F4
Chatsworth Ct L7 53 D3
Chatsworth Dr
Liverpool L7 68 B8
Widnes WA8 72 C3
Chatsworth Rd
Birkenhead CH42 67 A2
Heswall CH61 76 F5
Rainhill L35 57 B4
Southport PR8 7 B6
Chatteriss Ct WA10 43 D1
Chatterton Rd L14 54 C4
Chaucer Dr L12 40 F2
Chaucer Rd WA10 43 D6
Chaucer St
Bootle L20 38 A4
Liverpool L3 52 D3
Cheadle Ave L13 53 F4
Cheapside
Formby L37 10 A2
Liverpool L2 90 A4
Cheapside Alley [4] L2 90 A4
Cheddar Cl L25 69 F2
Cheddar Gr
Burtonwood WA5 59 F7
Kirkby L32 40 E7
Cheddon Way CH61 76 E4
Chedworth Dr WA8 72 C4
Chedworth Rd L14 54 E4
Cheldon Rd L12 40 C2
Chelford Ave WA3 47 D8
Chelford Cl CH43 65 C7
Chellowdene L23 27 A6
Chelmarsh Ave WN4 35 C3
Chelmsford Cl [8] L4 52 D7
Chelsea Ct L12 54 E8
Chelsea Lea L9 38 F6
Chelsea Rd
Bootle L21 38 B6
Liverpool L9 39 A6
Cheltenham Ave L17 68 D6
Cheltenham Cl L10 28 E1
Cheltenham Cres
Huyton-w-R L36 55 D1
Wallasey CH46 49 E3
Cheltenham Dr
Longshaw WN5 25 D2
Newton-le-W WA12 46 C5
Cheltenham Rd CH45 50 E6
Cheltenham Way PR8 4 F3
Chelwood Ave L14, L16 54 E1
Chelwood Pk WA12 35 B1
Chemical St WA12 46 B3
Chemistry Rd L24 82 C6
Chenotrie Gdns CH43 65 D5
Chepstow Ave CH44 51 C4
Chepstow Cl WA5 60 E3
Chepstow St L4 38 F1
Chequer Cl WN8 24 F5
Chequer La WN8 24 F6
Chequers Gdns L19 68 F1
Cheriton Ave CH48 63 D2
Cheriton Cl L26 82 E9
Cheriton Pk PR8 4 E3
Chermside Rd L17 68 E1
Cherry Ave L4 39 B1
Cherrybank CH44 51 B2
Cherry Cl
Liverpool L4 39 B1
Newton-le-W WA12 45 F4
Cherrycroft WN8 24 E6
Cherrydale Rd L18 69 A4
Cherryfield Cres L32 29 E2
Cherryfield Dr L32 29 E2
Cherryfield Prim Sch L32 40 E7
Cherry Gdns
Hoylake CH47 63 B7
Kirkby L32 40 F7
Cherry Gn L39 13 B1
Cherry La L4 53 D8
Cherry Rd PR8 7 D2
Cherry Sq [2] CH44 51 B4
Cherrysutton WA8 72 B3
Cherrysutton Mews WA8 72 B4
Cherry Tree Ave WA5 74 F4
Cherry Tree Cl
Hale L24 83 E1
Haydock WA11 45 A5
Prescot L35 56 D3
Cherry Tree Cotts WA11 33 A2
Cherry Tree Dr WA9 45 A2
Cherry Tree La
Billinge WA11 33 A2
Ormskirk L39 13 B1
Cherry Tree Mews [3] CH60 86 A8
Cherry Tree Rd
Birkenhead CH46 64 F8
Golborne WA3 47 F8
Huyton-w-R L36 70 E8
Cherry Vale L25 70 B3
Cherry View L33 30 A5
Cherrywood Ave L26 71 B1
Cherwell Cl WA2 61 D2
Cheryl Dr WA8 73 D1
Cheshire Acre CH49 65 A2
Cheshire Ave L10 40 B7
Cheshire Cl WA12 46 E3
Cheshire Gdns WA10 43 E2
Cheshire Gr CH46 64 E7
Cheshire Lines Path L39 10 E6
Cheshire Way CH61 76 F3
Chesnell Gr L33 29 F5
Chesney Cl L8 67 E6
Chesnut Gr
Birkenhead CH42 66 D4
Bootle L20 38 B4
Chesnut Rd L21 37 F8
Chester Ave
Golborne WA3 47 D8
Litherland L30 27 F1
Southport PR9 4 F8
Chester Cl L23 27 B4
Chester Ct CH63 78 F4
Chester Dr WN4 35 D2
Chesterfield Cl PR8 7 C4
Chesterfield Dr L33 29 E5
Chesterfield High Sch L23 27 A4
Chesterfield Rd
Bebington CH62 88 D4
Crosby L23 27 A4
Southport PR8 7 C5
Chesterfield St L8 90 C1
Chester High Rd CH64 86 E4
Chester La WA9 58 B4
Chester Rd
Heswall CH60, CH64 86 C6
Hooton CH66 89 A1
Huyton-w-R L36 56 A4
Liverpool L6 53 D5
Southport PR9 4 F8
Chester Row WA12 60 D8
Chester St
Birkenhead CH41 66 F6
Liverpool L8 90 C1
Prescot L34 56 D6
Wallasey CH44 51 A3
Widnes WA8 73 B1
Chesterton Dr WA2 61 A5
Chesterton St L19 81 C4
Chester Wlk L36 56 A4
Chestnut Ave
Crosby L23 26 F6
Huyton-w-R L36 70 D8
St Helens WA11 44 F5
Warrington WA5 74 F6
Widnes WA8 73 B2
Chestnut Cl
Birkenhead CH49 64 C2
Prescot L35 56 E4
Chestnut Ct
Bootle L20 38 B4
[3] Ormskirk L39 13 F6
Widnes WA8 72 D1
Chestnut Gr
Ashton-in-M WN4 35 D4
Bebington CH62 88 C8
Bootle L20 38 B5
Golborne WA3 47 F8
Liverpool L15 69 A8
St Helens WA11 44 D7
Chestnut Grange L39 13 D3
Chestnut Ho [1] L20 38 B4
Chestnut Lodge Specl Sch WA8 72 E1
Chestnut Rd L9 39 C3
Chestnut St
Liverpool L7 52 F1
Southport PR8 4 C5
Chestnut Tree Sch L23 26 E4
Chestnut Way L37 9 C1
Chestnut Wlk L31 29 A4
Cheswood Cl L35 56 E2
Cheswood Ct [4] CH49 65 A2
Chetham Ct WA2 61 A3
Chetwode Ave WN4 35 B1
Chetwood Ave L23 26 F5
Chetwood Cl WA12 46 B5
Chetwood Dr WA8 72 F4
Chetwynd Cl CH43 65 F4
Chetwynd Rd CH43 66 A5
Chetwynd St L17 68 B3
Chetwyn Ho [5] CH48 63 B1
Chevasse Wlk L25 70 C3
Cheverton Cl CH49 65 B3
Chevin Rd L9 39 A5
Cheviot Ave
St Helens WA9 44 F3
Warrington WA2 61 A3
Cheviot Cl CH42 66 D1
Cheviot Rd
Birkenhead CH42 66 D1
Liverpool L7 53 E2
Cheviot Way L33 29 F6
Cheyne Cl L23 26 A3
Cheyne Gdns L19 80 F8
Cheyne Wlk WA9 57 F6
Chichester Cl L15 68 D8
Chidden Cl CH49 64 C3
Chigwell Cl L12 40 E3
Chilcott Rd L14 54 C3
Childers St [1] L13 54 A3
CHILDWALL 69 E7
Childwall Abbey Rd L16 69 E7
Childwall Ave
Birkenhead CH46, CH49 64 D7
Liverpool L15 68 D7
Childwall Bank Rd L16 69 D7
Childwall CE Prim Sch L16 69 D5
Childwall Cl CH46 64 D7
Childwall Cres L16 69 D7
Childwall Five Ways L15 69 C7
Childwall Gn CH49 65 A2
Childwall La
Huyton-w-R L14 55 A2
Liverpool L16, L25 69 F6
Childwall Mount Rd L16 69 D7
Childwall Par L14 55 A2
Childwall Park Ave L16 69 E6
Childwall Priory Rd L16 69 D7
Childwall Rd L15 69 B7
Childwall Sch L15 69 C7
Childwall Valley Prim Sch L25 70 A7
Childwall Valley Rd L16, L25, L27 70 C6
Chilhem Cl [3] L8 67 F4
Chilington Ave WA8 84 D8
Chillerton Rd L12 54 D8
Chillingham St [1] L8 68 A3
Chiltern Cl
Ashton-in-M WN4 35 C2
Kirkby L32 29 C4
Liverpool L12 40 F2
Chiltern Cres WA2 61 A3
Chiltern Dr L32 29 C4
Chiltern Pl WA2 61 A3
Chiltern Rd
Birkenhead CH42 66 C1
Southport PR8 7 B6
St Helens WA9 45 A3
Warrington WA2 61 A3
Chilton Cl L31 20 D1
Chilton Ct L31 20 D1
Chilton Mews L31 20 D1
Chilwell Cl WA8 72 D4
Chimes Rd WN4 34 F6
China Farm La CH48 63 E3
Chindit Cl L37 9 D2
Chippenham Ave CH49 64 C3
Chipping Ave PR8 7 A5
Chirkdale St L4 38 E1
Chirk Way CH46 64 F7
Chirton Cl WA11 45 D7
Chisenhale St L3 52 C4
Chisledon Cl WA11 45 D7
Chislehurst Ave L25 70 B6
Chislet Ct WA8 72 E4
Chisnall Ave WA10 43 C4
Chiswell St L7 53 C2
Cholmley Dr WA12 46 E2
Cholmondeley Rd CH48 63 B2
Cholsey Cl CH49 64 F4
Chorley Cl PR9 2 F5
Chorley Rd L34 56 B6
Chorley's La WA8 73 E3
Chorley St WA10 43 F4
Chorley Way CH63 79 A1
Chorlton Cl L16 69 F8
Chorlton Gr CH45 50 D5
Christ Church CE Prim Sch
Birkenhead CH41 66 C5
Birkenhead, Moreton CH46 64 E8
Bootle L20 38 D4
Christchurch Rd CH43 66 B4
Christiana Hartley Maternity Hospl PR8 4 D5
Christian Fellowship Sch L7 68 B8
Christian St L3 52 E3
Christie Cl CH66 89 A2
Christie St WA8 73 D1
Christleton Cl CH43 65 D2
Christmas St L20 38 D1
Christopher Cl
Liverpool L16 69 D8
Rainhill L35 57 B2
Christopher Dr CH62 89 A5
Christophers Cl CH61 77 A4
Christopher St L4 52 F8
Christopher Taylor Ho L31 28 D8
Christopher Way L16 69 D8
Christowe Wlk L11 40 C5

Creek The CH45 50 E8
Cremona Cnr 3 L22 26 E1
Cremorne Hey L28 55 B7
Crescent Ave
Ashton-in-M WN4 35 A4
Formby L37 9 E1
Crescent Ct 6 L21 38 A6
Crescent Gn L39 13 B1
Crescent Rd
Crosby L23 26 B5
Liverpool L9 39 B4
Seaforth L21 38 A6
Southport PR8 3 F3
Wallasey CH44 51 C4
Crescents The L35 57 A4
Crescent The
Bebington CH63 78 E5
Birkenhead CH49 64 D3
Bootle L20 38 E6
Crosby, Thornton L23 27 A6
Crosby, Waterloo L22 26 E1
Heswall, Gayton CH60 86 B6
Heswall, Pensby CH61 76 F6
Huyton-w-R L36 56 B2
Liverpool L24 82 C5
Maghull L31 28 C6
Prescot L35 56 F4
Southport PR9 2 C3
West Kirby CH48 63 A2
Cressida Ave CH63 78 E7
Cressingham Rd 2 CH45 51 B8
Cressington Ave CH42 66 D1
Cressington Espl L19 81 A6
CRESSINGTON PARK 81 B6
Cressington Sta L19 81 A7
Cresson CH43 65 F5
Cresswell Cl
Liverpool L26 71 A1
Warrington WA5 60 D2
Cresswell St 7 L6 53 A4
Cresstor Rd L25 69 F3
Creswell St WA10 43 E3
Cretan Rd L15 68 D7
Crete Twr L5 52 E6
Crewe Gn CH49 65 A2
Cricket Cl L19 81 D4
Cricket Path
Formby L37 9 F5
Southport PR8 3 F3
Cricklade Cl L20 38 B4
Cringles Dr L35 71 A7
Crispin Rd L27 70 E5
Crispin St WA10 43 E3
Critchley Rd L24 83 A3
Critchley Way L33 29 F5
Crockett's Wlk WA10 43 B5
Crockleford Ave PR8 4 E3
Crocus Ave CH41 65 F7
Crocus Gdns WA9 59 A7
Crocus St L5 52 D7
Croft Ave
Bebington CH62 79 D1
Golborne WA3 35 F2
Orrell WN5 25 D5
Croft Ave E CH62 79 D2
Croft Bsns Pk CH62 79 E2
Croft Cl CH43 65 E4
Croft Ct PR9 2 C4
Croft Dr
Birkenhead CH46 64 F7
West Kirby CH48 75 C7
Croft Dr E CH48 75 E6
Croft Dr W CH48 75 C7
Croft Edge CH43 66 B3
Croft End WA9 44 F1
Crofters La L33 30 A5
Crofters The CH49 64 D4
Croft Field L31 20 E1
Croft Gn CH62 79 D3
Croft Heys L39 13 B1
Croft La
Bebington CH62 79 D1
Liverpool L9 39 D7
Croftlands WN5 25 D4
Crofton Cres L13 54 B3
Crofton Rd
Birkenhead CH42 66 E3
Liverpool L13 54 B3
Runcorn WA7 84 E1
Croftson Ave L39 13 F7
Croft St WA3 47 A8
Croftsway CH60 85 D8
Croft The
Birkenhead CH49 64 D2
Huyton-w-R L28 55 A8
Kirkby L32 40 F7
Liverpool L12 54 B7
Maghull L31 20 B5
Orrell WN5 25 D3
St Helens WA9 44 F1
Croft Way L23 27 B5
Croftwood Gr L35 56 E2
Cromarty Rd
Liverpool L13 53 F3
3 Wallasey CH44 50 F4
Cromdale Gr WA9 44 E2
Cromdale Way WA5 74 E6
Cromer Dr CH45 51 A5
Cromer Rd
Hoylake CH47 63 A7
Liverpool L17 68 E1
Southport PR8 3 E2
Cromer Way L26 82 F7
Cromfield L39 13 C2
Cromford Rd L36 55 E5
Crompton Ct
Ashton-in-M WN4 35 B2
Crompton Ct *continued*
Liverpool L18 69 D5
Crompton Dr
Liverpool L12 40 E3
Winwick WA2 61 A6
Cromptons La L16, L18 69 D5
Crompton St L5 52 D5
Cromwell Cl
Newton-le-W WA12 46 A4
Ormskirk L39 13 C2
Cromwell Rd 6 L4 38 F2
Crondall Gr L15 69 B7
CRONTON 72 D5
Cronton Ave
Prescot L35 56 C1
Wallasey CH46 49 F3
Cronton CE Prim Sch
WA8 72 C6
Cronton Farm Ct WA8 72 E4
Cronton La
Rainhill L35, WA8 57 B1
Widnes WA8 72 F5
Cronton Park Ave WA8 72 C6
Cronton Park Cl WA8 72 C6
Cronton Rd
Cronton L35, WA8 72 C5
Huyton-w-R L35, L36 71 B7
4 Liverpool L15 69 A5
Cronulla Dr WA5 74 E7
Crookall St WN4 35 C4
Crookhurst Ave WN5 33 D6
Croome Dr CH48 63 D2
Croppers Hill WA10 43 E3
Croppers Hill Ct WA10 43 E3
Cropper's La L39 14 A1
Croppers Rd WA2 61 F3
Cropper St L1 90 C3
Cropton Rd L37 9 F3
CROSBY 26 D6
Crosby Cl CH49 64 F6
Crosby Gn L12 54 A7
Crosby Gr
St Helens WA10 43 D1
Willaston CH64 88 B1
Crosby High Sch L23 26 E6
Crosby Rd PR8 4 A3
Crosby Rd N L22 26 E1
Crosby Rd S L21 37 F7
Crosender Rd L23 26 C3
Crosfield Cl 5 L7 53 C1
Crosfield Rd
Liverpool L7 53 C1
Prescot L35 56 F4
Wallasey CH44 51 C3
Crosfield Wlk 4 L7 53 C1
Crosgrove Rd L4 39 C1
Crosland Rd L32 30 A1
Crossacre Rd L25 70 B7
Cross Barn La L38 18 E3
Crossdale Rd
Bebington CH62 88 D5
Crosby L23 26 C3
Crossdale Way WA11 33 B1
CROSSENS 2 C4
Crossens Way PR9 2 C6
Cross Farm Prim Sch
L27 70 F4
Cross Farm Rd WA9 44 C1
Crossfield Rd WN8 24 C8
Crossford Rd L14 55 A5
Crossgates WA8 73 F3
Cross Gn L37 10 A2
Cross Green Cl L37 10 A2
Crosshall Brow L40 14 C4
Cross Hall Ct L39 14 A4
Crosshall St L1, L2 90 B4
Cross Hey L21 27 B2
Cross Hey Ave CH43 65 D5
Cross Hillocks La L35,
WA8 71 E3
Crossings The WA12 46 C3
Cross La
Bebington CH63 78 F4
Newton-le-W WA12 46 B4
Orrell WN5 25 D3
Prescot L35 56 D4
Wallasey CH45 50 D4
Crossledge Way L16 69 F7
Crossley Dr
Heswall CH60 85 D8
Liverpool L15 69 B8
Crossley Rd WA10 43 D1
Cross Meadow Ct WA9 44 C2
Cross Pit La WA11 31 F6
Cross St
Bebington CH62 79 B5
Birkenhead CH41 66 F6
Crosby L22 26 D1
Golborne WA3 47 A7
Prescot L34 56 E7
Southport PR8 4 B6
6 St Helens WA10 44 A3
Widnes WA8 73 C1
Cross The
Bebington CH62 79 D1
Ince Blundell L38 18 E4
Crossvale Rd L36 55 E1
Crossway
Birkenhead CH43 65 E8
Widnes WA8 84 D8
Crossway Cl WN4 35 E5
Crossways
Bebington CH62 79 D3
Liverpool L25 69 F6
Crossway The CH63 87 C4
Crosswood Cres L36 55 C3
Crosthwaite Ave CH62 88 F4
Croston Ave L35 57 B5
Croston Cl WA8 72 C3
Croston's Brow PR9 1 F3
Crouch St
9 Liverpool L5 53 A6
St Helens WA9 58 D8
Crowe Ave WA2 61 B2
Crow La WN8 16 F3
Crowland Cl PR9 5 A6
Crowland St PR9 5 A6
Crowland Way L37 10 B2
Crow Lane E WA12 46 C4
Crow Lane W WA12 46 A4
Crowmarsh Cl CH49 64 F4
Crown Acres Rd L25 82 C9
Crown Ave WA8 84 B8
Crown Bldgs
3 Crosby L23 26 E4
Southport PR8 7 F8
Crown Cl L37 10 A2
Crown Fields Cl WA12 46 B5
Crown Gdns WA12 46 B4
Crown Park Dr WA12 46 B5
Crown Rd L12 54 C7
Crown St
Liverpool, Edge Hill L7,
L8 68 A8
Liverpool L7 53 A1
Newton-le-W WA12 46 A3
St Helens WA9 57 D7
Crown Station Pl L8 68 A8
Crownway L36 55 D4
Crow Orchard Prim Sch
WN8 15 F2
Crow St L8 67 D6
Crowther St WA10 43 E3
CROW WOOD 73 D3
Crow Wood La WA8 73 D2
Crow Wood Pl WA8 73 D3
Crow Wood Rd WA3 36 D1
Croxdale Rd L14 55 A6
Croxdale Rd W
Huyton-w-R L14 55 A7
Liverpool L14 54 F7
CROXTETH 40 C4
Croxteth Ave
Bootle L21 38 B7
Rainford WA11 31 F7
Wallasey CH44 51 B4
Croxteth Cl L31 20 E3
Croxteth Com Comp Sch
L11 40 C5
Croxteth Com Prim Sch
L11 40 D4
Croxteth Ct 4 L8 68 B6
Croxteth Ctry Pk* L12 40 D2
Croxteth Dr L17 68 D5
Croxteth Gate L17 68 C5
Croxteth Gr L8 68 C6
Croxteth Hall* L12 40 D1
Croxteth Hall La L11,
L12 40 C2
Croxteth La L28, L34 41 C1
Croxteth Rd
Bootle L20 38 B5
Liverpool L8 68 B5
Croxteth View L32 40 F6
Croyde Cl PR9 2 B5
Croyde Pl WA9 58 C4
Croyde Rd L24 83 A3
Croydon Ave L18 68 F5
Croylands St L4 52 E8
Crucian Way L12 40 D3
Crump St L1 90 C1
Crutchley Ave CH41 66 B8
Crystal Cl L13 54 A2
Cubbin Cres L5 52 D6
Cubert Rd L11 40 D4
Cuckoo Cl L25 70 A4
Cuckoo La L25 70 A5
Cuckoo Way L25 70 A4
Cuerden St L3 90 B4
CUERDLEY CROSS 74 A2
Cuerdley Gn WA5 74 A2
Cuerdley Rd WA5 74 C3
Cullen Ave L20 38 D5
Cullen Cl CH63 88 C4
Cullen Dr L21 38 A7
Cullen St L8 68 C7
Culme Rd L12 53 F7
Culzean Cl L12 40 E3
Cumber La L35 56 F3
Cumberland Ave
Birkenhead CH43 66 A2
Litherland L30 27 C3
Liverpool L17 68 D6
St Helens WA10 57 B8
Cumberland Cl L6 53 D7
Cumberland Cres
WA11 45 A6
Cumberland Gate L30 28 A3
Cumberland Rd
Southport PR8 4 D5
Wallasey CH45 51 C7
Cumberland St L1 90 A4
Cumbria Ct PR9 4 C7
Cumbria Way L12 40 C2
Cummings St L1 90 C2
Cummins Ave L37 9 E5
Cumpsty Rd L21 27 C1
Cunard Ave CH44 51 D5
Cunard Cl CH43 65 C6
Cunard Rd L21 38 B7
Cunliffe Ave WA12 46 B5
Cunliffe St L2 90 A4
Cunningham Cl
Warrington WA5 74 F5
West Kirby CH48 75 C6
Cunningham Dr
Bebington CH63 88 C7
Runcorn WA7 84 E1
Cunningham Rd
Liverpool L13 54 A2
Widnes WA8 84 D8
Cunscough La L31, L39 21 D3
Cuper Cres L36 55 D4
Curate Rd L6 53 C7
Curlender Cl CH41 50 E1
Curlender Way L24 83 E2
Curlew Ave CH49 64 D6
Curlew Cl
Birkenhead CH49 64 D6
Golborne WA3 47 D8
Curlew Ct CH46 49 C1
Curlew Gr L26 70 E1
Curlew Way CH46 49 C1
Currans Rd WA2 61 B2
Curran Way L33 29 D5
Curtana Cres L11 40 C3
Curtis Rd L4 39 C1
Curwell Cl CH63 79 B3
Curzon Ave
Birkenhead CH41 66 B7
1 Wallasey CH45 51 B7
Curzon Rd
Birkenhead CH42 66 B2
Crosby L22 26 E1
Hoylake CH47 63 A7
Southport PR8 4 E5
Curzon St 5 WA7 84 F1
Cusson Rd L33 30 B1
Custley Hey L28 55 B8
Cut La
Haskayne L39, L40 12 F6
Kirkby L33 41 F7
Cygnet Cl L39 13 C2
Cygnet Ct L33 30 A2
Cynthia Rd WA7 84 F1
Cypress Ave WA8 73 B2
Cypress Cl L31 29 A3
Cypress Croft CH63 79 B3
Cypress Gdns L35 57 C7
Cypress Rd
Huyton-w-R L36 70 D8
Southport PR8 4 F6
Cyprian's Way L30 27 E3
Cyprus Gr 5 L8 68 A4
Cyprus St L34 56 D6
Cyprus Terr 6 CH45 51 B7
Cyril Gr L17 68 E2

D

Dacre Ct 7 CH42 66 F1
DACRE HILL 78 F8
Dacre's Bridge La L35 71 D6
Dacre St
Birkenhead CH41 66 E6
Liverpool L20 38 B1
Dacy Rd L5 53 A6
Daffodil Cl WA8 73 E4
Daffodil Gdns WA9 59 A7
Daffodil Rd
Birkenhead CH41 65 F7
Liverpool L15 69 B7
Dagnall Ave WA5 60 F2
Dagnall Rd L32 29 D1
Dahlia Cl
Liverpool L9 39 B4
St Helens WA9 59 A7
Dailton Rd WN8 25 A7
Daintith Ct 9 CH42 66 F2
Dairy Farm Rd WA11 31 C7
Dairylands Cl L16 69 C6
Daisy Ave WA12 46 C2
Daisy Bank Rd WA5 74 F4
Daisy Mews L21 38 B6
Daisy Mount L31 28 E8
Daisy St L5 52 D7
Daisy Way PR8 4 C2
Dakin Wlk L33 29 F2
Dakota Dr L19 81 E3
Dalby Cl WA11 44 C5
Dale Acre Dr L21, L30 27 C3
Dale Ave
Bebington CH62 88 D8
Heswall CH60 76 F1
Dalebrook Cl L25 70 B7
Dale Cl
Maghull L31 20 C2
Widnes WA8 84 A8
Dale Cres WA9 58 D6
Dalecrest WN5 25 D1
Dale Ct
Heswall CH60 76 F1
Heswall CH60 85 F8
Dale End Rd CH61 77 C4
Dalegarth Ave L12 40 F1
Dale Gdns CH60 76 D1
Dalehead Pl WA11 33 B1
Dale Hey
Hooton CH66 88 E2
Wallasey CH44 51 B3
Dalehurst Cl CH44 51 D4
Dale La L33 30 B4
Dalemeadow Rd L14 54 D3
Dale Mews L25 70 B4
Dale Rd
Bebington CH62 88 D6
Golborne WA3 47 A7
Dale St (Queensway) L1,
L2 90 A4
Daleside Ave WN4 35 A8
Daleside Cl CH61 76 F6
Daleside Rd L33 29 F3
Daleside Wlk L33 29 F3
Dales Row L36 56 B2
Dale St L19 81 C5
Dalesway CH60 85 E8
Dales Wlk L37 10 A6
Dale The WA5 74 F5
Dale View WA12 46 E4
Dale View Cl CH61 77 A5
Dalewood L12 40 E3
Dalewood Gdns L35 56 F2
Daley Pl L20 38 E7
Daley Rd L21 27 C1
Dallam Com Prim Sch
WA5 60 F1
Dallas Gr 3 L9 39 A6
Dallington Ct 3 L13 54 B2
Dalmeny St L17 68 B3
Dalmorton Rd CH45 51 C8
Dalry Cres L32 40 F7
Dalrymple St L5 52 D5
Dalry Wlk L32 40 F7
Dalston Dr WA11 33 B1
DALTON 16 C5
Dalton Cl L12 40 C2
Dalton Gr WN4 35 A4
Dalton Rd CH45 51 C7
Dalton St Michael's CE
Prim Sch WN8 16 D5
Daltry Cl L12 54 A7
Damerham Mews L25 70 A7
Damfield La L31 28 D8
Damian Dr WA12 46 A5
Dam La
Ashton-in-M WN4 35 F3
Winwick WA3 61 F7
Damson Rd L27 70 E6
Damwood Rd L24 82 E3
Danbers WN8 24 F6
Danby Cl L5 52 F5
Danby Fold L35 57 B3
Dane Cl CH61 76 F6
Dane Ct L35 57 C3
Danefield Pl L19 81 D8
Danefield Rd
Birkenhead CH49 64 C2
Liverpool L19 81 D8
Danefield Terr L19 81 D7
Danehurst Rd
Liverpool L9 39 B7
Wallasey CH45 50 F7
Danesbury Cl WN5 33 E4
Danescourt Rd
Birkenhead CH41 66 A8
Liverpool L12 54 C5
Danescroft WA8 72 B3
Daneshill Cl L17 80 F7
Dane St L4 38 F1
Daneswell Dr CH46 49 F1
Daneswell Rd L24 83 A2
Daneville Rd L4 39 D2
Daneway PR8 7 B6
Danger La CH46 49 F1
Daniel Cl L20 38 A6
Daniel Davies Dr L8 68 A7
Daniels La WN8 24 C7
Dannette Hey L28 55 C7
Dansie St L3 52 F1
Dan's Rd WA8 73 E2
Dante Cl L9 39 C8
Danube St L7, L8 68 C7
Dapple Heath Ave 1
L31 29 A3
Darby Gr L19 81 B6
Darby Rd L19 81 A8
D'Arcy Cotts CH63 87 B6
Darent Rd WA11 45 B7
Daresbury Ave PR8 7 A5
Daresbury Cl L32 29 C2
Daresbury Ct WA8 73 E3
Daresbury Expressway 5
WA7 84 F2
Daresbury Rd
St Helens WA10 43 B5
Wallasey CH44 51 A4
Darfield WN8 24 F7
Dark Entry L34 41 E1
Dark La
Maghull L31 20 E1
Ormskirk L40 14 C6
Darley Ave WA2 61 E3
Darley Cl WA8 72 B3
Darley Ct L12 54 C6
Darleydale Dr CH62 88 F5
Darley Dr L12 54 C6
Darlington Cl CH44 51 D4
Darlington St CH44 51 D4
Darmond Rd L33 30 A3
Darmond's Gn CH48 63 B3
Darmonds Green Ave
L6 53 D7
Darnley St L8 67 E5
Darrel Dr L7 68 C7
Darsefield Rd L16 69 E7
Dartford Cl L14 54 F6
Dartington Rd L16 69 D8
Dartmouth Ave L10 28 C2
Dartmouth Dr
Litherland L30 27 C3
St Helens WA10 43 C6
Darvel Ave WN4 34 C4
Darwall Rd L19 81 D8
Darwen Gdns WA2 61 E1
Darwen St L5 52 B5
Darwick Dr L36 71 A8
Darwin Gr WA9 57 E7

Daryl Rd CH60 .... 86 A8
Daulby St L3 .... 52 F2
Dauntsey Brow L25 .... 70 B7
Dauntsey Mews L25 .... 70 B7
Davenham Ave CH43 .... 65 F3
Davenham Cl CH43 .... 65 F2
Davenham Ct L15 .... 69 B7
Davenham Rd L37 .... 9 F3
Davenhill Pk L10 .... 28 C2
Davenport Cl CH48 .... 75 C6
Davenport Gr 3 L33 .... 29 E4
Davenport Rd CH60 .... 85 E7
Daventree Rd 4 CH45 .... 51 B5
Daventry Rd L17 .... 68 E2
Davidson Rd L13 .... 54 A3
David St L8 .... 67 F4
Davids Wlk L25 .... 70 C3
Davies Ave WA12 .... 46 C4
Davies St
Bootle L20 .... 38 D4
Liverpool L1, L2 .... 90 A4
St Helens WA9 .... 44 C4
Davis Rd CH46 .... 50 B3
Davy Cl WA10 .... 43 B5
Davy St L5 .... 53 A6
Dawber Cl 4 L6 .... 53 A4
Dawber St WN4 .... 35 D4
Dawley Cl WN4 .... 35 A3
Dawlish Cl L25 .... 82 C9
Dawlish Dr PR9 .... 2 A5
Dawlish Rd
Irby CH61 .... 76 C5
Wallasey CH44 .... 51 A4
Dawlish Way WA3 .... 35 F1
Dawn Cl WA9 .... 57 E7
Dawn Wlk L10 .... 40 B6
Dawpool CE Prim Sch CH61 .... 76 B6
Dawpool Cotts CH48 .... 76 A6
Dawpool Dr
Bebington CH62 .... 88 C7
Birkenhead CH46 .... 64 E8
Dawpool Farm CH61 .... 76 B5
Dawson Ave
Birkenhead CH41 .... 66 B8
Southport PR9 .... 2 C5
St Helens WA9 .... 58 D7
Dawson Gdns L31 .... 20 C2
Dawson Rd L39 .... 13 F7
Dawson St L1 .... 90 B3
Dawson Way 12 L1 .... 90 B3
Dawstone Ct CH60 .... 85 F8
Dawstone Rd CH60 .... 86 A7
Dawstone Rise CH60 .... 85 F7
Daybrook WN8 .... 24 F7
Dayfield WN8 .... 25 B7
Days Mdw 1 CH49 .... 64 C3
Day St L13 .... 54 A3
Deacon Cl L22 .... 37 D8
Deacon Ct
Liverpool L25 .... 70 B2
Seaforth L22 .... 37 D8
Deacon Rd WA8 .... 73 B1
Deacon Trad Est WA12 .... 46 A2
Deakin St CH41 .... 65 F8
Dealcroft L25 .... 69 F2
Deanacres L25 .... 70 A2
Dean Ave CH45 .... 50 E6
Dean Cl
Billinge WN5 .... 33 D3
Up Holland WN8 .... 25 C7
Dean Cres WA2 .... 61 B2
Dean Ct WA3 .... 47 A7
Dean Dillistone Ct L1 .... 90 C1
Deane Rd L7 .... 53 C2
Dean Ho L22 .... 37 D8
Dean Mdw WA12 .... 46 C4
Dean Patey Ct L1 .... 90 C1
Dean Rd WA3 .... 47 A7
Deansburn Rd L13 .... 53 E6
Deanscales Rd L11 .... 40 A2
Deans Ct L37 .... 9 F5
Deansgate La L37 .... 10 B5
Deansgate La N L37 .... 10 A6
Dean St L22 .... 37 D8
Deansway WA8 .... 84 C8
Deans Way CH41 .... 65 F8
Dean Way WA9 .... 58 B2
Dean Wood Ave WN5 .... 25 E8
Deanwood Cl L35 .... 56 F2
Dearden Way WN8 .... 25 A7
Dearham Ave WA11 .... 44 B7
Dearne Cl L12 .... 54 E5
Dearnford Ave CH62 .... 88 D6
Dearnford Cl CH62 .... 88 D6
Dearnley Ave WA11 .... 44 E5
Deauville Rd L9 .... 39 C7
Debra Cl L31 .... 29 B4
Dee Cl L33 .... 29 F6
Dee Ct L25 .... 70 C3
Dee Ho L25 .... 70 C3
Dee La CH48 .... 63 A2
Deeley Cl L7 .... 53 C1
Dee Park Cl CH60 .... 86 B6
Dee Park Rd CH60 .... 86 B5
Deepdale WA8 .... 72 C3
Deep Dale WA5 .... 74 F6
Deepdale Ave
Billinge WA11 .... 33 C1
Bootle L20 .... 38 A5
Deepdale Cl CH43 .... 65 C6
Deepdale Dr L35 .... 57 D3
Deepdale Rd L25 .... 70 A7
Deepfield Dr L36 .... 70 F8
Deepfield Rd L15 .... 68 F6
Deepwood Gr L35 .... 56 E2
Deerbarn Dr L30 .... 28 B4
Deerbolt Cl L32 .... 29 C3
Deerbolt Cres L32 .... 29 C3
Deerbolt Way L32 .... 29 C3
Deerbourne Cl L25 .... 69 F2
Dee Rd L35 .... 57 B3
Dee Side CH60 .... 85 C8
Deeside Cl CH43 .... 65 B6
Deeside Ct CH64 .... 86 B1
Dee View Cotts CH64 .... 86 D1
Dee View Rd CH60 .... 85 F8
De Grouchy St CH48 .... 63 B3
De-Haviland Way WN8 .... 24 E8
De Havilland Dr L24 .... 81 E3
Deighton Cl WN5 .... 25 E6
Deirdre Ave WA8 .... 73 A1
Dekker Rd L33 .... 29 E6
Delabole Rd L11 .... 40 D5
Delafield Cl WA2 .... 61 F3
Delagoa Rd L10 .... 39 F6
Delamain Rd L13 .... 53 E6
Delamare Pl 1 WA7 .... 84 F1
Delamere Ave
Bebington CH62 .... 88 E4
Golborne WA3 .... 47 E6
St Helens WA9 .... 58 A3
Widnes WA8 .... 72 C1
Delamere Cl
Bebington CH62 .... 88 E4
Birkenhead CH43 .... 65 B6
Liverpool L12 .... 40 D3
Delamere Ct CH62 .... 88 E4
Delamere Gr 3 CH44 .... 51 E2
Delamere Rd
Skelmersdale WN8 .... 15 F2
Southport PR8 .... 7 B5
Delamere Way WN8 .... 25 A7
Delamore Pl L4 .... 38 E1
Delamore St L4 .... 38 E1
De La Salle RC High Sch L11 .... 40 B2
De La Salle Sch WA10 .... 43 B4
Delavor CH43 .... 65 E4
Delavor Cl CH60 .... 85 E8
Delavor Rd CH60 .... 85 E8
Delaware Cres L32 .... 29 C3
Delaware Rd L20 .... 38 C4
Delfby Cres L32 .... 30 A1
Delf La
Haskayne L39 .... 12 A4
Liverpool, Hunt's Cross L24 .... 82 B6
Liverpool, Walton on the Hill L4 .... 39 A2
Dell Cl CH63 .... 88 B6
Dell Ct CH43 .... 65 F1
Dellfield La L31 .... 20 E1
Dell Gr CH42 .... 79 B8
Dell La CH60 .... 86 B7
Dellside Cl WN4 .... 34 D5
Dellside Gr 4 WA9 .... 58 C8
Dell St 2 L7 .... 53 C2
Dell The
Birkenhead CH42 .... 67 B1
Liverpool L12 .... 54 E8
Up Holland WN8 .... 25 B7
Delph Cl L39 .... 13 C1
Delph Common Rd L39 .... 13 C1
Delph Ct L21 .... 38 A8
Delph Hollow Way WA9 .... 58 B8
Delph La
Formby L37 .... 9 C3
Ormskirk L39 .... 13 C1
Prescot L35 .... 56 F5
Warrington, Houghton Green WA2 .... 61 E6
Winwick WA2 .... 61 A5
Delph Mdw Gdns WN5 .... 33 D4
Delph Park Ave L39 .... 13 B1
Delph Rd L23 .... 26 D8
Delphside Cl WN5 .... 25 D5
Delph Side Com Prim Sch WN8 .... 24 C8
Delphside Rd WN5 .... 25 D5
Delph Top L39 .... 14 A6
Delphwood Dr WA9 .... 44 B1
Delta Cres WA5 .... 60 C2
Delta Dr L12 .... 54 E8
Delta Rd
Bootle L21 .... 38 B7
St Helens WA9 .... 44 F4
Delta Rd E CH42 .... 67 B1
Delta Rd W CH42 .... 67 B1
Deltic Pl L33 .... 30 B1
Deltic Way
Kirkby L33 .... 30 B1
Liverpool L30 .... 39 A8
Delves Ave CH63 .... 78 F3
Delyn Cl CH42 .... 66 E1
Demesne St CH44 .... 51 E3
Denbigh Ave
Southport PR9 .... 1 F3
St Helens WA9 .... 58 C7
Denbigh Rd
Liverpool L9 .... 38 F3
Wallasey CH44 .... 51 D3
Denbigh St L5 .... 52 B5
Dencourt Rd L11 .... 40 B1
Dene Ave WA12 .... 45 F4
Denebank Rd L4 .... 53 B7
Denecliff L28 .... 55 B8
Dene Ct L9 .... 39 F4
Denefield Ho PR8 .... 4 B6
Denehurst Cl WA5 .... 74 F4
Deneshey Rd CH47 .... 63 C8
Denes Way L28 .... 55 A7
Denford Rd L14 .... 54 F5
Denham Cl 1 L12 .... 41 A3
Denholme
Skelmersdale WN8 .... 24 F7
1 Up Holland WN8 .... 25 A7
Denise Ave WA5 .... 74 E5
Denise Rd L10 .... 40 B7
Denison Gr WA9 .... 57 E7
Denison St L3 .... 52 B3
Denman Dr L6 .... 53 C4
Denman Gr 4 CH44 .... 51 E2
Denman St 7 L7 .... 53 B3
Denman Way L6 .... 53 C4
Denmark Rd PR9 .... 2 A2
Denmark St L22 .... 26 D1
Dennett Cl L31 .... 28 D7
Dennett Rd L35 .... 56 C4
Denning Dr CH61 .... 76 D7
Dennis Ave WA10 .... 57 C7
Denny Cl CH49 .... 64 F4
Densham Ave WA2 .... 61 B2
Denshaw WN8 .... 24 F7
Denston Cl CH43 .... 65 B7
Denstone Ave L10 .... 28 D3
Denstone Cl L25 .... 82 B9
Dentdale Dr L5 .... 52 E4
Denton Dr CH45 .... 51 C6
Denton Gr L6 .... 53 C5
DENTON'S GREEN 43 D5
Dentons Green La WA10 .... 43 E5
Denton St
Liverpool L8 .... 67 F4
Widnes WA8 .... 73 C1
Dentwood St L8 .... 68 A4
Denver Rd L32 .... 29 C1
Depot Rd L33 .... 30 D4
Derby Bldgs L7 .... 53 B1
Derby Cl WA12 .... 46 B3
Derby Ct L37 .... 9 E5
Derby Dr WA11 .... 32 A5
Derby Gr L31 .... 28 D6
Derby Hill Cres L39 .... 14 A5
Derby Hill Rd L39 .... 14 A5
Derby Ho 2 L39 .... 13 F5
Derby La L13 .... 54 A4
Derby Rd
Birkenhead CH41, CH42 .... 66 D4
Bootle L20 .... 38 B2
Formby L37 .... 9 E5
Golborne WA3 .... 47 C8
Huyton-w-R L36 .... 55 E2
Liverpool L20 .... 52 C7
Skelmersdale WN8 .... 23 C8
Southport PR9 .... 4 C7
Wallasey CH45 .... 51 A6
Widnes, Barrowís Green WA8 .... 73 D4
Widnes, Lunts Heath WA8 .... 73 B4
Derby Row WA12 .... 60 D8
Derby St W L39 .... 13 E5
DERBYSHIRE HILL 45 A2
Derbyshire Hill Rd WA9 .... 45 A2
Derby Sq
Liverpool L1 .... 90 A3
8 Prescot L34 .... 56 E6
Derby St
Huyton-w-R L36 .... 56 A2
Liverpool, Garston L19 .... 81 C4
Liverpool, Stanley L13 .... 53 F3
Newton-le-W WA12 .... 46 B3
Ormskirk L39 .... 13 F5
Prescot L34 .... 56 C6
Dereham Ave CH49 .... 65 A7
Dereham Cres L10 .... 39 F7
Derek Ave WA2 .... 61 E1
Derna Rd L36 .... 55 D3
Derringstone Cl WA10 .... 43 D1
Derrylea L9 .... 39 D7
Derwent Ave
Formby L37 .... 9 D2
Golborne WA3 .... 36 C1
Prescot L34 .... 56 F6
Southport PR9 .... 1 F1
Derwent Cl
Bebington CH63 .... 78 D5
Kirkby L33 .... 29 D4
Maghull L31 .... 20 F2
Rainhill L35 .... 57 B3
Derwent Dr
Bootle L21 .... 38 D8
Heswall CH61 .... 76 F4
Hooton CH66 .... 89 B2
Wallasey CH45 .... 51 A6
Derwent Ho L17 .... 68 C3
Derwent Rd
Ashton-in-M WN4 .... 35 E5
Bebington CH63 .... 78 D5
Birkenhead CH43 .... 66 B4
Crosby L23 .... 26 F2
Hoylake CH47 .... 63 E8
Orrell WN5 .... 25 F8
St Helens WA11 .... 44 B7
Widnes WA8 .... 72 C1
Derwent Rd E L13 .... 54 A4
Derwent Rd W L13 .... 53 F4
Derwent Sq L13 .... 54 A4
Desborough Cres L12 .... 54 A7
Desford Ave WA11 .... 44 D6
Desford Cl CH46 .... 49 B1
Desford Rd L19 .... 80 F8
Desilva St L36 .... 56 A2
Desmond Cl CH43 .... 65 C6
Desmond Gr L23 .... 26 F3
Desoto Rd WA8 .... 84 E5
Desoto Rd E WA8 .... 84 F6
Desoto Rd W WA8 .... 84 F6
Deva Cl L33 .... 29 E7
Deva Rd CH48 .... 63 A2
Deveraux Dr CH44 .... 51 C3
Deveraux Rd CH44 .... 51 C3
Deverell Gr L15 .... 54 B1
Deverell Rd L15 .... 54 B1
Deverill Rd CH42 .... 66 E1
Devilla Cl L14 .... 55 A5
De Villiers Ave L23 .... 26 E5
Devisdale Gr CH43 .... 65 C7
Devizes Dr CH61 .... 76 D7
Devoke Ave WA11 .... 33 A1
Devon Ave
Up Holland WN8 .... 25 B6
Wallasey CH44, CH45 .... 51 C5
Devon Cl L23 .... 26 A3
Devon Ct 12 L6 .... 53 A5
Devondale Rd L18 .... 69 A5
Devon Dr CH61 .... 76 E4
Devon Farm Way L37 .... 10 B3
Devonfield Rd L9 .... 38 F5
Devon Gdns
Birkenhead CH42 .... 66 F1
Liverpool L16 .... 69 E5
Devon Pl WA8 .... 73 B3
Devonport St L8 .... 67 F5
Devonshire Cl
Birkenhead CH43 .... 66 B5
4 Kirkby L33 .... 29 E4
Devonshire Gdns WA12 .... 46 C2
Devonshire Mews L8 .... 68 B5
DEVONSHIRE PARK 66 D3
Devonshire Park Prim Sch CH42 .... 66 C2
Devonshire Pl
Birkenhead CH43 .... 66 A5
Liverpool L5 .... 52 E6
Devonshire Rd
Birkenhead CH43 .... 66 B5
Birkenhead, Upton CH49 .... 64 E5
Crosby L22, L23 .... 26 C3
Heswall CH61 .... 76 E4
Liverpool L8 .... 68 A5
Southport PR9 .... 5 A8
St Helens WA10 .... 43 D5
Wallasey CH44 .... 51 B4
West Kirby CH48 .... 63 C1
Devonshire Rd W L8 .... 68 A5
Devon St
Liverpool L3, L6 .... 52 F2
St Helens WA10 .... 43 D4
Devonwall Gdns L8 .... 68 B5
Devon Way
Huyton-w-R L36 .... 56 A4
Liverpool L16 .... 69 E6
Dewberry Cl 3 CH42 .... 66 D4
Dewberry Fields WN8 .... 25 B7
Dewey Ave L9 .... 39 B8
Dewlands Rd L21 .... 37 F8
Dewsbury Rd L4 .... 53 C7
Dexter St L8 .... 67 E6
Dexter Way WN8 .... 25 B6
Deycroft Ave L33 .... 30 A4
Deycroft Wlk L33 .... 30 A4
Deyes Ct L31 .... 20 E1
Deyes End L31 .... 20 E1
Deyes High Sch L31 .... 20 D1
Deyes La
Maghull L31 .... 20 D1
Maghull, Moss Side L31 .... 20 E1
Deysbrook La L12, L28 .... 54 F8
Deysbrook Side L12 .... 54 C6
Deysbrook Way L12 .... 54 D8
Dial Rd CH42 .... 66 D3
Dial St 5 L7 .... 53 C2
Diamond Bsns Pk WA11 .... 32 B4
Diamond St L3, L5 .... 52 D4
Diana Rd L20 .... 38 D7
Diana St L4 .... 53 A8
Diane Rd WN4 .... 35 E5
Dibbinsdale Rd CH63 .... 88 B7
Dibbins Gn CH63 .... 88 B7
Dibbins Hey CH63 .... 79 B2
Dibbinview Gr CH63 .... 79 B2
Dibb La L23 .... 26 C7
Dicconson's La L39 .... 12 D4
Dicconson St WA10 .... 44 A4
Dicconson Way L39 .... 14 A5
Dickens Ave CH43 .... 65 F1
Dickens Cl
Birkenhead CH43 .... 65 F1
Liverpool L32 .... 40 D8
Dickens Dr WN2 .... 36 C8
Dickenson St L1 .... 90 B2
Dickens Rd WA10 .... 57 C8
Dickens St L8 .... 67 F6
Dicket's Brow L40 .... 14 F3
Dicket's La L40, WN8 .... 15 A2
Dickinson Cl
Formby L37 .... 9 F2
Haydock WA11 .... 45 A6
Dickinson Ct PR8 .... 4 A2
Dickinson Rd L37 .... 9 F2
Dick's La L40 .... 14 F4
Dickson St L3 .... 52 B4
Didcot Cl L25 .... 82 D9
Didsbury Cl L33 .... 29 F2
Digg La CH46 .... 49 D1
DIGMOOR 24 D6
Digmoor Dr WN8 .... 24 C7
Digmoor Rd
Kirkby L32 .... 40 F7
Skelmersdale WN8 .... 24 D6
Dignum Mead L27 .... 70 E5
Dilloway St WA10 .... 43 E4
Dinaro Cl L25 .... 70 C4
Dinas La L36 .... 55 B4
Dinesen Rd L19 .... 81 C7
DINGLE 68 A3
Dingle Ave
Newton-le-W WA12 .... 45 F2
Up Holland WN8 .... 25 C8
Dinglebrook Rd L9 .... 39 D3
Dingle Brow L8 .... 68 A3
Dingle Cl L39 .... 13 C1
Dingle Gr L8 .... 68 A4
Dingle Grange 5 L8 .... 68 A3
Dingle La L17, L8 .... 68 A3
Dingle Mount L8 .... 68 A3
Dingle Rd
Birkenhead CH42 .... 66 C4
Liverpool L8 .... 68 A3
Up Holland WN8 .... 25 B7
Dingle Vale L17, L8 .... 68 A3
Dingley Ave L9 .... 38 F6
Dingwall Dr CH49 .... 64 E3
Dinmore Rd CH44 .... 51 B4
Dinnington Ct WA8 .... 72 E3
Dinorwic Rd
Liverpool L4 .... 53 A6
Southport PR8 .... 4 A2
Dinsdale Rd CH62 .... 79 E2
Discovery Rd L19 .... 81 D4
District CE Prim Sch The WA12 .... 46 A4
Ditchfield L37 .... 10 A2
Ditchfield Pl WA8 .... 84 B8
Ditchfield Rd
Warrington WA5 .... 74 E3
Widnes WA8 .... 84 B8
DITTON 84 C8
Ditton CE Prim Sch WA8 .... 72 A1
Ditton La CH46 .... 49 E3
Ditton Prim Sch WA8 .... 72 E1
Ditton Rd
Widnes WA8 .... 84 D6
Widnes WA8 .... 84 F6
Dixon Ave WA12 .... 46 C5
Dixon Cl WA11 .... 46 A8
Dixon Mews L30 .... 27 E5
Dixon Rd L33 .... 41 B8
Dobbs Dr L37 .... 10 A4
Dobson Ct L6 .... 53 B5
Dobson St L6 .... 53 A4
Dock Rd
Liverpool L19 .... 81 B5
Wallasey CH41, CH44 .... 51 C1
Widnes WA8 .... 84 F5
Dock Rd N CH62 .... 79 C6
Dock Rd S CH62 .... 79 D4
Doctor's La L37 .... 10 E2
Dodd Ave
Birkenhead CH49 .... 64 D3
St Helens WA10 .... 43 C4
Doddridge Rd 6 L8 .... 67 E5
Dodd's La L31 .... 20 D2
Dodleston Cl CH43 .... 65 D4
Dodman Rd L11 .... 40 D5
Dodson Cl WN4 .... 35 C3
Dodworth Ave PR8 .... 4 E5
Doe Park Ctyd L25 .... 82 B9
Doe's Meadow Rd CH63 .... 88 B7
DOG & GUN 40 B2
Dolan Ct L25 .... 69 F8
Dolly's La PR9 .... 5 D8
Dolomite Ave L24 .... 81 F6
Domar Cl L32 .... 29 F1
Dombey St L8 .... 67 F6
Domingo Dr L33 .... 29 D5
Dominic Cl L16 .... 69 E8
Dominic Rd L16 .... 69 E8
Dominion St L6 .... 53 C5
Domville L35 .... 56 E2
Domville Dr CH49 .... 65 A3
Domville Rd L13 .... 54 A1
Donaldson St L5 .... 53 A6
Donalds Way L17 .... 68 E1
Doncaster Dr CH49 .... 64 F6
Donegal Rd 1 L13 .... 54 B2
Donne Ave CH63 .... 79 A3
Donne Cl CH63 .... 79 A3
Donnington Cl L36 .... 70 D8
Donnington Lo PR8 .... 3 F6
Donsby Rd L9 .... 39 B6
Dooley Dr L30 .... 28 B4
Doon Cl L4 .... 52 E8
Dorbett Dr L23 .... 26 F2
Dorchester Cl CH49 .... 64 F4
Dorchester Dr L33 .... 30 A5
Dorchester Pk CH43 .... 65 D3
Dorchester Rd
Liverpool L25 .... 70 B6
Up Holland WN8 .... 25 A7
Dorchester Way WA5 .... 59 F6
Doreen Ave CH46 .... 64 D8
Dorgan Cl L35 .... 57 C4
Doric Gn WN5 .... 25 D3
Doric Rd L13 .... 54 A4
Doric St
4 Birkenhead CH42 .... 66 F2
Seaforth L21 .... 37 F7
Dorien Rd L13 .... 53 F2
Dorincourt CH43 .... 66 A4
Dorking Gr L15 .... 69 B6
Dorney Ct L12 .... 54 D7
Dorothy St
Liverpool L7 .... 53 B1
St Helens WA9 .... 57 E8
Dorothy Wlk WN2 .... 35 F8

Esplanade
Birkenhead CH42 67 B2
Southport PR8 3 F7
Esplanade The
Birkenhead CH42 67 B1
4 Bootle L20 38 C3
Seaforth L22 37 D8
Esplen Ave L23 26 F5
Essex Rd
Huyton-w-R L36 56 B4
Southport PR8 8 A8
West Kirby CH48 63 C3
Essex St L8 67 F5
Essex Way L20 38 D4
Esthwaite Ave WA11 44 C8
Estuary Banks L24 81 F4
Estuary Bvd L24 81 F4
Estuary Commerce Pk L24 81 F4
Etal Cl 3 L11 40 B1
Ethelbert Rd CH47 63 C8
Ethel Rd CH44 51 D3
Etna St L13 53 F3
Eton Ct
Liverpool L18 69 D5
Southport PR9 1 C1
Eton Dr
Aintree L10 28 D2
Heswall CH63 86 F6
Eton Hall Dr WA9 58 C7
Eton St L4 38 F1
Eton Way WN5 25 F8
Etruria St L19 81 C4
Etruscan Rd L13 54 A4
Ettington Dr PR8 7 A5
Ettington Rd L4 53 B7
Ettrick Cl L33 29 D6
Eurolink WA9 57 F4
Europa Bvd
Birkenhead CH41 66 E6
Warrington WA5 60 D3
Euston Gr CH43 66 C5
Euston St L4 38 F2
Evans Cl WA11 45 F7
Evans Rd
Hoylake CH47 63 B7
Liverpool L24 82 C6
Evans St L34 56 D7
Evellynne Cl L32 29 D2
Evelyn Ave
Prescot L34 56 E6
St Helens WA9 44 E3
Evelyn Com Prim Sch L34 56 E7
Evelyn Rd CH44 51 C3
Evelyn St
Liverpool L5 52 D6
St Helens WA9 44 E3
Evenson Way L13 54 A4
Evenwood
Skelmersdale WN8 16 D1
5 St Helens WA9 58 C6
Evenwood Ct WN8 16 C1
Everard Rd PR8 4 D4
Everdon Wood L33 29 F3
Evered Ave L9 39 A4
Everest Rd
Birkenhead CH42 66 D2
Crosby L23 26 E4
Evergreen Cl
Birkenhead CH49 64 E6
Liverpool L27 70 E6
Evergreens The L37 9 D4
Evergreen Way WA9 59 A7
Everite Rd WA8 84 B7
Everite Road Ind Est WA8 84 B7
Everleigh Cl CH43 65 B7
Eversleigh Dr CH63 79 A4
Eversley
Skelmersdale WN8 16 D1
Widnes WA8 72 B2
Eversley Pk CH43 66 B3
Eversley St L8 68 A7
EVERTON 52 F5
Everton Brow L3, L5 52 E4
Everton Gr WA11 44 D5
Everton Rd
Liverpool L6 52 F4
Southport PR8 4 A4
Everton St WN4 34 D5
Everton Valley L4, L5 52 E7
Everton View L20 38 B2
Every St L6 53 B4
Evesham Cl L25 69 F2
Evesham Rd
Liverpool L4 39 D1
Wallasey CH45 50 F6
Evington WN8 16 D1
Ewanville L36 55 E1
Ewart Rd
Huyton-w-R L16 70 A8
Seaforth L21 38 A7
St Helens WA11 44 B6
Ewden Cl L16 69 E7
Exchange Pas E 2 L2 90 A4
Exchange Pas W 1 L2 90 A4
Exchange Pl L35 57 C3
Exchange St E L2 90 A4
Exchange St W 4 L2 90 A3
Exchange St 8 WA10 44 A3
Exeley L35 56 E2
Exeter Cl L10 28 E1
Exeter Rd
Bootle L20 38 C2
Wallasey CH44 51 C5
Exeter St WA10 43 D3
Exford Rd L12 54 D8
Exmoor Cl
Heswall CH61 76 F5
Southport PR9 2 B6
Exmouth Cl CH41 66 D6
Exmouth Gdns 3 CH41 66 D6
Exmouth St CH41 66 D6
Exmouth Way
1 Birkenhead CH41 66 D6
Burtonwood WA5 59 F6
Express Ind Est WA8 84 A7
Expressway Bsns Pk 10 CH42 66 F3
Extension View WA9 58 D8

F

FACT (Mus) L1 90 C2
Factory La WA8 73 B3
Factory Row WA10 43 E1
Fairacre Rd L19 81 A8
Fairacres Rd CH63 79 A4
Fairbairn Rd L22 26 E1
Fairbank St L15 68 E7
Fairbeech Ct CH43 65 C7
Fairbeech Mews CH43 65 C7
Fairbourne Cl WA5 60 E3
Fairbrook Dr CH41 50 E1
Fairbrother Cres WA2 61 D2
Fairburn WN8 16 B3
Fairburn Cl WA8 73 E3
Fairburn Rd L13 53 E6
Fairclough Cl L35 57 B3
Fairclough Cres WA11 45 A6
Fairclough La CH43 66 B4
Fairclough Rd
Huyton-w-R L36 55 C5
Rainhill L35 57 B3
St Helens WA10 43 C4
Fairclough St
Burtonwood WA5 59 E6
Liverpool L1 90 B3
Newton-le-W WA12 46 B3
Fairfax Pl L11 39 D2
Fairfax Rd
Birkenhead CH41 66 E4
Liverpool L11 39 E2
FAIRFIELD 53 E3
Fairfield L23 26 E4
Fairfield Ave L14, L36 55 A2
Fairfield Cl
Huyton-w-R L36 55 A2
Ormskirk L39 13 E7
Fairfield Cres
Birkenhead CH46 64 D8
Huyton-w-R L36 55 A2
Liverpool L6 53 D4
Fairfield Dr
Ormskirk L39 13 E7
West Kirby CH48 63 E3
Fairfield Gdns WA11 32 E2
Fairfield High Sch WA8 73 B3
Fairfield Hospl WA11 32 E2
Fairfield Inf Sch WA8 73 B2
Fairfield Jun Sch WA8 73 B2
Fairfield Rd
Birkenhead CH42 66 E2
Southport PR8 7 C5
St Helens WA10 43 D5
Widnes WA8 73 B2
Fairfield St L7 53 E3
Fairford Cres L14 54 B4
Fairford Rd L14 54 B4
Fairhaven
Kirkby L33 29 E5
Skelmersdale WN8 16 C3
Fairhaven Cl CH42 66 F2
Fairhaven Dr CH63 88 C5
Fairhaven Rd
Southport PR9 2 B4
Widnes WA8 73 C2
Fairholme L19 80 F6
Fairholme Ave
Ashton-in-M WN4 35 B4
Eccleston Park L34 57 A6
Neston CH64 86 D1
Fairholme Cl L12 54 A8
Fairholme Mews L23 26 E4
Fairholme Rd L23 26 E4
Fairhurst Terr 10 L34 56 E6
Fairlawn Cl CH63 88 A6
Fairlawn Ct CH43 65 F5
Fairlawne Cl 9 L33 29 E5
Fairlie WN8 16 C3
Fairlie Cres L20 38 D7
Fairlie Dr L35 57 D2
Fairmead Rd
Liverpool L11 39 E2
Wallasey CH46 49 F1
Fairoak Cl CH43 65 C7
Fairoak Mews CH43 65 C7
Fairstead WN8 16 C3
Fairthorn Wlk L33 30 A3
Fair View WN5 33 D5
Fairview Ave CH45 51 B5
Fair View Ave WN5 33 D5
Fairview Cl
Ashton-in-M WN4 35 B4
Birkenhead CH43 66 B3
Fair View Pl 3 L8 68 A4
Fairview Rd CH43 66 B3
Fairview Way CH61 76 F3
Fairway
Huyton-w-R L36 56 A4
Southport PR9 1 C2
St Helens WA10 43 C5
Fairway Cres CH62 79 D4
Fairway Ct CH47 63 A6
Fairway N CH62 79 D3
Fairways
Bebington CH42 78 B8
Birkenhead CH43 65 E5
Crosby L23 26 D5
Fairway S CH62 79 D3
Fairways Cl L25 82 B9
Fairways Ct L37 9 C5
Fairways The
Garswood WN4 34 D2
Liverpool L25 82 D9
Skelmersdale WN8 16 D3
West Kirby CH48 75 D6
Fairway The L12 54 D4
Fairway Trad Est WA8 84 E6
Faith Prim Sch L5 52 E4
Falcon Cres L27 70 F4
Falcondale Rd WA2 61 B6
Falconers Gn WA5 60 B2
Falconer St L20 38 A6
Falconhall Rd L9 39 F4
Falcon Hey L10 40 A6
Falcon Rd CH41, CH43 66 C4
Falkirk Ave WA8 72 F3
Falkland WN8 16 C3
Falkland Dr WN4 34 C4
Falkland Rd
Southport PR8 4 D5
Wallasey CH44 51 D4
Falklands App L11 39 E2
Falkland St
Birkenhead CH41 66 A8
Liverpool L3 52 F2
Falkner Sq L8 68 A7
Falkner St L1, L7, L8 67 F8
Fallbrook Dr L12 40 B1
Fallow Cl 6 WA9 58 C4
Fallowfield L33 29 E4
Fallowfield Rd L15 69 A6
Fallows Way L35 71 C8
Falmouth Dr WA5 74 E3
Falmouth Rd L11 40 D5
Falstaff St L20 52 C8
Faraday Rd
Knowsley L33 41 B7
Liverpool L13 53 E1
Faraday St L5 53 A5
Farefield Ave WA3 35 F2
Fareham Cl CH49 64 D6
Fareham Rd L7 53 D2
Faringdon Cl L25 82 B7
Farley Ave CH62 79 C1
Farley La WN8 16 F3
Farlow Rd CH42 66 F1
Farmbrook Rd L25 70 B7
Farm Cl
Birkenhead CH49 64 C4
Southport PR9 5 A8
St Helens WA9 58 D3
Farmdale Cl L18 69 B2
Farmdale Dr L31 20 E1
Far Meadow La CH61 76 D7
Farmer Pl L20 38 E7
Farmer's La WA5 60 A6
Farmfield Dr CH43 65 C7
Farm Meadow Rd WN5 25 E5
FAR MOOR 25 D4
Far Moss Rd L23 26 B6
Farm Pk* L39 11 F1
Farm Rd WA9 58 D3
Farmside CH46 49 F3
Farm View L21 27 B2
Farmview Cl L27 70 C7
Farm Way WA12 46 E1
Farnborough Gr L26 70 F1
Farnborough Rd PR8 7 F8
Farnborough Road Inf & Jun Schs PR8 8 A8
Farndale WA8 73 A5
Farndale Cl WA5 74 F7
Farndale Gr WN4 35 C2
Farndon Ave
St Helens WA9 58 B4
Wallasey CH45 50 E6
Farndon Dr CH48 63 E3
Farndon Way CH43 65 F4
Farnham Cl L32 29 F1
Farnside Ct L17 80 F7
FARNWORTH 73 A3
Farnworth Ave CH46 49 F4
Farnworth CE Prim Sch WA8 73 A4
Farnworth Cl WA8 73 B4
Farnworth Ct WA8 73 B3
Farnworth Gr 7 L33 29 E5
Farnworth Rd WA5 74 C4
Farnworth St
Liverpool L6 53 B3
St Helens WA9 44 C4
Widnes WA8 73 B4
Farrar St L13 53 E7
Farrell Cl L31 29 B4
Farr Hall Dr CH60 85 E7
Farr Hall Rd CH60 85 F8
Farrier Rd L33 30 A2
Farriers Way
Birkenhead CH48 64 B2
Bootle L30 38 F8
Farrier Wlk WA9 58 C4
Farringdon Cl WA9 57 F6
Farringdon Rd WA2 61 B6
Farrington Dr L39 13 E6
Farthing Cl L25 82 B8
Farthingstone Cl L35 57 A6
Fatherside Dr L30 27 C3
Faulkner Cl PR8 7 C6
Faulkner Gdns PR8 7 C6
Faversham Rd L11 39 E3
Fawcett WN8 16 B3
Fawcett Rd L31 20 D3
Fawley Rd
Liverpool L18 69 C2
Rainhill L35 57 E1
FAZAKERLEY 39 D5
Fazakerley Cl L9 39 A4
Fazakerley High Sch L10 39 F7
Fazakerley Prim Sch L10 39 F7
Fazakerley Rd
Liverpool L9 39 A4
Prescot L35 56 E4
Fazakerley St L3 52 B2
Fazakerley Sta L9 39 D7
Fearnhead Cross WA2 61 F2
Fearnley Rd CH41 66 D5
Fearnley Way WA12 46 C1
Fearnside St L7 68 C8
Feather La CH60 85 F8
Feathers The WA10 43 D3
Feeny St WA9 58 B2
Feilden Rd CH63 79 A4
Felcroft Way L33 29 F3
Felicity Gr CH46 49 D1
Fell Gr WA11 44 A8
Fell St
Liverpool L7 53 B2
Wallasey CH44 51 E2
Felltor Cl L25 69 F3
Fell View PR9 2 D6
Fellwood Gr L35 56 E3
Felmersham Ave L11 39 F3
Felspar Rd L32 40 F7
Felstead WN8 16 B2
Felstead Ave L25 70 C2
Felsted Dr L10 28 E1
Felthorpe Cl CH49 65 B7
Felton Cl CH46 64 C8
Felton Ct L17 68 C3
Felton Gr L13 53 F3
Feltons WN8 16 B2
Feltwell Rd L4 53 B6
Feltwood Cl L12 54 F7
Feltwood Manor L12 54 F7
Feltwood Rd L12 54 F8
Feltwood Wlk L12 54 F7
Fendale Ave CH46 50 A1
Fender Ct CH49 65 D1
Fender Hts CH46 50 A1
Fender La CH43, CH46 50 B1
Fender Prim Sch CH49 65 C3
Fenderside Rd CH43 65 C8
Fender View Rd CH46 65 A8
Fender Way
Birkenhead CH43 65 B7
Heswall CH61 77 A4
Fenham Dr WA5 74 F4
Fenney Ct WN8 16 C1
Fenton Cl
Liverpool, Warbreck Pk L30 39 B8
Speke L24 82 D4
St Helens WA10 43 F4
Widnes WA8 72 C3
Fenton Gn L24 82 D3
Fenwick St L2 90 A3
Ferguson Ave CH49 64 D3
Ferguson Dr WA2 61 D1
Ferguson Rd
Litherland L21 27 C1
Liverpool L11 53 E8
Fern Ave WA12 46 D2
Fern Bank
Maghull L31 20 E1
Rainford WA11 31 E7
Fernbank Ave L36 55 D2
Fernbank Dr L30 28 A4
Fernbank La CH49 64 F7
Fern Cl
Kirkby L33 29 F4
Liverpool L27 70 E4
Skelmersdale WN8 15 E1
Ferndale WN8 16 C2
Ferndale Ave
Birkenhead CH48 64 B1
Wallasey CH44 51 C4
Ferndale Cl
Bold Heath WA8 73 E7
Liverpool L9 39 A7
Ferndale Rd
Crosby L22 26 E2
Hoylake CH47 63 B8
Liverpool L15 68 E6
Fern Gdns L34 56 F7
Fern Gr
Birkenhead CH43 65 D4
Bootle L20 38 C4
Liverpool L8 68 C6
Fern Hey L23 27 B5
Fernhill 10 CH45 51 B8
Fernhill Ave L20 38 E3
Fernhill Cl L20 38 E3
Fernhill Dr L8 68 A6
Fernhill Gdns L20 38 E3
Fernhill Mews E L20 38 E3
Fernhill Mews W L20 38 E3
Fernhill Rd L20 38 E4
Fernhill Sports Ctr L20 38 D6
Fernhill Way L20 38 E3
Fernhill Wlk WA9 58 C3
Fernhurst Gate L39 13 B1
Fernhurst Rd L32 29 C1
Fernie Cres L8 67 F5
Fernlea Ave WA9 57 D7
Fernlea Gr WN4 34 D5
Fernlea Mews 5 CH43 65 C8
Fernlea Rd CH60 86 A8
Fernleigh Rd L13 54 B3
Fernley Rd PR8 4 A5
Fern Lo L8 68 C6
Ferns Cl CH60 76 C1
Ferns Rd CH63 78 D5
Fernwood Dr L26 82 E9
Fernwood Rd L17 68 E3
Ferny Brow Rd CH49 65 B3
Ferny Knoll Rd WA11 23 F4
Ferrer St WN4 34 F6
Ferrey Rd L10 40 A7
Ferries Cl CH62 79 B8
Ferry Rd CH62 89 A6
Ferryside CH44 51 E2
Ferryside La PR9 2 C5
Ferry View Rd CH44 51 E2
Festival Ave WA2 61 D2
Festival Cres WA2 61 D2
Festival Ct L11 40 B3
Festival Rd WA11 32 A5
Ffrancon Dr CH63 78 F7
FIDDLER'S FERRY 2 D6
Fiddler's Ferry Rd WA8 73 D1
Fidler St WA10 43 D1
Field Ave L21 38 A8
Field Cl
Bebington CH62 79 C8
St Helens WA9 58 D3
Fieldfare Cl
Golborne WA3 47 D8
Liverpool L25 70 A5
Fieldgate WA8 84 B6
Field Hey La CH64 88 B1
Field Ho L12 54 A7
Fielding St L6 53 A3
Fieldings The L31 20 B4
Field La
Litherland L21 38 A8
Liverpool L10 40 B7
Fieldlands PR8 5 A2
Field Rd
St Helens WA9 58 D3
Wallasey CH45 51 B7
Field's End L36 70 E8
Fieldsend Cl L27 70 E4
Fieldside Rd CH42 66 E2
Field St
Liverpool L3 52 E3
Skelmersdale WN8 15 D2
Fieldton Rd L11 40 B3
Fieldview 2 WN8 25 A7
Field View L21 27 A1
Fieldview Dr WA2 61 C1
Fieldway
Bebington CH63 78 D8
Heswall CH60 77 C1
Hoylake CH47 63 F7
Huyton-w-R L36 70 F8
Liverpool L15 69 C8
Maghull L31 28 E7
Wallasey CH45 51 A5
Widnes WA8 73 E2
Field Way L35 57 C5
Fieldway Ct CH41 66 C8
Field Wlk
Crosby L23 27 B5
Ormskirk L39 14 B5
Fifth Ave
Aintree L9 39 D7
Birkenhead CH43 65 B7
Liverpool, Fazakerley L9 39 E7
Filbert Cl L33 29 F6
Filby Gdns WA9 57 E6
Fillmore Gr WA8 72 F3
Filton Rd L14 55 B6
Finborough Rd L4 39 C1
FINCHAM 55 B5
Fincham Cl L14 55 B5
Fincham Gn L14 55 B5
Fincham Rd L14 55 A5
Fincham Sq L14 55 A5
Finch Ave WA11 32 A5
Finch Cl WA9 58 D3
Finch Ct CH41 66 D7
Finchdean Cl 3 CH49 64 C4
Finch Dene L14 54 F6
Finch La
Halewood L26 83 B7
Huyton-w-R L14 55 A6
Liverpool, Mill Yard L14 54 F5
Finch Lea Dr L14 55 A5
Finchley Dr WA11 44 C7
Finchley Rd L4 53 B7
Finch Meadow Cl L9 39 F4
Finch Pl L3 52 F2
Finch Rd L14 55 A6
Finch Way L14 54 F5
Findlay Cl WA12 46 C2
Findley Dr CH46 49 F3
Findon WN8 16 C2
Findon Rd L32 40 F8
Fine Jane's Way PR9 5 B8
Fingall Rd L15 69 B6
Finger House La WA8 58 D1
FINGER POST 44 D3
Fingland Rd L15 68 F7
Finlan Rd WA8 84 F7
Finlay Ave WA5 74 E3
Finlay Ct L30 27 F4
Finlay St L6 53 C3

Garstang Rd PR9 2 A5
GARSTON 81 C5
Garston CE Prim Sch L19 81 D6
Garston Ind Est L19 81 C4
Garston Old Rd L19 81 C7
Garston Way L19 81 C6
GARSWOOD 34 C3
Garswood Ave WA11 32 A7
Garswood Cl
- Maghull L31 20 E3
- Wallasey CH46 49 E4
Garswood Cres WN5 33 E4
Garswood Old Rd WA11, WN4 33 E1
Garswood Prim Sch WN4 34 C4
Garswood Rd
- Billinge WN5 33 F4
- Garswood WA11, WN4 34 C3
Garswood St
- Ashton-in-M WN4 35 B3
- Liverpool L8 67 F3
- St Helens WA10 44 A4
Garswood Sta WN4 34 D3
Garter Cl L11 40 C3
Garth Bvd CH63 78 E8
Garth Ct L22 26 E1
Garthdale Rd L18 69 B4
Garth Dr L18 69 C4
Garthowen Rd L7 53 D2
Garth Rd L32 41 A8
Garth The
- Birkenhead CH43 65 F5
- Huyton-w-R L36 55 E3
Garth Wlk 6 L32 41 A8
Garton Dr WA3 36 E1
Gartons La WA9 58 C3
Garway L25 70 C3
Garwood Cl WA5 60 C1
Gascoyne St L3 52 C3
Gaskell Ct WA9 44 F3
Gaskell Rake L30 27 D5
Gaskell's Brow WN4 34 E5
Gaskell St WA9 44 D2
Gaskill Rd L24 82 D5
Gatclif Rd L13 53 E7
GATEACRE 70 B5
Gateacre Brow L25 70 B4
Gateacre Com Comp Sch L25 70 A5
Gateacre Ct L25 69 F7
Gateacre Park Dr L25 69 F6
Gateacre Rise L25 70 B4
Gateacre Vale Rd L25 70 B3
Gategill Gr WN5 25 D3
Gateside Cl L27 70 E5
Gates La L29 19 C1
Gateway Complex L19 81 C5
Gathurst Ct WA8 84 D8
Gathurst Rd WN5 25 E8
Gatley Dr L31 28 E7
Gatley Wlk L24 82 F5
Gautby Rd CH41 50 E1
Gavin Rd WA8 84 B7
Gaw Hill La L39 13 B3
Gaw Hill View L39 13 B3
Gawsworth Cl
- Birkenhead CH43 65 F3
- St Helens WA10 43 B3
Gawsworth Rd WA3 35 F1
Gaybeech Cl CH43 65 B8
Gayhurst Ave WA2 61 F2
Gayhurst Cres L11 40 A2
Gaynor Ave WA11 45 F7
GAYTON 86 B6
Gayton Ave
- Bebington CH63 78 C8
- Wallasey CH45 51 B8
Gayton Farm Rd CH60 86 A5
Gayton La CH60 86 B6
Gayton Mill Cl CH60 86 B7
Gayton Parkway CH60 86 C5
Gayton Prim Sch CH60 86 A6
Gayton Rd CH60 86 A6
Gaytree Ct CH43 65 C7
Gaywood Ave L32 40 F8
Gaywood Cl
- Birkenhead CH43 65 C7
- 5 Kirkby L32 40 F8
Gaywood Ct L23 26 B3
Gaywood Gn 4 L32 40 F8
Gellings La L34 41 A5
Gellings Rd L34 41 A5
Gelling St L8 67 F5
GEMINI 60 D3
Gemini Bsns Pk WA5 60 E3
Gemini Cl L20 38 B4
Gemini Dr L14 54 F4
Gem St L5 52 C5
General Dr L12 54 D7
Geneva Cl L36 55 D4
Geneva Rd
- Liverpool L6 53 C3
- Wallasey CH44 51 D2
Genista Cl L9 39 A3
Genoa Cl L25 70 B7
Gentwood Par L36 55 D4
Gentwood Rd L36 55 D3
George Dr PR8 7 E5
George Hale Ave L34 55 E6
George Harrison Cl 1 L6 53 B3
George Moore Ct L23 27 C6
George Rd CH47 63 C6
George's Dock Gates L2, L3 52 B1
Georges Dockway L3 52 B1
George's La PR9 2 F8
Georges Par L3 52 B1
Georges Pierhead L3 52 B1
George's Prec WA5 74 D6
Georges Rd L6 53 C5
George St
- Ashton-in-M WN4 35 C4
- Birkenhead CH41 66 E7
- Liverpool L2 90 A4
- Newton-le-W WA12 46 A4
- St Helens WA10 44 A3
George Terr WN5 25 D5
George Trad Est PR8 4 B4
Georgia Ave
- Bebington CH62 79 E3
- Kirkby L33 29 D6
Georgia Cl 9 L20 38 C3
Georgian Cl
- Eccleston Park L35 57 A6
- Liverpool L26 82 F7
Georgian Pl L37 9 E1
Geraint St L8 67 F6
Gerald Rd CH43 66 A4
Gerard Ave CH45 51 A7
Gerard Corr Ho CH45 51 C6
Gerard Ctr The WN4 35 B3
Gerard Rd
- Wallasey CH45 50 F6
- West Kirby CH48 63 B3
GERARD'S BRIDGE 44 A5
Gerards Ct WA11 44 C8
Gerards La WA9 58 D7
Gerard St
- Ashton-in-M WN4 35 B3
- Liverpool L3 90 C4
Germander Cl L26 70 E1
Gerneth Cl L24 82 C5
Gerneth Rd L24 82 B5
Gerosa Ave WA2 61 B8
Gerrard Pl WN8 23 F7
Gerrard Rd WN5 33 E5
Gerrard's La L26 70 F3
Gertrude Rd L4 53 B6
Gertrude St
- Birkenhead CH41 66 F6
- St Helens WA9 57 D7
Geves Gdns L22 26 E1
Ghyll Gr WA11 33 B1
Gibbons Ave WA10 43 C3
Gibbon's Rd WN4 34 D3
Gibraltar Row L3 52 B2
Gibson Cl
- Heswall CH61 76 F3
- 10 Kirkby L33 29 D5
Gibson Rd L8 67 F6
Gibson Terr CH44 51 D5
Giddygate La L31 29 B7
Gidlow Rd L13 53 F3
Gidlow Rd S L13 53 F2
Gilbert Cl CH63 78 F2
Gilbert Ho WA7 84 E3
Gilbert Rd L35 56 F5
Gilbert St L1 90 B2
Gilbrook Sch CH41 66 F6
Gildarts Gdns L3 52 C4
Gildart St L3 52 F2
Gilead St L7 53 B2
Gilescroft Ave L33 30 A4
GILLAR'S GREEN 42 E2
Gillars Green Dr WA10 43 A3
Gillar's La WA10 42 E3
Gillbrook Sq 4 CH41 65 F8
Gilleney Gr L35 57 A5
Gillibrands Rd WN8 24 A7
GILLMOSS 40 C6
Gillmoss Cl L11 40 C4
Gillmoss Ind Est L10, L11 40 B6
Gillmoss La L11 40 C5
Gills La CH61 77 B4
Gill St L3 52 F2
Gilman St 3 L4 53 A7
Gilmartin Gr L6 53 A3
Gilmour Jun Sch L19 81 B7
Gilmour Mount CH43 66 B4
Gilmour (Southbank) Inf Sch L19 81 B7
Gilpin Ave L31 20 E2
Gilroy Rd
- Liverpool L6 53 B3
- West Kirby CH48 63 D3
Giltbrook Cl WA8 72 F3
Gilwell Ave CH46, CH49 64 E7
Gilwell Cl CH46 64 E7
Ginnel The CH62 79 B5
Gipsy Gr L18 69 E5
Gipsy La L16, L18 69 E5
Girton Ave
- Ashton-in-M WN4 34 F4
- Bootle L20 38 E2
Girtrell Cl CH49 64 D5
Girtrell Rd CH49 64 D5
Girvan Cres WN4 34 D4
Gisburn Ave WA3 35 F2
Givenchy Cl L16 69 E8
Givenchy Ct 1 L17 68 C2
Gladden Pl WN8 23 E8
Glade Park Ct L8 68 B4
Glade Rd L36 55 E4
Gladeswood Rd L33 30 B1
Glade The CH47 48 D1
Gladeville Rd L17 68 E3
Gladica Cl L36 56 B2
Gladstone Ave
- Huyton-w-R L16 70 A8
- 2 Seaforth L21 37 F7
Gladstone Cl CH41 66 C6
Gladstone Hall Rd CH62 79 B4
Gladstone Rd
- 5 Birkenhead CH42 66 F3
- Liverpool, Edge Hill L7 53 B1
- Liverpool, Garston L19 81 C6
- Liverpool, Walton L9 39 A3
- Seaforth L21 37 F7
- Southport PR9 4 F6
- Wallasey CH44 51 D3
Gladstone St
- 1 Liverpool, Vauxhall L3 52 C3
- Liverpool, Woolton Hill L25 69 F2
- St Helens WA10 43 D3
Gladstone Way WA12 46 B4
Gladsville Rd L27 70 F4
Glaisdale Cl WN4 35 C3
Glaisdale Dr PR8 4 F3
Glaisher St L5 53 A6
Glamis Cl CH43 65 D3
Glamis Dr PR9 2 B3
Glamis Gr WA9 58 C7
Glamis Rd L13 53 E6
Glamorgan Cl WA10 43 F2
Glan Aber Pk L12 54 E8
Glasier Rd CH46 49 C1
Glaslyn Way L9 39 A3
Glasshouse Farm WA9 57 F5
Glassonby Cres L11 40 A1
Glassonby Way 3 L11 40 A1
Glastonbury Cl L6 53 D7
Glasven Rd L33 29 F3
Gleadmere WA8 72 C2
Gleaner Cl WA7 84 F3
Gleaston Cl CH62 79 D1
Gleave Cres L6 53 A4
Gleave Rd WA5 59 F6
Gleave St WA10 44 A5
Glebe Ave WN4 35 C2
Glebe Cl L31 20 B1
Glebe End L29 27 F7
Glebe Hey L27 70 E5
Glebe Hey Rd CH49 65 A3
Glebe La WA8 73 B5
Glebelands Rd CH46 64 E8
Glebe Pl PR8 4 B7
Glebe Rd
- Skelmersdale WN8 24 A8
- Wallasey CH45 51 A6
Gleggside CH48 63 C2
Glegg St L3 52 B4
Glegside Rd L33 30 A2
Glenacres L25 70 A3
Glenalmond Rd CH44 51 D4
Glenathol Rd L18 69 C2
Glenavon Rd
- Birkenhead CH43 66 A1
- 3 Liverpool L16 54 C1
Glenbank L22 26 C2
Glenbank Cl L9 39 A5
Glenburn Ave CH62 88 E4
Glenburn Rd
- Skelmersdale WN8 15 F2
- Skelmersdale WN8 16 A1
- Wallasey CH44 51 D3
Glenburn Sports Coll WN8 24 B8
Glenby Ave L23 26 F2
Glencairn Rd L13 53 F3
Glencoe Rd CH45 51 C6
Glenconner Rd L16 54 E1
Glencourse Rd WA8 73 A5
Glencoyne Dr PR9 2 B5
Glencroft Cl L36 55 C5
Glendale Ave WN4 35 C4
Glendale Cl L8 67 F3
Glendale Gr
- Bebington CH63 79 B2
- Kirkby L33 30 A5
Glendale Rd WA11 44 A7
Glendale Way L37 9 F2
Glendevon Rd
- Huyton-w-R L36 55 E1
- Liverpool L16 54 D1
Glendower Ct 3 L23 26 B3
Glendower Rd L22 26 E1
Glendower St L20 38 C1
Glendyke Rd L18 69 C3
Gleneagles Cl
- Golborne WA3 47 F7
- Heswall CH61 76 F3
- Kirkby L33 29 D6
Gleneagles Dr
- Haydock WA11 45 A5
- Southport PR8 7 C3
- Widnes WA8 73 B5
Gleneagles Rd L14, L16 54 D1
Glenfield Cl
- Birkenhead CH43 65 C8
- Wallasey CH46 49 B1
Glenfield Rd 2 L15 69 A6
Glengariff St L13 53 E7
Glenham Cl CH47 63 E8
Glenhead Rd L19 81 B8
Glenholm Rd L31 28 C7
Glenluce Rd L19 69 B1
Glenlyon Rd L15, L16 69 C8
Glenmarsh Cl
- Bebington CH63 78 D5
- Liverpool L12 54 C6
Glenmarsh Way L37 10 B3
Glenmaye Cl L12 40 E2
Glenmore Ave L18 69 A3
Glenmore Rd CH43 66 A4
Glenn Bldgs 2 L23 26 E5
Glenn Pl WA8 72 E1
Glenpark Dr PR9 2 B4
Glen Park Rd CH45 51 A7
Glen Rd L13 54 B2
Glen Ronald Dr CH49 64 D5
Glenrose Rd L25 70 A3
Glenrose Terr PR8 4 A5
Glenside L18 69 C2
Glen The
- Bebington CH63 79 C3
- Liverpool L18 69 C3
Glentrees Cl CH49 64 D5
Glentrees Rd L12 54 B8
Glentworth Cl L31 28 D7
Glenville Cl L25 70 B4
Glen Vine Cl L16 69 F8
Glenway L33 29 F6
Glenway Cl L12 40 F4
Glenwood Cl L35 56 F2
Glenwood Dr CH61 76 E7
Glenwyllin Rd L22 26 F1
Globe Rd L20 38 B4
Globe St L4 52 E7
Gloucester Ave WA3 47 B8
Gloucester Ct 18 L6 53 A3
Gloucester Rd
- Bootle L20 38 D4
- Huyton-w-R L36 56 A3
- Liverpool L6 53 D5
- Southport PR8 3 F5
- Wallasey CH45 50 E6
- Widnes WA8 73 B3
Gloucester Rd N L6 53 D6
Gloucester St WA9 44 D2
Glover Pl L20 38 B4
Glover's Brow L32 29 C4
Glovers Ct 1 L32 29 C3
Glover's La L30 27 E4
Glover St
- Birkenhead CH42 66 C4
- Newton-le-W WA12 46 C3
- St Helens WA10 43 F3
Glyn Ave CH62 88 E7
Glynne Gr L16 70 A8
Glynne St L20 38 D6
Glynn St L15 68 F8
Glyn Rd CH44 51 B5
Godetia Cl L9 39 F4
Godshill Cl WA5 74 D7
GOLBORNE 47 B7
Golborne Dale Rd WA3, WA12 47 A5
Golborne Enterprise Pk WA3 36 A1
Golborne Jun & Inf Sch WA3 47 A8
Golborne Rd
- Ashton-in-M WN4 35 E4
- Golborne WA3 47 C8
- Winwick WA12, WA2 61 A7
Golborne St WA12 46 E4
Golbourne High Sch WA3 36 C1
Goldcliff Cl WA5 60 D3
Goldcrest Cl L12 40 F4
Goldcrest Mews L26 70 E1
Golden Gr 3 L4 39 A1
Goldfinch Cl L26 70 E1
Goldfinch Farm Rd L24 82 C4
Goldie St L4 52 F7
Goldsmith Rd 1 CH43 65 F1
Goldsmith St
- Bootle L20 38 A4
- Liverpool L6 53 B3
Goldsmith Way 2 CH43 65 F1
Goldsworth Fold L35 57 B3
Gold Triangle Complex WA8 84 C5
Golf Links Rd CH42 78 B8
Golf Rd L37 9 E5
Gondover Ave L9 38 F6
Gonville Rd L20 38 D2
Gooch Dr WA12 46 D2
Goodacre Rd L9 39 B7
Goodakers Ct 10 CH49 65 A2
Goodaker's Mdw 2 CH49 65 A2
Goodall Pl L4 52 E8
Goodall St L4 38 E1
Goodban St WA9 58 E8
Goodison Ave L4 52 F8
Goodison Park (Everton FC)* L4 52 F8
Goodison Pl L4 38 F1
Goodison Rd L4 38 F1
Goodlass Rd L24 82 A7
Goodleigh Pl WA9 58 C5
Good Shepherd Cl L11 40 B2
Goodwood Cl L36 55 D1
Goodwood Ct WA9 57 D6
Goodwood Dr CH46 49 F3
Goodwood St L5 52 D5
Goose Green The CH47 48 D1
Goostrey Cl CH63 79 B1
Gordale Cl
- 26 Liverpool L8 68 A4
- Warrington WA5 74 F7
Gordon Ave
- Bebington CH62 88 E7
- Birkenhead CH49 64 E3
- Crosby L22 26 C2
- Garswood WN4 34 E4
- Haydock WA11 45 F7
- Maghull L31 20 C3
- Southport PR9 1 C1
Gordon Ct CH49 64 E3
Gordon Dr
- Huyton-w-R L14 54 E3
- Liverpool L19 81 A7
Gordon Pl L18 69 A3
Gordon Rd
- Seaforth L21 37 F6
- Wallasey CH45 51 C7
Gordon St
- Birkenhead CH41 66 C6
- Liverpool L15 68 E7
- Southport PR9 4 C8
Gordonstoun Cres WN5 25 F7
Gore Dr L39 13 E3
Gores La
- Crank WA11 32 F6
- Formby L37 9 F5
Gore's La WA11 33 A5
Gores Rd L33 30 C1
Gore St L8 67 E6
Gorleston Mews 10 L32 40 F8
Gorleston Way L32 29 F1
Gorse Ave L12 40 B1
Gorsebank Rd L18 68 E5
Gorsebank St CH44 51 C3
Gorseburn Rd L13 53 E6
Gorse Cres CH44 51 C2
Gorsedale Pk CH44 51 D2
Gorsedale Rd
- Liverpool L18 69 A4
- Wallasey CH44 51 C2
Gorsefield
- Formby L37 10 A6
- St Helens WA9 57 D7
Gorsefield Ave
- Bebington CH62 88 D5
- Crosby L23 27 A5
Gorsefield Cl CH62 88 D5
Gorsefield Rd CH42 66 C3
Gorse Hey Ct L12, L13 54 A5
Gorsehill Rd
- Heswall CH60 77 A1
- Wallasey CH45 51 A8
Gorse La CH48 63 E1
Gorselands Ct L17 68 D2
Gorse Rd CH47 63 D8
Gorse Way L37 9 C4
Gorsewood Cl L25 70 C5
Gorsewood Gr L25 70 C5
Gorsewood Rd L25 70 B5
Gorsey Ave L30 27 C3
Gorsey Brow WN5 33 E5
Gorsey Brow Cl WN5 33 D5
Gorsey Cop Way L25 70 A6
Gorsey Croft L34 56 F7
Gorsey La
- Haskayne L39 11 B7
- Hightown L38 18 B2
- Litherland L21 27 C2
- St Helens WA5, WA9 59 C5
- Wallasey CH41, CH44 51 B2
- Widnes WA8 73 E1
Gorsey Pl WN8 24 B7
Gorseyville Cres CH63 78 E5
Gorseyville Rd CH63 78 E5
Gorst St 11 L4 52 F7
Gorton Rd L13 54 B2
Gort Rd L36 55 E3
Goschen St
- 6 Liverpool, Everton L5 52 F7
- Liverpool, Stanley L13 53 F3
Gosford St L8 67 F4
Gosforth Rd PR9 4 F8
Gosport Cl WA2 61 F1
Gostins Bldg 16 L1 90 B3
Goswell St L15 68 E8
Gotham Rd CH63 79 B3
Gothic St CH42 66 F2
Gough Ave WA2 61 B2
Gough Rd L13 53 E7
Gourley Rd L13 54 B1
Gourley's La CH48 63 D1
Government Rd CH47 63 B7
Govett Rd WA9 57 D7
Gower St
- Bootle L20 38 B5
- Liverpool L1, L3 90 A2
- St Helens WA9 44 D1
Gowrie Gr L21 38 B7
Goyt Hey Ave WN5 33 E5
Graburn Rd L37 9 F4
Grace Ave L10 40 A7
Grace Cl CH45 51 B5
Grace Rd L9 39 A6
Grace St
- Liverpool L8 67 F4
- St Helens WA9 58 C8
Gradwell St L1 90 B3
Graeme Bryson Ct L11 39 F1
Grafton Cres L8 67 E6
Grafton Dr
- Birkenhead CH49 65 B4
- Southport PR8 7 A5
Grafton Gr L8 67 E4
Grafton Rd CH45 51 B7
Grafton St
- Birkenhead CH43 66 B5
- Liverpool, Dingle L8 67 F3
- Liverpool L8 67 E4
- Liverpool L8 67 E6
- Liverpool, Toxteth L8 67 E5
- Newton-le-W WA12 46 B3
- St Helens WA10 43 D3

Grafton Wlk CH48 63 C2
Graham Cl WA8 72 C1
Graham Dr L26 83 A8
Graham Rd
West Kirby CH48 63 A3
Widnes WA8 84 C8
Graham's Rd L36 55 F2
Graham St WA9 44 C4
Grainger Ave
Birkenhead CH43 65 F1
Bootle L20 38 E5
West Kirby CH48 63 B3
Grain Ind Est L8 67 E4
Graley Cl L26 82 F7
Grammar School La
CH48 63 D1
Grampian Ave CH46 64 E8
Grampian Rd L7 53 E2
Grampian Way
Bebington CH62 88 E4
Birkenhead CH46 64 E8
Golborne WA3 36 D1
Granams Croft L30 27 D4
Granard Rd L15 69 A6
Granary Way L3 67 D6
Granborne Chase L32 29 B3
Granby Cl PR9 1 F3
Granby Cres CH63 79 A2
Granby St L8 68 A6
Grandison Rd L4 39 C1
Grand National Ave L9 28 B1
GRANGE 63 D2
Grange Ave
Halewood L25 82 D8
Liverpool, Mill Yard L12 54 E5
Southport PR9 4 E8
Wallasey CH45 51 B6
Grange Ave N L12 54 F5
Grange Cl WA3 47 C6
Grange Cotts CH63 78 A6
Grange Cres CH66 89 A1
Grange Cross Cl CH48 63 E1
Grange Cross Hey
CH48 63 E1
Grange Cross La CH48 63 E1
Grange Ct
Birkenhead CH43 66 A3
Liverpool L15 68 F7
Grange Dr
Heswall CH60 76 F2
St Helens WA10 57 B8
Thornton Hough CH63 87 A7
Widnes WA8 72 D1
Grange Farm Cres
CH48 63 E3
Grangehurst Ct L25 70 B4
Grange La
Formby L37 9 E5
Liverpool L25 70 A5
Grangemeadow Rd
L25 70 A5
Grange Mews L25 70 B4
Grange Mount
Birkenhead CH43 66 C5
Heswall CH60 76 F1
West Kirby CH48 63 D2
Grange Old Rd CH48 63 C2
GRANGE PARK 57 C8
Grange Park Rd WA10 57 C8
Grange Pk L31 28 F7
Grange Pl CH41 66 C6
Grange Prim Sch The
L30 27 E5
Grange Rd
Ashton-in-M WN4 34 F6
Birkenhead CH41 66 D6
12 Birkenhead CH41 66 E6
Haydock WA11, WA12 45 D5
Heswall CH60 76 F2
Hightown L38 17 E6
Litherland L30 28 B2
Southport PR9 4 E7
West Kirby CH48 63 B2
Grange Rd E 8 CH41 66 E6
Grange Rd W CH41,
CH43 66 C6
Grangeside L25 70 A5
Grange St L6 53 D5
Grange Terr L15 68 F7
Grange The
Southport PR9 2 C3
Wallasey CH44 51 C4
Grange Vale CH42 67 A1
Grange Valley WA11 45 D6
Grange Valley Prim Sch
WA11 45 D5
Grange View 15 CH43 66 C5
Grange Way L25 70 A5
Grange Weint L25 70 B4
Grange Wlk CH48 63 D1
Grangewood L16 54 F1
Granite Terr 9 L36 56 A2
Granston Cl WA5 60 E2
Grant Ave L15 68 F6
Grant Cl
Huyton-w-R L14 55 A3
St Helens WA10 43 E4
Warrington WA5 60 D1
Grant Ct 11 L20 38 C3
Grantham Cl
Heswall CH61 76 E4
Southport PR8 4 A1
Grantham Cres WA11 44 D5
Grantham Rd
Kirkby L33 29 E5
Grantham Rd *continued*
Southport PR8 4 A1
Grantham St L6 53 B3
Grantham Way L30 28 B4
Grantley Rd L15 69 B6
Grantley St WN4 35 A5
Granton Cl L37 9 E3
Granton Rd L5 53 A6
Grant Rd
Huyton-w-R L14 55 A4
Wallasey CH46 50 C4
Grantwood WN4 35 A5
Granville Ave L31 20 C2
Granville Cl
Ormskirk L39 21 B8
Wallasey CH45 50 E6
Granville Ct
Southport PR9 1 D1
3 Wallasey CH45 50 E6
GRANVILLE PARK 21 C8
Granville Pk L39 21 C8
Granville Pk W L39 21 B8
Granville Rd
Liverpool, Garston L19 81 C6
Liverpool L15 68 D7
Southport PR8 3 D4
Granville St WA9 44 D3
Grappenhall Way CH43 65 C7
Grasmere Ave
Birkenhead CH43 65 C5
Orrell WN5 25 F8
Prescot L34 56 F6
St Helens WA11 44 B7
Up Holland WN8 25 B7
Warrington WA2 61 E3
Grasmere Cl
Kirkby L33 29 D4
St Helens WA11 44 B7
Grasmere Ct
9 Birkenhead CH41 66 C5
St Helens WA11 44 B7
Grasmere Dr
Ashton-in-M WN4 35 B5
Bootle L21 38 E8
Wallasey CH45 51 A6
Grasmere Fold WA11 44 B7
Grasmere Gdns L23 26 F3
Grasmere Ho
Huyton-w-R L36 55 E2
Liverpool L17 68 D2
Grasmere Rd
Formby L37 9 D3
Hightown L38 18 A4
Maghull L31 20 D2
Grasmere St L5 53 B5
Grasmere Terr WN2 36 B8
GRASSENDALE 81 A8
Grassendale Ct L19 81 A7
Grassendale Espl L19 80 F6
Grassendale La L19 81 A7
Grassendale Rd L19 81 A7
Grassington Cres L25 70 C2
Grassmoor Cl CH62 88 E8
Grasswood Rd CH49 65 C3
Grass Wood Rd CH49 65 C3
Grasville Rd CH42 66 E3
Gratrix Rd CH62 88 D8
Gratton Pl WN8 24 A8
Gravel Cl PR9 2 F5
Gravel La PR9 2 F5
Grave-Yard La L39 22 A6
Gray Ave WA11 45 D6
Gray Gr L36 70 F8
Graylands Pl L4 39 C1
Graylands Rd
Bebington CH62 79 C6
Liverpool L4 39 C2
Grayling Dr L12 40 D3
Grays Ave L35 56 F6
Grayson Mews CH41 66 F7
Graysons Rd WA11 31 F8
Grayson St L1 90 B2
Gray St L20 38 A5
Grayston Ave WA9 58 D6
GREASBY 64 D2
Greasby Inf Sch CH49 64 C2
Greasby Jun Sch CH49 64 C1
Greasby Rd
Birkenhead CH49 64 E4
Wallasey CH44 51 A4
GREAT ALTCAR 10 E1
Great Ashfield WA8 72 D3
Great Charlotte St
Liverpool L1 90 B3
Liverpool L1 90 B4
GREAT CROSBY 26 D4
Great Crosby RC Prim Sch
L23 26 E4
Great Crosshall St L3 90 B4
Great Delph WA11 45 D7
Great George Pl L1 90 C1
Great George Sq L1 90 C1
Great George's Rd L22 37 E8
Great George St L1 90 C1
Great Hey L30 27 D5
Great Homer St L5 52 E5
Great Howard St L3, L5 52 B4
Great Meols Prim Sch
CH47 48 E1
Great Mersey St L5 52 D6
Great Nelson St L3, L5 52 D4
Great Newton St L3 52 F1
Great Orford St L3 52 F1
Great Richmond St L3 52 E3
Great Sankey High Sch
WA5 74 E7
Greaves St L8 67 F5
Grebe Ave WA10 57 B7
Grecian St L21 37 F8
Grecian Terr L5 52 F6
Gredington St L8 68 A4
Greek St
Liverpool L3 90 C4
Runcorn WA7 84 F3
Greenacre L40 14 E4
Greenacre Cl L25 82 C9
Greenacre Dr CH63 88 C7
Greenacre Rd L25 82 C9
Greenacres 4 L22 26 D1
Greenacres Cl CH43 65 C8
Greenacres Ct 6 CH43 65 C8
Greenall Ave WA5 74 D4
Greenall Ct 15 L34 56 D6
Greenall St
Ashton-in-M WN4 35 B5
St Helens WA10 43 E4
Greenbank
Abram Brow WN2 36 B7
Ormskirk L39 13 C2
Seaforth L22 37 E8
GREEN BANK 43 F2
Green Bank CH63 78 A2
Greenbank Ave
Maghull L31 20 C3
Orrell WN5 25 D3
2 Wallasey CH45 51 B7
Greenbank Cres WA10 43 F3
Greenbank Ct L17 68 E5
Greenbank Dr
Heswall CH61 77 A3
Liverpool, Gillmoss L10 40 B7
Liverpool L15, L17 68 E5
Southport PR8 3 E2
Greenbank High Sch
PR8 3 E1
Greenbank La L17, L18 68 E5
Greenbank Prim Sch
L18 68 F5
Greenbank Rd
Birkenhead CH42 66 C3
Liverpool L18 68 F5
West Kirby CH48 63 C4
Greenburn Ave WA11 33 C1
Greencroft Rd CH44 51 C3
Greendale Rd
Bebington CH62 79 B5
Liverpool L25 69 F4
Green End La WA9 58 C8
Green End Pk L12 54 A7
Greene's Rd L35 56 D2
Greenfield Cl PR9 2 A3
Greenfield Ct L18 69 C1
Greenfield Dr L36 70 F8
Greenfield Gr L36 70 F8
Greenfield La
Heswall CH60 76 C2
Litherland L21 27 A1
Greenfield Rd
Liverpool L13 54 A3
Southport PR8 5 C1
St Helens WA10 43 E5
Greenfields Ave CH62 88 C7
Greenfields Cl WA12 46 C4
Greenfields Cres
Ashton-in-M WN4 35 B4
Bebington CH62 88 C7
Greenfield View WN5 33 D4
Greenfield Way
Liverpool L18 69 C1
3 Wallasey CH44 51 B4
Greenfield Wlk L36 55 F1
Greenfinch Cl 1 L12 40 F3
Greenfinch Gr L26 70 E1
Greenford Cl WN5 25 D6
Greenford Rd PR8 7 C4
Greengables Cl 7 L8 68 A5
Green Gates L36 55 E6
Greengates Com Prim Sch
L26 82 F8
Greenham Ave L33 29 F6
Greenhaven WN8 25 B7
Greenhaven Cl L10 40 A7
Greenheath Way CH46 49 F3
Green Hey Dr L30 27 D3
Greenhey Pl WN8 23 F8
Greenheys Ct 5 L8 68 B6
Green Heys Dr L31 20 F1
Greenheys Gdns 7 L8 68 B6
Greenheys Rd
Irby CH61 76 C5
Liverpool L8 68 B6
Wallasey CH44 51 B4
Greenhill Ave L18 69 C4
Greenhill Cl L18 69 B2
Greenhill Cres WN5 33 F5
Greenhill Pl L36 55 E1
Greenhill Rd
Billinge WN5 33 F5
Liverpool, Grassendale
L19 81 C8
Liverpool, Mossley Hill
L18 69 B2
Greenholme Cl L11 40 A3
Greenhow Ave CH48 63 B3
Green Jones Brow
WA5 59 F6
Green La
Bebington CH63 79 A5
Birkenhead CH41 66 E4
Burtonwood WA5 59 E7
Crosby, Thornton L23 27 B6
Crosby, Waterloo L22 26 C2
Formby L37 9 F5
Litherland L21 27 B2
Liverpool, Calderstones
L18 69 B5
Green La *continued*
Liverpool, Childwall L16,
L18 69 C5
Liverpool L3 90 C3
Liverpool, Stanley L13 53 F4
Maghull L31 20 A2
Maghull L31 20 C1
Ormskirk L39 13 E6
Orrell WN5 25 D3
Rainford WA11 32 A5
Seaforth L21 38 A7
Skelmersdale L40 16 A6
Skelmersdale L40, WN8 15 F6
St Helens WA10 42 F5
Wallasey CH45 50 D6
Wallasey CH45, CH46 50 C5
Widnes WA8 72 E1
Winwick WA2 61 A7
Greenlake Rd L18 69 B2
Green La N L16 69 D6
Greenlands L36 55 E1
Greenland St L1 90 B1
Green Lane Ave L39 13 E6
Green Lane Cl WA2 61 A7
Green Lane Sta CH41 66 F4
Green Lawn
Birkenhead CH42 66 F1
Huyton-w-R L36 56 A4
Green Lawn Gr CH42 66 F1
GREEN LEACH 44 A7
Green Leach Ave
WA11 44 B7
Green Leach Ct WA11 44 B7
Green Leach La WA11 44 B7
Greenlea Cl
Bebington CH63 78 F6
Orrell WN5 25 D5
Greenleaf St L8 68 C7
Greenleas Cl CH45 50 D5
Greenleas Prim Sch
CH45 50 D6
Greenleas Rd CH45 50 D5
Greenleigh Rd L18 69 B2
Green Link L31 20 B2
Greenloon's Dr L37 9 C3
Greenloon's Wlk L37 9 C2
Green Mdws WA3 47 E5
Green Mount CH49 65 A5
Green Oaks Way WA8 73 C1
Greenock Mews WA8 72 E3
Greenock St L3 52 B3
Greenodd Ave L12 40 C1
Greenore Dr L24 83 D2
Greenough Ave L35 57 C5
Greenough St L25 69 F2
Green Park Dr L31 20 B1
Green Park Prim Sch
L31 20 B2
Green Pk L30 27 F5
Green Rd L34 56 C7
Greensbridge La
Halewood L26 83 A8
Liverpool L26, L35 71 B2
Greenshank Cl WA12 46 C4
Greenside L6 52 F3
Greenside Ave
Aintree L10 28 E2
Liverpool L15 69 A7
Greenside Cl L33 30 A6
Green's La L31 12 C1
Greenslate Ct WN5 25 E3
Greenslate Rd WN5 25 E3
Green St L3, L5 52 C4
Greens Wlk L17 68 E3
Green The
Bebington CH62 79 D5
Crosby L23 26 D5
Hale L24 83 D1
Liverpool L13 54 C2
Prescot L34 56 F7
Thornton Hough CH63 87 C4
West Kirby CH48 75 D7
Greenville Cl CH63 78 F5
Greenville Dr L31 20 C1
Greenville Rd CH63 78 F5
Greenway
Ashton-in-M WN4 35 A4
Bebington CH62 79 D3
Birkenhead CH49 64 E5
Crosby L23 27 A5
Heswall CH61 76 E4
Neston CH64 86 B2
Warrington WA5 74 E7
Green Way L36 55 B4
Greenway Ave WN8 24 B8
Greenway Cl WN8 15 E2
Green Way Cl L36 55 B4
Greenway Ct WA9 44 C3
Greenway Rd
Birkenhead CH42 66 D3
Runcorn WA7 84 F1
Speke L24 83 A3
Widnes WA8 73 B1
Greenways WN5 25 D3
Greenways Ct CH62 88 C6
Greenways Specl Sch
L19 80 F7
Greenway The L12 54 E4
Greenwell Rd WA11 45 C6
Greenwich Ave WA8 73 D4
Greenwich Ct L9 39 B8
Greenwich Rd L9 39 B7
Green Wlk PR8 7 D5
Greenwood Cl
Ormskirk L39 13 C1
Prescot L34 56 E6
Greenwood Cres WA2 61 E2
Greenwood Ct 7 WA9 58 C4
Greenwood Dr WA12 46 D2
Greenwood Gdns PR8 4 A5
Greenwood La CH44 51 C5
Greenwood Rd
Birkenhead CH49 65 B3
Hoylake CH47 63 E8
Liverpool L18 69 B1
Greetby Hill L39, L40 14 A6
Greetby Pl WN8 24 A8
Greetham St L1 90 B2
Gregory Cl L16 69 E8
Gregory Way L16 69 E8
Gregson Ct CH45 51 C8
Gregson Rd
Prescot L35 56 D5
Widnes WA8 73 C1
Gregson's Ave L37 9 E5
Gregson St L6 52 F3
Grenfell Cl CH64 86 C1
Grenfell Pk CH64 86 C1
Grenfell Rd L13 53 E8
Grennan Ct 9 CH45 51 B8
Grennan The CH45 51 B8
Grenville Cres CH63 88 C7
Grenville Dr CH61 76 E3
Grenville Rd
4 Birkenhead CH42 66 F3
Neston CH64 86 F1
Grenville St S L1 90 C2
Grenville Way CH42 66 F3
Gresford Ave
Birkenhead CH43 66 A2
Liverpool L17 68 E6
West Kirby CH48 63 C3
Gresford Cl
Prescot L35 56 F3
Warrington WA5 60 E1
Gresham St L7 53 E2
Gresley Cl 6 L7 53 C1
Gressingham Rd L18 69 C2
Gretton Rd L14 55 B5
Greyfriars WN4 34 F4
Greyfriars Rd PR8 7 B6
Greyhound Farm Rd
L24 82 C5
Grey Rd
Ashton-in-M WN4 35 A4
Liverpool L9 39 A4
Grey St L8 67 F6
Greystoke Cl CH49 64 F4
Greystokes L39 13 D2
Greystone Cres L14 54 E3
Greystone Pl L10 39 F7
Greystone Rd
Huyton-w-R L14 54 E2
Liverpool L10 39 F7
Warrington WA5 74 F4
Gribble Rd L10 40 A7
Grierson St L8 68 B7
Grieve Rd L10 40 A7
Griffin Ave CH46 64 E8
Griffin Cl
Liverpool L11 40 C4
St Helens WA10 42 F4
Griffin Mews WA8 73 B3
Griffin St WA9 58 E7
Griffiths Cl CH49 64 C3
Griffiths Dr PR9 4 F8
Griffith's Rd L36 55 E2
Griffiths St L1 90 C2
Griffon Ho PR9 1 F2
Grimrod Pl WN8 24 A7
Grimshaw Ct WA3 36 A1
Grimshaw La L39 13 E7
Grimshaw Rd WN8 24 D8
Grimshaw St
Bootle L20 38 B2
Golborne WA3 36 A1
St Helens WA9 58 C6
Grinfield St L7 53 A1
Grinshill Cl L8 68 A6
Grinstead Cl PR8 3 F1
Grinton Cres L36 55 D2
Grisedale Ave WA2 61 B3
Grisedale Cl L37 9 E3
Grisedale Rd CH62 88 F8
Grizedale WA8 72 B2
Grizedale Ave WA11 44 B8
Groarke Dr WA5 74 D5
Groes Rd L19 81 B7
Grogan Sq L20 38 D6
Gronow Pl L20 38 E6
Grosmont Rd L32 40 F8
Grosomont Rd 1 L32 41 A8
Grosvenor Ave
Crosby L23 26 E2
3 Golborne WA3 47 D8
West Kirby CH48 63 B2
Grosvenor Cl
Litherland L30 27 F3
Southport PR8 3 E3
Grosvenor Ct
1 Birkenhead CH43 66 B5
Liverpool L18 68 E3
Prescot L34 56 D6
Southport PR8 3 E3
Grosvenor Dr CH45 51 B8
Grosvenor Gdns
Newton-le-W WA12 46 C2
Southport PR8 3 F3
Grosvenor Pl
Birkenhead CH43 66 A5
Southport PR8 3 F3
Grosvenor Rd
Birkenhead CH43 66 B5
Haydock WA11 45 B7
Hoylake CH47 63 B6

- Grosvenor Rd *continued*
  - Liverpool, Cressington Park L19 81 A6
  - Liverpool L15 68 E7
  - 7 Liverpool, Walton on the Hill L4 38 F2
  - Maghull L31 28 D7
  - Prescot L34 56 D6
  - Southport PR8 3 E4
  - St Helens WA10 43 D2
  - Wallasey CH45 51 B8
  - Widnes WA8 73 B5
- Grosvenor St
  - Liverpool L3 52 D3
  - Wallasey CH44 51 B4
- Grosvenor Terr L8 68 B4
- Grove Ave CH60 76 F1
- Grovedale Dr CH46 50 A1
- Grovedale Rd L18 68 F5
- Grove Ho L8 68 C6
- Grovehurst Ave L14 54 F4
- Groveland Ave
  - Hoylake CH47 63 B7
  - Wallasey CH45 50 D6
- Groveland Rd CH45 50 D6
- Grovelands L7 68 A8
- Grove Mans 5 CH45 50 E6
- Grove Mead L31 20 F1
- Grove Park Ave L12 54 B8
- Grove Pk
  - Liverpool L8 68 C6
  - Ormskirk L39 13 F7
  - Southport PR9 4 F8
- Grove Pl
  - Hoylake CH47 63 B7
  - Liverpool L4 52 E7
- Grove Rd
  - Birkenhead CH42 66 F2
  - Hoylake CH47 63 B7
  - Liverpool L6 53 D3
  - Up Holland WN8 25 C8
  - Wallasey CH45 50 F7
- Groveside CH48 63 A2
- Grove Side L7 68 A8
- Grove Sq CH62 79 A7
- Grove St
  - Ashton-in-M WN4 35 A4
  - Bebington CH62 79 B7
  - Bootle L20 38 A4
  - Liverpool, Edge Hill L7, L8 68 A8
  - Liverpool, Wavertree L15 68 F8
  - Runcorn WA7 84 F3
  - Southport PR8 4 A4
- Groves The
  - Birkenhead CH43 66 A5
  - Kirkby L32 40 E7
- Grove Street Prim Sch CH62 79 B7
- Grove Terr
  - Hoylake CH47 63 B7
  - Southport PR8 4 A5
- Grove The
  - Bebington CH63 79 A5
  - Birkenhead CH43 66 B3
  - Golborne WA3 36 D1
  - Huyton-w-R L28 55 C7
  - Liverpool L13 53 F5
  - Ormskirk L39 21 C7
  - St Helens WA10 43 C5
  - Wallasey CH44 51 C3
  - Warrington WA5 74 F4
- Grove Way L7 68 A8
- Grovewood PR8 3 E5
- Grovewood Ct CH43 66 B3
- Grovewood Gdns L35 56 E3
- Grundy Cl
  - Southport PR8 4 E5
  - Widnes WA8 72 F3
- Grundy St
  - Golborne WA3 47 A7
  - Liverpool L5 52 C6
- Guardian Ct CH48 63 B1
- Guelph St L7 53 A2
- Guernsey Rd
  - Liverpool L13 54 A4
  - Widnes WA8 73 E3
- Guffitts Cl CH47 48 E1
- Guffitt's Rake CH47 48 E1
- Guildford Ave L30 27 F1
- Guildford Rd PR8 8 A8
- Guildford St CH44 51 D4
- Guildhall Rd L9 39 A6
- Guild Hey L34 41 D4
- Guillemot Way L26 70 E1
- Guilsted Rd L11 40 A2
- Guinea Gap CH44 51 E3
- Guion Rd L21 38 B7
- Guion St L6 53 B4
- Gullivers World Theme Pk* WA5 60 E1
- Gulls Way CH60 85 E7
- Gunning Ave WA10 43 B5
- Gunning Cl WA10 43 B5
- Gurnall St 13 L4 52 F7
- Gutticar Rd WA8 72 B1
- Guy Cl CH41 66 E4
- Gwendoline Cl CH61 77 A5
- Gwendoline St L8 67 F6
- Gwenfron Rd 10 L6 53 B3
- Gwent Cl L6 53 B5
- Gwent St L8 68 A6
- Gwladys St L4 38 F1
- Gwladys Street Prim Sch L4 39 A1
- Gwydir St L8 68 A5
- Gwydrin Rd L18 69 C5

H

- Hackett Ave L20 38 D6
- Hackins Hey L2 90 A4
- Hackthorpe St L5 52 F7
- Hadassah Gr L17 68 C4
- Hadden Cl L35 57 A4
- Haddock St L20 38 B1
- Haddon Ave L9 38 F6
- Haddon Dr
  - Heswall CH61 76 F4
  - Widnes WA8 72 C3
- Haddon Rd
  - Birkenhead CH42 67 A2
  - Golborne WA3 36 D2
- Haddon St 5 WN4 34 F5
- Haddon Wlk L12 40 E3
- Hadfield Ave CH47 63 B7
- Hadfield Cl WA8 73 E2
- Hadfield Gr L25 70 C3
- Hadleigh Cl WA5 74 E5
- Hadleigh Rd L32 29 F1
- Hadley Ave CH62 79 C1
- Hadstock Ave L37 9 D1
- Hadwens Bldgs L3 90 A4
- Haggerston Rd L4 39 A2
- Hague Bush Cl WA3 36 E1
- Hahnemann Rd L4 38 E2
- Haig Ave
  - Birkenhead CH46 64 F8
  - Southport PR8 4 E5
- Haigh Cres L31 20 C4
- Haigh Ct PR8 4 F6
- Haigh Rd L22 26 E1
- Haigh St L3, L6 52 F3
- Haig Rd WA8 73 A1
- Haileybury Ave L10 28 D2
- Haileybury Rd L25 82 B9
- Hailsham Rd L19 80 F8
- Halby Rd L9 39 B6
- Halcombe Rd L12 54 D7
- Halcyon Rd CH41 66 C4
- Haldane Ave CH41 65 F7
- Haldane Rd L4 39 A2
- HALE 83 D1
- HALE BANK 84 A4
- Hale Bank CE Prim Sch WA8 84 A5
- Halebank Rd WA8 83 F5
- Hale Bank Terr WA8 84 A4
- Hale CE Prim Sch L24 83 E1
- Hale Ct WA8 84 A4
- Hale Dr L24 82 E3
- Halefield St WA10 43 F4
- Hale Gate Rd
  - Hale WA8 83 F3
  - Widnes WA8 84 A3
- Hale Gr WN4 34 F5
- HALE HEATH 83 A1
- Hale Rd
  - Hale L24 83 B2
  - Liverpool, Kirkdale L4 38 E1
  - Speke L24 82 C4
  - Speke L24 82 E3
  - Wallasey CH45 51 C6
  - Widnes WA8 84 C7
- Hale Road Ind Est WA8 84 B4
- Hale St L2 90 A4
- Hale View Rd L36 56 A2
- HALEWOOD 82 F9
- Halewood Ave WA3 35 F1
- Halewood CE Prim Sch L26 71 A1
- Halewood Cl L25 70 B4
- Halewood Coll L26 82 E8
- Halewood Dr
  - Liverpool L25 70 B2
  - Liverpool L25 70 C2
- Halewood Lane Ends L26 83 A8
- Halewood Pl L25 70 C3
- Halewood Rd L25 70 C3
- Halewood Sta L26 82 F9
- Halewood 'Triangle' Ctry Pk L26 82 E9
- HALEWOOD VILLAGE 83 A8
- Halewood Way L25 70 C2
- Haley Rd N WA5 59 E6
- Haley Rd S WA5 59 E5
- Half Crown St L5 52 C6
- Halfpenny Cl L19 81 B7
- Halftide Wharf L3 90 A1
- Halidon Ct L20 38 A4
- Halifax Cl WA2 61 D2
- Halifax Cres L23 27 B6
- Halifax Rd PR8 7 C5
- Halkirk Rd L18 69 C1
- Halkyn Ave L17 68 D6
- Halkyn Dr L5 53 A5
- Hallam Wlk 3 L7 53 C1
- Hall Ave WA8 72 A1
- Hallbridge Gdns WN8 25 B8
- Hall Brow Cl L39 14 B4
- Hallcroft WN8 16 C2
- Hall Dr
  - Birkenhead CH49 64 C2
  - Kirkby L32 29 E3
- Hall Farm CH62 89 A4
- Hallfields Rd WA2 61 D1
- Hall Gn WN8 25 B7
- HALL GREEN 25 A7
- Hall Green Cl WN8 25 B7
- Hall La
  - Bickerstaffe L39 22 E4
  - Cronton L35 72 C7
  - Huyton-w-R L36 56 A2
  - Ince Blundell L38 18 F3
- Hall La *continued*
  - Kirkby L32 29 E2
  - Kirkby L33 30 A8
  - Liverpool, Kensington L7 53 A2
  - Liverpool, Walton L9 39 B6
  - Maghull L31 28 D8
  - Maghull, Lydiate L31 20 B7
  - Newton-le-W WA5 60 B8
  - Orrell WN5 25 F4
  - Prescot L34, L35 56 D5
  - Skelmersdale L40 15 A6
  - St Helens WA9 59 A4
- Hallmoor Cl L39 13 E2
- Hall Nook WA5 74 F3
- Hallows Ave WA2 61 D1
- Hall Rd WA11 45 E7
- Hall Rd E L23 26 B6
- Hall Rd W L23 26 A6
- Hall Road Sta L23 26 A6
- Hallsands Rd L32 40 E8
- Hall's Cotts WA10 43 D6
- Hallside Cl L19 81 A8
- Hall St
  - Ashton-in-M WN2 35 E7
  - Southport PR9 4 C7
  - St Helens, Pocket Nook WA10 44 B4
  - St Helens WA9 58 E3
- Hall Terr WA5 74 E7
- Halltine Cl L23 26 A6
- Hallville Rd L18 69 B5
- Hall Wood Ave WA11 34 F1
- HALSALL 12 B8
- Halsall Bldgs 6 PR9 4 C8
- Halsall Cl L23 26 E5
- Halsall Ct L39 13 D6
- Halsall Gn CH63 79 B1
- Halsall La
  - Formby L37 9 F3
  - Haskayne L39 12 D6
  - Ormskirk L39 13 D6
- Halsall Rd
  - Bootle L20 38 C5
  - Southport PR8 8 A8
- Halsall's Cotts WA8 83 E5
- Halsall St L34 56 D7
- Halsbury Rd
  - Liverpool L6 53 C3
  - Wallasey CH45 51 B6
- Halsey Ave L12 53 F7
- Halsey Cres L12 53 F7
- Halsnead Ave L35 56 C1
- Halsnead Cl L13 54 A1
- Halsnead Com Prim Sch L35 56 D2
- Halstead Rd
  - Liverpool L9 38 F6
  - Wallasey CH44 51 C3
- Halstead Wlk 5 L32 29 C1
- Halton Chase L40 14 E4
- Halton Cres CH49 64 B3
- Halton Hey L35 56 D1
- Halton Rd
  - Maghull L31 20 D3
  - 9 Wallasey CH45 51 A6
  - Warrington WA5 74 F6
- Halton St WA11 45 E6
- HALTON VIEW 73 C1
- Halton View Rd WA8 73 C1
- Halton Wlk L25 70 C6
- Halton Wood L32 29 B3
- Halville Rd CH44 51 C3
- Halyard Ho CH60 76 C2
- Hambledon Dr CH49 64 D4
- Hamble Dr WA5 74 F3
- Hambleton Cl
  - Liverpool L11 40 B4
  - Widnes WA8 72 C3
- Hamblett Cres WA11 44 B6
- Hamer Ho CH45 50 E5
- Hamer St WA10 43 F4
- Hamil Cl CH47 48 E1
- Hamilton Cl CH64 86 B2
- Hamilton Ct L23 26 B4
- Hamilton La CH41 66 E7
- Hamilton Rd
  - Garswood WN4 34 D4
  - Liverpool L5 52 F5
  - St Helens WA10 43 C6
  - Wallasey CH45 51 A8
- Hamilton Sq CH41 66 F7
- Hamilton Square Sta CH41 66 F7
- Hamilton St CH41 66 F6
- Hamlet Ct L17 68 C3
- Hamlet Rd CH45 50 F6
- Hamlin Rd L19 81 D6
- Hammersley Ave WA9 58 C3
- Hammersley St WA9 58 C3
- Hammersmith Way WA8 73 D4
- Hammill Ave WA10 43 E6
- Hammill St WA10 43 D5
- Hammond Rd L33 30 C3
- Hammond St WA9 44 D2
- Hamnett Rd L34 56 E7
- Hampden Gr CH42 66 E4
- Hampden Rd CH42 66 E4
- Hampden St L4 38 F2
- Hampshire Ave L30 27 C3
- Hampshire Gdns WA10 43 F2
- Hampson Cl WN4 35 B2
- Hampson St L6 53 C5
- Hampstead Rd
  - Liverpool L6 53 C4
  - Wallasey CH44 51 C3
- Hampton Chase CH43 65 D3
- Hampton Cl WA8 73 E3
- Hampton Court Rd L12 54 D5
- Hampton Court Way WA8 73 D4
- Hampton Dr WA8 72 C5
- Hampton Pl WA11 44 B6
- Hampton Rd
  - Formby L37 9 E1
  - Southport PR8 4 C5
- Hampton St L8 67 F7
- Hanbury Rd L4 53 D8
- Handel Ct L8 68 B6
- Handel Rd L27 70 C6
- Handfield Pl 5 L5 53 A5
- Handfield Rd L22 26 E1
- Handfield St L5 53 A5
- Handford Ave CH62 88 F5
- Handley Ct L19 80 F8
- Handley Dr WA2 61 E1
- Handley St WA7 84 F3
- Hands St L21 38 B6
- Handsworth Wlk PR8 4 F3
- Hanford Ave L9 38 F6
- Hankey Dr L20 38 E5
- Hankey St 2 WA7 84 F2
- Hankinson St L13 54 A1
- Hankin St L5 52 D5
- Hanley Cl WA8 72 C1
- Hanley Rd WA8 72 C1
- Hanlon Ave L20 38 D6
- Hanmer Rd L32 29 B2
- Hannah Cl CH61 76 E3
- Hannan Rd L6 53 C3
- Hanns Hall Rd CH64 87 D1
- Hanover Cl CH43 65 F6
- Hanover St L1 90 B3
- Hansard Ct WA9 57 D7
- Hansby Cl WN8 24 E8
- Hansby Dr L24, L25 82 C6
- Hanson Pk CH43 65 E5
- Hanson Rd L9 39 C5
- Hanson Road Bsns Pk L9 39 C5
- Hans Rd 9 L4 39 A1
- Hanstock Cl WN5 25 E5
- Hants La L39 13 E6
- Hanwell St L6 53 B6
- Hanworth Cl L12 40 E3
- Hapsford Rd L21 38 B6
- Hapton St L5 52 E6
- Harbern Cl L12 54 D6
- Harbord Rd L22 26 C1
- Harbord St L7 53 B1
- Harbord Terr L22 26 C1
- Harborne Dr CH63 78 F2
- Harbreck Gr L9 39 D3
- Harbury Ave PR8 7 A4
- Harcourt Ave CH44 51 E3
- Harcourt St
  - Birkenhead CH41 66 C7
  - Liverpool L4 52 D7
- Hardacre St L39 13 F6
- Hardie Ave CH46 49 C1
- Hardie Cl WA9 58 A3
- Hardie Rd L36 56 A3
- Harding Ave
  - Bebington CH63 79 A4
  - Warrington WA2 61 E1
- Harding Cl L5 53 A5
- Hardinge Rd L19 81 D8
- Hardknott Rd CH62 88 E8
- Hard La WA10 43 E6
- Hardman St L1 90 C2
- Hardshaw Ctr WA10 44 A3
- Hardshaw St
  - St Helens WA10 44 A3
  - St Helens WA10 44 A4
- Hardwick Rd WN4 35 A5
- Hardy St
  - Liverpool, Garston L19 81 D4
  - Liverpool L1 90 B1
  - Liverpool L1 90 C2
- Harebell Cl
  - Formby L37 9 F1
  - Widnes WA8 72 E4
- Harebell St L5 52 D7
- Hare Croft L28 54 F8
- Harefield Gn L24 82 D4
- Harefield Rd L24 82 D4
- HARESFINCH 44 B7
- Haresfinch Cl 3 L26 71 A1
- Haresfinch Rd WA10, WA11 44 B6
- Haresfinch View WA11 44 B6
- Hares La PR8 5 D1
- Harewell Rd L11 40 A1
- Harewood Ave PR8 7 C6
- Harewood Cl L36 55 E3
- Harewood Rd CH45 51 A7
- Harewood St 3 L6 53 A4
- Harford Cl WA5 74 F4
- Hargate Rd L33 29 F2
- Hargate Wlk 3 L33 29 F2
- Hargrave Ave CH43 65 E3
- Hargrave Cl CH43 65 E3
- Hargrave La
  - Bebington CH64 88 A4
  - Thornton Hough CH63, CH64 87 F5
- Hargreaves Ct WA8 73 D1
- Hargreaves Ho 5 WA8 73 D1
- Hargreaves Rd L17 68 C3
- Hargreaves St
  - Southport PR8 4 C6
  - St Helens WA9 44 E3
- Harington Cl L37 9 D3
- Harington Gn L37 9 D3
- Harington Rd L37 9 D4
- Harker St L3 52 E3
- Harke St L7 68 B8
- Harland Dr WN4 35 C3
- Harland Gn
  - Liverpool L24 82 F4
  - Speke L24 83 A3
- Harland Rd CH42 66 D4
- Harlech Cl WA5 60 E2
- Harlech Ct CH63 78 F4
- Harlech Rd L23 26 C3
- Harlech St
  - Ashton-in-M WN4 34 F5
  - Liverpool L4 38 F1
  - Wallasey CH44 51 E2
- Harleston Rd L33 30 A3
- Harleston Wlk L33 30 A3
- Harley Ave CH63 78 C8
- Harley Bldgs 11 L3 90 A4
- Harley St 2 L9 39 A6
- Harlian Ave CH46 64 D7
- Harlow Cl WA9 57 F7
- Harlow St L8 67 F4
- Harlyn Cl L26 82 E7
- Harlyn Gdns WA5 74 D3
- Harmony Way L13 54 A1
- Harold Ave WN4 35 A5
- Haroldene Gr L34 55 F5
- Harold Rd WA11 45 F7
- Harper Rd L9 39 A4
- Harpers Pond La L15 69 A8
- Harper St 3 L6, L7 53 A2
- Harp's Croft L30 27 C3
- Harptree Cl L35 56 E3
- Harradon Rd L9 39 B7
- Harridge La L39 12 F8
- Harrier Dr
  - Liverpool L26 70 E1
  - Skelmersdale WN8 24 E8
- Harrier Rd WA2 61 F2
- Harringay Ave L18 68 F5
- Harrington Ave CH47 63 C7
- Harrington Chambers L2 90 A3
- Harrington Rd
  - Crosby L23 26 D4
  - Litherland L21 27 D1
  - Liverpool L3 67 E4
- Harrington St L2 90 A3
- Harris Cl CH63 79 A2
- Harris Dr L20, L30 38 D7
- Harris Gdns WA9 44 B1
- Harris Grange WA10 43 C1
- Harrismith Rd L10 39 F6
- Harrison Dr
  - Bootle L20 38 E3
  - Haydock WA11 45 A6
  - Rainford WA11 31 F8
  - Wallasey CH45 50 E7
- Harrison Hey L36 55 E1
- Harrison Sq WA5 60 F1
- Harrison St WA8 84 B6
- Harrison Way
  - Liverpool L3 67 E4
  - Newton-le-W WA12 46 C4
- Harris St
  - St Helens WA10 43 E4
  - Widnes WA8 73 C1
- Harrocks Cl L30 27 D5
- Harrock Wood Cl CH61 76 E6
- Harrod Dr PR8 3 E3
- Harrogate Cl
  - Bebington CH62 88 D4
  - Warrington WA5 60 A1
- Harrogate Dr L5 52 F5
- Harrogate Rd
  - Bebington CH62 88 D4
  - Bebington, Dacre Hill CH42 79 A8
- Harrogate Way PR9 2 C6
- Harrogate Wlk CH42 79 A8
- Harron Cl 5 L32 29 C2
- Harrops Croft L30 27 E4
- Harrowby Cl L8 68 A7
- Harrowby Rd
  - Birkenhead CH42 66 D4
  - Seaforth L21 37 F7
  - Wallasey CH44 51 E4
- Harrowby Rd S CH42 66 C4
- Harrowby St 4 L8 68 A7
- Harrow Cl
  - Litherland L30 27 F2
  - Orrell WN5 25 F8
  - Wallasey CH44 50 F5
- Harrow Dr L10 28 D2
- Harrow Gr CH62 88 E8
- Harrow Rd
  - Liverpool L4 53 B6
  - Wallasey CH44 50 F5
- Harsnips WN8 16 C2
- Harswell Cl WN5 25 E5
- Hartdale Rd
  - Crosby L23 27 B6
  - Liverpool L18 69 A4
- Hartford Cl CH43 65 F3
- Harthill Ave L18 69 B4
- Harthill Mews CH43 50 C1
- Harthill Rd L18 69 C4
- Hartington Ave CH41 66 B7
- Hartington Rd
  - Liverpool, Garston L19 81 D6
  - Liverpool L8 68 C6
  - Liverpool, Sandfield Park L12 54 C6
  - St Helens WA10 43 D5

James Court Apartments L25 ... 70 B2
James Ct L25 ... 70 B2
James Dunne Ave L3, L5 ... 52 C5
James Gr WA10 ... 43 E2
James Holt Ave L32 ... 29 D2
James Hopkins Way 1 L4 ... 52 D7
James Larkin Way L4 ... 52 D7
James Rd
Haydock WA11 ... 45 F7
Liverpool L25 ... 70 B2
James Simpson Way L30 ... 27 F4
James St
Ashton-in-M WN2 ... 35 E7
Birkenhead CH43 ... 66 C4
Liverpool, Garston L19 ... 81 C6
Liverpool L2 ... 90 A3
St Helens WA9 ... 58 D3
7 Wallasey CH44 ... 51 E2
James Street Sta L2 ... 90 A3
Jamieson Ave L23 ... 27 A4
Jamieson Rd L15 ... 68 E7
Jane's Brook Rd PR8 ... 4 E4
Jane St WA9 ... 58 F7
Janet St L7 ... 53 B1
Japonica Gdns WA9 ... 59 A7
Jarrett Rd L33 ... 30 A4
Jarrett Wlk L33 ... 30 A4
Jarrow Cl CH43 ... 66 B4
Jasmine Cl
Birkenhead CH46, CH49 ... 64 D7
Liverpool L5 ... 52 F4
Jasmine Ct L36 ... 55 F5
Jasmine Gdns WA9 ... 59 A7
Jasmine Gr WA8 ... 84 D8
Jasmine Mews L17 ... 68 A3
Jason St L5 ... 52 E6
Jason Wlk L5 ... 52 E6
Java Rd L4 ... 39 D1
Jean Wlk L10 ... 40 B6
Jedburgh Dr L33 ... 29 D6
Jeffereys Cres L36 ... 55 B2
Jeffereys Dr L36 ... 55 A2
Jefferson Gdns WA8 ... 72 F3
Jeffreys Dr CH49 ... 64 D5
Jellicoe Cl CH48 ... 75 D6
Jenkinson St L3 ... 52 E3
Jenner Dr CH46 ... 50 A2
Jennet Hey WN4 ... 34 F6
Jennings Park Ave WN2 ... 36 C7
Jericho Cl L17 ... 68 D2
Jericho Farm Cl L17 ... 68 D1
Jericho Farm Wlk L17 ... 68 D1
Jericho La L17 ... 68 D1
Jermyn St L8 ... 68 B6
Jerningham Rd L11 ... 39 D3
Jersey Ave L21 ... 27 B1
Jersey Cl L20 ... 38 C3
Jersey St
Bootle L20 ... 38 C3
St Helens WA9 ... 58 C3
Jesmond St L15 ... 68 D8
Jessamine Rd CH42 ... 66 E3
Jessop Ho WA7 ... 84 E3
Jet Cl L6 ... 53 B4
Jeudwine Cl L25 ... 70 B1
Joan Ave
Birkenhead, Greasby CH49 ... 64 E4
Birkenhead, Moreton CH46 ... 64 D8
Jocelyn Cl CH63 ... 79 A3
John Bagot Cl L5 ... 52 E5
John Hunter Way L30 ... 27 F3
John Lennon Dr L6 ... 53 B3
John Middleton Cl L24 ... 83 E2
John Moores Cl L7 ... 68 A8
John Moores Uni L3 ... 52 F1
John Moores Univ
Liverpool, Edge Hill L7 ... 67 F8
Liverpool L1 ... 90 C2
Liverpool L3 ... 90 B4
Liverpool L3 ... 90 C3
Liverpool, Vauxhall L3 ... 52 D3
John Moores Univ Avril Roberts Ctr L3 ... 90 A4
John Moores Univ IM Marsh Campus L17 ... 68 F1
Johns Ave WA11 ... 45 E7
John Smith Ho L20 ... 38 B5
Johnson Ave
Newton-le-W WA12 ... 46 B5
Prescot L35 ... 56 D4
Johnson Gr L14 ... 54 E5
Johnson Rd CH43 ... 65 F1
Johnson's La WA8 ... 73 E1
Johnson St
Liverpool L1, L2, L3 ... 90 B4
Southport PR9 ... 4 B8
St Helens WA9 ... 44 C4
Johnson Wlk 10 L7 ... 53 C1
John St
Ashton-in-M WN4 ... 35 D5
Birkenhead CH41 ... 66 F7
Golborne WA3 ... 47 A8
Liverpool L3 ... 52 F3
Johnston Ave L20 ... 38 E6
Jones Farm Rd L25 ... 70 C4
Jones St L3 ... 90 C3
Jonson Rd CH64 ... 86 E1
Jonville Rd L9 ... 39 C7
Jordan St L1 ... 90 B1
Joseph Gardner Way L20 ... 38 B5
Joseph Lister Cl L30 ... 27 F3
Joseph St
St Helens WA9 ... 58 E7
Widnes WA8 ... 73 C2
Joshua Cl L5 ... 52 E6
Joyce Wlk L10 ... 40 C7
Joy La
Burtonwood WA5 ... 59 E4
St Helens WA8, WA9 ... 58 E2
Joy Wlk WA9 ... 58 E3
Jubilee Ave
Liverpool L14 ... 54 D1
Ormskirk L39 ... 13 F6
Orrell WN5 ... 25 D4
Warrington WA5 ... 74 E4
Jubilee Cres
Bebington CH62 ... 79 B5
Haydock WA11 ... 45 F7
Jubilee Ct
Birkenhead CH43 ... 66 A5
Golborne WA3 ... 36 A1
Jubilee Dr
Litherland L30 ... 28 A1
Liverpool L7 ... 53 B2
Prescot L35 ... 56 D2
Skelmersdale WN8 ... 23 E8
West Kirby CH48 ... 63 B3
Jubilee Rd
Bootle L21 ... 38 B7
Crosby L23 ... 26 C3
Formby L37 ... 9 D1
Jubilee Way WA8 ... 72 E1
Jubits La
St Helens WA8, WA9 ... 58 B2
Widnes WA8 ... 73 A8
Juddfield St WA11 ... 45 A7
Judges Dr L6 ... 53 C4
Judges Way L6 ... 53 C4
Julian Way WA8 ... 72 F4
Julie Gr L12 ... 54 F5
Juliet Ave CH63 ... 78 E7
Juliet Gdns CH63 ... 78 E7
July Rd L6 ... 53 D5
July St L20 ... 38 C5
Junction La
Newton-le-W WA12 ... 46 B3
St Helens WA9 ... 58 F7
Junction One Ret Pk CH44 ... 50 D3
Junction Rd WA11 ... 31 E8
June Ave CH62 ... 88 E8
June Rd L6 ... 53 D5
June St L20 ... 38 C4
Juniper Cl
Birkenhead CH49 ... 64 C2
Huyton-w-R L28 ... 55 B8
St Helens WA10 ... 43 D4
Juniper Gdns L23 ... 27 B6
Juniper St L20 ... 52 C8
Jurby Ct WA2 ... 61 F1
Justene Cl WA3 ... 36 A2
Justin Way L35 ... 57 B5
Juvenal Pl L3 ... 52 E4
Juvenal St L3 ... 52 D4

K

Kaigh Ave L23 ... 26 D5
Kale Cl CH48 ... 63 B1
Kale Gr L33 ... 30 A5
Kara Cl L20 ... 38 C3
Karan Way L31 ... 29 B3
Karen Cl WA5 ... 60 A6
Karonga Rd L10 ... 39 F7
Karonga Way L10 ... 39 F7
Karslake Rd
Liverpool L18 ... 68 F5
Wallasey CH44 ... 51 D3
Katherine Wlk L10 ... 40 C7
Kearsley Cl L4 ... 52 E7
Kearsley St L4 ... 52 E7
Keates St WA9 ... 58 F8
Keats Ave
Longshaw WN5 ... 25 D1
Prescot L35 ... 56 F3
Keats Cl WA8 ... 84 F8
Keats Gn L36 ... 56 A1
Keats Gr WA2 ... 61 C2
Keats St L20 ... 38 B5
Keats Terr PR8 ... 4 F6
Keble Dr
Aintree L10 ... 28 C3
Wallasey CH45 ... 50 D6
Keble Rd L20 ... 38 C2
Keble St L6, L7 ... 53 A3
Kedleston St L8 ... 68 A4
Keegan Dr CH44 ... 51 E2
Keele Cl CH43 ... 50 C2
Keel Hey CH64 ... 88 B1
Keel Wharf
Liverpool L3 ... 90 A1
Liverpool L3 ... 90 A2
Keenan Dr L20 ... 38 E5
Keene Ct L30 ... 27 D4
Keepers La CH63 ... 78 B5
Keighley Ave CH45 ... 50 E5
Keightley St 8 CH41 ... 66 D7
Keir Hardie Ave L20 ... 38 E5
Keith Ave
5 Liverpool L4 ... 39 A1
Warrington WA5 ... 74 E6
Keith Ct 4 L4 ... 38 F1
Keith Dr CH63 ... 88 D5
Keithley Wlk L24 ... 82 E5
Kelbey Cl 18 L8 ... 68 A4
Kelbrook Cl WA9 ... 58 D6
Kelburn Gr L12 ... 54 D8
Kelda Ct L25 ... 70 A6
Kelday Cl L33 ... 29 E2
Kelk Beck Cl L31 ... 20 F2
Kellet's Pl CH42 ... 66 F3
Kellett Rd CH46 ... 50 B3
Kellitt Rd L15 ... 68 E7
Kelly Dr L20 ... 38 E5
Kelly St L34 ... 56 E6
Kelmscott Dr CH44 ... 50 E4
Kelsall Ave
Bebington CH62 ... 88 F3
St Helens WA9 ... 58 B4
Kelsall Cl
Bebington CH62 ... 88 E3
Birkenhead CH43 ... 65 F3
Widnes WA8 ... 72 D1
Kelsey Cl WA10 ... 43 D4
Kelso Cl L33 ... 29 D6
Kelso Rd L6 ... 53 C3
Kelton Gr L17 ... 68 E2
Kelvin Cl WN4 ... 34 D4
Kelvin Ct CH44 ... 51 E1
Kelvin Gr L8 ... 68 A6
Kelvin Pk CH44 ... 51 E1
Kelvin Rd
Birkenhead CH41 ... 66 E4
Wallasey CH41, CH44 ... 51 E1
Kelvinside
Crosby L23 ... 26 F3
Wallasey CH44 ... 51 E1
Kemberton Dr WA8 ... 73 A5
Kemble St
Liverpool L7 ... 53 B2
Prescot L34 ... 56 D6
Kemlyn Rd L4 ... 53 A7
Kempsell Way L26 ... 83 A7
Kempsell Wlk L26 ... 83 A7
Kempsey Gr WA9 ... 57 E7
Kempson Terr CH63 ... 78 F4
Kempston St L3 ... 52 F2
Kempton Cl
Huyton-w-R L36 ... 55 D1
Newton-le-W WA12 ... 46 D5
Kempton Park Fold PR8 ... 4 F3
Kempton Park Rd L10 ... 28 E2
Kempton Rd
Bebington CH62 ... 79 B8
Liverpool L15 ... 68 D8
Kemsley Rd L14 ... 54 F4
Kenbury Cl L33 ... 30 A4
Kenbury Rd L33 ... 30 A4
Kendal Ave WA2 ... 61 C2
Kendal Cl
Bebington CH63 ... 78 F6
Rainford WA11 ... 23 F2
Kendal Dr
Maghull L31 ... 20 E2
Rainford WA11 ... 23 F2
Rainhill L35 ... 57 A4
St Helens WA11 ... 44 B8
Kendal Gr WN4 ... 35 B4
Kendal Pk L12 ... 54 D6
Kendal Rd
Kirkby L33 ... 29 D4
Liverpool L16 ... 69 E7
Wallasey CH44 ... 51 A2
Widnes WA8 ... 72 C1
Kendal St 15 CH41 ... 66 E6
Kendal Way PR8 ... 7 B3
Kendrick's Cross L35 ... 57 C3
Kendricks Fold L35 ... 57 B3
Kenham Ct 9 CH45 ... 51 A8
Kenilworth Cl L25 ... 69 E3
Kenilworth Dr CH61 ... 76 F5
Kenilworth Gdns
Birkenhead CH49 ... 64 E6
Newton-le-W WA12 ... 46 C1
Kenilworth Rd
Crosby L23 ... 26 C3
Golborne WA3 ... 47 E7
Liverpool L16 ... 69 D7
Southport PR8 ... 7 B4
Wallasey CH44 ... 51 E3
Kenilworth St 2 L20 ... 38 B3
Kenilworth Way L25 ... 69 E3
Kenley Ave WA8 ... 72 D5
Kenmare Rd L15 ... 68 E6
Kenmay Way L33 ... 30 A3
Kenmore 7 L22 ... 26 E1
Kenmore Gr WN4 ... 34 D4
Kenmore Rd CH43 ... 65 E1
Kennelwood Ave L33 ... 29 F3
Kennessee Cl L31 ... 28 E8
Kenneth Cl L30 ... 27 E3
Kenneth Rd WA8 ... 84 C8
Kennet Rd
Bebington CH63 ... 78 D5
Haydock WA11 ... 45 C6
Kennford Rd L11 ... 40 C5
Kennington Pk WA8 ... 72 E4
KENSINGTON ... 53 B2
Kensington L6, L7 ... 53 B2
Kensington Ave WA9 ... 58 C7
Kensington Cl WA8 ... 73 D4
Kensington Com Prim Jun Sch L7 ... 53 B2
Kensington Ct 1 L37 ... 10 A3
Kensington Dr L34 ... 56 A5
Kensington Gdns CH46 ... 64 E8
Kensington Ind Pk PR9 ... 4 C6
Kensington Rd
Formby L37 ... 9 E1
Southport PR9 ... 4 C6
Kensington St L6, L7 ... 53 A2
Kent Ave
Formby L37 ... 10 A1
Kent Ave *continued*
Litherland L21 ... 38 C8
Kent Cl
Bebington CH63 ... 88 B8
Bootle L20 ... 38 D4
Kentmere Ave WA11 ... 33 C1
Kentmere Dr CH61 ... 76 F4
Kentmere Pl WA2 ... 61 A3
Kenton Cl
Formby L37 ... 9 F6
Liverpool L25 ... 70 B7
Kenton Rd L26 ... 83 A7
Kent Rd
Formby L37 ... 10 A1
Southport PR8 ... 4 A4
St Helens WA9 ... 58 D7
Wallasey CH44 ... 51 A3
Kents Bank L12 ... 40 C1
Kent St
Birkenhead CH43 ... 66 B4
Liverpool L1 ... 90 B2
Widnes WA8 ... 73 B1
Kent Way WA12 ... 46 C1
Kentwell Gr L12 ... 54 D7
Kenview Cl WA8 ... 84 A4
Kenway WA11 ... 32 A6
Kenwood Cl L27 ... 70 F5
Kenworthys Flats PR9 ... 4 B8
Kenwright Cres WA9 ... 58 D8
Kenwyn Rd CH45 ... 51 B5
KENYON ... 47 F3
Kenyon Ave WA5 ... 74 E5
Kenyon Cl L33 ... 29 F6
Kenyon Ct 4 L8 ... 67 F6
Kenyon La
Golborne, Kenyon WA3 ... 47 F3
Golborne WA3 ... 47 F5
Kenyon Rd L15 ... 69 A5
Kenyons La L31 ... 20 E3
Kenyon's La L37 ... 10 A3
Kenyons La N WA11 ... 45 F8
Kenyon's La S WA11 ... 45 F7
Kenyons Lo L31 ... 20 E3
Kepler St L21 ... 38 A6
Keppel St L20 ... 38 B1
Kerfoot's La WN8 ... 23 C8
Kerman Cl L12 ... 40 B1
Kerr Cl 2 L33 ... 29 E6
Kerr Gr WA9 ... 44 E3
Kerris Cl L17 ... 68 C2
Kerrysdale Cl 4 WA9 ... 58 D7
Kersey Rd L32 ... 40 F8
Kersey Wlk L32 ... 40 F8
Kershaw Ave L23 ... 26 F3
Kershaw St WA8 ... 72 D1
Kershaw Way WA12 ... 46 C5
Kerslake Way L38 ... 18 A4
Kerswell Cl WA9 ... 58 D6
Kerton Row PR8 ... 3 F4
Keston Wlk L26 ... 82 F7
Kestral Dene L10 ... 40 A6
Kestrel Ave CH49 ... 64 D6
Kestrel Cl
Birkenhead CH49 ... 64 D6
St Helens WA11 ... 44 B6
Kestrel Ct PR9 ... 4 D7
Kestrel Dr WN4 ... 35 C6
Kestrel Gr L26 ... 70 D1
Kestrel Mews WN8 ... 16 C4
Kestrel Pk WN8 ... 16 C4
Kestrel Rd
Birkenhead CH46 ... 64 C8
Heswall CH60 ... 86 C7
Keswick Ave
Bebington CH63 ... 88 C4
Warrington WA2 ... 61 C2
Keswick Cl
Maghull L31 ... 20 E2
Southport PR8 ... 7 C3
Widnes WA8 ... 72 C1
Keswick Cres WA2 ... 61 C2
Keswick Dr L21 ... 38 E8
Keswick Gdns CH63 ... 88 C5
Keswick Pl CH43 ... 50 D1
Keswick Rd
Liverpool L18 ... 69 D2
St Helens WA10 ... 43 E5
Wallasey CH45 ... 50 E7
Keswick Villas L16 ... 70 A8
Keswick Way
Huyton-w-R L16 ... 70 A8
Rainford WA11 ... 23 F2
Ketterer Ct WA9 ... 44 C2
Kettering Rd PR8 ... 7 B5
Kevelioc Cl CH63 ... 78 F3
Kew Gardens Cl WA8 ... 73 D4
Kew House Dr PR8 ... 5 A2
Kew Rd
Formby L37 ... 9 D1
Southport PR8 ... 4 B3
Kew Ret Pk PR8 ... 5 A4
Kew St L5 ... 52 D5
Kew Woods Prim Sch PR8 ... 4 F3
Keybank Rd L12 ... 54 A8
Kiddman St L4 ... 38 F3
Kid Glove Rd WA3 ... 36 B1
Kidstone Cl 6 WA9 ... 58 D7
Kielder Cl WN4 ... 34 F7
Kilbuck La WA11 ... 46 A8
Kilburn Ave
Ashton-in-M WN4 ... 35 D4
Bebington CH62 ... 88 E6
Kilburn Gr WA9 ... 57 E7
Kilburn Rd WN5 ... 25 C5
Kilburn St L21 ... 38 B6
Kildale Cl L31 ... 20 C2
Kildare Cl L24 ... 83 D2
Kildonan Rd L17 ... 68 E2
Kilford Cl WA5 ... 60 E2
Kilgarth Sch CH41 ... 66 B8
Kilgraston Gdns L17 ... 68 F1
Killarney Gr 3 CH44 ... 51 A3
Killarney Rd L13 ... 54 B3
Killester Rd L25 ... 70 B4
Killington Way L4 ... 52 E8
Kilmalcolm Cl CH43 ... 65 F4
Kilmore Cl L9 ... 39 C8
Kilmory Ave L25 ... 70 C2
Kiln Cl WA10 ... 43 C5
Kiln Hey L12 ... 54 C5
Kiln La
Skelmersdale WN8 ... 15 E1
St Helens WA10 ... 43 C5
Kiln Rd CH49 ... 65 A3
Kilnyard Rd L23 ... 26 D4
Kilrea Cl L11 ... 53 F8
Kilrea Lo L11 ... 53 F8
Kilrea Rd L11 ... 53 E8
Kilsail Rd 3 L32 ... 41 A7
Kilsby Dr WA8 ... 73 E2
Kilshaw Rd WA5 ... 59 F6
Kilshaw St L6 ... 53 A4
Kilsyth Cl WA2 ... 61 F4
Kimberley Ave
Crosby L23 ... 26 D3
St Helens WA9 ... 57 F7
Kimberley Cl L8 ... 68 A7
Kimberley Dr L23 ... 26 D3
Kimberley Pl WN4 ... 35 C3
Kimberley Rd CH45 ... 51 B6
Kindale Rd CH43 ... 65 E1
Kinder Gr WN4 ... 34 F6
Kinder St L6 ... 52 F3
King Ave L20 ... 38 E5
King David High Sch L15 ... 69 C7
King David Prim Sch L15 ... 69 C7
King Edward Cl L35 ... 57 B4
King Edward Ind Est L3 ... 52 B2
King Edward Rd
Rainhill L35 ... 57 B4
St Helens WA10 ... 43 E6
King Edward's Dr CH62 ... 79 B6
King Edward St L3 ... 52 B2
Kingfield Rd L9 ... 38 F5
Kingfisher Bsns Pk L20 ... 38 C7
Kingfisher Cl
Kirkby L33 ... 29 E6
Liverpool L27 ... 70 F5
Kingfisher Ct
Ashton-in-M WN4 ... 35 B6
Maghull L31 ... 20 B4
Southport PR9 ... 4 D8
Kingfisher Dr WA11 ... 44 B6
Kingfisher Gr L12 ... 40 F1
Kingfisher Ho
Birkenhead CH41 ... 67 A6
Liverpool L13 ... 54 A1
Kingfisher Pk WN8 ... 16 C4
Kingfisher Way CH49 ... 64 D6
King George Cl WN4 ... 35 B3
King George Dr CH44, CH45 ... 51 D6
King George Rd WA11 ... 46 A7
King George's Dr CH62 ... 79 B6
King George V Coll PR8 ... 4 E5
Kingham Cl
Liverpool L25 ... 70 C2
3 Widnes WA8 ... 73 D1
Kingham Mews L25 ... 70 C2
Kinglake Rd CH44 ... 51 D5
Kinglake St L7 ... 53 B1
Kinglass Rd CH63 ... 79 B3
King's Ave
Golborne WA3 ... 47 F7
Hoylake CH47 ... 63 D8
Kingsbrook Way CH63 ... 78 D8
King's Brow CH63 ... 78 D6
King's Bsns Pk L34 ... 56 A5
Kingsbury CH48 ... 63 D2
Kingsbury Cl PR8 ... 7 B4
Kingsbury Ct WN8 ... 16 C4
Kingsbury Prim Spec Sch WN8 ... 15 D1
Kingsbury Rd WA8 ... 73 D4
Kings Cl
Bebington CH63 ... 78 D7
Formby L37 ... 9 E2
2 Liverpool L17 ... 68 C2
Kingscourt Rd L12 ... 54 C5
Kings Ct CH47 ... 63 A7
King's Ct
Bebington CH63 ... 78 D6
Birkenhead CH43 ... 66 B4
Kingsdale Ave
Birkenhead CH42 ... 66 D2
Rainhill L35 ... 57 D3
Kingsdale Rd
Liverpool L18 ... 69 A5
Warrington WA5 ... 74 F7
Kings Dock St L1 ... 90 B1
Kingsdown Rd
Abram Brow WN2 ... 36 B7
Liverpool L11 ... 40 B1
Kingsdown St CH41 ... 66 E4
Kings Dr
Huyton-w-R L34 ... 56 A5
Liverpool, Netherley L27 ... 70 D5
Liverpool, Woolton L25 ... 70 B2

116 Kin–Lar

King's Dr
Heswall CH61 76 F6
West Kirby CH48 75 D8
Kingsfield Rd L31 28 C7
King's Gap The CH47 63 A6
Kingsheath Ave L14 54 F5
Kings Hey Dr PR9 1 F1
King's La CH63 78 E8
Kingsland Bldgs CH42 66 C4
Kingsland Cres L11 39 E3
Kingsland Rd
Birkenhead CH42 66 C4
Liverpool L11 39 E3
Kingsley Ave CH62 88 E3
Kingsley Cl
Heswall CH61 77 A3
Maghull L31 20 C5
Kingsley Com Sch L8 68 B7
Kingsley Rd
Liverpool L8 68 B7
St Helens WA10 43 D6
Wallasey CH44 51 B3
Kingsley St CH41 66 A8
Kings Mdw PR8 7 D3
Kingsmead Dr L25 82 B8
Kingsmead Gr CH43 65 F5
Kings Meadow Prim Sch PR8 7 D3
Kingsmead Rd
Birkenhead CH43 65 F5
Wallasey CH46 49 F2
Kingsmead Rd N CH43 65 F5
Kingsmead Rd S CH43 65 F5
Kingsmead Sch CH47 63 C8
KINGS MOSS 32 E7
King's Moss La WA11 32 F7
Kings Mount CH43 66 C4
Kingsnorth L35 56 F2
Kings Par L3 90 A1
King's Par
Wallasey CH45 37 A1
Wallasey CH45 50 E8
Kings Pk L21 37 F7
Kings Rd
Crosby L23 26 D4
Formby L37 9 F2
Golborne WA3 47 A7
St Helens WA10 43 D2
King's Rd
Ashton-in-M WN4 35 A5
Bebington CH63 78 D7
Bootle L20 38 C1
King's Sq CH41 66 F6
King St
Birkenhead CH42 67 A1
Crosby L22 26 D1
Liverpool L19 81 C4
Newton-le-W WA12 46 B3
Southport PR8 4 A6
St Helens WA10 43 F4
Wallasey CH44 51 D4
Kings Terr L20 38 C1
Kingsthorne Pk L25 82 C7
Kingsthorne Rd L25 82 C7
Kingston Ave WA5 74 E6
Kingston Cl
Birkenhead CH46 64 E8
Liverpool L12 54 E5
Kingston Cres PR9 2 C5
Kingston Lo 2 CH43 66 C5
King's View CH47 62 F6
Kingsville Rd CH63 78 E5
Kingsway
Bebington CH63 78 D7
Crosby L22, L23 26 E2
Heswall CH60 86 C6
Huyton-w-R L36 55 D4
Newton-le-W WA12 46 C2
Prescot L34, L35 56 E5
Southport PR8 4 A7
St Helens WA11 44 A8
Wallasey CH45 51 A6
Widnes WA8 73 A1
Kingsway Ct 4 L3 52 D4
Kingsway Ind Pk L3, L5 52 D4
Kingsway Par L36 55 C4
Kingsway Prim Sch CH44 51 D2
Kingsway (Tunnel) L3, CH44 52 B3
Kingswell Cl L7 68 B8
Kings Wharf CH44 51 F1
Kings Wlk
Birkenhead CH42 67 A1
West Kirby CH48 63 C2
KINGSWOOD 60 B2
Kingswood
Huyton-w-R L36 55 D3
Warrington WA5 60 B2
Kingswood Ave
Crosby L22 26 F2
Liverpool L9 39 B7
Kingswood Bvd CH63 78 E8
Kingswood Ct 3 L33 29 F4
Kingswood Dr L23 26 D3
Kingswood Ho PR8 3 F5
Kingswood Pk PR8 3 F5
Kingswood Rd
4 Wallasey CH44 51 C5
Warrington WA5 60 A2
Kington Rd CH48 63 A3
Kinley Gdns L20 38 E5
Kinloch Cl L26 83 A7
Kinloch Way L39 13 D6
Kinloss Rd CH49 64 C3
Kinmel Cl
Birkenhead CH41 66 D7
Liverpool L4 53 D8
Kinmel St
Liverpool L8 68 A5
St Helens WA9 58 C8
Kinnaird Rd CH45 51 A6
Kinnaird St L8 68 A3
Kinnerton Cl CH46 64 B8
Kinnock Pk WA5 59 E6
Kinross Ave WN4 34 C4
Kinross Cl WA2 61 F4
Kinross Rd
Liverpool L10 39 F7
Seaforth L22 37 E8
Wallasey CH45 50 D6
Kinsman Ho L19 80 F7
Kintbury St WN2 35 F7
Kintore Cl CH63 88 C4
Kintore Dr WA5 74 D6
Kintore Rd L19 81 B7
Kipling Ave
2 Birkenhead CH42 66 F1
Huyton-w-R L36 71 A8
Warrington WA2 61 C1
Kipling Cres WA8 84 F8
Kipling Gr WA9 58 A3
Kipling St L20 38 A5
Kirby Cl CH48 63 C1
Kirby Mount CH48 75 C8
Kirby Park Mans 2 CH48 63 B1
Kirby Pk CH48 63 C1
Kirby Rd L20 38 D6
Kirby's Cotts L31 21 B3
Kirkacre Ave WA12 60 C8
Kirkbride Cl L27 71 A4
Kirkbride Lawn L27 71 A4
Kirkbride Wlk L27 71 A4
Kirkburn Cl 13 L8 67 F4
KIRKBY 29 E1
Kirkby Bank Rd L33 30 C2
Kirkby CE Prim Sch L32 29 E2
KIRKBY PARK 29 C3
Kirkby Row L32 29 D3
Kirkby Row Cotts 3 L32 29 C3
Kirkby Sta L32 29 C3
Kirkcaldy Ave WA5 74 D6
KIRKDALE 52 E8
Kirkdale Gdns WN8 25 A7
Kirkdale Rd L5 52 E6
Kirkdale St Lawrence CE Prim Sch L4 52 D8
Kirkdale Sta L20 38 D1
Kirkdale Vale L4, L5 52 E7
Kirket Cl CH63 79 A4
Kirket La CH63 79 A4
Kirkfield Gr CH42 67 A1
Kirkham Ave WA3 47 E6
Kirkham Rd
Southport PR9 2 A4
Widnes WA8 73 C2
Kirkham St WN2 36 B8
Kirklake Bank L37 9 C2
Kirklake Rd L37 9 D2
Kirkland Ave CH42 66 D2
Kirkland Cl L9 38 F7
Kirkland Rd CH45 51 C8
Kirkland St WA10 43 F4
Kirklands The CH48 63 C2
Kirklees Rd PR8 3 F1
Kirkmaiden Rd L19 81 B8
Kirkman Fold L35 57 B3
Kirkmore Rd L18 69 A2
Kirkmount CH49 65 A5
Kirk Rd L20 38 C6
Kirkside Cl L12 40 D3
Kirk St L5 52 E6
Kirkstall Dr L37 10 B2
Kirkstall Rd PR8 3 F2
Kirkstead Way WA3 47 A8
Kirkstead Wlk L31 29 B3
Kirkstone Ave
St Helens WA11 44 C8
Warrington WA2 61 C2
Kirkstone Rd N L21 27 C1
Kirkstone Rd S L21, L30, L20 38 D8
Kirkstone Rd W L21 27 B2
Kirkway
Bebington CH63 78 D7
Birkenhead, Greasby CH49 64 E4
Birkenhead, Upton CH49 64 F5
Wallasey CH45 51 B7
Kitchener Dr L9 38 F6
Kitchener St WA10 43 E4
Kitchen St L1 90 B1
Kitling La L34 41 B5
Kitling Rd L34 41 C5
Kiverley Cl L18 69 E3
Kiveton Dr WN4 35 C2
Knap The CH60 86 A6
Knaresborough Rd CH44 50 F4
Knighton Rd L4 39 D1
Knight Rd WA5 59 F6
Knightsbridge Cl WA8 73 D4
Knightsbridge Ct CH43 65 D3
Knightsbridge Wlk L33 29 D6
Knights Grange WA9 44 C4
Knight St L1 90 C2
Knightsway L22 26 F2
Knightswood Ct L18 81 C8
Knob Hall Gdns PR9 1 F3
Knob Hall La PR9 1 F3
Knoclaid Rd L13 53 E7
Knolle Park Mews L25 69 F3
Knoll The CH43 66 A3
KNOTTY ASH 54 C3
Knotty Ash Prim Sch L14 54 D4
Knotty Cross L25 70 C3
Knotty Mews L25 70 C3
Knowle Ave PR8 7 C6
Knowle Cl L12 40 C2
Knowles House Ave WA10 42 F3
Knowles St
Birkenhead CH41 66 C7
2 Widnes WA8 73 C2
Knowle The 5 L23 26 B3
Knowl Hey Rd L26 83 A6
KNOWSLEY 41 C4
Knowsley Ave WA3 36 B1
Knowsley Bsns Pk L34 41 B6
Knowsley Cl CH42 67 A1
Knowsley Com Coll (Kirkby Campus) L32 29 D2
Knowsley Comm Coll L36 55 D3
Knowsley Ct CH42 67 A1
Knowsley Expressway
Halewood L35, WA8 83 F8
Tarbock Green L35 71 D4
Knowsley Hey Sch L36 55 F2
Knowsley Hts L36 55 E5
Knowsley Ind Pk
Kirkby L33 30 C2
Knowsley L33 41 B7
Knowsley La
Huyton-w-R L34, L36 55 D6
Knowsley L34 41 C4
Knowsley Park La L34 56 C7
Knowsley Rd
Birkenhead CH42 67 A1
Bootle L20 38 B5
Liverpool L19 81 A6
Ormskirk L39 13 F5
Rainhill L35 57 D2
Southport PR9 1 C1
St Helens WA10 43 D3
Wallasey CH45 51 A6
Knowsley Safari Pk* L34 42 C2
Knowsley St 1 L4 38 F2
Knowsley View WA11 31 E8
Knowsley Village Sch L34 41 C3
Knox Cl CH62 79 B6
Knox St CH41 66 F6
Knutsford Cl WA10 43 B2
Knutsford Gn CH46 49 E1
Knutsford Rd CH46 49 E1
Knutsford Wlk L31 20 D4
Kramar Wlk 1 L33 29 F2
Kremlin Dr L13 54 A5
Kylemore Ave L18 69 A2
Kylemore Cl CH61 76 E3
Kylemore Ct L26 82 E8
Kylemore Dr CH61 76 F3
Kylemore Rd CH43 66 A4
Kylemore Way
Heswall CH61 76 E3
Liverpool L26 82 E8
Kynance Rd L11 40 D5

L

Laburnum Ave
Huyton-w-R L36 70 E8
St Helens WA11 44 D7
Laburnum Cres L32 29 D3
Laburnum Ct 14 L8 68 A4
Laburnum Dr WN8 15 D1
Laburnum Gr
Irby CH61 76 D6
Liverpool L15 69 A8
Maghull L31 20 F1
Southport PR8 4 F7
Laburnum La WA5 74 C5
Laburnum Pl L20 38 D3
Laburnum Rd
Birkenhead CH43 66 C4
Golborne WA3 47 F7
Liverpool L7 53 D3
Wallasey CH45 51 B7
Laburnum St WN4 35 B2
Lace St L3 90 B4
Lacey Rd L34 56 E5
Lacey St WA10 57 D8
Laddock Cl L4 53 C7
Lady Alice's Dr L40 14 E8
Ladybarn Ave WA3 46 F7
Ladybower Cl
Birkenhead CH49 64 E6
Liverpool L7 68 B8
Lady Chapel Cl L1 90 C1
Ladyewood Rd CH44 51 C3
Ladyfield CH43 65 C7
Ladyfields L12 54 B5
LADY GREEN 18 D4
Lady Green Ct L38 18 E3
Lady Green La L38 18 D4
Lady Lever Art Gall The* CH62 79 B6
Ladymount RC Prim Sch CH61 76 F3
Ladypool L24 83 C2
Ladysmith Ave WN4 35 C3
Ladysmith Rd L10 39 F6
Lady's Wlk L40 14 C6
Ladywood Rd WA5 60 D1
LAFFAK 44 D7
Laffak Rd WA11 44 D7
Lafford La WN8 25 C8
Lagan Ho CH46 49 E4
Laggan St L7 53 B2
Lagrange Arc 9 WA10 44 A3
Laird Cl CH41 65 F8
Lairds Pl L3 52 D4
Laird St CH41 66 A8
Laithwaite Cl WA9 58 B3
Lakeland Ave WN4 35 C4
Lakeland Cl L1 90 B2
Lakemoor Cl WA9 58 D7
Lakenheath Rd L26 82 E7
Lake Pl CH47 63 B7
Lake Rd
Hoylake CH47 63 B7
Liverpool L15 69 A7
Lakes Dr WN5 25 E6
Lakeside Ave WN5 25 E3
Lakeside Cl WA8 84 A8
Lakeside Ct
Rainford WA11 32 A6
Wallasey CH45 51 C8
Lakeside Gdns WA11 32 A6
Lakeside Lawn L27 71 A3
Lakeside View L22 37 D8
Lakes Rd L9 39 D7
Lake St 5 L4 53 A7
Lake View L35 71 E8
Lakeview Ct PR9 4 B8
Lake View Ct L4 39 A2
Laleston Cl WA8 84 E8
Lambert St L3 90 C4
Lambert Way L3 90 C4
Lambeth Ct CH47 63 A7
Lambeth Rd L4, L5 52 D7
Lambeth Wlk L4 52 D7
Lambourn Ave WA8 72 C5
Lambourne WN8 16 B4
Lambourne Gr WA9 45 A4
Lambourne Rd L4 39 D1
Lambrigg Row 18 L4 52 F7
Lambshear La L31 20 C4
Lambton Rd L17 68 B3
Lamerton Cl WA5 74 D4
Lammermoor Rd L18 69 A2
Lampeter Cl WA5 60 E2
Lampeter Rd L6 53 C6
Lamport Cl WA8 73 E3
Lamport St 2 L8 67 E5
Lanark Cl WA10 43 F2
Lanark Gdns WA8 72 E3
Lancashire Gdns WA10 43 F2
Lancaster Ave
Crosby L23 26 D3
Golborne WA3 47 C8
Liverpool L17 68 D6
Prescot L35 56 D3
Wallasey CH45 51 C5
Widnes WA8 72 A2
Lancaster Cl
Bebington CH62 79 B6
Liverpool L5 52 D6
Maghull L31 20 F1
Newton-le-W WA12 45 F4
Southport PR8 3 E4
Warrington WA2 61 F2
Lancaster Cres WN8 15 E1
Lancaster Dr PR9 2 F5
Lancaster Gate PR9 2 F5
Lancaster Gdns PR8 3 E4
Lancaster Ho PR8 3 E4
Lancaster Rd
Formby L37 9 E1
Huyton-w-R L36 56 A4
Southport PR8 3 E4
Widnes WA8 73 B3
Lancaster St
Liverpool L5 52 D6
Liverpool, Walton L9 38 F3
Lancaster Wlk L36 56 A4
Lance Cl L5 52 F5
Lancefield Rd L9 38 F5
Lance Gr L15 69 A7
Lance La L15 69 A7
Lancelyn Ct CH63 79 A3
Lancelyn Terr CH63 78 F4
Lancing Ave WA2 61 A4
Lancing Cl L25 70 D1
Lancing Dr L10 28 D2
Lancing Rd L25 70 D1
Lancing Way L25 70 D1
Lancots La WA9 58 D8
Land End L31 21 C1
Lander Rd L21 38 C6
Lander Road Prim Sch L21 38 C6
Landford Ave L9 39 E4
Landford Pl L9 39 E4
LAND GATE 35 A8
Landgate Ind Est WN4 35 A8
Land Gate La WN4 35 B8
Landgate Sch WN4 35 A7
LANDICAN 77 C8
Landican La CH43, CH49, CH63 77 E7
Landican Rd CH49, CH61 77 B7
Land La PR9 2 D4
Landor Cl
Golborne WA3 47 E8
Liverpool L3 52 C5
Landseer Rd L5 52 F5
Lane Ends WA8 83 D5
LANE HEAD 47 E6
Lane Head Ave WA3 47 F8
Lanfranc Cl L16 69 E8
Lanfranc Way L16 69 E8
Langbar L35 56 E2
Langdale Ave
Formby L37 9 D2
Golborne WA3 36 C1
Heswall CH61 76 F4
Langdale Cl
Formby L37 9 D2
Kirkby L32 29 F1
Warrington WA2 61 E2
Widnes WA8 84 C8
Langdale Cres WN2 36 B8
Langdale Dr L31 20 E2
Langdale Gdns PR8 3 F1
Langdale Gr WA11 44 B7
Langdale Rd
Bebington CH63 78 F4
Liverpool L15 68 E6
Wallasey CH45 51 A7
Langdale St L20 38 D3
Langfield WA3 47 E7
Langfield Gr CH62 88 D5
Langford L24 83 C2
Langford Rd L19 80 F8
Langham Ave L17 68 C3
Langham Ct L4 52 F8
Langham St Ind Est L4 52 F8
Langham St L4 52 F8
Langholme Hts L11 39 F4
Langholm Rd WN4 34 C4
Lang La CH48 63 B3
Langland Cl
Liverpool L4 53 D8
Warrington WA5 60 E2
Lang Lane S CH48 63 C2
Langley Ave WA12 46 C1
Langley Cl
Bebington CH63 79 A2
Golborne WA3 36 C1
Hightown L38 17 F2
Liverpool L12 40 F3
Langley Rd CH63 79 A2
Langley St L8 67 E6
Langrove St L5 52 E5
Langsdale St
Liverpool L3 52 E3
Liverpool L3, L6 52 F3
Langshaw Lea L27 70 F4
Langstone Ave CH49 64 C3
Langton Cl
Newton-le-W WA12 46 A4
Widnes WA8 72 B3
Langton Rd
Kirkby L33 29 F5
Liverpool L15 68 D7
Langtree WN8 16 B3
Langtree St WA9 44 C3
Langtry Cl L4 52 D8
Langtry Rd L4 52 D8
Lansbury Ave WA9 44 E3
Lansbury Bridge Sch WA9 44 E3
Lansbury Rd L36 56 A2
Lansdown L12 54 A6
Lansdowne Cl CH41 66 A8
Lansdowne Ct 6 CH43 65 F8
Lansdowne Ho CH41 66 F6
Lansdowne Pl
5 Birkenhead CH43 65 F8
Liverpool L5 52 F6
Lansdowne Rd
Birkenhead CH41, CH43 65 F8
Southport PR8 4 E6
Wallasey CH45 50 F7
Lansdowne Way L36 55 E2
Lanville Rd L19 69 B1
Lanyork Rd L3 52 B3
Lapford Cres L33 30 A4
Lapford Wlk L33 30 A4
Lapwing Cl
Golborne WA3 47 D8
Liverpool L12 40 F1
Newton-le-W WA12 46 C3
Lapwing Ct L26 70 E1
Lapwing Rise CH60 85 F6
Lapworth Cl 3 CH46 64 B8
Lapworth St L5 52 D6
Larch Ave
Newton-le-W WA12 46 C2
Warrington WA5 74 E5
Widnes WA8 73 B2
Larch Cl
Billinge WN5 33 D5
Golborne WA3 47 F6
Liverpool L19 80 F7
Skelmersdale WN8 15 E1
Larch Ct 13 L8 68 A4
Larchdale Gr L9 39 B4
Larchfield Rd L23 27 B5
Larch Gr
Birkenhead CH43 65 E8
Liverpool L15 54 A1
Larch Lea 2 L6 53 B5
Larch Rd
Birkenhead CH41 66 D5
Haydock WA11 45 E7
Huyton-w-R L36 55 D2
Larch St PR8 4 E6
Larchtree Mews L12 54 E8
Larch Way L37 9 D4
Larchwood Ave L31 28 C7
Larchwood Cl
Heswall CH61 76 F3
Liverpool L25 70 B5
Larchwood Dr CH63 78 F7
Larcombe Ave CH49 64 F5

Larkfield Cl L17 ... 68 C2
Larkfield Ct PR9 ... 2 A3
Larkfield Gr L17 ... 68 C2
Larkfield La PR9 ... 2 A3
Larkfield Prim Sch PR9 ... 2 A3
Larkfield Rd L17 ... 68 C2
Larkfield View L15 ... 68 E8
Larkhill WN8 ... 16 B4
Larkhill Ave CH49 ... 65 A7
Larkhill Cl L13 ... 53 E7
Larkhill Gr L38 ... 17 F3
Larkhill La
Formby L37 ... 9 C4
Liverpool L13 ... 53 E7
Larkhill Pl L13 ... 53 F7
Larkhill View L13 ... 53 F7
Larkhill Way CH49 ... 65 A7
Larkin Cl CH62 ... 79 A7
Lark La L17 ... 68 C4
Larkspur Cl 3 PR8 ... 4 D6
Larkspur Ct 5 L31 ... 29 A3
Larksway CH60 ... 86 B8
Lark Way L17 ... 68 C3
Larne Ct WA8 ... 72 E2
Larton Farm Cl CH48 ... 63 E3
Larton Rd CH48 ... 63 E3
Lartonwood CH48 ... 63 E3
Lascelles Rd L19 ... 81 D7
Lascelles St WA9 ... 44 C3
Latchford Rd CH60 ... 86 B6
Late Moffatt Rd W L9 ... 39 B7
Latham Ave
Newton-le-W WA12 ... 46 C4
Ormskirk L39 ... 14 A5
Latham Ct L7 ... 53 D2
Latham Ho WA12 ... 46 B4
Latham St L5 ... 52 D6
Latham Way CH63 ... 79 B2
Lathbury La L17 ... 68 E5
Lathom Ave
2 Seaforth L21 ... 37 F6
Wallasey CH44 ... 51 B4
Lathom Cl
Huyton-w-R L36 ... 56 A6
1 Seaforth L21 ... 37 F6
Lathom Dr
Maghull L31 ... 20 E3
Rainford WA11 ... 31 F7
Lathom High Sch WN8 ... 15 F3
Lathom Ho L40 ... 15 B7
Lathom La L40 ... 14 C7
LATHOM PARK ... 15 C7
Lathom Rd
Bickerstaffe L39 ... 22 F8
Bootle L20 ... 38 C5
Huyton-w-R L36 ... 55 E2
Southport PR9 ... 1 C1
Lathum Cl L35 ... 56 E5
Latimer Cl 2 WN5 ... 25 F7
Latimer St L5 ... 52 D5
Latrigg Rd L17 ... 68 E2
Lauder Cl L33 ... 29 D6
Launceston Dr WA5 ... 74 E3
Laund The CH45 ... 50 F5
Laurel Ave
Bebington CH63 ... 78 E4
Heswall CH60 ... 76 F1
Newton-le-W WA12 ... 46 D3
Laurel Bank WA8 ... 73 A3
Laurelbanks CH60 ... 76 E1
Laurel Ct WA11 ... 44 B7
Laurel Dr
Skelmersdale WN8 ... 15 E2
St Helens WA10 ... 42 F4
Willaston CH64 ... 88 B1
Laurel Gr
Ashton-in-M WN4 ... 35 B4
Crosby L22 ... 26 D2
Golborne WA3 ... 47 D8
Huyton-w-R L36 ... 70 E8
Liverpool L8 ... 68 C6
Southport PR8 ... 4 E7
Laurelhurst Ave CH61 ... 77 A4
Laurel Rd
Birkenhead CH42 ... 66 D4
Liverpool L7 ... 53 D2
Prescot L34 ... 56 E6
St Helens, Blackbrook WA11 ... 44 F5
St Helens, West Park WA10 ... 43 D2
Laurels The CH46 ... 49 E3
Laurence Deacon Ct 1 CH41 ... 66 D7
Lauren Cl L36 ... 56 B2
Lauren Ho L35 ... 56 F5
Lauriston Rd L4 ... 39 C1
Laurus Cl L27 ... 70 F5
Lavan Cl L6 ... 53 A3
Lavan St 3 L6 ... 53 A3
Lavender Cres 7 L34 ... 56 E6
Lavender Gdns
Crosby L23 ... 27 B5
St Helens WA9 ... 59 A7
Lavender Way L9 ... 39 B4
Lavender Wlk WN4 ... 34 D5
Lavrock Bank L8 ... 67 E4
Lawford Dr CH60 ... 86 C8
Lawler Gr L34 ... 56 E7
Lawler St L21 ... 38 B6
Lawnhurst Gr L17 ... 80 E8
Lawns Ave
Bebington CH63 ... 88 B6
Orrell WN5 ... 25 C5
Lawnside Cl CH42 ... 66 F1
Lawns The
Birkenhead CH43 ... 65 D7
6 Crosby L23 ... 26 B3
Lawns The *continued*
Southport PR9 ... 1 F2
Lawrence Cl L19 ... 81 A7
Lawrence Com Prim Sch L15 ... 68 D7
Lawrence Ct WN2 ... 36 B8
Lawrence Gr L15 ... 68 E7
Lawrence Rd
Liverpool L15 ... 68 E7
St Helens WA10 ... 43 C6
Lawrenson St WA10 ... 43 E3
Lawson St PR9 ... 5 A7
Lawson Wlk L12 ... 40 D3
Lawswood L37 ... 9 E5
Lawton Ave L20 ... 38 E5
Lawton Rd
Crosby L22, L23 ... 26 D2
Huyton-w-R L36 ... 55 C1
Rainhill L35 ... 57 D2
Lawton St L1 ... 90 C3
Laxey St L8 ... 67 E6
Laxton Rd L25 ... 82 C8
Layford Cl L36 ... 55 D6
Layford Rd L36 ... 55 D5
Layton Ave CH43 ... 65 F1
Layton Cl L25 ... 70 C2
Layton Rd L25 ... 70 C2
Lazenby Cres WN4 ... 34 F3
Lazonby Cl 4 CH43 ... 65 C8
Leach Croft L28 ... 55 A7
Leach La
St Helens, Sutton Leach WA9 ... 58 D5
St Helens WA9 ... 58 D6
Leach St 4 WA10 ... 43 F4
Leach Way CH61 ... 76 C6
Lea Cl CH43 ... 65 E4
Lea Cres L39 ... 13 F7
Leacroft WN4 ... 34 F6
Lea Cross Gr WA8 ... 72 C3
Lea Ct L39 ... 13 E7
Leadenhall Cl L5 ... 52 F6
Leafield Cl CH61 ... 76 F6
Leafield Rd L25 ... 82 B7
Leagate L10 ... 39 F8
LEA GREEN ... 57 F5
Lea Green Bsns Pk WA9 ... 57 F4
Lea Green Ind Est WA9 ... 58 A3
Lea Green Rd WA9 ... 58 A4
Lea Green Sta WA9 ... 58 B5
Leamington Ave
Newton-le-W WA12 ... 46 C1
Southport PR8 ... 7 D5
Leamington Com Prim Sch L11 ... 39 D2
Leamington Rd
Liverpool L11 ... 39 D2
Southport PR8 ... 7 D5
Leander Rd CH45 ... 51 A5
Lea Rd CH44 ... 51 D5
LEASOWE ... 50 A4
Leasowe Ave CH45 ... 50 E6
Leasowe Gdns CH46 ... 49 E4
Leasowe Prim Sch CH46 ... 50 B3
Leasowe Rd
Liverpool L9 ... 39 B7
Wallasey CH45, CH46 ... 50 C5
Leasoweside CH46 ... 50 A4
Leasowe Sta CH46 ... 50 A2
Leas Pk CH47 ... 63 A4
Leas The
Heswall CH61 ... 77 B6
Wallasey CH45 ... 50 E7
Leatherbarrows La
Kirkby L31 ... 29 A6
Maghull L31 ... 28 F7
Leather La L2 ... 90 A4
Leather's La L26 ... 82 F8
Leathwood L31 ... 28 E8
Leaway CH49 ... 64 D4
Leawood Gr CH46 ... 64 F8
Leckwith Rd L30 ... 28 B2
Leda Gr 3 L17 ... 68 C4
Ledburn WN8 ... 16 B3
Ledbury Cl
Birkenhead CH43 ... 65 E2
Liverpool L12 ... 40 F4
St Helens WA10 ... 43 B3
Ledger Rd WA11 ... 45 A5
Ledmore Gr WN4 ... 34 D3
Ledsham Cl CH43 ... 65 E4
Ledsham Rd L32 ... 29 C2
Ledsham Wlk 7 L32 ... 29 C2
Ledson Gr L39 ... 21 B7
Ledson Pk L33 ... 29 F6
Ledsons Gr L31 ... 29 A3
Leece St L1 ... 90 C2
Lee Cl L35 ... 57 D1
Leecourt Cl L12 ... 54 D5
Lee Ct WA2 ... 61 C2
Leeds St L3 ... 52 C3
Lee Hall Rd L25 ... 70 C5
Lee La WN2 ... 36 B8
Leeming Cl L19 ... 81 C5
Lee Park Ave L25 ... 70 C5
Lee Rd CH47 ... 63 C7
Lees Ave CH42 ... 66 F2
Leeside Ave L32 ... 29 F1
Leeside Cl L32 ... 29 F1
Lees La
Liverpool L12 ... 54 D7
Skelmersdale WN8 ... 16 E7
Lees Rd L33 ... 30 B2
Lee St WA9 ... 58 E8
Leeswood
6 Crosby L22 ... 26 E1
Skelmersdale WN8 ... 16 B3
Leeswood Rd CH49 ... 65 A4
Lee Vale Rd L25 ... 70 C4
Leeward Dr L24 ... 82 A5
Legh Ct WA3 ... 47 A8
Legh Rd
Bebington CH62 ... 79 B7
Haydock WA11 ... 45 B6
Legh St
Ashton-in-M WN4 ... 35 B2
Golborne WA3 ... 47 A8
Newton-le-W WA12 ... 46 A3
Legh Vale Prim Sch WA11 ... 45 B6
Legion La CH62 ... 79 D1
Legion Rd WA10 ... 57 D8
Leicester Ave L22 ... 26 D2
Leicester Rd L20 ... 38 D4
Leicester St
Southport PR9 ... 4 B8
St Helens WA9 ... 57 D8
Leigh Ave WA8 ... 73 A1
Leigh Bridge Way L5 ... 52 C5
Leigh Green Cl 4 WA8 ... 84 C8
Leigh Pl L1 ... 90 B3
Leigh Rd CH48 ... 63 B3
Leighs Hey Cres L32 ... 29 F2
Leigh St L1 ... 90 B3
Leighton Ave
Hoylake CH47 ... 63 E8
Maghull L31 ... 20 D2
Leighton Chase CH64 ... 86 D1
Leighton Cotts CH64 ... 86 D5
Leighton Rd
Birkenhead CH41 ... 66 E4
Neston CH64 ... 86 D2
Leighton St L4 ... 38 E1
Leinster Gdns WA7 ... 84 F3
Leinster Rd L13 ... 54 B3
Leinster St WA7 ... 84 F3
Leison St L4 ... 52 D7
Leiston Cl CH61 ... 76 E7
Lemon Cl L7 ... 53 C1
Lemon Gr L8 ... 68 C6
Lemon St L5 ... 52 D6
Lemon Tree Wlk WA10 ... 43 D1
Lendel Cl L37 ... 9 E3
Lenfield Dr WA11 ... 44 F6
Lenham Way L24 ... 82 B5
Lennox Ave CH45 ... 51 B7
Lennox La CH43 ... 50 C1
Lenthall St L4 ... 38 F2
Lenton Ave L37 ... 9 D4
Lenton Rd L25 ... 70 C5
Lentworth Ct L17 ... 80 F7
Leo Cl L14 ... 54 F4
Leominster Rd CH44 ... 51 B4
Leonard Cheshire Dr L30 ... 27 F3
Leonards Cl L36 ... 55 D6
Leonard St WA9 ... 58 F7
Leon Cl WA5 ... 74 D7
Leopold Gr WA9 ... 58 C5
Leopold Rd
Crosby L22 ... 26 C2
Liverpool L7 ... 53 B2
Leopold St CH44 ... 51 E3
Lesley Rd PR8 ... 4 E7
Leslie Ave CH49 ... 64 D3
Leslie Rd WA10 ... 57 C8
Lesseps Rd L8 ... 68 C7
Lessingham Rd WA8 ... 72 F3
Lester Cl L4 ... 52 E7
Lester Dr
Irby CH61 ... 76 C7
St Helens WA10 ... 43 A5
Lester Gr L36 ... 55 F4
Lestock St L8 ... 90 C1
Leta St
Liverpool L4 ... 38 F1
Liverpool L4 ... 39 A1
Letchworth St L6 ... 53 C5
Lethbridge Cl L5 ... 52 D6
Lethbridge Rd PR8 ... 4 D5
Letitia St L8 ... 67 F5
Levens Hey CH46 ... 64 D8
Leven St L4 ... 52 E8
Levens Way 1 WA8 ... 84 C8
Lever Ave 11 CH44 ... 51 E2
Lever Cswy CH63 ... 78 B7
Leveret Rd L24 ... 83 A3
Leverhulme Ct CH63 ... 79 A4
Lever St WA9 ... 58 D3
Lever Terr CH42 ... 66 E3
Leveson Rd L13 ... 54 B1
Lewis Ave WA5 ... 60 F2
Lewis Ct PR9 ... 4 D8
Lewis Gr WA8 ... 72 D1
Lewisham Rd
Bebington CH62 ... 79 C6
Liverpool L11 ... 40 A1
Lewis St WA10 ... 43 E3
Lewis Wlk 4 L33 ... 29 E6
Lexham Rd L14 ... 54 C3
Lexington Way L33 ... 29 D6
Lexton Dr PR9 ... 2 B3
Leybourne Ave PR8 ... 7 F7
Leybourne Cl L25 ... 70 A6
Leybourne Gn L25 ... 70 A6
Leybourne Gr L25 ... 70 A5
Leybourne Rd L25 ... 70 A6
Leyburn Cl L32 ... 40 E7
Leyburn Rd CH45 ... 50 F6
Ley Cl WA9 ... 58 C4
Leyfield Cl L12 ... 54 D6
Leyfield Ct L12 ... 54 D6
Leyfield Rd L12 ... 54 D6
Leyfield Wlk L12 ... 54 D6
Leyland Cl PR9 ... 2 E5
Leyland Gr WA11 ... 45 B6
Leyland Green Rd WN4 ... 34 C5
Leyland Rd
Rainford WA11 ... 31 F6
Southport PR9 ... 1 C1
Leyland St 8 L34 ... 56 D6
Leyland Way L39 ... 13 F5
Liberton Ct 10 L5 ... 53 A6
Liberty St L15 ... 68 E7
Libra Cl L14 ... 55 A5
Library St 3 WA10 ... 44 A3
Lichfield Ave
Crosby L22 ... 26 D3
Golborne WA3 ... 47 D8
Lichfield Cl L30 ... 28 A1
Lichfield Gr WN4 ... 35 C2
Lichfield Rd
Halewood L26 ... 82 E7
Liverpool, Wavertree Green L15 ... 69 A6
Lichfield St CH45 ... 51 C7
Lickers La L35 ... 56 E2
Liddell Ave L31 ... 29 B4
Liddell Ct CH45 ... 50 D5
Liddell Rd L12 ... 53 F7
Lidderdale Ct L15 ... 68 E6
Lidderdale Rd L15 ... 68 E6
Lidgate Cl L33 ... 29 F5
Liege Ho CH49 ... 64 F6
Lifeboat Rd L37 ... 9 B1
Liffey St L8 ... 68 B7
Lifton Rd L33 ... 30 A2
Lightbody St L5 ... 52 C5
Lightburn St 6 WA7 ... 84 F1
Lightfoot Cl CH60 ... 86 B7
Lightfoot La CH60 ... 86 B7
Lighthorne Dr PR8 ... 7 A4
Lighthouse La L37 ... 10 A1
Lighthouse Rd CH47 ... 63 B6
Lightoaks Dr L26 ... 71 B1
Lightshaw La WA3 ... 36 B4
Lightwood Dr 3 L7 ... 68 C8
Lightwood St 5 L7 ... 68 C8
Lilac Ave
Downall Green WN4 ... 34 D5
Southport PR8 ... 7 D2
Widnes WA8 ... 73 B2
Lilac Gr
Billinge WN5 ... 33 D4
Huyton-w-R L36 ... 70 D8
Skelmersdale WN8 ... 15 E1
St Helens WA11 ... 44 F5
Lilac Rd WA3 ... 36 A1
Lilford Ave L9 ... 38 F6
Lilford Dr WA5 ... 74 F6
Lilley Ct L7 ... 53 D3
Lilley Rd L7 ... 53 D2
Lillian Rd L4 ... 53 B6
Lillie Cl 3 CH43 ... 65 C8
Lillyfield CH60 ... 85 F6
Lilly Gn L4 ... 39 B1
Lilly Gr L4 ... 39 B1
Lilly Vale L7 ... 53 D3
Lily Ave WA12 ... 46 D2
Lily La WN2 ... 35 F7
Lily Pl WN4 ... 35 C2
Lily Rd L21 ... 38 B6
Lily St WN4 ... 35 E5
Limbo La CH49 ... 76 D8
Lime Ave
Bebington CH63 ... 78 D4
3 Widnes WA8 ... 73 B2
Lime Cl
Abram Brow WN2 ... 36 C7
Liverpool L13 ... 54 A4
Lime Ct
Liverpool L1 ... 90 C3
Skelmersdale WN8 ... 15 E1
Limedale Rd L18 ... 69 B5
Limefield Dr WN8 ... 24 E7
Lime Gr
Bootle L21 ... 38 A6
Golborne WA3 ... 47 E6
Liverpool L8 ... 68 C6
Rainford WA11 ... 31 F6
Skelmersdale WN8 ... 15 E1
Limehurst Gr CH62 ... 88 D6
Limekiln La
Burtonwood WA5 ... 59 E3
1 Liverpool L3 ... 52 D3
Liverpool L3, L5 ... 52 D4
Wallasey CH41, CH44 ... 51 A2
Limerick Cl WA8 ... 72 E3
Lime St
Liverpool L1 ... 90 B4
Southport PR8 ... 4 E6
Limes The
Birkenhead CH49 ... 64 F5
Golborne WA3 ... 47 D6
Lime Street Sta L3, L1 ... 90 C4
Lime Tree Cl L9 ... 39 B4
Lime Tree Gr CH60 ... 86 C8
Lime Tree Way L37 ... 9 C2
Lime Vale Rd WN5 ... 33 C3
Limont Rd PR8 ... 7 D5
Linacre La
Bootle L20 ... 38 D5
Maghull L37 ... 19 B7
Widnes WA8 ... 72 E5
Linacre Prim Sch L20 ... 38 C5
Linacre Rd L20, L21 ... 38 B6
Linaker Dr L39 ... 12 B8
Linaker Prim Sch PR8 ... 4 B5
Linaker St PR8 ... 4 B5
Linbeck Gr WA3 ... 36 E1
Lincoln Ave WA3 ... 36 D1
Lincoln Cl
Huyton-w-R L36 ... 56 B3
Liverpool L6 ... 53 B4
Lincoln Cres WA11 ... 44 B6
Lincoln Ct L20 ... 38 C2
Lincoln Dr
Aintree L10 ... 28 D3
Ashton-in-M WN4 ... 35 D2
Wallasey CH45 ... 51 C6
Lincoln Gn L31 ... 28 B8
Lincoln Rd
Southport PR8 ... 4 A1
St Helens WA10 ... 43 D2
Lincoln Sq WA8 ... 73 B2
Lincoln St
Birkenhead CH41 ... 51 A1
Liverpool L19 ... 81 D4
Lincoln Way
Huyton-w-R L36 ... 56 B3
Rainhill L35 ... 57 D1
Lincombe Rd L36 ... 55 C4
Lindale Cl CH46 ... 50 A1
Lindale Dr 11 WA9 ... 58 C4
Lindale Rd L7 ... 53 E3
Lindby Cl L32 ... 41 A8
Lindby Rd L32 ... 41 A8
Linden Ave
Ashton-in-M WN4 ... 34 F5
Crosby L23 ... 26 C4
Litherland L30 ... 27 F2
Orrell WN5 ... 25 E6
Linden Ct
1 Crosby L23 ... 26 B3
Orrell WN5 ... 25 E6
Widnes WA8 ... 72 F4
Linden Dr
Birkenhead CH43 ... 65 E1
Huyton-w-R L36 ... 70 E8
Linden Gr
Billinge WN5 ... 33 C3
Orrell WN5 ... 25 E6
Wallasey CH45 ... 51 B7
Linden Rd L27 ... 70 E5
Lindens WN8 ... 16 B4
Lindens The
3 Birkenhead CH43 ... 66 C5
Maghull L31 ... 28 C7
Linden Way
St Helens WA10 ... 43 B4
Widnes WA8 ... 72 F4
Linden Wlk WN5 ... 25 E6
Lindenwood 6 L32 ... 40 F8
Lindeth Ave CH44 ... 51 B3
Lindfield Cl 4 L8 ... 67 F4
Lindholme WN8 ... 16 C3
Lindisfarne Ct WA8 ... 72 F6
Lindisfarne Dr L12 ... 41 A3
Lindley Ave WN5 ... 25 C5
Lindley Cl 6 L7 ... 68 C8
Lindley St L7 ... 68 C8
Lindrick Cl L35 ... 57 A4
Lindsay Rd L4 ... 53 D8
Lindsay St WA9 ... 58 E3
Lind St L4 ... 38 F1
Lindwall Cl CH43 ... 50 C1
Linear Pk CH46 ... 49 C1
Linear View WA12 ... 46 C1
Lineside Cl L25 ... 70 B5
Linford Gr WA11 ... 44 C5
Lingdale Ave CH43 ... 65 F6
Lingdale Ct
Birkenhead CH43 ... 65 F7
Hoylake CH48 ... 62 F3
Lingdale Rd
Birkenhead CH41, CH43 ... 65 F7
West Kirby CH48 ... 63 A3
Lingdale Rd N CH41 ... 65 F7
Lingdales L37 ... 10 B5
Lingfield Cl
Huyton-w-R L36 ... 55 D1
Litherland L30 ... 28 A1
Lingfield Gr L14 ... 54 D2
Lingfield Rd
Liverpool L14 ... 54 D2
Runcorn WA7 ... 84 E1
Lingford Cl L27 ... 70 F4
Lingham Cl CH46 ... 49 D2
Lingham La
Wallasey CH46 ... 49 C3
Wallasey, Moreton CH46 ... 49 D1
Lingham Prim Sch CH46 ... 49 D1
Lingholme Rd WA10 ... 43 E4
LINGLEY GREEN ... 74 C7
Lingley Green Ave WA5 ... 74 D8
Lingley Mere Bsns Pk WA5 ... 74 D8
Lingley Rd WA5 ... 74 D6
Lingmell Ave WA11 ... 33 C1
Lingmell Rd L11, L12 ... 54 B8
Ling St L7 ... 53 B2
Lingtree Rd L32 ... 29 B3
Lingwell Ave WA8 ... 72 D2
Lingwell Pk WA8 ... 72 E2
Lingwood Rd WA5 ... 74 F6
Linhope Way L17 ... 68 C3
Link 25 Bsns Pk WN4 ... 34 F8
Link Ave
Crosby L23 ... 27 A5
St Helens WA11 ... 44 E5

Linkfield Cl L27 70 D6
Link Rd L36 56 B1
Links Ave PR9 1 F3
Links Cl
Bebington CH63 88 B6
Wallasey CH45 50 F7
Links Hey Rd CH48 75 E6
Linkside CH63 78 D7
Linkside Ave WA2 61 B6
Linkside Ct L23 26 A5
Linkside Rd L25 70 C1
Links Rd L32 30 A1
Links The CH43 65 F5
Linkstor Rd L25 69 F3
Links View
Birkenhead CH43 65 E5
Wallasey CH45 50 F8
Linksway CH45 50 F7
Linkway WA10 43 B6
Linkway Ave WN4 35 E5
Linkway E WA10, WA9 44 B2
Linkway W WA10 44 A2
Linner Rd L24 82 D4
Linnet Cl
Liverpool L17 68 C5
Newton-le-W WA12 46 C3
Warrington WA2 61 D3
Linnet Ct L17 68 C4
Linnet Ho L8 68 B5
Linnet La L17 68 C4
Linnets Way CH60 85 E8
Linnet Way L33 29 E7
Linslade Cl L33 29 F4
Linslade Cres 2 L33 29 F4
Linton Ave WA3 35 F2
Linton Pl L32 29 C3
Linton St 1 L4 38 F1
Linum Gdns WA9 59 B7
Linville Ave L23 26 B4
Linwood Gr L35 56 E2
Linwood Rd CH42 66 E3
Lionel St WA9 58 F7
Lions Cl 2 CH43 65 F6
Lipton Cl L20 38 C2
Lisburn La L13 53 E7
Lisburn Rd L17 68 E2
LISCARD 51 B6
Liscard Cres CH44, CH45 51 B4
Liscard Gr CH44, CH45 51 A4
Liscard Ho 4 CH44 51 B4
Liscard Prim Sch CH44, CH45 51 C5
Liscard Rd
Liverpool L15 68 D7
Wallasey, Liscard CH44 51 C4
Wallasey, Seacombe CH44 51 D3
Liscard Village CH45 51 B5
Liscard Way CH44 51 B4
Lisleholme Cl L12 54 C6
Lisleholme Cres L12 54 C6
Lisleholme Rd L12 54 C6
Lismore Ct L23 26 C4
Lismore Pk PR8 3 E4
Lismore Rd L18 69 A2
Lister Cres L7 53 C2
Lister Dr L13, L6 53 E4
Lister Jun & Inf Schs L13 53 E5
Lister Rd L7 53 C2
Liston St L4 38 F2
Litcham Cl CH49 65 A7
Litchborough Gr L35 57 A6
LITHERLAND 27 D1
Litherland Ave CH46 49 D1
Litherland Cres WA11 44 C7
Litherland High Sch L21 27 D2
Litherland Moss Prim Sch L21 27 D1
Litherland Pk L21 38 B8
Litherland Rd
Bootle L20 38 C4
Bootle L20 38 C5
Lithou Cl L5 52 D5
Little Acre L31 28 E8
LITTLE ALTCAR 10 A1
Little Barn Hey L30 27 D5
Little Bongs L12 54 D4
Little Brewery La L37 9 F6
Little Brook La L32 40 D8
Little Canning St 5 L8 67 F7
Little Catharine St L8 67 F7
Littlecote Cl 16 WA9 58 C4
Little Croft L35 56 D3
LITTLE CROSBY 26 D8
Little Crosby Mus★ L23 26 D7
Little Crosby Rd L23 26 E6
Little Ct L3 52 C4
Littledale L14 54 D3
Littledale Rd
Wallasey CH44 51 D3
Warrington WA5 74 F7
Little Delph WA11 45 C7
Little Digmoor Prim Sch WN8 24 B6
Little Hardman St 2 L1 90 C2
Little Heath Rd L24 82 E4
Little Heyes St L5 53 A6
Little Hey La L37 10 B4
Little Howard St L3 52 B4
Little Huskisson St L8 67 F7
Little La
Neston CH64 86 C1
Southport PR9 2 B1
Littlemore Cl CH49 64 D5
Little Moss Hey L28 55 C7
Little Parkfield Rd L17 68 B4
Littler Rd WA11 45 A5
Little St Bride St 12 L7, L8 67 F8
Little St WA9 44 E1
Littlestone Cl WA8 73 A4
LITTLE STORETON 78 A6
Little Storeton La CH63 78 A6
Littleton Cl CH43 65 E4
Littlewood Cl L35 56 E2
Little Woolton St L69 53 A1
Littondale Ave L35 57 D2
Liver Ind Est L9 39 C4
Livermore Ct L8 68 C6
LIVERPOOL 90 A1
Liverpool Ave PR8 7 D5
Liverpool Coll L18 68 F4
Liverpool Com Coll
Liverpool L1 90 C2
Liverpool L3 52 C3
Liverpool L3 90 C3
Liverpool Com Coll (Bankfield) L13 53 F5
Liverpool Com Coll (Old Swan Ctr) L13 54 A3
Liverpool Com Coll The Arts Ctr L7 67 F8
Liverpool Film Acad L4 38 E1
Liverpool Hope Univ L16 69 D6
Liverpool Hope Univ Coll L3 52 F3
Liverpool Inst (Blackburne House) L8 67 F8
Liverpool Inst for the Performing Arts L1 90 C2
Liverpool Int Bsns Pk L24 81 E3
Liverpool John Lennon Airport L24 82 C2
Liverpool Mus & Planetarium★ L3 90 B4
Liverpool One L2 90 A3
Liverpool Pl WA8 72 C1
Liverpool Rd
Ashton-in-M WN4 35 A3
Bickerstaffe L39 22 C5
Birkdale Hills PR8 7 E6
Crosby L22, L23 26 E3
Formby L37 10 A1
Garswood WA11, WN4 34 D2
Haydock, Stanley Bank WA11 45 A7
Hightown L37 18 A8
Huyton-w-R L36 55 D4
Maghull L31 20 D4
Neston CH64 86 F1
Ormskirk L39 13 B2
Royal Oak L39 21 F4
Skelmersdale WN8 23 C8
Southport PR8 4 A3
St Helens WA10 43 F3
Warrington WA5 74 E6
Widnes WA8 72 C1
Liverpool Rd N L31 20 C2
Liverpool Rd S
Maghull L31 20 C1
Maghull L31 28 C7
Liverpool Row WA12 60 D8
Liverpool South Parkway Sta L19 81 D6
Liverpool St WA10 43 F3
Liverpool Womens Hospl L8 68 A8
Liversidge Rd CH42 66 D4
Liver St L1 90 A2
Livesley's La
Great Altcar L37 10 F2
Haskayne L37 11 A2
Livingston Ave L17 68 C4
Livingston Ct L17 68 C3
Livingston Dr L17 68 C3
Livingston Dr N L17 68 C3
Livingston Dr S L17 68 C3
Livingstone Gdns CH41 66 C7
Livingstone Rd CH46 50 B4
Livingstone St
2 Ashton-in-M WN4 35 A5
Birkenhead CH41 66 C7
Llanrwst Cl L8 67 E5
Lloyd Ave CH41 66 B7
Lloyd Cl L6 52 F4
Lloyd Cres WA12 45 F3
Lloyd Dr CH49 64 D3
Lloyd Rd L34 56 E7
Lloyd St WA11 44 F6
Lobelia Ave L9 39 B4
Lochinvar St L9 38 F3
Lochmore Rd L18 69 B1
Lochryan Rd L19 81 B8
Locker Ave WA2 61 B2
Lockerbie Cl WA2 61 E3
Lockerby Rd L7 53 D2
Locker La WN4 35 F4
Locker Pk CH49 64 C4
Locke St L19 81 C4
Lockett Bsns Pk WN4 35 C5
Lockett Rd
Ashton-in-M WN4 35 C6
Widnes WA8 73 B3
Lockfields View L3, L5 52 C5
Lockington Cl 22 L8 68 A4
Lock Rd CH62 89 A8
Lock St WA9 44 C5
Lockton Rd L34 41 B5
Loddon Cl CH49 65 B7
Lodge La
Bebington CH62 79 B6
Haydock WA11, WA12, WN4 46 B8
Liverpool L8 68 B7
Rainford L39, WA11 23 D1
Widnes WA8 72 B4
Lodge Rd
Orrell WN5 25 E4
Widnes WA8 84 B8
Lodge The CH43 65 D6
Lodwick St L20 38 B1
Lofthouse Gate WA8 72 F4
Logan Rd CH41 51 B1
Logfield Dr L19 81 D4
Lognor Rd L32 29 C2
Lognor Wlk L32 29 C2
Logwood Rd L36 71 A8
Lois Ct CH45 51 C6
Lombard Rd CH46 49 F2
Lombardy Ave CH49 64 B2
Lomond Gr CH46 64 F8
Lomond Rd L7 53 E2
Londonderry Rd L13 53 E7
London Fields WN5 33 E5
London La PR8 8 D8
London Rd
Liverpool L3 52 F2
Liverpool L3 90 C4
London Row WA12 60 D8
London Sq 2 PR8 4 B7
London St PR8, PR9 4 B7
Longacre PR9 1 F3
Longacre Cl CH45 50 D5
Longacres CH46 64 D5
Long Acres Rd CH64 86 E2
Long Ave L9 39 B6
Longborough Rd L34 41 C2
Longcliffe Dr PR8 7 C4
Longcroft Ave L19 81 E7
Longcroft Sq L19 81 E7
Longdale La L29 27 D8
Longden Rd WN4 35 A3
Longdown Rd L10 40 B6
Longfellow Cl L32 40 D8
Longfellow Dr CH62 79 A7
Longfellow St
Bootle L20 38 A5
Liverpool L8 68 C7
Longfield L37 10 B5
Longfield Ave L23 26 E6
Longfield Cl CH49 64 D4
Longfield Pk WA9 58 D4
Longfield Rd
Bootle L21 38 B6
Warrington WA2 61 C1
Longfield Wlk L23 26 E6
Longfold L31 20 E1
LONGFORD 61 B1
Longford Dr WA8 72 E2
Longford Rd PR8 4 A2
Longford St L8 68 A3
Longhey WN8 16 C4
Long Hey L35 56 D2
Long Hey Rd CH48 75 E7
Long Heys or Back La WN8 16 F5
Long La
Bickerstaffe L39 22 B7
Crosby L23, L29 27 A8
Formby L37 9 E4
Liverpool, Garston L19 81 C7
Liverpool, Hartley's Village L9 39 C5
Liverpool, Norris Green L9 39 E4
Liverpool, Wavertree L15 68 F8
Maghull L29 19 B1
Ormskirk L39 21 F8
Skelmersdale WN8 24 E3
Warrington WA2 61 B1
Longland Rd CH45 51 B6
Long Mdw
Heswall CH60 85 F6
St Helens WA10 43 B4
Longmead Ave WN4 35 C4
Longmeadow Rd L34 41 D4
Long Meanygate PR9 5 F8
Longmoor Cl L10 39 E7
Longmoor Com Prim Sch L9 39 B6
Longmoor Gr L9 39 B6
Longmoor La L10, L9 39 D7
Long Moss L30 27 C2
Longreach Rd L14 54 F3
Longridge Ave
Birkenhead CH49 64 E6
St Helens WA11 44 D5
Longridge Wlk 10 L4 52 E8
LONGSHAW 25 E1
Longshaw Ave WN5 25 E1
Longshaw Cl WN5 25 E1
Longshaw Comm
Billinge WN5 33 E8
Longshaw WN5 25 E1
Longshaw Old Rd WN5 25 E1
Longshaw St WA5 60 F1
Longstone Wlk L7 68 B8
Longton Ave WA3 47 C7
Longton Ct PR8 7 C5
Longton Dr L37 10 A6
Longton La L35 57 B4
Longton Lane Com Prim Sch L35 57 B5
LONGVIEW 55 F4
Longview Ave
Rainhill L35 57 A4
Wallasey CH45 51 B5
Longview Com Sch L36 55 E6
Longview Cres L36 55 F3
Longview Dr L36 56 A3
Longview La L36 55 F4
Longview Rd
Huyton-w-R L36 55 F3
Rainhill L35 57 A4
Longville St L8 67 E5
Longwood Cl WA11 32 C1
Longworth Way L25 70 A3
Lonie Gr WA10 57 C8
Lonsboro Rd CH44 51 C3
Lonsdale Ave
Ormskirk L39 13 F7
St Helens WA10 57 B7
Wallasey CH45 51 A6
Lonsdale Cl
Litherland L21 27 B2
Warrington WA5 74 F8
3 Widnes WA8 84 C8
Lonsdale Mews L21 27 B2
Lonsdale Rd
Formby L37 9 F3
Litherland L21 27 B2
Liverpool L26 82 E7
Southport PR8 4 D4
Lonsdale Villas CH45 51 A6
Looe Cl WA8 72 E2
Looe Rd L11 40 D5
Looms The CH64 86 B2
Loomsway CH61 76 D6
Loraine St L5 52 F5
Lordens Cl L14 55 A5
Lordens Rd L14 55 A5
Lord Nelson St L1, L3 90 C4
Lord St W PR8 4 A6
Lords Ave CH43 65 C8
Lord Sefton Way L37 10 E2
Lords Fold WA11 31 E7
Lord St
Ashton-in-M WN4 35 D4
Birkenhead CH41 66 E7
Liverpool, Garston L19 81 D4
Liverpool L2 90 A3
Newton-le-W WA12 46 A3
Runcorn WA7 84 F3
Southport PR8, PR9 4 B7
St Helens WA10 44 A5
Loreburn Rd L15 69 B6
Lorenzo Dr L11 53 F8
Loretto Dr CH49 65 A6
Loretto Rd CH44 50 F4
Lorn Ct 17 CH41 66 E6
Lorne Ct CH43 66 B4
Lorne Rd
Birkenhead CH43 66 A5
Crosby L22 26 D1
Lorne St L7 53 E3
Lorn St CH41 66 E6
Lorton Ave WA11 44 A8
Lorton St L8 68 B7
Lostock Cl WN5 33 E5
Lothair Rd L4 53 A7
Lothian St L8 68 A5
Lotus Gdns WA9 59 A7
Loudon Gr L8 68 A6
Lough Gn CH63 79 A2
Loughlin Dr L33 30 A5
Loughrigg Ave WA11 33 B1
Louis Braille Cl L30 27 F4
Louis Pasteur Ave L30 27 F4
Lourdes Hospl L18 68 F5
Love La
Liverpool L3 52 B4
Wallasey CH44 51 B3
Lovelace Rd L19 81 B7
Lovel Rd L24 82 D4
Lovel Terr WA8 84 B5
Lovel Way L24 82 D4
Lovett Dr L35 56 E5
Low Bank Rd WN4 34 F4
Lowbridge Ct L19 81 D6
Lowcroft WN8 16 C3
Lowden Ave L21 27 B1
Lowell St L4 38 F1
Lower Alt Rd L38 17 F4
Lower Appleton Rd WA8 73 B1
Lower Bank View L20 38 B1
LOWER BEBINGTON 79 A5
Lower Breck Rd L6 53 C5
Lower Carr La L37 19 B7
Lower Castle St L2 90 A3
Lower Cl L26 83 A8
Lower Farm Rd L25 70 A7
Lower Flaybrick Rd CH43 65 E8
Lower Gill St L3 52 F2
Lower Gn CH49 65 A3
Lower Hey L23 27 B5
LOWER HOUSE 84 E8
Lower House La
Liverpool L11 40 A3
Widnes WA8 84 F8
Lower La L10, L9 39 F6
Lower Lee Sch L25 69 E4
Lower Mersey View L20 38 B1
Lower Prom
Southport PR8 4 A7
Southport PR9 4 B8
Lower Rd
Bebington CH62 79 B6
Halewood L26, WA8 83 C7
Lower Sandfield L25 70 B4
Lowerson Cres L11 53 E8
Lowerson Rd L11 53 E8
Lower Thingwall La CH61 77 C5
Lowe St S WA10 43 F3
Lowes Gn L37 10 B3
Lowe's La WN8 15 F8
Lowe St
Golborne WA3 47 A8
St Helens WA10 43 F4
Lowestoft Dr L19 81 B6
Loweswater Cl WA2 61 B3
Loweswater Cres WA11 45 A6
Loweswater Way L33 29 D4
Lowfield Ind Est WA9 57 F5
Lowfield La WA9 57 F5
Lowfield Rd L14 54 C3
Lowfields Ave CH62 88 E3
Lowfields Cl CH62 88 E3
Low Hill L6 53 A3
Lowlands Rd 6 WA7 84 F2
Lowndes Rd L6 53 D6
Lowry Bank CH44 51 E3
Lowry Cl L33 29 E6
Lowther Ave
Aintree L10 28 D2
Maghull L31 20 F2
Lowther Cres WA10 57 B8
Lowther Dr L35 57 C3
Lowther St L8 68 A7
LOWTON 47 E8
Lowton Gdns WA3 47 B5
LOWTON HEATH 47 C6
Lowton Rd WA3 36 C1
LOWTON ST MARY'S 47 F8
Lowton West Prim Sch WA3 47 D8
Lowwood Gr CH41 66 D5
Low Wood Gr CH61 77 C4
Lowwood Rd CH41 66 D5
Low Wood St 10 L6 53 A2
Loxdale Cl 23 L8 68 A4
Loxley Rd PR8 4 D4
Loxwood Cl L25 70 B7
Loyola Hey L35 72 E8
Lucania St L19 81 C4
Lucan Rd L17 68 E2
Lucerne Rd CH44 51 D2
Lucerne St L17 68 C3
Lucius Cl L9 38 F7
Lucknow St 4 L17 68 C4
Ludlow WN8 16 C4
Ludlow Ct 1 CH48 63 B1
Ludlow Dr
Ormskirk L39 13 D7
West Kirby CH48 63 B1
Ludlow Gr CH62 79 D1
Ludlow St L4 38 F1
Ludwig Rd 7 L4 53 B6
Lugard Rd L17 68 E2
Lugsmore La WA10 43 D1
Luke St
Ashton-in-M WN4 35 D5
Liverpool L8 67 F6
Wallasey CH44 51 E2
Lulworth WN8 16 C4
Lulworth Ave L22 26 C1
Lulworth Lo PR8 3 F5
Lulworth Rd
Liverpool L25 70 C5
Southport PR8 3 F5
Lumber La WA5 59 F8
Lumina CH62 79 E1
Lumley Rd CH44 51 D3
Lumley St L19 81 B7
Lumley Wlk L24 83 E1
Lunar Dr L30 27 F4
Lunar Rd L9 39 B6
Lunds Cl L40 14 E4
Lune Ave L31 20 E2
Lunehurst 12 WA3 47 E8
Lunesdale Ave 3 L9 39 B7
Lune St L23 26 E4
Lune Way WA8 72 C1
Lunsford Rd L14 54 F4
LUNT 27 D8
Lunt Ave
Litherland L30 28 A2
Prescot L35 56 E3
Lunt La L29 27 D8
Lunt Rd
Bootle L20 38 C5
Lunt L29 27 D8
Maghull L29 19 C1
LUNTS HEATH 73 A5
Lunts Heath Prim Sch WA8 73 B5
Lunt's Heath Rd WA8 73 B5
Luntswood Gr WA12 46 A4
Lupin Dr WA11 45 F6
Lupton Dr L23 27 A4
Luscombe Cl L26 83 A8
Lusitania Rd L4 39 B2
Luther Gr WA9 45 B2
Luton Gr L4 52 F8
Luton St L5 52 C6
Lutyens Cl 2 L4 52 F7
Luxmore Rd L4 39 A1
Lycett Rd
Liverpool L4 53 C7
Wallasey CH44 50 E5
Lyceum Pl 15 L1 90 B3
Lydbrook Cl 6 CH42 66 F3

Market St *continued*
Southport PR8 4 B7
[11] St Helens WA10 44 A3
Market Way
[8] Liverpool L1 90 B3
[6] Ormskirk L39 13 E5
Markfield Cres
Liverpool L25 70 C1
St Helens WA11 44 C5
Markfield Rd L20 38 C5
Markham Dr PR8 4 E2
Markham Gr CH43 65 F8
Mark Rake CH62 79 D1
Mark Rd L38 17 F4
Mark St L5 52 E7
Marksway CH61 77 A4
Marland WN8 16 A4
Marlborough WN8 16 A4
Marlborough Ave
Litherland L30 28 A2
Maghull L31 20 D3
Marlborough Cres
WA8 73 A5
Marlborough Ct [1]
WN8 16 B4
Marlborough Gdns [5]
PR9 4 C8
Marlborough Gr CH43 66 C4
Marlborough Pl [5] L3 52 C3
Marlborough Rd
Crosby L23 26 D3
Liverpool L13 53 E6
Prescot L34 56 E7
Seaforth L22 37 E8
Southport PR9 4 C7
Wallasey CH45 51 C7
Marlborough St [4] L3 52 C3
Marlborough Way
WA11 45 E8
Marlbrook Rd L25 70 B6
Marlcroft Dr L17 80 E7
Marldon Ave L23 26 E2
Marldon Rd L11, L12 54 B8
Marled Hey L28 55 A8
Marley Cl L35 57 E1
Marlfield La CH61 77 A4
Marlfield Rd L12 54 B6
Marl Gr WN5 25 D4
Marline Ave CH63 88 C6
Marling Pk WA8 72 B1
Marlowe Cl
Liverpool L19 81 C5
Widnes WA8 72 F1
Marlowe Dr L12 54 A6
Marlowe Rd CH44 51 A4
Marl Rd
Kirkby L33 30 C3
Litherland L30 28 B3
Marlsford St L6 53 C3
Marlston Ave CH61 76 F6
Marlwood Ave CH45 50 E5
Marmaduke St L7 53 B1
Marmion Ave L20 38 E7
Marmion Cl WA3 36 E1
Marmion Rd
Hoylake CH47 63 B7
Liverpool L17 68 C4
Marmonde St L4 52 E8
Marnock Cl WN2 36 F8
Marnwood Rd L32 29 D1
Marnwood Wlk [6] L32 29 C1
Marple Cl CH43 65 E3
Marquis St
Bebington CH62 79 B7
Birkenhead CH41 66 E4
Liverpool L3 90 C4
Marram Cl CH46 50 A1
Marron Ave WA2 61 B2
Marryat Cl WA2 61 A6
Marsden Ave WA10 43 D4
Marsden Cl CH44 51 D5
Marsden Ct
[13] Wallasey CH45 51 B7
Widnes WA8 72 E4
Marsden Rd
Liverpool L26 82 F7
Southport PR9 4 E7
Marsden St [12] L6 53 A3
Marsden Way [13] L6 53 A3
Marshall Ave
[5] St Helens WA9 58 C8
Warrington WA5 60 F2
Marshall Cl L33 29 F5
Marshall Pl L3 52 C4
Marshallsay L37 10 A2
Marshall's Cl L31 20 C4
MARSHALL'S CROSS 58 B5
Marshalls Cross Rd
WA9 58 B7
Marshall St CH41 66 C8
Marsham Cl CH49 65 A7
Marsham Rd L25 70 C5
Marsh Ave L20 38 E6
Marsh Brows L37 9 E2
Marshfield Cl L36 55 F3
Marshfield Ct CH46 49 E3
Marshfield Rd L11 40 B1
Marshgate WA8 84 B6
Marshgate Rd L12 40 C2
Marsh Hall Pad WA8 73 B4
Marsh La
Bebington CH63 78 C7
Bootle L20 38 C4
Hightown L37, L38 18 E6
Marsh La *continued*
Warrington, Penketh
WA5 74 C2
Marshlands Rd [1]
CH45 50 E6
MARSHSIDE 1 E4
Marshside Cl L8 67 F5
Marshside Nature
Reserve* PR9 1 E5
Marshside Prim Sch
PR9 2 A5
Marshside Rd PR9 1 F4
Marsh St
Liverpool L20 38 D1
St Helens WA9 44 C3
Marshway Dr WA12 46 B5
Marsland Gr WA9 58 E8
Marston Cl
Bebington CH62 88 E3
Birkenhead CH43 65 F3
Marston Cres L38 18 A2
Marsworth Dr [7] L5 52 F4
Marten Ave CH63 88 C7
Martensen St L7 53 B1
Martham Gdns WA9 57 E6
Martin Ave
Newton-le-W WA12 46 C5
St Helens WA10 43 F6
Warrington WA2 61 E1
Martin Cl
Irby CH61 76 C6
Liverpool L18 69 A1
Rainhill L35 57 A4
Martindale Rd
Bebington CH62 79 E1
Billinge WA11 33 C2
Liverpool L18 69 D5
Martine Cl L31 29 B4
Martin Gr L35 56 E5
Martinhall Rd L9 39 F4
Martin Rd L18 69 A1
Martins La WN8 24 D7
Martin's La CH44 51 C4
Martland Ave
Aintree L10 28 E2
Golborne WA3 47 E2
Martland Rd L25 70 C4
Martlesham Cres CH49 64 B3
Martlett Rd L12 54 D5
Martock L35 56 F2
Marton Cl L24 82 D4
Marton Gn L24 82 D3
Marton Rd L36 55 E6
Marvin St L6 53 A3
Marwood Twrs L5 52 E6
Mary Ave PR8 7 E6
Marybone L3 52 D3
Maryfield L23 26 E3
Maryfield Cl WA3 47 A7
Maryland Ho [8] L20 38 C3
Maryland La CH46 49 D1
Maryland St L1 90 C2
Marylebone Ave WA9 57 F6
Maryport Cl L5 52 F6
Mary Rd L20 38 D6
Mary St WA9 58 E3
Mary Stockton Ct [5]
L21 38 A6
Maryton Grange L18 69 D2
Maryville Rd L34 56 E6
Marywell Cl WA9 58 D7
Masefield Ave WA8 84 F8
Masefield Cl CH62 79 A7
Masefield Cres L30 38 D8
Masefield Dr WA2 61 A5
Masefield Gr
Liverpool L16 69 F8
St Helens WA10 43 D5
Masefield Pl L30 38 E8
Masefield Rd L23 27 C6
Maskell Rd L13 53 F3
Mason Ave WA8 73 B4
Mason Cl WN4 35 D4
Mason St
Abram WN2 36 B8
Crosby L22 26 D1
Liverpool L7 53 A1
Liverpool, Woolton L25 70 A2
Wallasey CH45 51 B8
Massam Cl WA11 32 A6
Massam's La L37 9 F6
Massey Ave WA5 60 F2
Massey Pk CH45 51 A5
Massey St
Birkenhead CH41 66 D8
St Helens WA9 58 C8
Masters Way L19 81 D4
Matchwood Cl L19 81 D5
Matchworks The L19 81 E5
Mather Ave
Golborne WA3 47 E6
Liverpool L18, L19 69 C2
St Helens WA9 44 E3
Mather Ct [3] CH43 66 B5
Mather Rd CH43 66 B5
Mathew St L2 90 A3
Mathieson Rd WA8 84 E5
Matlock Ave
[7] Liverpool L9 39 A6
Southport PR8 4 B4
Matlock Cl
Southport PR8 4 B4
Warrington WA5 60 A1
Matlock Cres PR8 4 B4
Matlock Rd PR8 4 B4
Matthew Arnold Prim Sch
L8 68 A3
Matthew Cl [16] CH44 51 E2
Matthew St CH44 51 E2
Maud Roberts Ct L21 38 A8
Maud St L8 68 A6
Maunders Ct L23 27 A5
Maureen Wlk L10 40 B7
Mauretania Rd L4 39 A2
Maurice Jones Ct
CH46 49 E1
Mavis Dr CH49 65 A3
Mawdsley Cl L37 10 B3
Mawdsley Terr L39 13 F7
Max Rd L14 54 F6
Maxton Rd L6 53 C3
Maxwell Cl CH49 65 A6
Maxwell Cl [5] CH42 66 C3
Maxwell Pl L13 53 F6
Maxwell Rd L13 53 F6
Maxwell St WA10 43 E3
May Ave
Abram Brow WN2 36 C7
Wallasey CH44 51 D2
Maybank Cl PR9 2 A1
Maybank Gr L17 68 F1
Maybank Rd CH42 66 D4
Maybury Way L17 68 C2
May Cl L21 38 B6
Mayer Ave CH63 78 F4
Mayew Rd CH61 76 F6
Mayfair Ave
Crosby L23 26 E5
Huyton-w-R L14 54 F3
Mayfair Cl
Hightown L38 17 F2
[1] Liverpool L6 53 B4
Warrington WA5 74 D7
Mayfair Ct [1] CH43 66 C3
Mayfair Gr WA8 72 D1
Mayfayre Ave L31 20 B5
Mayfield L4 52 E8
Mayfield Ave
Formby L37 9 C1
St Helens WA9 57 E8
Widnes WA8 72 B1
Mayfield Cl L12 54 C6
Mayfield Ct
Formby L37 9 F5
Widnes WA8 73 A2
Mayfield Dr CH62 89 B6
Mayfield Gdns
Liverpool L19 81 A7
Neston CH64 86 E1
Mayfield Rd
Bebington CH63 79 A3
Liverpool L19 81 A7
Up Holland WN8 25 B7
Wallasey CH45 50 F5
Mayfields Ho CH62 79 B7
Mayfields N CH62 79 B7
Mayfields S CH62 79 B7
Mayfield St WN4 35 A3
Mayflower Ave L24 82 A7
Mayflower Ind Est L37 10 A1
Mayford Cl L25 70 B6
Mayhall Ct L31 20 D2
May Pl L13 54 A2
Maypole Ct
Knowsley L34 41 C5
Litherland L30 27 D5
May Rd CH60 86 A8
May St
Bootle L20 38 C5
Golborne WA3 36 B2
Liverpool L3 90 C3
Maytree Cl L27 70 C6
Maytree Wlk WN8 16 B4
Mayville Rd L18 69 B5
Mazzini Cl L5 52 E4
Mead Ave L21 38 C8
Meade Cl L35 57 D1
Meade Rd L13 53 E6
Meadfoot Rd CH46 49 D1
Meadow Ave
Southport PR8 4 C4
St Helens WA9 58 D3
Meadow Bank
Maghull L31 20 B2
[6] Ormskirk L39 13 F5
Meadowbank Cl L12 54 E5
Meadowbarn Cl [3] L32 29 E1
Meadowbridge Cl L40 14 E4
Meadow Brook Cl L10 40 B7
Meadowbrook Rd
CH46 64 D7
Meadow Brow PR9 2 D5
Meadow Cl
Newton-le-W WA12 45 F3
Skelmersdale WN8 24 D7
Westhead L40 14 E4
Widnes WA8 72 D3
Meadow Clough WN8 16 B4
Meadow Cres CH49 65 B2
Meadowcroft
Ashton-in-M WN4 34 F6
Formby L37 9 F2
Heswall CH60 77 C1
Skelmersdale WN8 16 B4
St Helens WA9 58 C6
Meadowcroft Pk L12 54 D4
Meadowcroft Rd CH47 48 E1
Meadow Ct
Liverpool, Croxteth L11 40 B4
Liverpool, Woolton L25 70 B3
Meadow Dr
Huyton-w-R L36 70 F8
Ormskirk L39 13 C2
Meadowfield [3] WN8 25 A7
Meadowfield Cl
[3] Birkenhead CH42 66 F2
Meadowfield Cl *continued*
Liverpool L9 39 A7
Meadow Hey L20 38 A6
Meadow Hey Cl L25 70 B3
Meadow La
Birkenhead CH42 66 F2
Liverpool L11, L12 54 B8
Maghull L31 20 F1
Southport PR8 7 D3
St Helens WA9 44 F2
Willaston CH64 87 E1
Meadow Oak Dr L25 70 A4
Meadow Pk [2] CH42 66 F2
Meadow Rd CH48 63 F3
Meadowside CH46 50 B4
Meadowside Ave WN4 35 A8
Meadowside Com Prim
Sch WA2 61 B1
Meadowside Dr L33 29 F6
Meadowside Rd CH62 88 D8
Meadowside Sch CH49 65 B2
Meadow St CH45 51 A8
Meadows The
Bebington CH62 88 D7
Maghull L31 20 D1
Rainhill L35 57 C3
Meadow The CH49 65 B3
Meadow View
Litherland L21 27 B3
Southport PR8 4 D4
Meadow Way L12 40 B1
Meadow Wlk CH61 76 E3
Meads The L34 57 A7
Meadway
Bebington CH62 79 C2
Birkenhead CH49 65 B6
Golborne WA3 47 D8
Heswall CH60 85 F6
Litherland L30 28 A2
Liverpool L15 69 C8
Maghull L31 28 B7
Prescot L35 56 F4
Skelmersdale WN8 16 A4
Wallasey CH45 51 A5
Widnes WA8 72 A1
Mealors Weint CH64 86 B1
Meander The L12 40 E1
Measham Cl WA11 44 C5
Measham Way L12 40 E3
Medbourne Cres L32 40 F8
Medbourne Ct [12] L32 40 F8
Meddowcroft Rd [5]
CH45 51 A6
Medea Cl L5 52 E6
Medlar Way WN4 34 F5
Medlock Ct CH43 66 A5
Medlock St L4 52 E7
Medway [2] L20 38 C3
Medway Cl
Ashton-in-M WN4 34 F6
Warrington WA2 61 E2
Medway Ct WA9 44 F3
Medway Rd CH42 67 A2
Meeting La WA5 74 E5
Melbourne Cl L24 82 B5
Melbourne St
St Helens WA9 57 E7
Wallasey CH45 51 A8
Melbreck WN8 16 A4
Melbreck Rd L18 69 B1
Melbury Rd L14 55 C6
Melda Cl [8] L6 52 F3
Meldon Cl L12 40 C2
Meldreth Cl L37 9 C1
Meldrum Rd L15 69 B6
Melford Dr
Ashton-in-M WN4 35 A4
Birkenhead CH43 65 E1
Orrell WN5 25 D3
Melford Gr L6 53 D6
Meliden Gdns WA9 58 F7
Melksham Dr CH61 76 D7
MELLING 28 F5
Melling Ave L9 39 B7
Melling Ct CH45 51 C7
Melling Dr L32 29 E3
Melling La L31 28 F7
MELLING MOUNT 29 C7
Melling Prim Sch L31 29 B4
Melling Rd
Bootle L20 38 C5
Liverpool L9 39 C8
Southport PR9 4 E7
Wallasey CH45 51 C7
Mellings Ave WN5 25 E1
Melling Way L32 29 E3
Melloncroft Dr CH48 75 C7
Melloncroft Dr W
CH48 75 C7
Mellor Cl L35 71 A7
Mellor Rd CH42 66 C2
Mellors Cl PR8 4 F5
Melly Rd [5] L17 68 B3
Melmerby Cl WN4 34 F3
Melrose CH46 65 A8
Melrose Ave
Burtonwood WA5 59 F7
Crosby L23 26 E3
Hoylake CH47 63 B7
Southport PR9 2 B5
St Helens WA10 43 B5
Melrose Cres WN4 34 C3
Melrose Gdns [5] CH43 65 F1
Melrose Pk [3] L22 37 E8
Melrose Rd
Kirkby L33 29 D6
Liverpool L4, L5 52 D8
Seaforth L22 37 E8
Melton Cl CH49 64 E5
Melverley Rd L32 29 B2
Melville CH42 67 B1
Melville Ave CH42 67 A1
Melville Cl
St Helens WA10 43 D4
[2] Widnes WA8 73 D1
Melville Gr L8 68 A8
Melville Pl L7 68 A8
Melville Rd
Bebington CH63 78 E5
Bootle L20 38 C7
Melville St L8 68 A5
Melwood Dr L12 54 C7
Menai Mews [5] L34 56 E6
Menai Rd L20 38 D6
Menai St CH41 66 C6
Mendell Cl CH62 88 E8
Mendell Prim Sch
CH62 88 E8
Mendip Ave WA2 61 B3
Mendip Cl
Birkenhead CH42 66 C1
Liverpool L26 82 E8
Mendip Gr WA9 44 F3
Mendip Rd
Birkenhead CH42 66 C1
Liverpool L15 69 A6
Menivale Cl PR9 2 B5
Menlo Ave CH61 76 F6
Menlo Cl CH43 65 F4
Menlove Ave L18, L25 69 D4
Menlove Ct L18 69 C5
Menlove Gdns N L18 69 C5
Menlove Gdns S L18 69 B5
Menlove Gdns W L16,
L18 69 B5
Menlove Mans L18 69 C6
Menstone Rd L13 53 F4
Mentmore Cres L11 40 B1
Mentmore Rd L18 69 A2
MEOLS 63 D8
Meols Cl
Formby L37 9 E2
Hale L24 83 E2
Meols Cop High Sch
PR8 4 F5
Meols Cop Rd PR8, PR9 4 F4
Meols Cop Retail Pk
PR9 5 A4
Meols Cop Sta PR9 4 F7
Meols Ct CH47 63 A6
Meols Dr CH47, CH48 63 A4
Meols Par CH47 48 D1
Meols Sta CH47 63 E8
Meols View Cl PR8 5 A3
Mercer Ave L32 29 C1
Mercer Ct
[10] Bootle L20 38 C3
Liverpool L12 54 E5
Maghull L31 20 A3
Mercer Dr L4 52 E8
Mercer Rd
Birkenhead CH43 65 E8
Haydock WA11 45 D6
Mercer's La L39 22 B4
Mercer St
Burtonwood WA5 59 E6
Liverpool L19 81 C5
Newton-le-W WA12 46 D4
Merchants Cres WA3 36 E1
Merchants Ct L1 90 A3
Merchant Taylors' Boys'
Sch L23 26 E3
Merchant Taylors' Sch for
Girls L23 26 E4
Mercury Way WN8 24 E8
Mere Ave CH63 88 B6
Merebank CH43 65 E4
Mere Bank L17 68 E4
Merebrook Gr L33 29 F5
Mere Cl WN8 15 F2
Merecliff L28 55 B8
Merecroft Ave CH44 51 C2
Meredale Rd L18 69 A4
Meredith St L19 81 E5
Mere Farm Gr CH43 65 F4
Mere Farm Rd CH43 65 F4
Merefield Sch PR8 7 B4
Mere Gn L4 39 A1
Mere Gr WA11 33 B1
Mere Hall CH43 65 E4
Mereheath CH46 49 E3
Mereheath Gdns CH46 49 E3
Mere Hey WA10 43 A3
Mere La
Heswall CH60 76 E2
Liverpool L5 52 F6
Wallasey CH45 50 E7
Mereland Cl WN5 25 E6
Mereland Way WA9 44 F2
Merepark Dr PR9 2 B4
Mere Park Rd CH49 64 C3
Mere Pk L23 26 D4
Mere Rd
Ashton-in-M WN4 35 C4
Formby L37 9 D2
Newton-le-W WA12 46 F4
Meres Rd L9, L10 39 E7
Meres Way PR8 4 B2
Mereview Cres L12 40 D3
Merewood
[8] Kirkby L32 40 F8
Skelmersdale WN8 16 A4
Merewood Cl WA2 61 D3
Mereworth CH48 75 D6
Meribel Cl L23 27 A5
Meriden Ave CH63 79 A1

Meriden Cl
Southport PR8 7 B5
St Helens WA11 44 D6
Meriden Rd L25 70 B6
Merlewood Ave PR9 2 B3
Merlin Ave CH49 64 D6
Merlin Cl
Birkenhead CH49 64 D6
St Helens WA11 44 B6
Merlin Ct L26 70 D1
Merlin Rd 3 CH42 66 C3
Merlin St L8 67 F6
Merrick Cl WA2 61 E3
Merrills La CH49 65 A5
Merrilocks Gn L23 26 A5
Merrilocks Rd L23 26 B5
Merrilox Ave L31 20 D3
Merrion Cl L25 69 F3
Merritt Ave CH41 66 B8
Merrivale Rd L25 70 C2
Merrydale Dr L11 40 C3
Mersey Ave
Formby L37 9 E6
Liverpool L19 80 F8
Maghull L31 20 F2
Merseybank Ho CH62 79 B8
Mersey Bank Rd CH62 79 B7
Mersey Cotts L19 81 D5
Mersey Ct
Crosby L23 26 C3
14 Wallasey CH44 51 E2
Mersey Ho 3 L20 38 B4
Mersey La S CH42 67 A2
Mersey Park Prim Sch CH42 66 D3
Mersey Rd
Birkenhead CH42 67 A2
Crosby L23 26 C3
Liverpool L17 80 E8
Orrell WN5 25 F7
Runcorn WA7 84 F3
Merseyside Maritime Mus★ L3 90 A2
Merseyside Mounted Police HQ L18 69 C1
Merseyside Police Training Coll L18 69 C1
Mersey St
St Helens WA9 45 A3
2 Wallasey CH44 51 E2
Mersey View
Bebington CH63 78 D6
Crosby L22 26 C2
Liverpool L19 81 C6
Mersey View Rd WA8 84 B4
Mersham Ct WA8 72 F4
Merstone Cl L26 82 F8
Merthyr Gr L16 54 E1
Merton Bank Prim Sch WA9 44 C4
Merton Bank Rd WA11, WA9 44 C5
Merton Cl L36 55 B2
Merton Cres L36 55 B2
Merton Dr
Birkenhead CH49 65 A3
Huyton-w-R L36 55 A2
Merton Gr
Bootle L20 38 C3
Crosby L23 26 C3
Merton Pl CH43 66 C6
Merton Rd
Bebington CH65 89 B3
Bootle L20 38 C3
Wallasey CH45 51 B5
Merton St WA9 44 C5
Merton Twrs L20 38 D3
Mesham Cl CH49 64 E5
Metcalf Cl L33 29 D6
Meteor Cres WA2 61 D2
Methuen St
Birkenhead CH41 66 A8
Liverpool L15 68 E8
Metquarter L1 90 B3
Metropolitan Cath of Christ The King★ L3 52 F1
Mews The
Burtonwood WA5 59 E6
1 Crosby L23 26 E3
Huyton-w-R L28 55 C7
Liverpool L17 68 F1
Southport PR8 4 A5
St Helens WA9 58 D4
Meyrick Cl WA12 46 A3
Meyrick Rd L11 39 E2
Micawber Cl L8 67 F5
Michael Dragonette Ct L3 52 C4
Michaels Cl L37 9 E3
Michael's La L39 8 C3
Michigan Cl L27 70 E5
Mickering La L39 21 C5
Micklefield Rd L15 68 F6
Mickleton Dr PR8 7 A5
Middlecot Cl 2 WN5 25 E5
Middlefield Com Prim Sch L24 82 F4
Middlefield Rd L18 69 E3
Middleham Cl L32 29 C1
Middlehey Rd L34 41 D4
Middlehurst Ave WA10 43 F4
Middlehurst Cl L34 57 A7
Middlemass Hey L27 70 E5
Middle Moss La
Great Altcar L37 10 F3
Haskayne L37 11 A2
Middlesex Rd L20 38 D4
Middleton Ct L24 82 E3
Middleton Rd
Crosby L22 26 F2
Liverpool L7 53 E3
Middle Way L11 40 D5
Middle Withins La L37, L38 19 A7
Middlewood
Golborne WA3 47 E8
7 Kirkby L32 40 F8
Skelmersdale WN8 16 A4
Middlewood Cl L39 21 C7
Middlewood Dr L39 21 C7
Middlewood Rd L39 21 C7
Midghall St L3 52 C3
Midhurst Dr PR8 7 B4
Midhurst Rd L12 41 A3
Midland St
17 Birkenhead CH41 66 C5
Widnes WA8 73 B1
Midland Terr L22 26 D1
Midlothian Dr L23 26 C3
Midway Rd L36 55 F4
Milbrook Cres L32 29 E3
Milbrook Dr L32 29 E3
Milbrook Wlk L32 29 E3
Mildenhall Rd L25 70 B7
Mildenhall Way L25 70 B7
Mildmay Rd
Bootle L20 38 B5
Liverpool L11 39 E2
Mile End L5 52 D4
Miles Cl CH49 64 C2
Miles La CH49 64 C2
Miles St L8 68 A4
Milestone Hey L28 55 B8
Milford Cl L37 9 C1
Milford Dr L12 40 E3
Milford St L5 52 C6
Milk St 7 WA10 44 A3
Millachip Ct L6 53 B4
Milland Cl L11 40 C3
Millar's Pace PR9 2 B5
Mill Ave WA5 74 E7
Mill Bank L13 53 F6
Millbank Ct L9 39 D8
Millbank La L31, L39 20 F3
Mill Bank Rd CH44 51 A3
Millbeck Cl 6 L32 29 E4
Millbeck Gr WA11 33 B2
Millbridge Gdns WA12 46 E3
Millbrook Bsns Pk WA11 32 C3
Millbrook Cl WN8 15 E2
Millbrook Com Prim Sch L32 29 D3
Millbrook Ct
Knowsley L34 41 C5
Warrington WA2 61 B2
Millbrook La WA10 43 B4
Millbrook Rd CH44 51 B1
Mill Brow
Bebington CH63 78 D6
Haskayne L39 12 A7
St Helens, Eccleston WA10 43 B4
St Helens WA9 58 D5
Widnes WA8 73 C1
Mill Brow Cl WA9 58 D5
Millbutt Cl CH63 78 D6
Mill Cl
Birkenhead CH42 66 D4
Crosby L23 26 E6
Warrington WA2 61 E4
Mill Cotts CH64 87 F1
Millcroft
Crosby L23 27 A5
Neston CH64 86 E1
Millcroft Ave WN5 25 D5
Millcroft Pk CH49 64 B3
Millcroft Rd L25 70 C1
Mill Ct L30 27 D5
Mill Dam La L40 14 D8
Millennium Ct
Crosby L22 26 E2
Neston CH64 86 E2
Millennium Rd L8 68 A6
Miller Ave L23 26 D5
Miller's Bridge L20 38 B2
Millers Cl 7 CH46 64 B8
Millerscroft L32 29 C4
Millers Ct L39 13 F5
Millersdale 13 WA9 58 C4
Millersdale Ave 5 L9 39 B7
Millersdale Cl CH62 88 F5
Millersdale Rd L18 69 A4
Millers Fold WA10 43 B4
Millersmede 6 L5 52 D5
Millers Nook WN8 25 B7
Millers Way CH46 64 C8
Mill Farm Cl WA2 61 E3
Millfield CH64 86 E1
Millfield Bsns Ctr WA11 45 E8
Millfield Cl
Bebington CH63 78 D5
Liverpool L13 54 A6
Millfield La WN4, WA11 34 E1
Millfield Rd WA8 73 C2
Millfields WA10 43 B3
Millfields Prim Sch CH62 88 E4
Millgreen Cl
Liverpool L12 40 E3
Up Holland WN8 25 A7
Mill Green La WA8 73 E5
Mill Green Sch WA12 46 E3
Mill Hey L35 57 E1
Mill Hey Rd CH48 75 D6
Mill Hill CH43 66 A3
Mill Hill Rd CH61 76 C7
Millhouse Cl CH46 49 B1
Millhouse Ct L12 54 A6
Millhouse La CH46 49 B1
Millhouse Lo PR8 7 D5
Mill House View WN8 25 C7
Millingford Ave WA3 35 F2
Millingford Gr WN4 35 B3
Millingford Ind Est WA3 47 A8
Millington Cl
Birkenhead CH43 65 E1
Widnes WA8 84 F8
Mill La
Birkenhead CH49 64 C2
Bold Heath WA8 73 D6
Bootle L20 38 D3
Cronton WA8 72 D6
Haskayne L39 12 F1
Heswall CH60 86 B8
Kirkby L32 29 D4
Knowsley L34 41 D5
Liverpool L3 90 B4
Liverpool, Olive Mount L13, L15 54 A1
Liverpool, Sandfield Park L12 54 A6
Newton-le-W WA12 46 E3
Rainford WA11 32 C4
Rainhill L35 57 C1
Skelmersdale, Elmers Green WN8 16 F1
Skelmersdale, Pennylands WN8 15 F2
Skelmersdale, Tawd Valley Park WN8 16 A3
Southport PR9 2 A1
St Helens WA9 58 D5
Up Holland WN8 25 A8
Wallasey CH44 51 A3
Warrington, Houghton Green WA2 61 E4
Warrington WA2 60 F4
Willaston CH64 87 F1
Mill Lane Cres PR9 2 A1
Mill Mdw WA12 46 E3
Millom Ave L35 57 B4
Millom Gr
Liverpool L12 40 C1
St Helens WA10 57 C8
Mill Park Dr CH62 88 E3
Mill Rd
Bebington CH62 79 D3
Bebington, Higher Bebington CH63 78 D6
Heswall CH61 77 A6
Liverpool L6 52 F4
Liverpool L6 53 A4
Orrell WN5 25 D5
Southport PR8 7 D5
Millrose Cl WN8 15 F2
Mill Spring Ct L20 38 D3
Mill Sq L10 28 E2
Mill St
Ashton-in-M WN4 35 C2
Birkenhead CH42 66 D4
Golborne WA3 47 A8
Liverpool, Toxteth L8 67 E5
Liverpool, Woolton L25 70 A2
Ormskirk L39 13 F5
Prescot L34 56 D6
Southport PR8 4 C6
St Helens WA10 43 F4
Millstead Rd L15 69 B8
Millstead Sch L15 69 B8
Millstead Wlk L15 69 A8
Millthwaite Ct 4 CH44 50 F4
Millthwaite Rd CH44 50 F4
Millvale St L6 53 C3
Mill View 4 L8 67 E5
Mill View Ct L39 22 E7
Mill View Dr CH63 78 C6
Millway Rd L24 83 A4
Millwood CH63 78 D6
Mill Wood Ave WA10 42 F3
Millwood Cl WN4 35 A5
Millwood Ct L24 83 A4
Millwood Gdns L35 56 F2
Millwood Rd L24 82 F4
MILL YARD 54 E4
Mill Yd CH61 77 B6
Milman Cl
Birkenhead CH49 64 F4
Ormskirk L39 13 D3
Milman Ct L25 69 E3
Milman Rd L4 39 A1
Milner Cop CH60 86 A8
Milne Rd 5 L13 53 E8
Milner Rd
Heswall CH60 86 A8
Liverpool L17 68 E1
Milner St CH41 66 A8
Milnthorpe Cl 11 L4 52 E8
Milnthorpe Rd WA5 59 E6
Milnthorpe St L19 81 C6
Milroy St L7 53 B1
Milton Ave
Huyton-w-R L14 54 F2
Newton-le-W WA12 46 B3
Prescot L35 56 F3
Widnes WA8 84 F8
Milton Cl L35 56 E3
Milton Cres CH60 77 A1
Milton Dr L39 14 A4
Milton Gn CH61 77 B6
Milton Gr
Longshaw WN5 25 D1
Milton Gr *continued*
Orrell WN5 25 F6
Milton Pavement 7 CH41 66 D6
Milton Rd
Birkenhead CH42 66 C4
Crosby L22 26 E2
Golborne WA3 47 D7
Liverpool L7 53 E2
Liverpool, Walton on the Hill L4 38 E2
Wallasey CH44 51 D2
West Kirby CH48 63 A3
Widnes WA8 84 F8
Milton Rd E CH42 66 D4
Milton St
Bootle L20 38 B4
Southport PR9 5 A7
St Helens WA9 58 B2
Milton Way L31 20 B1
Milvain Dr WA2 61 C1
Milverny Way WA9 44 A2
Milverton St L6 53 C4
Mimosa Rd L15 69 B7
Mindale Rd L15 68 F8
Minehead Gr WA9 58 D5
Minehead Rd L17 80 E8
Miners Way L24 83 A3
Mines Ave L17 80 F8
Mine's Ave L34 56 E6
Mine Way WA11 45 F7
Minshull St L7 53 A1
Minstead Ave L33 30 A2
Minster Ct L7 68 A8
Minstrel Cl WN2 36 B7
Minto Cl L7 53 C2
Minto Ho CH47 63 C8
Minton Cl L12 40 F3
Minton Way WA8 73 B5
Mintor Rd L33 30 A2
Minto St L7 53 B2
Minver Rd L12 54 D7
Miranda Ave CH63 78 E7
Miranda Pl L20 38 D1
Miranda Rd L20 38 D1
Miranda Rd S 4 L20 38 D1
Mirfield Cl
Golborne WA3 47 D7
Liverpool L26 82 F7
Mirfield St L6 53 C3
Miriam Pl 2 CH41 65 F8
Miriam Rd L4 53 A6
Miskelly St L20 52 C8
Missouri Rd L13 53 D7
Mistle Thrush Way 2 L12 40 F3
Miston St L20 52 C8
Misty Cl WA8 72 C2
Mitchell Ave WA5 59 E5
Mitchell Cres L21 38 B8
Mitchell Pl L1 90 C3
Mitchell Rd
Billinge WN5 33 E5
Prescot L34 56 C6
St Helens WA10 43 C1
Mitchell St
Ashton-in-M WN4 35 C2
Golborne WA3 47 A8
Mithril Cl WA8 73 E3
Mitre Cl L35 56 D1
Mitten's La L37 10 A4
Mitten's La L37 10 B3
Mitylene St L5 52 E6
Mobberley Way CH63 79 A3
Mockbeggar Dr CH45 50 D8
Mockbeggar Wharf CH45 50 E7
Modred St L8 67 F5
Moel Famau View L17 68 B2
Moffatdale Rd L4 53 C8
Moffat Rd L9 39 C7
Moira Sephton Ct CH43 65 D4
Molesworth Gr L16 54 F1
Molineux Ave L14 54 D1
Molland Cl L12 54 D8
Mollington Ave L11 39 F2
Mollington Link CH41 66 F5
Mollington Rd
Kirkby L32 29 C2
Wallasey CH44 51 C3
Mollington St CH41 66 E5
Molly's La L33 41 D7
Molton Rd L15, L16 69 C8
Molyneux Cl
Birkenhead CH49 64 F5
Huyton-w-R L36 55 F2
Prescot L35 56 D4
Molyneux Ct
Liverpool, Broad Green L14 54 D1
Liverpool, Dog & Gun L11 40 B3
Molyneux Dr
Prescot L35 56 D4
Wallasey CH45 51 C8
Molyneux Rd
Crosby L22 26 E2
Liverpool L6 53 B3
Liverpool, Mossley Hill L18 68 F4
Maghull L31 28 F7
Ormskirk L39 21 C7
Molyneux Way L10 28 C3
Monaghan Cl L9 39 A7
Monarchs Quay L3 90 A1
Monash Cl L33 29 E6
Monash Rd L11 53 F8
Mona St
Birkenhead CH41 65 F7
Bootle L20 38 D6
St Helens WA10 43 D3
Monastery La WA9 58 E7
Monastery Rd
4 Liverpool L6 53 C6
St Helens WA9 58 E7
Mond Rd
Liverpool L10 40 A7
5 Widnes WA8 73 A1
Monfa Rd
Bootle L20 38 C6
Bootle L20 38 D6
Monica Dr WA8 73 A5
Monica Rd L25 70 B1
Monica Terr WN4 35 B2
Monkfield Way L19 81 D4
Monk Rd CH44, CH45 51 B4
Monks Carr La L37, L38 19 A6
Monks Cl L37 10 A1
Monksdown Prim Sch L11 40 A1
Monksdown Rd L11 40 A1
Monks Dr L37 10 A1
Monks Ferry CH41 66 F6
Monksferry Wlk L19 80 F7
Monk St
Birkenhead CH41 66 F6
Liverpool L5 52 F6
Monks Way
Bebington CH63 78 F4
Liverpool L25 70 B2
Monk's Way CH48 63 C2
Monkswell Dr L15 69 A8
Monkswell St L8 68 A3
Monkswood Cl WA5 60 E2
Monmouth Cres WN4 35 D2
Monmouth Dr L10 28 F1
Monmouth Gr WA9 44 D2
Monmouth Rd CH44 50 F4
Monro Cl L8 67 F4
Monro St L8 67 F4
Mons Sq 5 L20 38 C3
Montague Rd
Liverpool L13 54 A2
Widnes WA8 84 A6
Montagu Mews L37 9 E5
Montagu Rd L37 9 E5
Montclair Dr L18 69 B6
Monterey Rd L13 54 B2
Montfort Dr L19 81 A7
Montgomery Ave PR9 5 B6
Montgomery Cl L35 56 D2
Montgomery Hill
Birkenhead CH48 64 A1
Irby CH48 76 A8
Montgomery Ho 8 L21 37 F7
Montgomery Rd
Huyton-w-R L36 55 E4
Liverpool L9 39 A7
Widnes WA8 84 D8
Montgomery Way 3 L6 53 B4
Montpelier Dr 8 L8 67 F4
Montpellier Cres CH45 51 A8
Montpellier Ct 7 CH45 51 A8
Montpellier Ho 5 CH45 51 A8
Montreal Rd L27 70 E5
Montreal St WN7 36 E4
Montrey Cres WN4 34 C3
Montrose Ave CH44 51 E1
Montrose Cl WA2 61 F4
Montrose Ct
Hoylake CH47 63 B6
Liverpool L12 54 F7
Montrose Dr PR9 1 F1
Montrose Pl L26 82 F7
Montrose Rd L13 53 E6
Montrose Way L13 53 F2
Montrovia Cres L10 39 F6
Monville Rd L9 39 C7
Moorbridge Cl L30 28 A5
Moor Cl
Crosby L23 26 F5
Southport PR8 7 D2
Moor Coppice L23 26 F5
Moorcroft Rd
Huyton-w-R L36 55 E5
Liverpool L18 69 D1
Wallasey CH45 50 D5
Moor Ct L10 40 A7
Moor Dr
Crosby L23 26 F4
Skelmersdale WN8 24 D7
Moore Ave
Birkenhead CH42 66 E2
St Helens WA9 45 B3
Moore Cl WA8 73 D2
Moore Dr WA11 45 F6
Moore's Ho 11 L4 38 F2
Moore St L20 38 B5
Mooreway L35 57 E1
Moorfield L33 29 F5
Moorfield Ctr The L33 29 F6
Moorfield Dr CH64 86 C1
Moorfield Prim Sch WA8 73 D3
Moorfield Rd
Crosby L23 27 A5
St Helens WA10 43 D5
Widnes WA8 73 D3

Moorfields L2 90 A4
Moorfields Ave CH43 65 D4
Moorfields Sta L2 90 A4
Moorfoot Rd WA9 44 F3
Moorfoot Road Ind Est
WA9 44 F4
Moorfoot Way L33 29 D6
Moorgate L39 13 E4
Moorgate Ave L23 26 F4
Moorgate La 8 L32 41 A8
Moorgate Rd L32 41 A7
Moorgate St 8 L7 53 B1
Moorhead Cl L21 38 A7
Moorhey Rd L31 28 D6
Moor Ho 4 L23 26 E5
Moorhouses L38 17 F3
Moorings Cl CH64 86 B1
Moorings The
6 Birkenhead CH41 66 D5
Heswall CH60 85 C8
Maghull L31 20 B4
West Kirby CH48 63 A2
Moor La
Crosby L23 26 F5
Heswall CH60 85 F8
Ince Blundell L38, L23 18 E2
Liverpool L10 40 A7
Liverpool L32 40 B8
Liverpool, Walton L4 39 A2
Maghull L29 19 D1
Southport PR8 7 C2
Widnes WA8 84 F7
Moorland Ave L23 26 E5
Moorland Cl CH60 86 A7
Moorland Pk CH60 86 A7
Moorland Rd
Ashton-in-M WN4 35 E5
Birkenhead CH42 66 E3
Maghull L31 28 D6
Moorlands Rd L23 27 B6
Moor La S WA8 84 F7
MOOR PARK 26 F6
Moor Pl L3 90 C4
Moor Rd WN5 25 E6
Moorside Cl L23 26 F4
Moorside Com Prim Sch
WN8 24 E7
Moorside Ct WA8 84 F7
Moorside Rd L23 26 F4
Moor St
Liverpool L2 90 A3
Ormskirk L39 13 F5
Moorway CH60 86 B8
Moorwood Cres WA9 58 C4
Moray Cl WA10 43 E5
Morcott La L24 83 D2
Morden Ave WN4 35 B3
Morden St L6 53 C3
Morecambe St L6 53 C5
Morecroft Rd CH42 67 A1
Morella Rd L4 53 C8
Morello Cl WA10 43 F5
Morello Dr CH63 79 B2
Moret Cl L23 27 A5
MORETON 49 D1
Moreton Ave 1 WA9 58 C4
Moreton Cl WA3 35 F1
Moreton Gr CH45 50 E6
Moreton Rd CH49 64 F6
Moreton Sta CH46 49 E2
Morgan Ave WA2 61 C2
Morgan Mews L30 27 D3
Morgan St WA9 44 D3
Morland Ave CH62 88 D6
Morley Ave CH41 66 B8
Morley Ct L14 54 E4
Morley Rd
Southport PR9 4 E8
Wallasey CH41, CH44 51 A3
Morley St
Liverpool L4 52 E7
St Helens WA10 43 F5
Morley Way 1 WA10 43 F4
Morningside L23 26 F3
Morningside Pl L11 39 F1
Morningside Rd L11 53 F8
Morningside View L11 53 F8
Morningside Way L11 53 F8
Mornington Ave L23 26 E2
Mornington Rd
Southport PR9 4 C7
Wallasey CH45 51 B6
Mornington St L8 67 E5
Morpeth Cl CH46 64 B8
Morpeth Rd CH47 63 A5
Morpeth St L8 67 F7
Morpeth Wharf CH41 66 F8
Morris Cl WA11 45 A5
Morris Ct CH43 65 F5
Morris Rd WN8 25 A7
Morrissey Cl WA10 43 D4
Morris St WA9 44 E1
Morston Ave L32 40 E8
Morston Cres L32 40 E8
Morston Wlk L32 40 E8
Mortar Mill Quay CH44 51 E1
Mortimer St CH41 66 F6
Mortlake Cl WA8 72 C3
Morton St L8 67 F5
Morvah Cl 2 L12 40 C2
Morval Cres L4 38 E2
Morven Cl WA2 61 E3
Morven Gr PR8 4 E7
Moscow Dr
Liverpool L13 53 F5
Moscow Dr *continued*
Liverpool L13 54 A5
Mosedale Ave WA11 33 B1
Mosedale Rd
Bebington CH62 79 E2
Liverpool L9 39 A5
Moseley Ave CH44,
CH45 51 A4
Moseley Rd CH63 79 A1
Moses St L8 67 F4
Mosley St PR8 4 B4
Moss Ave WN5 25 D3
MOSS BANK 33 A1
Moss Bank L39 13 D2
Moss Bank Ct L39 13 D2
Moss Bank Pk L21 38 A8
Moss Bank Rd WA11 33 B2
Mossborough Hall La
WA11 31 C2
Mossborough Rd
WA11 31 E4
Moss Brow WA11 31 E7
Mossbrow Rd L36 55 E4
Moss Cotts L40 15 A3
Mosscraig L28 55 C7
Mosscroft Cl L36 56 A4
Mosscroft Prim Sch
L36 56 A3
Mossdale Dr L35 57 D3
Mossdale Rd
Ashton-in-M WN4 35 A8
Kirkby L33 29 F5
Moss Delph La L39 13 C1
Mossdene Rd CH44 50 F4
Moss End Way L33 30 D3
Mossfield Rd L9 38 F6
Moss Gate Gr L14 55 A3
Moss Gate Rd L14 55 A3
Moss Gdns PR8 4 C2
Mossgiel Ave PR8 7 B5
Moss Gn L37 10 B4
Moss Gr
Birkenhead CH42 66 C2
Liverpool L8 68 C6
Moss Green Way WA9 45 A1
Mosshill Cl L31 20 C3
Moss La
Bickerstaffe L39 22 F2
Birkenhead CH42 66 B2
Crank WA11 32 E5
Formby L37, L39 10 E5
Golborne WA3 47 B5
Hightown L38, L23 18 C2
Kirkby L33 29 F7
Kirkby, Northwood L33 30 B3
Litherland L21 27 D1
Liverpool L9, L20 38 F6
Maghull L31 20 E2
Maghull, Lydiate L31 20 D5
Skelmersdale WN8 23 F6
Southport PR9 5 B8
St Helens, Moss Nook
WA9 45 A1
St Helens WA11 43 B7
Mosslands WA10 43 A4
Mosslands Dr CH44,
CH45 50 E4
Mosslands Sch The
CH45 50 E4
Moss Lane View WN8 23 F6
Mosslawn Rd L32 30 A1
Mosslea Pk L18 68 F4
Mossley Ave
Bebington CH62 88 D8
Liverpool L18 68 F5
Mossley Ct L18 69 A3
MOSSLEY HILL 69 A3
Mossley Hill Dr L17 68 E4
Mossley Hill Hospl L18 68 E3
Mossley Hill Rd L18,
L19 68 F2
Mossley Hill Sta L18 69 A3
Mossley Rd CH42 66 E3
MOSS NOOK 44 F1
Moss Nook L39 13 C2
Moss Nook La
Kirkby L31 29 B7
Rainford WA11 31 E6
Rainford WA11 31 F5
Moss Pits Cl L10 39 F7
Mosspits Jun & Inf Schs
L15 69 B6
Moss Pits La
Liverpool, Fazakerley
L10 39 E7
Liverpool, Wavertree Green
L15 69 B7
Moss Rd
Orrell WN5 25 D3
Southport PR8 4 C2
MOSS SIDE 21 A1
Moss Side
Formby L37 10 B4
Huyton-w-R L14 55 A3
Moss St
Liverpool, Garston L19 81 C6
Liverpool L3, L6, L7 52 F2
Prescot L34 56 D7
Moss View
Litherland L21 38 C8
Maghull L31 20 F1
Ormskirk L39 13 E4
Mossville Cl L18 69 A2
Mossville Rd L18 69 B2
Moss Way L11 40 C4
Mossy Bank Rd CH44 51 D4
Mostyn Ave
Aintree L10 28 C2
Mostyn Ave *continued*
Heswall CH60 85 C8
Liverpool L19 81 D8
West Kirby CH48 63 B1
Mostyn Cl L4 52 E7
Mostyn Gdns CH64 86 B1
Mostyn Hall L15 68 E7
Mostyn House Sch
CH64 86 C1
Mostyn Sq CH64 86 B1
Mostyn St CH44 51 B2
Motherwell Cl WA8 72 E3
Motherwell Cres PR8 4 F3
Mottershead Rd WA8 73 A1
Mottram Cl L33 29 F2
Moughland La WA7 84 F1
Mould St L5 52 D5
Mounsey Rd CH42 66 D5
Mount Ave
Bebington CH63 78 D7
Bootle L20 38 D7
Heswall CH60 85 F8
Mount Carmel Sch
L39 13 D2
Mount Cl L32 29 C4
Mount Cres
Kirkby L32 29 C4
Orrell WN5 25 F6
Mount Ct
3 Heswall CH60 85 F8
8 Wallasey CH45 51 A8
Mount Dr CH63 78 D7
Mountfield Ct WN5 25 F7
Mount Gr CH41 66 C5
Mount Grove Pl 5
CH41 66 C5
Mount Haven Cl CH49 65 A5
Mount House Cl L37 10 B5
Mount House Rd L37 10 B5
Mount Mews CH60 85 F8
Mount Olive CH43 66 A3
Mount Park Ct L25 70 A3
Mount Pk
Bebington CH63 78 D7
Liverpool L25 70 A3
Mount Pleasant
Birkenhead CH43 66 B3
Crosby L22 26 D1
Liverpool L1, L3, L7 90 C3
Liverpool L3, L7 52 F1
Widnes WA8 73 B2
Mount Pleasant Ave
WA9 45 B3
Mount Pleasant Cl
CH45 51 B7
Mount Pleasant Flats 6
L22 26 D1
Mount Pleasant Rd
CH45 51 B7
Mount Prim Sch CH45 51 A7
Mount Rd
Bebington CH63 78 D5
Birkenhead, Egerton Park
CH42 66 D1
Birkenhead, Upton CH49 65 A5
Kirkby L32 29 B3
Wallasey CH45 51 A7
West Kirby CH48 63 C1
Mount St
Crosby L22 26 D1
Liverpool L1 90 C2
Liverpool, Woolton L25 70 A2
Southport PR9 4 D7
Widnes WA8 73 B1
Mount The
Heswall CH60 85 F8
Skelmersdale WN8 24 B8
Wallasey CH44 51 C4
Mount Vernon L7 53 A1
Mount Vernon Gn 9
L7 53 A2
Mount Vernon Rd L7 53 A1
Mount Vernon St 6
L7 53 A2
Mount Vernon View 7
L7 53 A2
Mountview Cl 5 L8 68 A5
Mountway CH63 78 D7
Mountwood WN8 16 A4
Mountwood Lo PR8 7 C5
Mount Wood Rd CH42 78 C8
Mowbray Ave WA11 44 C5
Mowbray Ct 1 L20 38 C1
Mowbray Gr
Liverpool L13 54 A1
Liverpool L13 54 A1
Mowcroft La WA5 74 B3
Moxon St WA10 43 D2
Moxon Way WN4 35 D4
Moyles Cl WA8 72 D2
Mozart Cl L8 68 B6
Much Woolton RC Prim
Sch L25 70 B2
Muirfield Cl L12 54 E6
Muirfield Dr PR8 7 C4
Muirfield Rd L36 55 C1
Muirhead Ave L13 53 F7
Muirhead Ave E L11,
L12 40 B1
Mulberry Ave
Golborne WA3 47 F7
St Helens WA10 43 C3
Mulberry Cl L33 29 F6
Mulberry Gr CH44 51 D3
Mulberry Lo L36 55 E3
Mulberry Pl L7 67 F8
Mulberry Rd CH42 66 F2
Mulberry St L7 67 F8
Mulcrow Cl WA9 44 D4
Mulgrave St L8 68 A7
Mullberry St L7 52 F1
Mullein Cl WA3 47 D8
Mullen Cl WA5 60 F1
Mulliner St L7 68 C7
Mullins Ave WA12 46 C5
Mullion Cl
Liverpool L26 82 E9
Southport PR9 2 B5
Mullion Rd L11 40 C5
Mullion Wlk L11 40 C5
Mullrea Cl L27 70 C6
Mullwood Cl L12 40 F3
Mulrankin Ct 4 L13 54 B2
Mulveton Rd CH63 78 F3
Mumfords Gr CH47 48 E1
Mumfords La CH47 48 E1
Muncaster Cl CH62 79 D1
Muncaster Dr WA11 32 B6
Munro Ave WN5 25 E6
Munster Rd L13 54 B3
Murat Gr L22 26 D1
Murat St L22 26 D1
Murcote Rd L14 54 F5
Muriel Cl WA5 74 D6
Muriel St L4 53 A8
Murphy Gr WA9 44 E4
Murrayfield Dr CH46 49 F4
Murrayfield Hospl
CH61 77 D5
Murrayfield Rd L25 70 B6
Murrayfield Wlk L25 70 B6
Murray Gr CH48 63 A3
Musker Ct L23 26 F3
Musker Dr L30 27 C3
Musker Gdns L23 26 F3
Musker St L23 26 F3
Muspratt Rd L21 38 A6
Muttocks Rake L30 27 D5
Myddleton La WA2 61 C6
Myers Ave L35 57 A5
Myerscough Ave L20 38 E5
Myers Ct L23 26 F2
Myers Rd E L23 26 E3
Myers Rd W L23 26 D3
Mynsule Rd CH63 78 F3
Myrtle Ave
Ashton-in-M WN4 34 F6
Haydock WA11 45 B7
Newton-le-W WA12 46 C2
Myrtle Gr
Billinge WN5 33 D4
Crosby L22 26 D2
Southport PR9 4 E7
Wallasey CH44 51 E3
Widnes WA8 84 D8
Myrtle Par L7 67 F8
Myrtle St L7, L8 68 A8
Myrtle Way CH49 65 B4
Mystic Mews 9 L39 13 E5

N

Naburn Dr WN5 25 E5
Naburn Gr CH46 64 E7
Nairn Ave WN8 16 B5
Nairn Cl CH63 88 D4
Nansen Gr 4 L4 39 A1
Nant Park Ct CH45 51 C8
Nantwich Cl CH49 65 A2
Napier Cl WA10 43 E3
Napier Dr CH46 64 F8
Napier Rd CH62 79 B8
Napier St
Bootle L20 38 B1
St Helens WA10 43 E3
Napier Terr PR8 4 A5
Naples Rd CH44 51 D3
Napps Cl L25 69 F7
Napps Way
Heswall CH61 77 A2
Liverpool L25 69 F8
Napps Wlk L25 69 F7
Nares Cl WA5 60 C1
Narrow Croft Rd L39 13 B1
Narrow La L39 13 B1
**Narrow Lane (Clieves
Hills)** L39 12 E6
Narrow Moss La L39,
L40 13 E8
Naseby Cl CH43 65 C4
Naseby St L4 38 F2
Natal Rd L9 39 B6
Nathan Dr WA11 45 E6
Nathan Gr L33 29 F4
National Wildflower Ctr
The★ L16 54 F1
Naughton Lea WA8 72 D3
Navigation Cl L30 28 A4
Navigation Wharf L3 67 D5
Naylor Ave WA3 47 B8
Naylor Rd
Birkenhead CH43 65 E8
Widnes WA8 73 D1
Naylorsfield Dr L27 70 C6
Naylor's Rd
Liverpool L25 70 D5
Liverpool L27 70 D7
Naylor St L3 52 D3
Nazareth House La
WA8 84 C7
Nazeby Ave L23 27 A3
N Brooke Way CH49 65 A3
Neale Dr CH49 64 E3
Neales Fold PR9 2 D5
Neasham Cl L26 82 F9
Nedens Gr L31 20 C3
Nedens La L31 20 C3
Needham Cres CH43 65 D4
Needham Rd L7 53 C2
Needham Way WN8 16 B5
Needwood Dr CH63 78 F3
Neills Rd WA5 59 B6
Neilson Rd L17 68 C3
Neilson St L17 68 B3
Neil St WA8 73 C2
Nell's La L39 20 F5
Nelson Ave L35 56 E2
Nelson Ct
Birkenhead CH42 67 A1
Southport PR8 3 F4
Wallasey CH45 37 B1
Nelson Dr CH61 76 E3
Nelson Ho CH42 67 A1
Nelson Pl L35 56 E2
Nelson Rd
Birkenhead CH42 67 A1
Bootle L21 38 B7
Liverpool L7 53 B1
Nelson's Croft CH63 79 A3
Nelson St
Bootle L20 38 B2
Liverpool L1 90 B1
Liverpool L1 90 C2
Liverpool, Wavertree
L15 68 E8
Newton-le-W WA12 46 A3
Southport PR8 4 A6
Wallasey CH45 51 C7
Nelville Rd L9 39 C7
Neptune Ent Ctr CH41 66 D8
Neptune St CH41 66 D8
Ness Gr L32 29 C2
NESTON 86 D2
Neston Ave WA9 58 B4
Neston Gdns CH41 66 B8
Neston High Sch CH64 86 F1
Neston Rd CH63, CH64 86 F5
Neston Road Cotts
CH63 87 A6
Neston St L4 38 F1
Netherby St L8 67 F4
Netherfield WA8 84 E8
Netherfield Cl CH43 65 C4
Netherfield Rd N L5 52 E6
Netherfield Rd S L5, L6 52 F4
NETHERLEY 70 D5
Netherley Rd L35, L27 71 C3
NETHERTON 28 A5
Netherton Gn L30 27 F5
Netherton Grange L30 28 B3
Netherton Ind Est L30 38 F8
Netherton La L30 27 E5
Netherton Moss Prim Sch
L30 27 E3
Netherton Park Rd
L21 38 D8
Netherton Rd
Birkenhead CH46 64 E8
Bootle L20 38 D6
Liverpool L18, L19 69 A1
Netherton Way L20, L21,
L30 38 E8
Netherwood Rd L11 39 E2
Netley St L4 52 E8
Nettle Hill CH48 63 B3
Nettlestead Rd L11 40 A1
Neva Ave CH46 64 D8
Neverstitch Cl WN8 15 F2
Neverstitch Rd WN8 15 D2
Neville Ave
St Helens WA9 45 B2
Warrington WA2 61 D1
Neville Cl CH43 65 C4
Neville Rd
Bebington CH62 88 E8
Crosby L22 26 E1
Wallasey CH44 51 A4
Neville St WA12 46 A3
Nevill St PR8 4 B7
Nevin St 10 L6 53 A3
Nevison St 12 L7 53 B1
Nevitte Cl L28 55 A8
New Acres Cl CH43 65 C8
Newark Cl
Birkenhead CH43 65 C4
Huyton-w-R L36 55 D6
Litherland L30 28 B5
Newark St L4 38 F1
New Bank Pl WA8 72 B1
New Bank Rd WA8 72 B1
New Barn Ave WN4 35 C3
New Barnet WA8 72 F4
New Bartram Ct 9
L17 68 C4
New Bird St L1 90 B1
Newbold Cres CH48 63 E3
New Bold Ct WA9 59 A7
Newbold Gr L12 40 F2
Newborough Ave
Crosby L23 27 A4
9 Liverpool L18 68 F5
Newborough Cl WA5 60 E2
Newborough Sch L25 69 F3
NEW BOSTON 45 E7
Newbridge Cl
Birkenhead CH49 65 B3
Garswood WN4 34 D3
Warrington WA5 60 D2
NEW BRIGHTON 51 B8
New Brighton Prim Sch
CH45 51 C8
New Brighton Sta
CH45 51 A8

Newburn CH43 66 B5
Newburn Cl WN8 16 B5
Newburns La CH43 66 B3
Newburn St 7 L4 39 A2
Newbury Cl
  Huyton-w-R L36 55 D1
  Widnes WA8 73 A3
Newbury Rd WN8 16 B5
Newbury Way
  Liverpool L12 54 E5
  Wallasey CH46 49 F3
Newby Ave L35 57 A4
Newby Cl PR8 7 B3
Newby Ct L37 9 F3
Newby Dr
  Huyton-w-R L36 55 C3
  Skelmersdale WN8 16 B5
Newby Gr L12 40 C2
Newby Pl WA11 44 A8
Newby St L4 52 F8
New Carr La L31 19 E7
Newcastle Rd L15 69 A6
New Century Bldg 14 L3 90 A4
New Chester Rd
  Bebington CH42, CH62 79 C5
  Bebington, Eastham CH62 88 E7
  Birkenhead CH41, CH42 66 F4
Newchurch Cl L27 70 F4
Newcombe St L6 53 B5
New Cotts L12 54 E8
New Court Way L39 13 F5
Newcroft Rd L25 69 F4
New Cross St
  Prescot L34 56 D7
  6 St Helens, Cowley Hill WA10 43 F4
  1 St Helens WA10 43 F3
New Cswy L37, L38 18 B8
New Cut Cl PR8 8 A8
New Cut La
  Knowsley L34 42 A8
  Rainford L33, WA11 31 B1
  Shirdley Hill L39, PR8 8 D6
Newdales Cl CH43 65 C8
Newdown Rd L11 40 D5
Newdown Wlk L11 40 D5
Newell Rd CH44, CH45 51 B5
Newenham Cres L14 54 E3
NEW FERRY 79 B7
New Ferry By-Pass CH62 79 B7
New Ferry Rd CH62 79 B8
Newfield Cl L23 27 C6
Newfields WA10 43 D4
Newfield Sch L23 27 B5
New Fold WN5 25 C4
New Fort Way L20 38 A6
New Foul La PR8 5 A4
NEWGATE 25 A6
Newgate Rd WN8 24 F7
New Glade Hill WA11 44 E6
New Grey Rock Cl 4 L6 53 B4
New Hall L10 39 F8
New Hall Dr PR8 5 C1
Newhall La CH47 63 B6
New Hall La L11 39 E1
New Hall Manor CH64 86 E6
Newhall St L1 90 C1
Newhaven Rd
  Wallasey CH45 51 C7
  Warrington WA2 61 B4
New Hedley Gr L5 52 C5
New Henderson St L8 67 E5
New Hey L12 54 B5
New Heyes CH64 86 E1
New Hey Rd CH49 65 C3
NEW HEYS 69 D1
New Heys Comp Sch L19 69 D1
New Heys Dr L18 69 D1
Newholme Cl L12 40 E3
Newhope Rd CH41 66 C7
Newhouse Rd L15 68 D7
New Hutte La L26 82 F7
Newick Pk 8 L32 29 C1
Newick Rd L32 29 C1
Newington L1 90 C3
New Islington L3 90 C4
New La
  Haskayne L39 11 E3
  Ormskirk L39 13 E2
  Southport PR9 2 E3
Newland Cl WA8 72 C3
Newland Ct L17 68 C3
Newland Dr CH44, CH45 51 A4
Newlands Ct CH44 51 D4
Newlands Dr WA3 47 D8
Newlands Rd
  Bebington CH63 79 B4
  St Helens WA11 44 C7
Newling St CH41 66 C7
Newlyn Ave
  Litherland L21 27 B1
  Maghull L31 20 E1
Newlyn Cl CH47 48 E2
Newlyn Dr
  Ashton-in-M WN4 35 B1
  Skelmersdale WN8 24 D7
Newlyn Gdns WA5 74 D3
Newlyn Gr WA11 44 D7
Newlyn Rd
  Hoylake CH47 48 E2
  Liverpool L11 40 D5
Newlyn Wlk L11 40 D5
New Manesty's La L1 90 B3
Newman St L4 52 D7
Newmarket Gdns WA9 57 C6
New Market Rd L21 38 B7
New Meadow La L37 18 F8
New Mersey Ret Pk L24 81 F5
New Mill Stile L25 70 A3
Newmorn Ct L17 68 C2
New Park Prim Sch L6 53 B3
Newport Ave CH45 50 D7
Newport Cl CH43 65 C4
Newport Ct L5 52 C5
New Quay L3 52 B2
New Rd
  Formby L37 10 A5
  Liverpool L13 53 E5
  Prescot L34 56 E7
New Red Rock View L6 53 B4
New Road Ct L13 53 E5
New School La CH66 89 B1
Newsham Cl WA8 72 B4
Newsham Dr L6 53 D5
Newsham Rd L36 71 A8
Newsham St L5 52 D5
News La WA11 23 F2
Newspaper Ho WA5 74 D3
New St
  Ashton-in-M WN4 35 C4
  Haskayne L39 12 B8
  St Helens WA9 58 C7
  Wallasey CH44 51 E2
Newstead Ave L23 26 B3
Newstead Dr WN8 16 B5
Newstead Rd
  Hale WA8 83 F6
  Liverpool L8 68 C7
Newstet Rd L33 30 C2
NEWTON 63 E2
Newton Bank Sch WA12 46 E4
Newton Cl L12 54 B8
Newton Com Hospl WA12 46 B2
Newton Cross La CH48 63 E2
Newton Ct L13 53 E1
Newton Dr
  Skelmersdale WN8 16 B5
  West Kirby CH48 63 E2
Newton Gr WA2 61 F3
Newton La WA12 46 E6
NEWTON-LE-WILLOWS 45 E3
Newton-le-Willows Com High Sch WA12 46 D5
Newton-le-Willows Prim Sch WA12 46 C3
Newton-le-Willows Sta WA12 46 E3
Newton Park Dr WA12 46 F3
Newton Park Rd CH48 63 E2
Newton Rd
  Billinge WN5 33 F6
  Golborne, Town of Lowton WA12, WA3 47 D5
  Hoylake CH47 63 C7
  Liverpool L13 53 E3
  St Helens WA9 45 A3
  Wallasey CH44 51 A4
  Winwick WA2 61 A5
Newton St
  Birkenhead CH41 66 C7
  Southport PR9 5 A7
Newton Way
  Birkenhead CH49 64 F5
  Liverpool L3 52 F1
Newton Wlk 4 L20 38 B4
New Tower Ct CH45 51 C8
NEWTOWN 43 D4
Newtown Gdns L32 29 E2
Newway L14 55 A5
New Way L39 22 C2
New Way Bsns Ctr CH44 51 D2
Nicander Rd L18 68 F5
Nicholas Ct 8 L23 26 B3
Nicholas Rd
  Crosby L23 26 B3
  Widnes WA8 84 C8
Nicholas St 3 L3 52 D3
Nicholl Rd WA10 43 A5
Nicholls Dr CH61 76 F4
Nicholson St WA9 44 E4
Nickleby Cl L8 67 F5
Nickleford Hall Dr WA8 72 F6
Nicola Ct CH45 51 C6
Nicol Mere Dr WN4 35 A5
Nicol Mere Sch WN4 35 A5
Nicol Rd WN4 35 B5
Nidderdale Ave L35 57 D3
Nigel Rd CH60 86 C8
Nightingale Cl
  Kirkby L32 29 B3
  Liverpool L27 70 F5
Nightingale Rd L12 40 F3
Nimrod St L4 38 F1
Nine Tree Prim Sch L28 41 A1
Ninth Ave L9 39 D7
Nipe La WN8 24 B5
Nithsdale Rd L15 68 E6
Nixons La WN8 24 D7
Nixon's La PR8 7 E7
Nixon St L4 38 F2
NOCTORUM 65 E5
Noctorum Ave CH43 65 C4
Noctorum Dell CH43 65 D4
Noctorum La CH43 65 E5
Noctorum Rd CH43 65 E5
Noctorum Way CH43 65 D3
Noel Gate L39 13 B1
Noel St L8 68 C7
Nolan St PR8 4 C5
Nook La
  Golborne WA3 47 B8
  St Helens WA9 44 F1
Nook Rise L15 69 B8
Nook The
  Birkenhead CH43 66 B5
  Birkenhead, Frankby CH48 64 B2
  Liverpool L25 70 C3
  St Helens WA10 43 B6
Noonan Cl L9 38 F4
Noon Ct WA12 46 B1
Norbeck Ave L14 54 F2
Norbreck Ave L14 54 F2
Norburn Cres L37 9 F2
Norbury Ave
  Bebington CH63 78 E5
  Billinge WN5 33 D6
  8 Liverpool L18 68 F5
Norbury Cl
  Bebington CH63 78 F5
  Kirkby L32 29 D2
  Southport PR9 2 C5
  Widnes WA8 73 E1
Norbury Fold L35 57 E1
Norbury Rd L32 29 D2
Norbury Wlk L32 29 D2
Norcliffe Rd L35 57 B4
Norcote Lo L37 9 E4
Norcott Dr WA5 59 F6
Norfield L39 13 F5
Norfolk Cl
  Birkenhead CH43 65 C4
  Bootle L20 38 D4
Norfolk Dr
  Warrington WA5 74 E6
  West Kirby CH48 63 C1
Norfolk Gr PR8 3 F1
Norfolk Pl
  Bootle L21 38 A7
  Widnes WA8 84 C8
Norfolk Rd
  Longshaw WN5 25 E1
  Maghull L31 28 C7
  Southport PR8 3 F1
  St Helens WA10 43 D1
Norfolk St L1 90 B1
Norgate St 16 L4 52 F7
Norlands Ct CH42 66 E1
Norland's La L35, WA8 72 F7
Norlands Pk WA8 72 F6
Norland St WA8 73 D1
Norley Ave CH62 88 E3
Norley Dr WA10 43 B3
Norley Pl L26 82 E7
Norman Ave
  Haydock WA11 46 A7
  Newton-le-W WA12 46 E3
Normandale Rd L4 39 D1
Normandy Rd L36 55 D3
Normanhurst L39 14 A4
Norman Pannell Sch L27 70 E5
Norman Rd
  Bootle L20 38 C7
  Crosby L23 26 D3
  Wallasey CH44 51 E2
Norman Salisbury Ct 1 WA10 44 A4
Normans Rd WA9 58 F7
Norman St CH41 65 F8
Normanston Cl CH43 66 B4
Normanston Rd CH43 66 B4
Normanton Ave L17 68 C3
Norma Rd L22 26 E1
Normington Cl L31 20 C4
Norris Cl CH43 65 C4
NORRIS GREEN 39 F2
Norris Green Cres L11 39 F1
Norris Green Rd L12 54 B6
Norris Green Way 6 L11 40 A1
Norris House Dr L39 21 C8
Norris Rd L34 56 C6
Norris Way L37 10 B3
Norseman Cl L12 54 B8
Northam Cl PR9 2 A5
NORTH ASHTON 34 E6
North Atlantic Cl L36 55 E4
North Ave
  Aintree L10 28 E2
  Golborne WN7 36 F4
  Liverpool L24 82 A7
North Barcombe Rd L16 69 D7
North Breeze Hill 8 L4, L9 38 F2
Northbrook Cl L8 68 A7
North Brooke Way CH49 65 A3
Northbrook Rd CH44 51 D3
Northbrook St L8 68 A7
North Cantril Ave L12 54 F8
North Cheshire Trad Est CH43 77 E8
North Cl CH62 79 C2
Northcote Cl 1 L5, L6 52 F4
Northcote Prim Sch L9 39 A3
Northcote Rd
  Liverpool L9 38 F3
Northcote Rd *continued*
  Wallasey CH45 50 D5
Northdale Rd L15 68 F8
North Dingle
  Liverpool L4 52 D8
  Liverpool L4 52 E7
North Dr
  Heswall CH60 86 A7
  Liverpool, Sandfield Park L12 54 B6
  Liverpool, Victoria Park L15 69 A8
  Wallasey CH45 50 F8
North Dunes L38 17 F4
NORTH END 18 B6
North End La
  Hightown L38 18 A6
  Liverpool L26 70 E3
Northern La WA8 72 A3
Northern Perimeter Rd L30 28 B5
Northern Rd L24 82 E5
Northern Rd The L23 26 F4
Northfield WN8 16 B4
Northfield Cl
  Kirkby L33 30 A4
  St Helens WA9 58 D3
Northfield Ct WN3 36 C1
Northfield Rd L20 38 E6
NORTH FLORIDA 45 D8
North Florida Rd WA11 45 D8
North Front L35 56 E1
Northgate Rd L13 54 A5
North Gr L18 69 C1
North Hill St L8 68 A6
North John St
  Liverpool L2 90 A3
  St Helens WA10 43 F3
  3 St Helens WA10 44 A4
North Leach Dr PR8 7 A5
North Linkside Rd L25 70 C1
North Liverpool Acad L4 53 B7
North Manor Way L25 70 C2
North Meade L31 20 C2
Northmead Rd L19 81 E7
North Mersey Bsns Ctr L33 30 D4
North Moor La L39 12 F8
North Moss La L37 10 D7
North Mossley Hill Rd L17, L18 68 F3
North Mount Rd L32 29 C4
Northolt Ct WA2 61 E1
Northop Rd 8 CH45 51 A6
North Par
  Hoylake CH47 63 B7
  Kirkby L32 29 E2
  Liverpool L24 82 E4
  Neston CH64 86 B2
North Park Brook Rd WA5 60 E1
Northpark Ct CH44 51 E3
North Park Rd L32 29 C4
North Parkside Wlk L12 54 A8
North Perimeter Rd L33 30 D4
North Rd
  Bebington CH65 89 E3
  Birkenhead CH42 66 D3
  Halewood L26 82 E6
  Liverpool, Broad Green L13, L14 54 C2
  Liverpool, Cressington Park L19 81 A6
  Southport PR9 2 C4
  St Helens WA10 43 F5
  West Kirby CH48 63 A2
Northridge Rd CH61 77 A5
North St
  Ashton-in-M WN4 35 D5
  Haydock WA11 45 E6
  Liverpool L1, L2, L3 90 B4
  Newton-le-W WA12 45 F4
  Southport PR9 4 C8
North Sudley Rd L17 68 E2
Northumberland Gr L8 67 D5
Northumberland St L8 67 E5
Northumberland Terr L5 52 E6
Northumberland Way L30 27 C3
North View
  Huyton-w-R L36 56 A2
  Liverpool L7 53 A1
  Warrington WA5 74 E7
Northway
  Heswall CH60 77 D1
  Liverpool L15 54 B1
  Maghull L31, L39 20 E4
  Ormskirk L39 13 A1
  Skelmersdale WN8 16 B2
  Warrington WA2 61 B2
  Widnes WA8 72 D1
Northway Prim Sch
  Liverpool L15 54 B1
  Maghull L31 20 E3
Northways CH62 79 D3
Northwich Cl L23 27 B6
North William St 5 CH44 51 E2
North Wirral Coastal Pk* CH46 49 E4
NORTHWOOD 30 A3
Northwood Ave WA12 46 F3
Northwood Rd
  Birkenhead CH43 65 F1
  Huyton-w-R L36 55 F4
Norton Ave WA5 74 E5
Norton Dr CH61 76 C7
Norton Gr
  Maghull L31 28 D6
  St Helens WA9 57 D7
Norton Rd CH48 63 A3
Norton St
  Bootle L20 38 B5
  Liverpool L3 90 C4
Norton Terr L20 38 B5
Norville Rd L14 54 C2
Norwich Ave
  Ashton-in-M WN4 35 D3
  Golborne WA3 47 D8
Norwich Dr CH49 65 A7
Norwich Rd L15 69 A6
Norwich Way L32 29 E2
Norwood Ave
  Ashton-in-M WN4 34 F6
  Golborne WA3 47 F7
  Litherland L21 27 B1
  Southport PR9 4 E7
Norwood Cres PR9 4 E7
Norwood Ct CH49 64 D3
Norwood Gdns PR9 4 F7
Norwood Gr
  2 Liverpool L6 53 B4
  Rainford WA11 32 A6
Norwood Prim Sch PR9 4 E7
Norwood Rd
  Birkenhead CH49 64 D4
  Southport PR8, PR9 4 F6
  Wallasey CH44 51 B2
Norwyn Rd L11 39 E2
Nostell Rd WN4 35 A5
Notre Dame RC Coll L5 52 F7
Nottingham Cl L35 57 C5
Nottingham Rd L36 55 C1
Nowshera Ave CH61 76 F5
Nuffield Cl CH49 64 F4
Nugent House Sch WN5 33 D4
Nun Cl CH43 66 B3
Nunn St WA9 44 D3
Nunsford Cl L21 27 D2
Nunthorpe Rd L34 41 B5
Nurse Rd CH61 77 B6
Nurseries The L37 10 A2
Nursery Ave L39 14 A6
Nursery Cl
  Birkenhead CH43 66 C3
  Liverpool L25 82 C9
  Widnes WA8 73 D3
Nursery Dr L37 9 F2
Nursery La L19 81 C7
Nursery Rd
  Maghull L31 20 C4
  St Helens WA9 57 D7
NUTGROVE 57 D6
Nutgrove Ave WA9 57 D7
Nutgrove Hall WA9 57 D6
Nutgrove Hall Dr WA9 57 D6
Nutgrove Methodist Prim Sch WA9 57 D7
Nutgrove Rd WA9 57 D7
Nuthall Rd PR8 4 F3
Nut St WA9 57 D7
Nuttall St L7 53 C1
Nyland Rd L36 55 E5

O

Oak Ave
  Abram Brow WN2 36 C7
  Birkenhead CH49 64 D6
  Golborne WA3 47 B8
  Haydock WA11 45 E7
  Liverpool L9 39 B6
  Newton-le-W WA12 46 D3
  Ormskirk L39 13 D4
Oak Bank CH41 66 C5
Oakbank Rd L18 68 E5
Oakbank St CH44 51 C3
Oakbourne Cl 5 L17 68 C2
Oak Cl
  Birkenhead CH46 64 D7
  Liverpool L12 40 F1
  Prescot L35 56 E3
Oak Cres WN8 15 D1
Oakcross Gdns L25 70 C2
Oak Ct 15 L8 68 A4
Oakdale Ave CH44 51 D2
Oakdale Cl 7 L32 29 C1
Oakdale Dr CH49 64 C2
Oakdale Rd
  Crosby L22 26 D2
  Liverpool L18 69 A5
  Wallasey CH41, CH44 51 D2
Oakdene Cl CH62 88 D5
Oakdene Ct L35 57 D2
Oakdene Prim Sch L35 57 D2
Oakdene Rd
  Birkenhead CH42 66 C3
  Liverpool L4 53 B7
Oakenden Cl WN4 35 A6
Oakenholt Rd
  Birkenhead CH46 64 E8
  2 Wallasey CH46 49 E1
Oakes St L3 52 F2

Oak Farm L25 . . . 82 A8
Oakfield L4 . . . 53 B6
Oakfield Ave
Golborne WA3 . . . 35 F1
Liverpool L25 . . . 70 A4
Oakfield Cl WA9 . . . 57 D7
Oakfield Com Prim Sch WA8 . . . 84 B8
Oakfield Dr
Formby L37 . . . 9 D4
Huyton-w-R L36 . . . 70 F8
Widnes WA8 . . . 84 A8
Oakfield Gr L36 . . . 70 F8
Oakfield Rd
Bebington CH62 . . . 88 C8
Hightown L38 . . . 17 F2
Liverpool L4 . . . 53 A6
Oakfields L39 . . . 14 A5
Oakgate Cl L11 . . . 40 B3
Oak Gn L39 . . . 13 F5
Oak Grange L26 . . . 82 F9
Oakham Ct PR9 . . . 4 C8
Oakham Dr
Aintree L10 . . . 28 F1
Wallasey CH46 . . . 49 B1
Oakham St L8 . . . 67 E6
Oakhill Cl
Liverpool L12 . . . 40 D3
Maghull L31 . . . 20 D2
Oakhill Cottage La L31 . . . 20 D4
Oakhill Dr L31 . . . 20 D4
OAKHILL PARK . . . 54 B2
Oakhill Pk L13 . . . 54 B2
Oakhill Rd
Liverpool L13 . . . 54 B3
Maghull L31 . . . 20 D3
Oakhurst Cl L25 . . . 70 B5
Oak La L12 . . . 40 C2
Oak La N L11, L12 . . . 40 D2
Oakland Cl L21 . . . 38 C6
Oakland Ct CH43 . . . 66 A5
Oakland Dr CH49 . . . 65 A6
Oakland Rd L19 . . . 80 F8
Oaklands
Bebington CH62 . . . 88 D6
Rainhill L35 . . . 57 C3
Oaklands Ave L23 . . . 26 E5
Oaklands Ct WA9 . . . 58 C4
Oaklands Dr
Bebington CH63 . . . 79 A6
Heswall CH61 . . . 77 A1
Oaklands Rd WA3 . . . 47 F7
Oaklands Terr CH61 . . . 77 A2
Oakland Vale CH45 . . . 51 C8
Oakleaf Mews CH43 . . . 65 D5
Oaklea Rd CH61 . . . 76 F6
Oaklee Gr L33 . . . 30 A4
Oakleigh WN8 . . . 24 D2
Oak Leigh L13 . . . 53 E5
Oakleigh Gr CH63 . . . 78 F6
Oakley Ave WN5 . . . 33 E6
Oakley Cl L12 . . . 40 E3
Oak Meadows Ct L35 . . . 57 E1
Oakmere Cl
Liverpool L9 . . . 39 A7
Wallasey CH46 . . . 49 E4
Oakmere Dr
Birkenhead CH49 . . . 64 C4
Warrington WA5 . . . 74 F3
Oak Rd
Bebington CH63 . . . 78 F7
Hooton CH66 . . . 88 E1
Huyton-w-R L36 . . . 70 D8
Prescot L35 . . . 56 E3
Warrington WA5 . . . 74 F3
Oakridge Cl CH62 . . . 79 C2
Oakridge Rd CH62 . . . 79 C2
Oaks Cl WA9 . . . 58 D3
Oaks Gdns WA5 . . . 74 E4
Oaks La CH61 . . . 77 A4
Oaksmeade Cl L12 . . . 40 F2
Oak St
Bootle L20 . . . 38 C4
Southport PR8 . . . 4 E6
St Helens WA9 . . . 58 E8
Oaks The
Bebington CH62 . . . 88 C8
Liverpool L12 . . . 40 F3
Southport PR8 . . . 3 F6
St Helens WA9 . . . 58 D4
Widnes WA8 . . . 73 D4
Oakston Ave L35 . . . 57 D2
Oaksway CH60 . . . 86 C6
Oak Terr L7 . . . 53 C2
Oakthorn Gr WA11 . . . 45 C6
Oak Tree Ct WN8 . . . 16 D3
Oaktree Pl CH42 . . . 66 F3
Oaktree Rd WA10 . . . 43 A5
Oak Vale L13 . . . 54 B2
OAK VALE PARK . . . 54 B2
Oak View L24 . . . 83 A3
Oakwood WN8 . . . 16 D3
Oakwood Ave
Ashton-in-M WN4 . . . 35 A2
Southport PR8 . . . 7 D6
Oakwood Cl L25 . . . 70 B5
Oakwood Dr
Birkenhead CH43 . . . 65 E8
Huyton-w-R L36 . . . 55 F1
Southport PR8 . . . 7 E5
Oakwood Pk CH62 . . . 88 D5
Oakwood Rd L26 . . . 82 F8
Oakworth Cl L33 . . . 29 E4
Oakworth Dr
Bebington CH62 . . . 79 C7
Oakworth Dr *continued*
Huyton-w-R L36 . . . 71 A7
Oarside Dr CH45 . . . 51 A6
Oatfield La L21 . . . 27 B2
Oatlands Rd L32 . . . 29 C2
Oatlands The CH48 . . . 63 C1
Oban Dr
Garswood WN4 . . . 34 C4
Heswall CH60 . . . 86 A8
Oban Rd L4 . . . 53 B6
Oberon St L20 . . . 38 C1
O'Brien Gr WA9 . . . 44 E4
Observatory Rd CH43 . . . 65 E8
Oceanic Rd L13 . . . 53 F2
Ocean Pk CH44 . . . 51 D1
Ocean Plaza PR8 . . . 4 A8
Ocean Rd L21 . . . 38 B7
Ocean View [10] CH45 . . . 51 A8
O'Connell Cl WA11 . . . 45 C6
O'Connell Rd L3 . . . 52 D4
O'Connor Gr L33 . . . 29 E6
Octavia Ct L36 . . . 55 F1
Octavia Hill Rd L21 . . . 27 C1
October Dr L6 . . . 53 D6
Odsey St L7 . . . 53 C2
Odyssey Ctr CH41 . . . 66 C8
Off Botanic Rd PR9 . . . 2 A1
Ogden Cl L11 . . . 54 A8
Ogle Cl L35 . . . 56 E5
OGLET . . . 82 E1
Oglet La L24 . . . 82 E1
Ogle Way L36 . . . 55 E5
Oil St L3 . . . 52 B4
O'Keeffe Rd WA9 . . . 44 C4
Okehampton Rd L16 . . . 69 D8
Okell Dr L26 . . . 70 D1
Old Acre L38 . . . 17 F3
Old Alder La WA2, WA5 . . . 60 D5
Old Barn Rd
[6] Liverpool L4 . . . 53 B6
Wallasey CH44 . . . 51 A3
Old Bidston Rd CH41 . . . 66 B8
OLD BOSTON . . . 46 A8
Old Boston WA11 . . . 46 A7
Old Boston Trad Est WA11 . . . 46 B8
Old Boundary Way L39 . . . 13 F6
Oldbridge Rd L24 . . . 82 F4
Old Chester Rd
Bebington CH42, CH63 . . . 78 F8
Birkenhead CH41, CH42 . . . 66 F2
Old Church Cl L9 . . . 39 B7
Old Church Yd
[1] Liverpool L2 . . . 90 A3
Liverpool L3 . . . 52 B1
Old Clatterbridge Rd CH63 . . . 78 F2
Old Coach Rd WA7 . . . 84 F3
Old College Pl L7 . . . 53 C1
Old Colliery Rd L35 . . . 56 D3
Old Colliery Yd WN4 . . . 34 C3
Old Court House Rd CH62 . . . 79 D5
Old Dover Rd L36 . . . 70 C8
Old Eccleston La WA10 . . . 43 C3
Old Engine La WN8 . . . 15 C2
Oldershaw Sch The CH45 . . . 51 A5
Old Farm Rd
Crosby L23 . . . 26 F4
Kirkby L32 . . . 40 F8
Oldfield L35 . . . 56 F4
Oldfield Cl CH60 . . . 76 E2
Oldfield Cotts CH60 . . . 76 C2
Oldfield Dr CH60 . . . 76 D2
Oldfield Gdns CH60 . . . 76 D1
Oldfield La CH48 . . . 64 A5
Oldfield Rd
Heswall CH60 . . . 76 D1
Liverpool L19 . . . 81 A8
Wallasey CH45 . . . 50 F6
Oldfield St WA10 . . . 43 F5
Oldfield Way CH60 . . . 76 E1
Old Fire Station The [12] L17 . . . 68 C4
Oldgate WA8 . . . 84 C7
Old Gorsey La CH41, CH44 . . . 51 C1
Old Greasby Rd CH49 . . . 64 F5
Old Hall L35 . . . 71 E8
Old Hall Cl L31 . . . 28 D7
Old Hall Dr WN4 . . . 35 A2
Old Hall Farm Bsns Pk PR9 . . . 5 A5
Old Hall Gdns WA11 . . . 32 A7
Old Hall La L32 . . . 29 D2
Old Hall Rd
Bebington CH62 . . . 79 F1
Maghull L31 . . . 28 D7
Old Hall St L2, L3 . . . 90 A4
Oldham Pl L1 . . . 90 C3
Oldham St L1 . . . 90 C2
Old Haymarket L1 . . . 90 B4
Old Hey Wlk WA12 . . . 46 C1
Old Higher Rd WA8 . . . 83 D5
Old Hutte La L26 . . . 83 A6
Old Kennel Cl L12, L14 . . . 54 F8
Old La
Formby L37 . . . 9 F6
Haskayne L39 . . . 11 E3
Heswall CH60 . . . 86 D8
Maghull L31 . . . 20 E4
Prescot L34, L35 . . . 56 F6
Rainford WA11 . . . 31 F7
Rainhill L35 . . . 57 B3
Old Leeds St L3 . . . 52 B2
Old Links Cl PR9 . . . 5 B8
Old Lodge Cl L12 . . . 54 B8
Old Maryland La CH46 . . . 49 E1
Old Mdw L34 . . . 41 C4
Old Meadow Rd CH61 . . . 76 E4
Old Mill Ave WA9 . . . 58 D5
Old Mill Cl
Heswall CH60 . . . 86 B7
Liverpool L15 . . . 69 A8
Old Mill Hill L39 . . . 13 D3
Old Mill La
Formby L37 . . . 9 F4
Knowsley L34 . . . 41 E4
Liverpool L15 . . . 69 A8
Old Mill Lane Cotts L34 . . . 41 E4
Old Moss La L39 . . . 11 C5
Old Nook La WA11 . . . 44 E6
Old Orch L35 . . . 56 E1
Old Park La PR9 . . . 5 A8
Old Penny La WA11 . . . 46 B8
Old Post Office Pl [1] L1 . . . 90 B3
Old Prescot Cl L31 . . . 21 C2
Old Pump La CH49 . . . 64 C3
Old Quarry The L25 . . . 70 A2
Old Racecourse Rd L31 . . . 28 B8
Old Rd WN4 . . . 35 A4
Old Rectory Gn
Aughton L39 . . . 21 A7
Sefton L29 . . . 27 F7
Old Riding L14 . . . 54 F5
Old Roan Sta L30 . . . 28 B3
Old Ropery [6] L2 . . . 90 A3
Old Rough La L33 . . . 29 F2
Old Sch L31 . . . 29 A5
Old School House La WA2 . . . 61 A7
Old School Pl WN4 . . . 35 A3
Old School The L29 . . . 27 E6
Old School Way CH41 . . . 65 E7
OLD SWAN . . . 54 A3
Old Thomas La L14 . . . 54 D1
Old Town Cl WN8 . . . 23 D8
Old Town Ct L37 . . . 9 E4
Old Town La L37 . . . 9 E4
Old Town Way WN8 . . . 23 D8
Old Upton La WA8 . . . 72 E4
Old Wargrave Rd WA12 . . . 46 C3
Old Whint Rd WA11 . . . 45 A6
Old Wood Rd CH61 . . . 76 F3
Oleander Dr WA10 . . . 43 C4
Olga Rd WA9 . . . 58 C7
OLGET . . . 82 E1
Olinda St CH62 . . . 79 B7
Olive Cl L31 . . . 29 A2
Olive Cres CH41 . . . 66 E4
Olivedale Rd L18 . . . 68 F5
Olive Gr
Huyton-w-R L36 . . . 55 D2
Litherland L30 . . . 28 A1
Liverpool L15 . . . 54 A1
Skelmersdale WN8 . . . 15 E1
Southport PR8 . . . 4 E7
Olive La L15 . . . 69 A8
OLIVE MOUNT . . . 54 A1
Olive Mount
Birkenhead CH41 . . . 66 E4
St Helens WA10 . . . 43 D2
Olive Mount Hts L15 . . . 69 A8
Olive Mount Rd L15 . . . 69 A8
Olive Mount Wlk L15 . . . 69 B8
Olive Rd L22 . . . 37 E8
Oliver La CH41 . . . 66 E6
Oliver Lyme Ho [6] L34 . . . 56 E6
Oliver Lyme Rd L34 . . . 56 E6
Oliver Rd WA10 . . . 57 C8
Oliver St E CH41 . . . 66 E6
Oliver St CH41 . . . 66 D6
Olivetree Rd L15 . . . 54 B1
Olive Vale L15 . . . 68 F8
Olivia Cl CH43 . . . 65 C4
Olivia Mans [4] L36 . . . 56 A2
Olivia Mews CH43 . . . 65 C4
Olivia St L20 . . . 38 D1
Olivia Way L36 . . . 56 B2
Ollerton Cl CH43 . . . 65 C4
Ollerton Pk WA5 . . . 59 E7
Ollery Gn L30 . . . 28 B4
Olney St L4 . . . 38 F2
Olton St L15 . . . 68 E8
Olympia St L6 . . . 53 A3
Olympic Way L30 . . . 39 B8
Omega Bvd WA5 . . . 59 D1
O'Neill St L20 . . . 38 B4
Onslow Cres PR8 . . . 4 A2
Onslow Rd
Bebington CH62 . . . 79 B8
Liverpool L6 . . . 53 C3
[11] Wallasey CH45 . . . 51 B8
Ontario Cl L27 . . . 70 E5
Opal Cl
Litherland L21 . . . 38 C8
Liverpool L6 . . . 53 B4
Opco Complex L24 . . . 82 B6
Openfields Cl L26 . . . 70 E2
Oppenheim Ave WA10 . . . 57 C8
Orange Gr
Liverpool L8 . . . 68 C6
Warrington WA2 . . . 61 E2
Orange Tree Cl L28 . . . 55 B8
Oran Way L36 . . . 55 D3
Orb Cl L11 . . . 40 C3
Orb Wlk [3] L11 . . . 40 C4
Orchard Ave L14, L16 . . . 54 D1
Orchard Cl
Eccleston Park L34 . . . 57 A7
Orchard Cl *continued*
Prescot L35 . . . 56 E1
St Helens WA11 . . . 44 D7
Orchard Ct
Birkenhead CH41 . . . 66 F3
Maghull L31 . . . 20 F1
Orrell WN5 . . . 25 D3
Orchard Dale L23 . . . 26 F4
Orchard Dene L35 . . . 57 C3
Orchard Gdns L35 . . . 71 E8
Orchard Grange CH46 . . . 64 C7
Orchard Hey
Litherland L30 . . . 28 B4
Maghull L31 . . . 28 E8
St Helens WA10 . . . 43 A3
Orchard La PR8 . . . 7 D4
Orchard Lo [1] L39 . . . 13 F6
Orchard Rd CH46 . . . 49 E1
Orchard St WN4 . . . 35 C3
Orchards The
[3] Orrell WN5 . . . 25 E5
Southport PR8 . . . 7 D4
Orchard The
Huyton-w-R L36 . . . 55 E2
Liverpool L17 . . . 68 F1
Ormskirk L39 . . . 13 D5
Wallasey CH45 . . . 51 A7
Orchard View L39 . . . 13 D1
Orchard Way
Bebington CH63 . . . 78 D6
Widnes WA8 . . . 72 A3
Orchid Cl WN8 . . . 25 B6
Orchid Gr L17 . . . 67 F3
Orchid Way WA9 . . . 59 B7
O'Reilly Ct L3 . . . 52 C4
ORFORD . . . 61 D2
Orford Cl
Golborne WA3 . . . 47 A7
Hale L24 . . . 83 E2
Orford Gn WA2 . . . 61 D1
Orford St L15 . . . 68 F8
Oriel Cl
Aintree L10 . . . 28 D3
[2] Liverpool L2 . . . 90 A3
Oriel Cres L20 . . . 38 C1
Oriel Dr L10 . . . 28 D3
Oriel Lo L20 . . . 38 C2
Oriel Rd
Ashton-in-M WN4 . . . 34 F4
Birkenhead CH42 . . . 66 E3
Bootle L20 . . . 38 C2
Liverpool L20 . . . 38 C1
Oriel St L3 . . . 52 C3
Orient Dr L25 . . . 70 B3
Origen Rd L16 . . . 54 D1
Oriole Cl WA10 . . . 57 B7
Orion Bvd WA5 . . . 59 E1
Orith Ave WA10 . . . 42 F3
Orkney Cl
St Helens WA11 . . . 44 D7
Widnes WA8 . . . 73 E3
Orlando Cl CH43 . . . 65 C4
Orlando St L20 . . . 38 C1
Orleans Rd L13 . . . 54 A3
Ormande St WA9 . . . 44 B1
Orme Ho L39 . . . 14 A5
Ormerod Ct CH63 . . . 79 A5
Ormesby Gdns WA9 . . . 57 E6
Ormesby Gr CH63 . . . 88 B6
Ormiston Rd CH45 . . . 51 B7
Ormond Ave L40 . . . 14 E4
Ormond Cl WA8 . . . 72 C2
Ormonde Ave L31 . . . 28 C7
Ormonde Cres L33 . . . 30 A2
Ormonde Dr L31 . . . 28 C8
Ormond Mews CH43 . . . 65 C4
Ormond St
Liverpool L3 . . . 90 A4
Wallasey CH45 . . . 51 B5
Ormond Way CH43 . . . 65 C4
Ormsby St L15 . . . 68 E7
Ormside Gr [7] WA9 . . . 58 D7
ORMSKIRK . . . 13 C6
Ormskirk Bsns Pk [2] L39 . . . 13 F6
Ormskirk CE Prim Sch L39 . . . 14 A6
Ormskirk Coll L39 . . . 13 E5
Ormskirk & District General Hospl L39 . . . 14 A4
Ormskirk Ind Pk L39 . . . 14 A6
Ormskirk Lathom Park CE Prim Sch L40 . . . 15 A8
Ormskirk Old Rd L39 . . . 22 F7
Ormskirk Rd
Aintree L10, L30, L9 . . . 28 B2
Bickerstaffe L39 . . . 22 E7
Knowsley L34 . . . 41 D4
Rainford WA11 . . . 23 D1
Rainford WA11 . . . 31 E7
Skelmersdale, Tanhouse WN8 . . . 24 D7
Skelmersdale WN8 . . . 15 C1
Up Holland WN8 . . . 25 A7
Ormskirk Sch L39 . . . 14 B5
Ormskirk St WA10 . . . 44 A3
Ormskirk Sta L39 . . . 13 F5
Orms Way L37 . . . 9 E3
Orphan Dr
Liverpool L6, L3 . . . 53 D4
Liverpool L7 . . . 53 D3
Orphan St L7 . . . 68 A8
ORRELL
Bootle . . . 38 D6
Wigan . . . 25 D6
Orrell Gdns WN5 . . . 25 F6
Orrell Hey L20 . . . 38 D7
Orrell Hill La L38 . . . 18 C4
Orrell Holgate Prim Sch WN5 . . . 25 E5
Orrell La L20, L9 . . . 38 F7
Orrell Lo L20 . . . 38 E6
Orrell Mount L20 . . . 38 C7
Orrell Newfold Com Prim Sch WN5 . . . 25 D4
ORRELL PARK . . . 38 F5
Orrell Park Sta L9 . . . 39 A6
ORRELL POST . . . 25 E7
Orrell Rd
Bootle L20, L21 . . . 38 C7
Orrell WN5 . . . 25 E7
Wallasey CH45 . . . 51 C7
Orrell St WA9 . . . 44 C3
Orrell Sta WN5 . . . 25 E4
Orrell Water Pk* WN5 . . . 25 E4
Orret's Meadow Rd CH49 . . . 65 B3
Orrets Meadow Sch CH46 . . . 64 F8
Orrysdale Rd CH48 . . . 63 A3
Orry St L5 . . . 52 D5
Orsett Rd L32 . . . 40 F8
Orston Cres CH63 . . . 79 B2
Ortega Cl CH62 . . . 79 C7
Orthes St L3 . . . 52 F1
Orton Rd L16 . . . 69 C8
Orton Way WN4 . . . 34 F3
Orville St WA9 . . . 58 F7
Orwell Cl
Formby L37 . . . 9 D1
St Helens WA9 . . . 58 A3
Orwell Rd L4 . . . 52 D8
Osbert Rd L23 . . . 26 B4
Osborne Ave
Wallasey CH45 . . . 51 B7
Warrington WA2 . . . 61 D1
Osborne Ct
Bebington CH62 . . . 79 B6
St Helens WA10 . . . 57 C8
Osborne Gr
Huyton-w-R L34 . . . 56 A5
Wallasey CH45 . . . 51 B6
Osborne Ho L15 . . . 69 A8
Osborne Rd
Ashton-in-M WN4 . . . 35 A4
Birkenhead CH43 . . . 66 B5
Formby L37 . . . 9 E1
Golborne WA3 . . . 47 E7
Litherland L21 . . . 27 C1
Liverpool L13 . . . 53 E6
Southport PR8 . . . 7 B6
St Helens WA10 . . . 43 A5
Wallasey CH45 . . . 51 C7
Osborne Vale [8] CH45 . . . 51 B7
Osborne Wood L17 . . . 68 D1
Osbourne Cl CH62 . . . 88 E7
Osmaston Rd CH42 . . . 66 A1
Osprey Cl
Liverpool L27 . . . 70 F5
Warrington WA2 . . . 61 E3
Ossett Cl CH43 . . . 65 C4
Osterley Gdns L9 . . . 38 F6
O'Sullivan Cres WA11 . . . 44 E5
Oteley Ave CH62 . . . 88 D8
Othello Cl L20 . . . 38 C1
Otterburn Cl CH46 . . . 64 B8
OTTERSPOOL . . . 68 D1
Otterspool Dr L17 . . . 80 D8
Otterspool Rd L17 . . . 68 D1
Otterton Rd L11 . . . 40 C5
Ottery Cl PR9 . . . 2 A5
Ottley St L6 . . . 53 C3
Oulton Cl
Birkenhead CH43 . . . 65 E2
Maghull L31 . . . 20 B4
Oulton Gdns WA9 . . . 57 E6
Oulton La L36 . . . 70 D8
Oulton Rd L16 . . . 69 D6
Oulton Way CH43 . . . 65 E3
Oundle Dr L10 . . . 28 C3
Oundle Pl L25 . . . 82 B8
Oundle Rd CH46 . . . 49 E1
Our Lady Immaculate RC Prim Sch
Downall Green WN4 . . . 34 E6
Liverpool L5 . . . 52 E6
Our Lady of Compassion RC Prim Sch L37 . . . 10 A3
Our Lady of Good Help RC Prim Sch L15 . . . 69 A8
Our Lady of Lourdes RC Prim Sch PR8 . . . 4 A1
Our Lady of Lourdes RC Sch CH46 . . . 50 B4
Our Lady of Mount Carmel RC Prim Sch L8 . . . 67 F5
Our Lady of Perpetual Succour RC Prim Sch WA8 . . . 84 A8
Our Lady of Pity RC Prim Sch CH49 . . . 64 D2
Our Lady of the Assumption RC Prim Sch L25 . . . 70 B6
Our Lady of Walsingham RC Prim Sch L30 . . . 27 F2
Our Lady Queen of Peace RC High Sch WN8 . . . 15 F4
Our Lady Queen of Peace RC Prim Sch L21 . . . 27 B2
Our Lady & St Edward's RC Prim Sch CH41 . . . 66 B8
Our Lady & St Philomena's RC Prim Sch L9 . . . 39 F4
Our Lady & St Swithin's RC Prim Sch L11 . . . 40 C5

Peasefield Rd L14 ... 55 A4
PEASLEY CROSS ... 44 C1
Peasley Cross La WA9 ... 44 C2
Peatwood Ave L32 ... 40 F7
Peckers Hill Rd WA9 ... 58 E7
Peckforton Cl L13 ... 53 E6
Peckmill Gn L27 ... 70 F4
Pecksniff Cl 4 L8 ... 67 F5
Peebles Ave WA11 ... 44 E6
Peebles Cl
Garswood WN4 ... 34 C4
Kirkby L33 ... 29 D6
Peel Ave CH42 ... 66 F3
Peel Cl L35 ... 56 E3
Peel Ho L15 ... 68 E7
Peel House La WA8 ... 73 B2
Peel Pl
Liverpool L8 ... 67 F7
St Helens WA10 ... 44 A5
Peel Rd
Bootle L20 ... 38 A5
Skelmersdale WN8 ... 24 E5
Peel St
Liverpool L8 ... 68 A4
Newton-le-W WA12 ... 46 A3
Runcorn WA7 ... 84 F3
Southport PR8 ... 4 F6
Peel Wlk L31 ... 20 B2
Peet Ave
Ormskirk L39 ... 13 D4
St Helens WA10 ... 43 C3
Peet's La PR9 ... 2 A1
Peet St L7 ... 53 B1
Pelham Gr L17 ... 68 C4
Pelham Rd CH44 ... 51 A3
Pemberton Rd
Birkenhead CH49 ... 65 B2
Liverpool L13 ... 54 A3
Windy Arbour WN5 ... 34 A8
Pembertons Ct 9 L34 ... 56 E6
Pemberton St WA10 ... 43 E3
Pembrey Way L25 ... 82 D9
Pembroke Ave CH46 ... 64 E7
Pembroke Cl WA10 ... 43 E2
Pembroke Ct CH41 ... 66 E4
Pembroke Gdns L3 ... 52 F2
Pembroke Ho L6 ... 53 C4
Pembroke Pl L3 ... 52 F2
Pembroke Rd L20 ... 38 C2
Pembroke St L3 ... 52 F2
Pembury Cl L12 ... 40 E3
Penarth Cl L7 ... 68 B8
Pencombe Rd L36 ... 55 C4
Penda Dr L33 ... 29 E6
Pendennis Rd CH44 ... 51 C3
Pendennis St L6 ... 53 B5
Pendine Cl
Liverpool L6 ... 53 C4
Warrington WA5 ... 60 C2
Pendle Ave WA11 ... 44 D5
Pendlebury St WA9 ... 58 C3
Pendle Cl CH49 ... 64 E6
Pendle Ct WN8 ... 24 D3
Pendle Dr
Litherland L21 ... 27 C4
Ormskirk L39 ... 14 A6
Pendle Pl WN8 ... 24 D4
Pendle Rd WA3 ... 36 C1
Pendleton Gn L26 ... 82 E8
Pendleton Rd 8 L4 ... 39 A2
Pendle View L21 ... 27 C4
Pendle Villas L21 ... 27 C3
Penfold L31 ... 20 E1
Penfold Cl L18 ... 69 D5
Pengwern Gr L15 ... 68 D8
Pengwern St 3 L8 ... 68 A5
Pengwern Terr CH45 ... 51 C7
Penhale Cl L17 ... 68 B2
Peninsula Cl CH45 ... 50 E8
PENKETH ... 74 D4
Penketh Com Prim Sch
WA5 ... 74 D4
Penketh Ct WA5 ... 74 D4
Penketh Gn L24 ... 82 E5
Penketh High Sch
WA5 ... 74 F5
Penketh Pl WN8 ... 24 C5
Penketh South Com Prim
Sch WA5 ... 74 E3
Penkett Ct CH45 ... 51 C6
Penkett Gdns CH45 ... 51 C6
Penkett Gr CH45 ... 51 C6
Penkett Rd CH45 ... 51 C6
Penkford La WA5 ... 45 D2
Penkford Sch WA12 ... 45 E2
Penkford St WA12 ... 45 E3
Penlake Ind Est WA9 ... 58 E6
Penlake La WA9 ... 58 F7
Penley Cres L32 ... 29 B2
Penlinken Dr L6 ... 53 C4
Penmann Cl L26 ... 82 F8
Penmann Cres
Halewood L26 ... 83 A7
Liverpool L26 ... 82 F8
Penmark Cl WA5 ... 60 C2
Penmon Dr CH61 ... 76 F3
Pennant Ave L12 ... 40 C1
Pennard Ave L36 ... 55 D5
Pennine Cl WA9 ... 44 E3
Pennine Dr WA9 ... 44 F3
Pennine La WA3 ... 36 C1
Pennine Pl WN8 ... 24 B6
Pennine Rd
Bebington CH42 ... 78 C8
Wallasey CH44 ... 50 F4
Pennine Rd *continued*
Warrington WA2 ... 61 E2
Pennine Way L32 ... 29 C4
Pennington Ave
Bootle L20 ... 38 E6
Ormskirk L39 ... 13 E6
Pennington Ct 4 L39 ... 13 F6
Pennington Dr WA12 ... 46 E3
Pennington Flash Ctry
Pk★ WN7 ... 36 F4
Pennington La WA5,
WA9 ... 45 D2
Pennington Rd L21 ... 38 C6
Pennington St 2 L4 ... 38 F2
Penn La WA7 ... 84 F1
Pennsylvania Rd L13 ... 53 D7
Pennyford Dr L18 ... 68 E3
Penny La
Collins Green WA5 ... 45 D1
Cronton L35, WA8 ... 72 B6
Haydock WA11 ... 46 B7
Liverpool L18 ... 68 F5
PENNYLANDS ... 15 E1
Penny Lane
Neighbourhood Ctr
L15 ... 69 A6
Pennystone Cl CH49 ... 64 D6
Pennywood Dr L35 ... 56 E2
Penpoll Ind Est L20 ... 38 C6
Penrhos Rd CH47 ... 63 A6
Penrhyd Rd CH61 ... 76 D5
Penrhyn Ave
Bootle L21 ... 38 B7
Heswall CH61 ... 77 A6
Penrhyn Rd L34 ... 41 B6
Penrhyn St L5 ... 52 D5
Penrith Ave
Southport PR8 ... 7 C3
Warrington WA2 ... 61 C2
Penrith Cres
Ashton-in-M WN4 ... 35 B4
Maghull L31 ... 20 E2
Penrith Rd WA10 ... 57 B7
Penrith St CH41 ... 66 C5
Penrose Ave E L14 ... 54 F2
Penrose Ave W L14 ... 54 E2
Penrose Gdns WA5 ... 74 D3
Penrose Pl WN8 ... 24 E4
Penrose St L5 ... 52 F6
Penryn Ave WA11 ... 44 D7
Penryn Cl WA5 ... 74 E3
Pensall Dr CH61 ... 76 F2
Pensarn Gdns WA5 ... 60 D2
Pensarn Rd L13 ... 53 F2
PENSBY ... 76 F4
Pensby Cl CH61 ... 77 A5
Pensby Hall La CH61 ... 76 F2
Pensby High Sch for Boys
CH61 ... 76 D4
Pensby High Sch for Girls
CH61 ... 76 E3
Pensby Inf Sch CH61 ... 76 F3
Pensby Jun Sch CH61 ... 76 F3
Pensby Park Prim Sch
CH61 ... 76 E4
Pensby Rd CH61 ... 77 A4
Penshaw Cl L14 ... 55 A6
Pentire Ave WA10 ... 43 B6
Pentire Cl L10 ... 40 B6
Pentland Ave
6 Liverpool L4 ... 39 A1
St Helens WA9 ... 44 F3
Warrington WA2 ... 61 B3
Pentland Pl WA2 ... 61 B3
Pentland Rd L33 ... 30 A4
Penuel Rd 10 L4 ... 38 F2
Penvalley Cres L6 ... 53 C4
Penwell Fold WN8 ... 24 E8
Peony Gdns WA9 ... 59 B7
Peover St L3 ... 52 D3
Peploe Rd L4 ... 39 D2
Peplow Rd L32 ... 29 B2
Pepper St L24 ... 83 D1
Pera Cl 16 L6 ... 53 A3
Perch Pool La PR9 ... 5 F4
Perch Rock★ CH45 ... 37 B2
Percival Ct 2 PR8 ... 4 A6
Percival La WA7 ... 84 E2
Percival Way WA10 ... 43 D4
Percy Rd CH44 ... 51 E2
Percy St
Bootle L20 ... 38 B5
Liverpool L8 ... 67 F7
St Helens WA9 ... 58 F7
Percy Villas L9 ... 39 A4
Perimeter Rd L33 ... 30 E2
Perriam Rd L19 ... 81 D8
Perrin Rd CH45 ... 50 E5
Perrins Rd WA5 ... 59 F6
Perrybrook Wlk WN4 ... 35 D4
Perrygate Cl L7 ... 68 B8
Perry St L8 ... 67 D6
Pershore Gr PR8 ... 7 A4
Pershore Ho CH42 ... 66 B1
Pershore Rd L32 ... 40 E8
Perth Ave WA9 ... 57 E7
Perth Cl
Kirkby L33 ... 29 D6
Warrington WA2 ... 61 F3
Perth St L6 ... 53 A3
Peterborough Dr L30 ... 27 F4
Peterborough Rd L15 ... 69 A6
Peterhouse Sch PR9 ... 2 B3
Peterhouse Wlk WN4 ... 34 F4
Peterlee Cl WA9 ... 57 F7
Peterlee Way L30 ... 28 A1
Peter Mahon Way L20 ... 38 B4
Peter Price's La CH63 ... 78 E4
Peter Rd
Liverpool L4 ... 38 E1
Liverpool L4 ... 38 F2
Petersfield Cl L30 ... 28 A1
Peter's La L1 ... 90 B3
Peter St
Ashton-in-M WN4 ... 35 C3
Golborne WA3 ... 47 A8
Liverpool L1 ... 90 B4
St Helens WA10 ... 43 F4
8 Wallasey CH44 ... 51 E2
Peterstone Cl WA5 ... 60 D2
Peterwood CH42 ... 67 A1
Petham Ct WA8 ... 72 E4
Petherick Rd L11 ... 40 C5
Petre Ct L4 ... 53 C7
Petunia Cl
Huyton-w-R L14 ... 55 A4
St Helens WA9 ... 59 A7
Petworth Ave WA2 ... 61 B3
Petworth Cl L24 ... 82 B5
Petworth Rd PR8 ... 7 B6
Peveril St L9 ... 38 F3
PEWFALL ... 34 C1
Pex Hill Ct WA8 ... 72 E5
Pex Hill Visitor Ctr★
WA8 ... 72 E6
Pharmacy Rd L24 ... 82 C6
Pheasant Field L24 ... 83 C2
Pheasant Gr L26 ... 70 E1
Philbeach Rd L11, L4 ... 39 D2
Philharmonic Ct 5 L8 ... 67 F8
Philip Dr PR8 ... 7 F6
Philip Gr WA9 ... 58 C7
Philip Leverhulme Lo 4
CH62 ... 79 B6
Philip Rd WA8 ... 84 B8
Philips Dr WA5 ... 74 E7
Phillimore Rd L6 ... 53 C3
Phillip Gr L12 ... 54 F5
Phillips Cl L23 ... 27 B6
Phillip's Cl L37 ... 9 F2
Phillip's La L37 ... 9 F2
Phillips St L3 ... 52 C3
Phillips Way CH60 ... 85 E8
Phipps' La WA5 ... 59 E7
Phoenix Ave WA5 ... 60 F2
Phoenix Brow WA9 ... 44 B3
Phoenix Dr L14 ... 55 B5
Phoenix Prim Sch L7 ... 53 E2
Physics Rd L24 ... 82 C6
Phythian Cl L6 ... 53 B3
Phythian Cres WA5 ... 74 F4
Phythian St
Liverpool L6 ... 53 A3
St Helens WA11 ... 44 F6
Picadilly WN5 ... 33 E5
Pickerill Rd CH49 ... 64 D3
Pickering Rake L30 ... 27 D5
Pickering Rd CH45 ... 51 B8
Pickering's Pasture
(Nature Reserve)★
WA8 ... 84 B3
Pickerings Rd WA8 ... 84 B5
Pickering St L6 ... 53 A5
Pickmere Dr
Bebington CH62 ... 88 F3
Bebington CH62 ... 88 F4
Pickop St 6 L3 ... 52 C3
Pickwick St L8 ... 67 F6
Pickworth Way L31 ... 29 B3
Picow Farm Rd WA7 ... 84 E1
Picow St 2 WA7 ... 84 F1
Picton Cl
Bebington CH62 ... 88 E3
Birkenhead CH43 ... 65 F4
Picton Cres L15 ... 68 E8
Picton Gr L15 ... 68 D8
Picton Rd
Crosby L22 ... 26 D1
Liverpool L15 ... 68 E8
Piele Rd WA11 ... 45 E8
Piercefield Ct L37 ... 10 A5
Piercefield Rd L37 ... 9 F5
Pighue La
Liverpool L13 ... 54 A1
Liverpool L13, L7 ... 53 F1
Pigot St WA10 ... 43 E3
Pigotts Rake L30 ... 27 D5
Pike House Rd WA10 ... 43 A5
Pikelaw Pl WN8 ... 24 C5
Pike Pl WA10 ... 43 B4
Pikes Bridge Fold
WA10 ... 43 A4
Pikes Hey Rd CH48 ... 75 F7
Pilch Bank Rd L14 ... 54 E4
Pilch La L14, L36 ... 54 F3
Pilch La E L36 ... 55 A2
Pilgrim Cl WA2 ... 61 A6
Pilgrim St
Birkenhead CH41 ... 66 F6
Liverpool L1 ... 90 C2
Pilkington Rd PR8 ... 4 D5
Pilkington St WA11 ... 31 F6
Pilkington Tech Ctr
L40 ... 15 C6
Pilling Cl PR9 ... 1 F5
Pilling La L31 ... 20 A5
Pilling Pl WN8 ... 24 C5
Pilot Gr L15 ... 68 D8
Pimblett Rd WA11 ... 45 E7
Pimblett St WA3 ... 47 A7
Pimbley Gr E L31 ... 28 C6
Pimbley Gr W L31 ... 28 C6
Pimbo La WN8 ... 24 F3
Pimbo Rd
Crank WA11, WN8 ... 32 E7
Skelmersdale WN8 ... 24 C5
Pimhill Cl L8 ... 68 A6
Pimlico Rd WA7 ... 84 E2
Pincroft Way 3 L4 ... 52 D7
Pine Ave
Bebington CH63 ... 78 F3
Newton-le-W WA12 ... 46 D2
Ormskirk L39 ... 13 F7
St Helens WA10 ... 43 F6
4 Widnes WA8 ... 73 B2
Pine Cl
Haydock WA11 ... 45 C6
Huyton-w-R L36 ... 55 D4
Kirkby L32 ... 29 C3
Prescot L35 ... 56 E3
Skelmersdale WN8 ... 15 F1
Pine Crest L39 ... 13 B2
Pine Ct
Birkenhead CH41 ... 66 D6
11 Liverpool L8 ... 68 A4
Pine Dale WA11 ... 31 E7
Pinedale Cl CH43 ... 65 D4
Pine Dr L39 ... 13 F6
Pine Gr
Bootle L20 ... 38 D4
Crosby L22 ... 26 D2
Golborne WA3 ... 47 C8
Ormskirk L39 ... 13 F7
Southport PR9 ... 4 D7
Pinehey CH64 ... 86 D1
Pinehurst Ave
Crosby L22 ... 26 C2
Liverpool L4 ... 53 C7
Pinehurst Prim Sch L4 ... 53 C7
Pinehurst Rd L4 ... 53 C7
Pine Lo L4 ... 53 B8
Pine Mews L1 ... 90 C1
Pinemore Rd L18 ... 69 A2
Pine Rd CH60 ... 86 C8
Pineridge Cl CH62 ... 79 C2
Pines The
Bebington CH63 ... 79 B3
Liverpool L12 ... 40 F4
Southport PR8 ... 3 F6
Widnes WA8 ... 73 D4
Pinetop Cl L6 ... 53 C4
Pine Tree Ave CH43 ... 65 C4
Pinetree Cl
Birkenhead CH46 ... 64 F8
Litherland L30 ... 27 F3
Pinetree Ct CH45 ... 50 F5
Pinetree Dr CH48 ... 63 D1
Pinetree Gr CH46 ... 64 F8
Pine Tree Rd L36 ... 70 D8
Pine View Dr CH61 ... 77 A3
Pine Walks
Bebington CH42 ... 78 B8
Birkenhead CH42 ... 66 B1
Pinewalks Ridge CH63 ... 78 C8
Pine Way CH60 ... 76 E2
Pine Wlks CH48 ... 63 D1
Pinewood
Ashton-in-M WN4 ... 35 A2
Skelmersdale WN8 ... 16 D3
Pinewood Ave
Formby L37 ... 9 D1
Liverpool L12 ... 40 D3
Pinewood Cl
Abram Brow WN2 ... 36 C7
Formby L37 ... 9 D2
Liverpool L27 ... 70 E6
Southport PR8 ... 5 C1
Pinewood Cres WN5 ... 25 E6
Pinewood Dr CH60 ... 86 B8
Pinewood Gdns L33 ... 29 E5
Pinewood Rd WA5 ... 59 F7
Pinfold CH47 ... 63 A4
Pinfold Cl
Litherland L30 ... 27 E5
Southport PR8 ... 7 B3
Pinfold Cres L32 ... 41 A8
Pinfold Ct
3 Crosby L23 ... 26 D5
Prescot L35 ... 56 E3
Pinfold Dr WA10 ... 43 A3
Pinfold La
Knowsley L34 ... 41 C3
Southport PR8 ... 7 B3
West Kirby CH48 ... 63 A4
Pinfold Pl WN8 ... 24 D4
Pinfold Rd L25 ... 82 C8
Pingot Rd WN5 ... 33 E5
Pingwood La L33 ... 30 A5
Pinnington Pl L36 ... 55 E2
Pinnington Rd L35 ... 56 E3
Pintail Cl WA11 ... 44 B6
Piper's Cl CH60 ... 85 D8
Piper's End CH60 ... 85 D8
Piper's La CH60 ... 76 C1
Pipers The
Golborne WA3 ... 47 F8
Heswall CH60 ... 76 D1
Pipistrelle Rise CH43 ... 65 E4
Pipit Ave WA12 ... 46 C3
Pipit Cl L26 ... 70 E2
Pirrie Rd L9 ... 39 D3
Pitch Cl CH49 ... 64 D4
Pit Hey Pl WN8 ... 24 C5
Pit La WA8 ... 73 A4
Pit Pl L25 ... 70 A2
Pitsmead Rd L32 ... 29 E1
Pitts House La PR9 ... 5 B8
Pitt St
Liverpool L1 ... 90 B2
Southport PR9 ... 4 F6
St Helens WA9 ... 44 C3
St Helens WA9 ... 44 C4
Pitville Ave L18 ... 69 A3
Pitville Cl L18 ... 69 A2
Pitville Gr L18 ... 69 A3
Pitville Rd L18 ... 69 A3
Pitville Terr WA8 ... 84 C7
Plane Cl L9 ... 39 C3
Plane Tree Gr WA11 ... 46 A7
Planetree Rd L12 ... 54 F8
Plane Tree Rd CH63 ... 78 E5
Plantation Bsns Pk
CH62 ... 79 F2
Plantation Prim Sch
L26 ... 82 F9
Plantation Rd CH62 ... 79 F2
Planters The
Birkenhead CH49 ... 64 C4
Litherland L30 ... 28 A4
Platt Gr CH42 ... 79 A8
Platts St WA11 ... 45 A6
Plattsville Rd L18 ... 69 A5
Playfield Rd L12 ... 54 F7
Playfield Wlk L12 ... 54 F7
Pleasance Way WA12 ... 46 D4
Pleasant Hill St L8 ... 67 D6
Pleasant St
Bootle L20 ... 38 B2
Liverpool L3 ... 90 C3
Wallasey CH45 ... 51 B7
Pleasant Street Prim Sch
L3 ... 90 C3
Pleasant View L20 ... 38 B2
Pleasington Cl CH43 ... 65 E4
Pleasington Dr CH43 ... 65 E4
Plemont Rd L13 ... 54 A5
Plex La L39 ... 12 C5
Plex Moss La
Haskayne L39 ... 11 D8
Southport PR8, L39, L37 ... 7 E1
Plimsoll St 6 L7 ... 53 B1
Plough La L40 ... 15 A4
Plover Cl WA12 ... 46 C3
Plover Way WA3 ... 47 E8
Pluckington Rd L36 ... 56 B3
Plumbers Way L36 ... 55 F2
Plumer St
Birkenhead CH41 ... 66 A8
Liverpool L15 ... 68 E8
Plumley Gdns WA8 ... 72 A1
Plumpton Cross 6
WA8 ... 73 B2
Plumpton La L39 ... 8 E2
Plumpton St L6 ... 52 F4
Plum Tree Cl
Eccleston Park L35 ... 57 A6
Huyton-w-R L28 ... 55 B8
Plymyard Ave CH62 ... 88 D5
Plymyard Cl CH62 ... 88 D5
Plymyard Ct CH62 ... 88 C6
POCKET NOOK ... 44 C4
Pocket Nook St WA9,
WA10 ... 44 C4
Pocklington Ct WA2 ... 61 F1
Podium Rd L13 ... 54 A4
Poets Cnr CH62 ... 79 B5
Poets Gn L35 ... 56 F3
Poleacre Dr WA8 ... 72 D2
Polinda Gdns WA10 ... 57 C8
Pollard Rd L15 ... 54 A1
POLL HILL ... 76 F1
Poll Hill Rd CH60 ... 76 F1
Pollitt Cres WA9 ... 58 C3
Pollitt Sq CH62 ... 79 C8
Polperro Cl
Liverpool L11 ... 40 D5
Warrington WA5 ... 74 E3
Pomfret St L8 ... 68 A6
Pomona St L3 ... 90 C3
Pond Cl L6 ... 53 C4
Pond Green Way WA9 ... 44 F1
Pond View Cl CH60 ... 86 C8
Pondwater Cl 2 L32 ... 29 E1
Pond Wlk WA9 ... 45 A1
Ponsonby Rd CH45 ... 50 E5
Ponsonby St L8 ... 68 A6
Pontville Sch L39 ... 13 D3
Pool Bank CH62 ... 79 B6
Poolbank Rd CH62 ... 79 B7
Poole Ave WA2 ... 61 B2
Poole Cres WA2 ... 61 B2
Pool End WA9 ... 44 F2
Poole Rd CH44 ... 51 D5
POOL HEY ... 5 B3
Pool Hey L28 ... 55 B8
Pool Hey La PR8, PR9 ... 5 B3
Pool La
Bebington CH62 ... 79 D5
Birkenhead, Woodchurch
CH49 ... 65 A2
Poolside Wlk PR9 ... 2 C4
Pool St
Birkenhead CH41 ... 66 D7
Southport PR9 ... 2 D5
Poolwood Rd CH49 ... 65 B3
Pope St L20 ... 38 B5
Poplar Ave
Birkenhead CH49 ... 64 F5
Crosby L23 ... 26 F5
Downall Green WN4 ... 34 D5
Newton-le-W WA12 ... 46 D3
St Helens WA10 ... 43 A4
Warrington WA5 ... 74 E3
Poplar Bank
Huyton-w-R L36 ... 55 E2
Southport PR9 ... 1 D1
Poplar Cl L26 ... 71 A1
Poplar Ct 7 L8 ... 68 A4
Poplar Dr
Bebington CH63 ... 79 A4
Kirkby L32 ... 29 D3
Liverpool L5 ... 53 A5

R

RABY 87 C4
Raby Ave CH63 88 B6
Raby Cl
Bebington CH63 88 A7
Heswall CH60 85 F7
Widnes WA8 73 E2
Raby Ct CH60 77 A1
Raby Dr
Bebington CH63 88 A6
Birkenhead CH46 64 D7
Raby Gr CH63 78 D8
Raby Hall Rd CH63 88 A6
RABY MERE 88 B7
Raby Mere Rd CH63 87 D5
Raby Park Rd CH64 86 F1
Raby Rd CH63 87 B5
Rachel St L5 52 D4
Radburn Cl L23 27 B5
Radburn Rd L23 27 B5
Radford Ave CH63 79 B2
Radford Cl WA8 84 C7
Radlett Cl WA5 74 E3
Radley Dr
Aintree L10 28 C3
Heswall CH63 86 F6
Radley La WA2 61 E4
Radley Rd CH44 50 F5
Radley's Ct 3 L8 67 F6
Radley St WA9 57 E7
Radmore Rd L14 54 D3
Radnor Ave CH60 76 F1
Radnor Cl L26 82 E7
Radnor Dr
Bootle L20 38 E4
Southport PR9 1 F3
Wallasey CH45 51 C6
Widnes WA8 72 D2
Radnor Pl
Birkenhead CH43 66 C6
Liverpool L6 53 D5
Radstock Gr WA9 58 D5
Radstock Rd
Liverpool L6 53 C3
Wallasey CH44 50 E5
Radway Rd L36 55 F5
Raeburn Ave
Bebington CH62 88 E6
West Kirby CH48 63 C3
Raeburn Prim Sch CH62 88 D6
Raffles Rd CH42 66 D5
Raffles St L1 90 C1
Rafter Ave L20 38 E6
Raglan St L19 81 C5
Railbrook Hey L13 54 A1
Rail Cl WA11 23 F2
Railside Ct L5 52 C5
Railton Ave L35 57 D2
Railton Cl L35 57 D2
Railton Rd L11 39 E2
Railway App L39 13 F5
Railway Ave PR9 2 F5
Railway Bldgs CH47 63 B6
Railway Cotts
Hooton CH66 88 E1
Liverpool L25 82 C8
Railway Path L39 13 E4
Railway Rd
Birkenhead CH42 67 A1
Golborne WA3 36 B1
Ormskirk L39 13 F5
Skelmersdale WN8 23 E8
Railway St
Liverpool L19 81 C5
Newton-le-W WA12 46 B3
Southport PR8 4 B5
St Helens WA10 44 B4
Railway Terr PR8 4 A5
Railway View WA5 45 D1
Rainbow Cl WA8 72 C3
Rainbow Dr
Kirkby L31 29 B4
Liverpool L26 82 E9
Raines Cl CH49 64 E4
RAINFORD 32 B6
Rainford Ave L20 38 E5
Rainford Brook Lodge Com Prim Sch WA11 32 A7
Rainford By-Pass WA11 32 B3
Rainford CE Prim Sch WA11 32 A6
Rainford Gdns 14 L2 90 B3
Rainford High Tech Coll WA11 32 A8
Rainford Ind Est WA11 32 C4
RAINFORD JUNCTION 23 F2
Rainford Rd
Billinge WA11, WN5 33 C5
Skelmersdale L39, WA11 23 C4
St Helens WA10, WA11 43 C6
Rainford Sta WA11 23 F2
Rainham Cl L19 81 C8
RAINHILL 57 D3
Rainhill High Sch L35 57 E2
Rainhill Rd L35 57 C5
Rainhill Sta L35 57 C3
RAINHILL STOOPS 57 E1
Rake Cl CH49 65 A4
Rake Hey CH46 64 B8
Rake Hey Cl CH46 64 C8
Rake La
Birkenhead CH49 65 A4
Wallasey CH45 51 B6
Rakersfield Ct CH45 51 C8
Rakersfield Rd CH45 51 C8
Rake The CH62 88 C8
Raleigh Ave L35 56 D2
Raleigh Cl WA5 60 D1
Raleigh Rd
Neston CH64 86 F1
Wallasey CH46 50 B4
Raleigh St L20 38 B1
Ralph's Wife's La PR9 2 E6
Rame Cl L10 40 B6
Ramford St WA9 44 D2
Ramilies Rd L18 68 F5
Ramleh Pk L23 26 B3
Rampit Cl WA11 45 F7
Ramsbrook Cl L24 82 C5
Ramsbrook La L24, WA8 83 C3
Ramsbrook Rd L24 82 C5
Ramsey Cl
Ashton-in-M WN4 35 B2
Liverpool L19 81 D8
Prescot L35 56 E3
Widnes WA8 73 E3
Ramsey Ct CH48 63 B1
Ramsey Rd L19 81 D8
Ramsfield Rd L24 83 A4
Ramsons Cl L26 70 E1
Randall Cl WA12 46 B4
Randall Dr L30 27 C3
Randle Ave WA11 31 E8
Randle Brook Ct WA11 31 E8
Randle Cl CH63 79 A2
Randles Rd L34 41 A5
Randolph Ho CH41 66 F6
Randolph St 12 L4 52 F7
Randon Gr 5 WA10 43 F4
Ranelagh Ave L21 38 A8
Ranelagh Dr PR8 7 F7
Ranelagh Dr N L19 81 A8
Ranelagh Dr S L19 81 A8
Ranelagh Pl L1 90 C3
Ranelagh St L1 90 B3
Ranfurly Rd L19 81 B7
Range High Sch L37 17 C8
Rangemore Rd L18 69 A1
Rankin St CH44 51 A2
Rankin Way CH62 79 E1
Ranleigh Dr WN8 16 A8
Ranmore Ave WN4 34 D4
Ranslett Ct L37 10 A3
Ranworth Cl L11 39 E3
Ranworth Dr WA3 47 E7
Ranworth Gdns WA9 57 D6
Ranworth Pl L11 39 F3
Ranworth Rd WA5 74 E6
Ranworth Sq L11 39 F3
Ranworth Square Prim Sch L11 39 F3
Ranworth Way L11 39 F3
Rappart Rd CH44 51 D3
Rashid Mufti Ct 6 L8 68 A6
Ratcliff Pl L35 57 B4
Rathbone Rd
Hightown L38 17 F4
Liverpool L15, L13 68 F8
Rathlin Cl WA8 73 E3
Rathmore Ave L18 69 A3
Rathmore Cl CH43 66 A3
Rathmore Cres PR9 2 B3
Rathmore Dr CH43 66 A4
Rathmore Rd CH43 66 A4
Raven Cl 15 L6 53 A3
Ravendale Cl CH43 65 D4
Ravenfield Cl L26 82 E9
Ravenfield Dr WA8 72 C3
Ravenglass Ave L31 20 D2
RAVENHEAD 43 E1
Ravenhead Ave L32 40 E7
Ravenhead Dr WN8 25 A7
Ravenhead Foyer WA9 44 B1
Ravenhead Rd WA10 43 E1
Ravenhead Ret Pk WA9 44 A2
Ravenhead Way WN8 24 F6
Ravenhill Cres CH46 49 F4
Ravenhurst Way L35 56 D1
Raven Meols Hills Nature Reserve* L37 17 B7
Raven Meols La L37 9 F2
Raven Meols Lo L37 9 E2
Ravenna Rd L19 81 D8
Ravenscourt L26 82 F8
Ravenscroft L37 9 F2
Ravenscroft Ave L39 13 E4
Ravenscroft Com Prim Sch L33 29 E5
Ravenscroft Rd 1 CH43 66 C5
Ravensdale Cl WA2 61 D3
Ravens The L37 9 F2
Ravensthorpe Gn L11 39 F3
Ravenstone Cl CH49 64 F7
Ravenstone Dr WA9 58 D7
Ravenstone Rd L19 81 B8
Ravenswood Ave CH42 78 F8
Ravenswood Rd
Heswall CH61 77 A2
6 Liverpool L13 54 A3
Rawcliffe Cl WA8 72 F4
Rawcliffe Rd
3 Birkenhead CH42 66 D5
Liverpool L9 39 A4
Rawlinson Cres L26 83 B8
Rawlinson Ct PR9 4 D8
Rawlinson Gr PR9 1 F1
Rawlinson Rd
Liverpool L13 54 A2
Southport PR9 1 E1
Rawlins St L7 53 D3
Rawson Cl L21 37 F7
Rawson Rd L21 37 F7
Raydale Cl
Golborne WA3 36 E1
Liverpool L9 39 A3
Raymond Ave L30 28 A1
Raymond Pl L5 52 D4
Raymond Rd CH44 51 C3
Raynham Rd L13 53 F2
Reach The L3 52 C3
Reade Cl CH63 79 A1
Reading Cl L5 52 D7
Reading St L5 52 D7
Reads Ct L9 38 F6
Reapers Way L30 28 A4
Reay Ct CH44 51 E3
Reay St WA8 73 C2
Rebecca Gdns WA9 58 C7
Recreation Ave WN4 35 D4
Recreation Dr WN5 33 E5
Recreation St WA9 44 D4
Rector Rd L6 53 C7
Rectory Ave WA3 47 C8
Rectory CE Prim Sch WN4 34 D5
Rectory Cl
Birkenhead CH42 66 D4
Heswall CH60 85 F7
Winwick WA2 61 A6
Rectory Dr L26 71 A1
Rectory Gdns WA9 58 C6
Rectory La
Heswall CH60 85 E7
Winwick WA2 61 A6
Rectory Rd
Downall Green WN4 34 D5
Southport PR9 2 A1
West Kirby CH48 63 B1
Red Bank Ave WA12 46 F1
Red Barnes L37 9 F5
Red Barn Rd WN5 33 C6
Redbourne Ave L26 82 F7
Redbourne Dr WA8 72 B4
Redbourn St L6 53 C6
Redbridge High Sch L10 39 F8
Redbrook Cl CH62 88 D6
Redbrook St L6 53 C6
Redbrow Way 1 L33 29 E4
Redburn Cl 2 L8 68 A4
Redcap Cl CH45 50 E8
Redcar Cl PR8 4 F3
Redcar Dr CH62 88 D5
Redcar Mews 7 L6 53 C6
Redcar Rd CH45 50 D6
Redcar St L6 53 C6
Red Cat La WA11 32 F5
Redcliffe CH45 37 A1
Redcliffe Gdns L39 13 E3
Redcote Ct CH48 63 A1
Redcourt-St Anselm's Sch CH43 66 A5
Redcroft 2 CH49 64 C3
Red Cross St L2, L3 90 A3
Red Cut La L33 41 F8
Red Dale CH60 76 F1
Red Delph La WA11 23 E1
Redditch Cl CH49 64 C4
Redesdale Cl WA2 61 E2
Redfern St L20 52 C8
Redfield Cl CH44 51 D4
Red Fold L39 13 C2
Redford Cl CH49 64 C4
Redford St L6 53 C6
Redgate
Formby L37 10 A2
Ormskirk L39 13 E1
Redgate Ave L23 27 A4
Redgate Dr
Formby L37 10 B2
St Helens WA9 44 D3
Redgate Prim Sch L37 10 A2
Redgate Rd WN4 35 B6
Redgrave St 4 L7 53 C2
Redhill Ave L32 41 A8
Red Hill Rd CH63 78 B5
Redhills Dr PR8 4 F3
Redhouse Bank CH48 63 A3
Redhouse La CH48 63 A3
Redington Rd L19 81 E8
Redland Ct WN2 35 E7
Redland Rd L9 39 B8
Red Lion Cl L31 20 C1
Red Lion Sh Ctr L31 20 C1
Red Lomes L30 27 D5
Redmain Gr WA3 47 E8
Redmain Way L12 40 F2
Redmayne Cl WA12 46 B4
Redmere Dr CH60 86 D8
Redmires Cl L7 68 B8
Redmond St CH41 66 E4
Redmoor Cres 3 L33 29 E5
Redoaks Way L26 71 A1
Redpoll Gr L26 70 E2
Red Rock St L6 53 B4
Red Rum Cl L9 39 D8
Redruth Ave WA11 44 D7
Redruth Rd L11 40 D5
Red Sands L39 13 D3
Redshank Cl WA12 46 C4
Redstart Cl 7 WA3 47 E8
Redstone Cl CH47 63 D8
Redstone Dr CH60 76 C1
Redstone Pk 3 CH45 51 A8
Redstone Rise CH43 65 D6
Redtail Cl WA7 84 F3
Redvers Ave CH66 89 A2
Redvers Dr L9 38 F6
Redwald Cl L33 29 F6
Redwing La L25 70 A4
Redwing Way L26 70 D2
Redwood Ave L31 20 C3
Redwood Cl
Birkenhead CH43 65 F2
Liverpool L25 70 B5
Redwood Ct 8 L8 68 A4
Redwood Dr
Ormskirk L39 13 D4
St Helens WA11 44 F5
Redwood Gr L20 38 C4
Redwood Rd L25 70 B5
Redwood Way L33 29 F6
Reedale Cl L18 69 A4
Reedale Rd L18 69 A4
Reeds Ave E CH46 50 A3
Reeds Ave W CH46 49 F3
Reeds Brow WA11 32 B8
Reeds La CH46 49 F3
Reed's La WA11 32 A3
Reeds Rd L36 55 E4
Reeds The L39 13 D6
Reedville CH43 66 B5
Reedville Gr CH46 49 F2
Reedville Rd CH63 78 F5
Reeve Ct WA9 57 C6
Reeves Ave L20 38 E5
Reeves St WA9 44 E3
Regal Cres WA8 84 B8
Regal Ct PR8 7 D5
Regal Dr WA10 43 C5
Regal Rd L11 40 C3
Regal Wlk L4 52 F7
Regency Gdns PR8 3 E4
Regent Ave
Ashton-in-M WN4 34 F5
Haydock WA11 45 B7
Huyton-w-R L14 54 E2
Litherland L30 27 F3
Regent Cl PR8 3 F4
Regent Ct 12 PR9 4 C8
Regent Mews PR8 3 F4
Regent Pk L36 55 E5
Regent Rd
Bootle L20, L5 38 B1
Crosby L23 26 D4
Liverpool L20, L5 52 B6
Southport PR8 3 F4
Wallasey CH45 50 D6
Widnes WA8 73 B1
Regents Cl CH61 77 B6
Regents Rd WA10 43 C1
Regent St
Liverpool L3 52 B4
Newton-le-W WA12 46 A3
Regents Way CH63 78 D8
Regina Ave L22 26 C2
Reginald Rd WA9 58 E6
Reginald Rd Ind Pk WA9 58 E6
Regina Rd L9 39 A6
Reigate Cl L25 70 C3
Reins Croft CH64 86 E1
Renacres La L39 8 F6
Renaissance Way L24 82 D6
Rendal Cl L5 53 A5
Rendcombe Gn L11 39 F3
Rendel Cl WA12 46 D2
Rendelsham Cl CH49 64 E5
Rendel St CH41 66 D7
Renfrew Ave
Bebington CH62 88 E5
St Helens WA11 44 E7
Renfrew St L7 53 A2
Renfrey Cl L39 13 E8
Rennell Rd L14 54 C3
Rennie Ave WA10 43 C4
Renown Way L24 82 A7
Renshaw St L1 90 C3
Renville Rd L14 54 C2
Renwick Ave L35 57 A4
Renwick Rd L9 39 B5
Renwick Sq WN4 34 F3
Repton Gr L10 28 C2
Repton Rd L16 69 D8
Reservoir Rd
Birkenhead CH42 66 B1
Liverpool L25 69 F3
Reservoir Rd N CH42 66 B1
Reservoir St
Liverpool L6 53 A4
St Helens L35 57 C7
Rest Hill Rd CH63 78 C5
Retford Rd L33 30 A2
Retford Wlk 5 L33 29 F2
Reva Rd L14 54 F3
Revesby Cl WA8 72 D2
Rex Cohen Ct L17 68 E5
Rexmore Rd L18 69 A2
Rexmore Way L15 68 E7
Reynolds Ave WA9 45 B2
Reynolds Cl L6 53 A4
Reynolds Way L25 70 A3
Rhiwlas St L8 68 A5
Rhodesia Rd L9 39 C6
Rhodesway CH60 86 B7
Rhona Cl CH63 88 C4
Rhona Dr WA5 74 E6
Rhosesmor Cl L32 40 F6
Rhosesmor Rd L32 40 F6
Rhuddlan Cl L13 53 F2
Rhyl St
Liverpool L8 67 F5
Widnes WA8 84 F7
Rialto Cl 11 L8 67 F7
Ribble Ave
Maghull L31 20 E2
Rainhill L35 57 C3
Southport PR9 2 C4
Ribble Cl WA8 73 F3
Ribble Cres WN5 33 C3
Ribbledale Rd L18 69 A4
Ribble Ho L25 70 C3
Ribble Rd L25 70 C3
Ribbler's La
Kirkby L32 40 E7
Kirkby L34 40 F6
Ribblesdale Ave 2 L9 39 B7
Ribblesdale Cl CH62 88 F5
Ribble St CH41 50 F1
Ribchester Way L35 71 A7
Rice Hey Rd CH44 51 C4
Rice La
Liverpool L9 39 A4
Wallasey CH44 51 D4
Rice Lane Jun Sch L9 39 A5
Rice Lane Sta L9 39 A5
Rice St L1 90 C2
Richard Allen Way 5 L6 52 F4
Richard Chubb Dr CH44, CH45 51 D6
Richard Gr L12 54 F5
Richard Hesketh Dr L32 29 C2
Richard Kelly Cl L4 53 D8
Richard Kelly Dr L4 39 D2
Richard Kelly Pl L4 53 D8
Richard Martin Rd L21 27 C1
Richard Rd L23 26 A5
Richards Gr WA9 44 E4
Richardson Rd CH63 78 E8
Richardson St L7 68 C7
Richland Rd L13 53 F5
Richmond Ave
Haydock WA11 45 B7
Litherland L21 38 A8
Richmond Cl
Bebington CH63 79 A6
Hightown L38 17 F2
St Helens WA10 42 F4
Richmond Cres L30 27 F3
Richmond Ct
Bootle L21 38 B7
5 Crosby L23 26 E5
Widnes WA8 73 D4
Richmond Gdns WA12 46 C2
Richmond Gr L31 20 E3
Richmond Pk L6 53 C5
Richmond Rd
Ashton-in-M WN4 34 F5
Bebington CH63 78 F6
Crosby L23 26 E5
Southport PR8 3 F2
Richmond Row L3 52 E3
Richmond St
Liverpool L1 90 B3
Wallasey CH45 37 B1
Widnes WA8 73 C1
Richmond Terr L6 53 B5
Richmond Way
Heswall CH61 76 F2
Heswall, Thingwall CH61 77 A6
Huyton-w-R L35 71 A7
Rich View CH43 66 B3
Rickaby Cl CH63 88 C8
Rickman St L4 52 D7
Rickman Way L36 70 F8
Riddock Rd L21 38 B6
Rides The WA11 45 D6
Ridgeborne Cl WA5 60 D2
Ridge Cl PR9 2 C5
Ridgefield Rd CH61 76 F5
Ridgemere Rd CH61 76 F5
Ridge The CH60 76 D2
Ridgetor Rd L25 70 A3
Ridgeview Rd CH43 65 D5
Ridgeway WA3 47 E7
Ridgeway Dr L31 20 E3
Ridgeway High Sch CH43 65 D4
Ridgeway The
Bebington CH63 78 D8
Cronton WA8 72 C6
Heswall CH60 86 B7
Hoylake CH47 63 E7
Liverpool L25 70 A3
Ridgewell Ave 4 WA3 47 D8
Ridgewell Cl L21 38 A7
Ridgewood Dr
Heswall CH61 76 F5
St Helens WA9 58 D6
Ridgewood Way L9 39 A7
Ridgmont Ave L11 39 F2
Riding Cl
Haskayne L39 11 F4
St Helens WA9 58 C4
Riding Fold L26 70 D2
Riding Hill Rd L34 41 D2
Riding Hill Wlk L34 41 D2
Riding La
Ashton-in-M WN4 35 F5
Haskayne L39 11 E4
Ridings Hey CH43 65 D4
Riding St
Liverpool L3 52 F2
Southport PR8 4 B6
Ridings The
Birkenhead CH43 65 D5

Ridings The continued
Southport PR9 2 A3
Ridley Gr CH48 63 A3
Ridley La L31 20 D1
Ridley Rd L6 53 C3
Ridley St CH43 66 C5
Ridsdale [2] WA8 84 C8
Ridsdale Lawn L27 71 A3
Riesling Dr L33 29 E5
Rigby Dr CH49 64 D2
Rigby Rd L31 20 B3
Rigby St
Ashton-in-M WN4 35 A3
Golborne WA3 47 A8
Liverpool L3 90 A4
St Helens WA10 43 F4
Riley Ave L20 38 D5
Rimington Ave WA3 36 C1
Rimmer Ave L16 55 A1
Rimmerbrook Rd L25 70 B7
Rimmer Cl L21 38 B7
Rimmer Gn PR8 5 D1
Rimmer Gr WA9 44 E3
Rimmer's Ave
Formby L37 9 E6
Southport PR8 4 B6
Rimmers Ct CH41 65 F7
Rimmer St L3 90 C4
Rimmington Rd L17 68 E2
Rimrose Bsns Pk L20 38 A4
Rimrose Rd L20 38 A4
Rimrose Valley Country Pk* L23 27 A3
Rimrose Valley Rd L23 27 B4
Rimsdale Cl L17 80 E7
Ringcroft Rd L13 54 B2
Ringley Ave WA3 35 F1
Ringo Starr Dr [4] L6 53 B3
Ringsfield Rd L24 83 A2
Ringway CH64 86 E1
Ringway Rd L25 70 C4
Ringways CH62 79 D3
Ringwood CH43 66 A3
Ringwood Ave L14 54 F2
Ringwood Ct CH43 66 A3
Rio Ct L34 56 D7
Rio Ho [8] L36 56 A2
Ripley Ave L21 27 B1
Ripley Cl L31 20 E1
Ripon Ave WA3 47 D8
Ripon Cl
Huyton-w-R L36 56 B3
Litherland L30 27 F1
Newton-le-W WA12 46 C5
Southport PR8 4 F3
Ripon Dr WN4 35 D2
Ripon Rd CH45 50 F6
Ripon St
Birkenhead CH41 66 E4
Liverpool L4 38 F1
Risbury Cl L11 39 F2
Rishton Cl [10] L5 53 A5
Rishton St [8] L5 53 A5
Ritchie Ave L9 39 C6
Ritherup La L35 57 C4
Ritson St L8 68 B6
Rivacre Rd CH62, CH65, CH66 89 C2
River Avon St
[3] Liverpool L8 68 B7
[1] Liverpool L8 68 C7
Riverbank Cl CH60 85 F6
Riverbank Rd
Bebington CH62 79 F4
Heswall CH60 85 E6
Liverpool L19 81 A7
River Cl L37 10 B1
River Gr CH62 79 B8
Rivermeade PR8 4 D4
Riverpark Gdns L8 67 E6
Riversdale Cl [8] L33 29 F4
Riversdale Ct
Liverpool L19 80 F8
West Kirby CH47 63 A3
Riversdale Mews
Liverpool L19 80 F8
West Kirby CH48 63 A2
Riversdale Rd
Liverpool L17, L19 80 F7
[3] Seaforth L21 37 F7
Wallasey CH44 51 D4
West Kirby CH48 63 A2
Riverside
Bebington CH62 79 B5
Hightown L38 17 F4
Liverpool L12 40 E1
West Kirby CH48 75 B8
Riverside Cl L20 38 A5
Riverside Coll Halton Runcorn Campus WA7 84 E3
Riverside Dr L17 68 B2
Riverside Gr WA9 58 D7
Riverside Prim Sch CH44 51 E3
Riverside Trad Est WA5 74 D1
Riverside View L17 68 C1
Riverslea Rd L23 26 B2
Rivers St WN5 25 E6
River St CH41 66 D6
Riverview CH49 65 A1
River View
Bebington CH62 79 C8
[9] Crosby L22 26 C2
Riverview Gdns [8] CH42 66 F2
Riverview Rd CH44 51 E3
Riverview Wlk [9] L8 67 F4
Riverwood Rd CH62 79 F1
Riviera Dr
Birkenhead CH42 66 D1
Liverpool L11 40 C4
Rivington Ave
Birkenhead CH43 65 E4
Golborne WA3 36 C1
St Helens WA10 43 F6
Rivington Cl PR8 4 A3
Rivington Dr
Bickershaw WN2 36 F8
Up Holland WN8 25 C7
Rivington Prim Sch WA10 43 E5
Rivington Rd
St Helens WA10 43 D4
Wallasey CH44 51 D3
Rivington St WA10 43 D3
RL Hughes Prim Sch WN4 35 A3
Roadside Ct WA3 47 C8
Roadwater Cl L25 70 B7
Robarts Rd L4 53 B6
Robbin's Bridge L31 20 E5
Robeck Rd L13 54 B1
Robert Dr CH49 64 E3
Robert Gr L12 54 E5
Roberts Ave WA11 45 A5
Roberts Dr L20 38 E7
Robertson St L8 67 E5
Roberts St L3 52 B3
Robert St
[4] Birkenhead CH41 66 D7
Widnes WA8 73 B1
Robina Rd WA9 58 D8
Robins La WA9 58 D8
Robin's La WA11 33 A8
Robins Lane Com Prim Sch WA9 58 C8
Robinson Mews CH41 66 F6
Robinson Pl WA9 44 D3
Robinson Rd L21 27 C1
Robin Way CH49 65 B2
Rob La WA12 46 E5
Robsart St L5 52 E5
Robson Pl WN2 36 B8
Robson St
Liverpool, Everton L5 52 F6
Liverpool, Old Swan L13 54 A1
Robson Way [3] WA3 47 F8
ROBY 55 C2
Roby Cl L35 57 C4
Roby Ct L36 55 D1
Roby Mount Ave L36 55 D2
Roby Park Prim Sch L36 55 A3
Roby Rd
Huyton-w-R, Bowring Park L14, L36 54 F1
Huyton-w-R L36 55 C2
Roby St
Bootle L20 38 C4
Liverpool L15 68 E7
St Helens WA10 43 D1
Roby Sta L36 55 C2
Roby Well Way WN5 33 D5
Rocastle Cl [17] L6 53 A3
Rochester Ave L30 27 F1
Rochester Cl WA3 47 A8
Rochester Gdns WA10 43 D1
Rochester Rd CH42 67 A1
Rock Ave CH60 76 F1
Rock Bank CH49 65 A5
Rockbank Rd L13 53 F5
Rockbourne Ave L25 69 F5
Rockbourne Gn L25 69 F5
Rockbourne Way L25 69 F5
Rock Cl CH42 66 F2
ROCK FERRY 66 F1
Rock Ferry By-Pass CH42 67 A2
Rock Ferry High Sch CH42 78 F8
Rock Ferry Prim Sch CH42 66 F2
Rock Ferry Sta CH42 66 F2
Rockfield Cl WA8 72 D2
Rockfield Gdns [2] L31 20 C2
Rockfield Rd L4 53 A7
Rockford Ave L32 40 E7
Rockford Cl L32 40 E7
Rockford Wlk L32 40 E7
Rock Gr L13 54 A3
Rockhill Rd L25 70 B2
Rockhouse St L6 53 C5
Rockingham Ct [4] L33 29 F4
Rock La
Aintree L31 28 F5
Widnes WA8 72 F4
Rock La E CH42 67 A2
Rockland Rd
Crosby L22 26 E2
Wallasey CH45 50 F7
Rocklands Ave CH63 79 A7
Rocklands La CH63 87 C8
Rock La W CH42 66 F1
Rockley St [8] L4 52 E8
Rock Mount Cl L25 69 F3
Rock Mount Pk L25 69 F3
Rockmount Rd L17 68 F1
ROCK PARK 67 B1
Rock Park Rd CH42 67 B1
Rockpoint Ave CH45 51 C7
Rock Ret Pk CH41 66 F5
Rockside Rd L18 69 A1
Rock St
Golborne WA3 36 A2
Rock St continued
Liverpool L13 54 A3
St Helens WA10 57 C8
Rock View
Kirkby L31 29 A4
Liverpool L5 52 E6
Rockville Rd L13, L14 54 C1
Rockville St CH42 66 F2
Rockwell Cl L12 54 D8
Rockwell Rd L12 54 E8
Rocky Bank Rd CH42 66 D3
Rocky La
Heswall CH60 85 F8
Liverpool, Anfield L6 53 C5
Liverpool, Childwall L15, L16 69 D8
Rocky La S CH60 86 A8
Roderick Rd [1] L4 39 A2
Roderick St [3] L3 52 E3
Rodick St L25 69 F2
Rodmell Rd L9 39 B6
Rodney Ct CH45 37 B1
Rodney St
Birkenhead CH41 66 E5
Liverpool L1 90 C2
St Helens WA10 43 E4
Roe Alley L1 90 B3
Roeburn Way WA5 74 D3
Roedean Cl
Liverpool L25 82 B9
Maghull L31 20 D2
Roehampton Dr L23 26 C6
Roe La PR9 4 E8
Roemarsh Cl L11 40 B2
Roe-Park Mews PR9 4 D8
Roe St L1 90 B4
Roften Ind Est CH66 88 D1
Roger Arden Ct L20 38 D4
Rogers Ave L20 38 E5
Rogerson's Gn L26 70 E2
Rokeby Ave WA3 36 D1
Rokeby Cl L3 52 E3
Rokeby St L3 52 E3
Rokeden WA12 46 D4
Roker Ave [6] CH44 51 A3
Rokesmith Ave L7 68 C8
Roklis Ct CH49 65 A4
Roland Ave
Bebington CH63 78 E6
Runcorn WA7 84 F1
St Helens WA11 44 C7
Roleton Cl L30 28 B4
Rollesby Gdns WA9 57 E6
Rolleston Dr
Bebington CH63 79 A4
Wallasey CH45 50 F6
Rolling Mill La WA9 58 F8
Rollo St L4 52 E7
Roman Cl WA12 46 C2
Roman Rd
Ashton-in-M WN4 35 A5
Bebington CH43, CH63 78 A8
Hoylake CH47 48 D1
Rome Cl L36 55 D3
Romer Rd L6 53 C3
Romford Way L26 82 F7
Romiley Dr WN8 15 F2
Romilly St L6 53 B3
Romley St L4 38 F1
Romney Cl WA8 73 E2
Romsey Ave L37 10 B2
Romulus St L7 53 D2
Ronald Cl L22 26 F1
Ronald Rd L22 26 F1
Ronald Ross Ave L30 27 F3
Ronaldshay WA8 73 E2
Ronald St L13 53 F3
Ronaldsway
Birkenhead CH49 64 F6
Crosby L23 27 A6
Halewood L26 83 A8
Heswall CH60 85 F6
Liverpool L10 40 A7
Ronan Cl L20 38 A4
Ronan Rd WA8 84 E5
Rone Cl CH46 64 D8
Roofers Way [1] L36 56 A2
Rookery Ave WN4 35 B2
Rookery Dr
Liverpool L19 80 F8
Rainford WA11 32 A5
Rookery La WA11 32 B5
Rookery Rd PR9 1 F1
Rookery The WA12 46 D4
Rookley Cl L27 70 F4
Rooks Way CH60 85 E8
Rooley The L36 55 D1
Roosevelt Dr L9 39 B8
Ropers Bridge Cl L35 56 D2
Roper St
Liverpool L8 67 F5
St Helens WA9 44 C4
Ropewalks Sq [4] L1 90 C2
Rosalind Ave CH63 78 E7
Rosalind Way L20 38 D1
Rosclare Dr CH45 50 F6
Roscoe Ave WA12 46 E3
Roscoe Cl L35 71 A7
Roscoe Inf Sch L13 53 E7
Roscoe Jun Sch L13 53 E7
Roscoe La L1 90 C2
Roscoe Pl L1 90 C2
Roscoe St
Liverpool L1 90 C2
St Helens WA10 43 D3
Roscommon St L5 52 E4
Roscommon Way WA8 72 E3
Roscote Cl CH60 85 F7
Roscote The CH60 85 F7
Roseacre CH48 63 A3
Roseate Ct CH45 50 E8
Rose Ave
Abram Brow WN2 36 B7
Bootle L20 38 C7
Haydock WA11 45 E6
St Helens WA9 58 C7
Rosebank Rd L36 55 C5
Rose Bank Rd L16 69 D7
Rosebank Way L36 55 C5
Rosebay Cl L37 10 A3
Roseberry Rd WN4 35 A5
Rosebery Ave
Crosby L22 26 C2
Wallasey CH44 51 C4
Rosebery Ct CH44 51 C4
Rosebery Gr CH42 66 B2
Rosebery Rd WA10 43 D5
Rosebery St
Liverpool L8 68 A7
Southport PR9 5 A6
Rosebourne Cl L17 68 C2
Rose Brae L18 69 B4
Rose Brae Ct CH60 77 A1
Rose Brow L25 70 A4
Rose Cl L26 83 A7
Rose Cres
Skelmersdale WN8 15 E1
Southport PR8 7 C2
Widnes WA8 84 F7
Rosecroft CH62 88 C6
Rosecroft Cl L39 13 E6
Rosecroft Ct CH47 63 A6
Rose Ct
[9] Birkenhead CH41 66 D6
Liverpool L15 68 E7
Rosedale Ave
Crosby L23 26 F4
Golborne WA3 47 C7
Rosedale Cl L9 39 B4
Rosedale Rd
Birkenhead CH42 66 E3
Liverpool L18 69 B5
Rose Dr WA11 32 A5
Rosefield Ave CH63 78 E7
Rosefield Rd L25 70 C1
Rosegarth Gn L14 54 B4
Roseheath Dr L26 83 A6
ROSE HILL 34 F7
Rose Hill
Liverpool L3 52 D3
Southport PR8, PR9 4 D6
Rosehill Ave WA9 59 B5
Rosehill Bsns Pk [1] PR9 4 D6
Rosehill Ct L25 70 A4
Rosehill Dr L39 13 C2
Rosehill Mans L39 13 C2
Rose Hill View WN4 34 F7
Rose La L18 69 A3
Roseland Cl L31 20 B4
Roselands Ct CH42 66 E1
Rose Lea Cl WA8 73 A4
Roselea Dr PR9 2 C4
Rosemary Cl
Birkenhead CH43 65 E8
Liverpool L7 68 A8
Rosemary Ct L37 9 F3
Rosemary Dr WA12 46 F3
Rosemary La
Formby L37 9 F3
Haskayne L39 12 B4
Rosemead Ave CH61 77 A4
Rosemont Rd L17 68 F2
Rosemoor Dr L23 27 A5
Rosemoor Gdns L11 40 A2
Rose Mount
Birkenhead CH43 66 B4
Crosby L22 26 C1
Rosemount Cl CH43 66 A3
Rosemount Cotts WA2 61 B8
Rose Mount Dr CH45 51 A6
Rosemount Pk CH43 66 A3
Rose Path L37 10 A2
Rose Pl
Birkenhead CH42 66 D4
Liverpool L3 52 D3
Liverpool L3 52 E3
Ormskirk L39 13 D2
Rainford WA11 32 A5
Roseside Dr L27 70 F6
Rose St
Liverpool L1 90 B4
Liverpool, Woolton Hill L25 69 F2
Widnes WA8 84 F7
Rose Terr L18 69 A4
Rose Vale L5 52 E5
Rose View Ave WA8 73 A2
Rose Villas L15 69 A7
Rosewarne Cl L17 68 B2
Rosewell Ct L28 55 B6
Rosewood Cl
Abram Brow WN2 36 B7
Huyton-w-R L28 55 B7
Liverpool L27 70 E5
Rosewood Dr CH46 64 B8
Rosewood Farm Ct WA8 72 E4
Rosewood Gdns [1] L11 40 B1
Rosewood Gr WA8 84 B8
Roseworth Ave L9 39 A7
Rosina Cl WN4 34 F6
Roskell Rd L25 82 C8
Roslin Ct CH43 66 B4
Roslin Rd
Birkenhead CH43 66 B4
Roslin Rd continued
Irby CH61 76 D6
Roslyn St CH42 66 F3
Rossall Ave L10 28 D3
Rossall Cl L24 83 E2
Rossall Ct CH46 49 F2
Rossall Rd
Liverpool L13 54 B2
Wallasey CH46 49 F1
Widnes WA8 73 D2
Ross Ave CH46 50 C4
Ross Cl
Billinge WN5 33 E6
Knowsley L34 41 D3
Ross Ct CH62 79 B7
Rossendale Cl CH43 65 D4
Rossett Ave L17 68 E6
Rossett Cl WA5 60 E2
Rossett Rd L23 26 C3
Rossett St L6 53 C5
Rossini St L21 38 A6
Rosslyn Ave L31 28 B8
Rosslyn Cres CH46 64 E8
Rosslyn Dr CH46 64 E8
Rosslyn Pk [1] CH46 64 E7
Rosslyn St L17 68 B3
Rossmore Gdns L4 53 C8
Ross St WA8 73 B1
Ross Tower Ct CH45 51 C8
Rostherne Ave
Golborne WA3 47 D8
Wallasey CH44 51 A3
Rostherne Cres WA8 72 D2
Rosthwaite Gr WA11 33 B1
Rosthwaite Rd L12 54 C6
Rostron Cres L37 9 E1
Rosyth Cl WA2 61 F3
Rothay Dr WA5 74 D3
Rothbury Cl CH46 64 C8
Rothbury Ct WA9 58 B2
Rothbury Rd L14 54 F6
Rotherham Cl L36 55 F4
Rotherwood CH43 65 D5
Rotherwood Cl CH63 78 D6
Rothesay Ct CH63 78 F4
Rothesay Dr
Bebington CH62 88 E4
Crosby L23 26 F3
Rothesay Gdns [3] CH43 65 F1
Rothley Ave PR8 7 A4
Rothsay Cl WA11 44 E6
Rothwell Cl L39 13 D5
Rothwell Dr
Ormskirk L39 13 B2
Southport PR8 7 A4
Rothwell Rd WA3 36 C1
Rothwells La L23 27 B7
Rothwell St [5] L6 53 A4
Rotten Row PR8 3 F6
Rotunda St L5 52 D5
Roughdale Ave
Kirkby L32 40 F7
St Helens WA9 58 B4
Roughdale Cl L32 40 F7
Roughsedge Ho L28 55 B8
Roughwood Dr L33 29 F3
Roundabout The WA8 72 D6
Round Hey L28 55 A8
Round Meade The L31 20 C2
Roundway The L38 17 F3
Roundwood Dr WA9 44 B1
Routledge St WA8 73 B1
Rowan Ave
Golborne WA3 47 F7
Liverpool L12 40 F1
Rowan Cl
St Helens, Blackbrook WA11 44 F5
St Helens, Laffak WA11 44 D7
Warrington WA5 74 F6
Rowan Ct
Bebington CH63 78 D6
Birkenhead CH49 64 C2
Liverpool L17 68 E2
Rowan Dr L32 29 D3
Rowan Gr
Bebington CH63 78 E4
Huyton-w-R L36 70 D8
Rowan La WN8 16 B4
Rowan Park Sch L21 27 D2
Rowans The
Aughton L39 21 A7
Widnes WA8 73 D4
Rowan Tree Cl CH49 64 B3
Rowena Cl L23 26 F4
Rowlings Way [11] L32 40 F8
Rowsley Gr L9 39 B7
Rowson Ct [7] CH45 51 B8
Rowson St
Prescot L34 56 D7
Wallasey CH45 51 B7
Row The CH47 63 B7
Rowthorn Cl WA8 84 E8
Rowton Cl CH43 65 F3
Roxborough Cl WA5 60 A6
Roxborough Wlk L25 70 C3
Roxburgh Ave
Birkenhead CH42 66 D2
Liverpool L17 68 C3
Roxburgh St L20, L4 38 E1
Royal Ave WA8 72 A1
Royal Birkdale Golf Links PR8 3 D3
Royal Cl L37 10 A1

130 Roy–St H

Royal Cres L37 10 A1
Royal Croft L12 54 B4
Royal Gr WA10 43 D1
Royal Liver Building L3 52 B1
Royal Liverpool Univ Dental Hospl L3 52 F2
Royal Liverpool Univ Hospl L3, L7 52 F2
Royal Mail St L3 90 C3
ROYAL OAK 21 F4
Royal Pk PR8 3 E4
Royal Pl WA8 84 B8
Royal Quay L3 90 A2
Royal School for the Blind The L15 69 A7
Royal St L4 52 E7
Royal Standard Ho 9 CH42 66 F3
Royal Standard Way 8 CH42 66 F3
Royal Terr PR8 4 A7
Royal The CH47 62 F6
Royden Ave CH44 51 D5
Royden Cres WN5 33 E5
Royden Ho CH41 66 C7
Royden Pk* CH48 64 A1
Royden Pk Visitor Ctr* CH48 76 B8
Royden Rd
Billinge WN5 33 E5
Birkenhead CH49 64 E6
Royden Way L3 67 E3
Royhsay Cl L5 52 F4
Roysten Gdns WA9 44 D2
Royston Ave CH44 51 D4
Royston Cl 2 WA3 47 E8
Royston St L7 53 B1
Royton Rd L22 26 F2
Rubbing Stone CH48 75 D6
Ruby Cl L21 38 C8
Ruby St L8 68 A3
Rudd Ave WA9 45 B2
Ruddington Rd PR8 4 E2
Rudd St CH47 63 B7
Rudgate L35 56 E2
Rudgrave Cl CH43 65 D4
Rudgrave Mews CH44 51 D5
Rudgrave Pl CH44 51 D5
Rudgrave Sq CH44 51 D5
Rudley Wlk L24 82 F3
Rudloe Ct WA2 61 F1
Rudston Jun & Inf Schs L16 69 D8
Rudston Rd L16 69 D7
Rudyard Cl L14 54 C3
Rudyard Rd L14 54 D3
Ruff La L39, L40 14 B4
Rufford Ave L31 20 E3
Rufford Cl
Liverpool L10 39 F8
Prescot L35 56 F5
Widnes WA8 72 C2
Rufford Dr PR9 2 F5
Rufford Rd
Bootle L20 38 C5
Liverpool L6 53 D3
Rainford WA11 31 F8
Southport PR9 2 C4
Wallasey CH44 51 C3
Rufford St 4 WN4 34 F5
Rufford Wlk WA11 44 E6
Ruffwood Sch L33 29 F3
Rugby Cl WN5 25 E5
Rugby Dr
Aintree L10 28 F1
Orrell WN5 25 F8
Rugby Rd
Liverpool L9 39 B8
Wallasey CH44 50 F4
Ruislip Cl L25 70 C2
Ruislip Ct WA2 61 F1
Rullerton Rd CH44, CH45 51 A4
Rumford Pl L2, L3 90 A4
Rumford St L2 90 A3
Rumney Pl L4 52 E8
Rumney Rd L4 52 E8
Rumney Rd W L4 52 D8
RUNCORN 84 D2
Runcorn Docks Rd WA7 84 E2
Runcorn Sta WA7 84 F2
Rundle Rd L17 68 E1
Rundle St CH41 66 A8
Runic St L13 53 F2
Runnell's La L23 27 C5
Runnell The CH64 86 D4
Runnymede L36 55 D4
Runnymede Cl L25 70 A4
Runnymede Ct 2 WA8 73 C1
Runnymede Dr WA11 45 A6
Runnymede Gdns 5 WA8 73 C1
Runnymede Wlk 3 WA8 73 C2
Runton Rd L25 70 C5
Rupert Dr L6 53 A3
Rupert Rd L36 55 D3
Ruscar Cl L26 70 E2
Ruscolm Cl WA5 74 D7
Ruscombe Rd L14 55 A5
Rushden Rd L32 30 A1
Rushey Hey Rd L32 29 F1
Rushgreen Cl CH43 65 C7
Rushlake Dr L27 70 D5
Rushmere Rd L11 39 F2
Rushmoor Ave WN4 35 E4
Rusholme Cl L26 83 A6
Rushton Ave WA12 46 B4
Rushton Cl
Burtonwood WA5 59 F7
Widnes WA8 72 F3
Rushton Pl L25 70 A2
Rushton's Wlk L30 27 D4
Rushy View WA12 46 A4
Ruskin Ave
Birkenhead CH42 66 F1
Newton-le-W WA12 46 C4
Wallasey CH44 51 A3
Warrington WA2 61 C2
Ruskin Cl L20 38 C3
Ruskin Dr WA10 43 D5
Ruskin St L4 38 E1
Ruskin Way
Birkenhead CH43 65 E3
Huyton-w-R L36 55 D1
Rusland Ave CH61 76 F4
Rusland Rd L32 40 F8
Russel Ct WA8 73 B4
Russell Ave PR9 5 A7
Russell Ct PR9 2 B4
Russell Pl L3 90 C3
Russell Rd
Birkenhead CH42 67 A2
Huyton-w-R L36 56 B2
Liverpool, Garston L19 81 C6
Liverpool L18 68 F5
Runcorn WA7 84 E1
Southport PR9 5 A6
Wallasey CH44 50 E5
Russell St
Birkenhead CH41 66 E7
Liverpool L3 90 C3
Russet Cl
Liverpool, Netherley L27 70 E5
St Helens WA10 43 F5
Russian Ave L13 53 F5
Russian Dr L13 53 F5
Rutherford Cl L13 53 E1
Rutherford Rd
Liverpool L18 69 B6
Maghull L31 28 E7
St Helens WA10 43 C6
Rutherglen Ave L23 26 F2
Ruth Evans Ct L35 57 A4
Ruthin Cl WA5 60 E3
Ruthven Ct L21 38 A7
Ruthven Rd
Litherland L21 38 A7
Liverpool L13 54 B1
Rutland Ave
Golborne WA3 47 D7
Halewood L26 83 A8
Liverpool L17 68 D6
Rutland Cl 4 L5 53 A5
Rutland Cres L39 13 E7
Rutland Dr WN4 35 C4
Rutland Ho
Crosby L23 26 B3
Liverpool L17 68 D5
Rutland Rd PR8 4 D5
Rutland St
Bootle L20 38 D4
1 Runcorn WA7 84 F2
St Helens WA10 43 F5
Rutland Way L36 56 B3
Rutter Ave WA5 60 F2
Rutter St L8 67 E5
Ryburn Rd L39 13 E4
Rycot Rd L24 82 C5
Rycroft Rd
Hoylake CH47 63 E8
Liverpool L10 39 E7
Wallasey CH44 51 C2
Rydal Ave
Birkenhead CH43 65 C5
Crosby L23 26 F2
Formby L37 9 D3
Orrell WN5 25 F7
Prescot L34 56 F6
Rydal Bank
Bebington CH63 79 A7
Wallasey CH44 51 C4
Rydal Cl
Aintree L10 28 F2
Ashton-in-M WN4 35 C4
Heswall CH61 76 F4
Kirkby L33 29 D4
Rydal Gr WA11 44 A7
Rydal Pl WN2 36 B8
Rydal Rd L36 55 E1
Rydal St
Liverpool L5 53 A5
Newton-le-W WA12 46 C3
Rydal Way WA8 72 C1
Rydecroft L25 69 F2
Ryder Cl
Ormskirk L39 13 C2
Rainhill L35 57 A4
Ryder Cres
Ormskirk L39 13 C1
Southport PR8 7 E7
Ryder Rd WA8 73 B4
Rydinge The L37 10 A6
Rye Cl WA9 58 D4
Ryecote L32 40 E7
Ryecroft L21 27 B3
Ryecroft Ave WA3 36 E1
Ryecroft Rd CH60 86 C7
Ryedale Cl L8 68 B7
Ryefield La L21 27 B3
Ryegate Rd L19 81 B8
Rye Gr L12 54 E6
Ryeground La L37 10 A5
Rye Hey Rd L32 29 F2
Rye Moss La L37 19 B8
Ryland Pk CH61 77 A5
Rylands Hey CH49 64 D4
Ryleys Gdns L2 90 A4
Rymer Gr 2 L4 39 A1
Rymers Gn L37 9 E4

S

Sables Ct 4 CH45 51 A8
Sackville Rd WA10 43 C6
Sacred Heart RC Coll L23 26 E3
Sacred Heart RC Prim Sch
Liverpool L7 53 A2
Wallasey CH46 49 F1
Saddle Cl L9 39 D8
Saddlestone Gr 5 L8 67 E5
Sadler's La WA11 42 E7
Sadler St WA8 73 C1
Saffron Cl WA3 47 E8
Saffron Gdns WA9 44 D2
Saffron Mews L23 27 B6
Sagar Fold L39 21 D8
St Aelred's RC Tech Coll WA12 46 D4
St Agnes RC Prim Sch L36 55 F1
St Agnes Rd
Huyton-w-R L36 55 F2
Liverpool L4 52 D8
St Aidan's CE Com Prim Sch WN5 33 E5
St Aidan's Cl WN5 33 E6
St Aidans Ct WA9 58 E3
St Aidan's Ct CH43 65 F6
St Aidans Dr WA8 72 F6
St Aidan's Gr L36 55 C7
St Aidan's RC Prim Sch L36 55 F3
St Aidan's Terr 1 CH43 65 F6
St Aidan's Way L30 27 E3
St Alban Rd WA5 74 E5
St Albans L6 53 B5
St Albans Cl WA11 46 A7
St Albans Ct L5 52 C5
St Alban's RC Prim Sch CH44 51 B4
St Alban's Rd
Birkenhead CH43 66 A6
Bootle L20 38 C3
Wallasey CH44 51 B4
St Alban's Sq L20 38 C2
St Albert's RC Prim Sch L28 55 A8
St Alexander Cl 3 L20 38 D1
St Aloysius RC Prim Sch L36 55 C4
St Ambrose Barlow RC Coll L30 28 A5
St Ambrose Croft L30 27 E4
St Ambrose Gr L4 53 B6
St Ambrose RC Prim Sch L24 83 A2
St Ambrose Rd WA8 73 C1
St Ambrose Way 6 L5 52 F4
St Andrew Gdns L3 90 C4
St Andrew Rd L4 53 B6
St Andrews Ave L12 54 E6
St Andrew's CE Prim Sch
Bebington CH63 78 F6
Warrington WA2 61 C3
St Andrews Ct
Birkenhead CH43 65 D6
Seaforth L22 37 E8
Southport PR8 4 B6
St Andrew's Dr L23 26 C6
St Andrew's Dr L36 55 C7
St Andrews Gr WA11 44 B6
St Andrew's Gr L30 27 C3
St Andrew's Maghull CE Prim Sch L31 20 D1
St Andrews Pl L17 68 C3
St Andrew's Pl PR8 4 B6
St Andrews Rd
Bebington CH63 79 A4
Bootle L20 38 C6
St Andrew's Rd
Birkenhead CH43 66 B6
Crosby L23 26 B6
St Andrew St L3 52 F1
St Andrew's View 8 L33 29 E5
St Andrews Villas L36 55 B3
St Andrew The Apostle RC Prim Sch L26 82 D8
St Anne Gr CH41 66 C8
St Anne's Cl
6 Birkenhead CH41 66 D7
Formby L37 9 F6
St Anne's Cotts L14 54 C3
St Annes Ct
Liverpool, Aigburth L17 68 E1
Liverpool L3 52 E3
St Anne's Ct L13 53 F3
St Annes Gdns L17 68 F1
St Annes Gr L17 68 F1
St Anne's Path L37 9 F6
St Anne's Pl CH41 66 C8
St Anne's RC Prim Sch
Bebington CH42 78 F8
Huyton-w-R L36 55 D1
St Anne's RC Prim Sch continued
Liverpool L7 68 B8
Ormskirk L39 13 E4
St Helens WA9 58 E7
St Annes Rd PR9 1 F4
St Anne's Rd
Formby L37 9 F6
Huyton-w-R L36 55 F1
Liverpool L17 68 F1
Ormskirk L39 13 D4
Widnes WA8 73 B2
St Anne's (Stanley) JMI Sch L13 54 A3
St Anne St
Birkenhead CH41 66 C8
5 Birkenhead CH41 66 D7
Birkenhead CH41 66 D7
Liverpool L3 52 E3
St Annes Way CH41 66 D7
St Anne Terr CH41 66 C7
St Ann Pl L35 57 C4
St Ann's CE Prim Sch L35 57 C3
St Anns Rd WA10 43 C3
St Anselm's Coll CH43 66 A6
St Anthony of Padua RC Prim Sch L18 68 F4
St Anthony Pl WA2 61 B6
St Anthony's Cl L36 55 C7
St Anthony's Gr L30 27 D3
St Anthony's Rd L23 26 B4
St Anthony's Sh Ctr 5 L5 52 D5
St Asaph Dr WA5 60 E3
St Asaph Gr L30 27 F1
St Augustine of Canterbury RC High Sch WA11 44 E5
St Augustine St 1 L5 52 D5
St Augustine's Way L30 27 E4
St Austel Cl WA5 74 E3
St Austell Cl CH46 49 B1
St Austells Rd L4 38 E2
St Austin's RC Prim Sch
Liverpool L19 81 A7
St Helens WA9 57 D7
St Bartholomew's RC Prim Sch L35 57 E1
St Basil's RC Prim Sch WA8 72 A2
St Bedes Cl L39 13 D3
St Bede's RC High Sch L39 13 D4
St Bede's RC Inf Sch WA8 73 A1
St Bede's RC Jun Sch WA8 73 A1
St Benedicts Coll L19 81 D6
St Benet's RC Prim Sch L30 27 F4
St Benet's Way L30 27 E3
St Bernard's Cl
Litherland L30 27 D3
7 Liverpool L8 68 B7
St Bernard's Dr L30 27 D3
St Brendan's Cl L36 55 C7
St Brides Cl WA5 74 E3
St Bride's Rd CH44 51 D5
St Bride St 10 L8 67 F8
St Bridget's CE Prim Sch CH48 63 B1
St Bridgets Cl WA2 61 F3
St Bridget's Gr L30 27 D3
St Bridget's La CH48 63 B1
St Bridget's RC Prim Sch WA2 61 E3
St Brigid's Cres L5 52 C5
St Brigid's RC Prim Sch L28 55 A7
St Catherines Cl L36 55 E1
St Catherines Gdns CH42 66 D4
St Catherine's Hospl CH42 66 D3
St Catherine's RC Prim Sch WA3 47 E7
St Catherine's Rd L20 38 C3
St Cecilia's RC Inf Sch L13 53 E5
St Cecilia's RC Jun Sch L13 53 E5
St Chad's Dr L32 29 E2
St Chad's Par L32 29 E2
St Charles RC Prim Sch L17 68 C2
St Christopher's Ave L30 27 D4
St Christopher's Dr L36 55 C7
St Christopher's RC Prim Sch L24 82 D5
St Clair Dr PR9 2 A1
St Clares RC Prim Sch L15 68 E6
St Cleopas' CE Jun Mix & Inf Sch L8 67 F4
St Columba's Cl CH44 51 D5
St Columba's RC Prim Sch L36 55 E5
St Cuthbert's Cl
3 Liverpool L12 40 E3
Southport PR9 2 A2
St Cuthbert's RC Com Coll WA9 44 F1
St Cuthbert's RC Prim Sch L13 53 F3
St Cuthbert's Rd PR9 2 A2
St Cyrils Cl L27 70 C6
St Cyrils Ct L27 70 C6
St Damian's Croft L30 27 E3
St David Rd
Bebington CH62 89 A6
Birkenhead CH43 66 A6
St Davids Cl L35 57 C4
St Davids Dr WA5 60 E2
St Davids Gr L30 27 D2
St Davids La CH43 65 D5
St Davids Rd L14 55 B5
St David's Rd 5 L4 53 B6
St Domingo Gr L5 53 A6
St Domingo Rd L5 52 E6
St Domingo Vale L5 53 A6
St Dominic's RC Jun & Inf Sch L14 55 B6
St Dunstan's Gr L30 27 D3
St Edmond's Rd L20 38 C2
St Edmund Arrowsmith RC High Sch
Ashton-in-M WN4 35 B2
Prescot L35 56 F5
St Edmund of Canterbury RC High Sch L14 55 B6
St Edmund's RC Prim Sch WN8 15 F1
St Edmunds Rd CH63 78 F5
St Edmund's & St Thomas' RC Prim Sch L22 26 D1
St Edwards Cl CH41 66 B8
St Edward's Coll L12 54 B5
St Edwards Mews CH41 66 B8
St Elizabeth's RC Prim Sch L21 38 C6
St Elmo Rd CH44 51 D5
SS Peter & Paul RC High Sch WA8 72 F2
SS Peter & Paul's RC Prim Sch L33 29 F5
St Finbar's RC Prim Sch L8 68 A3
St Francis de Sales RC Inf Sch L4 38 E2
St Francis de Sales RC Jun Sch L4 38 E1
St Francis of Assisi RC Prim Sch WN8 24 D7
St Francis of Assisi RC Prim Sch, Garston L19 81 C6
St Francis Xavier's Coll L25 69 F4
St Gabriel's Ave L36 56 A2
St Gabriel's CE Prim Sch L36 56 A2
St George of England Specialist Engineering Coll L20 38 D6
St Georges Ave CH42 66 D2
St George's Ave WA10 43 C5
St Georges Ct L31 28 D8
St George's Ct WA8 84 D8
St Georges Gr
Birkenhead CH46 64 D8
Litherland L30 27 D2
St George's Hill L5 52 F5
St George's Mount CH45 51 B8
St George's Pk CH45 51 B8
St George's Pl
Liverpool L1 90 B4
Southport PR9 4 B7
St George's Prim Sch CH45 50 F5
St George's Prim Sch (Annexe) CH45 50 F6
St George's RC Prim Sch L31 28 D7
St Georges Rd WA10 43 D2
St George's Rd
Formby L37 9 E4
Hightown L38 17 F5
Huyton-w-R L36 55 E5
Wallasey CH45 50 E6
St George's Way
11 Liverpool L1 90 B3
Thornton Hough CH63 87 A7
St Gerard's Cl L5 52 D6
St Gregory's Croft L30 27 E4
St Gregory's RC Prim Sch
Liverpool L27 70 E5
Maghull L31 20 C4
ST HELENS 44 B5
St Helens Central Sta WA10 44 B3
St Helen's Cl CH43 66 B6
St Helens Coll WA10 43 F3
St Helens Coll Newton Campus WA12 46 B4
St Helens Coll (Tech Campus) WA9 44 B4
St Helens Hospl WA9 44 C1
St Helens Junction Sta WA9 58 F7
St Helens Linkway L35, WA9 57 F4
St Helens Rd
Ormskirk L39 14 A2
Prescot L34, WA10 56 E7
Rainford WA11 32 B1
St Helens Ret Pk WA9 44 B3
St Helens RLFC WA10 43 C3
St Hilary Brow CH44 50 F4
St Hilary Dr CH45 50 F5

Shadowbrook Dr L24 82 B7
Shadwell St L5 52 B5
Shaftesbury Ave
Southport PR8 8 A8
Warrington WA5 74 E2
Shaftesbury Gr PR8 4 A1
Shaftesbury Rd
Crosby L23 26 D4
Southport PR8 4 A1
Shaftesbury St L8 67 E6
Shaftesbury Terr L13 54 A3
Shaftesbury Way WA5 59 F7
Shaftsbury Ave L33 29 E5
Shaftway Cl WA11 45 F7
Shakespeare Ave
Birkenhead CH42 66 F1
Kirkby L32 29 D1
Shakespeare Cl L6 53 A4
Shakespeare Gr WA2 61 C2
Shakespeare Rd
Neston CH64 86 E1
St Helens WA9 58 A3
Wallasey CH44 51 D2
Widnes WA8 73 A1
Shakespeare St
Bootle L20 38 A5
Liverpool L19 81 C4
Liverpool L19 81 C5
Southport PR8 4 B5
Shalcombe Cl L26 83 A7
Shaldon Cl 3 L32 41 A8
Shaldon Gr 2 L32 41 A8
Shaldon Rd L32 41 A8
Shaldon Wlk 5 L32 41 A8
Shalem Ct CH63 78 D6
Shalford Gr CH48 63 D2
Shallcross Ct L6 53 A4
Shallcross Pl 1 L6 53 A4
Shallmarsh Cl CH63 78 D5
Shallmarsh Rd CH63 78 D5
Shalom Ct L17, L18 68 E5
Shamrock Rd CH41 65 F7
Shand St L19 81 C4
Shanklin Cl WA5 74 C6
Shanklin Rd L15 53 F1
Shankly Ct L4 53 A7
Shannon Gr WA8 72 E2
Shannon Ho CH46 49 E4
Shannons La L34 41 C1
Shannon St CH41 50 F1
Shard Cl L11 40 B5
Shard St WA9 58 E7
Sharon Sq WN2 35 F8
Sharpeville Cl 9 L4 52 D7
Sharples Cres L23 27 A3
Sharrock St 7 PR8 4 B7
Sharwood Rd L27 70 F4
Shavington Ave CH43 65 F3
Shawbury Ave CH63 78 D7
Shaw Cl L39 8 F6
Shaw Cres L37 10 B3
Shawell Ct WA8 73 E2
Shaw Entry L35, WA8 72 A7
Shaw Hill St L1 90 B4
Shaw La
Birkenhead CH49 64 C2
Haskayne L39 11 E6
Prescot L35 56 E4
Shaw Rd L24 82 D6
Shaws Alley L1 90 B2
Shaw's Ave PR8 4 A1
Shaws Dr CH47 63 D8
Shaws Garth L39 8 F6
Shaw's Rd PR8 4 A1
Shaw St
Ashton-in-M WN4 35 B5
Birkenhead CH41 66 D5
Haydock WA11 45 E6
Hoylake CH47 63 B7
Liverpool L3, L6 52 F3
Runcorn WA7 84 F2
St Helens WA10, WA9 44 B4
Shawton Rd L16 69 D8
Shearman Cl CH61 77 A4
Shearman Rd CH61 77 A4
Shearwater Cl L27 70 F4
Sheen Rd CH45 51 C7
Sheffield Row WA12 60 D8
Sheila Wlk L10 40 B6
Sheilings The WA3 47 F8
Sheil Pl L6 53 C3
Sheil Rd L6 53 C3
Shelagh Ave WA8 73 A1
Sheldon Cl CH63 79 A1
Sheldon Rd L12 54 D8
Shelley Cl L36 56 A1
Shelley Ct L32 40 D8
Shelley Dr L39 13 D6
Shelley Gr
Liverpool L19 81 C5
Southport PR8 4 F6
Shelley Pl L35 56 F3
Shelley Rd WA8 73 A1
Shelley St
Bootle L20 38 B4
St Helens WA9 58 B2
Shelley Way CH48 75 B8
Shellfield Rd PR9 2 A4
SHELL GREEN 73 E1
Shellingford Rd L14 55 A4
Shelmore Dr 5 L8 67 F4
Shelton Cl
Liverpool L13 54 A2
Widnes WA8 73 F3
Shelton Dr PR8 7 A4
Shelton Rd CH45 51 A6
Shenley Cl CH63 78 F6
Shenley Rd L15 69 C8
Shenley Way PR9 2 D5
Shenstone St L7 53 B1
Shenton Ave WA11 44 D6
Shepherd Cl CH49 64 C4
Shepherds Fold Cl 4 L8 68 A6
Shepherd's La L39 12 E5
Shepherd St L6, L7 52 F2
Sheppard Ave L16 70 A8
Shepston Ave 7 L4 39 A1
Shepton Rd L36 55 D6
Sherborne Ave
Litherland L30 27 E4
Liverpool L25 82 D9
Sherborne Rd CH44 50 F5
Sherborne Sq L36 55 E2
Sherbourne Way WA5 59 F6
Sherbrooke Cl L14 54 E4
Sherburn Cl L9 39 D8
Sherdley Bsns Pk WA9 58 B8
Sherdley Park Dr WA9 58 B7
Sherdley Prim Sch WA9 58 C6
Sherdley Rd
St Helens, Peasley Cross WA9 44 B1
St Helens, Sutton Heath WA9 57 F7
St Helens WA9 58 A8
Sherford Cl L27 70 F4
Sheridan Ave WA3 47 D7
Sheridan Pl WA2 61 A5
Sheri Dr WA12 46 E2
Sheriff Cl 3 L5 52 E4
Sheringham Cl
Birkenhead CH49 65 A7
St Helens WA9 44 D3
Sheringham Rd WA5 74 E6
Sherlock Ave WA11 45 E7
Sherlock La CH44 51 A2
Sherman Dr L35 57 D1
Sherrat St WN8 15 D1
Sherringham Rd PR8 3 E2
Sherry Ct L17 68 E5
Sherry La CH49 65 A2
Sherwell Cl L15 54 A1
Sherwood Ave
Ashton-in-M WN4 35 C4
Crosby L23 26 D5
Irby CH61 76 C7
Ormskirk L39 13 C2
Sherwood Cl
Rainhill L35 57 C5
Widnes WA8 72 C1
Sherwood Cres WA5 59 E6
Sherwood Ct
Huyton-w-R L36 55 F2
Liverpool L12 40 F3
Sherwood Dr
Bebington CH63 78 E7
Prescot L35 56 F2
Skelmersdale WN8 16 D3
Sherwood Gr CH47 63 F7
Sherwood Ho PR8 7 C5
Sherwood Lo PR8 3 F5
Sherwood Rd
Crosby L23 26 C5
Hoylake CH47 63 F8
Wallasey CH44 51 C3
Sherwood Row L26 82 E7
Sherwood's La L10 39 F8
Sherwood St L3 52 B4
Sherwyn Rd L4 53 C8
Shetland Cl
Warrington WA2 61 E4
Widnes WA8 73 E3
Shetland Dr CH62 88 E8
Shevington Cl
St Helens WA9 58 C7
Widnes WA8 73 E3
Shevington's La L33 29 E6
Shevington Wlk WA8 73 E3
Shewell Cl CH42 66 D4
Shiel Rd CH45 51 B7
Shimmin St L7 53 A1
Shipley Wlk L24 82 D5
Shipton Cl
Birkenhead CH43 65 E1
Liverpool L19 81 B8
Widnes WA8 72 D3
Shirdley Ave L32 40 F7
Shirdley Cres PR8 7 C3
SHIRDLEY HILL 8 F6
Shirdley Wlk L32 40 F7
Shirebourne Ave WA11 44 B7
Shireburn Rd L37 9 D5
Shiregreen 6 WA9 58 C6
Shires The WA10 43 F2
Shirewell Rd WN5 25 E5
Shirley Rd L19 81 C8
Shirley St CH44 51 E3
Shirwell Gr WA9 58 C4
Shobdon Cl L12 40 F4
Shop La L31 20 C1
Shop Rd L34 41 C4
Shore Bank CH62 79 C8
Shore Dr CH62 79 C6
Shorefields CH62 79 C7
Shorefields Ho CH62 79 C7
Shorefields Sch L8 68 A3
Shorefields Village L8 67 F3
Shore Rd
Birkenhead CH41 66 E7
Birkenhead CH41 66 F7
Seaforth L21 37 F5
Southport PR8 7 B6
West Kirby CH48 75 C7
Shore Road Pumping Sta Mus* CH41 66 F7
Shoreside Prim Sch PR8 7 B4
Short Cl WA12 45 E3
Shortfield Rd CH49 65 A4
Shortfield Way CH49 65 A4
Short St
Golborne WA3 36 B1
Haydock WA11 45 E6
Newton-le-W WA12 45 E3
Shortwood Rd L14 54 F3
Shorwell Cl WA5 74 C7
Shottesbrook Gn L11 39 F3
Shrewsbury Ave
Aintree L10 28 D2
Crosby L22 26 D3
Shrewsbury Cl 3 CH43 65 F6
Shrewsbury Dr CH49 65 A6
Shrewsbury Mews L25 82 D9
Shrewsbury Pl L19 81 C6
Shrewsbury Rd
Birkenhead CH43, CH41 66 A5
Heswall CH60 77 A1
Liverpool L19 81 C6
Wallasey CH44 50 F5
West Kirby CH48 63 A1
Shrewton Rd L25 70 B7
Shropshire Cl L30 28 A4
Shropshire Gdns WA10 43 F2
Shuttle Hillock Rd WN2 36 F7
Sibford Rd L12 54 D5
Sibley Ave WN4 35 D4
Siddall St WA10 43 F7
Siddeley Dr WA12 45 F4
Siddeley St L17 68 C3
Sidgreave St WA10 43 E3
Siding La
Kirkby L33 30 C7
Rainford WA11 23 C1
Sidings The CH42 66 F2
Sidlaw Ave WA9 44 F3
Sidmouth Cl
St Helens WA10 43 C6
Warrington WA5 74 E4
Sidney Ave CH45 51 A8
Sidney Cl CH64 86 F1
Sidney Ct CH42 66 E4
Sidney Pl L7 68 A8
Sidney Powell Ave L32 29 C2
Sidney Rd
Birkenhead CH42 66 E4
Bootle L20 38 D2
Neston CH64 86 F1
Southport PR9 4 F8
Sidney St
Birkenhead CH41 66 E7
St Helens WA10 43 D4
Sidwell St L19 81 C5
Sienna Cl L27 70 C6
Signal Works Rd L9, L10 39 E8
Silcock St WA3 36 A1
Silcroft Rd L32 40 E8
Silkstone Cl
Liverpool L7 68 B8
St Helens WA10 43 D3
Silkstone St WA10 43 D3
Silver Ave WA11 45 A5
Silverbeech Ave L18 69 B4
Silverbeech Rd CH44 51 C3
Silverbirch Gdns CH44 50 E5
Silver Birch Gr WN4 35 A5
Silver Birch Way L31 20 B5
Silverbrook Rd L27 70 D7
Silverburn Ave CH46 49 E1
Silverdale PR8 3 E4
Silverdale Ave L13 53 E5
Silverdale Cl L36 70 E8
Silverdale Ct PR8 4 E4
Silverdale Dr L21 38 D8
Silverdale Gr WA11 44 A8
Silverdale Rd
Bebington CH63 78 F7
Birkenhead CH43 66 A4
Newton-le-W WA12 46 B4
Silverlake Cl L9 39 A3
Silverlea Ave CH45 51 B5
Silver Leigh L17 68 D1
Silverlime Gdns L35 57 C7
Silverstone Dr L36 70 D8
Silverstone Gr L31 20 B4
Silverthorne Dr PR9 1 F1
Silverton Rd L17 80 E8
Silverwell Rd L11 40 D5
Silverwell Wlk L11 40 D5
Silvester St L5 52 D5
Simms Ave WA9 44 E3
SIMM'S LANE END 34 B5
Simm's Rd L6 53 D6
Simnel Cl L25 70 B6
Simon Ct CH48 63 A2
Simonsbridge CH48 75 D6
Simons Cl L35 71 D8
Simon's Croft L30 27 C3
Simonside WA8 72 C2
Simonstone Gr 5 WA9 58 D7
Simonswood Ind Pk L33 30 B6
Simonswood La
Kirkby L33 30 A2
Royal Oak L39 21 F3
Simonswood Prim Sch L33 29 F2
Simonswood Wlk L33 30 A2
Simpkin St WN2 36 C8
Simpson St
Birkenhead CH41 66 D6
Liverpool L1 90 B1
Sim St L3 52 E3
Sinclair Ave
Prescot L35 56 F5
Warrington WA2 61 B2
Widnes WA8 84 F8
Sinclair Cl L35 56 F6
Sinclair Dr L18 69 B6
Sinclair St L19 81 C4
Sineacre La L33, L39 30 E8
Singleton Ave
Birkenhead CH42 66 C3
St Helens WA11 44 D5
Singleton Dr L34 41 D3
Sir Alfred Jones Meml Hospl L19 81 C6
Sirdar Cl L7 68 B8
Sir Howard St 13 L8 67 F8
Sir Howard Way 14 L8 67 F8
Sir Thomas St L1 90 B4
Siskin Cl WA12 46 C3
Siskin Gn L25 70 A4
Sisters Way CH41 66 D6
Sixpenny La L37 7 D1
Sixth Ave
Aintree L9 39 D7
Liverpool, Fazakerley L9 39 D7
Skeffington L35 56 E2
Skelhorne St L1, L3 90 C3
SKELMERSDALE 16 A1
Skelmersdale Coll (Westbank Campus)
Skelmersdale WN8 16 B1
Skelmersdale WN8 24 B8
Skelmersdale Rd L39, WN8 23 B7
Skelmersdale Sports Ctr WN8 24 C7
Skelton Cl WA11 44 A7
Skelton St WN4 34 F6
Skerries Rd L4 53 A7
Skiddaw Rd CH62 79 E2
Skipton Ave PR9 2 C6
Skipton Rd
Huyton-w-R L36 56 B3
Liverpool L4 53 B7
Skirving Pl L5 52 D6
Skirving St L5 52 E6
Skye Cl WA8 73 E3
Sky Lark Rise WA9 45 A3
Slackey La PR9 2 C4
Slag La
Golborne WA3 36 F2
Haydock WA11 45 B7
Slaidburn Cres
Golborne WA3 35 F2
Southport PR9 2 B5
Slaidburn Ind Est PR9 2 B5
Slate La WN8 15 C2
Slater Pl L1 90 B2
Slater St L1 90 B2
Slatey Rd CH43 66 B5
Sleaford Rd L14 55 B6
Sleepers Hill L4 52 F7
Slessor Ave CH48 63 D3
Slim Rd L36 55 E3
Slingsby Dr CH49 65 A4
Small Ave WA2 61 C2
Small Cres WA2 61 C2
Small La
Ormskirk, Clieves Hills L39 13 A3
Ormskirk L39 13 F4
Small La S L39 12 D6
Smallridge Cl CH61 76 E4
Smallshaw Cl WN4 35 A2
Smallwoods Mews CH60 76 E1
Smeaton St L4 38 E1
Smethurst Hall Pk WN5 25 C2
Smethurst Rd WN5 25 C2
Smilie Ave CH46 49 C1
Smith Ave CH41 66 B8
Smithdown Gr L7 68 B8
Smithdown La L7 53 A1
Smithdown Pl 5 L15 69 A5
Smithdown Prim Sch L7 68 B8
Smithdown Rd L15, L7 68 D7
Smith Dr L20 38 E5
Smithfield St
Liverpool L2, L3 90 A4
St Helens WA9 44 D2
Smithford Wlk L36 71 B7
Smith Pl L5 52 D6
Smith Rd WA8 84 F7
Smith St
Liverpool L5 52 E6
2 Prescot L34 56 E6
Skelmersdale WN8 15 D1
St Helens WA9 58 E7
Smithy Brow WA3 61 F7
Smithy Cl
Cronton WA8 72 C5
Formby L37 10 B4
Smithy Glen Dr WN5 25 E4
Smithy Gn L37 10 B4
Smithy Hey CH48 63 C2
Smithy Hill CH63 87 A6
Smithy La
Aughton L39 21 A6
Cronton WA8 72 C5
Haskayne L39 12 A6
Smithystone Cl L15 69 A7
Smock La WN4 34 C4
Smollett St
Bootle L20 38 B6
Liverpool L7 53 B2
Smugglers Way CH45 50 E8
Smythe Croft PR9 2 A2
Smyth Rd WA8 73 D2
Snaefell Ave L13 53 E5
Snaefell Gr L13 53 E5
Snape Gn PR8 5 E1
SNAPE GREEN 5 E1
Snave Cl L21 38 B5
Snowberry Cl WA8 73 E4
Snowberry Rd L14 55 A7
Snowden Rd CH46 64 C8
Snowdon Cl WA5 74 E6
Snowdon Gr WA9 58 C7
Snowdon La L5 52 C5
Snowdon Rd CH42 66 D2
Snowdrop Ave CH41 65 F7
Snowdrop Mews L21 38 B6
Snowdrop St L5 52 D7
Soane Cl WN4 35 D3
Soho Pl L3 52 E3
Soho St L3 52 E3
Solar Rd L9 39 B6
Solly Ave CH42 66 E2
Solomon St L7 53 B2
Solway Cl
Ashton-in-M WN4 35 A4
Warrington WA2 61 F4
Solway St E L8 68 B7
Solway St W L8 68 B7
Solway St CH41 51 A1
Soma Ave L21 38 C8
Somerford Ho 9 L23 26 B3
Somerford Rd L14 55 A4
Somerford Wlk WA8 73 E3
Somerley Cl L12 54 D8
Somerset Dr PR8 7 C3
Somerset Pl L6 53 D5
Somerset Rd
Bootle L20 38 D4
Crosby L22 26 C2
Heswall CH61 76 E4
Wallasey CH45 50 E5
West Kirby CH48 63 C3
Somerset St WA9 44 D2
Somerton St L15 68 E8
Somerville CH44 51 C3
Somerville Cl CH63 88 B6
Somerville Gr L22 26 D2
Somerville Prim Sch CH44 51 D3
Somerville Rd
Crosby L22 26 D2
Widnes WA8 84 D8
Sommer Ave L12 54 A7
Sonning Ave L21 27 B1
Sonning Rd L4 39 D2
Sorany Cl L23 27 B6
Sorogold St WA9 44 C3
Sorrel Cl CH43 65 D5
Sougher's La WN4 34 F7
Sougher's Lane End WN4 34 E6
South Albert Rd L17 68 C4
South Ave
Golborne WN7 36 F4
Prescot L34 56 C5
South Bank CH43 66 B3
Southbank Rd PR8 4 C5
South Bank Rd
Liverpool, Elm Park L7 53 D2
Liverpool, Grassendale L19 81 B7
South Bank Terr WA7 84 F3
South Barcombe Rd L16 69 E7
South Boundary Rd L33 41 C8
Southbourne Rd CH45 50 D5
Southbrook Rd L27 70 C7
Southbrook Way L27 70 C6
South Cantril Ave L12 54 F7
South Chester St L8 67 F6
Southcroft 7 L33 29 E4
Southcroft Rd CH45 50 D5
South Dale WA5 74 F5
Southdale Rd
Birkenhead CH42 66 E2
Liverpool L15 68 F8
Southdean Rd L14 55 B6
SOUTHDENE 40 E8
South Dr
Birkenhead CH49 65 A6
Heswall CH60 86 A7
Irby CH61 76 C5
Liverpool, Sandfield Park L12 54 B5
Liverpool, Victoria Park L15 69 A8
Southern Cres L8 67 E5
Southern Rd
Liverpool L24 82 E3
Southport PR8 4 A6
Southern's La WA11 32 A6
Southey Cl WA8 84 F8
Southey Gr L31 28 D6
Southey Rd WA10 57 C8
Southey St
Bootle L20 38 B4
Liverpool L15 68 E7
South Ferry Quay L3 67 D5
Southfield Rd L9 38 F6

Tatton Rd
Birkenhead CH42 66 D5
Liverpool L9 39 A6
Taunton Ave WA9 58 D5
Taunton Dr L10 28 F2
Taunton Rd
Huyton-w-R L36 56 B2
Wallasey CH45 50 E6
Taunton St L15 68 E8
Taurus Pk WA5 60 D3
Taurus Rd L14 55 A4
Tavener Cl CH63 88 C5
Tavington Rd L26 71 A1
Tavistock Dr PR8 7 B6
Tavistock Rd
Wallasey CH45 50 E6
Warrington WA5 74 E4
Tavlin Ave WA5 60 F1
Tavy Rd L6 53 A4
TAWD BRIDGE 24 B7
Tawd Rd WN8 24 C8
Tawd St L4 52 E8
TAWD VALLEY PARK 16 A2
Taylforth Cl L9 39 A5
Taylor Ave L39 14 A5
Taylor Cl WA9 58 E8
Taylor Rd WA11 45 F7
Taylors Cl L4 38 E3
Taylors La L9 38 F3
Taylor's La WA5 74 A2
Taylor St
Birkenhead CH41 66 E7
Golborne WN3 36 C1
Liverpool L5 52 E5
Skelmersdale WN8 15 C1
St Helens WA9 58 E8
Widnes WA8 73 C1
Taylor Street Heritage Ctr* CH41 66 E7
Taylor Street Ind Est L5 52 E5
Teakwood Cl L6 53 B5
Teal Cl
Ormskirk L39 13 C2
St Helens WA11 44 B6
Warrington WA2 61 E3
Teal Gr L26 70 E1
Teals Way CH60 85 E8
Tears La WN8 15 F8
Teasville Rd L18 69 E4
Tebay Cl L31 20 F2
Tebay Rd CH62 88 E8
Teck St L7 53 A2
Tedburn Cl L25 70 C4
Tedbury Cl L32 40 E8
Tedbury Wlk L32 40 E8
Tedder Ave PR9 5 A7
Tedder Sq WA8 84 D8
Teehey Cl CH63 78 D6
Teehey Gdns CH63 78 D6
Teehey La CH63 78 D6
Tees Cl L4 38 D1
Teesdale Cl WA5 74 F7
Teesdale Rd
Bebington CH63 78 E4
Haydock WA11 45 C7
Tees Pl L4 38 D1
Tees St
Liverpool L4 38 E1
Wallasey CH41 50 F1
Teigh Cl L6 53 A4
Teilo St L8 68 A5
Telary Cl L5 52 C5
Telegraph Ho 3 L23 26 E5
Telegraph Rd
Heswall CH60 86 A7
Irby CH48, CH60, CH61 76 C4
West Kirby CH48 75 F7
Telegraph Way L32 29 E2
Telford Cl
Birkenhead CH43 66 B4
Widnes WA8 72 D4
Telford Ct L7 53 B1
Telford Dr WA9 58 F7
Tempest Hey L2 90 A4
Temple Ct L2 90 A3
Temple La L2 90 A3
Templemartin 2 WN8 15 F2
Templemore Ave L18 69 A3
Templemore Rd CH43 66 A4
Temple Rd CH42 66 C2
Temple Sq 6 L2 90 A4
Temple St L2 90 A4
Templeton Cres L12 40 B1
Tenbury Cl WA5 60 A1
Tenbury Dr WN4 35 A4
Tenby 2 WN8 15 E2
Tenby Ave L21 27 A1
Tenby Cl WA5 60 C2
Tenby Dr CH46 64 F8
Tenby St 5 L5 53 A6
Tennis St N WA10 43 E5
Tennis St WA10 43 E5
Tennyson Ave 3 CH42 66 F1
Tennyson Dr
Longshaw WN5 25 D1
Ormskirk L39 13 D6
Warrington WA2 61 C2
Tennyson Rd
Huyton-w-R L36 71 A8
Widnes WA8 73 A1
Tennyson St
Bootle L20 38 B5
St Helens WA9 58 B2
Tennyson Way L32 29 D1
Tensing Rd L31 20 D1
Tenterden St L5 52 D4
Tenth Ave L9 39 D7
Terence Rd L16 69 D6
Terminus Rd
Bebington CH62 79 D3
Huyton-w-R L36 55 C5
Tern Cl
Kirkby L33 29 E7
Widnes WA8 73 B4
Ternhall Rd L9 39 F4
Ternhall Way L9 39 F4
Tern Way
St Helens WA10 57 A7
Wallasey CH46 49 B1
Terret Croft L28 55 B7
Tetbury St CH41 66 C5
Tetlow St L4 52 F8
Tetlow Way L4 52 F8
Teulon Cl 1 L4 52 F7
Teversham WN8 15 F2
Teviot 5 WN8 15 E2
Tewit Hall Cl L24 82 C4
Tewit Hall Rd L24 82 C4
Tewkesbury 4 WN8 15 E2
Tewkesbury Cl
Liverpool, Croxteth L12 40 F4
Liverpool L25 70 D2
Tewkesbury Rd WA3 47 B8
Teynham Ave L34 41 D4
Teynham Cres L11 39 F2
Thackeray Cl L8 67 F6
Thackeray Ct 7 L8 67 F6
Thackeray Gdns L30 38 D8
Thackeray Sq L8 67 F6
Thackeray St 8 L8 67 F6
Thackray Rd WA10 57 D8
Thames Cl WA2 61 D2
Thames Dr WN5 25 F7
Thames Rd WA9 58 C6
Thames St L8 68 B6
Thanet WN8 15 F2
Thatchers Mount WA5 45 D1
THATTO HEATH 57 E8
Thatto Heath Com Prim Sch WA9 57 E8
Thatto Heath Rd WA10, WA9 57 D8
Thatto Heath Sta WA9 57 D8
Thealby Cl WN8 15 E2
Thermal Rd CH62 79 E4
Thetford Rd WA5 74 E6
Thickwood Moss La WA11 32 A5
THINGWALL 77 B5
Thingwall Ave L14 54 D3
Thingwall Dr CH61 77 A6
Thingwall Grange CH61 77 B6
Thingwall Hall Dr L14 54 D2
Thingwall La L14 54 E3
Thingwall Prim Sch CH61 77 A6
Thingwall Rd
Irby CH61 76 E6
Liverpool L15 69 B8
Thingwall Rd E CH61 77 A7
Third Ave
Aintree L9 39 D7
Birkenhead CH43 65 B6
Crosby L23 26 D4
Liverpool, Fazakerley L9 39 E7
Thirlmere Ave
Abram WN2 36 B8
Ashton-in-M WN4 35 C4
Birkenhead CH43 65 C5
Bootle L21 38 D8
Formby L37 10 A2
1 Orrell WN5 25 F7
St Helens WA11 44 B8
Up Holland WN8 25 B7
Warrington WA2 61 C3
Thirlmere Cl L31 20 E2
Thirlmere Ct L5 53 A5
Thirlmere Dr
Bootle L21 38 D8
Southport PR8 7 B3
Wallasey CH45 51 B5
Thirlmere Gn L5 53 A5
Thirlmere Rd
Golborne WA3 36 C1
Hightown L38 18 A4
Liverpool L5 53 A5
Thirlmere Way WA8 84 C8
Thirlmere Wlk L33 29 D4
Thirlstane St 2 L17 68 B3
Thirsk WN8 15 E2
Thistledown Cl 3 L17 68 A3
Thistleton Ave CH41 65 F8
Thistleton Mews 3 PR9 4 C8
Thistlewood Rd L7 53 E2
Thistley Hey Rd L32 29 F2
Thomas Cl L19 81 C5
Thomas Ct L14 54 D3
Thomas Dr
Liverpool L14 54 C2
Prescot L35 56 C4
Thomas Gray Prim Sch
Bootle L20 38 B4
Bootle L20 38 B5
Thomas La
Liverpool, Broad Green L14 54 D2
Liverpool L1 90 A3
Thomas St
Birkenhead CH41 66 E5
7 Birkenhead CH41 66 E6
Golborne WA3 47 A8
Thomaston St L5 52 E6
Thomas Winder Ct L5 52 D6
Thompson Ave L39 14 B5
Thompson Cl WA12 46 C1
Thompson St
Ashton-in-M WN4 35 D4
Birkenhead CH41 66 E4
St Helens WA10 43 D1
Thomson Rd L21 38 A7
Thomson St L6 53 B4
Thorburn Cl CH62 79 B8
Thorburn Cres CH62 79 B8
Thorburn Ct CH62 67 B1
Thorburn Lo CH62 67 B1
Thorburn Rd CH62 79 B8
Thorburn St L7 53 B1
Thorley Cl L15 54 A1
Thornaby Gr WA9 57 D6
Thornbeck Ave L38 17 F3
Thornbeck Cl 3 L12 40 F3
Thornber 1 WN8 15 F2
Thornbridge Ave L21 38 D8
Thornbrook Cl L12 54 D7
Thornbury WN8 15 F2
Thornbury Ave WA3 47 E7
Thornbury Rd L4 53 C7
Thornbush Cl WA3 36 E1
Thornby 3 WN8 15 F2
Thorn Cl WA5 74 F3
Thorncliffe Rd CH44 51 A3
Thorncroft Dr CH61 77 B4
Thorndale 4 WN8 15 F2
Thorndale Rd L22 26 D2
Thorndyke Cl L35 57 E1
Thornes Rd 11 L6 53 B3
Thorness Cl CH49 64 C2
Thorneycroft St CH41 66 A8
Thornfield Cl WA3 47 C8
Thornfield Hey CH63 79 A2
Thornfield Rd
Crosby L23 27 A6
Liverpool L9 38 F5
Thornham Ave WA9 58 C8
Thornham Cl CH49 65 A7
Thornhead La L12 54 D6
Thornhill L39 21 B8
Thornhill Cl L39 21 B8
Thornhill Rd
Garswood WN4 34 C4
Liverpool L15 69 A7
Thornhills WA8 72 A3
Thornholme Cres L11 40 A1
Thornhurst L32 40 E7
Thornleigh Ave CH62 88 F3
Thornley Rd CH46 64 C7
Thorn Rd WA10 43 C3
Thornridge CH46 65 A8
Thorns Dr CH49 64 C2
Thornside Wlk L25 70 B4
Thorns The L31 20 B2
THORNTON 27 B6
Thornton
Skelmersdale WN8 15 F2
Widnes WA8 84 E8
Thornton Ave
Bebington CH63 78 D8
Bootle L20 38 D7
Thornton Cl WN4 34 F4
Thornton Common Rd CH63 87 D7
Thornton Cres CH60 86 B6
Thorntondale Dr WA5 74 F7
Thornton Gr CH63 78 D8
Thornton Ho CH63 87 B6
THORNTON HOUGH 87 A7
Thornton Hough Prim Sch CH63 87 B7
Thornton Prim Sch L23 27 B6
Thornton Rd
Bebington CH63 78 D8
Bootle L20 38 C5
Liverpool L16 54 F1
Southport PR9 4 F7
4 Wallasey CH45 51 A6
Thornton St
Birkenhead CH41 66 A8
Bootle L21 38 B6
Thorntree Cl L17 68 A3
Thorn Tree Cl L24 83 E2
Thornvale WN2 36 C7
Thornwood WN8 15 F2
Thornwood Cl 4 L6 53 B5
Thornycroft Rd L15 68 D7
Thorpe WN8 15 F2
Thorpe Bank CH42 78 F8
Thorstone Dr CH61 76 C7
Thorsway
Birkenhead CH42 66 F2
West Kirby CH48 75 D8
Threadneedle Ct WA9 58 F8
Three Acres Cl L25 69 E3
Three Butt La L12, L13 54 A7
Three Lanes End CH48 64 B5
Three Pools PR9 2 C3
Three Sisters Rd WN4 35 B7
Three Sisters Recn Area* WN4 35 C7
Three Tuns La L37 9 F3
Threlfall's La PR9 1 F2
Threlfall St L8 68 A4
Thresher Ave 4 CH49 64 C4
Threshers The L30 28 A4
Throne Rd L11 40 C3
Throne Wlk 2 L11 40 C4
Thurcroft Dr WN8 15 E2
Thurlby Cl WN4 35 D4
Thurlow WA3 47 E7
Thurne Way L25 70 A6
Thurnham St L6 53 C5
Thursby Cl
2 Kirkby L32 40 F8
Southport PR8 7 B3
Thursby Cres 1 L32 40 F8
Thursby Rd CH62 79 E2
Thursby Wlk 3 L32 40 F8
THURSTASTON 76 A5
Thurstaston Rd
Heswall CH60 85 F8
Irby CH61 76 C6
Thurston WN8 15 E2
Thurston Rd L4 53 B6
Tibbs Cross La WA8 73 D8
Tichbourne Way 2 L6 53 B5
Tickle Ave WA9 44 E3
Tideswell Cl L7 68 B8
Tide Way CH45 50 E8
Tilbrook Dr WA9 58 D6
Tilcroft WN8 15 E2
Tillotson Cl L8 67 E5
Tilney St L9 39 A6
Tilstock Ave CH62 79 B8
Tilstock Cl L26 71 A2
Tilstock Cres CH43 65 F2
Tilston Cl L9 39 D3
Tilston Rd
Kirkby L32 29 C2
Liverpool L9 39 D4
6 Wallasey CH45 51 A6
Time Pk L35 56 F5
Timmis Cres WA8 73 A1
Timms Cl L37 9 F5
Timms La L37 9 F5
Timon Ave L20 38 E5
Timor Ave WA9 57 E8
Timpron St L7 68 C8
Timway Dr L12 54 E8
Tinas Way CH49 65 A5
Tinling Cl 3 L34 56 E6
Tinsley Ave PR8 4 E3
Tinsley Cl L26 70 E2
Tinsley's La PR8 5 A1
Tinsley St 4 L4 53 A7
Tintagel WN8 15 E2
Tintagel Rd L11 40 D5
Tintern Ave WN4 35 D3
Tintern Cl WA5 60 E2
Tintern Dr
Birkenhead CH46 64 E8
Formby L37 10 B2
Tiptree Cl L12 40 F4
Titchfield St L3, L5 52 D4
Tithebarn Cl CH60 85 F7
Tithebarn Dr CH64 86 B2
Tithebarn Gr L15 69 A7
Tithebarn La
Kirkby, Melling L31 29 A5
Kirkby, Westvale L32 29 D1
Tithebarn Rd
Crosby L23 26 F4
Garswood WN4 34 D2
Knowsley L34 41 D4
Southport PR8 4 E6
Tithebarn St
Liverpool L2, L3 90 A4
Up Holland WN8 25 B7
Titherington Way L15 68 D6
Tiverton Ave
Skelmersdale WN8 15 E2
1 Wallasey CH44 51 B4
Tiverton Cl
Huyton-w-R L36 56 B3
Widnes WA8 72 C3
Tiverton Rd L26 82 E7
Tiverton Sq WA5 74 E4
Tiverton St L15 68 E8
Tivoli Villa's CH45 37 C1
Tobermory Cl WA11 45 A5
Tobin Cl L3 52 C4
Tobin St CH44 51 D4
Tobruk Rd L36 55 D4
Todd Rd WA9 44 B3
Toft Cl WA8 72 F1
Toft St L7 53 C2
Toftwood Ave L35 57 D1
Toftwood Gdns L35 57 D1
Tokenspire Pk L33 41 B8
Toleman Ave CH63 79 A5
TOLL BAR 43 C1
Toll Bar Cnr CH62 79 B7
Toll Bar Pl WA2 61 A4
Toll Bar Rd WA2 61 A3
Tollemache Rd CH41 65 E7
Tollemache St CH45 37 C1
Tollerton Rd L12 54 A7
Tolpuddle Rd L25 69 F2
Tolpuddle Way L4 52 D8
Tolver Ho 4 WA10 44 A4
Tolver St WA10 44 A4
Tom Mann Cl L3 52 D3
Tonbridge Cl L24 82 B5
Tonbridge Dr L10 28 D3
Tongbarn WN8 15 E2
TONTINE 25 D5
Tontine WN5 25 C5
Tontine Mkt WA10 44 A3
Tontine Rd WN5, WN8 25 C6
Toothill Cl WN4 35 B5
Top Acre Rd WN8 24 C7
Topaz Cl L4 38 E2
Topcliffe Gr L12 41 A3
Topgate Cl CH60 86 B8
Topham Dr L9 28 B1
Topsham Cl L25 70 C4
Torcross Cl PR9 2 A5
Torcross Way
Halewood L26 70 F1
Liverpool, Gateacre L25 70 C4
Tordelow Cl L6 53 A4
Toronto St CH44 51 E3
Torquay Dr WN5 33 E8
Torr Dr CH62 89 A7
Torrington Dr
Heswall CH61 77 B7
Liverpool L26 82 E7
Torrington Gdns CH61 77 B7
Torrington Rd
Liverpool L19 81 B7
Wallasey CH44, CH45 51 A4
Torrisholme Rd L9 39 D3
Torr St L5 52 E6
Torus Rd L13 54 A4
Tor View Rd L15 69 A6
Torwood CH43 65 D6
Totland Cl
Liverpool L27 70 F4
Warrington WA5 74 C7
Totnes Ave L26 70 F1
Totnes Dr PR9 2 A5
Totnes Rd L11 40 C5
Tourney Gn WA5 60 A2
Towcester St L21 38 B6
Tower Bldg L3 52 B1
Tower Bldgs 11 PR9 4 C8
Tower Coll L35 57 D1
Tower Dene Sch PR9 1 F2
Tower End L37 9 C5
Tower Gdns L3 90 A3
TOWER HILL 29 F5
Tower Hill
Birkenhead CH42 66 D3
Ormskirk L39 14 A5
Tower Hill Rd WN8 25 B6
Towerlands St L7 53 B1
Tower Nook WN8 25 A5
Tower Prom CH45 37 C1
Tower Quays CH41 66 E8
Tower Rd
Birkenhead CH41 66 E8
Birkenhead, Devonshire Park CH42 66 D3
Birkenhead, Prenton CH42 66 B1
Tower Rd N CH60 76 F2
Tower Rd S CH60 76 F1
Towers Ave L31 20 C2
Towers Rd L16 69 C6
Tower St L3 67 E4
Towers The CH42 66 D2
Tower Way L25 70 A3
Tower Wharf CH41 66 E8
TOWN CENTRE 16 C1
Towneley Ct WA8 73 A1
TOWN END 72 C6
Town End Cl L39 13 D4
Townfield Ave WN4 35 B2
Townfield Cl CH43 65 E3
Townfield Ct CH43 66 A4
Townfield Ctr CH43 65 E3
Townfield Gdns CH63 78 F7
Townfield La
Bebington CH63 78 F7
Birkenhead CH43 65 F3
Townfield Prim Sch CH43 65 E3
Townfield Rd CH48 63 B2
Townfields WN4 35 A3
Town Fields 2 CH45 50 E6
Towngate Bsns Ctr WA8 84 B7
TOWN GREEN
Ashton-in-Makerfield 35 C4
Ormskirk 21 D7
Town Green Ct L39 21 C8
Town Green Gdns L39 21 C8
Town Green La L39 21 C8
Town Green Sta L39 21 C8
Town La
Bebington CH63 78 E7
Hale L24, WA8 83 E2
Southport PR8 4 E3
Town Lane Inf Sch CH63 78 E6
Town Lane (Kew) PR8 4 E3
Town Meadow La CH46 49 C1
TOWN OF LOWTON 47 B5
Town Rd CH42 66 E3
Town Row L12 54 B6
Townsend Ave L11, L4 39 E2
Townsend La L13, L6 53 C6
Townsend St
Liverpool L5 52 C6
Wallasey CH41 50 F1
Townsend View
Litherland L21 27 B2
Liverpool L11 39 E3
Townsfield La WA2 61 A5
Townshend Ave CH61 76 D4
Town View 13 CH41, CH43 66 C5
Town View Mews 14 CH43 66 C5
Towson St L5 52 F6
TOXTETH 67 E5
Toxteth Com Coll L7 67 F8
Toxteth Gr L8 68 A4
Toxteth St L8 67 F5
Tracks La WN5 25 D3
Tracy Dr WA12 46 E3
Tradewind Sq L1 90 B2
Trafalgar Ave CH44 51 D5
Trafalgar Ct PR8 3 F3

Waywell Cl WA2 61 F3
Weardale Rd L15 68 E6
Wearhead Cl WA3 46 F7
Weasdale Cl WA9 58 D7
Weates Cl WA8 73 F3
Weatherhead High Sch & Media Arts Coll CH44 50 F3
Weaver Ave
  Kirkby L33 29 F6
  Rainhill L35 57 C3
Weaver Ct L25 70 C3
Weaver Gr WA9 45 A3
Weaver Ho L25 70 C3
Weaver Ind Est L19 81 C3
Weavers La L31 28 F6
Weaver St L4 38 F3
Webb Cl 8 L7 53 C1
Webb Dr WA5 59 F6
Webber Rd L33 30 C1
Webb St
  Liverpool L7 68 C7
  St Helens WA9 44 D1
Webster Ave
  Bootle L20 38 E4
  Wallasey CH44 51 D6
Webster Dr L32 29 E2
Webster Rd L15, L7 68 D7
Websters Holt CH49 64 F6
Webster St
  Bootle L21 38 C6
  Liverpool L3 90 B4
Wedge Ave WA11 45 A5
Wedgewood Gdns WA9 57 C6
Wedgewood St L7 53 B2
Wedgwood Dr WA8 73 B4
Wednesbury Dr WA5 74 F6
Weedon Ave WA12 46 B5
Weightman Gr 4 L9 39 A6
Weirside WA9 58 D6
Welbeck Ave
  Liverpool L18 68 F5
  Newton-le-W WA12 46 D2
Welbeck Ct 3 L22 26 D1
Welbeck Rd
  Ashton-in-M WN4 35 C4
  Southport PR8 4 A4
Welbeck Terr PR8 4 A4
Welbourne WN8 15 D1
Welbourne Rd L16 54 C1
Welburn Cl WN5 25 E5
Weldale Ho 5 PR8 3 F4
Weld Blundell Ave L31 20 B5
Weld Dr L37 9 D4
Weldon Dr L39 13 F4
Weldon St L4 38 F2
Weld Par 2 PR8 3 F4
Weld Rd
  Crosby L23 26 C3
  Southport PR8 3 F5
Welfield Pl L8 68 A4
Welford Ave
  Birkenhead CH43 65 F2
  Golborne WA3 47 C7
Welland Cl L26 82 E7
Welland Rd
  Ashton-in-M WN4 35 E5
  Bebington CH63 78 D5
Wellbank Dr L26 71 A1
Wellbrae Cl CH49 64 D5
Wellbrook Cl L24 82 D5
Wellbrooke Cl WN4 35 C3
Wellbrook Gn L24 82 D4
Well Brow Rd L4 39 A2
Wellcroft Rd L36 55 F4
Wellcross Rd WN8 25 B6
Weller St L8 67 F5
Weller Way 6 L8 68 A4
Wellesbourne Com Prim Sch L11 39 F2
Wellesbourne Pl L11 40 A2
Wellesbourne Rd L11 40 A3
Wellesley Cl WA12 46 B5
Wellesley Gr CH63 79 A6
Wellesley Rd
  Liverpool L8 68 A4
  Wallasey CH44 51 B4
Wellfarm Cl L9 39 D3
Wellfield
  Rainford WA11 32 A4
  Widnes WA8 73 A3
Wellfield Ave L32 29 F1
Wellfield La L40 14 C3
Wellfield Rd L9 39 A4
Wellgreen Rd L25 70 A7
Wellgreen Wlk L25 70 A7
Wellington Ave L15 68 E7
Wellington Cl
  Aintree L10 28 C3
  Bebington CH63 79 A6
  Newton-le-W WA12 46 A3
  Skelmersdale WN8 24 E8
  Warrington WA2 61 F2
Wellington Ct CH43 66 A4
Wellington Fields L15 68 D6
Wellington Gate L24 83 E2
Wellington Gdns
  5 Crosby L22 26 D1
  Newton-le-W WA12 46 A3
Wellington Gr L15 68 F8
Wellington Rd
  Bebington CH63 79 A6
  Birkenhead CH43 66 A4
  Bootle L21 38 A7
  Liverpool L8 67 F4
  Liverpool, Wavertree L15 68 E7
  Wallasey CH45 37 A1
Wellington St
  Crosby L22 26 D1
  Liverpool, Garston L19 81 C6
  2 Liverpool L3 52 D3
  Newton-le-W WA12 46 A3
  1 Southport PR8 4 A6
Wellington Terr
  Birkenhead CH41 66 D5
  2 Liverpool L8 68 A5
  St Helens WA10 44 A5
Well La
  Bebington CH63 78 D6
  Birkenhead, Greasby CH49 64 C3
  Birkenhead, Tranmere CH42 66 E2
  Bootle L20 38 D3
  Haskayne L39 11 E6
  Heswall CH60 86 B6
  Liverpool L16, L25 69 F7
  Warrington WA5 74 F3
Well Lane Gdns L20 38 D3
Well Lane Prim Sch CH42 66 E3
Wells Ave WN5 33 D6
Wells St L15 68 F8
Wellstead Cl L15 69 A8
Wellstead Rd L15 69 A8
Wellstead Wlk L15 69 A8
Welsby Cl WA2 61 F3
Welshpool Cl WA5 60 D2
Welsh Rd CH66 89 A1
Welton Ave CH49 64 F5
Welton Cl L24 82 D4
Welton Gn L24 82 D4
Welton Rd CH62 79 E3
Welwyn Ave PR8 7 E6
Welwyn Cl WA9 57 F6
Wembley Gdns L9 38 F6
Wembley Rd
  Crosby L23 26 F3
  Liverpool L18 69 B5
Wendell St L8 68 C7
Wendover Ave L17 68 C3
Wendover Cl
  Birkenhead CH43 65 D4
  Haydock WA11 45 D7
Wendron Rd L11 40 D5
Wenger Rd WA8 73 B5
Wenlock Ct L26 82 E8
Wenlock Dr L26 82 E8
Wenlock Rd L4 53 B7
Wenning Ave L31 20 E2
Wennington Rd PR9 4 F7
Wensley Ave L26 82 F8
Wensleydale L9 39 A7
Wensleydale Ave
  Bebington CH62 88 E5
  Rainhill L35 57 D3
Wensleydale Cl
  Maghull L31 20 B2
  Warrington WA5 74 F8
Wensley Rd
  Golborne WA3 47 E7
  Liverpool L9 39 A7
Wentworth Ave CH45 51 B7
Wentworth Cl
  Birkenhead CH43 65 D4
  Southport PR8 7 C4
  Widnes WA8 73 A5
Wentworth Dr
  Bebington CH63 88 C5
  Liverpool L5 52 F4
Wentworth Gr L36 55 B2
Wentworth Rd WN4 35 A5
Wernbrook Cl CH43 65 D4
Wernbrook Rd L4 53 C7
Wervin Cl CH43 65 E2
Wervin Rd
  Birkenhead CH43 65 E2
  Kirkby L32 29 D1
Wescoe Cl WN5 25 E5
Wesley Ave
  Haydock WA11 45 F7
  Wallasey CH44 51 C5
Wesley Gr CH44 51 E3
Wesley Grange CH49 65 B3
Wesley Hall Gdns WA9 57 D6
Wesley Pl L15 68 F8
Wesley St
  Seaforth L22 37 D8
  Southport PR8 4 B7
West Albert Rd L17 68 B4
West Alfred Ct 23 CH43 66 C5
West Allerton Sta L18 69 B1
West Ave WA3 36 B1
Westbank Ave CH45 51 C7
West Bank Dock Est WA8 84 E5
Westbank Rd CH42 66 C3
West Bank Rd L7 53 E2
Westbourne Ave
  Crosby L23 27 B6
  West Kirby CH48 63 B2
Westbourne Gdns PR8 3 D4
Westbourne Gr CH48 63 B2
Westbourne Rd
  Birkenhead CH43 66 C5
  Southport PR8 3 D4
  Wallasey CH44 50 F4
  West Kirby CH48 63 B2
Westbourne Sch CH45 51 C6
West Bridge L31 20 C1
Westbrook Ave L34 56 B6
WESTBROOK CENTRE 60 B1
Westbrook Cres WA5 60 B2
Westbrook Ctr WA5 60 C1
Westbrook Rd
  Birkenhead CH46 64 C7
  Liverpool L25 70 C5
Westbrook Way WA5 60 B1
West Brow Gdns CH43 65 C8
Westbury Cl
  Liverpool L25 82 D9
  Liverpool, Otterspool L17 68 C1
Westbury St CH41 66 E4
West Cl
  Birkenhead CH43 65 D5
  Eccleston Park L34 57 A7
Westcliffe Ct
  Southport PR8 3 F5
  Widnes WA8 73 B4
Westcliffe Rd
  Liverpool L12 54 A7
  Southport PR8 3 F5
Westcombe Rd L4 53 C7
Westcott Rd L4 53 B6
Westcott Way CH43 65 D3
Westdale Rd
  Birkenhead CH42 66 E2
  Liverpool L15 68 F8
Westdale View L15 68 F8
Westdene PR9 1 D1
WEST DERBY 54 D7
West Derby Rd
  Liverpool L6 53 B4
  Liverpool, Tuebrook L13, L6 53 E5
West Derby Sch L13 54 A5
West Derby Sch (Bankfield Wing) L13 53 F6
West Derby St L7 53 A2
West Derby Village L12 54 B7
West Dr
  Birkenhead CH49 65 A5
  Heswall CH60 86 A7
West End Gr WA11 45 A6
West End Prim Sch L39 13 E7
West End Rd
  Haydock WA11 45 A6
  St Helens WA11 44 F6
West End Terr PR8 4 A7
Westerhope Way WA8 72 F3
Westerings The CH62 88 C6
Western Approaches Mus* L2 90 A4
Western Ave
  Bebington CH62 79 D3
  Huyton-w-R L36 55 B3
  Liverpool L24 82 C4
Western Dr L19 81 A7
Westerton Rd L12 54 E6
Westfield Ave
  Ashton-in-M WN4 35 A4
  Huyton-w-R L14 54 E2
Westfield Cres WA7 84 E1
Westfield Dr L12 40 E3
Westfield Mews WA7 84 F1
Westfield Prim Sch WA7 84 E1
Westfield Rd
  Liverpool L9 38 E6
  Runcorn WA7 84 E1
  Wallasey CH44 51 D1
Westfield St WA10 43 F3
Westfield Wlk
  Kirkby L32 29 B1
  Kirkby L32 29 B2
Westgate
  Skelmersdale WN8 23 D8
  Widnes WA8 84 B7
Westgate Dr WN5 25 D5
Westgate Rd
  Bebington CH62, CH63 79 B4
  3 Liverpool L15 69 A5
WEST GILLIBRANDS 23 E8
West Gillibrands Ind Est WN8 23 E8
West Gr CH60 85 F8
Westhaven PR9 4 D8
Westhaven Cres L39 13 C1
WESTHEAD 14 D4
Westhead Ave
  Golborne WA3 36 E1
  Kirkby L33 29 F2
Westhead Cl L33 30 A1
Westhead Lathom St James' CE Prim Sch L40 14 E4
Westhead Wlk L33 29 F2
Westholme Ct PR9 1 C1
Westhouse Cl CH63 88 C5
WEST KIRBY 63 B2
West Kirby Gram Sch CH47 63 A3
West Kirby Prim Sch CH47 63 A3
West Kirby Rd CH46, CH48 64 C6
West Kirby Residential Sch CH47 63 A3
West Kirby Sta CH48 63 A2
West La L37 9 F6
Westland Dr WA2 61 E2
Westlands Cl CH64 86 F1
Westleigh Pl WA9 58 C5
West Lodge Dr CH48 63 A3
West Mains L24 83 A3
West Meade L31 20 B2
Westminster Ave L30 27 F4
Westminster Cl
  Liverpool L4 38 E1
  Widnes WA8 84 B8
Westminster Ct CH43 65 F5
Westminster Dr
  Bebington CH62 88 D7
  Haydock WA11 45 F7
  Southport PR8 7 A4
Westminster Gr L34 56 A5
Westminster Rd
  Liverpool L4 52 E8
  Wallasey CH44 51 B4
Westmoreland Pl 3 L5 52 D5
Westmoreland Rd
  Southport PR8 4 D5
  Wallasey CH45 51 C7
Westmorland Ave
  Litherland L30 27 C3
  Widnes WA8 73 B1
Westmorland Dr L3 52 C3
Westmorland Rd L36 55 E2
West Mount WN5 25 F6
West Oakhill Pk L13 54 A2
Westonby Ct WN4 35 D3
Weston Ct L23 26 B3
Weston Gr
  Halewood L26 83 A6
  Maghull L31 28 D6
Weston Point Expressway WA7 84 E2
Weston Rd WA7 84 F1
West Orchard La L9 39 D7
Westover Cl L31 20 C1
Westover Rd L31 20 C1
WEST PARK 43 D2
West Park Cl WN8 23 D8
West Park Gdns CH43 65 C8
West Park Rd WA10 43 D2
WEST PIMBO 24 D4
West Pimbo Ind Est WN8 24 D4
West Pk PR9 1 D1
Westport Bsns Pk L20 52 C7
West Quay Rd WA2 60 F3
West Rd
  Birkenhead CH43 65 D5
  Liverpool, Broad Green L14 54 C2
  Liverpool, Walton L9 38 F3
Westry Cl CH46 64 B8
West Side WA9 44 C2
West Side Ave WA11 45 A6
Westside Ind Est WA9 44 C2
West St
  Prescot L34 56 C6
  Southport PR8 4 A7
  St Helens WA10 43 D1
  Wallasey CH45 51 B5
WESTVALE 29 C2
Westvale Prim Sch L32 29 B2
West View
  Birkenhead CH41 66 F4
  Huyton-w-R L36 56 B2
  1 Ormskirk L39 13 F5
  Rainford WA11 31 F6
  Warrington WA2 61 F1
West View Ave L36 56 B2
Westview Cl CH43 65 D4
West View Cl L36 56 B2
Westward Ho CH48 75 D6
Westward View
  Crosby L22 26 B2
  Liverpool L17 68 A3
Westway
  Birkenhead, Greasby CH49 64 E4
  Birkenhead, Noctorum CH43 65 D4
  Heswall CH60 85 F6
  Hightown L38 17 F4
  Liverpool L15 69 B8
  Maghull L31 20 C2
West Way CH46 49 E1
Westway Sq CH46 49 E1
Westwick Pl L36 55 B3
Westwood Cl PR8 4 E3
Westwood Ct
  Birkenhead CH43 65 F5
  Neston CH64 86 E2
Westwood Gr 2 CH44 51 A4
Westwood Rd
  Birkenhead CH43 65 C6
  Liverpool L18 81 C8
Wetherby Ave CH45 50 E5
Wetherby Cl WA12 46 C5
Wetherby Ct L36 55 C5
Wethersfield Rd CH43 65 E4
Wetstone La CH48 63 C1
Wexford Ave L24 83 D2
Wexford Cl
  Birkenhead CH43 65 E4
  Haydock WA11 45 D7
Wexford Rd CH43 65 F4
Wexford Wlk CH43 65 F4
Wexwood Gr L35 56 F2
Weybourne Cl CH49 65 A7
Weyman Ave L35 56 E3
Weymoor Cl CH63 78 F2
Weymouth Ave WA9 44 F1
Weymouth Cl L16 69 F8
Weymouth Rd WA5 59 F6
Whaley La CH61 76 F6
Whalley Ave
  Rainford WA11 31 F6
  St Helens WA10 43 E7
Whalley Ct L30 27 D4
Whalley Dr
  Formby L37 10 A2
  Ormskirk L39 21 D8
Whalley Gr WA8 73 D3
Whalley Rd 2 CH42 66 D5
WHALLEYS 16 A5
Whalleys Rd WN8 16 B5
Whalley St L8 67 F4
Wharfedale Ave CH42 66 B2
Wharfedale Dr
  Bebington CH62 88 F5
  Rainhill L35 57 D3
Wharfedale Rd CH45 50 F6
Wharfedale St L19 81 E5
Wharf Rd WA12 45 E2
Wharf St CH62 79 C5
Wharmby Rd WA11 45 E6
Wharncliffe Rd L13 54 A3
Wharton Cl CH49 64 D6
Wharton St WA9 44 B1
Wheatacre WN8 23 E8
Wheatcroft Rd L18 69 D2
Wheatear Cl L27 70 E4
Wheatfield Cl
  Birkenhead CH46 64 F7
  Litherland L30 28 B3
Wheatfield Rd WA8 72 C5
Wheatfield View L21 27 B2
Wheat Hill Rd L27, L36 70 E8
Wheathills Ind Est L27 70 E6
Wheatland Bsns Pk CH44 51 D2
Wheatland Cl WA9 58 C4
Wheatland La CH44 51 D2
Wheatland Rd CH60 86 C7
Wheatley Ave
  Bootle L20 38 E5
  Newton-le-W WA12 46 C5
Wheatsheaf Ave WA9 58 D6
Wheatsheaf Wlk 4 L39 13 E5
Wheeler Dr L31 29 B4
Whelan Gdns WA9 57 E6
Wheldon Rd WA8 83 F7
Whernside WA8 72 C3
Whetstone Ct 4 CH41 66 D5
Whetstone La CH41, CH42 66 D5
Whickham Cl WA8 72 F3
Whimbrel Ave WA12 46 C3
Whimbrel Pk L26 70 E1
Whinberry Dr L32 29 D1
Whinbury Ct 15 WA9 58 C4
Whinchat Ave WA12 46 C4
Whinchat Cl WA3 47 E7
Whincraig L28 55 C7
Whinfell Rd L12 54 C5
Whinfield Rd
  Crosby L23 27 B6
  Liverpool L9 38 F6
Whinhowe Rd L11 40 B2
Whinmoor Cl CH43 65 D6
Whinmoor Rd
  Liverpool L10 40 A7
  Liverpool, Sandfield Park L12 54 C5
Whinney Gr E L31 28 C6
Whinney Gr W L31 28 C6
WHISTON 56 E4
WHISTON CROSS 56 D3
Whiston Hospl L35 56 F4
Whiston La L36 56 B4
WHISTON LANE ENDS 56 C2
Whiston Sta L35 56 E3
Whiston Willis Com Prim Sch L35 56 E3
Whitburn WN8 15 D1
Whitburn Cl WN4 34 D4
Whitburn Rd L33 30 A4
Whitby Ave
  Southport PR9 2 D6
  Wallasey CH45 50 E5
  Warrington WA2 61 D2
Whitby St L6 53 D6
Whitcroft Rd L6 53 D3
Whitebeam Cl L33 29 F6
Whitebeam Dr L12 40 D3
Whitebeam Gdns WA9 57 C6
Whitebeam Wlk CH49 64 B2
Whitechapel L1 90 B3
Whitecroft Ave WA3 36 E1
Whiteeside Cl CH49 65 A4
Whitefield Ave
  Liverpool L4 52 E8
  Newton-le-W WA12 46 E2
Whitefield Cl
  Birkenhead CH49 65 B3
  Golborne WA3 47 A8
  Hightown L38 17 F2
Whitefield Dr L32 29 C1
Whitefield La L35 71 A6
WHITEFIELD LANE END 71 B8
Whitefield Prim Sch L6 53 A4
Whitefield Rd
  Liverpool L6 53 B5
  St Helens WA10 43 D5
Whitefield Way 2 L6 53 A4
Whitefriars WA10 43 A4
Whitegate Cl L34 41 D4
Whitegates Cl CH64 87 E1
Whitegates Cres CH64 87 E1
Whitehall Cl L4 38 E1

Whitehart Cl L4 39 B1
Whitehaven Cl PR8 7 B3
Whitehaven Rd L5 52 F6
Whiteheath Way CH46 49 F3
Whitehedge Rd L19 81 B7
Whitehey WN8 23 E8
Whitehey Rd WN8 23 E8
Whitehorn Dr L28 55 B8
White House Ave L37 10 A3
White House Cl WA11 45 B6
Whitehouse La
  Formby L37 10 A3
  Heswall CH60, CH63 77 D1
Whitehouse Rd L13 54 B2
Whitelands Mdw CH49 64 E5
Whiteledge Rd WN8 24 B6
Whiteleys La L40 14 D2
White Lodge Ave L36 55 D3
White Lodge Cl CH62 88 D5
White Lodge Dr WN4 35 D4
Whitely Gr L33 30 A6
White Meadow Dr L23 27 A6
WHITE MOSS 23 F7
Whitemoss Bsns Pk WN8 23 F6
White Moss Rd WN8 23 C7
White Moss Rd S WN8 23 D7
White Oak Lo L19 80 F7
Whiterails Dr L39 13 D6
Whiterails Mews L39 13 D6
White Rock St L6 53 B4
Whiteside Ave WA11 44 E5
Whiteside Cl
  Birkenhead CH49 65 A4
  Liverpool L5 52 D5
Whiteside Rd WA11 45 B6
White St L1 90 B2
Whitestock WN8 23 E8
Whitestone Cl L34 41 C2
Whitethorn Ave WA5 74 F5
White Thorn Sch L9 39 D7
Whitewell Dr CH49 64 F7
Whitewood Cl WN4 35 A6
Whitewood Pk L9 39 D6
Whitfield Ct [1] CH42 66 D4
Whitfield Gr WA11 45 A6
Whitfield La CH60 77 A1
Whitfield Lodge WA9 58 D4
Whitfield Rd L9 39 A5
Whitfield St CH42 66 D4
Whitford Rd CH42 66 D4
Whitham Ave L23 26 F3
Whithorn St L7 68 D8
Whitland Rd L6 53 D3
Whitledge Gn WN4 35 A5
Whitledge Rd WN4 35 A5
Whitley Cres WN2 36 B7
Whitley Dr [1] CH44, CH45 51 C5
Whitley St L3 52 B4
Whitlow Ave WA3 35 F1
Whitman St L15 68 E7
Whitmoor Cl L35 57 E1
Whitney Pl L25 70 C2
Whitney Rd L25 70 C2
Whitstable Pk WA8 72 E4
Whitstone Cl L18 69 E2
Whitstone Dr WN8 24 D7
Whittaker Ave WA2 61 D2
Whittaker Cl L13 53 F1
Whittaker St WA9 44 D1
Whittier St L8 68 C7
Whittle Ave
  Haydock WA11 45 A5
  Warrington WA5 60 A1
  Warrington WA5 74 F8
Whittle Cl L5 52 E6
Whittle Dr L39 13 E7
Whittle Hall La WA5 74 F6
Whittle St
  Liverpool L5 52 E6
  St Helens WA10 43 D1
Whittlewood Ct L33 29 F4
Whitwell Cl WA5 74 D7
Wicket Cl L11 40 D5
Wickham Cl CH44 51 E2
Wicks Cres L37 9 C4
Wicks Gdns L37 9 D3
Wicks Gn L37 9 C3
Wicks Green Cl L37 9 C3
Wicks La L37 9 D3
Widdale Ave L35 57 D3
Widdale Cl WA5 74 F7
Widgeons Covert CH63 86 F5
Widmore Rd L25 70 C4
WIDNES 72 F2
Widnes Rd
  Cuerdley Cross WA5, WA8 73 F2
  Warrington WA5 74 C3
Widnes Sta WA8 73 A3
Wiend The
  Bebington CH63 79 A5
  Birkenhead CH42 66 D1
Wigan Rd
  Ashton-in-M WN4 35 A5
  Billinge WN5 33 F7
  Golborne WA3 36 B3
  Ormskirk L39 14 A5
  Skelmersdale WN8 23 F8
  Westhead L40 14 E4
Wightman Ave WA12 46 C5
Wightman St L6 53 B3
Wight Moss Way PR8 4 D3
Wignall Cl L32 40 E7
Wignalls Mdw L38 17 F3
Wigston Cl PR8 7 B4
Wilberforce Rd L4 39 B2
Wilbraham Pl [4] L5 52 D5
Wilbraham St
  [19] Birkenhead CH41 66 E6
  Liverpool L5 52 D5
  St Helens WA9 58 E3
Wilburn St L4 38 F1
Wilbur St WA9 58 E7
Wilcock Cl L5 52 D5
Wilcock Rd WA11 46 B8
Wilcote Cl WA8 73 C4
Wilcove WN8 15 F1
Wild Arum Cl [8] WA3 47 E8
Wildbrook Dr CH41 50 D1
Wildcherry Gdns L35 57 C7
Wilde St L3 90 C4
Wild Pl L20 38 E7
Wilfer Cl [4] L7 68 C8
Wilfred Owen Dr CH41 65 E7
Wilkes Ave CH46 50 B3
Wilkie St L15 68 E7
Wilkinson Ct L15 68 E8
Wilkinson St [18] CH41 66 C5
Wilkin St L4 52 E7
Willan St CH43 66 B4
Willard Ave WN5 25 D3
Willard St L20 38 D6
WILLASTON 88 A1
Williston Dr L26 83 A6
Willaston Rd
  Liverpool L4 39 B1
  Thornton Hough CH63, CH64 87 D4
  Wallasey CH46 49 D1
Willedstan Ave L23 26 E3
William Beamont Com High Sch WA2 61 C1
William Brown St L3 90 B4
William Ct CH64 86 F2
William Gladstone CE Sch L21 38 A7
William Harvey Cl L30 27 F3
William Henry St
  Bootle L20 38 B2
  Liverpool L3, L6 52 E3
William Jessop Way L3 52 B2
William Morris Ave L20 38 E5
William Moult St L5 52 D5
William Penn Cl WA5 74 E5
William Rd WA11 44 F6
William Roberts Ave L32 29 C2
Williams Ave
  Bootle L20 38 E5
  Newton-le-W WA12 46 C5
Williamson Art Gall & Mus★ CH43 66 B5
Williamson Ct
  [4] Liverpool, Halewood Village L26 71 A1
  Liverpool, Woolton L25 70 C1
Williamson Sq [13] L1 90 B3
Williamson St
  Liverpool L1 90 B3
  St Helens WA9 44 C4
Williamson Student Village L7 53 A1
Williamson Tunnels Heritage Ctr★ L7 53 A1
Williams St L34 56 D6
William St
  Birkenhead CH41 66 E6
  [2] St Helens WA10 44 A4
  Wallasey CH44 51 E2
  Widnes WA8 73 C1
William Wall Rd L21 27 B2
Willingdon Rd L16 54 E1
Willington Ave CH62 88 E3
Willink Rd WA11 44 C7
Willis Cl L35 56 D2
Willis La L35 56 D2
Williton Rd L16 69 E5
Willmer Rd
  Birkenhead CH42 66 D5
  Liverpool L4 53 B7
Willoughby Cl WA5 60 C1
Willoughby Dr WA10 57 B8
Willoughby Rd
  Crosby L22 26 E1
  Huyton-w-R L14 54 F2
  Wallasey CH44 51 A4
Willow Ave
  Huyton-w-R L36 70 E8
  Kirkby L32 29 C3
  Newton-le-W WA12 46 E4
  Prescot L35 56 E3
  [2] Widnes WA8 73 B2
Willowbank Cl L36 55 C5
Willow Bank Est WA12 46 F4
Willowbank Holiday Home & Touring Pk PR8 7 B2
Willowbank Rd
  [2] Bebington CH62 79 B6
  Birkenhead CH42 66 D3
Willowbrow Rd CH63, CH64 87 D3
Willow Cl L14 54 E2
Willowcroft Rd CH44 51 C2
Willow Ct
  Bebington CH63 78 D6
  Bootle L20 38 C2
  [17] Liverpool L8 68 A4
  Newton-le-W WA12 46 D4
  St Helens WA9 58 D4
Willow Ct *continued*
  [14] Wallasey CH45 51 B8
  Warrington WA2 60 F3
Willowdale WA12 46 E3
Willowdale Rd
  Liverpool, Hartley's Village L9 39 A4
  Liverpool L18 68 F5
Willowdene Ct L11 40 D5
Willow Dr WN8 15 E1
Willowfield Gr WN4 35 A2
Willow Gn
  Liverpool L25 69 F4
  [5] Ormskirk L39 13 F5
Willow Gr
  Ashton-in-M WN4 35 E5
  Birkenhead CH46 64 D7
  Formby L37 9 F4
  Golborne WA3 36 A1
  Liverpool L15 69 A8
  Prescot L35 56 E5
  Southport PR9 4 E7
Willow Grove Prim Sch WN4 35 E5
Willowherb Cl L26 70 D2
Willowhey PR9 1 F4
Willow Hey
  Maghull L31 28 E7
  Skelmersdale WN8 15 F1
Willow Ho [7] L21 38 A6
Willow La CH63, CH64 87 D3
Willow Lea CH43 66 A4
Willowmeade L11 40 B3
Willow Moss Cl CH46 50 A2
Willow Pk
  Birkenhead CH49 64 C4
  Southport PR8 4 A5
Willow Rd
  Haydock WA11 45 E7
  Liverpool L15 68 E8
  Newton-le-W WA12 46 E4
  St Helens WA10 43 C3
Willows The
  Newton-le-W WA12 46 D4
  Southport PR8 3 F6
  [3] St Helens WA9 58 C4
  Wallasey CH45 50 E7
  Warrington WA5 74 F5
Willow Tree Ave WA9 58 D4
Willow Tree Ct WA8 73 D2
Willow Tree Prim Sch WA9 58 D4
Willow Way
  Crosby L23 26 E5
  Liverpool L11 40 D6
Willow Wlk WN8 16 B4
Wills Ave L31 20 C2
Willsford Ave L31 29 B3
Wilmcote Gr PR8 7 B4
Wilmere La WA8 73 A6
Wilmot Ave WA5 74 F6
Wilmot Dr WA3 46 F7
Wilne Rd [3] CH45 51 A6
Wilsden Rd WA8 72 B1
Wilsford Cl WA3 36 B1
Wilsham Rd WN5 25 E5
Wilshaw Terr CH63 87 B6
Wilson Ave CH44 51 E4
Wilson Cl
  St Helens WA10 43 F3
  [4] Widnes WA8 73 D1
Wilson Gr L19 81 C6
Wilson Rd
  Huyton-w-R L36 56 A1
  Prescot L35 56 D4
  Wallasey CH44 51 E4
Wilsons La L21 38 B8
Wilstan Ave CH63 78 D5
Wilstone Cl [8] L5 52 F4
Wilton Gr [6] L13 54 A2
Wilton Grange CH47 63 A4
Wilton Rd
  Birkenhead CH42 67 A1
  Huyton-w-R L36 55 D1
Wiltons Dr L34 41 D3
Wilton St
  Liverpool L3 90 C4
  [6] Wallasey CH44 51 B4
Wiltshire Dr L30 27 D3
Wiltshire Gdns WA10 43 F2
Wimbald Cl L25 70 C5
Wimbledon St
  Liverpool L15 68 E7
  Wallasey CH44, CH45 51 B5
Wimborne Cl L14 55 B6
Wimborne Pl L14 55 B5
Wimborne Rd L14 55 B5
Wimborne Way CH61 76 D7
Wimbourne Ave CH61 77 A5
Wimbrick Cl
  Birkenhead CH46 64 F8
  Ormskirk L39 13 D4
Wimbrick Cres L39 13 D3
Wimbrick Ct CH46 64 F8
Wimbrick Hey CH46 65 A8
Wimpole St L7 53 B2
Winchester Ave
  Aintree L10 28 D3
  Ashton-in-M WN4 35 A3
  [1] Crosby L22 26 D3
Winchester Cl
  Liverpool L25 82 B8
  [4] Orrell WN5 25 F7
Winchester Dr CH44, CH45 51 A5
Winchester Pl WA8 84 C8
Winchester Rd
  Ashton-in-M WA11 34 E1
Winchester Rd *continued*
  Liverpool L6 53 C6
  Longshaw WN5 25 D2
Winchfield Rd L15 68 F6
Windbourne Rd L17 68 C2
Windermere Ave
  St Helens WA11 44 B8
  Warrington WA2 61 D3
  Widnes WA8 73 B4
Windermere Cres PR8 7 C3
Windermere Ct [8] CH41 66 C5
Windermere Dr
  Kirkby L33 29 D4
  Liverpool L12 40 C1
  Maghull L31 20 E2
  Rainford WA11 23 F2
Windermere Ho L17 68 D2
Windermere Pl WA11 44 A8
Windermere Rd
  Abram WN2 36 B8
  Birkenhead CH43 65 C5
  Haydock WA11 45 B6
  Hightown L38 18 A4
  Orrell WN5 25 F8
Windermere St
  Liverpool L5 53 B5
  Widnes WA8 73 B4
Windermere Terr L8 68 B5
Windfield Cl L33 30 A6
Windfield Gn L19 81 D3
Windfield Rd L19 81 D4
Windgate WN8 15 F1
Windle Ash L31 20 C2
Windle Ave L23 27 A3
Windlebrook Cres WA10 43 B6
Windle City WA10 43 F6
Windle Ct CH64 86 E2
Windle Gr WA10 43 C6
Windle Hall Dr WA10 43 E7
WINDLEHURST 43 F6
Windlehurst Ave WA10 43 E6
Windleshaw Rd WA10 43 E5
Windle Smithies WA10 43 C7
Windle St WA10 43 F5
Windle Vale WA10 43 E5
Windmill Ave
  Crosby L23 26 F5
  Ormskirk L39 13 F5
Windmill Cl [2] L33 29 E5
Windmill Gdns
  Birkenhead CH43 65 C8
  St Helens WA9 44 D4
Windmill Ho PR9 1 F2
Windmill Hts WN8 25 A8
Windmill La WA5 74 E5
Windmill Rd WN8 24 F7
Window La L19 81 C4
Windrows WN8 15 F1
Windsor Ave
  Litherland L21 38 A8
  Newton-le-W WA12 46 D2
Windsor Cl
  Bebington CH62 79 A7
  Birkenhead CH49 64 D3
  Litherland L30 27 F5
Windsor Com Prim Sch L8 67 F6
Windsor Ct
  [1] Bootle L20 38 E5
  [6] Liverpool L8 67 F6
  Southport PR8 3 E4
Windsor Day Hospl L8 67 F7
Windsor Dr WA11 46 A7
Windsor Mews CH62 79 A7
Windsor Park Rd L10 28 E3
Windsor Rd
  Ashton-in-M WN4 35 C1
  Billinge WN5 33 F5
  Bootle L20 38 E5
  Crosby L23 26 D5
  Formby L37 9 F1
  Golborne WA3 47 C8
  Huyton-w-R L36 55 B3
  Liverpool, Tuebrook L13 53 D6
  [5] Liverpool, Warbreck Pk L9 39 A6
  Maghull L31 28 C8
  Prescot L35 56 F4
  Southport PR9 4 D7
  St Helens WA10 43 D4
  Up Holland WN8 25 A8
  Widnes WA8 73 A4
Windsor St
  Birkenhead CH41 66 C5
  Liverpool L8 67 F6
  Wallasey CH45 37 B1
Windsor View L8 68 B7
Windus St WA10 43 E3
Windward Dr L24 82 A5
WINDY ARBOR 71 C8
Windy Arbor Brow L35 71 C8
Windy Arbor Cl L35 56 D1
Windy Arbor Rd L35 56 D1
WINDY ARBOUR 34 B8
Windy Bank CH62 79 B6
Windy Bank Ave WA3 47 E8
Windy Harbour Rd PR8 7 E7
Wineva Gdns L23 26 F3
Winford St CH44 51 D3
Winfrith Cl CH63 78 F2
Winfrith Dr CH63 78 F2
Winfrith Rd L25 70 C4
Wingate Ave WA9 57 D6
Wingate Cl CH43 65 E4
Wingate Rd
  Bebington CH62 88 E5
Wingate Rd *continued*
  Kirkby L33 29 F3
  Liverpool L17 68 E2
Wingate Wlk L33 30 A3
Wingfield Cl L29 27 D8
Wingrave Way L11 40 B1
Winhill L25 70 A4
Winhill Lo L25 70 A4
Winifred La L39 21 B8
Winifred Rd L10 40 B7
Winifred St L7 53 B1
Winkle St [1] L8 67 F5
Winmoss Dr L33 30 A5
Winnard St WA3 36 B2
Winnington Rd CH47 63 A4
Winnipeg Dr L27 70 E5
Winsford Cl WA11 45 F7
Winsford Dr WA5 59 E7
Winsford Rd L13 53 F6
Winsham Cl L32 40 F8
Winsham Rd L32 40 F8
Winskill Rd L11 40 A1
Winslade Ct L4 39 B2
Winslade Rd L4 39 B2
Winslow St L4 52 F8
Winstanley Coll WN5 25 F3
Winstanley Ho
  Bebington CH62 79 B7
  [1] Crosby L22 26 E1
Winstanley Ind Est WA2 61 B1
Winstanley Rd
  Ashton-in-M WN2 35 F8
  Bebington CH62 79 B7
  Crosby L22 26 E2
  Garswood WN4, WN5 34 B6
  Orrell WN5 25 F3
  Skelmersdale WN8 23 F8
Winster Dr L27 71 A3
Winsters The WN8 15 F1
Winston Ave
  Newton-le-W WA12 46 C3
  St Helens WA9 45 B2
Winston Cres PR8 4 E2
Winston Dr CH43 65 C5
Winstone Rd L14 55 A4
Winston Gr CH46 64 E8
Winterburn Cres L12 54 D7
Winter Gr WA9 45 B3
Winterhey Ave CH44 51 B3
Winterlea Dr L26 83 A6
Winter St [9] L6 53 A3
Winthrop Pk CH43 65 E5
Winton Cl CH45 51 A8
Winton Rd WA3 47 E6
WINWICK 61 A6
Winwick CE Prim Sch WA2 61 B6
Winwick La WA3 47 E3
Winwick Link Rd WA2, WA3 61 C6
Winwick Park Ave WA2 61 A5
WINWICK QUAY 61 A3
Winwick Rd
  Newton-le-W WA12 46 F1
  Warrington WA2 61 A2
Winwick View WA5 45 D1
Winwood Hall L25 70 A1
Wirral Bsns Ctr CH41 51 C1
Wirral Bsns Pk The CH49 64 F3
Wirral Cl CH63 78 F3
Wirral Country Pk★ CH48 75 D5
Wirral Ctry Pk★ CH60 76 B2
Wirral Gdns CH63 78 F3
Wirral Gram Sch for Boys CH63 78 F4
Wirral Gram Sch for Girls CH63 78 F4
Wirral International Bsns Pk CH62 79 E3
Wirral L Pk CH62 79 E3
Wirral Metropolitan Coll CH62 89 A7
Wirral Mount
  Wallasey CH45 50 F5
  West Kirby CH48 63 D3
Wirral Mus★ CH41 66 F6
Wirral View L19 80 F6
Wirral Villas CH45 50 E6
Wirral Way CH43 65 C5
Wisteria Way WA9 59 A7
Witham Cl L30 28 A4
Witham Rd WN8 15 D1
Withburn Cl CH49 64 E5
Withensfield CH45 51 B6
Withen's La CH44, CH45 51 C5
Withens Rd L31 20 D3
Withens The L28 55 B8
Withert Ave CH63 78 D8
Withill Wlk [4] WN4 35 A5
Withington Rd
  Liverpool L24 82 F4
  Wallasey CH44 51 D3
Withins Field L38 17 F3
Withins La L37 19 A7
Withins Rd WA11 45 F8
Within Way L24 83 E1
Withnell Cl L13 54 B2
Withnell Rd L13 54 B2
Withycombe Rd WA5 74 E4
Witley Ave CH46 49 E1
Witley Cl CH46 49 E1
Witney Cl CH49 64 C3
Wittenham Cl CH49 64 F4
Wittering La CH60 85 D7

Addresses

Name and Address	Telephone	Page	Grid reference

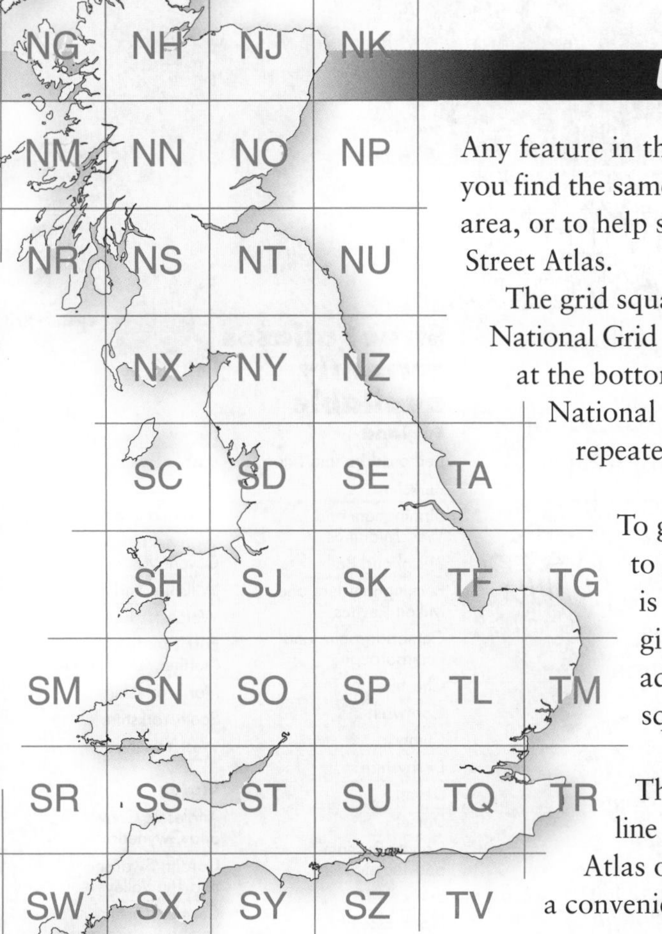

Any feature in this atlas can be given a unique reference to help you find the same feature on other Ordnance Survey maps of the area, or to help someone else locate you if they do not have a Street Atlas.

The grid squares in this atlas match the Ordnance Survey National Grid and are at 500 metre intervals. The small figures at the bottom and sides of every other grid line are the National Grid kilometre values (**00**°to°**99** km) and are repeated across the country every 100°km (see left).

To give a unique National Grid reference you need to locate where in the country you are. The country is divided into 100 km squares with each square given a unique two-letter reference. Use the administrative map to determine in which 100 km square a particular page of this atlas falls.

The bold letters and numbers between each grid line (**A**°to°**F**,°**1**°to°**8**) are for use within a specific Street Atlas only, and when used with the page number, are a convenient way of referencing these grid squares.

Example   The railway bridge over DARLEY GREEN RD in grid square B1

Step 1: Identify the two-letter reference, in this example the page is in **SP**

Step 2: Identify the 1 km square in which the railway bridge falls. Use the figures in the southwest corner of this square: Eastings **17**, Northings **74**. This gives a unique reference: **SP 17 74**, accurate to 1°km.

Step 3: To give a more precise reference accurate to 100 m you need to estimate how many tenths along and how many tenths up this 1 km square the feature is (to help with this the 1 km square is divided into four 500 m squares). This makes the bridge about **8** tenths along and about **1** tenth up from the southwest corner.

This gives a unique reference: **SP 178 741**, accurate to 100°m.

Eastings (read from left to right along the bottom) come before Northings (read from bottom to top). If you have trouble remembering say to yourself Along the hall, THEN up the stairs !

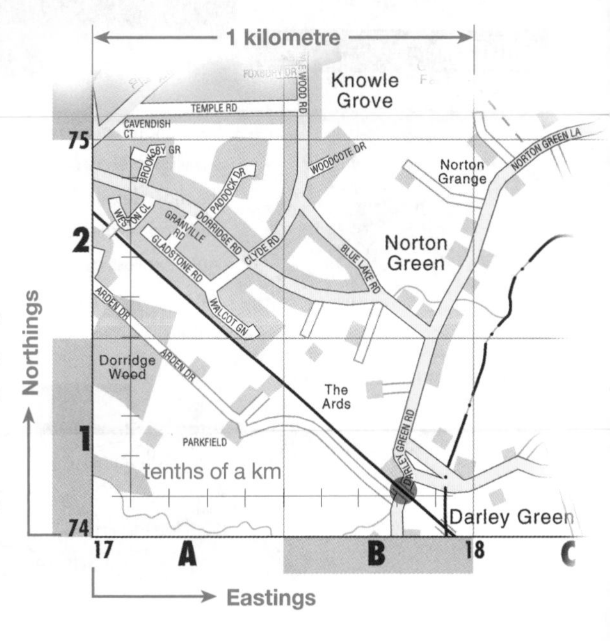

PHILIP'S MAPS

the Gold Standard for drivers

◆ **Philip's street atlases cover every county in England, Wales, Northern Ireland and much of Scotland**

◆ Every named street is shown, including alleys, lanes and walkways

◆ Thousands of additional features marked: stations, public buildings, car parks, places of interest

◆ Route-planning maps to get you close to your destination

◆ Postcodes on the maps and in the index

◆ Widely used by the emergency services, transport companies and local authorities

Street atlases currently available

England

Bedfordshire and Luton	Surrey
Berkshire	East Sussex
Birmingham and West Midlands	West Sussex
Bristol and Bath	Tyne and Wear
Buckinghamshire and Milton Keynes	Warwickshire and Coventry
Cambridgeshire and Peterborough	Wiltshire and Swindon
Cheshire	Worcestershire
Cornwall	East Yorkshire Northern Lincolnshire
Cumbria	North Yorkshire
Derbyshire	South Yorkshire
Devon	West Yorkshire
Dorset	
County Durham and Teesside	**Wales**
Essex	Anglesey, Conwy and Gwynedd
North Essex	Cardiff, Swansea and The Valleys
South Essex	Carmarthenshire, Pembrokeshire and Swansea
Gloucestershire and Bristol	Ceredigion and South Gwynedd
Hampshire	Denbighshire, Flintshire, Wrexham
North Hampshire	Herefordshire Monmouthshire
South Hampshire	Powys
Herefordshire Monmouthshire	
Hertfordshire	**Scotland**
Isle of Wight	Aberdeenshire
Kent	Ayrshire
East Kent	Dumfries and Galloway
West Kent	Edinburgh and East Central Scotland
Lancashire	Fife and Tayside
Leicestershire and Rutland	Glasgow and West Central Scotland
Lincolnshire	Inverness and Moray
Liverpool and Merseyside	Lanarkshire
London	Scottish Borders
Greater Manchester	
Norfolk	**Northern Ireland**
Northamptonshire	County Antrim and County Londonderry
Northumberland	County Armagh and County Down
Nottinghamshire	Belfast
Oxfordshire	County Tyrone and County Fermanagh
Shropshire	
Somerset	
Staffordshire	
Suffolk	

For national mapping, choose **Philip's Navigator Britain** the most detailed road atlas available of England, Wales and Scotland. Hailed by Auto Express as 'the ultimate road atlas', the atlas shows every road and lane in Britain.

How to order

Philip's maps and atlases are available from bookshops, motorway services and petrol stations. You can order direct from the publisher by phoning **0207 531 8473** or online at **www.philips-maps.co.uk**
For bulk orders only, e-mail philips@philips-maps.co.uk